The Gulf Conflict
1990–1991

*Diplomacy and War
in the New World Order*

Lawrence Freedman and
Efraim Karsh

Princeton University Press
Princeton, New Jersey

Library of Congress Cataloging-in-Publication Data

Freedman, Lawrence.
    The Gulf conflict, 1990-1991 : diplomacy and war in
the new world order / Lawrence Freedman and Efraim Karsh.
       p.   cm.
    Includes bibliographical references and index.
    ISBN 0-691-08627-3
    ISBN 0-691-03772-8 (pbk.)
    1. Persian Gulf War, 1991.   I. Karsh, Efraim.
II. Title
    DS79.72.F74 1992
    956.704'42—dc20   92-38995

First published in Great Britain by Faber and Faber Limited

Third printing, and first paperback printing, 1994

The Gulf Conflict
1990–1991

For Judith and Inari

Contents

List of Illustrations

List of Tables

Acknowledgements

Our thanks are very much due to our research assistants David Boren, Yossi Meckelberg and Michael McNerney. The data base organized by David which is to be deposited with the Liddell Hart Centre for Military Archives at King's College will be a great boon to future historians. Marie-France Desjardines provided some translations. Richard Ullman read an early version of the manuscript with great care and the final version has benefited enormously from his constructive criticism and advice. We wish to acknowledge the readiness of Brian Lapping Associates to let us use materials gathered for their documentary series on the conflict. Lastly we would like to thank our editors, Susanne McDadd at Faber and Walter Lippincott at Princeton, for their encouragement from the earliest stages of this project and their tolerance of the book's widening scope and length.

LF and EK
April 1992

Dramatis Personae

Algeria

Chadly Benjedid, President
Ahmad Ben-Bella, former President

Arab League

Chadly Klibi, Secretary-General

Britain

Lt.-General Sir Peter de la Billière, British Forces Commander, Middle East
General Sir John Chapple, Chief of the General Staff
Brigadier Patrick Cordingley, Commander, 7th Armoured Brigade
Sir David Hannay, Ambassador to the United Nations (from October 1990)
Air Chief Marshal Sir Patrick Hine, Commander-in-Chief, Operation Granby
Sir Geoffrey Howe, Deputy Prime Minister (until November 1990)
Douglas Hurd, Foreign Secretary
Tom King, Defence Secretary
John Major, Chancellor of the Exchequer, then Prime Minister (from November 1990)
Charles Powell, Foreign Policy Adviser to the Prime Minister
Margaret Thatcher, Prime Minister (until November 1990)
Sir Crispin Tickell, Ambassador to the United Nations (until October 1990)

Egypt

Dr Boutrus Ghali, Minister of State for Foreign Affairs
Husni Mubarak, President

France

Claude Cheysson, former Minister of Foreign Affairs
Jean-Pierre Chevènement, Minister of Defence (until January 1991)
Roland Dumas, Minister of Foreign Affairs
Pierre Joxe, Interior Minister then Defence Minister (from January 1991)
Admiral Jacques Lanxade, Chief-of-Staff in the Elysée Palace
François Mitterrand, President
Edgar Pisani, Director of the Institute of the Arab World
Michel Rocard, Prime Minister

Germany

Willy Brandt, former West German Chancellor
Hans-Dietrich Genscher, Foreign Minister
Helmut Kohl, Chancellor
Hans Stercken, Chairman of the Bundestag's Foreign Affairs Committee
Gerhard Stoltenberg, Defence Minister

Iran

Ali Akbar Hashemi-Rafsanjani, President

Iraq

Lt.-Colonel Walid Saud Muhammad Abdallah, Foreign Minister, provisional Kuwaiti Government
Lt.-General Sa'di Tumah Abbas, Chief-of-Staff, then Minister of Defence
Akram Abd al-Qader Ali, Justice Minister
Abd al-Amir al-Anbari, Ambassador to the United Nations
Tariq Aziz, Foreign Minister and Deputy Prime Minister
Isam Abd al-Rahim al-Chalabi, Oil Minister
Dr Sa'dun Hammadi, Deputy Prime Minister, then Prime Minister
Nizar Hamdoon, Under Secretary of State for Foreign Affairs
Abd al-Razzaq al-Hashimi, Ambassador to Paris
Saddam Hussein, President
Izzat Ibrahim, Vice-President
Latif Nusseif Jasim, Minister of Information
Barzan al-Tikriti, Ambassador to the UN, Geneva
Ali-Hassan al-Majid, Governor of Kuwait, then Minister of the Interior

Hussein Kamil Hassan al-Majid, Minister of Production and Military Industry, then Minister of Defence
Taha Yasin Ramadan, First Deputy Prime Minister
Sa'di Mehdi Saleh, Speaker of the Iraqi Parliament

Israel

Moshe Arens, Minister of Defence
Major-General Ehud Barak, Deputy Chief-of-Staff
Major-General Avihu Bin-Nun, Air Force Commander
David Levy, Foreign Minister
Shimon Peres, Head of Labour Party, Leader of the Opposition
Yitzhak Rabin, former Prime Minister
Yitzhak Shamir, Prime Minister
Ariel Sharon, Minister for Housing
Lt.-General Dan Shomron, Chief-of-Staff

Italy

Giulio Andreotti, Prime Minister
Gianni de Michelis, Foreign Minister

Japan

Akihito, Emperor
Toshiki Kaifu, Prime Minister
Taro Nakayama, Foreign Minister
Yasuhiro Nakasone, former Prime Minister

Jordan

Crown Prince Hassan
King Hussein

Kuwait

Sheikh Jaber al-Ahmad al-Sabah, Emir of Kuwait
Sheikh Sa'd Abdallah al-Sabah, Crown Prince
Sheikh Saud Nasir al-Sabah, Ambassador to the United States

Libya

Mu'amar Gaddafi, President

Luxembourg

Jacques Poos, Foreign Minister

Palestinian Liberation Organization

Yasser Arafat, Chairman
Salah Khalaf (Abu Iyad), Chief of Security

Saudi Arabia

Crown Prince Abdallah Ibn-Abd-al-Aziz
King Fahd Ibn-Abd-al-Aziz
Prince Bandar Ibn Sultan, Ambassador to Washington
Lt.-General Khalid Ibn Sultan, Commander, Saudi Forces
Prince Saud al-Faisal, Foreign Minister
Prince Sultan Ibn-Abd-al-Aziz, Minister of Defence

Soviet Union

Alexander Bessmertnykh, Foreign Minister (from January 1991)
Mikhail Gorbachev, President
Yevgeny Primakov, Special Envoy to the Middle East
Eduard Shevardnadze, Foreign Minister (until January 1991)
Sergei Tarasenko, Head of Planning Department, Foreign Office
Vitaly Vorontsov, Ambassador to the United Nations
Dimitri Yazov, Minister of Defence

Syria

Hafiz Asad, President
Abd al-Khalim Khaddam, Vice-President
Farouq al-Shara, Foreign Minister
Mustafa Tlas, Minister of Defence

Turkey

Turgut Ozal, President

United Nations

Javier Perez de Cuellar, Secretary-General
Prince Sadruddin Aga Khan, High Commissioner for Refugees

United States

Les Aspin, Chairman of the House Armed Services Committee
James Baker, Secretary of State
George Bush, President
Henry Catto, Ambassador to the Court of St James
Richard Cheney, Secretary of Defense
Robert Dole, Senate Republican Minority leader
General Michael J. Dugan, Air Force Chief-of-Staff (until September 1990)
Lawrence Eagleburger, Under Secretary of State
Marlin Fitzwater, White House Spokesman
Thomas Foley, Speaker of the House of Representatives
Charles Freeman, Ambassador to Riyadh
Robert Gates, Deputy Adviser on National Security Affairs
April Glaspie, Ambassador to Baghdad
Brigadier General 'Buster' Glossan, Targeting Director, Operation Desert Storm
Richard Haass, Special Assistant to the President for Near East and South Asian Affairs
Lt. General Charles Horner, CENTCOM Air Commander
Marine Major General Robert B. Johnston, Chief-of-Staff to General Schwarzkopf
John Kelly, Assistant Secretary of State for Near Eastern and South Asian Affairs
Robert Kimmitt, Under Secretary of State for Political Affairs
General Merrill McPeak, Air Force Chief-of-Staff (from September 1990)
Sam Nunn, Chairman of the Senate Armed Services Committee
Colin Powell, Chairman, Joint Chiefs-of-Staff
Thomas Pickering, Ambassador to the United Nations
Dan Quayle, Vice-President
Dennis Ross, Director State Department Policy Planning Staff

General Norman Schwarzkopf, Commander-in-Chief, Central Command
General Brent Scowcroft, National Security Adviser
John Sununu, White House Chief-of-Staff
Margaret Tutwiler, State Department Spokesperson
General Carl Vuono, Army Chief-of-Staff
William Webster, Director, Central Intelligence Agency
Joseph Wilson, Chargé d'Affaires in Baghdad
Paul Wolfowitz, Under Secretary of Defence for Policy

Maps

1. The Gulf Region

2. Iraq and Kuwait

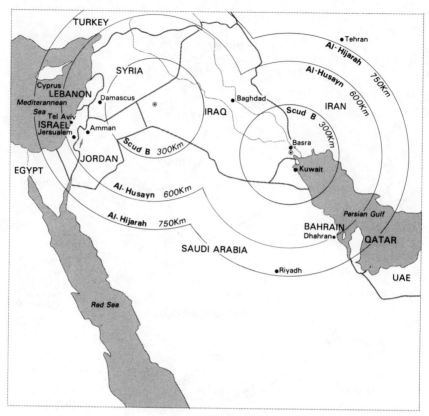

3. Scud Missile Range

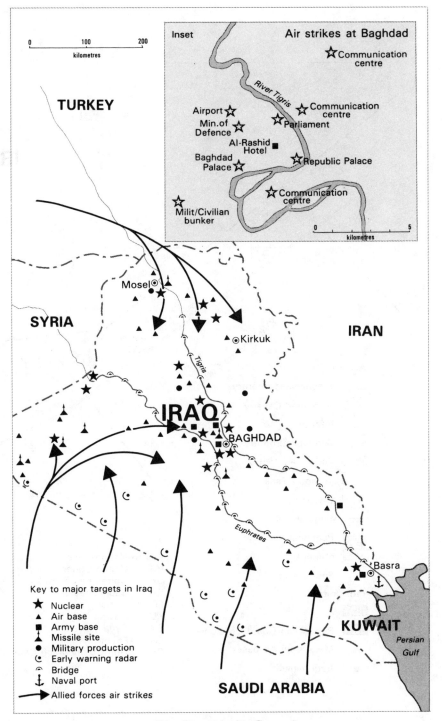

Inset — Air strikes at Baghdad

☆Communication centre

River Tigris

Airport ☆
Min.of ☆
Defence
Al-Rashid ■
Hotel
Baghdad ☆
Palace

☆Communication centre
☆Parliament

☆Republic Palace

☆Communication centre

☆
Milit/Civilian
bunker

0   5
kilometres

0   100   200
kilometres

TURKEY

SYRIA

Mosel ◉
★

★

◀

▼

★ ▶

▲◉Kirkuk
▲

IRAN

Tigris

★

★

▲

●

●

IRAQ ◀

■ ■
★ ●BAGHDAD
★★
■

■

Euphrates

●Basra ⚓

Key to major targets in Iraq
★ Nuclear
▲ Air base
■ Army base
⊥ Missile site
● Military production
☾ Early warning radar
⌒ Bridge
⊥ Naval port
➤ Allied forces air strikes

KUWAIT

Persian Gulf

SAUDI ARABIA

4. The Strategic Air Campaign

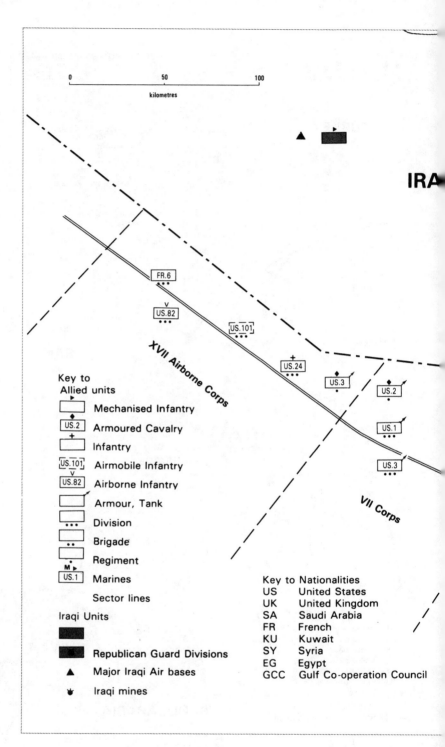

0   50   100

kilometres

IRA

FR.6

US.82

US.101

US.24

US.3

US.2

US.1

US.3

XVII Airborne Corps

VII Corps

**Key to
Allied units**

Mechanised Infantry

US.2   Armoured Cavalry

Infantry

US.101   Airmobile Infantry

US.82   Airborne Infantry

Armour, Tank

Division

Brigade

Regiment

US.1   Marines

Sector lines

Iraqi Units

Republican Guard Divisions

▲   Major Iraqi Air bases

☙   Iraqi mines

Key to Nationalities
US   United States
UK   United Kingdom
SA   Saudi Arabia
FR   French
KU   Kuwait
SY   Syria
EG   Egypt
GCC   Gulf Co-operation Council

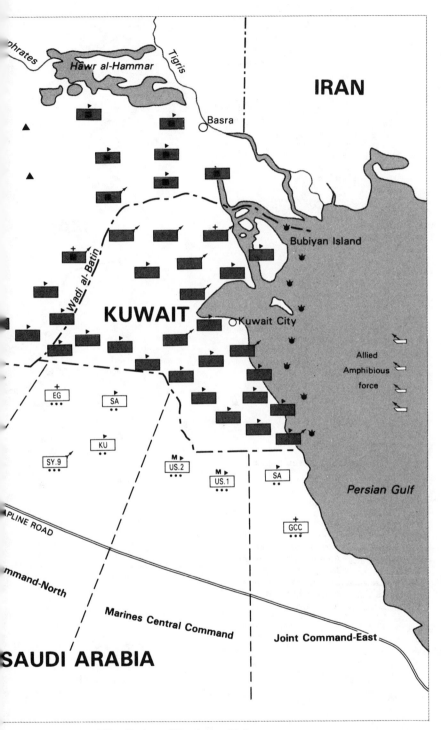

5. The Order of Battle: 23 February 1991

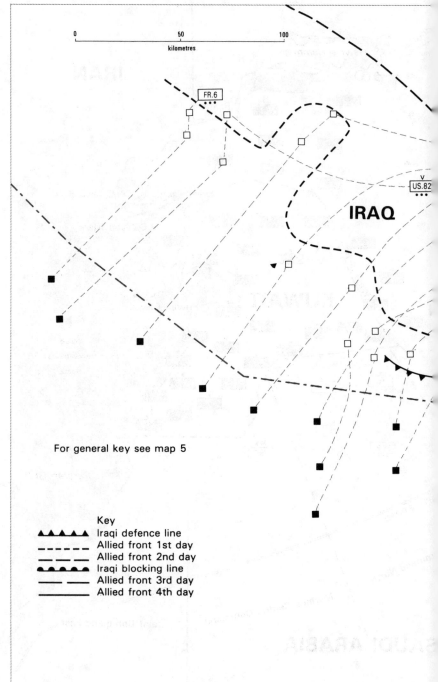

IRAN

0   50   100
kilometres

FR.6

US.82

IRAQ

For general key see map 5

Key
▲▲▲▲▲ Iraqi defence line
– – – – – Allied front 1st day
– · – · – Allied front 2nd day
●●●●● Iraqi blocking line
—— · —— Allied front 3rd day
———— Allied front 4th day

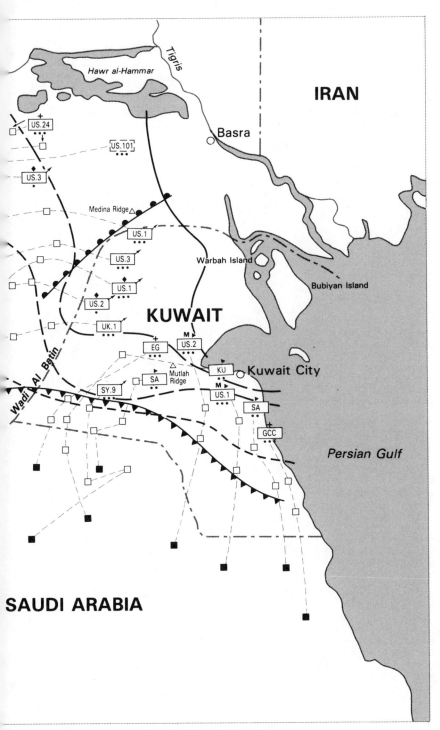

6. The Coalition Offensive

Introduction: The New World Order

> What is at stake is more than one small country: it is a big idea: a new world order – where diverse nations are drawn together in common cause, to achieve the universal aspirations of mankind: peace and security, freedom and the rule of law.[1]

A crisis involving the whole world is inevitably complex in its ramifications; yet it is likely to be simple in its origins, for only a stark challenge can jolt the whole world into action. The Iraqi occupation of Kuwait was a textbook case of aggression. If international law and norms of behaviour are to mean anything, then aggression must be opposed. But the meaning of international norms in such cases is always moot, for the capacity of the world community to enforce them is inherently limited. The United Nations depends on agreement among members of the Security Council if there is to be any action. These may be reluctant to act either because they do not want to accept the consequences or because it will mean turning against an ally or client. It was Saddam Hussein's misfortune that 1990 found the United Nations with a rare will and capacity for action, largely because the United States and the Soviet Union were able to act in concert.

Not long after Iraq seized Kuwait, President Bush spoke of this challenge as both a test and an opportunity. If the international community could only act now with resolution then the best hopes of the post-cold-war era might be realized. Should Iraq be successfully expelled, it would be possible to speak optimistically of a 'new world order' in creation. For once, a regional conflict had not served as a proxy for superpower confrontation, the United Nations Security Council had functioned as intended and nations from all around the world had joined together against an aggressor.[2]

The idealistic gloss and progressive aspirations conveyed by the President were contrasted by the more cynical with evidence of old world practices and double standards.[3] The United States's intervention in the Gulf, it was argued, had nothing to do with its concern for world order. It suited the

Americans to take up this particular crime because it happened to interfere with a basic interest – oil – while comparable outrages were ignored when perpetrated by American friends. Even Saddam Hussein had been accorded undue tolerance when his brutality was directed inwards against his own people and Washington wished to curry favour. The talk of a new world order was therefore dismissed as at best mistaking a unique example of international co-operation for a long-term trend or, at worst, a code for a Pax Americana.

Thus from the start a critical feature of the Gulf conflict was that it went far beyond the immediate clash between Iraq and Kuwait to raise issues at the heart of contemporary international affairs. To use another favourite Bush phrase, the conflict could be seen as a 'defining moment', for it was both shaped by the fundamental changes taking place in global politics and, through the precedents set, influenced its emerging character.

The world in January 1990 was not particularly orderly, as its most pronounced feature was the liberation of hitherto suppressed political forces. However, following two months of revolution in Eastern Europe it was certainly 'new'. The Middle East, settling after a tumultuous decade of war and tension, was unsettled again by the winds of change generated by the collapse of European communism. There were very particular reasons why Saddam Hussein seized Kuwait, not least a chronic indebtedness, but his calculations were shaped by his understanding of the meaning of these larger changes for the stability of his regime. Equally the initial American inattention to the simmering crisis in the Gulf reflected its complete absorption in European developments while its subsequent crisis management was shaped by a keen sense of the options for working through the UN and with the Soviet Union, as Moscow sought to maintain some international standing through co-operation rather than confrontation. The removal of the threat along NATO's central front allowed for the transfer of American and British armoured divisions and strike aircraft from Europe to the Gulf.

The crisis went beyond American interests to impact on every region, from the European Community's attempt to turn itself into as substantial a force in global political affairs as in economic affairs, to Eastern Europe's programme of post-communist reconstruction, to Japan's sense of its international obligations, to China's attempt to ingratiate itself back into the international community, to North Africa's political and economic neuroses, as well as the whole gamut of Middle Eastern disputes.

Against this backdrop, an examination of the crisis provides a remarkable snapshot of the international system at the start of the 1990s, and an opportunity to explore the wider significance of the break-up of the Soviet empire in Europe and its implications for the conduct of diplomacy and the role of military force. It is tempting to turn the Gulf conflict into a prize-fight between George Bush and Saddam Hussein, but only an analysis that places it firmly in its wider context can do full justice to its many strands.

The major problem posed by the occupation of Kuwait was not one of ends. Few disputed the need for Iraq to withdraw: even Iraq's friends did not attempt to make a case for Kuwait's annexation. The problem was one of means. What would it take to force Iraq out of Kuwait and was the principle at stake worth the costs of such measures? Much of this book is inevitably concerned with the available measures – economic sanctions, diplomatic deals, military force – and the manner in which they were chosen and implemented.

For a while great hopes were invested in an embargo, simply because Iraq's dependence on the oil trade led to the belief that it was susceptible to economic coercion. Following this through raised questions of patience, and the durability of a variegated international coalition, and the morality of putting pressure on Saddam through imposing hardship on his people. With military pressure the questions were whether there was any point signalling displeasure with a token display of force or would the only effective signal be based on a threat of credible military action? Should airpower be used in support of ground forces or in such a way as to make a decisive impact on its own? There was also a familiar ring to the debates on diplomatic solutions, and the search for the line between 'not rewarding aggression' and helping the aggressor acknowledge his mistake through peaceful means with some 'face-saving' concessions.

The coalition asserted that there could be no reward for aggression but that there need not necessarily be a punishment other than the loss of its fruits. This moderate position was necessary to reassure its more hesitant members. Yet it was contradicted by the rhetoric which stressed the sinister character of both Saddam and the regime over which he presided in order to justify a call to arms, as well as by the commonsensical view that the matter could not be closed until the criminal himself was brought to book.

Here we come up against a basic difference between national and international law. A national police force will seek to deal with the crime by apprehending the criminal and bringing him to justice. The international community has no government and no police force – just institutions, rules and instruments that can be used to deal with the worst offenders but only if the major powers are prepared to make the effort and can agree on a course of action, or are prepared to stand aside while one power enforces its version of the rules on its own. It may often be too much bother to reverse the crime, never mind punish the criminal. This is inherently frustrating and it became doubly so in the Iraqi case because of the demonic character of Iraq's leader.

Saddam Hussein had long posed a challenge to the international community. He had initiated war with Iran, repressed his own people and in particular the Kurds, used chemical weapons, and circumvented the nuclear non-proliferation treaty. This challenge had not been met because other countries saw him as serving a useful purpose in taking on revolutionary Iran (which was perceived as being the main threat to the regional system) and as a lucrative client, and also because the extent of his wrongdoing was not fully appreciated. Even when the nature of his regime became more recognized, action was inhibited because of doubts with regard to both the possibility of getting collective action and the efficacy of the most available means – economic sanctions and diplomatic isolation.

When his conduct became wholly unacceptable as a result of naked aggression against a small, hapless neighbour it was natural to demand a solution to the 'Saddam problem' as part of the solution to the 'Kuwait problem'. This was easier said than done. It was always evident that the least painful settlement for Kuwait would involve sparing Saddam. Also, the Saddam problem was bound up with the 'Iraq problem' in that a determination to remove one regime required some clear views as to a realistic replacement. Lastly, replacing Saddam and sustaining an alternative regime would involve an effort far beyond that required to liberate Kuwait and would not have been acceptable to many members of the coalition. It would have been tempting fate and a source of dissension to make the 'liberation' of Iraq an explicit war aim.

This is why the separation of the Kuwait problem from the Saddam/Iraq problem was considered essential to the construction of an international coalition sufficient to force Iraq out of Kuwait. But in practice the separation was not so easy, if for no other reason than that mobilizing support for the liberation of Kuwait also involved a stress on the horrors perpetrated by Saddam and even a comparison with Hitler. As a result, the failure to remove Saddam from power after the war was taken to qualify the validity of the whole exercise, and was widely attributed to a loss of nerve at the end of the war and an over-hasty agreement to a cease-fire.

This criticism, however, is largely misconceived. It had never been intended to remove Saddam by direct means. This does not mean that there was no desire to see Saddam toppled, only that it was hoped to achieve this by indirect methods. This is where the separation of the Saddam problem from the Iraq problem became difficult. Economic pressure was seen both before and after the main conflict as the most appropriate means to weaken

Saddam's grip on power. But while it was possible to cut off trade effectively, sanctions raised a basic dilemma: when confronting a regime indifferent to the sufferings of its own people, is it acceptable to seek to undermine it by intensifying this suffering and encouraging insurrection, and if insurrection takes place is there not an obligation to support it?

In this book we have attempted to reconstruct the strategic calculations of the main participants in the light of how the unfolding drama will have appeared to them at the time. We have been interested to note the extent to which decisions could be based on judgements – for example, about the importance of the 'Israel question' to Arab countries or the tolerance of casualties in the West – that sometimes owed as much to myth as to evidence, and the influence of 'lessons' drawn from the recent history of crisis management. In the United States the shadow of Vietnam was very evident but so too was the memory of pushing things too far in Korea, entanglements in Lebanon and the hunt for Noriega in Panama. The British and Soviet Governments drew conclusions from their very different experiences in the Falklands and Afghanistan. Saddam Hussein based his strategy for dealing with a Western military offensive on one that he judged to have served him well against Iran.

This was also a remarkably transparent crisis, a consequence in itself of important shifts in the conduct of contemporary diplomacy. This was partly a function of American leadership, for Washington is a city where crisis transparency is a presumption, partly the necessity to hold together a wide coalition, which required a constant stream of reassurances, and, lastly, the result of remarkable developments in modern communications. Diplomats of previous generations would have been astonished at the speed with which information reached them from foreign capitals or distant battlefields, and at which they would be expected to respond and their responses made public. Even diplomats from earlier in the television age would have been surprised at the extent to which a single news source – Cable Network News (CNN) – was employed in all capitals, and the influence of raw and undigested information as it was transmitted instantaneously around the globe, reaching public and policy-makers at the same moment. Here was a war in which pilots were shown taking off to bomb an enemy capital – where cameras were waiting to broadcast the results. Places where there were no cameras – which included all of Kuwait – could have little influence on the developing perceptions of the rights and wrongs of the conflict, and assessments of its likely outcome.

There was considerable official sensitivity to these perceptions and the impact of images of war and diplomacy upon them. Saddam appeared at times to be waging a media rather than a military campaign, as if the key to success lay in unsettling public opinion in the West and creating a heroic reputation in the Arab world. Western strategy was shaped throughout with one eye on its presentation – diplomatic initiatives to persuade a reluctant Congress that no stones were being left unturned in the quest for peace, military briefings intended to stress the precision of air strikes and that everything was under control. This public relations strategy also acted as an important inhibitor on secret diplomacy, for at some point every substantive initiative was going to have to be revealed and be subjected to critical media analysis.

Even now, with the benefit of a series of 'inside stories' written by top investigative reporters, it is hard not to be struck by just how much of the detail was known at the time. The conflict was covered by the international media to an extraordinary extent. It was front page news for seven months, and there is therefore a wealth of information to be found by reading the daily reports, and also the commentary and analysis of those who were attempting to make sense of, and even influence, the unfolding events.

In the United States decision-makers readily co-operate with reconstructions of their deliberations. As a result, there are already in the public domain numerous accounts of the conflict from the perspective of members of the Bush Administration. It is of course frustrating that the sources are often not named. Some accounts are obviously highly speculative. However, sufficient are authentic to be an invaluable resource to any contemporary historian. We have been fortunate ourselves to have had access to a number of interviews with top American policy-makers who participated in a television series on the war for which Lawrence Freedman served as a consultant.[4] We have also spoken with those involved from other countries, in Europe and in the Middle East, in the decision-making and in the prosecution of the war.

There is always the temptation to go for revelation rather than relevance when using interviews – to turn history into a sensational news story by headlining new 'facts' uncovered by assiduous reporters. We have tried to resist this temptation though we believe that we have uncovered new evidence. We prefer to emphasize more the scope and originality of our analysis, which requires pulling together evidence from *all* available sources – Government and other official documents, newspaper files, academic analyses as well as interviews. It is perhaps one difference between academics and journalists that, whereas the latter are frustrated when someone else gets a good 'story', the former are delighted if it helps to build a more complete picture. We also firmly believe that wherever possible we should indicate where our evidence came from, although in some cases it has been necessary to respect the confidentiality requested by our sources.

Another problem with the 'inside story' approach is that it produces accounts heavily weighted towards Washington, where officials are more naturally loquacious. Because the United States was obviously leading the international coalition this encourages the tendency to look no further than the White House. Unfortunately this has led to a neglect of European, Soviet and Middle Eastern decision-making. We hope that one of the contributions of this book will be to remedy this deficiency by producing a comprehensive account which demonstrates the interaction between all the parties involved.

Unlike the authors of the 'first wave' of books on the Gulf conflict we have been able to take account of the work of others and form views less influenced by the excitement and passions of the campaign itself. Inevitably much of the 'first wave' was written to make a point – from the brilliance of the military operation to the inflexibility of Bush to the error in letting Saddam Hussein off the hook. We cannot pretend to have been indifferent observers of the crisis and the war, but we do believe that coming to terms with these events requires some detachment and understanding of how they appeared to those making the critical decisions at the time. This book is neither a celebration nor an indictment. It is based on the conviction that it is possible to apply the historian's method of detached and systematic inquiry to contemporary international affairs, without losing the sense of drama inherent in such events.

PART ONE
Origins of the Crisis

CHAPTER I
New World, New Middle East?

As Iraqi troops began to mass on the border with Kuwait during July 1990, the major powers were fixated with Europe. So it had been since the revolutions of 1989 when one communist regime after another had succumbed to popular discontent and the Berlin Wall had been breached. Now they were digesting the implications of a deal struck between German Chancellor Helmut Kohl and Soviet President Mikhail Gorbachev. Gorbachev had suddenly consented to the unification of Germany within NATO in return for promises to cut the German armed forces and substantial economic assistance.

This breakthrough after weeks of stalemate reinforced the best hopes for the future in which developments of historic significance could be agreed peaceably and amicably, so long as the West used its effective victory in the cold war in a responsible and non-provocative manner. The next event to look forward to was a gathering in Paris in November of all the countries of the Conference on Security and Co-operation in Europe (CSCE), and the signature of a new arms control treaty cutting conventional forces in Europe.

The Kohl–Gorbachev meeting was symbolic in another way. Although President George Bush and his Secretary of State James Baker had been active proponents of German unification and played a key role in its realization, the final deal was struck by the Federal Chancellor alone. This seemed to confirm the ascent of Germany as the pre-eminent regional power and potentially one of global stature, with its influence drawn from its economic rather than its military strength.

This ascent was watched with some trepidation. Gorbachev was well aware of the dismay of many in Moscow at the collapse of the old strategic concept by which this traditional enemy had been kept divided and then at arm's length through the buffer zone provided by the Eastern Bloc. France saw itself being displaced as the natural leader of Western Europe, while in Britain, Prime Minister Margaret Thatcher did not hide her reservations with regard to German unification or her irritation at the Bush Administration's transfer of its affections from London to Bonn.

3

In all of this the Americans seemed relaxed. While the Administration was stressing its willingness to continue to play a major role in European affairs it seemed reasonable to assume that the decline of the Soviet threat would lead to progressive disengagement from global responsibilities. So much of its past involvement had been justified by a need to arrest the advance of communism. With communism everywhere in retreat the occasions for interventionism had been correspondingly reduced. The withdrawal of the Soviet military from its former East European garrisons would allow for major reductions in forces based in Europe.

There were, of course, still areas of concern. Despite the early optimism concerning the capacity of the Soviet Union to metamorphose from a stagnant, totalitarian communism into advanced liberalism and a thriving economy, all signs pointed to a steep decline and intensifying demands for secession from the Baltic and Caucasian Republics. Even the states of Central and Eastern Europe, after the initial excitement of the 1989 revolution, were now coming to terms with the harsh realities of the crumbling communist legacy, and their own ethnic and national tensions. The risk of total war which had dominated European politics throughout the twentieth century had suddenly and dramatically abated. But in its wake had come a growing risk of widespread low-intensity conflict, with similar characteristics to those which had proved to be so vexatious in the Third World.

For this reason the chancelleries of Europe and America were busy during the summer of 1990 attempting to construct a new set of security arrangements which would allow conflicts to be handled in a sensitive and efficient manner. A variety of proposals were canvassed to reinforce the CSCE, revive the Western European Union, revamp the European Community to give it a defence role, and restructure NATO to give it a more political role. Amid all this there was a debate under way on the future of economic and political union in the European Community.

The restructuring of Europe thus dominated the diplomatic agenda in the first half of 1990, and left little time for much else. It encouraged the general presumption that at last the world community might find means to transcend the settlement of disputes through violent methods. Conflicts in the Third World should be easier to resolve because of the new possibilities opened up for strategic co-operation between the West and the Soviet Union. At any rate, for the same reason, any conflicts that did occur would be of far less strategic significance.

American power and the Third World

This euphoric mood was in stark contrast to the atmosphere a decade earlier. The 1980s had begun with warnings of a global Soviet challenge. Days before the previous decade had closed, Soviet forces had moved in to Afghanistan to prop up a failing Marxist regime, crudely removing the head of government in the process. This caused outrage in the West. The more alarmist asserted that the intervention had little to do with Afghanistan and was merely an attempt by the Soviets to establish themselves closer to the oilfields of the Gulf. Conservative geo-politicians pointed to the Soviet footholds in Angola, the Horn of Africa, and the Yemen – and the resultant risk to critical trade routes from the Middle East.

Anxiety was doubly high because of the 1979 revolution in Iran, which had overthrown the staunchly pro-Western Shah and led to a correspondingly anti-Western Islamic Government led by the zealous Ayatollah Ruhollah Khomeini. The hostage crisis, in which forty-four American diplomats were held by militants with the connivance of the revolutionary Government for 444 days until the end of the Carter presidency, underlined America's multiple vulnerabilities in the Third World. The abortive attempt to rescue the hostages in June 1980, which ended in a tragic fiasco, reinforced this sense of weakness. The American public watched helplessly while an Iranian cleric taunted them around the dead bodies of their soldiers who had died in the desert on a futile mission.

President Jimmy Carter had begun his tenure warning against 'paranoia' with regard to the Soviet Union. By its close the Persian Gulf had been declared a 'vital' American interest and a Rapid Deployment Force (RDF) was being created to allow for a proper assertion of military strength. The concept of rapid deployment suffered from the start because the regional powers, such as Saudi Arabia, were uncertain as to whether the American efforts were geared towards the Soviet threat to the region, towards radical Islam, or simply towards the protection of Western oil interests against any challenge from any direction. Their consequent reluctance to get too close to the Americans meant that the RDF would not be able to use local ground bases but would have to rely on mobilization of men from the United States meeting up with pre-positioned stocks kept on ships in the general vicinity.

Ronald Reagan exploited the sense of malaise over America's international standing during the 1980 election campaign. He then presided over a remarkable increase in the size of the defence budget. His Administration gained a hawkish reputation by supporting particular anti-communist groups, such as the Mujaheddin in Afghanistan, UNITA in Angola and the

5

Contras in Nicaragua, but when it came to direct military intervention there was more caution. It either came in areas where resistance would be minimal, as in the Caribbean island of Grenada in 1983 following a coup, or was confined to air strikes, such as the 1986 raid against the Libyan capital of Tripoli in reprisal for acts of state-sponsored terrorism.

The most difficult operation had been the dispatch of a peace-keeping force to Beirut in 1983. This left under a cloud in early 1984 after taking heavy casualties and failing to achieve peace. The débâcle led to an intense debate within the Reagan Administration over the prerequisites for successful military intervention. The State Department still saw the readiness to use force as an essential underpinning of all diplomacy. This view was countered by the Secretary of Defence, Caspar Weinberger, who argued forcefully that the United States should not engage in conflicts which it could lose and certainly not without the full backing of the American people.

All evidence suggested that such support was unlikely to be forthcoming. Vietnam had rendered the global role unpopular. Public opinion saw little reason to accept all the costs and risks of a high defence budget and overseas commitments when the domestic economy was in difficulty and US allies in Western Europe and Japan did not accept their fair share of the burden of maintaining international order. By the time of the 1988 election the talk was of economic and political decline resulting in part from 'over-stretch' in overseas commitments.

In the event it was Soviet power which experienced a far steeper decline. A deep crisis in the communist system, which had been brewing for many years, dominated Soviet politics through the 1980s. A series of elderly, ailing figures were succeeded in March 1985 by Mikhail Gorbachev. Gorbachev determined that he could not make much progress in domestic reform until he put his country's external affairs in order. He would not get economic co-operation from Western countries unless he convinced them that he no longer represented a threat. Nor would he be able to reduce the heavy burden of military expenditure before calming the arms competition which, with Reagan at the White House, was more intense than ever. The Americans set Gorbachev tests on political liberties and arms control on which he scored far higher than his predecessors. For the most substantial progress they looked less to Moscow relinquishing control over Eastern Europe, which until 1989 was judged to be largely a rhetorical objective, but more to co-operation on what were described as 'regional issues'.

In particular there was an American demand on the table to leave Afghanistan. It was one Gorbachev planned to accept. Soviet forces had their hands full coping with the Mujaheddin guerrillas in a war that was costly, unpopular and without prospect of victory. In general the global interventionism of the 1970s had proved to be an expensive mistake. The regimes backed by Moscow were not thriving, and many suffered from civil war, thus imposing a drain on scarce Soviet resources. Even before Brezhnev died in 1982 greater caution had begun to enter Soviet calculations. It took Gorbachev to reverse direction fully. In 1988 agreement was reached on a Soviet pull-out from Afghanistan, and the Americans noted a growing readiness to co-operate on what had been in the past the most intractable disputes. This began to influence the work of the United Nations Security Council, which for most of its forty-five years had been inhibited by the antagonism between its two leading members. A vivid illustration of this evolving trend of US–Soviet collaboration over regional disputes within the United Nations framework was Security Council Resolution 598 of 18 July 1988 on a cease-fire to the Iran–Iraq War.

A new order in the Middle East?

This cease-fire created hopes that the Middle East was experiencing its own shift towards greater moderation. The 1980s had been one of the most violent decades in the region's modern history. The war in Afghanistan, the Iranian revolution and the ensuing eight-year Iran–Iraq War, the Israeli invasion of Lebanon, and the eruption of the *intifada*, the Palestinian uprising in the West Bank and the Gaza Strip, had all rocked its socio-political edifice. And yet the turbulence had also triggered a painful process of disillusionment with armed force as a foreign policy instrument. This was reinforced by widespread regional apprehensions over the implications for the Middle East of the momentous events in Eastern Europe. Slowly the region was moving in the direction of a more 'orderly' system, based on a growing readiness – albeit constrained, shaky, and far from complete – to come to terms with its diversity.

A decade earlier, the main new threat to regional order had been the Islamic Republic of Iran, which had just overthrown the Pahlavi monarchy and was committed to the subversion of the existing status quo and its replacement by an Islamic order. 'The Iranian Revolution is not exclusively that of Iran,' stated Ayatollah Khomeini,

> because Islam does not belong to any particular people. We will export our revolution throughout the world because it is an Islamic revolution. The struggle will continue until the call 'there is no god but God and Muhammad is the messenger of God' is echoed all over the world.[1]

7

He made good on his promise: in November 1979 and February 1980 widespread riots erupted in the Shi'ite towns of the oil-rich Saudi province of Hasa, exacting dozens of casualties. Similar disturbances occurred in Bahrain during the summer of 1979 and the spring of 1980, while Kuwait became the target of a sustained terrorist and subversive campaign.

A minority faction of approximately one third of the Middle Eastern (and one tenth of the global) Muslim population, the Shi'ites have been traditionally ruled as an underprivileged class by their Sunni counterparts, even in those few countries (such as Iraq) where they constitute the absolute majority. In the decade following the overthrow of the Iraqi monarchy in 1958, the Sunnis occupied 80 per cent of the top Government posts, while Shi'ites held merely 16 per cent. Syria, too, has been ruled during the past few decades by the tiny Alawite community (about 12 per cent of the total population), who are not universally accepted as Shi'ites. Only in Iran, where they enjoy an overwhelming majority of 90 per cent of the population, do Shi'ites exercise unequivocal political control. This has made Iran a strong claimant to Shi'ite spiritual leadership and a potential threat to its neighbouring Sunni regimes.

In 1979 the Iranian regime hoped that the Iraqi community, which had always viewed itself as deprived and disenfranchised, would emulate its example and rise against its own Sunni 'oppressors'. These expectations were fuelled by the location of the holiest Shi'ite shrines – Karbala, Najaf, Kazimain – on Iraqi territory, a potentially powerful weapon in the hands of the clerics in Tehran. The primary hindrance was the Ba'th regime in Baghdad and its absolute leader, Saddam Hussein. The nationalist and secularist ideology of the Ba'th challenged the ideological credentials of the Islamic Republic by offering an alternative path to 'spiritual salvation', while Iraq's position as the strongest Arab military power in the Gulf threatened in practical terms the 'spread of the revolution'. In the words of a militant member of the Iranian leadership, Hujjat al-Islam Sadiq Khalkhali:

> We have taken the path of true Islam and our aim in defeating Saddam Hussein lies in the fact that we consider him the main obstacle to the advance of Islam in the region.[2]

This candid statement of intention was accompanied by a vehement propaganda campaign which called upon the Iraqi people to rise up and overthrow the 'Saddamite regime'. In addition, Iran gave substantial support to the Iraqi Kurds in their longstanding struggle against the central Government (which had been severely disrupted in 1975) and to underground Shi'ite movements in Iraq and, last but not least, initiated terrorist attacks against prominent Iraqi officials.

In September 1980 Saddam, after imposing ruthless counter-measures against his own Shi'ites, concluded that he had little choice but to invade Iran. Khomeini, for his part, wholeheartedly embraced 'the imposed war' as a means of consolidating his regime and furthering his influence throughout the region. The heretic Ba'th Party in Iraq had sown disunion among Muslims for years by propagating the themes of race and nationalism, he argued. Now that Iran was attacked by this aggressive regime, the time had come to put the record straight and to establish the Islamic order in the Middle East. There was no way back and the struggle had to continue until a change of regime had been effected in Baghdad: 'until the complete attainment of the legitimate conditions of the Islamic Republic of Iran and the downfall of the regime governing Baghdad we shall continue the slogan "war, war until victory".'[3]

Eventually, the exorbitant human toll and economic dislocation of the Iran–Iraq War drove the Iranian leadership to more modest and less zealous objectives. Doubts regarding the 'export of the revolution' began surfacing as early as mid-1982, when a loose coalition of political and military figures questioned the logic of carrying on the war. Although these sceptical voices were dismissed by Khomeini, who considered the extension of the war into Iraq as a defensive move 'to protect Islam and the oppressed peoples of Iran and Iraq',[4] the moderates steadily reinforced their position. They were supported in this by the growing public disenchantment, illustrated by widespread demonstrations against the war and the Iranian Government, and a steep drop in the number of recruits for the battlefront. When Khomeini's reluctant order to cease hostilities came at last in July 1988, there was little left of Iran's revolutionary pretensions. The earlier call for the removal of the Gulf regimes – 'Islam proclaims monarchy and hereditary succession wrong and invalid'[5] – had been replaced by appeasing statements underlining the peaceful nature of the Iranian revolution and Tehran's good will towards the Gulf monarchies. The demand for the overthrow of the Ba'th regime in Iraq, in violation of the 1975 Algiers Agreement between the two countries, gave way to an open acceptance of the status quo established in the mid 1970s by that agreement.

Iran's militant version of non-alignment, widely known as the policy of 'neither East nor West', was another casualty of the war, as Tehran embarked on a vigorous campaign aimed at breaking its isolation and reincorporation into the mainstream of international politics. Excluding neither East nor West, this campaign led to the re-establishment of diplomatic relations with the major West European powers and the intensification of Iranian–Soviet relations.[6] Although this process suffered a temporary setback in 1989 following the 'Rushdie affair',[7] the Iran–Iraq War exerted a profoundly sobering effect on Iran's zeal by providing a devastating proof of the limits of armed force as a foreign policy instrument.

With the Ba'th regime still in power in Baghdad, and with its revolutionary message spurned by the decisive majority of Middle Eastern Muslims, including the Iraqi Shi'ites who preferred to fight alongside their compatriots against their co-religionist 'liberators', the Islamic regime's regional outlook had turned a full circle – from the vision of 'the permanent revolution' to the notion of 'Islam in one country'. Khomeini's vision of a universal Islamic community transcending national borders (*umma*) did not disappear altogether from the Iranian political vocabulary after his demise in 1989, but the far-reaching goal of subverting the regional order had succumbed to eight years of futile conflict, and was replaced by acceptance of those conventional 'rules of the game' to which the Islamic Republic had been so adamantly opposed.

The Arab–Israeli conflict

A similar process of disillusionment with respect to the utility of military force took place in Israel. As in the Iranian case, this process was triggered by a protracted and futile war. Instead of using the Iran–Iraq War, which pitted two of its enemies against each other, to try to pursue a negotiated settlement with its neighbours, Israel had sought to impose its own solution on the Arab world. On 6 June 1982 Israeli forces crossed the Lebanese border in strength with the declared aim of 'ensuring peace and security for the Galilee'.

As a preventive move designed to remove a military threat to the north, this was acceptable to many Israelis. Since its expulsion from Jordan in the bloody events of September 1970 (the 'Black September'), when King Hussein slaughtered thousands of Palestinians in a bitter struggle for control over the country, the PLO had managed to build a formidable military infrastructure in Lebanon and to use it as a springboard for successive attacks on civilian targets in the Galilee. With Israel retaliating in a heavy-handed manner, Palestinian–Israeli relations spiralled into a vicious circle, culminating in a full-scale conflagration along the Israeli–Lebanese frontier in the summer of 1981. Israeli settlements in the Galilee were subjected to heavy artillery bombardments. This was contained only with great difficulty through American mediation.

Although the 1981 hostilities were followed by a prolonged lull, Israeli decision-makers were determined to prevent this region from becoming a hostage to the vicissitudes of the Palestinian problem. This essentially preventive outlook was clearly reflected in the official enunciation of war aims, instructing the IDF (Israeli Defence Forces) 'to ensure that all the Galilean settlements were out of the range of terrorist artillery fire'.[8] It soon transpired that the Israeli Cabinet, including Premier Menachem Begin, had been manipulated by Minister of Defence Ariel Sharon, whose own plan was much more ambitious. This was to eliminate the PLO as an independent political factor, cut Syria down to size and neutralize it as a threat to Israel, install a sympathetic regime in Lebanon under the Christian leader Bashir Gumayel, strengthen co-operation with the United States while further undermining Soviet influence:

> In a single stroke, Sharon believed he would reap a historic yield and open glorious vistas before his country. A victory in Lebanon, so the theory went, would accord Israel absolute control over the West Bank by inaugurating an era of unchallenged Israeli domination and, at the same time, generate momentum for further initiatives to impose Israel's will on its neighbours.[9]

This combination of megalomaniacal war aims and their devious presentation to the Cabinet and to the public at large, doomed Sharon's grandiose vision from the outset. The nation could be rallied behind the idea of 'Peace for the Galilee', but most Israelis would have nothing to do with Sharon's dreams of a new regional order. Finding themselves bogged down in the Lebanese quagmire, fighting former friend and foe alike, the IDF began to lose any sense of purpose, and the Israeli public lost its patience. When the folly led to the Sabra and Shatila tragedy - when Lebanese militiamen were allowed into these refugee camps by the IDF to clear them of PLO guerrillas and massacred several hundred innocent civilians – the Cabinet ousted Sharon and gradually disassociated itself from his grand design. The disengagement was completed in 1985.

The collapse of this ill-conceived adventure set in motion a chain reaction which drove the Middle East into greater moderation. The futile war disabused many Israelis of the perception of military force as a be-all and end-all, discredited 'wars by choice' (as Premier Begin so proudly called the Lebanon War), and provided yet more proof that there was no military solution to the Arab–Israeli conflict. At the same time, the war had a sobering impact on the Arab world, best illustrated by the peace plan of the Fez Arab summit of September 1982 which, while still ambiguous about Israel's right to exist, called for a regional peace based on 'the guarantee of peace and security of all states in the region'. More concretely, by destroying the PLO's military infrastructure in Lebanon and denying it a territorial base for activities against Israel, the Lebanon War drove the Palestinians towards the political path, thereby sowing the seeds of the PLO's historic decisions in November and December 1988 to accept Security Council Resolutions 338 and 242 and to recognize Israel's right to exist.

At the same time, the magnitude of their military setback forced the Palestinians to resort to new modes of physical struggle. This culminated in the *intifada* which, in turn, accelerated the evolution of mutual war-weariness unleashed by the Lebanon War. The *intifada* was one of the major watersheds in Palestinian history. It did more to redeem Palestinian dignity and self-esteem than two and a half decades of armed struggle by the PLO. Frustrated with the longstanding neglect and manipulation of their cause by Arabs and Israelis alike, the Palestinians proved capable of becoming self-reliant and rebuffing the Israeli occupation in a fashion they had never done before. This fundamental transformation brought the Palestinian problem to the fore of the Arab–Israeli conflict, and enabled the PLO to cross the Rubicon of recognizing the State of Israel and accepting 'a two-state solution' – Israel, and a Palestinian state on the West Bank and the Gaza Strip. With the Palestinians in the occupied territories anxious to see progress on the diplomatic front that would make their sacrifice worth while, the PLO could hardly afford to remain entrenched in its rejectionist posture, which impressed neither the United States nor the Soviet Union, let alone Israel.

The more moderate stance adopted by the PLO led Washington to put pressure on Israel to open a serious dialogue with authentic Palestinian representatives. Within Israel the reaction to this challenge was mixed. On the one hand, the *intifada* was met by a defiant mood by the right wing (including influential figures within the ruling Likud Party), which viewed this development as the continuation by other means of the longstanding Arab desire to destroy Israel, and advocated a tough policy in the territories. On the other hand, the uprising brought home the mounting costs of the continued occupation, thereby reinforcing the evolving general recognition of the need for a historic compromise between Arabs and Jews. This awareness was clearly reflected in successive public opinion polls at the time, which indicated that nearly *two-thirds* of the Israeli public were willing to talk to the PLO, despite the vehement rejection of such a move by their own Government.

Prime Minister Yitzhak Shamir, despite himself, began to edge in a more conciliatory direction. In early 1989 he proposed elections in the occupied territories to choose representatives who could then discuss some future form of self-government, as a first stage towards a comprehensive settlement. He apparently hoped that such elections might generate a local leadership, unencumbered by the political baggage carried by PLO leader Yasser Arafat and his colleagues. The plan was vague in that neither the electorate nor the permissible subjects for discussion were precisely defined. Nevertheless it contained promise and excited some interest. This alarmed Shamir's own party, the Likud, and he began to backtrack. Meanwhile, the PLO was wary, insisting that the only purpose of elections would be to elect the leaders of a new and independent Palestinian state.

In an effort to break this deadlock, President Husni Mubarak of Egypt suggested that Israel and a select Palestinian delegation meet to discuss Shamir's proposals. The Palestinian delegation would be drawn from within and without the occupied territories but would not have formal PLO links. Capitalizing on the idea, US Secretary of State James Baker sought to move matters forward by identifying possible Palestinian interlocutors who might have the confidence of their own community as well as be tolerable to the Israelis. His efforts, however, came to naught as hardline circles within the Likud forced Shamir effectively to abandon his plan. The coalition with the Labour Party collapsed as a result.

The decline of communism and the Middle East

As the *intifada* subsided, its participants battered and exhausted by continual rioting, strikes and harsh Israeli policing, so did world interest in the Arab–Israeli conflict. This decline of interest was further affected by the end of the cold war, the growing turmoil inside the Soviet state, and the all-absorbing American preoccupation with Europe.

Both Arabs and Israelis were naturally wary of these developments. In the past they had sensed a reverse correlation between the state of global detente and the room for manoeuvre of the smaller actors: the warmer great power relations, the narrower the lesser actors' freedom of action. For this reason they have traditionally viewed with much alarm any manifestations of super-power detente. Special dissatisfaction with the thaw in superpower relations was voiced in Damascus, which did not attempt to disguise its abhorrence of Mikhail Gorbachev's 'new political thinking'. This Syrian concern was not difficult to understand. Mikhail Gorbachev's readiness to sacrifice longstanding Soviet interests – and allies – for the sake of superpower detente did not bypass the Middle East. In a marked departure from the traditional Soviet line which (while disagreeing with many Arab positions) unequivocally sided with the Arabs in their feud with Israel, Moscow's 'new political thinking' sought to portray the USSR as an impartial broker amenable to both parties to the conflict. Putting the Arab and the Israeli causes on a par, Soviet policy began to urge *both Arabs and Israelis* to

> renounce their rejectionist stance and reach a compromise solution, [based on a] constructive balance of interests ... which would provide assurance and guarantee of security for everyone, both for the Arab countries and Palestine, and for Israel.[10]

This change of heart was accompanied by unprecedentedly severe criticism of Syria's quest for 'strategic parity' with Israel (deplored by Moscow as 'diverting attention from the question of achieving security and peace in the Middle East'),[11] a visible drop in Soviet arms transfers to Damascus, and a perceptible improvement in Soviet–Israeli relations, including the initiation of a massive exodus of Soviet Jews to Israel.

With the crumbling of East European communism added to Gorbachev's 'new thinking', the radical regimes in the Middle East were ultimately convinced that the old 'rules of the game' had been irrevocably reversed to their detriment. Since the Soviet Union was no longer the superpower it had previously been, and since the unreserved support of the East European states could no longer be taken for granted, the commonplace conclusion in the Middle East was that the region had been left to the mercy of the only remaining superpower, the United States, and its 'lackeys', first and foremost Israel.

This gloomy assessment had an immediate impact on the Middle Eastern political map. Reluctant to compromise their hold on the levers of power, and fearful of a spillover of the revolutionary process in Eastern Europe to the Middle East, many regimes quickly adopted a series of preventive measures to shore up their position. The crumbling of the *ancien régime* in Eastern Europe was attributed to the socio-political ineptitude of communism, to which the Middle Eastern regimes (including the socialist Ba'th parties in Syria and Iraq) had never adhered. According to Saddam Hussein, the collapse of the Soviet Bloc lay in the fact that 'Communist thought chooses the temporary and easy way', as opposed to Arab socialism whose 'option is more complicated, because the easy solution is not always the correct one'.[12] The Iranians, for their part, interpreted the 'disintegration of the foundations of anti-God, anti-religious and anti-prophet structures throughout the world' as a proof that their piety was the only viable political course. In those Arab countries, such as Jordan and Algeria, where the hold on power was far from absolute, steps were taken towards liberalization of the political systems.

On the external front, the most remarkable outcome of the decline of Soviet power was the significant weakening of the militant Arab camp, illustrated most vividly by Egypt's reincorporation into the mainstream of Arab politics despite its peace treaty with Israel. In May 1989 Egypt took part in the all-Arab summit in Casablanca for the first time since its expulsion from the Arab League a decade earlier after the Camp David accord. Four months later the radical ruler of Libya, Mu'amar Gaddafi, paid an official visit to Egypt, and in December 1989 President Hafiz Asad of Syria, who for more than a decade had spearheaded the Arab campaign against the separate Egyptian–Israeli peace, swallowed his pride and restored full diplomatic relations with Egypt.

Worst of all for the Arabs was the mass exodus of Soviet Jews. New immigration laws denied them their former and generally preferred escape route to the United States, so they emigrated *en masse* to Israel. With up to 1 million Soviet Jews expected to travel to Israel during the 1990s and some 10,000 a month already arriving, the Arabs feared that Israel could retain the demographic advantage over the Palestinians and feel under no compulsion to yield at all on the occupied territories. Indeed, as Shamir incautiously noted, the territories might now be needed to settle the new immigrants. The Arabs suddenly had to contemplate Israel's position being strengthened rather than weakened over the long term.

Saddam Hussein gathered Arab leaders to address this crisis in May 1990. Arab bluster with regard to Jewish immigration had failed to have any impact, and they now sought to warn the international community that unless the flow of Soviet Jews was stemmed frustration could spill over into war. Yet none of the front-line Arab states appeared in any position to take on Israel nor was inclined to do so. The old divisions within the Arab world militated against a co-ordinated strategy, as illustrated by the absence of Syria and Algeria from the summit. Syria was still bogged down in Lebanon and weakened the most by the decline of its Soviet ally. President Mubarak of Egypt, though one of the first to warn of a possible war, honoured his country's peace treaty with Israel and was anxious to avoid gratuitous affront to the United States. He had therefore been searching desperately for evidence that Shamir had not completely closed the door on negotiations.

King Hussein of Jordan had long been considered by Israelis the most amenable of all Arabs, even though his domestic weakness has never permitted him to translate his interest in co-existence into a positive peace settlement. This domestic weakness was becoming chronic. Like other non-oil-producing Arab states, his economy was in trouble. A recent attempt to stem the bubbling domestic cauldron through a measure of democratization allowed a political breakthrough by Islamic Fundamentalists. He feared that Israel might seek to exploit this vulnerability – that a right-wing Likud government – which lacked the Labour Party's commitment to the preservation of the Hashemite dynasty – could adopt a deliberate policy of driving Palestinians into his country across the Jordan river to make way for the new immigrants.

King Hussein's weakness had led him to look to Iraq for support. Mutual vulnerability and dislike of Syria had encouraged close connections between the two already during the Iran–Iraq War, when the Jordanian port of Aqaba became Baghdad's main point of entry for military supplies. In the wake of the war this connection was expanded to include limited military co-operation. Here the King was walking a tightrope, since it was evident that any Iraqi military move towards the Jordanian–Israeli border would inevitably trigger a harsh Israeli response.

At this time, however, the Israeli political élite was focused less on these possibilities than on the formation of a new government. Since the Likud–Labour coalition had fallen apart in March 1990 over how to respond to US proposals for the peace process, first Shimon Peres of the Labour Party and then Yitzhak Shamir tried to put together a narrower coalition supported by the small parties. The process was unedifying, with very public bargaining over personalities, portfolios and policies. Shamir's eventual success produced the most right-wing government in Israel's political history.

This inevitably meant the renewal of pressure on Israel. Internally, the *intifada* showed signs of revival following the murder of seven Arabs by a deranged Israeli in May. Palestinian resentment and frustration were fed by the flow of new immigrants into Israel, although for the moment the number settling in the occupied territories was minimal. Even more disturbing than the continued hostility in the occupied territories was the evidence that Israel's Arabs were also becoming radicalized, a development with potentially dire consequences for Israel's internal security.

Also striking was the depth of American irritation with Israel. President Bush and Secretary of State Baker, who took these developments very personally, felt slighted by Shamir and were demonstrating increasing disregard for Israeli sensitivities. Baker raised the question of the legitimacy of Israel's position in East Jerusalem and the possible value of UN observers in the occupied territories. Congress was also becoming impatient. There were suggestions that the growing detente might allow a reduced US commitment to the Middle East – Israel no longer seemed such a great strategic asset. With funds for foreign aid limited by budgetary stringency and many new demands from former communist states, a loss of aid was a real possibility.

Special ire in Jerusalem was caused in January by the suggestion of Republican Senator Robert Dole that US military aid to Israel (as well as to Egypt, Turkey and Pakistan) be reduced by 5 per cent. The mere hint that US economic backing might be withdrawn could trigger a financial crisis in Israel. Actual loss of aid would make it harder both to keep the Israeli defence forces up to scratch and to absorb Soviet Jews.

There was now a growing consensus in the West blaming Israel for a lack of progress on a durable peace settlement. During the 1980s European attempts to map out a distinctive line on the Middle East had led to tensions in US–European relations. Divergent policies on the Middle East were as much a source of transatlantic dispute as the more familiar concerns over NATO doctrine and burden-sharing. However, the shift in PLO policy in 1988 leading to the opening of a US–PLO dialogue, bequeathed by Reagan to Bush, and then the coolness to the Shamir Government evident in the Bush Administration, narrowed the European–American gap.

When in the summer American peace efforts became unstuck with the break-up of the Israeli coalition and the termination of US–PLO links after the latter failed to condemn in sufficiently unequivocal terms an abortive attempt by one of its factions to carry out an indiscriminate attack on Israeli civilian targets, the Europeans tried to get things moving. In late July 1990 the European Community's 'troika' – Gerry Collins, Jacques Poos, and Gianni de Michelis, Foreign Ministers of Ireland, Luxembourg and Italy respectively (representing the immediate past, future and current Presidents of the Council of Ministers) – visited Israel and Tunis where they met the PLO leadership. They called for the resumption of Middle East peace efforts as a matter of urgency. Waving the stick and the carrot in front of Israel, de Michelis indicated that movement of the peace process might lead to improved access to the post-1992 Community, while in the case of deterioration in the Middle East 'co-operation on economic, social and cultural matters will become much more difficult'.

Western countries were no longer arguing among themselves on the Middle East as they had done so often in the past. The political assessments were similar. In the middle of 1990, they were frustrated by the lack of the sort of political breakthroughs that had become the norm in Europe, and especially exasperated by the intransigence of the Israeli Government. Yet they judged that the *intifada* provided its own punishment and were generally comforted by the lack of an evident dynamic towards war.

If there was one element in the equation which could upset this general stability it was the growing unpredictability of Iraqi policy. Since the spring of 1990 Saddam Hussein had been sending confusing signals of both extremism and moderation. For the moment Western leaders felt that it was worth reinforcing the latter tendency. They were soon to change their minds.

CHAPTER 2
Saddam's Crisis

Saddam Hussein was always an unlikely moderate. The use of physical force to promote his political ends had been the hallmark of the Iraqi leader's career from the start: his rise to power in July 1979, for example, was followed by a bloody purge in which hundreds of party officials and military officers, some of whom were close friends and associates, perished. Nevertheless, as far as Iraq's external relations were concerned, Saddam's bark had always been harsher than his bite, as he had preferred to pursue his goals with the lowest risk and greatest economy possible.

During the 1970s, while acting as Vice-President but the *de facto* 'strong man in Baghdad', he effectively pursued an overly pragmatic line which ran counter to his party's outspoken radicalism. In September 1970 he prevented Iraqi troops, then deployed on Jordanian soil, from intervening to stop the bloodshed between the Jordanian Army and the PLO. Similarly, Iraq's military support to the co-ordinated Egyptian–Syrian attack against Israel in October 1973 was extremely limited, and was withdrawn at the first available opportunity. Then, in March 1975, Saddam made a far-reaching concession to the Iranian Shah by concluding the so-called Algiers Agreement which settled the longstanding territorial dispute between the two countries over the Shatt al-Arab waterway on terms favourable to Iran. He observed this agreement throughout the latter part of the 1970s.

Indeed, contrary to the common wisdom, the hazardous move of invading Iran was not motivated by imperial dreams and megalomaniac aspirations. War in the autumn of 1980 could not have been more ill-timed for Saddam Hussein's political career. He assumed the presidency in July 1979, at a time when his country enjoyed unprecedented economic prosperity. Due to the world oil boom Iraqi export revenues had risen to $21 billion in 1979 and $26 billion in 1980, and during the months preceding the invasion these revenues were running at an annual rate of $33 billion, enabling Saddam to carry out ambitious development programmes.[1]

War could only put these achievements at risk and, in consequence, render Saddam's domestic standing more tenuous.

Hence, following the overthrow of the Shah in January 1979, Saddam did not attempt to take advantage of the civil strife in Iran to extract territorial or political concessions, but welcomed the revolutionary regime in Tehran, went out of his way to placate it, and emphasized his determination to continue to observe the status quo established by the Algiers Agreement. As late as the spring of 1980 Saddam was publicly airing his fears of Iraq's disintegration into Sunni, Shi'ite and Kurdish statelets.[2]

Only after his gestures of goodwill had been spurned by the Iranians did Saddam change tack. Initially he sought to counter Iranian-inspired Shi'ite restiveness within Iraq, by clamping down on the main Shi'ite underground organization, the *Da'wa* Party ('the Islamic call'), and launching a series of verbal attacks against Ayatollah Khomeini. He also supported Iranian separatist elements, such as the Kurds in northern Iran and the Arabs in the southern Iranian province of Khuzestan, and attempted to orchestrate the Arab Gulf states into a unified front against the Iranian threat.

These countermeasures were significantly upgraded after April 1980, following an abortive Iranian-sponsored attempt on the life of Iraq's Deputy Premier, Tariq Aziz. Deeply shaken by Tehran's ability to hit at the heart of his regime, Saddam resorted to draconian measures against the Shi'ite opposition. Within a fortnight, Iraq's most prominent Shi'ite religious authority, Ayatollah Muhammad Bakr al-Sadr, who had been under house arrest for several months, was executed, together with his sister, as were hundreds of Shi'ite political prisoners. Saddam effectively sealed the southern part of Iraq, denying foreign, particularly Iranian, worshippers any access to the Shi'i holy shrines. The extent of his anxiety was further illustrated by the expulsion of some 100,000 Iraqi Shi'ites from the country.[3]

As these measures failed Saddam invaded Iran, as a pre-emptive strike to shore up his personal rule. He apparently believed that a limited campaign would suffice to convince the revolutionary regime in Tehran to desist from its attempts to overthrow him, and did not intend to engage in a prolonged drawn-out conflict. If he entertained aspirations beyond the containment of the Iranian danger – as he may have done – they were not the reasons for launching the war but were incidental. As Foreign Minister Aziz put it: 'We want neither to destroy Iran nor to occupy it permanently, because this country is a neighbour with which we will remain linked by geographical and historical bonds and common interests.'[4]

Saddam's limited objectives were also demonstrated by his war strategy. Rather than dealing a mortal blow to the Iranian Army and seeking to topple the revolutionary regime, he sought to confine the war by restricting the Army's goals, means and targets. His territorial aims did not go beyond the Shatt al-Arab and a small portion of Khuzestan. As to means, the invasion was carried out by less than half of the Iraqi Army – five of twelve divisions. Saddam's initial strategy avoided targets of civilian and economic value in favour of attacks almost exclusively on military targets. Only after the Iranians escalated by attacking non-military targets did the Iraqis respond in kind. Most importantly, on 28 September, merely five days after the invasion, Saddam voluntarily halted his troops, while they were still moving forward, and announced his readiness to cease hostilities and to enter into peace negotiations.[5] Hence, when the war turned out to be a far more tortuous experience than he had ever feared, Saddam turned every stone and bent every principle in an attempt to survive this monster of his own making.

The outcome was further moderation in Iraq's regional and global outlook. In March 1979 Saddam had triumphantly hosted in Baghdad an all-Arab conference which expelled Egypt from the Arab League for making peace with Israel; a year later he was desperately pleading with the excommunicated Egyptian President, Anwar Sadat, for military support. During the following years, as Egypt developed into an important military provider, Saddam would toil tirelessly to pave the way for its return to the Arab fold.

Furthermore, whenever his personal survival so required, Saddam had no qualms about accommodating Israel which, for its part, seemed increasingly disillusioned with the prospects of the restoration of a favourable regime in Tehran.[6] In 1985 he sought to buy Israel's acquiescence in the laying of an Iraqi oil pipeline to the Jordanian port town of Aqaba by offering it $700 million over ten years. Covert overtures to Israel were paralleled by growing public indications of readiness to reach a political accommodation with the Jewish state. In 1982 Saddam participated in the Fez Arab summit, which tacitly accepted a two-state solution to the Arab–Israeli conflict. Subsequently, he even voiced public support for peace negotiations between the Arabs and Israel, emphasizing that 'no Arab leader looks forward to the destruction of Israel' and that any solution to the conflict would require 'the existence of a secure state for the Israelis'.[7]

This moderation was sustained into the post-war period. Having survived the deadliest threat to his personal rule, Saddam had no inclination to risk his regime by further foreign entanglements. Even though it was Tehran which eventually pleaded for a cease-fire, the end of the Iran–Iraq War did not imply a lull in Saddam's struggle for political survival. The nature of the threat to his regime had, of course, fundamentally changed as the mullahs in Tehran were no longer calling for his blood. Instead he faced the daunting task of reconstructing Iraq, so as to prove to his subjects that the eight-year war had been won. This, in turn, meant that Saddam's personal interest could be best served by moderation and collaboration rather than antagonism and confrontation, by domestic stability and a relaxed international atmosphere rather than turmoil and heightened tensions.

Hence, the end of the war was followed by unprecedented manifestations of political openness on Saddam's part, such as a public commitment to end the Ba'th's monopoly on power, to establish a democratic multi-party system in Iraq, and to hold direct free elections for the country's presidency. These measures were accompanied by greater liberalization of the Iraqi economy, a process begun in the mid 1970s and accelerated during the war. Price controls on all goods were lifted, and an attempt was made to attract capital from Gulf states and foreign companies. Many state-owned corporations were sold off to the private sector at very attractive prices, and there was much speculation about the eventual privatization of all state enterprises except oil and the military industry.

Equally indicative of Saddam's interest in tranquillity was the continuation of his moderate international policy. He did not revert to his pre-war radical rhetoric but sustained and expanded collaboration with moderate Arabs in an attempt to orchestrate them into a unified bloc that would resist Iranian hegemony, promote the Palestinian cause and pressure Syria. This objective was crowned with success in February 1989 with the formation of the Arab Co-operation Council (ACC) comprising Egypt, North Yemen, Jordan, and Iraq. A month later, during an official visit to Baghdad by King Fahd of Saudi Arabia, a bilateral non-aggression pact was concluded.

Saddam also sustained his positive approach towards a negotiated settlement of the Arab–Israeli conflict, playing an important role, together with President Mubarak of Egypt, in sponsoring the PLO's historic recognition of Israel's right to exist in November and December 1988. Were it not for Iraq's and Egypt's readiness to shield the PLO from Syrian wrath, the Palestinians' political room for manoeuvre would have been severely constrained. Saddam's growing acceptance of Israel was also underlined by the evolution of tacit Iraqi–Israeli collaboration against Syria's interests and its presence in Lebanon. This collaboration was mainly expressed in Israel's abstention from intercepting Iraqi arms shipments to the Christians in Beirut despite its ability to do so. There were also reports that the Israeli port of Haifa was used by Iraq as a transit station for shipping tanks and heavy equipment to General Michel Aoun, the self-styled Maronite President who declared 'a war of liberation' to drive the Syrians out of Lebanon.[8]

The West supports Saddam

France had taken the Western lead in courting Saddam. As early as 1963, when the war over Algeria was concluded, France under General de Gaulle had begun to reappraise its Middle Eastern policy, which in the past had been based on deep hostility towards Arab nationalism and close co-operation with Israel (to the point of helping create Israel's nuclear capability). It now went into complete reverse. De Gaulle judged that the future lay with the Arabs and turned against Israel at the time of the 1967 war.

The radical Arab regimes were outside the traditional British sphere of influence in the Middle East, which was still largely based on the monarchies. Taking up the cause of Arab nationalism softened what might otherwise have been stormy relations with France's old North African colonies. It also offered an acceptable alternative for radical regimes which did not wish to be completely dependent on the Soviet Union for arms. However, there were limits to success with this policy. During the 1970s, after the death of Nasser, Egypt under President Sadat gradually moved closer to the Americans. With Syria there were problems because of France's lingering sympathy for the Christian community in Lebanon. Iraq was thus a far more promising avenue and here French policy appeared to pay dividends.

It had been targeted from the moment of the Ba'thi takeover in July 1968. Saddam, for his part, quickly recognized the immense economic, military, and technological potential attending a closer relationship with France. Already in June 1972 he had paid an official visit to Paris, the first ever to a Western capital, where he agreed to sell France nearly a quarter of the oil produced by the Iraq Company for Oil Operations (ICOO). In the autumn of 1974 the French Prime Minister, Jacques Chirac, paid an official visit to Baghdad. The next year it was Saddam's turn in Paris; back came the French Premier, now Raymond Barre, to Baghdad in the summer of 1977. Before long France was Iraq's largest arms supplier after the Soviet Union. In 1976 France agreed to sell Iraq the Osiraq nuclear reactor, which was to be destroyed by the Israeli Air Force in a famous raid in June 1981.

Following the Iranian revolution the French stepped up their support for Saddam. They were fearful of Islamic fundamentalism and saw the Iraqi leader as a bulwark of secularism. This was in addition to his capacity to counter Syrian influence. With the outbreak of the Iran–Iraq War the arms relationship between the two countries grew ever closer – in the first six years of the war France gained some $15–17 billion in military contracts, with an additional $5 billion spent on civilian purchases. A special deal allowed the Iraqis to use French Étendard aircraft and Exocet missiles, while notionally on loan, to escalate the war with Iran into Gulf shipping.

The British had been somewhat more circumspect. They were aware of Saddam's ruthlessness towards his internal opponents and his brutal treatment of the Kurdish minority. But ruthlessness is a common attribute among successful Middle Eastern dictators, and positive tendencies had been identified in the talk of political reform, an evident tilt towards the West, a generally calm approach towards the Arab–Israeli dispute. In 1989, with the war over, there was hope that Iraq might now turn to domestic reconstruction and some lucrative orders for British companies. A dialogue was set in motion and the results were impressive: by 1990 Britain was Iraq's third largest trading partner. While mindful of the less attractive aspects of Saddam's regime, the Foreign Office was unconvinced of the utility of ostracizing Iraq. As an official briefing paper in September 1988 put it:

> We believe it better to maintain a dialogue with others if we want to influence their actions. Punitive measures such as unilateral sanctions would not be effective in changing Iraq's behaviour over chemical weapons, and would damage British interests to no avail.[9]

In July 1989 London had even considered breaking its previous self-denying ordinance not to sell weapons which could 'materially enhance the danger to each other' to the former disputants in the Iran–Iraq War. Actively encouraged by British Aerospace, as well as by the Ministries of Trade and Industry and of Defence, the Cabinet was asked to consider the sale of about sixty Hawk trainer aircraft to Baghdad. Though dressed up by time limits on both the initial delivery and the associated weapons, had the sale gone through it would have marked a major gesture in Saddam's direction. However, the sale was blocked by John Major, in one of the few decisions taken during his brief sojourn as Foreign Secretary.

Like its allies in London and Paris, the US Administration had gradually come to believe that Saddam could be progressively weaned away from his past militancy and that Iraq could become a source of reason and moderation as well as valuable contracts. For Washington Iraq's most promising feature was that it was Iran's enemy. Since the overthrow of the Shah and the hostage crisis of 1980–81 the regime led by the Ayatollah Khomeini had become something of an obsession for decision-makers in Washington. Hence, if Iraq could keep Iran in check then that in itself was a cause for commendation. So much the better that American friends in the region, such as Saudi Arabia, Jordan and Egypt, also viewed Iraq in the same light.

The first agricultural credits – which were to become the mainstay of the relationship – were agreed in 1982. Some $300 million was made available to buy American produce. At the same time, amid warnings from US intelligence agencies that Iraq was on the verge of defeat, satellite imagery and communications intercepts on Iranian dispositions were passed to Baghdad, and the next year an official blind eye was taken to the seepage of American arms into Iraq from Jordan and Kuwait, who were legitimate clients. As with France, an opportunity was seen to wean Iraq away from its traditional dependence on the Soviet Union, which at this time was unsuccessfully courting Iran as the most strategically significant of the two warring states.[10] By 1984 Iraq had done enough to allow the Reagan Administration to claim that it no longer sponsored acts of international terrorism and so diplomatic relations, severed in 1967 following the Six Day War, were restored. By 1987 Iraq had become one of the main US customers of agricultural and food products, being promised $1 billion credit, the largest loan of its kind to any single country worldwide.

A crisis developed between the two countries following the revelations of the extraordinary Iran–Contra affair, during which high-ranking officials in the Reagan Administration had conspired to get arms to Iran in return for the release of US hostages held by pro-Iranian groups in Lebanon. Embarrassment over this affair perhaps made Washington more willing than might otherwise have been the case to agree to a request from Kuwait (then seen as Iraq's ally) to reflag its ships and provide them with protection against Iranian attacks, which were themselves retaliation for Iraq's attempt to harass Iran's oil trade, and then to accept Saddam's apologies when one of his aircraft mistakenly attacked an American warship, USS *Stark*, in 1987, killing thirty-seven sailors.

Yet while the Reagan and then the Bush Administrations had a consistent policy of cultivating Saddam there was a tension in the relationship, resulting largely from indignation in Congress over Saddam's human rights record, and in particular his repression of the Kurds, including the use of chemical weapons. Saddam had turned on the Kurds with great brutality as the cease-fire with Iran came into effect, and in a number of cases had used chemical weapons. Senate Foreign Relations Committee staff members had been active in publicizing this activity, and it led to Senator Clairborne Pell initiating what was to become a familiar pattern of Congressional attempts to punish Iraq being countered by Administration resistance to sanctions. Pell's bill, starkly named *The Prevention of Genocide Act 1988*, was passed without opposition in the Senate but succumbed to delaying tactics in the House of Representatives and the close of the Congressional session on the eve of the

1988 presidential election. If passed, it would have required the President to impose a trade embargo on Baghdad until it could be certified that Iraq was no longer practising genocide. When the Bush Administration examined policy towards Iraq in its strategic review of 1989 it came to the same conclusion as its predecessor. By 1990 Iraqi loans under the agricultural credits scheme had exceeded $1 billion, while annual trade between Iraq and the United States had grown from around $500 million in the early 1980s to over $3.5 billion.

The message from friendly Arab states, such as Egypt and Saudi Arabia, was that Iraq was well worth some attention and could be turned towards a moderate posture. The Administration's disposition to accept this line was only slightly ruffled by a series of revelations from FBI and Federal Reserve Bank investigators who, after a raid on 4 August, had uncovered the role of the Atlanta branch of the Italian Banca Nazionale Lavoro (BNL) in financing the build-up of Iraq's military machine by diverting agricultural credits. The bank began in 1984 exploiting the US line of credit for agricultural exports to Iraq. In 1986 it had been caught when Italy decided to ban further credits to Iraq because of a dispute over payment on a major naval contract (eventually settled in 1989 on the basis of a substantial Italian loss). With the war going badly, Iraq was generally considered to be a bad risk at this time. BNL then began to lend money in secret, using its high credit rating to borrow money from other banks which it then lent to Iraq at a higher rate. In 1987 this moved into the funding of military projects. When the scandal broke there were some $4 billion of loans outstanding. News of these revelations generated immediate concern in State and CIA over their impact on US–Iraqi relations.

They were not, however, seen as a reason in themselves for reappraising these relations. The Administration's review came to orthodox conclusions, expressed in National Security Decision Directive 26 (NSDD-26), signed on 2 October. It judged that

> Normal relations between the US and Iraq would serve our longer-term interests in both the Gulf and the Middle East. The US government should propose economic and political incentives for Iraq to moderate its behaviour and to increase our influence with Iraq.
>
> As a means of developing access to and influence with the Iraqi defence establishment, the US should consider sales of non-lethal forms of military assistance, eg training courses and medical exchanges, on a case-by-case basis.

The only nod in the direction of anxieties over actual rather than potential Iraqi behaviour was a readiness to consider sanctions and urge allies to do so if Baghdad resumed use of chemical weapons, used biological weapons or tried to develop nuclear weapons.[11] The overall tenor was positive. It was assumed that Saddam would respond to inducements and also, as the intelligence community predicted at the time, that Iraq was so exhausted by its recent war that there was little risk of it turning aggressive toward its neighbours for two to three years.

A few days later, on 6 October, Iraqi Foreign Minister Tariq Aziz visited Secretary of State James Baker in Washington. Aziz accused the Administration of having a 'disturbing' policy towards Iraq, of which he saw evidence in the allegations of bribery and corruption emanating from the BNL scandal. Baker was conciliatory, insisting that no harm to Iraq was intended, that the United States desired good relations and that questions of chemical weapons and nuclear proliferation should be seen as a 'general' problem rather than one specific to Iraq. Aziz set a test. At that time the Agriculture Department was prepared to offer only $400 million new credits. Aziz was concerned that such a cut from the previous year would be seen as a vote of no confidence in Iraqi debt policy. Moreover, he told Baker that this was 'an explosive issue – a government must feed its people'.

Baker set the request for new guarantees worth $1 billion in motion. Those in charge of the BNL investigation were appalled and worked to persuade the Agriculture and State Departments to deny the Iraqi request. The case they produced was devastating. The money which had been made available to Iraq had not always been used to buy agricultural commodities but had been diverted to purchases of military hardware, and even nuclear-sensitive equipment. When agricultural goods were bought bribes were demanded from US businesses if they wished to secure orders. Even then many of the goods received were being bartered with the Soviet Union and other Eastern European states in return for military equipment.

When the issue was addressed at a meeting on 13 October in the Agriculture Department it was minuted that 'although additional research needs to be done, it appears more and more likely that CCC-guaranteed funds and/or commodities may have been diverted from Iraq to third parties in exchange for military hardware'. The same day, a State Department memo observed that the BNL investigation would 'blow the roof' off the Iraq food export programme. 'If smoke indicates fire, we may be facing a four-alarm blaze in the near future.' Even without this scandal, the Federal Reserve Bank's board opposed more credit guarantees for Iraq because of doubts over Iraq's general credit worthiness. It did not seem sensible to allocate one fifth of the credit scheme's fiscal year 1990 budget to a country with such a poor debt-servicing record.

Baker was not prepared to have his Iraq policy blown off course in this manner. His officials decided to assign blame to 'corrupt elements' in

Baghdad and put pressure on the Agriculture and Treasury Departments to authorize the new loans. The inclination was to see the BNL scandal as a storm that would blow over if Iraqi sensitivities were not too bruised, rather than as evidence of something rotten at the heart of Iraqi procurement and debt policy. Those who took this latter view received scant attention. Baker himself contacted Agriculture Secretary Clayton Yeutter to drop his objections. On 8 November 'on foreign policy grounds', another $1 billion loan programme was agreed. The only concession to concerns over Iraq's worthiness was that it was to be disbursed in two instalments.[12]

The arguments in London, Paris, Bonn and Washington remained the same: Iraq's war with Iran was over and it was a time for domestic reconstruction and thus good business opportunities. Saddam was undoubtedly ruthless, but at least he was no longer a Soviet client and he had shown a potential for flexibility on the Arab–Israeli dispute. There was no international support for ostracizing the regime – therefore the only logical policy was to cultivate it to advantage, claiming that this could encourage Saddam to stick to a more moderate path. Meanwhile they turned a blind eye to the intensive efforts being made by Iraqis to procure the most sensitive military technologies – especially from Europe.

The relationship deteriorates

Policies based on a hope of Iraqi moderation suffered a severe setback when in the spring of 1990 Saddam made an about-turn in a series of ruthless moves. The most sensational were the execution of the journalist Farzad Bazoft on charges of espionage in March 1990, followed on 2 April by a threat to use chemical weapons against Israel.

A common retrospective explanation of these moves is that they were designed to serve as a smoke-screen to disguise Saddam's aggressive designs against Kuwait, and to prepare the region for its occupation. It has even been argued that Saddam had already conceived of the invasion in the mid-1980s and made the final decision to occupy Kuwait in February 1990. He then engineered an acrimonious encounter with the West to rally the Arabs behind his regime, to secure American and Israeli assurances that he would not be attacked under any circumstances, and to build up the pressure on Kuwait, from which he was trying at the time to extract large sums of money to finance Iraq's economic reconstruction.[13]

This theory, however, fails to take account of Saddam's heavy dependence on the political goodwill and economic support of the West in his effort to revamp the Iraqi economy from the havoc left by the Iran–Iraq War. Rather than a ferocious confrontation with the West and Israel, a low profile and a conciliatory approach would have been more likely to help gain acquiescence in the occupation of Kuwait. The explanation for these events would seem to lie in Saddam's growing desperation during the first half of 1990.

Saddam had a paranoiac obsession with personal and political survival, natural for one operating in one of the region's most hazardous political systems. He had never lost sight of his predecessors' fate. When in July 1958 the pro-Western Hashemite dynasty, which had ruled Iraq since its inception in 1921, was overthrown by a military coup headed by General Abd al-Karim Qassem, the mutilated body of the Iraqi regent was dragged by a raging mob in the streets of Baghdad. Five years later, Qassem's bullet–ridden corpse was screened on television to the entire nation. Saddam was determined to use whatever means were required to avoid a similar fate. 'I know that there are scores of people plotting to kill me,' he told a personal guest shortly after assuming the presidency, 'and this is not difficult to understand . . . However, I am far cleverer than they are. I know they are conspiring to kill me long before they actually start planning to do so. This enables me to get them before they have the faintest chance of striking at me.'[14]

That this candid revelation reflected Saddam's mindset could be evidenced by the long trail of victims left during his years in power – both as the *de facto* leader under President Bakr and in the top spot. Pre-empting any dissent through systematic purges and subordinating all domestic and foreign policies to the ultimate goal of political survival, he had transformed the ruling Ba'th Party into an extension of his will and to cow his subjects into unquestioning submission. Yet the protracted war against Iran had somewhat loosened Saddam's grip over the officer corps, the main potential threat to his personal rule. In the late war years he confronted what nearly amounted to an open mutiny, when the military leadership questioned his ability to lead Iraq to victory. He survived this challenge because his Generals were not after political power (but rather after the freedom to run the war according to their professional judgement), and because he was sensible enough to give in to their demands – only to purge them at a later stage. But the barrier of fear had been broken, and after the war he apparently confronted several attempts on his life. The first took place in November 1988 and reportedly involved a plan to shoot down his plane on his way from a state visit to Egypt. Another attempt, which reportedly occurred in northern Iraq in late 1988 or early 1989, was ruthlessly suppressed with dozens, if not hundreds of officers executed. The attempt must have been particularly worrying for Saddam since it involved officers from the Republican Guard, his élite bodyguard force. A third coup attempt was aborted in September 1989, and in January

1990 he narrowly escaped an assassination attempt by army officers while he was riding in his car through Baghdad.

There was another major source of frustration. If Iraq did in fact win the war, as its people were urged to believe, the fruits of victory had to be formally sealed, the hatchets officially buried. Then the 65,000 war prisoners could return to their families, alongside hundreds of thousands of demobilized troops. Life would return to normal. Reconstruction would be under way. None of these things happened. The UN-orchestrated peace talks in Geneva quickly ran into a blind alley, as Iran would not negotiate directly with Iraq. In the lack of progress Saddam was forced to look to his guns. The formidable Army remained by and large mobilized, costing the destitute Iraqi treasury a fortune. The social consequences were no less worrying. An entire generation was lost: hundreds of thousands of young conscripts who had been eighteen when the war started were twenty-six by its end and still under arms. They had no private life; they could neither study nor work nor get married. Now that the war had been 'won' they began questioning the necessity of their continued mobilization. Saddam's attempt to defuse the boiling social problem by ordering partial demobilization in 1989 backfired, as it proved beyond the capacity of the shaky Iraqi economy to absorb the huge numbers of young men pouring into the labour market.[15]

There was little else in the foreign policy sphere to provide much comfort. Apart from the formation of the Arab Co-operation Council (ACC), which had boosted his prestige in the Arab world, Saddam's regional policy had little to show for itself. The clash he initiated with Syria in Lebanon brought no results, as his protégé, the maverick General Michel Aoun, made no headway towards his declared goal of 'liberating Lebanon from the Syrian occupation'. Moreover, at the Arab summit in Casablanca in May 1989 he suffered a public humiliation when his proposal for the replacement of the Syrian military presence in Lebanon by a genuine Arab League force was rejected in the face of tough opposition by the Syrian President Asad.

Looking beyond the Middle East, Saddam's anxiety over the stability of his regime was exacerbated by the historic changes in Eastern Europe. The various attempts on his life had been sufficient on their own to ring the strongest alarms in the mind of the ever-vigilant leader. But coming against the backdrop of the collapse of the communist regimes their impact was magnified several-fold. For the West, the events in Europe were a rare moment of spiritual elevation. For Saddam Hussein, like most Arab leaders, it was a development fraught with grave dangers. In his view, the decline of Soviet power and the disintegration of the Eastern Bloc had deprived the Arab world of its traditional allies and left the arena open for a US–Israeli 'diktat'. 'The USSR shifted from the balanced position with the United States in a practical manner, though it has not acknowledged it so far,' he argued at a summit meeting in Amman of the ACC in February 1990. 'It has become clear to everyone that the United States has emerged in a superior position in international politics. This superiority will be demonstrated in the US readiness to play such a role.'[16]

The fall of the Romanian dictator, Nicolae Ceauşescu, was particularly traumatic. Whether or not Saddam actually ordered the heads of his security services to study the videotapes of Ceauşescu's overthrow, as had been widely speculated in the West, this event undoubtedly made him wary. He must have been at least as informed as foreign diplomats in Baghdad that the events in Romania had left a strong impact even within one of the most sensitive centres of power, the officer corps, especially since some officers did not conceal their delight over the fate of the deposed dictator.

A suspicion by Saddam that the Americans, having seen off a succession of dictators in Eastern Europe, would now turn their attention to him may well have been the starting point for the steady decline in Iraq's relationship with the West. Such suspicions were heightened on 15 January 1990, when the Voice of America, in a broadcast celebrating the resurgence of democracy in Eastern Europe and encouraging the overthrow of remaining dictators, described Saddam as a 'tyrant'. Then on 21 February a State Department report was published that discussed human rights abuses in Iraq at length. This was followed by the Foreign Affairs Committee in the House of Representatives condemning Iraq for 'gross violations of human rights'.

Now Saddam was apprehensive, and in a speech to the ACC on 23 February he began to ventilate his anxieties. It was here that he not only spoke of the challenge posed by the Soviet decline but began to revert to an old tune, calling the Americans 'imperialists' and suggesting that their present interest in the Gulf was to support Israel and keep the oil price down. He asked that the residual American maritime force should leave the Gulf, though by now there were only a few ships present compared with the fifty deployed at the height of the war (essentially serving the Iraqi cause).

Israel

Another symptom of the collapse of communism in Europe was the influx of Soviet Jews to Israel which Saddam feared would boost the self-confidence of the Jewish state and would lure it into military adventures beyond its frontiers. Reports in the Western media at the time about secret meetings between Israeli and Syrian representatives in Europe were viewed by the

Iraqi President as further indications of 'a dangerous conspiracy' against Iraq.[17] In January 1990 he warned Israel that any attack on Iraq's scientific or military installations 'would be confronted by us with a precise reaction, using the means available to us according to the legitimate right to self-defence'.[18] A month later, during a visit to Baghdad, Ambassador Richard Murphy, former US Assistant Secretary of State for Near Eastern and South Asian Affairs, was told by his hosts that they had reliable information of an imminent Israeli strike against Iraq's non-conventional arms industry, modelled on the 1981 attack on Iraq's Osiraq reactor.[19] A similar message was delivered to the British Chargé d'Affaires in Baghdad in late March, during his meeting with Iraq's Under-Secretary of State for Foreign Affairs, Nizar Hamdoon.[20]

In Saddam's eyes, an Israeli strike against Iraq could be catastrophic. For him, nuclear weapons had always been more than the 'great equalizer', the weapons that could erode Israel's technological edge. They had been a personal obsession. They could be the symbol of Iraq's technological prowess, a prerequisite for regional hegemony, the ultimate guarantee for absolute security. Hence, not only could an Israeli attack on Iraq's nuclear reactor subvert his strategic plans, it would deal his political standing a devastating blow. 'If I am attacked by Israel now,' he told the Saudi Ambassador to Washington, Prince Bandar Ibn Sultan, on 5 April, 'I would not last six hours. When I was attacked the first time [1981], I was in war [with Iran] and could always say I was in war. And now if I am attacked, people will not understand why this happened.'[21]

Bandar had come to Baghdad to help smooth over the consequences of an incautious remark. On 2 April, in an address to the General Command of the Iraqi armed forces, Saddam had threatened Israel with harsh retaliation if it tried to repeat its 1981 attack on Iraq's nuclear installation. 'By God,' he said to the enthusiastic clapping of his audience, 'we will make fire eat half of Israel if it tries to do anything against Iraq.'[22] The statement was immediately deplored by President Bush. Israel, focusing on this threat and ignoring the conciliatory part of the speech, was said to have hinted that an Iraqi chemical attack might be met by a nuclear response.[23]

Though reluctant to lose the newly gained position of inter-Arab prominence, Saddam went out of his way to reassure decision-makers in Jerusalem and Washington that his bellicose statement should not be construed 'in the context of threats or demonstration of power'. Even in his speech he had taken care to underline the purely defensive nature of his threat. 'Everyone must know his limits,' he said within the same breath of issuing his 'burn Israel' threat, 'thanks be to God, we know our limits and we will not attack anyone.'[24] In the following months, this defensive theme was regularly reiterated. 'It should not be assumed,' argued the Iraqi media,

> that if the Arabs have a certain weapon, they will use it while others will not. We talked about using chemical weapons, should Israel threaten us or threaten any Arab nation militarily, including using nuclear weapons that it owns . . . when anyone threatens us with aggression, or tries to raise slogans of aggression, against Iraq or any part of the Arab homeland, then it would be natural for the Arabs to say to him: 'if you try to attack us, we will retaliate against your aggression with the weapons we have.'[25]

These public reassurances were accompanied by covert attempts to convince the Americans and the Israelis of Saddam's 'pure intentions'. In his extraordinary meeting with Prince Bandar, Saddam argued that his words had been misconstrued and that the United States was over-reacting. Vehemently denying any offensive designs, he admitted to his guest that he wished his speech 'had been phrased differently'. 'But you must understand the context in which it had been made,' he continued apologetically,

> it had been delivered to members of his armed forces at a public forum where emotions were running high, with people clapping and screaming. As we both know, it never hurt in the Arab world to threaten Israel, and so I had done it.[26]

Nonetheless, he emphasized that his threat had been made *only* in the context of an Israeli attack against Iraq. He then asked Bandar to assure President Bush and King Fahd that he would not attack Israel, and to request the Americans to secure an Israeli guarantee that it would not attack Iraq either. Having returned to Washington, Bandar conveyed Saddam's message to Bush who, in turn, contacted the Israelis and got their assurance that they were not going to move against Iraq in any way. This was then passed directly back to Saddam.

The Bazoft and 'supergun' affairs

Farzad Bazoft, an Iranian-born journalist working for the London weekly newspaper the *Observer*, had been arrested in September 1989 while probing into a mysterious explosion at a secret military complex near Baghdad. In March he was suddenly put on trial, given a death sentence and summarily executed. Saddam was using Bazoft to send two signals. To potential plotters at home it carried the message that the Iraqi leader was as adamant as ever on exacting the ultimate price from 'traitors'. To the West he was

33

demonstrating the futility of any attempts at coercion.[27]

The exposure of fabricated plots and the punishment of their 'perpetrators' had been one of Saddam's favourite methods of eliminating political dissent and deterring 'treacherous conspiracies' against the regime. However, while his other political victims had been Iraqis, which had enabled him to keep these purges internal affairs, and Bazoft's Iranian origins would not have endeared him to Saddam, he was carrying British travel documents which made his execution an international issue.[28] Whether Saddam might have avoided Bazoft's execution had he foreseen the intensity of Western indignation is difficult to say. His preoccupation with personal survival meant that all aspects of Iraq's domestic and foreign policy were subordinated to this objective. Saddam's meagre understanding of the West may have led him to believe that Bazoft's death might be a useful way of demonstrating his determination to survive without leading to a full confrontation.

This confrontation was particularly galling for Saddam, since it was not confined to expressions of public indignation with the appalling standards of Iraqi justice, but was apparently accompanied by a determined effort on the part of several Western governments to subvert his programme of non-conventional weapons, into which Bazoft had been apparently inquiring. On 22 March 1990 a Canadian ballistics expert, Dr Gerald Bull, was assassinated in Brussels. Since Bull was involved in developing a 'supergun' for Iraq that would supposedly be capable of launching non-conventional warheads for thousands of miles, the assumption was made by many that he was murdered by a Western security service, or possibly by Israel's Mossad. Soon afterwards, British Customs officials confiscated eight Iraqi-bound large steel tubes, manufactured by a Sheffield company and believed to be destined to form the barrel of Dr Bull's forty-ton 'supergun'. During the next few weeks other parts of the 'supergun' were intercepted in Greece and Turkey. Another blow to Iraq's non-conventional programme was dealt on 28 March, when a joint US–UK Customs operation culminated in the seizure at Heathrow Airport of forty electrical capacitors, devices designed to be used as nuclear triggers.

There was a common theme running through all these conflict points. The enormous resources put into building up Iraq's military power were starting to bear fruit. Determined to reduce his dependence upon overseas suppliers and not to be cowed by Israel's nuclear advantage, Saddam had set about creating an indigenous arms industry capable of producing not only 'conventional' guns and bombs but non-conventional missiles, chemical and nuclear weapons. This had been done by creating an intricate network of agents and companies in the West who had sought out the necessary high-technology equipment and found ways of obtaining finance and getting round export controls. By 1989 the extent of this effort was starting to be recognized and it was transforming international assessments of Iraqi strength. In February the US Government gave its first official warning that Iraq was attempting to become a nuclear power.[29] In April, an Arms Fair took place in Baghdad which displayed weapons manufactured by Iraq at some nineteen identifiable manufacturing plants, most of which had completely escaped the notice of the West.[30] In September there was the devastating explosion at the al-Hillah solid-fuel propellants plant, which had led Bazoft to seek his 'scoop'. In December Saddam boasted of the launch of his first long-range missile; two months later, US intelligence detected construction of five fixed-launch complexes in western Iraq, in range of Israeli cities.

Saddam was aware that the pressures would grow as his additional military strength became recognized – which is why he was becoming increasingly wary of an Israeli strike designed to destroy this strength before it was fully developed. The events which served to thwart the 'supergun' projects and impede his drive for a nuclear capability naturally came to be seen as part of a merging Israeli, American, British conspiracy.

In fact neither the British nor the American Government saw it in this way. They were getting more dubious with regard to Saddam's intentions, but they had not yet diverged from established policy. If anything, all the evidence that Saddam was up to no good convinced them that they must redouble their efforts to strengthen ties. Each Government looked around and was convinced that no other had an interest in a punitive policy. Without collective action such a policy was bound to fail, and the instigating Government would suffer a loss of contracts and influence. Better to persevere along established lines in the hope of steering Saddam back along the path of moderation and domestic reconstruction. Thus these Governments attempted to avoid provocation and insisted that there was no conspiracy and that amicable relations were still sought.

Britain, for example, sent back Ambassador Harold Walker to Baghdad in May after the 'supergun' affair began to blow over. Walker had only been in the post five weeks when the execution of Bazoft had led to him being recalled. In May his instructions were to get back into a dialogue. Saddam must be convinced that there was no UK campaign against Iraq, that the seizure of the capacitors at Heathrow was simply Customs men doing their duty, and that the derogatory comments found in a free press were not Government-inspired. Britain had no desire to rupture relations with yet another Middle Eastern regime. It had broken with Libya and Syria over terrorism and then Iran had broken with it over the Rushdie affair. Walker, therefore, had a developed plan for rebuilding relations, progressing from a scheduled visit by a serious non-Governmental figure, to a substantial showing in the Baghdad trade fair in the autumn, perhaps with a junior trade minister in attendance, and then possibly a visit by the Secretary of State in 1991. He was encouraged in this by the release of Daphne Parish, a nurse who had helped Bazoft and had been sentenced to a long prison term. This was taken as a signal of good will.

There had been a move in the United States to toughen policy on Iraq. To some extent this reflected a growing restlessness over the maltreatment of the Kurds, the use of chemical weapons and the generally repressive nature of the Iraqi state. However these issues were all toned down when on 17 January 1990 George Bush confirmed a policy based on detente and trade. On 12 February 1990 the Under Secretary of State for Near Eastern Affairs, John Kelly, visited Baghdad and met Saddam. He had the first tranche of the new credit but the Agriculture Department was starting to drag its feet on the second. Kelly warned that with relations so fragile such a cut would 'feed Saddam's paranoia'.[31] He told Saddam that he was a 'force for moderation in the region, and the United States wishes to broaden her relations with Iraq'.[32] Saddam's pleasure with this was then somewhat qualified by the Voice of America broadcast which followed three days later and the publication of the report on human rights abuses later in the month. Then came the 'burn Israel' speech of 2 April.

The United States described the threat as 'inflammatory, outrageous and irresponsible'. John Kelly argued against sanctions on Capitol Hill largely on the grounds that they would deny US exporters opportunities and they would not have much effect. Kelly insisted that if sanctions would work in modifying Iraq's behaviour then the Administration would support them, and agreed that Saddam's actions had raised new questions regarding his intentions. The question was how best to 'exercise a restraining influence'.[33] There was a review of policy on 16 April, chaired by Robert Gates, the Deputy Adviser on National Security Affairs. This review has been subject to much speculation, with references to suggestions from both the State and Commerce Departments for an end to favourable treatment on export licences and credits. The policy debate seems to have been half-hearted, with little confidence in the effects of a harder line and uncertainty over how to implement it. The position taken by the presidential National Security Adviser, Brent Scowcroft, was that there was no reason to change policy. As a result of the meeting a paper was prepared by the NSC staff a month later reviewing options. None looked promising. Those in the trade, credits and oil fields were either trivial or more likely to hurt the United States. The political measures could affect the conduct of business. Even the residual intelligence relationship – on Iran –

was deemed valuable because of the access provided to this segment of the Iraqi establishment. All that could be done was not to go forward with the second tranche of the agricultural credits, although even this political signal was moderated by a public rationale unrelated to foreign policy – the illegal 'kickbacks'.

In May it was decided not to proceed with the second half of the $1 billion loan guarantee, largely on the basis of the 'kickback' being received by Iraq from its favoured agricultural suppliers, which included such 'after-sale service' as armoured trucks. There was no desire to be seen to be using the 'food weapon' against Iraq. Even here, an attempt to impose a formal cut in credits was defeated in the Senate.[34]

To the fore in opposing any restraints in relations with Iraq was Senator Robert Dole from Kansas – a major exporter of grain to Iraq. It was Dole who led a group of five Senators, ten days after Saddam's threat to Israel, to meet the Iraqi leader at Mosul. They made it known that they handed over a letter denouncing attempts to get chemical and nuclear weapons. The Iraqis, however, as they did a number of times later to embarrass their past interlocutors, released their own transcript of the meeting. This had Dole reassuring Saddam that President Bush, who had encouraged the trip, did not support a campaign against Iraq, and that the Voice of America man had been sacked (which was not the case). Alan Simpson from Wyoming explained that the problems were with a 'haughty and pampered' press.[35]

The industrial and agricultural lobby were as enthusiastic as ever about a close relationship with Iraq. If sanctions were mentioned they had a well-rehearsed answer: we will be the only losers because nobody else will observe them and they will have no influence on Iraqi behaviour. There was, however, one argument for which they did not have a good answer: Iraq was running out of money.

Saddam's crisis

In the five years from 1984 Saddam had spent $14.2 billion in hard currency in high-technology imports from Britain, France, Germany, Italy and the United States. At the height of the war with Iran, in 1985, some 60 per cent of Iraq's gross oil revenues were being spent on military equipment and weapons manufacturing technology.[36] In 1989 the BNL scandal was instrumental in bringing out into the open details of Iraqi activities and making other lenders doubly cautious.

Increasingly the most practical issues for Western countries dealing with Iraq concerned lines of credit. Britain's trading position had been achieved in part by extending a line of credit throughout the war. As a result it was being slightly favoured, in that at least some of the debts were being repaid. Yet it was decided in 1990 only to give Iraq further credit to the amount required to turn over existing debts. In May Iraqi repayments fell behind the levels which automatically triggered a halt in new credit coverage from the Export Credits Guarantee Department (ECGD). There were outstanding debts of $100 million.

France had been Iraq's major arms supplier other than the Soviet Union. It had sold Iraq about $5 billion worth of arms, equivalent to about one quarter of the total arsenal. However, reports suggested that Iraq owed France FF28 billion, of which FF15 billion was for military equipment. In September 1989 the two countries had agreed to reschedule the debt so that FF5 billion would be repaid in 1990, but little had been done by Baghdad. An informal arms embargo was imposed and a more formal block on further arms sales was being considered. The French Coface export credit agency stopped covering Iraqi credits, frustrating efforts by Dassault to sell more than fifty Mirage 2000s to Iraq for FF22 billion.

Not even Jean-Pierre Chevènement, a left-winger and founder member in 1984 of the Iraqi–French Friendship Association, could help. He had made full use of his position as Defence Minister to promote the military relationship. In January 1990 he paid an official visit to Baghdad, the first Minister of Defence to do so for ten years, and spoke to Saddam of his intention to 'raise our bilateral relations to a higher level' and how the President enjoyed the respect and esteem of French leaders. Although he obtained some small deals, he was hampered by demands from Paris that all deals had cash up front. An aide to Finance Minister Beregovoy made an observation that was becoming widely shared:

> We note that an enormous share of Iraq's GNP is currently being devoted to military industrialization projects. We do not want to finance regional destabilization. Nor will we issue any more export credit guarantees until the Iraqis make good on the debt rescheduling deal we worked out.[37]

The greatest danger for Saddam in all of this was not simply that the flow of high technology into Iraq would be stemmed but that his creditors would get together to arrange a global rescheduling package which would involve a degree of international surveillance of his economy. This was a far greater danger than economic sanctions. Rescheduling had been mooted in 1988. Saddam dealt then with the challenge on a divide and rule basis. Western Governments were informed that if they resisted this move then they would be rewarded with excellent contracts. The West German Government, with high-technology exports to Iraq booming, was the first to break after Chancellor Kohl had been visited by Tariq Aziz in July 1988. Germany's attitude with regard to the ultimate Iraqi purpose behind the contracts remained relaxed, despite its elaborate domestic legislation aimed at preventing the export of weapons to crisis-ridden areas.[38]

In the first half of 1990, Western finance ministries were coming back to address the problem. Western Ambassadors in Baghdad found credit the abiding topic of conversations with their Iraqi hosts, with each Government being dealt with separately, desperately pitting one against the other to dissuade them from consolidating their interests. Only those prepared to make further loans could expect past loans to be repaid.

All this brought home to Saddam the awful state of his economy. Though Saddam invested huge efforts to depict the end of hostilities with Iran as a shining victory, it increasingly became evident that Iraq had emerged from the war a crippled nation. From a prosperous country with some $35 billion in foreign exchange reserve in 1980, Iraq had been reduced to dire economic straits, with $80 billion in foreign debt and shattered economic infrastructure. Western estimates put the cost of reconstruction at $230 billion.

Even if one adopted the most optimistic (and highly unrealistic) assumption that every dollar of oil revenues would be directed to the reconstruction effort, it would have required nearly two decades to repair the total damage. As things stood a year after the termination of hostilities, Iraq's oil revenues of $13 billion per annum barely covered the military budget. Unless rescheduling could be arranged, half of this would be required to service Iraq's non-Arab debt. With civilian imports approximating $12 billion ($3 billion for foodstuffs), military imports exceeding $5 billion, debt repayments totalling $5 billion, and transfers by foreign workers topping $1 billion, the regime needed an extra $10 billion per annum to balance its current deficit before it could even think about reconstruction. By mid-1990 cash reserves were available for only three months of imports. Yet it was upon this reconstruction that both Saddam's political survival and his long-term ambitions hinged, and it would have to be shelved.[39]

In order to reduce expenditures and to secure jobs for the first demobilized soldiers returning to the labour market, Saddam had begun by squeezing out of Iraq 2 million migrant workers, mainly Egyptians, and slashed the remittances they were allowed to send home. Intensive privatization measures were then introduced but they never stood any chance. With the oil industry, accounting for some 95 per cent of Iraq's income, remaining in the hands of the state, there was no viable basis for the creation of a significant private sector. Moreover, the repressive nature of the regime and its arbitrary convulsions left entrepreneurs wary, investing the barest minimum in future expansion and reaping as much profit as they could in the short term. The high expectations created among the various groups of the society were only matched by soaring inflation, forcing the reintroduction of price controls.[40]

As far as Saddam's personal position was concerned, an immediate economic breakthrough had become critical, for his domestic vulnerability would grow enormously if the state had to be declared bankrupt. On paper, the cure was strikingly simple: a decisive reduction in expenditures and a significant increase in revenues. As Saddam was not one to keep a 'tight ship' when it came to expenditure and the economy was unable to generate extra revenues this created something of a dilemma.

OPEC

At one time Saddam could have hoped to pay for his ambitious modernization plans by means of oil revenues. Not so in the late 1980s. The price of oil was falling. If there was to be any hope of meeting his requirements, Saddam had to find some way of reversing this trend. It was the basic laws of supply and demand which had forced the price down – the industrialized world had responded to artificially high prices as set by the Organization of Petroleum Exporting Countries (OPEC) in the 1970s by exploiting non-OPEC oil reserves and substituting other fuels for oil.

One way to get the price back up was to enforce dramatic cuts in production. Saudi Arabia, with the largest reserves, had been best placed to influence the market in this way, but by the mid-1980s it had become increasingly reluctant to play this role, which meant that it was obliged to accept a disproportionate decline both in production and revenues. To regain market share it decided to take advantage of its relatively cheap production costs by forcing prices even further down, thereby pushing high-cost producers out. At one point the price even went down to below $10 per barrel. In 1986 OPEC agreed to attempt to get the price back to $18 per barrel by sharing out the production cuts. The resulting quota system was complex from the start and honoured as much in the breach as in the observance. The price did not settle.[41]

At issue was as much economic philosophy and circumstances as OPEC discipline. The radical countries such as Iraq not only opposed Western market pressures in principle but, with massive expenditure plans, were desperate for extra revenue. They wanted higher prices but also an extra

quota for themselves and less for others. The low-reserve and small production producers were anxious to maximize prices while they could. The
Saudis believed that there was no point in pushing the price up too far, but
OPEC had given them considerable influence and they were not comfortable with the idea of a wholly unregulated market.

Kuwait, by contrast, was much more inclined to follow market pressures.
Only by allowing prices to fall could oil recapture its share of the world
energy market. This view was shared by the United Arab Emirates (UAE).
These countries did not even pretend to take the idea of quotas very
seriously, and refused in June 1989 to hold down production. To the extent
that there had to be quotas, they argued, they should be based on reserves
and spare capacity and not modernization plans. Also Kuwait had an interest
in downstream activities which meant that it had a natural cushion against
lower prices.

To the radical states the deliberate flouting of the quota system by Kuwait
and UAE was exasperating just as the idea of preserving markets through
price moderation was anathema. Yet in practice the economic philosophy of
the Kuwaitis was correct and the lower prices of 1986 did revive the demand
for OPEC oil, which was surging by the end of the decade. Instead of
enjoying the consequent hardening of the price, the major large-reserve
producers – mainly to be found in the Gulf – began to position themselves to
take a larger share of a growing market by expanding their production
capabilities. Inevitably this resulted in an excess of capacity. At the start of
1990, instead of total production by OPEC states sticking at the agreed level
of 22 million barrels per day it was approaching 24, with Kuwait and the
UAE accounting for 75 per cent of the excess. These two states were
pressing for the quota system to be abandoned. Meanwhile the price hawks
were becoming alarmed as prices fell once more – from $20.5 a barrel in
January to below $18 in March, with the threat of a complete collapse of
OPEC discipline.

Saddam's revenue problem was as a result becoming chronic. If he could
not get OPEC discipline from these small Gulf states then an alternative was
to go to them directly and demand the money with menaces – especially to
Kuwait, to which Iraq owed some $10 billion.

CHAPTER 3
Iraq Confronts Kuwait

After he had invaded and annexed the emirate of Kuwait, Saddam insisted that it had all been done in a noble cause – the elimination of 'a trace of Western colonialism' left in the Middle East since the turn of the century. 'Kuwait is part of Iraqi territory that was severed at some point in the past . . . by the British occupation authorities,' argued the Iraqi media, 'in order to weaken Iraq by depriving it of territory overlooking the Arabian Gulf that would strengthen its pan-Arab security and give it flexibility of movement, and also to put part of its petroleum resources outside the will of its population.' Hence, it was only natural for Iraq to acquiesce in the Kuwaiti appeal 'to approve the return of the sons to their family, the return of Kuwait to great Iraq, the motherland'.[1]

The idea that Kuwait was part of historic Iraq was an old theme and certainly made it a natural choice for appropriation. Until the turn of the twentieth century Kuwait had officially been part of the Ottoman Empire. Yet, since 1756, when the al-Sabah family established an autonomous sheikhdom in Kuwait, the Empire's rule had been nominal. In response to a bilateral British–Kuwaiti agreement, concluded on 23 January 1899, giving London responsibility for Kuwait's defence and foreign affairs,[2] the Ottoman Sultan declared Kuwait part of the *velayet* (province) of Basra and nominated the Sheikh of Kuwait as *qaimaqam*, district officer. However, in the 1913 treaty with Britain the Ottomans recognized the autonomy of the Sheikh of Kuwait, and undertook not to interfere in the principality's foreign and security affairs and to exercise any administrative measures only with the approval of the Kuwaiti Sheikh. Moreover, Iraq itself was not a unified political entity during the Ottoman era, but rather consisted of three disparate provinces: Mosul, Baghdad, and Basra. Hence, it later became subject to territorial demands from Turkey, which viewed the inclusion of the oil-rich province of Mosul in Iraqi territory as a historical wrong that ought to be rectified.

Nor is Iraq more of a nation than Kuwait. Rather, it is a land torn by ethnic and religious divisions, a land where the main non-Arab community, the Kurds (20 per cent of the total population), has been constantly suppressed, and where the majority of the population, the Shi'ites, have been ruled by a minority group, the Sunnis, less than one-third their number. These broad divisions have been further compounded (particularly in the Shi'ite case) by the lack of a cohesive leadership and social organization, as well as deep schisms between various communities, such as the inhabitants of the cities and the rural concentrations. It is a country which, in the words of its first modern ruler, King Faisal I, is no more than 'unimaginable masses of human beings, devoid of any patriotic idea, imbued with religious traditions and absurdities . . . and prone to anarchy'.[3]

And yet, since its inception as an independent state in 1932, Iraq had persistently challenged the right to sovereign existence of its tiny neighbour to the south. The Iraqi Premier Nuri al-Sa'id had recognized the Iraqi–Kuwaiti boundary set in the 1913 British–Ottoman 'Draft Convention on the Persian Gulf Area'.[4] However, Baghdad consistently pressured Kuwait to lease it the islands of Warba and Bubiyan which, according to its claim and contrary to the 1913 Treaty, belonged to Iraq, or sought to subvert the al-Sabah dynasty which had ruled Kuwait for some two centuries. In the late 1930s the Iraqi King Ghazi openly demanded the incorporation of the whole of Kuwait into Iraq.

The same demand was reiterated, with greater vehemence, by the radical Iraqi ruler Abd al-Karim Qassem, who in July 1958 overthrew the monarchy. In June 1961, the same month that Kuwait gained independence, he claimed that the sheikhdom had always been part of the *velayet* of Basra and therefore belonged to Iraq, and alluded to the possible use of armed force to redress this 'historical wrong', backing his threat by the deployment of troops along the joint border. The Kuwaitis quickly approached Britain with a request for military support. On 1 July 1961 British troops arrived while naval units patrolled the Gulf. Arab support came too, though more slowly: in September, after prolonged and arduous negotiations, the Arab League acquiesced to a Kuwaiti request and sent a multinational force comprising Saudi, Egyptian, Jordanian and Sudanese troops. Iraq's relations with the Arab League soured. In December Baghdad announced that it would 'reconsider' diplomatic relations with any state recognizing Kuwait. Thus, as Kuwait was recognized by a growing number of states, a procession of Iraqi ambassadors throughout the world made their way home.

An Arab contingent remained until February 1963, when Qassem was overthrown by a Ba'thi coup. By then, it had become clear that the aggressive policy towards Kuwait had brought Iraq nothing but isolation in the Arab world. Hence, without much delay, the regime changed tack and in October 1963 recognized Kuwait's independence. This concession was, reportedly, made in return for a substantial Kuwaiti financial contribution to Iraq.

This reconciliation proved short-lived. Before 1963 was over the Ba'th regime had been overthrown. Upon its return to power in July 1968, under the dual leadership of Ahmad Hasan al-Bakr and his deputy, Saddam Hussein, it was less kind to the Kuwaitis. In 1969 Baghdad requested that Kuwait allow Iraqi forces to assume positions on the Kuwaiti side of the common border in order to protect the Iraqi coastline against an alleged impending Iranian attack. Despite the evasive Kuwaiti response, the Iraqis deployed troops in a narrow strip along the border.[5] Having presented the Kuwaitis with a *fait accompli*, an Iraqi delegation arrived in Kuwait to gain the Government's formal approval. Although this was not granted, the Iraqi forces, augmented in spring 1973 by additional troops, remained on Kuwaiti territory for nearly a decade against Kuwait's wishes. Whenever the Kuwaitis requested the withdrawal of these forces, Iraq feigned innocence and declined on grounds that the troops could not be pulled out as long as the permanent border had not been delineated. When Kuwait sought to reach an agreement on the final status of its border with Iraq, the latter made it plain that it would recognize the 'de-facto borders only if the islands of Warba and Bubiyan be either included within Iraq or leased to it'.[6]

Iraq's attempts to cow Kuwait into surrendering control over the two islands, in one form or another, persisted throughout the 1970s and gained momentum during the Iran–Iraq War. Painfully aware of its limited access to the Gulf, Iraq approached Kuwait on several occasions with the request to lease the two islands, only to be rebuffed by the Kuwaitis who feared that by placing the islands under Iraqi control they would open the door for further territorial demands. The last occasion had been in February 1989, when the Kuwaiti Crown Prince visited Baghdad in the expectation that the border dispute would now be resolved out of gratitude for Kuwait's wartime support, only to find Iraq still demanding the islands. The presumption by Kuwait that Iraq should be the country to show gratitude rather than the other way around, along with the independence shown in Kuwait's foreign policy as it moved to mend fences with both Iran and Syria, served to irritate Saddam.

Despite all this, during the Iraqi campaign preceding the invasion of Kuwait, there was hardly any reference to Iraq's claim to Kuwait in general, or to the Warba and Bubiyan islands in particular. Even in the immediate wake of the invasion, the Iraqi media failed to mention Iraq's 'historic rights' over Kuwait, instead presenting the invasion as a temporary emergency measure taken at the request of the 'liberal regime' established in Kuwait instead of the 'reactionary' al-Sabah dynasty.

The economic campaign

The Iraqi interest in Kuwait had always less to do with legal or historical rights than with the fact that this tiny state possessed mammoth wealth, a large natural harbour and some 120 miles of Gulf coastline. In the first instance, Saddam's campaign in the summer of 1990 focused on Kuwait's wealth.

This picked up a theme that could also be traced back to the war with Iran. Then Saddam had pressed the Gulf states, Saudi Arabia and Kuwait in particular, to forgive their loans to Iraq. The war was not Iraq's private business, he told them, but rather a defence of the eastern flank of the Arab world against fundamentalist Islam. While the Gulf states were not asked to pay with rivers of blood for the protection of their own security, since Iraq did that on their behalf, they could not expect to take a 'free ride' on Iraq's heroic struggle.

At the summit meeting of the Arab Co-operation Council in Amman in February 1990, celebrating the organization's first anniversary, Saddam asked King Hussein of Jordan and President Mubarak of Egypt to inform the Gulf states that Iraq was not only adamant on a complete moratorium on its wartime loans, but urgently needed an immediate infusion of additional funds of some $30 billion. 'Let the Gulf regimes know,' he added, 'that if they do not give this money to me, I will know how to get it'; and this threat was accompanied by Iraqi military manoeuvres in the neutral zone on the Kuwaiti border.[7] The message was immediately passed on to Saudi Arabia by the Jordanian monarch.

The same month, during a working visit to Kuwait, the Iraqi Oil Minister, Isam Abd al-Rahim al-Chalabi, pressured his hosts to abide by the new oil quota set by OPEC earlier that year. Then he proceeded to Riyadh to deliver a personal message from Saddam Hussein to King Fahd. The Saudis must convince the rest of the Gulf states not to exceed their oil quotas. This had scant influence on Kuwait and the United Arab Emirates (UAE). Instead of reducing their oil quota to make more room for increased Iraqi production they continued to exceed their quotas by far, putting a downward pressure on world oil prices. In this they felt that they were doing no more than all the other OPEC states which had the option. Since Saddam was intent on pushing oil prices up without relinquishing his own plans for increased production, an immediate change in Kuwaiti and UAE policy became a matter of great urgency.

By May, when OPEC ministers met in Geneva, the oil price was falling and the frustration with Kuwait was making itself felt. Chalabi reiterated the need to adhere to the organization's established production quota of 22 million barrels a day (mbd) and urged his counterparts to raise oil prices to $18 a barrel. The Iraqi First Deputy Prime Minister, Taha Yasin Ramadan, was far more outspoken in his criticism of quota violations, which he deplored as 'detrimental to Iraqi interests'.[8] Saddam himself drove the point home forcibly during discussions at the Arab summit meeting in Baghdad in May 1990. In an extraordinary closed session with the visiting heads of states, he tabled his grievances against the Gulf oil states:

> For every single dollar drop in the price of a barrel of oil our loss amounts to $1 billion a year. Is the Arab nation in a position to endure a loss of tens of billions as a result of unjustified mistake by some technicians or non-technicians, especially as the oil markets, or let us say, the clients are, at least, prepared to pay up to $25 for the next two years, as we have learned or heard from the Westerners who are the main clients in the oil market?

The answer to this question, in Saddam Hussein's opinion, was an unequivocal 'no'. The continued violation of oil quotas by some Arab states amounted to a *declaration of war on Iraq*.

> War is fought with soldiers and much harm is done by explosions, killing, and coup attempts – but it is also done by economic means. Therefore, we would ask our brothers who do not mean to wage war on Iraq: this is in fact a kind of war against Iraq.

'Were it possible,' he concluded, 'we would have endured. But I believe that all our brothers are fully aware of our situation . . . we have reached a point where we can no longer withstand pressure.'[9]

Kuwait and the UAE were unmoved by Saddam's uncharacteristically candid admission of weakness and his blatant threat. While replacing his Oil Minister in an attempt to appease Saddam, the Emir of Kuwait would neither reduce oil production nor forgive his wartime loans to Iraq nor extend Baghdad additional grants. 'That is absurd. Kuwait does not have such a large amount available,' he responded angrily to a demand for a $10 billion contribution to Iraq, made during a visit to Kuwait in June 1990 by Dr Sa'dun Hammadi, Deputy Prime Minister of Iraq and Saddam's chief economic adviser. All the Emir was willing to contribute was a $500 million grant, spread over three years, as 'an act of charity to Iraq'. Hammadi's demand that Kuwait reduce its oil production quota was similarly spurned by the Emir, who made any Kuwaiti support for Iraq conditional on the resolution of the pending border issues between the two countries. 'Let's agree about our borders,' he told his guest, 'and then we can talk about other things.'[10]

In the following weeks Kuwait was to rebuff several tough warnings by Iraq's Oil Minister regarding its oil quota. Even a direct attack by Saddam on this policy as a 'conspiracy against the region's economy which serves Israel directly' failed to bend Kuwait into submission.[11] It was only on 10 July, during a co-ordination meeting of the Gulf Oil Ministers in Jeddah, that Kuwait and the UAE succumbed to combined Saudi, Iranian and Iraqi pressure and agreed to abide by their oil quotas. However, Saddam did not trust the Kuwaitis to stick to this agreement. He later complained to the American Ambassador in Baghdad, Ms April Glaspie, that two days after the Jeddah meeting the agreement had been contradicted by the Kuwaiti Oil Minister and that he had received intelligence that the Kuwaitis intended to stick to the agreement for only two months before their policy would be changed again.[12]

The crisis

By this time Saddam's frustration with Kuwait was intense. He was now determined to extract substantial grants plus a complete moratorium on war loans on top of adherence to OPEC quotas. The Kuwaiti indifference to his desperate needs amounted to 'stabbing Iraq in the back with a poisoned dagger'.[13] He had gone out of his way to plead the Iraqi case and further begging would only cause him (and, by extension, Iraq) an unendurable public humiliation.

He began to put his strategy in place in mid-July. On 15 July the build-up of armed forces began. A division of the élite Republican Guard began moving from central Iraq to the south-east of the country, just north of Kuwait. Within less than twenty-four hours some 10,000 men and 300 tanks were in place and a second division was making its appearance. By 19 July, 35,000 men from three divisions had been deployed ten to thirty miles from the Kuwaiti border, with their tanks facing outward in a coiled pattern, thereby facilitating both defence and supply.[14]

As the military build-up got under way the diplomatic offensive began. On 16 July the Iraqi Foreign Minister, Tariq Aziz, delivered a memorandum to the Secretary-General of the Arab League, Chadly Klibi, for distribution to the League's members. In this he set down the Iraqi indictment:

- Kuwait with the UAE had 'implemented an intentional scheme to glut the oil market with a quantity of oil that exceeded their quotas as fixed by OPEC'. This policy had a devastating impact on the Middle East: 'the drop in oil prices between 1981 and 1990 led to a loss of $500 billion by the Arab states, of which Iraq sustained $89 billion'.

- To add insult to injury, Kuwait had directly robbed the Iraqi treasury by 'setting up oil installations in the southern section of the Iraqi Rumaila oilfield and extracted oil from it'. The value of the oil 'stolen by the Kuwaiti Government from the Rumaila oilfield in this manner that conflicts with fraternal relations' amounted to $2.4 billion.

- The Gulf states had provided 'various kinds of assistance' to Iraq during the war, but this support covered merely a small fraction of Iraq's tremendous costs. Moreover, 'a simple calculation will show that the UAE and Kuwaiti loans to Iraq were not entirely from their treasuries but from the increases in their oil revenues as a result of the drop in Iraqi oil exports over the war years'.

- While Iraq had been distracted by the war with Iran, Kuwait had 'implemented a plot to escalate the pace of the gradual, systematic advance towards Iraqi territory'. The Kuwaiti Government set up military establishments, police posts, oil installations, and farms on Iraqi territory.

Stealing Iraq's territory and wealth, and so weakening it at a time when it was facing up to the imperialists and Zionists, was tantamount 'to a military aggression'. In order to rectify this and to help Iraq recover from the dire economic plight that it now faced due to its defence of 'the [Arab] nation's soil, dignity, honour and wealth', Aziz tabled several demands: the raising of oil prices to over $25 a barrel; the cessation of Kuwaiti 'theft' of oil from the Iraqi Rumaila oilfield and the return of the $2.4 billion 'stolen' from Iraq; a complete moratorium on Iraq's wartime loans; the formation of 'an Arab plan similar to the Marshall Plan to compensate Iraq for some of the losses during the war'.[15]

The next day Saddam escalated further. In an address to the nation on the twenty-second anniversary of the 'Ba'th Revolution', he accused Kuwait and the UAE yet again of conspiring with 'world imperialism and Zionism' to 'cut off the livelihood of the Arab nation', threatening that Iraq would not be able to put up with such behaviour for much longer, since 'one would be better off dead than having one's livelihood cut off'. The two states had therefore to come 'back to their senses', he said, preferably through peaceful means. However, he cautioned, 'if words fail to afford us protection, then we will have no choice but to resort to effective action to put things right and ensure the restitution of our rights'.[16]

While the failure to resolve the border issue was implied in the exchanges, Saddam's own speech concentrated on the question of the oil price and quotas. The specific demands were largely economic in nature. They were not new, but had been presented to the Kuwaiti and Arab Governments on several previous occasions. Yet by stating in public what had hitherto been said behind closed doors and by backing his demands by military moves, Saddam had changed the whole character of his dispute. He had committed himself to certain objectives in such a way that any compromise on his part would have been seen as a capitulation. There was no room left for bargaining or procrastination. Kuwait had to accept his demands in full or face the grave consequences.

The Kuwaiti Cabinet met the day after Saddam's speech. The prevailing view was that surrender to such extortionist methods would only lead to unlimited demands in the future. They suspected that some concessions might be necessary, but were determined to reduce them to the barest minimum. If they were going to do a deal with Iraq they wanted in return abandonment of Iraq's claim over Kuwait. However startled it may have been by the harsh Iraqi rhetoric, the Kuwaiti leadership remained complacent, interpreting Saddam's demands as a bargaining position rather than an ultimatum. They recognized that military action could not be ruled out but believed that it was extremely unlikely, and that in the worst case it would be confined to a small disputed area such as the Rumaila oilfield and the Bubiyan and Warba islands.[17] The state of alert on which Kuwaiti forces had been put when the first news came through of the Iraqi build-up was cancelled on 19 July. A Kuwaiti official was quoted as saying that: 'It was all a summer cloud that has been blown away.'[18]

Kuwait dispatched to the Secretary-General of the Arab League a strongly worded memorandum refuting the Iraqi accusations and expressing strong indignation at Iraq's behaviour. This was not the way to treat a sister country which had always been at the forefront of the Arab national struggle, it argued. The Iraqi expressions were

> out of line with the spirit of the existing fraternal relations between Kuwait and Iraq, and conflict with the most fundamental bases on which we all wish to govern our Arab relations. The sons of Kuwait, in good as well as in bad times, are people of principle and integrity. By no means will they yield to threat and extortion.[19]

Meanwhile they decided to gather their allies around them. They called an emergency meeting of the Gulf Co-operation Council in order to get the

Arab League fully involved. Chadly Klibi was brought to meet the Emir, and told of the injustice of the Iraqi demands but also that Kuwait was ready for a 'dialogue'. In addition the Kuwaitis wrote to the President of the United Nations Security Council and the UN Secretary-General, Javier Perez de Cuellar.

The Arab League chose Husni Mubarak of Egypt as a mediator. He arrived in Baghdad on 24 July for what turned out to be a crucial meeting. According to the Iraqi account, Saddam gave Mubarak a clear impression that he did not intend to invade but couched this in a carefully worded formula:

> As long as discussions last between Iraq and Kuwait, I won't use force. I won't intervene with force before I have exhausted all the possibilities for negotiation.

According to Mubarak there was no qualification, but, certainly, an agreement to negotiations in Saudi Arabia. At issue was the extent to which the Iraqi position was backed up by force. To Mubarak Saddam denied rumours of a substantial military build-up along the border – the troops in southern Iraq were 'Republican Guard units on a normal routine move with forces stationed there'. But he was not averse to scaring the Kuwaitis into concessions. He seems to have sought to co-opt the Egyptian leader as an accomplice. As Mubarak was going on to Kuwait, Saddam asked him not to tell the al-Sabahs this was only intimidation. This much Tariq Aziz later confirmed to James Baker. He recalled the two men emerging from their private meeting and Saddam saying to Mubarak: 'Brother Husni, don't let the Kuwaitis rest easy before the meeting.'

Mubarak did not play along. He was annoyed that the statement on the meeting issued by Iraq which was released by the time that he reached the emirate reported that there had been no discussion of the Kuwaiti issue. Instead of supporting what he presumed to be Saddam's game of bluff, he told the Kuwaitis that Saddam did not intend to invade. However, he still advised flexibility in the negotiations. When asked what Saddam wanted the Egyptian leader replied: 'It seems he needs some money.'[20]

The Western response

American spy satellites picked up the move of Iraqi troops to the Kuwaiti border almost immediately. The first assessment was that this was geared to intimidation rather than imminent action and did not match any manoeuvre previously observed in exercises. The United States kept this information to itself, so the news of the build-up did not become public until 20 July.[21]

When Saddam made his threat to Kuwait on 17 July the United States issued a public statement that it would defend its interests and friends in the region. Secretary of Defence Richard Cheney was asked about the threats on 19 July and repeated this. The Iraqi Ambassador in Washington was summoned to the State Department and told that the United States would continue to support the 'sovereignty and integrity of the Gulf states'. No position was taken on the Iraqi–Kuwaiti dispute, but the US insisted 'that disputes be settled peacefully and not by threats or intimidation'. Ambassador April Glaspie in Baghdad delivered the same message to Under Secretary of State for Foreign Affairs Nizar Hamdoon and asked for an explanation of Saddam's statement, though without success.[22]

The initial American response was therefore quite strong, to the extent that local Arab Governments became anxious lest it inflame the situation and provoke Iraqi action. They urged Washington to take a lower profile. One exception was the United Arab Emirates (UAE), the other recipient of Iraqi threats, which was sufficiently alarmed to ask for some practical support. Having experienced Iraqi intimidation before – in 1986, when Saddam felt that he was not getting enough support against Iran, he sent his aircraft over 600 miles to bomb two of the UAE's oil rigs[23] – the UAE was watching out for a repeat performance. This required maintaining a continual air patrol, which depended on aerial-refuelling tankers. It therefore asked the Americans secretly to supply two large KC-135 aircraft. By way of a cover for the KC-135s it was decided to announce a joint naval exercise with the UAE, which required pulling two ships out of port to join four other ships in the Gulf.

The Pentagon agreed but the State Department, aware of the entreaties from other Arab states on the need for a low profile, opposed. However, on 21 July President Bush backed the Pentagon. Three days later, on 24 July, the morning *National Intelligence Daily* (NID), circulated to top policy-makers in Washington, warned that 'Iraq now has ample forces and supplies available for military operations inside Kuwait', and during the day doubts grew as to whether Saddam really was bluffing. Bush was briefed on the danger by CIA Director William Webster.[24] The American stand was toughened. The naval exercise was announced on 24 July, but so were the KC-135s, and they were both justified as a signal of support for UAE and Kuwait – 'We remain strongly committed to supporting the individual and collective self-defence of our friends in the Gulf.' The announcement was linked to the long-standing defence of the 'principle of freedom of navigation and to ensure the free flow of oil through the Strait of Hormuz'. The same day the State

Department spokesperson Margaret Tutwiler asserted that 'Iraq and others know there is no place for coercion and intimidation in a civilized world.' She noted the lack of any 'defence treaties with Kuwait, and . . . special defence or security commitments', but when pressed reaffirmed a commitment to 'the individual and collective-defence of our friends in the Gulf with whom we have deep and longstanding ties'.[25]

Again the Americans were moving ahead of their friends in the Gulf. Now the UAE expressed anger at the disclosure: the object had been to facilitate surveillance, not to send a political signal.[26] Kuwait did not even go as far as the UAE. There were inconclusive discussions with American officials over what might be done under vaguely defined circumstances but no definite requests for support and, in the absence of such requests, no American proposals.

Even so Baghdad had complained about Kuwaiti contacts with the United Nations, warning that this was paving the way for 'inviting foreign troops to intervene in the region'.[27] Now, it took note of the unmistakable hardening of the American stance. At midnight Ambassador Glaspie received a protest over the announcement of the exercises with the UAE and was asked if the US fleet had been redeployed. The next morning – 25 July – the Iraqi press was complaining about 'foreign' threats.[28] After delivering a copy of Tutwiler's statement to the Foreign Ministry, Glaspie returned to her office when she was suddenly summoned back to the Ministry to meet Saddam Hussein. There had not been an opportunity to contact Washington for guidance – all she could do was work within the terms of established policy.

This background is critical to an understanding of this meeting, which is now judged to be one of the most controversial milestones on Iraq's road to Kuwait.[29] The Iraqi leader was suspicious. He began by asking, 'What can it mean when America says it will now protect its friends? It can only mean prejudice against Iraq. This stance plus manoeuvres and statements which have been made has encouraged the UAE and Kuwaitis.' Glaspie was treated to a lengthy exposition of Iraq's economic plight and his grievances against the Gulf states. The United States was supporting 'Kuwait's economic war against Iraq' at a time when it should be grateful to Baghdad for having contained fundamentalist Iran. He then went on to threaten the United States with terrorist retaliation should it sustain its hostile policy. 'You can come to Iraq with aircraft and missiles,' he said, 'but do not push us to the point where we will cease to take. If you use pressure, we will deploy pressure and force. We cannot come all the way to you in the United States but individual Arabs may reach you.' To emphasize his point, he observed that the Americans lacked Iraq's readiness to lose 10,000 men in a day's combat.

Glaspie appears to have interpreted this as a developing crisis in Iraqi–American relations and responded – somewhat defensively – with the reassuring line that the State Department had been following for some months. There was no hostility to Iraq nor a conspiracy. On the contrary, 'I have direct instruction from the President to seek better relations with Iraq.' Successive attempts by Congress to impose economic sanctions on Iraq had been blocked. 'President Bush is an intelligent man. He is not going to declare an economic war against Iraq.'

It was in this context that the Kuwait crisis was viewed. Here again Glaspie was conciliatory. The Administration fully understood Saddam's desperate need for funds; indeed, many Americans also had a stake in higher oil prices. She conceded that 'my own estimate after twenty-five years of serving in the area is that your aims [of ensuring that Kuwait did not cheat on its quota] should receive strong support from your brother Arabs'. This was an issue for the Arabs to solve among themselves. Nor did the United States have an 'opinion on inter-Arab disputes such as your border dispute with Kuwait . . . and Secretary of State Baker had directed our official spokesman to reiterate this stand'.[30] Also repeating official statements, she told Saddam that the United States 'could never excuse settlement of disputes by any but peaceful means'.[31] This message could not be backed up by any threat of American action. She had no authority to make one. If she had judged it necessary she would have had to go back to Washington for new instructions.

The natural interpretation for Saddam to put on this, especially in the light of his opening harangue, was that the United States was still offering him a hand of friendship while urging him to be good. However, he had not specifically said that he was going to invade Kuwait, and any reading he may have made of the Ambassador's remarks would have been distorted by the fact that he also encouraged her to believe that the crisis was blowing over.

According to Glaspie, after Saddam's diatribe on Iraqi rights he left to take a thirty-minute call from Mubarak. He returned in a more relaxed mood and told her that there was no problem because Iraq and Kuwait would meet in Jeddah the next week. He gave an 'unconditional pledge' not to use force against Kuwait, a pledge later repeated, in Glaspie's claim, by two top officials on 28 and 29 July. He appeared uninterested in her refutation of his original points and quickly closed the meeting. When Glaspie asked Saddam 'in the spirit of friendship, not of confrontation' his intentions regarding Kuwait, she was reassured with a clear preference for a peaceful resolution of the crisis, though he did not discount the military option as a means of last resort.

Interestingly, in the light of his own injunction to Mubarak on his

53

departure from Baghdad to Kuwait, Saddam reported the Egyptian's view that the Kuwaitis were 'scared'. His extortionate tactics were having the desired effect. Saddam explained that he had told Mubarak to

> assure the Kuwaitis and give them our word that we are not going to do anything until we meet with them. If, when we meet, we see that there is hope, nothing will happen. But if we are unable to find a solution, then it will be natural that Iraq will not accept death, even though wisdom is above everything else.

So relieved was the Ambassador that she told Saddam that she would revive her holiday plans – which she had shelved when the crisis had been escalating – and would return to Washington the following Monday (30 July). She reported back to Washington: 'His emphasis that he wants a peaceful settlement is surely sincere.'[32]

The view in Washington on 26 July was thus that the crisis had abated. Ambassador Glaspie got confirmation from Iraqi officials of Baghdad's apparently more conciliatory position, and the Iraqi propaganda machine, which had been going full blast for a week, was immediately switched off. The Kuwaitis were no longer being denounced daily by the media. She reported this relaxed assessment back to Washington – where it fitted in with the equally optimistic reports coming from the Egyptians and the Saudis. Her advice: 'ease off on public criticism of Iraq until we see how the negotiations develop'.[33]

The British view was similar. There was never any suggestion of British intervention and no emergency meetings. As the crisis built up over the second half of July 1990, there was consistent assessment from the Joint Intelligence Committee, strongly influenced by contacts with the Arabs, to the effect that this was merely a tough negotiation. As in the United States the technical intelligence gave a clear and accurate picture of the Iraqi build-up, but this was overshadowed by confident Arab statements. The Foreign Office did back the American line on 24 July: 'We continue to believe that the dispute should be settled by discussion and peaceful means. We would deplore any threat or use of force.'[34] However, when Mubarak sent word that there was no danger there was a general sigh of relief and return to other business. One piece of information received suggested that Saddam had sent all these forces to the border area because he wanted them away from Baghdad or in the south because of internal troubles at either location. This seemed perfectly plausible.

It was assumed that the crisis would end when the Kuwaitis handed over a substantial amount of cash. One official saw a Kuwaiti prince on a private visit to London and gained the impression that it was all 'a tiresome business but would be sorted out'. There were some worries that both Kuwait and the UAE were behaving in an incautious fashion. These concerns were communicated through normal diplomatic contacts. However, as one diplomat observed, this had little impact as the Kuwaitis were in their 'we know how to deal with the Iraqi mode'. The senior Foreign Office official dealing with the Middle East, David Gore-Booth, is said to have agreed with the Kuwaiti Ambassador, when they met on 25 July, that the crisis was blowing over and that it was largely over oil prices, an area where the Kuwaitis were urged not to be so 'cavalier'. In general he advised restraint, including in military deployments.[35]

This was followed by the only meeting Foreign Secretary Douglas Hurd had with his officials on the issue, which led to the only British initiative. Although the Arab process appeared to be working this time, instructions were sent to the delegation at the United Nations suggesting that the problem of borders would remain and that this should be raised among the five permanent members of the Security Council. There was no interest from the other members. No attempt was even made to co-ordinate with other states of the European Community.

The crisis persists

These rosy assessments were hardly supported by developments on the ground. Intelligence reports continued to inform of a rapidly expanding military build-up. On 27 July, eleven days after Saddam's public warning to Kuwait, eight Iraqi divisions of some 100,000 men from the best Iraqi units were poised on the joint border. Senior officials in Washington still judged this to be more consistent with intimidation than with preparations for an actual invasion, which would have required a far heavier communications traffic and more substantial artillery stocks, munitions and logistics 'tail'.[36] This view was reinforced by a personal message from Mubarak to Bush, assuring the Administration that there was no problem and encouraging the United States to keep a low profile. A message was thus sent from Bush to Saddam, promising him US friendship and asking for an Iraqi *quid pro quo*. It warned the Iraqi President not to pursue 'threats involving military force or conflict against Kuwait', but at the same time expressed a keen interest in improving relations with Baghdad.[37] The Americans also toned down their own remarks and heeded Arab advice to keep themselves detached from a problem that the Arabs now intended to solve among themselves.[38]

Yet, although Baghdad had said that there was an opportunity for a negotiated settlement, it had not toned down any of its demands. Indeed, in conversation with Chadly Klibi of the Arab League, Tariq Aziz had expressed his conviction that the Kuwaiti royal family should go. When Klibi briefed the Kuwaitis on the Iraqi view he stressed the importance of the impending summit and the determination of the Egyptians and the Saudis to ensure that it succeeded. King Hussein of Jordan urged them to take the Iraqi threats seriously. King Fahd wrote to the Emir making clear his expectation of a compromise, by expressing confidence that

> your wisdom and foresight will, God willing, achieve our aims, our brother Arabs: to reduce all difficulties and to ensure the love and understanding between the two sisterly states.[39]

The Emir was aware that the Saudi King did not necessarily have Kuwait's best interests at heart. He therefore treated Fahd's entreaties warily. The Saudis, he suspected, had their own agenda. A weak Kuwait would be less able to resist Saudi demands on the status of the demilitarized zone between the two countries as well as being vulnerable to recurring Iraqi pressures that were bound to come sooner or later.

The Emir accepted the idea of a Kuwaiti–Iraqi summit meeting in Jeddah but showed no inclination to make concessions to Iraq. Nor was he happy to concede that the next step after Jeddah should be Baghdad, where a Kuwaiti delegation would be at a political and psychological disadvantage. He was placing the risks of appeasing Saddam higher than those of failing to do so. A warning had been received on 25 July from their military attaché in Basra that Iraq's Republican Guard was planning to invade the whole of Kuwait.[40] However, this was probably discounted then in the light of the optimism attending Mubarak's mediation and his report that the Iraqis did not really intend to invade.

As news filtered out that Iraq had relaxed neither its demands nor its military pressure anxiety once more began to grow, and on 27 July the Americans warned Kuwait, Egypt and Saudi Arabia of ever greater concentrations of men and equipment. However, there was a ready explanation to be found for the Iraqi behaviour. That day in Geneva a meeting of OPEC Ministers was beginning. There the Iraqi Oil Minister set his objective as raising the current price from $18 a barrel to $25. This went against both prevailing market conditions, in which there was still a glut, and the Saudi determination to keep the price at a 'reasonable' level which would not trigger Western inflation. Working closely now with its former adversary, Iran, the Iraqis allowed themselves to be pulled down to a lower price only reluctantly – first to $23 and then finally to $21. In return they achieved what was assumed to be a critical agreement on OPEC's overall production quotas – of 22.5 million barrels a day – and promises of firm enforcement.[41]

When this agreement was achieved on 28 July it was widely assumed that the Iraqis had been rather clever in imposing some discipline into the cartel's affairs and had obtained a better OPEC agreement than they could have otherwise expected. Yet Saddam had no reason to take new Kuwaiti promises seriously. One source cites a conversation between the Kuwaiti and Iraqi oil ministers at the meeting, with the former 'rudely and publicly' saying that the new agreement meant nothing.[42] The pressure was sustained. That same day, using Yasser Arafat as an intermediary, Saddam passed on to Kuwait the message that at the Jeddah meeting scheduled for 31 July, he sought $10 billion 'as compensation for the use of the Rumaila oil wells', in return for which he promised only to reduce his troops. Meanwhile, he moved forward his artillery, logistics support and aircraft. On 30 July an analyst in the Defence Intelligence Agency (DIA) in Washington wrote that this was 'a force disproportionate to the task at hand, if it is to bluff'. If so, the only answer was that 'he intends to use it'.[43]

This stark warning was sent to senior US policy-makers but was treated with the disbelief that commonly accompanies a warning that another Government is about to break a basic international rule. When Bush spoke with King Hussein on 28 July, he expressed his hope that 'the situation will not exceed the limits of reason', to which the King replied: 'There is no possibility for this, and it will not reach this point.'[44] So the prevailing view – shared by the Kuwaitis, the other Arabs, the British and even the Israeli intelligence which had long been cautioning against Saddam's aggressive intentions[45] – was largely that the Iraqi objective was still intimidation and, if military action was taken, it would probably be confined to seizing part of the Rumaila oilfield or possibly the strategically located Warba and Bubiyan islands. It was assumed that Saddam would pull back from Kuwait once the islands were secured. A compelling strategic case was constructed as to why Iraq badly needed the islands.[46]

The only problem with this analysis was that this objective had never figured prominently in Saddam's public or private utterances, where the immediate Iraqi demand was focused on cash. Nevertheless, this notion of a limited strike was critical to American policy. If it had been appreciated that the logic of Iraqi military action was to take all of Kuwait, that might have produced a firm American response; the thought that it was geared only to wounding produced more reticence. A senior Administration official acknowledged later:

We were reluctant to draw a line in the sand. I can't see the American public supporting the deployment of troops over a dispute over twenty miles of desert territory and it is not clear that the local countries would have supported that kind of commitment. The basic principle is not to make threats you can't deliver on.[47]

Even if the United States had wished to take stronger action there were limits to what it could do. The Egyptians and the Saudis were relying on the forthcoming Jeddah meeting and wanted the Americans to do nothing that might undermine its success. There were limits to how far Washington could go ahead of its major Arab allies. Moreover, its coercive options were also constrained. Without local support it could not send ground troops into the area and, anyway, they would take weeks to arrive. The experience with the UAE warned of the problems of attempting to give states more military support than they dared acknowledge publicly.

Nor were economic sanctions, for which Congress was pressing, likely to have much effect. As Saddam had noted to Glaspie, non-agricultural trade was now minimal and subject to numerous restrictions. Total trade was barely an annual $2 billion. The most substantial was the agricultural credit guarantee programme but this was due to expire on 30 September and was not expected to be renewed in the current climate.

All the ambiguities in American policy towards the region and to Iraq itself were now surfacing. The Administration could not ignore the Iraqi pressure on Kuwait, but it did not want to jettison its previous policy. It still wanted to get Saddam's help in opposing terrorism and in promoting a moderate view on the Arab–Israeli dispute. Saddam's unpredictability and ruthlessness were recognized, yet there was hope that he would be rational in his basic calculations.

Crisis management had become a matter of working with the prevailing Arab view which was still intent on creating the optimum conditions for a successful negotiation. As a result, Administration officials found themselves walking a tightrope between sustaining a conciliatory line towards Iraq and deterring it from embarking on an aggression for which it seemed now geared. The outcome was an ambiguous policy combining threats with attempts at appeasement. When on 27 July the Senate voted eighty to sixteen to impose economic sanctions on Iraq, including the end of the $1.2 billion in loan guarantees, the Administration still objected. Representative Howard Berman reported being telephoned four times at the end of the month by senior State Department and White House people asking him to postpone a vote on the bill he had introduced in the House to cut off trade with Iraq.[48]

After being persistently questioned by Congressman Lee Hamilton on 31 July, John Kelly acknowledged:

> We don't have any defence treaty with the Gulf states. That's clear. We support the independence and security of all friendly states in the region. Since the Truman Administration, we've maintained naval forces in the area because its stability is in our interest. We call for a peaceful solution to all disputes, and we think that the sovereignty of every state in the Gulf must be respected.

When asked what would happen if Iraq crossed the Kuwaiti border, he said he could not enter into such hypothetical questions: 'Suffice it to say that we would be extremely concerned, but I cannot venture into the realms of hypothesis.' He then went on to confirm that the United States would be under no treaty obligation to use American forces. If Kelly had suggested a defence obligation he was unlikely to have received a favourable Congressional response. The prevailing view there was that economic sanctions but not military action were appropriate.

All this reinforced Saddam in his conviction that the US would remain aloof in the case of an Iraqi attack on Kuwait. His Ambassador to Washington, Muhammad al-Mashat, was reporting 'few risks of an American reaction in case of an intervention in Kuwait'. According to one account, US intelligence intercepted and decoded a telegram giving numerous examples of American passivity during international crises – Turkey and Cyprus, China and Tibet, the Soviet Union and Afghanistan.[49] Confident of American neutrality, Saddam proceeded to the promised negotiations with Kuwait.[50] The Kuwaitis arrived in Jeddah as defiant as ever regarding Iraq's financial demands,[51] but there was no doubting the hard Iraqi position on the eve of the talks. As the Iraqi press put it:

> Iraq attends the Jeddah meeting to regain its rights and not to hear new talk about 'fraternity and solidarity' which yields nothing.

In the evening hours of 31 July the two delegations met at Jeddah without a mediator present. They had been greeted by the Saudi Crown Prince, Abdallah Ibn-Abd-al-Aziz, but he left as the serious discussions began. Izzat Ibrahim, the Vice-President of Iraq's Revolutionary Command Council, read out a prepared statement laying out all the charges against Kuwait. Then the head of the Kuwaiti delegation, Crown Prince Sa'd Abdallah al-Sabah, replied, refuting the allegations. Eventually they got on to the money, and the haggling began. The Iraqis claim that Ibrahim asked for a $10 billion compensation for the use of the Rumaila oilfield, but was ready to settle for a loan if Kuwait was unable to give the money as a grant. However, in their account, the Kuwaitis were determined to humiliate Iraq by offering it 'only' $9 billion. Naturally, Ibrahim could not acquiesce in such an affront from a minor power, even when the Saudis offered to make up the difference.[52]

The Kuwaiti version has Ibrahim not contenting himself with the $10 billion but demanding surrender of some disputed territories to Iraq, as well as oil-pumping rights inside Kuwait.[53] These demands were declined by the Kuwaitis, who argued that they did not have such huge sums of money at hand. They agreed, nevertheless, to write off their wartime loans to Baghdad, but in return asked for the settlement of the longstanding Iraqi–Kuwaiti border dispute. As a token of goodwill, they even suggested that Iraq kept the forgiven loans in its books, so as to magnify its economic predicament and gain improved repayment terms from its international creditors. This outraged Ibrahim. Ignoring Kuwaiti pleas not to do so, he called off the summit and soon afterwards left Jeddah.[54]

The Kuwaitis did not expect the meeting to stop here. They had (reluctantly) agreed that they would go to Baghdad on 4 August and still believed that the issues would be picked up again then. Assuming that they were still engaged in an extended haggle during which they would identify the minimum price to be paid to Iraq to achieve their security, they were developing some ideas for a broader agenda designed to improve relations between the two countries. Their optimism was apparently reinforced by a statement by Sa'dun Hammadi that Kuwait had failed to take Iraq's demands seriously but that the meetings would continue in Baghdad.[55]

On 31 July the Americans had been alerted by King Hussein that the situation was serious. He told George Bush: 'The Iraqis are angry but I hope that something will take place in the interests of greater co-operation in the region.' The President asked: 'Without war?' and the King replied that yes, he hoped so. After talking on 1 August with King Fahd, the US issued a statement hoping that this next meeting would be more successful and that coercion and intimidation would have no future.[56] Behind the scenes the Americans had been in touch with the Kuwaitis, who were still nervous about calling on non-Arab forces. Washington did not want to be blamed for provoking a crisis. Both parties believed that they had more time. John Kelly saw Iraqi Ambassador Muhammad al-Mashat in the afternoon and expressed his concern. The Ambassador told him there was no need to worry. 'We are not going to move against anybody.'[57]

However, even before the collapse of the Jeddah talks, the three Iraqi armoured divisions facing Kuwait had uncoiled and moved forward to within three miles of the border, which was then closed. The tanks and artillery took up classic offensive positions and were joined by some eighty helicopters.[58] After Ibrahim had reported back to Saddam, the Iraqi President called an immediate meeting of the Revolutionary Command Council and launched his invasion of Kuwait.

Why the invasion?

The possibility of an Iraqi takeover had loomed over Kuwait for as long as the emirate had been independent. Although there is no evidence that Saddam had entertained serious thoughts in this direction prior to the summer of 1990, it has been suggested that planning for the occupation of Kuwait began up to five years before August 1990 and specific training two years before.[59] This may well be true. Military organizations habitually plan for a whole range of contingencies, some of which are inevitably fanciful. Even serious planning does no more than create an option for the political leadership. Once such an option is created, however, it plays on the politician's mind and he may begin to think of circumstances in which it might be exercised. Equally, once the option is known to be available, especially to the intended victim, then not to exercise it makes it difficult to revive in the future. We do not, however, believe that Saddam would have resorted to such a desperate measure if Iraq's economic condition had not been so dire.

When Saddam set in motion the military build-up in the middle of July 1990, he knew full well that he was initiating a process that would most probably end with the occupation of Kuwait. At the same time as the build-up began on the border with Kuwait, there were exercises in central Iraq to practise the helicopter-borne assault on Kuwait City by special forces with which the invasion began on 2 August. An advance party of commandos is said to have been part of a sports delegation on a pre-arranged visit. They were able to help guide the helicopters to their targets.[60]

It is doubtful that Saddam expected any invasion to be anything other than comprehensive. His needs from Kuwait, as clarified to the Kuwaitis time and again, were by no means confined to the Bubiyan and Warba islands, and there is no evidence of any interest in a limited 'land grab' which would allow the residual Kuwaiti state to continue to mobilize international opinion against Iraq. Whether he was determined to invade come what may is much more difficult to judge. According to Heikal he had set the invasion in motion two days earlier and it would have taken unexpected Kuwaiti concessions to stop it. He also reports that Saddam was convinced by this time there was no point in taking just islands and an oilfield. If the al-Sabah family were left in power they could turn Kuwait into an American military base. Conversely, he believed that once all of Kuwait had been swallowed, no Arab country would dare to ask for US support.[61]

We have described how relations between Iraq and Kuwait had been deteriorating for some time. Kuwaiti behaviour had become increasingly provocative to Saddam and it would have required a complete about-face on the part of the Emir for Saddam to forgo his campaign. If the Kuwaitis had taken a conciliatory line in immediate response to Saddam's demarche of 17 July and given in to his demands, then there might have been a peaceful resolution. The Kuwaitis were understandably nervous that an easy victory for Iraqi extortion at this point would invite regular repetition. Given the formidable economic obstacles confronting Iraq and Saddam's determination to cling to power at all costs, further demands that would make Kuwaiti sovereignty merely nominal were bound to come if Saddam's economic interests so required.

Nonetheless, Kuwait's failure to appease Saddam confirmed its fate. Not only was it taken by Saddam as a vindication of his longstanding perception of Kuwait as a parasitic state thriving on Iraq's heavy sacrifices, but it was also viewed as a personal affront from a minor neighbour. In Saddam's opinion, the Kuwaitis did not treat him (i.e. Iraq) with due respect, or take his word seriously. They were playing their devious game of procrastination, believing that they could yet again evade their responsibilities to Iraq.

By adding Kuwait's fabulous wealth to the depleted Iraqi treasury, Saddam hoped to slash Iraq's foreign debt and launch the ambitious reconstruction programmes he had promised his people in the wake of the war with Iran. Given Iraq's historic claim to Kuwait, its occupation could lift Saddam's national prestige by portraying him as the liberator of usurped Iraqi lands. Last but not least, the capture of Kuwait could make Iraq the leading power in the Arab world and give it a decisive say in the world oil market. In short, in one stroke his position would be permanently secured.

Saddam's public readiness to continue a dialogue with Kuwait must therefore be seen as largely a smoke-screen aimed at gaining international legitimization for the impending military action. If Kuwait had fully acceded to Iraqi demands on 31 July then Saddam might have found it difficult to launch an invasion the next day. In this sense the reassurances dispensed from 24 July on, the turning off of the media vitriol and the agreement to a negotiating process of which the Jeddah meeting was supposed to be just the beginning, ensured that no compromise was reached because the Kuwaitis were lulled into a false sense of security and persisted with their intransigence. At this stage Saddam did not search for a compromise or string the crisis out any longer. Rather he exercised his military option while he could and for maximum gain, accepting that if he waited much longer the option would decline and could be difficult to recreate in the future.

This raises the final question as to whether the United States – and the West in general – could have done more to prevent the invasion. It is important not to stress the Western role to the neglect of that played by such key Arab states as Saudi Arabia and Egypt. The American and British Governments had little choice but to take their cues from those most directly involved with Arab efforts at mediation. For its part, Kuwait assumed that if it came to the crunch it would have American support but was wary about being seen to be too close to Washington (especially perhaps as a conspiracy between the two was a constant theme in the Iraqi propaganda) and so failed to derive any deterrent effect by keeping the relationship ambiguous.

Less reasonable in American behaviour over this period was the determination to sustain a policy of good relations with a state which, on the most favourable interpretation, was engaged in extortion and in opposition to a number of central US foreign policy goals. The unfortunate message this conveyed was compounded by an insistence that the United States had no position on the particulars of the Iraq–Kuwait dispute. This is a common American practice on regional issues and reflects an understandable desire to avoid becoming embroiled in complex matters which inflame intense local passions. In this particular case, however, it suggested indifference and an inability to judge the quality of the cases presented by the disputants. Also unfortunate was the readiness to stress the lack of any defence commitment to Kuwait at such a critical juncture, even though it was difficult to assert one.

Saddam was certainly sensitive to the possibility of US interference. His response to intimations of American concern was to seek to deflect their anxieties while simultaneously warning them off intervention. He calmed down the propaganda onslaught and stressed the possibility of a negotiated outcome. At the same time he did not alter his position on any questions of substance nor put the military build-up into reverse gear. If his objective was to calm the Americans then he succeeded, and was rewarded with more evidence of Washington's determination to pursue good relations than of overt support for Kuwaiti sovereignty beyond general declarations. Saddam encouraged American self-delusion with regard to the crisis blowing over. Consequently, no attempt was made to provide explicit warning of the likely response to an overt act of aggression. As a result, Saddam in the end also deceived himself. The embryonic 'new world order' was thrown into its first major test.

PART TWO
Lines in the Sand

CHAPTER 4

Response to Invasion

The attack began at 01.00 exactly on 2 August 1990. It eventually involved some 140,000 Iraqi troops and 1,800 tanks but was initially spearheaded by two Republican Guard armoured divisions – the Hammurabi and the Medina. They moved rapidly south towards Kuwait City, while a special forces commando division attacked the city itself. Simultaneously, heliborne Iraqi units seized selected strategic sites throughout Kuwait, including the coveted islands of Bubiyan and Warba at the northern tip of the Persian Gulf. It was followed the next day by a mechanized division of the Republican Guard – the Tawakalna – with the task of securing the border with Saudi Arabia.

This operation was nothing like the agonizing invasion of Iran a decade earlier. The 16,000-strong Kuwaiti Army was not fully mobilized, in line with the Government's attempt not to provoke the Iraqis. It was no match for the overwhelmingly superior invading forces and was crushed within hours, though intermittent armed resistance continued for several days. The fiercest resistance was reported around the Emir's palace in Kuwait City, which was taken only after two hours of tough fighting involving heavy machine-gun fire and air strikes. The Kuwaiti Air Force managed to keep flying and attacking armoured columns until their base was overrun the next day. But this was the exception that proved the rule: within twelve hours of the invasion Kuwait was under Iraq's control.

There was no possibility of outside help. Some three hours after the invasion began, a request for aid was made by the Crown Prince, Sheikh Sa'd Abdallah al-Sabah, to the American Embassy. But there were no military options available to the United States. The Crown Prince, still apparently worried about creating the wrong impression, asked that the request 'not be made public or treated as official'. An hour later the request was repeated with this condition removed. Before there could be a reply the Crown Prince had joined the Emir on his flight to Saudi Arabia.[1] Of the royal family, only the Emir's brother died, resisting the assault on the Royal Palace.

Saddam apparently intended neither officially to annex the tiny emirate nor

67

to maintain a permanent military presence there. Instead, he sought to establish hegemony over Kuwait, ensuring its complete financial, political and strategic subservience to his wishes. This would have given Saddam everything he wanted from Kuwait, without incurring the attendant risks of outright annexation. Accordingly, the overthrow of the ruling dynasty in Kuwait was presented by the Iraqi mass media as an indigenous uprising, and the Iraqi intervention as a temporary measure, of days or weeks at the most, aimed at shoring up the new 'liberal regime' against external aggression. Once this external threat had dissipated there would be no further need for keeping Iraqi troops in Kuwait.[2]

If this was his objective then, in one important sense, the operation was a failure. That Saddam had intended to seize the Emir was evident in the determined effort to seize both the Dasman Palace, the Emir's seaside residence, and the main royal palace in Kuwait City at the start of the invasion. However, early warning had been received (from a radar carried on a balloon), giving the government a couple of hours' notice of the attack. The Emir and the royal family escaped to exile.

Had they been captured, Saddam could have physically annihilated them as traitors or agents of 'world imperialism', as he had done to numerous prominent figures in Iraq during his political career. Alternatively he could have forced the captive Kuwaiti leadership into an agreement that would have undermined its own legitimacy. As it was, the authority and legitimacy of the al-Sabah family remained intact. Within hours the Kuwaiti Crown Prince was appealing to his people in a clandestine radio broadcast, calling upon them to resist 'the Iraqi aggression'.

To make things worse for Saddam, he totally failed to predict the reaction of the Kuwaiti people to his predatory move. Not only did they not rise in large numbers to greet their self-styled liberators, but this peaceful, soft nation proved to be far more resilient than anticipated. Notwithstanding the immediate collapse of the Kuwaiti military, armed resistance continued throughout the principality, and clandestine radio broadcasts urged the Kuwaitis to resist. From a purely military point of view, this was no match for the formidable Iraqi contingent. Yet its political consequences were far-reaching: an unmistakable signal was sent to Saddam that his puppet regime stood no chance of survival unless propped up by Iraqi bayonets. Over the following months the resistance tied down an estimated two divisions of Iraqi troops, as well as providing intelligence to the coalition and harassing and sabotaging the occupation. The Kuwaiti Government later estimated that some 1,000 civilians were murdered during the occupation, with many more forcibly deported to Iraq.

Saddam's scheme turned sour also because, with few exceptions, the international reaction was one of condemnation. Instead of a simple, straightforward operation that overnight would close a chapter of Arab history, Saddam found himself in the middle of a major crisis. The conflict between Iraq and Kuwait turned into a feud between Iraq and almost the entire international community.

The failure of the 'Arab solution'

The internationalization of the crisis was particularly alarming. To counter this Saddam hurried to play the Arab card. Exploiting the deeply ingrained suspicion of any revival of Western colonialism in the Middle East, he propagated the idea of containing the crisis in the region and not allowing foreign powers to 'invade' the Middle East again.

For a short while this ploy seemed to work. No Arab regime dared to refer publicly to the possibility of external intervention. Even Kuwait's emotional plea for help from the international community was still coupled with a denial of any intention to internationalize the crisis and a stated preference for 'an Arab solution'.[3]

On 2 August, King Hussein of Jordan and President Husni Mubarak of Egypt met in Alexandria. The King had already spoken to Saddam, who had warned against 'a position of condemnation and accusation and a tough stance that might pave the way for outside intervention' – if this was the outcome, then 'we will tear each other's eyes out'. Hussein and Mubarak agreed that this was not the sort of crisis that could be solved at Foreign Minister level and that a summit of Arab leaders was required. They both spoke to President Bush, pleading with him to hold back on any American action to give the Arabs an ample chance to resolve the crisis on their own. They were told that they had a few days but that already the crisis 'had gone beyond simply a regional dispute because of the naked aggression'. Time was therefore limited. Then they telephoned Saddam and asked him to receive the King and attend an emergency Arab mini-summit in Jeddah, with the participation of Saudi Arabia, Egypt, Jordan, and the Kuwaiti Emir.[4]

As to what happened from this point on, there are fundamentally different versions. In the Jordanian account, King Hussein and President Mubarak instructed their Foreign Ministers to ask the Arab League Council, which at the time was holding a special emergency session in Cairo at the request of Kuwait, to delay any public reference to the Iraqi occupation, so as not to undermine the chances for convening a mini-summit. The fear was that such a reference would cause Saddam a public loss of face and drive him to become more intransigent. On 3 August the King met Saddam, who reportedly informed him of his consent to attend the mini-summit in Jeddah on 5 August and to withdraw his troops from Kuwait. At this stage, when the Jordanians felt that their mediation effort was making significant progress, the Arab League unexpectedly decided to bring things to a head and issued a condemnation of the Iraqi invasion, contrary to the earlier understanding. Having failed to forestall this move, the Jordanians felt they had no choice but to express their reservations 'from a pan-Arab premise based on our deep understanding of the perils of the internationalization of the Iraqi–Kuwaiti crisis'.[5]

The Egyptian account of these events is markedly different. According to Mubarak, he instructed King Hussein to inform Saddam that the mini-summit hinged on his unequivocal acceptance of two preconditions: 'the immediate withdrawal [of Iraqi forces] from Kuwait which is an independent and sovereign state', and the restoration of the al-Sabah family, 'because it is not a man's responsibility to change a system in a neighbouring country by force; this is the responsibility of the people'. Once Saddam had accepted these conditions and pulled out of Kuwait, a mini-summit would be convened to discuss the problems between Iraq and Kuwait. Egypt was willing to participate in an all-Arab peace-keeping force to act as a buffer between Iraq and Kuwait, should the need arise.

Most regrettably, argued Mubarak, the Jordanian King did not pursue the line agreed at Alexandria. He was simply too timid to raise the two preconditions with Saddam. 'On Friday, 3 August, at approximately 16.00, my brother King Hussein telephoned me and informed me that Saddam had accepted the summit,' Mubarak told a press conference on 8 August,

> I then asked on what basis the summit should be held? On the basis of these few points? He told me he had not been able to discuss details. I answered that I could not accept that. Could I contact the custodian of the two mosques [i.e. King Fahd] and invite him to attend a summit while we still did not know what we were going to achieve? Could we sit down and use invective against each other and then have the world say the summit had failed? The issue would worsen and deteriorate.

In these circumstances Mubarak felt that he could neither give the mini-summit a 'green light' nor continue to hold back the Arab League from publicly condemning the Iraqi invasion. The Syrians were pressing hard for condemnation, while the Saudis were becoming increasingly impatient. Yet, this did not mean the end of the quest for an Arab solution. The League's statement, while condemning the Iraqi occupation of Kuwait and demanding that it end immediately, rejected any external interference in the crisis and urged the Arab Kings and Presidents to convene an Arab summit after Iraq's unconditional withdrawal.[6]

King Hussein's allegation that the Arab League's statement and Mubarak's behaviour aborted Iraq's immediate withdrawal from Kuwait seems fanciful. Eager to prevent external interference, Saddam certainly preferred to confine the crisis to the Arab arena. It is also plausible that he told King Hussein he was ready to pull out of Kuwait: on the same day that the King arrived in Baghdad, Iraq's supreme decision-making body, the Revolutionary Command Council (RCC), publicly stated that 'the valiant armed forces [of Iraq] had completed their honest national and pan-Arab duties [of defending Kuwait]', and were to begin withdrawing from the principality on 5 August 'unless something emerges that threatens the security of Kuwait and Iraq'.[7]

By this time the Bush Administration was accusing Saddam of planning to attack Saudi Arabia. There was deep anxiety underlying the RCC's statement, illustrated by its vehement denial that the decision came in response to 'the empty hubris voiced here and there by tendentious parties to whom we attach no weight at all', and its warning that any attack against Kuwait or Iraq would be 'confronted by decisiveness that would sever its hand from its shoulder'.

The statement to the effect that the Iraqis were about to quit Kuwait was thus less to do with the Jordanian monarch than an attempt to avoid an escalation of the crisis. It did not reflect a sincere intention. American satellites did not detect any indications of a withdrawal. To the contrary, the 'popular Kuwaiti Army' which was to replace the regular Iraqi Army was simply a cover for a disguised Iraqi military presence.

Nor did the Arab League's statement on the Kuwaiti crisis seem to have added to Saddam's intransigence in any significant way. Contacts concerned with the proposed mini-summit continued even after the statement had been issued. The League was not even the first international Muslim or Arab body to condemn the invasion publicly.[8] Above all, even before the League's public condemnation of the invasion, Saddam appeared as defiant as ever, accompanying the appeasing melodies whispered in King Hussein's ears with harsh chords towards the rest of the Arab world. In his visit to Riyadh on 3 August to explain the Iraqi invasion, Izzat Ibrahim told his hosts that there was no way to reverse the clock and that Kuwait was past history.[9] Sa'dun Hammadi, who arrived in Cairo on 2 August for the extraordinary session of the Arab League, had an equally uncompromising message. 'The situation in Kuwait is not negotiable,' he told his audience.

> What happened in the emirate was an internal affair. There had been a popular uprising against the treacherous al-Sabah regime, and the provisional revolutionary government requested Iraq's assistance. Naturally, Baghdad complied with the request. There was nothing the Arab League could, and should, do in this respect.[10]

Saddam was using the so-called 'Arab solution' as a delaying tactic to cushion himself against international pressure while he pursued the satellization of Kuwait. The only value of the proposed mini-summit was the necessary time for and acquiescence in this task. Mubarak's preconditions were non-starters. As satellization was turning out to be far more demanding than originally conceived, requiring a substantially greater investment of time and repressive measures, immediate withdrawal from Kuwait was impossible. To have left before satellization was complete would have done nothing for Saddam's economic predicament and would have incurred an extremely humiliating loss of face which he was unable to afford.

The restoration of the al-Sabah family was unthinkable. Saddam drove this point home forcefully to the Saudis and the Egyptians;[11] he would not even have the al-Sabahs participate at the proposed meeting at Jeddah.[12] This position was unacceptable to the Arab leaders. The violation of Kuwait was tantamount to a declaration of war on the rest of the Gulf regimes. However unpopular the Kuwaiti ruling family might have been in Saudi Arabia, its violent removal set a precedent that threatened other monarchies in the Gulf and, hence, had to be rectified without delay. President Mubarak, with his personal trust in Saddam shattered following the latter's deception prior to the invasion, dreaded the idea of allowing the Iraqi leader gains that would transform him into the most powerful leader in the Arab world. This feeling was shared by President Asad of Syria, Saddam's arch-enemy for more than two decades.

The outcome of this contradictory balance of interests, desires, and passions was that the 'Arab solution' was a stillborn idea. The gap between Saddam and the other Arab leaders was simply too wide to bridge, and the two parties realized this fact. An immediate Iraqi withdrawal from Kuwait was an impossibility. An eventual evacuation depended on the readiness of other Arab leaders to sacrifice the al-Sabah family and to acquiesce in Iraqi hegemony over Kuwait. Since neither Saudi Arabia, nor Egypt, nor Syria was willing to accept such an eventuality, they became more receptive to the international alternative.

Bush takes the lead

In truth the crisis had been internationalized from the moment the first news of the invasion came in. The occupation of Iraq may have come as a surprise but it was such a textbook case of aggression that there was never any question that an elemental rule of international order had been broken. Iraq had been so ostentatious in the build-up to the occupation and so blatant in its execution that there was no possibility of giving it the benefit of the doubt. Baghdad's claim that the whole exercise was a response to requests from a revolutionary Government in Kuwait was such a patent fabrication, and so unrelated to Iraq's pre-occupation demands, that it stripped the action of any sort of legitimacy. It is basic to an understanding of everything that followed the Iraqi invasion of Kuwait that this action was immediately identified by the bulk of the international community as a blatant act of aggression without nuance or ambiguity. From the start the United Nations set itself the goal of getting Iraq out of Kuwait, and at no point thereafter was that goal ever judged to be secondary to the potential costs of achieving it.

Within the first day it was possible to see the three elements which ensured that pressure on Iraq would be serious and sustained: American leadership; the active co-operation of the Soviet Union; the close involvement of the United Nations.

It was during the afternoon of 1 August that senior officials in Washington began to conclude that an Iraqi invasion was imminent. By 19.00 (US time) the first news arrived that Iraqi forces had crossed the border. It was still unclear whether this was just a limited land-grab or a full-scale invasion. As more information came in, the seriousness of the situation became apparent. The 'Deputies Committee' – the crisis management group at the sub-Cabinet level – was convened. For the next seven months this group, with representatives from all key agencies, met regularly to discuss policy options.

A statement was issued calling for 'the immediate and unconditional withdrawal of all Iraqi forces'. The US Ambassador to the United Nations, Thomas Pickering, was notified and began to prepare a Security Council resolution. Measures were taken to deny Iraq access to its own and – more importantly because they were more substantial – to Kuwaiti assets overseas. The Kuwaiti Ambassador to Washington, Sheikh Saud Nasir al-Sabah, agreed on his own initiative. Other nations soon followed the American lead. Within hours Iraqi telexes were being sent in an attempt to get hold of Kuwaiti assets, but to no avail. The Iraqis managed nevertheless to lay their hands on $2 billion worth of booty from the Kuwaiti Central Bank.

President George Bush took naturally to a leadership role. He felt more comfortable generally with foreign than with domestic policy. His style in international affairs, and indeed politics in general, was based on cultivating personal relations. The risks were that this could lead to identifying friendship between individuals with the interests of states, as happened with King Hussein, and putting too much store on judgements gleaned from conversations rather than hard analysis. However, the personal touch undoubtedly could work effectively on the loyalties of other world leaders. Using his 'telephone diplomacy' – over the next six days he made more than twenty calls – he worked these contacts to gain a series of commitments to a tough stance against Iraq.

Questioned by reporters just before an 08.00 meeting of the National Security Council (NSC) on the day of the invasion, President Bush responded that he was neither discussing nor contemplating intervention, and that he did not believe any other countries were threatened. Yet he did not rule anything out and said that he wanted Iraq out of Kuwait.

This first NSC meeting was inconclusive, though it set the agenda for future debates. It confirmed that at issue were US interests as well as international law. Quick calculations revealed that Iraq now had access to 20 per cent of the world's known oil reserves. As this could be doubled by taking over Saudi Arabia, the vulnerability of that kingdom was identified as the most pressing security question. Treasury Secretary Nicholas Brady described how best to adapt to higher oil prices, prompting Bush to interject that he was not planning on 'adapting' and simply living with the new situation. However, whether or not Kuwait was now lost was to be determined; if it was, there was an immediate need to focus on the next threat. General Colin Powell, Chairman of the Joint Chiefs of Staff, asked whether the best option would be to 'draw a firm line with Saudi Arabia,' the main US interest, although this would leave Kuwait on the other side of the line.[13]

By the evening of 2 August, President Bush was at Aspen, Colorado. Standing beside the British Prime Minister, Margaret Thatcher, he was not so definite: 'We are not ruling any options in, but we are not ruling any options out.'

The special relationship

Mrs Thatcher had arrived the previous evening at Aspen to attend a high-level conference on international affairs. She was staying at the ranch of the American Ambassador to Britain, Henry Catto. The news of invasion came in almost as soon as she arrived. As in the White House, it took time to get clarification with regard to the scale of the invasion and the fate of the royal family. Her foreign policy adviser, Charles Powell, was also anxious to ensure that President Bush was still able to come to Colorado on his scheduled visit. Then Mrs Thatcher started her own phone calls to foreign leaders, starting with François Mitterrand of France. Powell interpreted.[14]

As the Western country with the closest links to the Gulf other than the United States, Britain's position was of crucial importance. It was inconceivable that Mrs Thatcher would be anything other than outraged by the Iraqi action. She saw Saddam as another in a series of dictators against whom Britain must react strongly and robustly. She had taken on Argentina over the Falkland Islands in 1982, as she reminded President Bush, and saw this as a similar sort of challenge. Bush's world view had also been forged by the failure of appeasement in stopping Hitler and the consequent need to uphold international law in the face of aggression. It is not so much the case, as was suggested at the time,[15] that Mrs Thatcher gave Bush backbone that he might otherwise be lacking, but that she reinforced his own inclinations to take a tough line with Iraq.

Bush arrived at the ranch mid-morning, accompanied by retired General Brent Scowcroft, his National Security Adviser. The first meeting took a couple of hours and concentrated mainly on the need to assemble the widest possible coalition in the United Nations, and on assessing progress on such measures as freezing assets and economic sanctions. Bush had already spoken to many leaders, including King Fahd and President Mubarak (but not President Mitterrand). King Hussein, he reported, was already blaming the Kuwaitis and the West for not listening to him. President Turgut Ozal of Turkey was more positive and recognized that Turkey was in a crucial position. Mrs Thatcher confirmed that France would support collective action. They were both concerned about the position of their nationals trapped in Kuwait. Military matters were not discussed but the basic geopolitical stakes – including the threat to the Saudis and oil – were. As President Bush explained in a brief appearance before the press: 'Prime Minister Thatcher and I are looking at it on exactly the same wavelength.'

After lunch they travelled by motorcade to the conference, where Bush gave his speech. It was one which had been long in gestation and was planned as a major announcement of a shift in defence policy away from global confrontation with the Soviet Union to a greater focus on regional disputes. In the event the substance passed unnoticed, although Bush was able to illustrate the thesis in the subsequent months.

Thatcher and Bush then went back to the ranch. The discussion was now moving on to the question of force, although entirely in terms of uncertainty over Saddam's ultimate objectives and the possible need to defend Saudi

Arabia. By this time the Iraqis were beyond Kuwait City. Britain had taken some small steps to increase naval presence in the Gulf, summoning ships from the Indian Ocean and the Far East. According to Brent Scowcroft, it was during this day of meetings that the two leaders determined that there was more at stake than the fate of Kuwait.[16]

Early next morning Bush and Scowcroft attended yet another meeting of the National Security Council. Fortified by the meeting with Thatcher at Aspen and still dissatisfied by the downbeat nature of the NSC's first meeting, Scowcroft was determined that a firm policy should emerge this time and that the logic must be to get the American flag into the region to deter Saddam from further aggression. He met with Defense Secretary Richard Cheney, Deputy Secretary of State Lawrence Eagleburger, standing in for James Baker who was in the Soviet Union,[17] and Richard Haass, Special Assistant to the President for Near East and South Asian Affairs. It was agreed that Scowcroft, Eagleburger and Cheney would open to set the tone of the meeting. Scowcroft dissuaded Bush from taking the chair and opening, as he had done at the first meeting, as there was more likely to be a free discussion if he had not made his own views clear.

The basic position adopted by all three was that here was an act of unprovoked aggression in an area of vital interest to the United States. It was therefore a far more important issue than Kuwait. As Eagleburger put it, the Iraqi aggression would set 'all the wrong standards' for the post-cold-war world – telling local dictators that now the rules of the game might have changed to make it possible to get away with aggression.[18] It was about oil, in that with access to Kuwaiti reserves, Saddam would be able to wield unprecedented influence over the world oil market. Inevitably too, any enhancement of Saddam's position would impinge on Israel, and so the United States would be unavoidably implicated. The discussion was still largely on the role of political and economic measures but the military issues were starting to loom larger – in terms of the vulnerability of Saudi Arabia and the possible need to enforce an embargo. Above all there was a growing sense that the occupation of Kuwait had to be reversed – in the long run it was insufficient simply to draw a line in the sand if Kuwait was left on the other side. There were no serious arguments among the participants. The tone had been set effectively. Haass later recalled ' a palpable sense of history in the room'.[19]

The Soviet connection

One notable absentee at the NSC meeting had been Secretary of State James Baker. As the crisis broke he had been meeting with his Soviet counterpart

Eduard Shevardnadze in Irkutsk in Siberia, about as far away as it was possible for a top policy-maker to be from home base in such circumstances. He had already had one day of meetings, talking about arms control and a variety of regional issues. The two men had not even talked about the threat Iraq had been posing to Kuwait. When Baker was warned by Washington that Iraqi forces were poised for an assault, he reported this to Shevardnadze who expressed disbelief:

> The man is perhaps sort of a thug, but he is not irrational, and this would be an irrational act and I don't think this is something that could happen.

At about 10.30 local time the news of the invasion came through. Shevardnadze appeared both 'embarrassed and surprised'.[20] His immediate reaction was that it must be a border incursion. The Iraqis had not forewarned their old patrons and Soviet intelligence had not picked up any hints of Saddam's plans. His best information had been that Saddam had only been posturing.

The news was a blow against what had been a favourable trend in Moscow's regional policy. In the two years since the termination of the Iran–Iraq War Moscow had managed to make steady inroads into the Gulf: it had deepened its relations with Iran, established working relationships with the Arab Gulf states including Saudi Arabia, and was busily mediating a peace settlement between Iran and Iraq. Moscow's relations with Kuwait prior to the invasion had also been better than with any other Gulf state, partly reflecting the Kuwaitis' own penchant for demonstrations of independence from traditional allies. Diplomatic relations had been established as early as 1964 and in the 1980s there were significant arms sales, including some missiles. When in 1987 the Kuwaitis approached the two superpowers with a request to protect their ships against Iranian attacks, it was Moscow which moved first to offer such protection, thereby prompting the United States to follow suit.[21] Kuwait reciprocated by showing understanding of the USSR's economic plight: merely three months before the Iraqi invasion it extended to Moscow a $300 million financial credit. Given the mounting turmoil in the Soviet Union's Asiatic republics throughout 1990, there was also reason to fear that any surge of nationalistic or religious fervour in the Gulf would entail grave consequences for the stability of these republics.

From the moment Saddam made his quarrel with Kuwait public in mid-July, the Soviets had stressed the merits of a negotiated settlement: 'The USSR is convinced that there are no conflicts, no matter how difficult, that cannot be settled across the negotiating table.'[22] When the Iraqi leader left the Soviet pleas unheeded and headed towards escalation, Moscow moved to direct criticism. 'If Saddam's threats against Israel last April could be justified, albeit with great difficulty, by the possibility of an Israeli attack, how can one explain and justify Saddam Hussein's remarks against one of his closest allies in the Iran–Iraq War?'[23]

Moscow found the Iraqi behaviour inexplicable. Like the Kuwaitis and the Americans the Soviets had failed to grasp the depth of Saddam's yearning for Kuwait's riches, assessing that the massive military build-up along the joint border was merely a show of force, designed to drive Kuwait into concessions. They did not rule out hostilities, but shared the consensus view at the time that these would be confined to disputed territories.[24] Hence, their reaction to the Iraqi invasion was one of unequivocal indignation. 'The Soviet Union believes that no contentious issues, no matter how complicated, justify the use of force,' read an official statement by the Soviet Government. 'Such events totally contradict the interests of the Arab states, create new, additional obstacles to the settlement of conflicts in the Middle East and run counter to the positive tendencies of improvement in international life.' Therefore,

> The Soviet Union is convinced that the elimination of dangerous tension in the Persian Gulf would promote the immediate and unconditional withdrawal of Iraqi troops from Kuwaiti territory. The sovereignty, national independence and territorial integrity of Kuwait must be fully restored and defended.[25]

From Irkutsk Baker was scheduled to go even further from the action – to Mongolia. As the information from the Gulf was still sketchy he decided to make his trip and then leave early. Dennis Ross, Director of the State Department's Planning Staff, was directed to fly back with the Soviet team to Moscow. In discussion with colleagues at the American Embassy, Ross decided that it would be helpful if Baker could return to Washington via Moscow, stopping off to deliver a joint statement with Shevardnadze. Baker agreed.

Ross then went to see his Soviet opposite number, Sergei Tarasenko. He was struck immediately that when Tarasenko wanted more information he would switch on Cable Network News (CNN) – already establishing itself as an international source of information – rather than seek out the latest Soviet intelligence. Tarasenko agreed that the crisis provided them with a good opportunity to demonstrate that the two old adversaries could co-operate on a major issue. It was also important to show that one of Iraq's most important sponsors was prepared to condemn an act of blatant illegality. In this

Tarasenko saw American pressure as a useful means of counteracting the influence of the Arabist lobby in Moscow.[26]

At the UN, the Soviet Ambassador was to the fore in securing the passage of Resolution 660 and the later resolutions on economic sanctions. The Soviet media, for their part, were castigating Saddam Hussein and his regime with a ferocity unknown in Soviet–Arab relations:

> Iraq's aggression is not merely a throwback to the era predating peres-
> troika, but rather to medieval fist law. Iraqi leaders have satisfied the
> bellicose ambitions of some of their subjects by targeting their aggres-
> sion against prosperous Kuwait, like the feudal lords who gave up
> prosperous trading cities for plunder.[27]

In this context it was not surprising that when the Foreign Minister received a draft text worked out by Ross and Tarasenko he agreed, and obtained President Gorbachev's agreement as well. Gorbachev had been in touch with Saddam, offering help in getting out of Kuwait to which he received a dusty response.

The draft text condemned the action and called for an immediate arms embargo, a point of no small significance given the Soviet role as Iraq's leading supplier. At the same time Ross checked the text with Baker and Scowcroft. At this point it ran into trouble. The Near East Department of the Soviet Foreign Ministry, as well as some influential figures in Gorba-chev's coterie, most notably Yevgeny Primakov, an academic turned active politician, still held to the old stereotypes of US–Soviet rivalry in the Middle East. In their view, giving the United States a blank cheque to lead the international coalition against Saddam would not only amount to an open admission of the USSR's decline from superpower status, but would also risk years of carefully nurtured relations with the Arab world. This view was shared by the military, frustrated with what they already saw as excessive concessions to the West in East Europe. Western military deployment in the region was a far less alarming development from the Soviet standpoint than it might have been during the 'cold war era', but was still highly undesir-able.[28] The critics pointed to the treaty with Iraq and in particular to the risk to the 8,000 Soviet citizens based there. This worried Alexander Belonogov, Shevardnadze's deputy, who saw the joint statement as causing more trouble than it was worth. Rather than endorse American policy, they argued it would be better to stress the importance of an 'Arab solution'.

By the morning of 3 August, the text had been completely rewritten and turned into something bland and without even a call for action. Ross rejected it on the grounds that it would not be worth Baker's return to Moscow. That morning the draft was discussed in the Foreign Ministry with all heads of departments and their deputies present – a group of two dozen known as the Sovnarkum (little Collegium). The general tenor was negative, but in the end Shevardnadze concluded that 'better a strong statement than a weak one'. However, even he was worried about the fate of Soviet personnel in Iraq and Kuwait – in private he was already calling them hostages. The phrase calling for international action was therefore bracketed. He knew he would probably have to agree but he wanted Baker to make the case. Then at least he could tell his hardline opponents that the Americans had insisted.

While all this was going on, Ross was finding it impossible to contact Baker, who was flying from Ulan Bator via Irkutsk back to Moscow. First there were communications problems. Then his plane was grounded in Irkutsk with a blown tyre and no power jacks (it had to be jacked up manually). The consequent two-hour delay helped Tarasenko get the draft through the Soviet machine. When Baker's aircraft finally arrived in Moscow, Ross went on board to explain the position and then the two Foreign Ministers met. Shevardnadze raised his concerns about the Soviet people in Iraq and the fears in Moscow that the Americans were being given a licence to use armed force. Baker responded by telling Shevardnadze:

> that we should condemn the action in any event; that we did not at that time have plans to move into Kuwait, but that we had a lot of American citizens in the region and we had interests there to protect, and therefore I couldn't give him any ironclad assurances.[29]

The two men stood together and called 'jointly ... upon the rest of the international community to join with us in an international cut off of all arms supplies to Iraq'. The next day Gorbachev made another appeal to Saddam, this time in slightly tougher language. There was no response other than curt comment in the Iraqi press.[30] Later, Shevardnadze stressed Baker's assurances when US troops were sent to the Gulf. The Soviet people were told that this was a temporary measure and that they would leave Saudi Arabia 'as soon as circumstances allow'.[31]

International action

The international response was already substantial. Within hours of the invasion, the UN Security Council met. On the evening of 1 August, the American Ambassador to the United Nations was having dinner with his British counterpart, Sir Crispin Tickell, when the news came through. After consultations between the two and their Governments, a draft text was ready for a Security Council resolution soon after midnight. Other members were summoned from their beds for an emergency meeting,[32] which began at 02.00. It would have ended quickly were it not for the fact that the Yemenis had not received any instructions. The vote was held up until eventually – at 06.00 – it had to be taken with a Yemeni abstention. Resolution 660, the first of many on the crisis, condemned Iraq's invasion and demanded that it 'withdraw immediately and unconditionally all its forces to the positions in which they were located on 1 August 1990'. There was no dissent: even Cuba supported it. By calling for 'intensive negotiations for the resolution of their differences' between Iraq and Kuwait the Council explicitly looked to the League of Arab States to arrange an early solution. However, the groundwork was laid for further action. The resolution invoked Articles 39 and 40 of Chapter 7 of the UN Charter. This chapter grants the Council sweeping powers to prevent 'acts of aggression' including economic sanctions or actions 'by air, sea or land forces as may be necessary to maintain or restore international peace and security'.

The next step was full economic sanctions. Most of the major powers moved quickly to stop all trade with Iraq, including oil supplies. The European Community's Foreign Ministers met two days after the invasion to co-ordinate a joint strategy, though individual members had already taken action on their own. The Italian Foreign Minister, Gianni de Michelis, speaking for Europe as Chairman of the Council of Ministers, insisted that 'we need actions of great firmness. Words are not enough.' He demanded 'concrete measures to exert the maximum possible pressure on the Iraqi government'. Thus, on Sunday 5 August, the Community agreed on a series of tough measures against Iraq, including an embargo on oil exports and a freeze on Iraqi and Kuwaiti assets.[33]

Japan appeared less enthusiastic. Officials from the Ministry of International Trade and Industry (MITI) were reportedly telling the press that sanctions would hurt exports, drive up oil prices and damage Japan's trade insurance fund. There were concerns that as there was no clear legal framework for imposing sanctions the Japanese Government might be sued by companies whose sales and profits were affected. Japan's exports to Iraq were running at $490 million each year with $670 million to Kuwait. Iraq was in arrears of about $2.56 billion on repayment of loans. Some of these repayments were being made in kind with oil: 12 per cent of Japan's supply came from this source. Yet despite these misgivings the reluctant Government judged that it had little choice but to follow the American lead, especially after a personal call to Prime Minister Kaifu from President Bush. Some comfort was drawn from the size of the oil stockpile that had been accumulated – 142 days' supply – which reduced Japan's vulnerability compared with previous oil crises. By 5 August, therefore, Japan had fallen in line.

Other countries which had substantial trade relations with Iraq were also unhappy at the prospect of sanctions. Brazil, for example, exported cars, arms and services to Iraq in return for oil. Almost half its oil requirements came from Iraq and Kuwait – 160,000 and 30,000 barrels per day (bpd) respectively. While it was disposed to sit out sanctions,[34] in practice it could do little on its own to sustain its trade if Iraq was being systematically isolated.

Iraq offered a special opportunity for sanctions because of its dependence upon one single commodity which represented some 95 per cent of its exports – oil. If Iraq could be prevented from supplying anyone, there was no need to worry about the identity of individual customers. By seizing Kuwait, Iraq had obtained control of 10 per cent of the world's oil supply and exports of 4 million bpd. Kuwaiti oil had traditionally been moved by supertankers, but Iraq transported only 400,000 bpd this way. The rest went through two pipelines, one across Turkey with a potential capacity of 1.7 million bpd and the other across Saudi Arabia, which could carry 800,000 bpd to a terminal on the Red Sea. Both pipelines had been built during the Iran–Iraq War as a means to circumvent Iran's naval blockade of the Persian Gulf and the closure of the Syrian pipeline as an act of support for Iran.

For both Saudi Arabia and Turkey, closing the pipelines would mean a loss of revenue and would further excite their restless neighbour. For Saudi Arabia the security considerations were paramount and it would therefore not decide on the pipeline until it had made up its mind on the larger question of an American guarantee and whether or not to host American forces. Turkey was more mindful of the financial questions: Iraq supplied a third of its oil and owed Ankara nearly $1 billion. However, as a member of NATO, it was better placed to withstand Iraqi pressure.

As early as 3 August Turkey indicated that it might support an economic blockade on Iraq. President Turgut Ozal chaired a meeting of the National Security Council that day which led to a demand for unconditional Iraqi withdrawal. There was no move on sanctions until the stance of other NATO states was known. The hint that Turkey might close the pipelines led Saddam to send an emissary to Ankara to warn against such a step. On 5 August, First Deputy Prime Minister Taha Yasin Ramadan arrived with a message from Saddam to Ozal. The Turks were aware that Iraq could stoke up Kurdish insurgency in the south-east of the country. The two countries were also in dispute over the allocation of water, with Iraq anxious over

Turkish dam and irrigation projects diverting water from the Euphrates. After his meeting Ramadan put on a brave face. 'There may be those who wish to cast a shadow over our relations with Turkey,' he said. 'Our belief that this will not happen is infinite.'[35]

His optimism was overdone. Ozal had given him no promises on keeping the pipeline open. He was also being contacted regularly by President Bush and was welcoming the sudden surge of attention from his Western allies. Like other Middle Eastern leaders, Ozal had been concerned that Turkey was being marginalized because of developments in Central and Eastern Europe. Also like other regional leaders, he was very optimistic that the sanctions would have an immediate effect on Saddam's calculations and could possibly do the trick in six to eight weeks. Such optimism led others to agree to measures about which they might have had second thoughts if they had realized how long matters were going to take.

In practice the issue was settled for Turkey through the success of the initial moves towards an embargo. Oil tankers were not loading at the end of the pipeline, so there was little point in the Iraqis pumping oil that they could not sell. So it was at Iraq's request that one of the two pipelines was shut down on the afternoon of 6 August and the flow reduced in the other. This was described as a 'marketing' decision. The same thing was happening with the Saudi pipeline. As a result the formal decisions by Ankara and Riyadh to close the terminals at the end of the pipelines were made easier than they might have expected.

By this time a full economic embargo of Iraq had been agreed by the United Nations. The move to sanctions was a natural response to Iraq's indifference to Resolution 660. This required in the first instance consensus among the five permanent members. The Western members were all agreed and the Soviet Union posed no objections. The Baker–Shevardnadze joint statement had succeeded in providing a stimulus to co-operation at the UN. China was initially anxious to give Iraq more time but, as the Arab League's efforts to resolve the crisis floundered, accepted that there was no evidence of any Iraqi readiness to comply.

The sanctions resolution was based on those adopted against Southern Rhodesia following its Unilateral Declaration of Independence in 1965. This was the only precedent. The only other sanctions had been the arms embargo against South Africa, though they had been threatened as a means to obtain cease-fires during the 1947–9 Arab–Israeli War and, in 1987, at the end of the Iran–Iraq War.

Resolution 661 was adopted on 6 August, with Cuba and Yemen abstaining. It prohibited all trade with Iraq or Kuwait and any transfer of funds. The only exception was 'supplies intended strictly for medical purposes, and, in humanitarian circumstances, foodstuffs'. Exactly what could be regarded as humanitarian provision of foodstuffs was not made clear, other than that luxury items would obviously be forbidden. This was left to national discretion, although the Security Council set up a committee to monitor the implementation of the resolution. It was a question that was to recur in later debates on sanctions.

So was the question of enforcement. The Americans and the British would have preferred some reference to enforcement in Resolution 661 but had judged that there was no chance of this being agreed. When news came through that the resolution had been passed on the morning of 6 August, Mrs Thatcher was meeting with President Bush and his advisers in the Oval Office. Her immediate reaction to the text was unfavourable for this reason. 'How are we going to enforce it?' she asked. Robert Kimmitt, the Under Secretary of State for Political Affairs, pointed to Article 51 of the UN Charter, which refers to the inherent right of self-defence.[36] This meant, he explained, that if the United States received a request from the Emir of Kuwait to take action to support the embargo they would have a sound basis in international law. The Prime Minister herself had good reason to recall Article 51. She had used it as the legal rationale for the campaign to recover the Falkland Islands in 1982, but she was dubious whether it would work in this case. However, on her return to London she checked with her Attorney-General and became convinced. Later she was a firm advocate of relying solely on Article 51 for enforcement - even when the political basis turned out to be less strong than the legal.

The passage of Resolution 661 was not the only news that President Bush and Mrs Thatcher received that morning. Bush also took a call from his Secretary of Defense, Richard Cheney, reporting from Riyadh that King Fahd was prepared to accept American troops on his territory. The military option was now pushing itself to the fore.

CHAPTER 5
Desert Shield

In military terms, the United States had no adequate response to the Iraqi invasion. All that was possible for it to do upon hearing the alarming news was to move one carrier task force, led by USS *Eisenhower*, to take up position in the Eastern Mediterranean while another, led by USS *Independence*, was moved from the Indian Ocean to a position close to the Strait of Hormuz, at the southern tip of the Persian Gulf. In the Gulf itself an eight-ship battle fleet was already deployed.

The armed forces necessary to force Iraq to leave Kuwait were simply not in place. The United States had nothing in the region capable of such a task. The Americans could, of course, use aircraft from carriers against a variety of targets within Iraq, related to either military power or the oil industry, but their impact would inevitably be limited.

The American Command responsible for military intervention in the Gulf was Central Command (CENTCOM), with its headquarters in Tampa, Florida. General Norman Schwarzkopf had taken over command in 1987. CENTCOM was composed of elements which could be taken from other commands in the event of the specific South-west Asian or Pacific Gulf contingencies to which it was geared. Its original goal, when established as the Rapid Deployment Force (RDF) by President Carter in the late 1970s, had been a Soviet move into the region, but this was now becoming daily less likely. The plan which had served as the starting point for operational planning during this crisis – Plan 1002-90 – reflected the fruits of this reappraisal. It identified Iraq as the most likely threat to the stability of the region, and as a result there had already been a number of limited analyses on how it might be necessary to respond to threats to other Gulf states. In June there had even been a headquarters exercise based on plans to deal with an Iraqi military challenge.[1] However, it was by no means complete: in July it was still undergoing its final review.

This scenario did not reflect any formal guidance from the Pentagon, nor was it approved by the State Department, who were worried about the signals being sent to Iraq. It was basically about defending Saudi Arabia from a determined attempt to seize its oilfields and did not consider the defence of Kuwait.[2]

When the Iraqi military build-up had first been detected in July Schwarzkopf was asked to examine military options. His initial thoughts were the basis of some preliminary discussions in the first Deputies' meeting on the night of 1 August and were largely concerned with shows of support for friendly countries or expressions of disapproval with Iraq. One was to send a tactical fighter squadron to Saudi Arabia as a display of solidarity. Schwarzkopf went to Washington for the first NSC meeting the next day, where he made a brief report on the state of planning. The serious options were already recognized as either an air strike from carriers or the introduction of ground forces, with the former carrying the risk of not hurting Saddam substantially while creating the risk of counter-strike against Saudi Arabia. Introducing ground forces would enable the US to take advantage of Plan 1002-90. This would involve sending up to 200,000 personnel to Saudi Arabia over a period of months and required the active co-operation of the desert kingdom.

Past experience suggested great reluctance in Riyadh when it came to even the most modest Western military presence. Discussions on the military situation with Saudi Arabia had opened very early, when, at about 02.00 Washington time on 2 August, William Webster of the CIA and John Kelly of the State Department met with the head of Saudi intelligence in Washington to assess the possible contingency of Iraq not stopping when it reached the Saudi border. However, the initial contacts gave few grounds for optimism about a viable military option. Nothing was agreed when President Bush first spoke to King Fahd on 2 August. An offer to dispatch as a matter of urgency two squadrons of F-15 combat aircraft received no response, and there were reports that the Saudis were turning down requests for extra US surveillance facilities.

The scope of the Iraqi action had initially been unclear because they had sent so many armoured vehicles into Kuwait City, where they had been slowed down. By 3 August other units were moving to the Saudi border, confirming Iraqi control of all of Kuwait and posing a threat to Saudi Arabia. With so many troops involved, the question became one of where the movement would end. Fearing further Iraqi advances, Washington was apprehensive lest the Saudis – like the Kuwaitis – would be so reluctant to ask for help that they would wait until it was too late. President Bush became convinced that the kingdom was vulnerable and that the United States could not afford to see an Iraqi takeover. He set about convincing Riyadh that it should host American troops. For this reason, one result of the second NSC meeting was that the President asked Colin Powell to begin to think through the various options presented by Schwarzkopf.

When President Bush met with Saudi Ambassador Prince Bandar Ibn Sultan on the afternoon of 3 August, one reason for Saudi reluctance became clear. They were fearful that the Americans might not be serious, that they might send over some aircraft as a gesture but then not follow it through, thereby leaving the Saudis to face the consequences alone. To take in large numbers of Western troops would be an unprecedented step for a regime charged with protecting Islam's holiest sites, yet to settle for half-measures would leave it exposed to accusations of defiling Islam's holy places and to retaliation while sending confusing signals to Saddam. The perception, as Lawrence Eagleburger put it later, was that the United States was 'short of breath', that it was prepared to get engaged but once hurt would pull out.[3] The two key items in the case for the prosecution were the Carter Administration's dispatch of some F-15s to Saudi Arabia as a show of force after the fall of the Shah of Iran in 1979, only for it to be announced when they were on their way that they were unarmed, and the minimal response and subsequent disengagement by the Reagan Administration following the 1983 attack on the Marine Barracks in Beirut.

It was therefore necessary to convince the Saudis that this time the Americans were serious. This was a recurrent theme in all communications between the two countries during this stage of the crisis. As it happened, there was little interest in token gestures in the Pentagon. The basic approach adopted by Schwarzkopf and Powell was to reject limited, symbolic options and to go for the force necessary for the task at hand. To start with, it would be possible to send only air power and light forces, but it was essential to make Saddam realize that he was entering the 'Big League'. This should be made clear by the fact that the first arrivals would carry the American flag and then by the scale of future deployments. In the Pentagon, too, part of the analysis of past failures was that there had been insufficient seriousness when it came to the use of the military instrument in the early stages of a crisis.

At the same time the Americans needed to be convinced that they could depend on the Saudis. Riyadh faced a stark choice: to rely on the United States or to appease Saddam. Just pursuing economic sanctions without US military backing was not an option. Ambassador Bandar understood clearly, in his meetings with the Administration on 3 August, that cutting the Iraqi pipeline which passed through the kingdom and resisting the inevitable Iraqi intimidation to come depended on confidence that a full defence was in place.

That afternoon, Cheney and Powell briefed Bandar. He was told that the

American preference was to insert ground forces and not dabble with limited air strikes. Most importantly, he was shown the latest satellite photography of the three Iraqi armoured divisions that had spearheaded the invasion. One was already moving through Kuwait and into the 'neutral zone' on the Saudi–Kuwaiti border, shared by the two neighbours, and was ten miles from the border. Others were following in a similar pattern to that observed prior to the invasion of Kuwait.

The 70,000-strong Saudi military was generally well equipped. The Air Force had both the air defence and the strike versions of Tornado, along with fifty-seven F-15s and ninety-eight F-5s. The Army, with two armoured, one mechanized and five infantry battalions, had some 550 tanks and 850 artillery pieces. However, it was extremely small compared to the Iraqi forces and lacked battle experience. Besides, all that faced Iraq at this point was the National Guard, a well-equipped brigade, which had been mobilized on 4 August. There was no way that it could cope without American forces. The CIA estimated that the capital, Riyadh, 275 miles away from Kuwait, could be reached within three days.[4]

The Iraqi capability was there, but what of Saddam's intentions? Bandar needed little convincing that Saddam was intent on invading Saudi Arabia. Shortly after the invasion he expressed the view that he who eats Kuwait for breakfast is likely to ask for something else for lunch.[5] Now his fears seemed to have been vindicated by the fact that the 140,000 Iraqi troops in Kuwait by far exceeded the number required simply to pacify the emirate (although the size of occupying forces always seems to be disproportionate to the task at hand). The units close to the border appeared to have supplies and weapons suitable for further offensive action.[6] Cheney and Powell gave Bandar an indication of the sort of US forces they judged necessary in order to organize a response. When Bandar asked what this meant in numbers, Powell said vaguely 100,000–200,000 men. The Ambassador smiled and acknowledged that this did show seriousness.

At 08.00 on 4 August at Camp David, Schwarzkopf and his planners, along with intelligence analysts, described to the President how 40,000 light forces could be got in within a few weeks. To implement fully Plan 1002-90 would take 250,000 men and four months. Although there was no doubt about air superiority, this would be, it was stressed, a defensive force, inadequate for offensive operations.[7] Whether it went depended on the Saudis.

Bandar had telephoned King Fahd on the evening of 3 August. Fahd was irritated with Saddam, with whom he had just had an unsatisfactory conversation about the proposed Arab League summit, and was worried about the situation on the border, where there had already been a few incidents, even though Saddam had dismissed his concerns. Nonetheless, and despite the urgency of the situation, he needed to be convinced that the threat was real. The Americans had cried wolf before on threats to the kingdom (for example, Iran), and these threats had not materialized. Inviting American forces into the kingdom was no small matter. The attitudes and behaviour of American servicemen were unlikely to fit naturally into a traditional Islamic monarchy. Another option would simply be to buy the Iraqis off as had been done in the past. Some consideration was given to this.

The Americans were getting anxious. Two sources mention a call from President Mubarak on Saturday 4 August to the effect that he had heard from Jeddah that the Saudis had rejected the idea of an American presence on their territory. Ambassador Bandar was a man of considerable influence, and his views were shared by the young generation of Saudi princes, but he was not a decision-maker himself and he was meeting considerable resistance in Riyadh, mainly from the King's brothers.[8] President Bush called King Fahd to tell him of his belief in the vulnerability of his kingdom and an American commitment to its defence. Faced with scepticism about the Iraqi threat, Bandar had suggested that Fahd should accept an American briefing team. Fahd now told Bush, who knew nothing of this idea, that he would like this briefing. The President quickly agreed.[9]

Although Fahd expected a low-level technical team, Bush wanted to send a senior figure who could be seen as a personal emissary of the President. This would be a means of putting pressure on the King to make up his mind. On the other hand, if such a figure were to be rebuffed then this would drive the two countries further apart rather than bring them closer together. So the make-up of the team took on critical importance: before it could be determined, the Americans needed some sense of the drift of Saudi thinking. To encourage the King, Bush stated publicly his readiness to respond if Saudi Arabia asked:

> If they ask for specific help, it obviously depends what it is, but I would be inclined to help in any way we possibly can. It's that serious.[10]

The King understood why Bush wanted to send a high-level team and for his part did not want to be pressured. By the afternoon of 5 August he had changed his mind. If he was not as yet persuaded of the need for American ground forces, he did accept that he needed to see the best American intelligence. His own army scouts had failed to detect any Iraqi troops heading towards the kingdom, but their range of vision was trivial compared with the American spy satellites. By that afternoon Secretary of Defense

Cheney, who combined seniority with the appropriate expertise, was in the air, accompanied by Robert Gates, the Deputy Adviser on National Security Affairs, and General Norman Schwarzkopf. Schwarzkopf was armed with the latest intelligence demonstrating that Iraqi troops had not moved out of Kuwait but were now being reinforced. There were now 70,000 troops near or closing to the Saudi border. Hundreds of tanks were dug in. Some Scud missile launchers were now in position close to Kuwait City, pointing in the Saudi direction.[11]

President Bush could now start to feel more confident that the political, economic and military aspects of his strategy were starting to fall into place. The remaining uncertainty concerned Cheney's reception in Riyadh. As the American team flew to Riyadh, Bush was pressed by reporters on the possibility of a military intervention. For the past two days speculation had been building up in the press, reflecting Pentagon briefings on the proximity of Iraqi forces to the Saudi border, the possibilities of limited air strikes and the logistics of getting 'heavy' US divisions to the Gulf.[12]

As the President's helicopter bringing him back from Camp David landed on the White House lawn, he was met by Richard Haass. Haass had hurriedly typed out a few notes reminding Bush of the main events of a busy few days: Saddam's claim that Iraqi forces were to withdraw from Kuwait and the fact that the opposite seemed to be taking place; the futile diplomacy in the Arab League and the efforts of King Hussein to find a compromise with Iraq. After reading the paper, Bush told reporters that while he was not going to discuss his options they were 'wide open' and they had better wait – 'watch and learn'. For the first time in public he then committed himself to the liberation of Kuwait: 'This will not stand, this aggression against Kuwait.' To insiders this was no more than a reflection of the trend of their deliberations of the past days. To many observers it seemed to change the terms of the debate.[13]

Saddam's rebuttal

Saddam noted the speculation about an impending Iraqi act of aggression against Saudi Arabia. He needed to dissuade Bush from taking this further and so he issued a denial. 'Some news agencies have reported fabricated news about what they called the approach of Iraqi forces towards the Saudi border,' read an official statement. 'Iraq categorically denies these fabricated reports. Causing confusion between the kingdom of Saudi Arabia, which is a fraternal country with which we have normal cordial relations, and Kuwait's case is tendentious.'[14]

This message was directly relayed by Saddam Hussein at a meeting with the US Chargé d'Affaires in Baghdad, Joseph Wilson, on 6 August. That morning the press had reported Cheney's trip and also that Bush was considering air attacks on Iraq in the event of an invasion of Saudi Arabia, directed against strategic and industrial centres as well as oil installations.[15]

With Glaspie in Washington, Wilson was now the senior American diplomat in Baghdad. He had been woken up by a call from the White House at 04.00 on 2 August, as Iraqi tanks were making their way inside Kuwait, and asked if he had Saddam's telephone number. Standing to attention stark naked, he searched for the requested number.[16] Two hours later the Iraqis cut the Embassy lines. He managed to meet Tariq Aziz at about 08.30 and laid out the American position, calling for immediate withdrawal. Aziz simply told him that the occupation had been in response to the breakdown in negotiations with the Kuwaitis. Thereafter Wilson had maintained intensive contact with Iraqi officials – largely with a view to safeguarding the position of US citizens.

On 6 August he was given his opportunity to meet Saddam. Like others he noted the 'ambience of intimidation' created by Saddam. He was lectured for some forty-five minutes on Kuwait's economic war against Iraq and the threat this posed to national interests. The al-Sabah family was history, Saddam told him. Nonetheless, the underlying message was more conciliatory than in his bellicose encounter with Ambassador Glaspie a fortnight earlier. 'Iraq is firmly willing to respect the United States's legitimate international interests in the Middle East,' he told Wilson, 'and is interested in establishing normal relations with the United States on the basis of mutual respect.' The fabricated reports on Iraqi military deployments along the Saudi border were 'pretexts to interfere in the region's affairs and to justify an aggression against Iraq'. Iraq harboured no ill-intentions whatsoever against Saudi Arabia. There was a fundamental difference between Iraq's relations with Saudi Arabia and its relations with Kuwait, he argued. Kuwait had been *sui generis*, an artificial entity with no real frontiers. Therefore, 'whatever happened with the entry of the Iraqi forces cannot be measured in the framework of the relationship between states in the Arab world'. In contrast, Iraq had excellent relations with Saudi Arabia since 1975, with a bilateral non-aggression treaty. There was consequently no reason for Saudi Arabia to fear an Iraqi attack.

Wilson's brief was to attempt to secure the opening of the borders for the departure of all foreigners who wished to leave. When he requested this, Saddam asked whether there was 'something that you know that I don't that causes you such concern about getting your citizens out so quickly'. Wilson assumed that he feared that B-52 bombers were about to come over Baghdad.[17]

The decision is taken

For Saddam to take on Saudi Arabia would have been to bite off far more than Kuwait, and there is no evidence that this was his intention. No plans were found as coalition forces sifted through the debris of the Iraqi military after the war. However, the intelligence agencies who had just been scarred by erring on the side of complacency were not going to be caught out again. They now tilted towards alarmism. The political mood had shifted in the same way. Disclaimers from Baghdad were discounted by those who felt misled by Saddam's previous claims of peaceful intent.

By this time American policy-making was far too advanced for Iraqi assurances to make much difference. The Bush Administration was now fully focused on Saudi Arabia, whose fate was critical to the whole regional balance of power. The question of an immediate strike was less important than the prospect of Iraqi forces remaining in a menacing position and putting Riyadh on permanent notice that it dare not annoy Baghdad. If it had not embraced Washington it would have been hard to avoid Baghdad's embrace – leading it to endorse an 'Arab solution' on Saddam's terms or, at least, fail to implement fully the UN sanctions by cutting off Iraq's oil pipeline running through Saudi territory.

This was the choice that Cheney and his team were to help King Fahd to make. After flying all night they arrived in Riyadh on the morning of Monday, 6 August. *En route* they had anticipated the main Saudi concerns: What were the Iraqi intentions? Were the Americans serious? Would they leave when this was all over? The American team decided not to overplay the satellite images of Iraqi forces – at least six divisions – moving towards the border. Rather than put too much stress on what the Iraqis might do next as this was unpredictable, they simply pointed out that they could be in Kuwait at one moment and in Saudi Arabia within twelve hours.

They met King Fahd and his advisers in the evening. Cheney had with him Schwarzkopf, Robert Gates of the National Security Council, Paul Wolfowitz, Under Secretary of Defense for Policy, and the US Ambassador to the kingdom, Charles Freeman. The King was flanked by the Crown Prince, Abdallah, and the Foreign Minister, Saud al-Faisal. For two hours the Americans took the Saudis through the available intelligence on what Saddam had done and the current disposition of Iraqi forces. They then described the sort of American deployments envisaged, emphasizing that they were not looking for a permanent base.

Cheney chose his words carefully, stressing the severity of the threat, the President's personal commitment to the security guarantee to Saudi Arabia, the intensity of the international diplomatic campaign now being conducted, the dangers if Saddam was left unchallenged. To prevent him from succeeding, economic measures would be important, but 'in future months, as Saddam Hussein begins to feel the pressure, he could lash out and attack'. The defence of Saudi Arabia was thus an important condition for a successful strategy of economic strangulation. The Americans were prepared to send in large forces sufficient to deter, and with the Saudis, if necessary, able to defeat Iraq in battle. But deployment must begin soon, before it was too late. Equally, promised Cheney, as soon as the crisis was over the Americans would leave. They had no intention of establishing a base on Saudi soil.

Although the Americans expected that they would have to wait for a Saudi decision, it came immediately. There was a brief consultation in front of the Americans. The Saudis had already had their debate over the previous weekend. There was a hint of this when Crown Prince Abdallah suggested waiting for an unambiguous warning. The King responded that the Emir had waited for such warnings: 'Now the Kuwaitis are a nation living in hotels.' Saddam had misled Fahd over Kuwait. Now he was pretending to withdraw when he was creating a new threat to Saudi Arabia. Iraq's vast expenditure on armaments reflected Saddam's basic instincts. 'Let's believe in God and do what has to be done,' the King told Cheney. 'We will proceed with the details.'[18] The decision was eased by the possibility of an 'Islamic cover' to broaden the military support beyond the United States. Cheney agreed that this was a good idea. In fact, President Bush had already contacted King Hassan of Morocco to urge him to offer a battalion to Saudi Arabia if King Fahd so wished. Mubarak was also forthcoming, though not quite so definite. The King had already received King Hassan's offer and accepted.

Cheney returned to his quarters and rang Bush. He asked for and was granted the go-ahead to begin the deployment of forces. The main concern now was that should Saddam decide to pre-empt, the American forces would be extremely vulnerable during the protracted period of deployment. While it would be impossible to devise an elaborate cover for such a major movement of forces, it was agreed to delay the announcement at least until the first American units were on Saudi soil.[19] The next day the 82nd Airborne Division was on the move along with the first fighter squadrons and the deployment was announced.

On 8 August President Bush spoke on national television. 'We seek the immediate, unconditional and complete withdrawal of all Iraqi forces from Kuwait.' Bush emphasized that the legitimate Government of Kuwait must be restored. He stressed the commitment to the security of the Gulf and that:

The mission of our troops is wholly defensive. Hopefully, they will not be needed long. They will not initiate hostilities, but they will defend themselves, the kingdom of Saudi Arabia, and other friends in the Persian Gulf.

The implementation of the presidential decision was prompt. Orders to prepare for the execution of Plan 1002-90, should this be deemed necessary, had been given already on 2 August. The first deployment order was issued at 21.50 on 6 August. Priority was to be given to fighter aircraft: 122 F-15s and F-16s were deployed in a week. Then the build-up continued gradually, as every type of reconnaissance, logistics, electronic warfare, refuelling and combat aircraft was introduced. By mid-September the air deployment was all but complete, with almost 700 aircraft in place.

The main concern was the vulnerability of American troops in the initial detachments. It would take seventeen weeks before they could defend themselves properly, and for the first month they could be in serious difficulty. To maximize the immediate deterrent effect, priority was given to combat units rather than logistics support. The initial Division Ready Brigade from the 82nd Airborne was only 2,300 men. As little as possible was therefore said about numbers and times of arrival. The plan was to send up to 250,000 troops, to be in place by 1 December. There was a tension between the assertions by top officials to the press that American forces were not excessively at risk and that the operation was going to be a long haul.[20] Three weeks after deployment began, General Schwarzkopf had available seven brigades, three carrier battle groups, fourteen tactical fighter squadrons, four tactical airlift squadrons, a strategic bomber squadron and a Patriot air defence umbrella. However, during August President Bush and his advisers had all sorts of nightmares about lightly armed members of the 82nd Airborne Division being caught by a chemical weapons attack or having to withdraw as they arrived because they were so outnumbered.

If the Iraqis chose to move forward there was little that could be done to stop them. Saddam Hussein, however, was well aware of the folly of attacking troops of the United States even if he could score an initial victory. As the first American troops moved in he ordered a shift in the Iraqi deployment. The Republican Guard and armoured divisions capable of striking into Saudi Arabia began to move back, to be replaced by more defensive deployments. A line had been drawn in the sand.

CHAPTER 6
Middle East Alignments

The Arabs go along

Once committed to the deployment of US troops in Saudi Arabia, there was no way back for King Fahd. His position could never be safe again unless Saddam was shamefully expelled from Kuwait, or – even better – overthrown. This last objective, of course, could not be spelled out openly lest it played into Saddam's hands by branding the royal family as a lackey of 'Western imperialism'. However, in private the Saudis made no secret of their conviction that as long as Saddam remained in power it would be impossible to restore stability to the Gulf. A special meeting of the Gulf Co-operation Council (GCC) on 7 August issued a strongly worded resolution, condemning Iraq.[1]

One person who required no reminder of the need to overthrow Saddam was the Syrian President, Hafiz Asad. His rivalry with Saddam dated back to the late 1960s, when the latter had engineered a rift between the Iraqi and the Syrian branches of the Ba'th Party. This evolved into an unbridgeable personal animosity. Both were young, dynamic, competent and harboured undisguised ambitions for championship of the Arab cause. For Saddam, Asad was a permanent reminder of his unfulfilled dreams. He was a military officer. This was an achievement the Iraqi leader had failed to emulate – in his eyes a disgrace for which he felt compelled to compensate throughout his career. Consequently, each considered his counterpart the most dangerous Arab rival and worked assiduously throughout the 1970s and the 1980s to ensure the other's premature demise.[2] Now that his arch-enemy had been trapped in a quagmire of his own making, Asad apparently reasoned that the time was ripe to deal him a mortal blow: were Saddam to emerge from the crisis intact, let alone victorious, he would be impossible to co-exist with.

This consideration was probably sufficient to drive Asad into the anti-Iraq coalition, but there were additional advantages. Prior to the crisis, Syria's regional standing had been at a particularly low ebb. With its international

95

protector, the Soviet Union, in disarray, its presence in Lebanon challenged by Saddam's protégé, General Michel Aoun, and its economy in malaise, Asad was grudgingly forced to settle for a secondary role for Syria and to lie in wait for better days. Now, suddenly, he was thrown into regional prominence. While the West's traditional ally, King Hussein of Jordan, as well as the PLO leader, Yasser Arafat, were ostracized for their support for Saddam, Damascus was courted by both Saudi Arabia and the United States into the international effort against Iraq. By mid August Assistant Secretary of State John Kelly had already paid two visits to Damascus, and President Bush called Asad on the phone to inform him of their congruent outlook on the crisis.[3]

Asad took his chance, but not before satisfying himself as to the extent of US commitment to the anti-Saddam crusade. In a meeting with Ambassador Bandar, who had been sent to Damascus by King Fahd shortly after the invasion of Kuwait to request Syrian help, Asad had only three questions: 'Are the Americans serious about stopping the Iraqis? Will they finish the job by going all the way? And do you trust them?'[4] Once reassured, he moved promptly. At the emergency Arab League summit, held in Cairo on 10 August, he supported a decision to send an inter-Arab force to Saudi Arabia, and four days later the first Syrian units arrived in the desert kingdom. On 13 September, during a visit to Damascus by Secretary of State James Baker, he promised to reinforce the 4,000 commando troops already deployed in Saudi Arabia by an additional 11,000-strong force, including an armoured division of some 300 tanks.[5] Nor was Asad deterred from signalling publicly where he stood: on the same day that Syrian troops began landing in Saudi Arabia he was host in Damascus to the deposed Kuwaiti Crown Prince, Sheikh Sa'd Abdallah al-Sabah, for an official visit. The twenty-one-gun salute greeting the Kuwaiti guest on his arrival was a symbol of Syria's commitment to the complete and unconditional liberation of Kuwait.

Furthermore, on 15 August Syrian Vice-President Abd al-Khalim Khaddam arrived in Tehran for talks with the Iranian authorities. A day earlier Saddam had made his surprising peace proposal to Iran, and the coalition was anxious to ensure that Iran was kept outside the crisis. Syria, as Tehran's staunchest Middle Eastern ally during the Iran–Iraq War, was the most suitable candidate for the delicate mission of pre-empting any Iraqi–Iranian alliance. During his talks in Tehran, Khaddam was assured that such an alliance was not in the making and that Syria and Iran would adopt 'a joint strategy to promote their goals'.[6]

To make the decision to collaborate with the West against a sister Arab state amenable to the Syrian people and the Arab world at large (after all, until the Kuwait crisis the West had been 'the source of all evil in the Middle East' as far as Syria was concerned), the deployment of Syrian troops was hailed as a bold pan-Arab and Islamic move to defend Saudi Arabia, the holy sites in particular, against an impending Iraqi aggression. 'Syria is not for the presence of foreign troops anywhere in the Arab world,' stated President Asad in a public speech explaining his decision;

> But the issue is not that of foreign troops, because the problem started before the foreign troops came into the area and it was the problem that brought us the foreign troops... The problem is the occupation of Kuwait.[7]

Besides, argued the Syrians, the dispatch of an expeditionary force to the Gulf did not imply collaboration with the West. On the contrary, this act reflected Damascus's conviction that the region 'should not be left for foreign troops' and that 'it is possible for Arab forces to replace foreign troops gradually and with the passage of time'.[8]

Since it must have been evident to Asad that the Syrian forces in Saudi Arabia were no substitute for a Western military presence in the Gulf, and that in the event of war they would at best play a secondary role, his real agenda behind joining the coalition was to cash the direct gains of Syria's unexpected rise to prominence: increased financial contributions from Saudi Arabia, Syria's reluctant financier in the past, and the opening of a completely new era in US–Syrian relations, with its immeasurable economic and political rewards. An indication of what such rewards could mean was given in October 1990 when the United States acquiesced in Syria's final (and brutal) drive against its opponents in Lebanon.[9]

A similar combination of practicality and personal animosity drove President Mubarak of Egypt into the anti-Iraq coalition. There were, of course, substantial political and economic gains to be reaped by such a move, primarily the consolidation of Egypt's relations with Saudi Arabia and the United States. Yet the personal dimension in Mubarak's reaction should not be underestimated. For years he had been Saddam's close ally, providing him with military and economic support during his war against Iran and co-establishing with him the Arab Co-operation Council in its wake. For his part, Saddam had generously reciprocated by becoming the chief advocate of Egypt's reincorporation into the Arab world despite its peace treaty with Israel. Saddam's false pledge not to attack Kuwait was therefore received by Mubarak not only as a public humiliation, but as a personal betrayal. As a result, a relationship built over nearly a decade was undone with one stroke.

A long memorandum, prepared for Mubarak by his presidential staff and the foreign ministry shortly after the invasion, accused Iraq of deliberately misleading Egypt regarding its intentions. Baghdad's support for the Arab Co-operation Council was viewed as an attempt to 'isolate Egypt' while preparing the invasion. The occupation of Kuwait was defined as 'a blow to Egyptian policy and interests'.[10]

This turn-about in Mubarak's position required that the Egyptian people be explained the nature of the fresh threat posed by the ally-turned-enemy. The occupation of Kuwait was portrayed as a predatory act endangering the stability of the entire world, and Saddam as worse than 'the most notorious tyrants in history – Genghis Khan, Hulegu, Nero, and Hitler'.[11] The arrival of foreign troops in the Gulf, it was argued, had nothing to do with Egypt. Quite the reverse in fact:

> Egypt has done a great deal to prevent the invasion from taking place, but Saddam failed to heed the voice of reason. When he defied the entire world, the world decided to stop the new Hitler, since he has become a danger to the region, to the Arabs, and to the world.[12]

This callous disregard of human norms and political conduct left Egypt with no choice but to put itself, in its capacity as the largest Arab state, at the forefront of the inter-Arab effort to end the Iraqi occupation of Kuwait. It was now up to the one person who had created this tragic situation, Saddam Hussein, to redress his mistake by withdrawing unconditionally from Kuwait. Failure to do so could only lead to a regional catastrophe of unprecedented proportions.

This doomsday scenario was not exclusively Egyptian; it had been widely used by King Hussein and Yasser Arafat in their attempts to defuse the crisis. But whereas the two were using this apocalyptic vision as a tool to force the coalition to back down so as to get Saddam off the hook, President Mubarak put the onus for de-escalation on the Iraqi leader. In a personal message to Saddam on 21 August, he pleaded to him to 'save mankind from a destructive war which would leave a scorched earth'. 'Only God knows the horrifying end of this war once it starts,' he wrote. 'It would take us backwards to darkness and loss.' The two were to exchange thirty-eight messages of decreasing civility during the crisis.[13]

Saddam's dismissive response – how did Mubarak, he asked, who came of an undistinguished Egyptian family, dare to question the behaviour of a direct descendant of the Prophet Muhammad[14] – did not dissuade Mubarak from continuing his public efforts to convince Saddam to back down.[15] Simultaneously, he steadily increased his support of the military coalition facing Saddam. By late August Egypt had already sent some 5,000 troops to Saudi Arabia, while Egyptian anti-aircraft batteries were being deployed in the United Arab Emirates. In early September, following a meeting with James Baker, Mubarak agreed to send another 15,000 troops.

The introduction of 'linkage'

If Saddam had ever planned, as he occasionally implied, to leave Kuwait some time after the invasion, this was no longer an option. Withdrawal after securing Kuwait as a satellite was one thing; an unconditional pullout in the face of American pressure would be a glaring and unaffordable admission of failure. Against a backdrop of mounting international and regional pressures, as well as ongoing popular defiance in Kuwait, Saddam felt that he had no alternative but to escalate. Fearing that he would have to face an American attack, he believed that his forces would be more inclined to fight 'unto death' if they were protecting their own territory: on 8 August, allegedly in acquiescence to a request by the 'Provisional Government in Kuwait', the Revolutionary Command Council announced the merger of Iraq and Kuwait.[16] If this move was designed to indicate to the anti-Iraq coalition the irreversibility of the situation, Saddam was to be quickly disillusioned. The next day the Security Council convened for yet another emergency session and issued its third resolution on the crisis. Resolution 662 declared the Iraqi annexation 'null and void', demanded that Baghdad 'rescind its action purporting to annex Kuwait', and called upon 'all states, international organizations and special agencies not to recognize that annexation, and to refrain from any action or dealing that might be interpreted as an indirect recognition of the annexation'.[17] This time even Cuba and Yemen gave their support.

The regional response was equally uncompromising. Not only did the Arab world fail to recognize the annexation of Kuwait, but an extraordinary Arab League summit, convened in Cairo on 10 August, adopted a resolution condemning the invasion and the ensuing annexation, and calling for Iraq's immediate withdrawal and the reinstatement of the pre-August status quo. It was this meeting which – particularly troubling for Saddam – provided for the dispatch of Arab troops as part of the multinational force confronting Iraq.[18] The first Egyptian troops began arriving in Saudi Arabia the day of the summit.

The summit had been scheduled to meet on 9 August but had been postponed to give Baghdad a last chance to accept the principle of an immediate withdrawal – to no avail. The Iraqi delegation, First Deputy

Premier Taha Yasin Ramadan and Foreign Minister Tariq Aziz, arrived in a bellicose mood. They would not sit at the same table with the former Kuwaiti rulers, since the emirate had always been an integral part of Iraq, and the al-Sabah family had been nothing but 'traitors and servants of world imperialism'. Nor should the 'return of Kuwait to the motherland' be part of the summit's agenda. Rather, the conference should address the 'overt US threats to the Arab nation and the clear preparations to carry out aggression against Iraq with US land, naval, and air forces which have taken up positions on Arab territories and waters to attack Iraq'. It was not Iraq which deserved condemnation but the kingdom of Saudi Arabia, which had allowed the deployment of foreign troops on Islam's holiest lands. This message was echoed by the Iraqi media, which explicitly called for uprisings in Egypt and Saudi Arabia, even while the meeting was in session.[19]

With the summit revealing an unbridgeable gap with other Arab regimes, Saddam sought to undermine them by rallying the masses behind his cause by 'Zionizing' the crisis. By linking his Kuwaiti venture to the Palestinian problem, he hoped to portray himself as the champion of the pan-Arab cause, thereby eradicating any conceivable opposition to his move in the Arab world. If the 'restoration of Kuwait to the motherland' was the first step towards 'the liberation of Jerusalem', how could any Arab leader be opposed to it? The aggressor would be transformed into a liberator and a hero.

Although the 'Zionization' of the Kuwaiti problem turned out to be one of Saddam's more powerful weapons in subsequent months, its adoption was more of a response to the tightening noose around Iraq than a premeditated grand design. A particularly sensitive accusation levelled at Saddam by his Arab opponents (first and foremost, the rival Ba'th regime in Damascus) was that the occupation of Kuwait had marginalized the Palestinian problem and divided the Arab world, thereby weakening its ability to resist Israel's 'expansionist machinations'. 'As usual, when inter-Arab relations become tense or suffer from a split or trouble,' responded the Syrian media to the Iraqi invasion,

> Israel tries to calculate so as to benefit from circumstances and exploit them in its favour in a way that serves its expansionist, hostile plan against the Arab nation, to escalate Arab differences, tarnish the Arabs' international reputation, and instil despair and frustration in Arab citizens . . . We are all, in all parts of the Arab homeland, in need of the maximum degree of caution and vigilance while this Zionist move is underway to seize the opportunity to exploit the Gulf events in the interest of the hostile Zionist plan.[20]

Anger that Saddam had given the United States an opportunity to establish itself in the Middle East and let Israel off the hook was a prevalent theme even among opposition groups in Egypt.[21]

This insinuation of serving Israel's interests was anathema to Saddam, and drove him to counter the Syrian propaganda by portraying the annexation of Kuwait as 'a dear pan-Arab goal, through which we would comprehensively, eternally and radically rectify what colonialism had imposed on our country'.[22] Similarly, once the first American units arrived in Saudi Arabia, Saddam quickly argued that Israeli pilots and troops (although disguised as American) had been deployed in the kingdom, and that the United States and Israel had 'divided aggressive duties among themselves'. Saddam claimed, however, that 'Iraq is vigilant and cannot be misled by the US markings on Zionist fighter planes ... It will respond in kind to any hostile action by Israel.'[23] Allegations of Israel's military contribution to the international coalition, and threats to attack Israel should hostilities break out, became a regular theme in Saddam's statements throughout the crisis.[24]

On 12 August, in the first official presentation of his 'peace initiative', Saddam revealed his optimum scenario for resolving the crisis. He linked the Kuwaiti issue to the Palestinian problem by suggesting a comprehensive solution for 'all issues of occupation, or the issues that have been depicted as occupation in the entire region'. In his view, such a solution should include 'the immediate and unconditional withdrawal of Israel from the occupied Arab territories in Palestine, Syria, and Lebanon, as well as the withdrawal of Syria from Lebanon, and the withdrawal of Iraq and Iran'. Only after all these outstanding problems had been settled, *in chronological order*, 'the formulation of provisions relating to the situation in Kuwait' could be arranged on a similar basis, 'taking into consideration the historic rights of Iraq to its territory and the choice of the Kuwaiti people'.[25]

Had this proposal been accepted, let alone implemented, it would have represented a great achievement for Saddam. With one stroke he would have projected himself as the architect of a new Middle Eastern order and the champion of the Palestinian cause, resolved the frustrating deadlock on the Iranian front, reversed fifteen years of Syrian efforts in Lebanon, and become the undisputed Arab leader, with the Arab world, the wealthy oil states in particular, more subservient than ever to his financial wishes. Above all, in making this proposal he risked precious little. Whatever the outcome of his initiative, he would emerge the winner since his sweeping demands articulated what were believed to be the cherished dreams of the majority of people in the Arab world. By leaving the resolution of the Kuwait crisis at the bottom of the list, Saddam gave himself ample time to change the demographic balance in the emirate (as he had done in Kurdistan in the early 1970s) so that when the 'Kuwaiti people would be given a chance to determine their own future', the outcome would be a foregone conclusion. Indeed, within months from the Iraqi invasion nearly a third of Kuwait's indigenous population had been forced into exile, while those who stayed behind were subjected to a systematic campaign of terrorism, aimed at extinguishing Kuwait as an independent nation – with everything distinctively Kuwaiti – including street names, identity documents and car number plates – eliminated.

Not surprisingly, Saddam's 'peace proposal' was dismissed by the Arab members of the coalition. By raising the 'linkage' between the Kuwaiti and the Palestinian problems, they had not intended to sanctify the Iraqi occupation of Kuwait but, rather, to reverse it. Now Saddam seemed to be turning the tables on his Arab rivals by twisting the 'linkage' so as to portray himself as the champion of the Palestinian cause. They determined not to allow him to get away with this. 'Saddam's initiative contravenes what the Arab and Islamic nations had agreed unanimously,' argued the Egyptian Minister of State for Foreign Affairs, Dr Boutrus Ghali, 'namely, an immediate Iraqi withdrawal from Kuwait.'[26] Damascus was far more pointed in its criticism: 'The appalling attempt to link the Iraqi withdrawal from Kuwait and the Israeli withdrawal from the occupied Arab territories,' argued the Syrian media, is a gross falsehood.

> After all, how can we equate Kuwait, the fraternal Arab country, with Israel, the Arab arch-enemy? Every Arab citizen knows that when Arab countries invade each other Israel will celebrate and perpetuate its occupation of the Arab lands. Linking withdrawal from Kuwait to Israel's withdrawal from the occupied Arab territories, therefore, is not only a falsehood but also a weak excuse for the continuation of the invasion.[27]

The seeds of 'linkage' had been sown, and during the following months Saddam would persistently strive, both directly and through his chief Arab advocates, Yasser Arafat and King Hussein of Jordan, to establish an inseparable bond between his personal predicament and the Palestinian problem.

Israel keeps out

In these circumstances it appeared vital for the cohesion of the Arab–Western coalition that Israel remained outside. This, in turn, required a high degree of self-restraint and political foresight which had never been the main trait of Middle Eastern regimes, particularly in such volatile situations.

On the face of it, the Israelis should not have been surprised by the Iraqi invasion of Kuwait. Since the end of the Iran–Iraq War they had followed with grave concern the military and political moves of Saddam Hussein: the significant expansion of Iraq's non-conventional arsenal, the intensifying military collaboration between Iraq and Jordan, the flurry of Iraqi activity in the Arab world in general, and in the Lebanese civil war in particular. Jerusalem had feared that once the Iranian threat had been essentially eradicated, the Iraqi leader might embark on a new adventure in which Israel would occupy the focal point. Such fears were significantly exacerbated by Saddam's 'burn Israel' speech in April 1990, and in the following months Israeli officials travelled to Western capitals in an attempt to alert them to this growing threat to regional stability.

And yet not only did the Israeli intelligence community fail to ring the alarm bells once Saddam began massing his troops along the Kuwaiti border, but the Military Intelligence, Israel's foremost institution for national security estimates, adhered to the common wisdom at the time that an overall Iraqi assault on the emirate was rather unlikely. This view was shared by the Mossad, which believed that in the worst case Iraq might try to seize the disputed oilfields of Rumaila and the islands of Warba and Bubiyan.[28] It was even assessed that the Iraqi troop concentrations might be a cover for an air strike against Israel to avenge the destruction of Iraq's nuclear reactor in 1981; the Israeli Air Force (IAF) was thus placed on high alert.[29]

In this context, it was hardly surprising that the official response to the Iraqi invasion reflected considerable confusion regarding its implications for Israel's security. Eager to redeem itself from its earlier mistake, Military Intelligence quickly cautioned that Israel had replaced Iran on Saddam's list of priorities, and that, given Saddam's brutish world-view and his belief that crude force was the best means for dealing with Israel, he could be expected to move against the Jewish state, either directly or by imposing his domination over Jordan. The Israeli Prime Minister, Yitzhak Shamir, seemed disposed to this view. 'There is a danger that Saddam Hussein will attack Israel next,' he said.

> We know that man's lust for power. We know that the wars he waged were meant to glorify him and to tighten his grip over Iraq and the entire region, and Israel has always been the trump card for those Arab leaders who aspire to become the champions of pan-Arabism.[30]

This assessment was challenged by an equally prominent school of thought which believed that Israel's strategic position had been boosted by the occupation of Kuwait, for no reason other than that this action changed the perception of almost everything in the region, above all the priorities in US–Israeli relations which, until then, had been undergoing a deep crisis due to differing perceptions regarding the Arab–Israeli peace process. By exposing Saddam's true nature, the invasion was believed to have exposed the unpredictability of Middle East leaders, to underscore the threat facing Israel, and to prove that the Arab–Israeli conflict was not the main source of regional instability. Now that the danger of Iraq had been underscored, the Americans could be expected to forget previous differences over the peace process, and to be more considerate of Israel's strategic needs.[31]

Whatever their initial assessment of the Iraqi intentions, it soon dawned upon the Israelis that Saddam would not leave them in peace. Israel's implication in the crisis was simply too valuable for his purposes, and offered him, in his own perception, the best way of collapsing the international coalition confronting him. Thus from 8 August when, for the first time, Saddam accused Israel of taking part in the anti-Iraq coalition, and all the more so after his 12 August 'peace initiative', Israeli policy towards the crisis was geared towards one and only one goal: escaping the gathering storm in the desert.

There was unanimity in Israel that the international community should not allow the Iraqi leader to get away with his aggression, lest he and his like would be vindicated in the belief that naked force was the most efficacious foreign policy instrument.[32] But what was the best way to achieve this objective? According to Western press reports, Israel sought to convince the Administration that time was working in Saddam's favour and that America's best option lay with an early massive air and missile strike against Iraq, in order to disarm Saddam of offensive capability and, better still, break the morale of his army.[33] Yet there was little in the official statements to substantiate such reports. To the contrary, the deciding 'triumvirate' – Prime Minister Shamir, Defence Minister Moshe Arens and Foreign Minister David Levy – believed that 'diplomatic, political, and economic measures . . . could stop Saddam Hussein dead in his tracks'.[34]

As far as the Israeli Government was concerned, calls for an immediate action against Iraq were confined to the extremist fringes, primarily Ariel Sharon, Minister of Housing, who did not believe for a moment that sanctions could force Saddam out of Kuwait.[35] Surprisingly enough, Sharon was supported in his view by some Labour figures who outflanked the ruling Likud Party from the right by suggesting extreme measures against Saddam Hussein. Yitzhak Rabin, a former Prime Minister and Minister of Defence, concluded that the momentous events in Eastern Europe significantly reduced the ability of both superpowers for political and military intervention in regional conflicts. Therefore, 'neither the United States nor the Soviet Union was capable of defeating the Iraqi Army, unless they employed non-conventional weapons'.[36] An equally forceful view was presented by another member of the Labour Party, Major General (res.) Avigdor Ben Gal, who advised the United States to use 'non-contaminating' tactical nuclear weapons against Iraq in order to destroy its military infrastructure.[37]

A similar unholy alliance between the extreme right and some Labour politicians was forged over the question of the Israeli attitude towards Jordan. From the beginning of the crisis there was a strong fear in Jerusalem that Saddam might try to provoke Israel by deploying Iraqi troops on Jordanian soil. An associated fear was that the Iraqi pressures on Jordan to violate the international trade embargo, and the overwhelming support for Saddam among the majority of Jordanians and the military leadership, would put King Hussein in an impossible position and could even endanger his throne. Not everybody in Israel was sympathetic to the King's predicament. Geula Cohen, a Deputy Minister of the right-wing Tehiya Party, viewed the crisis as an opportunity for promoting the cause of 'greater Israel'. In her view, Israel should warn the King that if he allowed the Iraqi Army to enter Jordan or undertook other 'irresponsible' measures, he would have to face the possibility of a mass expulsion of Palestinians from the occupied territories to Jordan, or, even worse, lose the eastern bank of the Jordan river to Israel. In the meantime the Gulf crisis should be the catalyst for annexing the West Bank and the Gaza Strip to Israel.[38] A Labour member of Knesset, Binyamin Ben-Eliezer, accused Jordan of violating the international sanctions by allowing goods to reach Iraq through the port of Aqaba, and called for Israeli moves against the Hashemite kingdom.[39]

The official position on this issue was far less bellicose. In a marked departure from the longstanding Likud line which had taken Jordan for a Palestinian state and implicitly (or explicitly, as in the case of Ariel Sharon and his supporters) advocated the replacement of the Hashemite dynasty by a Palestinian Government, the Israeli leadership went out of its way to allay King Hussein's fears of an Israeli aggression, going as far as to state publicly that the stability of his regime was in Israel's best interest. During his visit to Rome, Foreign Minister Levy asked his Italian counterpart, Gianni de Michelis, to reassure King Hussein of Israel's pure intentions. A similar reassurance was reportedly passed to the King by President Mubarak of Egypt. Premier Shamir announced that 'Israel's interest requires that Jordan remain stable under the complete control of King Hussein. Until now, there have been no indications of any erosion in his power.'[40]

While reassuring King Hussein, Israel sought to deter Saddam from either launching a direct attack against the Jewish state or endangering its security by entering Jordan. To this end a two-pronged strategy was adopted, combining vehement denials of any connection to the coalition with strong warnings aimed at underlining the exorbitant cost of any act of aggression. 'Israel has a variety of means to respond to an Iraqi threat,' said the Israeli Chief of Staff, Lieutenant-General Dan Shomron. 'I hope, and also believe, that Saddam Hussein is aware that he will pay dearly for attacking Israel, and will, therefore, refrain from carrying out his threats.'[41]

But how far was Israel willing to go in its retaliatory policy, and did it consider pre-empting an imminent Iraqi attack? Israeli statements in this respect left a thick cloud of ambiguity. Speaking to a Jewish–American group visiting Israel, Shamir said: 'If, God forbid, Israel fails to prevent war with Iraq, or to launch a pre-emptive strike, it won't have any other choice – it will have to win quickly and decisively.'[42] This last sentence was picked up by the foreign press as an indication of Israel's determination to mount a pre-emptive strike, only to be vehemently denied by the Prime Minister's office. Yet, when Defence Minister Arens was asked about the possibility of a pre-emptive strike, he would neither confirm nor deny that Israel was entertaining such an option.[43]

A similar uncertainty was left about the Israeli reaction to an Iraqi entry of Jordan. While Arens implied that any such move would trigger an immediate harsh response, Chief of Staff Shomron advocated a graduated, well-considered approach:

> We will first examine what Iraqi troops are sent to Jordan and why, and how Israeli intervention would affect the Western–Arab coalition in the Persian Gulf. The 'red line' does not mean that if an Iraqi soldier steps on it, an electric circuit will close and all sorts of things will start flying in the air.[44]

Still Shomron took care to emphasize that Israel retained the right to retaliate for an Iraqi attack and that, while preferring to co-ordinate a response with the coalition, Israel would 'go it alone' if necessary.[45]

This deterrent posturing notwithstanding, the general message coming from Jerusalem was one of moderation and restraint. The crisis was an essentially inter-Arab affair and therefore Israel was determined to keep out of it. Paradoxically, the Bush Administration was benefiting here from the same traits in Mr Shamir that had irritated them so much in the past, namely, extreme caution and lack of political initiative. An elderly politician who reached his country's top spot almost by default, following Premier

Begin's premature resignation in 1983, Shamir had become the longest serving Prime Minister in Israel's history after David Ben-Gurion. In achieving this he relied on his impeccable instincts for political survival, which advised him against any abrupt moves, both in domestic and foreign policy. As far as the Arab–Israeli peace process was concerned, this approach alienated the Administration and led to a severe crisis in US–Israeli relations. In the Gulf crisis, however, this caution was a welcome gift, as an abrupt Israeli response was exactly what Saddam was waiting for. Indeed, from the early stages of the crisis, Shamir expressed his preference for staying out of the crisis. 'Israel has no interest in aiding Saddam Hussein, who wants to involve us in the current confrontation,' he said in a televised interview. 'Israel will not play with its fate and those circles planning to attack us know that they will pay a terrible price for such an attack.'[46] This line was underscored by Moshe Arens, who hurried to discount expressions of eagerness in the military to collaborate with the coalition by stating unequivocally that Israel would not participate in the naval blockade since the crisis was not an Israeli problem.[47]

There were, however, anticipated rewards for this acquiescence in the American request. In his visit to Washington in early September, Foreign Minister Levy received a presidential undertaking to preserve Israel's 'qualitative edge', and a promise by Secretary Baker to supply Israel with Patriot anti-missile missiles. Yet his request that Israel's $4.5 billion military debt be forgiven, as had been the case with Egypt's $6.5 billion, received only an evasive reply. Egypt's debt was worthless and there was no desire to set a precedent for others. And Levy was made aware that the crisis was producing other regional pressures which could further weaken Israeli influence in Washington. Baker informed him that he was going to Damascus for a brief visit. He would not, however, visit Israel.[48] The Bush Administration had yet to warm to Israel. Numerous heads of government had received personal calls from George Bush since the start of the crisis: Yitzhak Shamir was still waiting.

Peace with Iran

Saddam also tried to ease his isolation by offering his old enemy Iran a significant carrot. The lack of any progress towards an enduring settlement with Iran had been a major impediment to Iraq's return to normalcy after the war, and consequently, a paramount concern for Saddam. Yet until 2 August there was virtually nothing he could do. He could not admit to his people that he had embroiled them in eight years of horrendous war only to save his

regime or concede that the war had not actually been won through concessions to Iran.

This dilemma was now eased. In order to resist the United States and its
lackeys, Saddam told his subjects, Iraq had to free itself of any possible
distraction, even if this involved a certain cost. On 14 August he conveyed a
message to the Iranian President, Ali Akbar Hashemi-Rafsanjani, suggesting
that the two countries accept the status quo established by the 1975 Algiers
Agreement, agree to exchange prisoners of war, and withdraw their forces
from occupied respective territories.

Bearing in mind the humiliating circumstances under which the Algiers
Agreement had been concluded, and the fact that the abrogation of this
treaty topped the list of the Iraqi demands from Iran following the 1980
invasion, Saddam's peace proposals were no minor concession. In a letter to
Rafsanjani only three days before the invasion of Kuwait, he had still been
adamant that sovereignty over the Shatt al-Arab waterway, the main bone of
contention between Iraq and Iran, should 'belong to Iraq as its lawful
historical right'.[49] Now, not only were these demands dropped altogether,
but the Iraqi people was told for the first time that 'the eight-year war was
not over the 1975 agreement, which the Iranians implicitly cancelled and
denounced'.[50]

The abruptness of the Iraqi initiative took the Iranian leadership by
complete surprise. Since the Kuwaiti–Iraqi dispute had erupted in mid July
the Iranians had followed Saddam's moves with mixed feelings. On the one
hand, given the desperate need of the Iranian economy for increased oil
revenues, the clerics in Tehran had few qualms about supporting the
pressures put by their former arch-enemy on Kuwait and the UAE to reduce
their oil production quotas.[51] On the other hand, they feared that Saddam's
bullying of Kuwait disguised wider expansionist ambitions. 'Iran despises the
Iraqi territorial ambitions against Kuwait,' wrote the daily *Tehran Times*, the
mouthpiece of the Iranian President, '[which] has its roots in Iraq's long-
held territorial ambitions against Kuwait, as well as in Baghdad leaders'
military and political aspirations.'[52]

The invasion of Kuwait was thus naturally interpreted by Tehran as
confirmation of Saddam's inherent bellicosity, and a move that could well
extend beyond the emirate. 'Iran rejects any form of resorting to force as a
solution to regional problems,' read an official statement of the Iranian
Foreign Ministry on 2 August:

> it considers Iraq's military action against Kuwait contrary to stability
> and security in the sensitive Persian Gulf region and . . . calls for the

immediate withdrawal of Iraqi troops to recognized international borders and for a peaceful solution to the dispute. Iran declares that, as the largest country in the region with the highest degree of interest in the Persian Gulf region, she cannot remain indifferent to developments that could endanger her national security and regional stability.[53]

The intensity of Tehran's anxiety over the occupation of Kuwait was further illustrated by its neutral, perhaps even positive response to President Bush's announcement of his decision to deploy US troops in Saudi Arabia. Rather than attacking this move as the latest manifestation of America's 'hegemonic machinations' and castigating the Saudis for defiling Islam's holy lands, the Iranians chose to describe the American deployment as part of a multinational effort to 'safeguard Arabia in the face of Iraqi threats'.[54] Given the unbounded hostility of the Islamic Republic towards the United States, this remarkably restrained response reflected Tehran's grim assessment that the threat of the Iraqi devil was far greater than that of the 'Great Satan', to use the late Ayatollah Khomeini's label for the United States. Indeed, when Saddam approached the Iranians following the Kuwaiti invasion, they feared that he was laying yet another devious trap. 'If Saddam Hussein fails to impose his expansionist demands on President Hashemi-Rafsanjani during their yet unscheduled future meeting,' commented the Iranian media on the Iraqi peace feelers, 'he will perhaps resort to another war against Iran in order to exert pressure on Tehran.'[55]

Nonetheless, realizing that it was Saddam's growing plight, and not unbridled ambition, which drove him to seek their friendship, the Iranians quickly seized the opportunity, and on 18 August the exchange of war prisoners began. If Saddam hoped that this settlement would allow the two radical regimes to work together to counter American influence, again he was to be disappointed: Tehran pocketed the concessions but still opposed the annexation of Kuwait and supported the international sanctions.

CHAPTER 7

Sharing the Burden

Beyond the Middle East the direct impact of the crisis was not so great, yet the international community as a whole still had to be engaged if sanctions were to stick. The addition of a military dimension meant that the United States was now anxious to show that it was not alone in being prepared to take drastic measures in opposing aggression. In Europe, as with so many other international issues, the question became one of European self-respect. Thus, Italian Foreign Minister Gianni de Michelis argued that while Europe wanted to 'contribute to burden sharing', this must be 'in a way that is autonomous and direct and not as support for the expenses of another country, even if it is an ally'. The Danish Foreign Minister, Uffe Ellemann Jensen, was quite explicit that the 'self-respect of Europeans means they cannot accept that the US should once again solve a crisis on their own doorstep'.[1] Nonetheless, the major European powers were prepared to accept that the issue was one of international order and not European self-respect.

Britain

Having been in the United States when the crisis broke, Prime Minister Margaret Thatcher was closely associated with the development of American policy from the start. The crisis provided an opportunity to reassert the 'special' Anglo-American relationship which had taken a battering with the retirement of Ronald Reagan and the inclination of the Bush Administration to focus on Germany, particularly during its unification process. Mrs Thatcher's advisers hoped that President Bush would see who his real friends were when it came to the crunch.

As a former imperial power there was also a natural tendency towards globalism in British foreign policy. This made it responsive to challenges to international order. A readiness to take on aggression was an important part of the national self-image. This tendency was further reinforced by a reasonable record in military interventions, with the unfortunate memory of the 1956 Suez campaign overtaken by the successful 1982 Falklands war. The Persian Gulf was an area in which Britain could claim long connections and expertise. In 1961 British troops had shielded Kuwait against an Iraqi threat to its newly gained independence. Close relations were maintained thereafter and Kuwaiti investments played a significant part in the British economy. One commentator observed 'For the British ... intervening East of Suez is like riding a bike: you never lose the knack.'[2]

In the absence of Mrs Thatcher, the first meeting of the Cabinet's Overseas and Defence Committee (on 3 August) was chaired by Deputy Prime Minister Sir Geoffrey Howe. The meeting endorsed full economic sanctions against Iraq but shared the prevailing uncertainty over the extent of the risks that Turkey or Saudi Arabia were likely to take in support. Mrs Thatcher's close association with President Bush in the first few days of the crisis made it inevitable that Britain would follow the American lead.

Britain's main move had been to strengthen the Armilla patrol, the Royal Navy's patrol in the Gulf region which had begun in 1980 and been stepped up during the threat to shipping in the late stages of the Iran–Iraq War. Since the end of the war it had been kept down to a minimum level. Now the one frigate in the Gulf, off Dubai, was to be supported by a frigate from Mombasa and another which had been in Malaysia.

The Prime Minister saw this crisis – as so many others – first and foremost as a matter of principle. She told her audience in Aspen on 5 August:

> Iraq's invasion of Kuwait defies every principle for which the United Nations stands. If we let it succeed, no small country can ever feel safe again. The law of the jungle would take over from the rule of law.[3]

She had intended to stay in the United States after 6 August but cut short her trip to get back to London. She stopped *en route* to give a press conference at which she was asked about a military option. 'The method we are using to try to get Iraq out of Kuwait,' she answered, 'is by the United Nations sanctions and by denying imports to Iraq and exports from Iraq.' She was not as sceptical as she had been about sanctions against South Africa or the Soviet Union, because of the extent of UN backing, the vulnerability of Iraq and the fundamental nature of the challenge. It was only in this context that she thought that force – in the form of a blockade – might have to be 'considered'. There was no mention of a threat to Saudi Arabia, although she knew by this time that King Fahd had accepted American forces.[4] However, speculation here was growing, as acknowledged by

Foreign Secretary Douglas Hurd who, while noting that Britain had 'no specific commitment' to the Saudis, added that 'I don't think it would be wise for Saddam Hussein to suppose that an attack upon Saudi Arabia would be an attack on Saudi Arabia alone.'[5]

On her return to London, Mrs Thatcher met with Douglas Hurd, Chancellor of the Exchequer John Major, and Defence Secretary Tom King. Before President Bush's announcement, the Cabinet was in session. It agreed in principle to contribute some forces to the anti-Iraq coalition. Afterwards the Prime Minister spoke to King Fahd, who formally requested British forces. Outside Downing Street, Hurd read out a statement:

> The Government will contribute forces to a multinational effort for the collective defence of the territory of Saudi Arabia and other threatened states in the area, and in support of the United Nations embargo. We are in urgent touch with the United States, our other allies, and our friends in the Gulf, on the contribution we can best make in response to a request.

Neither he nor Tom King would give full details of this contribution, though it was clear that it would be confined to air and naval forces. As naval forces were already in the Gulf, the key decision in principle was to send aircraft.[6] Here the modest start to the British military engagement was set at twelve Tornado F3 air defence fighters, twelve Jaguar ground attack aircraft with two Victor tankers, and three Nimrod maritime patrol aircraft. There would be 1,700 UK servicemen in the region.

Merely eight days before the invasion, Defence Secretary Tom King had announced the outlines of a programme of defence cuts following the end of the cold war,[7] and there was concern in Whitehall that an 'out of area' crisis might be used to obstruct these cuts. The initial inclination was therefore to find a level of contribution that achieved the maximum political profile with the minimum of risk. If there was a model it was the small UK contingent (100 men) sent to the Multi-National Force in Beirut in 1983–4, which was judged to have achieved an entrée into American decision-making at low cost. Eventually it was realized that the initial contribution was too small to be truly significant.

In September Parliament assembled for a rare debate during the summer recess. During the debate the Prime Minister announced, without elaboration, that 'some additional forces will be needed and their composition is under consideration'. Despite pressure from the Royal Navy to send a carrier to provide extra flexibility, the Chiefs saw little need to do so, since the American carrier fleet was already so large and it could provide no capability that could not be met from land. Since 8 August three mine-sweepers, extra support vessels, and most recently a second destroyer had been dispatched to the Gulf and, with so many other nations sending naval vessels, there was no case for any more. Two additional Tornado squadrons had also been sent in late August, bringing the numbers up from thirty-six to fifty-four, but these were the Tornado GR3s, strike aircraft which could be taken to demonstrate a more offensive inclination than the original air defence contribution. There was a sharp internal debate as to whether this would be sending the wrong message for a defensive force.

The most controversial question was whether the Army should now be sent. Unlike air and naval units, which were self-contained and could be extracted at will, ground forces indicated a significantly higher level of commitment. A range of options were under consideration, from sending an infantry battalion to Bahrain to protect the Tornado squadrons, to a lightly armed airborne brigade, to a full armoured brigade. It was soon decided that it would be pointless to send more light forces as there was a sufficiency of them already.

There was no doubt that the main need, in the eyes of American planners, was for more tanks. Secretary of State Baker made this explicit when he spoke to NATO Foreign Ministers at Brussels on 10 September. The Prime Minister was both anxious to respond to a real military need and aware that to dispatch a small force would be to send the wrong political signal. If it did become necessary to push Iraq out of Kuwait then substantial forces would be required, and even the French did not seem to be ruling that out. If Britain was making a greater military input then it could also expect to achieve a greater influence over the policy output.

Yet Mrs Thatcher was also nervous about the public reaction that might follow such a major stepping up of Britain's involvement. Furthermore, there were concerns about the logistical problem of sustaining such a large force, and anxiety with regard to the reliability of British tanks in desert conditions. They had a reputation for engine trouble, and this was embarrassing enough in exercises in Germany but could be catastrophic in an actual war. One alternative option was to send heavy artillery pieces. As the M-109 guns were of American origin they would be able to operate under the wing of the US Army, thereby keeping the number of support troops down and the total extra commitment to as few as 2,000 men.

Nonetheless, the Chief of the General Staff, General Sir John Chapple, wanted to send a substantial force. If tanks were to be sent it had to be a full armoured brigade – with half a brigade there would be far less than half effectiveness. In the light of events in Eastern Europe, the gap that would be left in NATO would not be as important as it would have been judged even a year earlier – and it was not far from the thoughts of some Army officers that the Gulf might do for armoured brigades – looking increasingly anomalous as the Warsaw Pact evaporated – what the Falklands had done for the Royal Navy after the 1981 Defence Review.

The Army argued that so long as sufficient back-up was provided the problems with the Challenger tank were exaggerated. This requirement, plus the lack of commonality in most ammunition and spare parts, except for the artillery, meant that the support effort would be considerable, with a force of 8,000 troops divided almost equally between 'teeth' and 'tail'.

By Tuesday 11 September the Overseas and Defence Committee took the decision in principle to send an armoured brigade. The next day Brigadier Patrick Cordingley, commanding the 7th Armoured Brigade in Germany, was told to prepare to move to Saudi Arabia. In London the Prime Minister was still seeking reassurances from the Army with regard to whether this force could be properly maintained in the field, while soundings were being taken to judge the likely response of both Conservative backbenchers and Opposition leaders to such a force. The response was encouraging, and the proposal was finally endorsed by the Overseas and Defence Committee on 14 September.

It was then announced that the 7th Armoured Brigade (the 'Desert Rats') would be sent to Saudi Arabia, consisting of two armoured regiments with 120 Challenger tanks, an infantry battalion equipped with armoured cars, an air defence battery, plus helicopters and anti-tank and anti-aircraft missiles. In addition extra Tornado squadrons would be sent. According to Tom King the purpose of these forces was:

> to ensure that Saddam Hussein understands that while we seek the implementation of the UN resolutions by peaceful means, other options remain available and, one way or another, he will lose.[8]

France

France, it may be recalled, had been Iraq's foremost Western ally. As far as the arms trade with Baghdad was concerned, it was second only to the USSR, having provided about one quarter of Iraq's total arsenal. These arms ranged from the Mirage F1 fighter aircraft, to Exocet anti-ship missiles, to advanced electronic gear for radar systems and equipment to increase the range and accuracy of Scud missiles.[9] Largely because of Iraq's indebtedness, this relationship was already starting to sour by the time of the crisis. President François Mitterrand responded firmly to Iraq's annexation of Kuwait on 8 August:

> France has for long had friendly relations with Iraq. You know that we continued to help it during the war with Iran. That allows us to say all the more clearly that we accept neither the aggression against Kuwait nor the annexation which followed.[10]

The developing French position was shaped less by its close relationship with Iraq than by its general attempt to develop special relations with the Arabs and its eagerness to demonstrate a distinctive national approach and, in particular, independence from the United States. In order not to be seen as slavishly following American policy, on 13 August Mitterrand announced that he was dispatching twelve envoys to twenty-four different countries. These were drawn from various sectors of political life and included a former Prime Minister, two former Foreign Ministers and the Secretary General of the Elysée Palace. Their mission was to emphasize that the actions taken in the Gulf were purely defensive and that there was no need to transform the international embargo against Iraq into a blockade.[11]

Interpreted as an attempt to save face after French foreign policy had been wrong-footed by the sudden emergence of one its close regional associates as a dangerous aggressor, this diplomatic offensive was generally acceptable to the French political system and the public at large. There was, however, a measure of scepticism. The foremost opposition to Mitterrand's initiative came from Jean-Marie Le Pen of the National Front, who said that the crisis was an Arab affair. There was also some equivocation from other leading French politicians who had had close association with Saddam, such as the former Prime Minister, Jacques Chirac. Defence Minister Jean-Pierre Chevènement indicated that he feared that the military build-up in the Gulf was heightening the risk of war. His view was shared by Interior Minister Pierre Joxe. They were lukewarm about getting involved militarily because of the effect on relations with the rest of the Arab world.[12]

Against this backdrop Mitterrand moved cautiously. The French military commitment was initially tentative and again geared to conveying French distinctiveness as much as opposition to the Iraqi action. On 9 August, after a meeting of the Executive Committee of the Council of Ministers, Mitterrand declared that France would not be associated with the multinational force proposed by Washington. France would, however, take its own steps.

At the time one warship was already on manoeuvres in the Gulf: it would now be reinforced by its intended replacement, and then joined quickly by the Exocet-carrying frigates, *Montcalm* and *Dupleix*. The main gesture was to send the aircraft carrier *Clemenceau*, accompanied by the battle cruiser *Colbert*, equipped with long-range missiles. The operation was said to involve 3,500 personnel.[13] In addition there was already a French garrison of 3,850 men at Djibouti.

Clemenceau was supposed to be a symbol of national pride. Its crew was 1,700 men plus one woman, but all that it was carrying was forty-two Gazelle and Super-Puma helicopters belonging to the Rapid Action Strike Force rather than the Exocet-carrying Super-Étendards. The symbolism, which was lost on most observers at the time, was to hint at a commitment of ground forces (to whom the helicopters were assigned) while maintaining diplomatic flexibility.[14] They would indicate that the French role was largely defensive and diplomatic rather than threatening.

Once it had unloaded its helicopters in Saudi Arabia and in the UAE and Oman, *Clemenceau* would have little or no further value. In practice, the carrier epitomized French weakness. One reason that the Super-Étendards had not been taken was that they were judged too antiquated to risk against superior Iraqi aircraft, which had themselves been supplied by France. The symbolism became even more unfortunate when trouble in the engine room of the thirty-year-old ship forced it to slow down to twenty-eight knots. After arriving in Djibouti on 22 August it sailed for Abu Dhabi six days later. It had been delayed also because there was uncertainty over where it should go next. The decision was that it should go to the Sea of Oman, with the possibility then of the helicopters being unloaded in Saudi Arabia. Two weeks later *Clemenceau* was diverted to the Saudi port town of Yanbu, 200 miles north of Jeddah, where the helicopters disembarked. The ship left Yanbu on 25 September but three days later was told to return to Toulouse – where it arrived on 5 October.

The senior French military were pushing for a more credible effort. Admiral Lanxade, the French Chief of Staff, wrote to President Mitterrand on 3 September that France could sustain its existing presence in the Gulf, letting 'the Americans and the British go in by themselves, while we would, for our part, simply cover the Saudi forces'. Alternatively, France could 'provide a significant contribution, with all the political and military risks that this entails'. He preferred the second option, with the forces on *Clemenceau* being used as the first units. 'When a symbolic game is being played,' he noted, 'then even the smallest moves have significance. Once French forces have landed on Saudi soil then the whole character of the French commitment would change.' Defence Minister Chevènement remained reluctant: 'We know how to land the troops, but we do not know in what conditions they would be able to leave.'[15]

But even then an excessively small force would also send a strange message – especially if it was outnumbered by journalists. It became evident to Mitterrand that French forces would have to be more substantial if they were to be taken seriously. However, there was at that time no particular pressure from the United States, which was focused on the enforcement of the embargo, for an increase in forces.

The opportunity to give France a more serious military presence was provided by the Iraqis in mid September. Saddam demanded the closure of all foreign embassies in Kuwait. Western Governments refused to acknowledge the annexation of the emirate and so maintained their embassies in Kuwait City. In one of Iraq's grosser errors, French diplomats suffered more than most. As with the British and Americans, the French Embassy was surrounded and cut off from water and electricity supplies. But the French Ambassador's residence in Kuwait was also entered, and four French citizens including the military attaché were kidnapped. Furious, Mitterrand decided to lay the matter before the Security Council, asking that

> a United Nations mission be sent to Kuwait to contribute to restore the normal functioning of the diplomatic missions and secure their inviolability.
>
> In the face of such an escalation, France reserves the possibility of taking any measure she will consider appropriate.

France also began to move towards the Anglo-American position by deciding to respond 'favourably to Saudi Arabia's request by stationing on her territory a precursory unit of the combat helicopter regiment embarked on the *Clemenceau*'.[16] On 16 September it was announced that among additional forces going to the Gulf would be 4,200 ground troops. This included half of the 6th Light Armoured Division (DLB), comprising an air-mobile brigade of three regiments; a regiment of forty-eight combat helicopters; a regiment of forty-eight AMX-10 armoured vehicles; the 1,100-strong 2nd Infantry Regiment of the Foreign Legion, with anti-tank weapons; an anti-aircraft section with high-performance ground-to-air Mistral missiles; and some thirty Mirage 2000, Mirage F-1 and Jaguar combat aircraft. The 5th Combat Helicopter Regiment, on *Clemenceau*, was now to form part of the Brigade and carry air-mobile forces with anti-tank weapons. The French contribution was designated 'Operation Daguet'.[17]

Gradually the character of the French commitment was changing and the gap with the Americans and British narrowing. On 18 September senior French ministers and military officers met with their American counterparts in Munich to sort out the role of French forces and their relationship with those of the other members of the coalition. Inevitably one of the first questions, raised by Chevènement, was one of command. President Mitterrand, while insisting that he maintained autonomy of decision, was well aware that autonomy of action would be impossible in these circumstances. Chevènement, still anxious to keep France's relations with Baghdad intact, voiced his fear that France would be trapped by some American provocation, only to be told by his superior – as President and Commander-in-Chief of French Armed Forces – that in the event of military action French forces would be under American command, and operating at the front rather than the rear.[18]

Germany

For Germany the crisis could not have come at a worse time. It erupted just as the date for unification had been agreed for 2 October 1990, to be followed by elections in December. German politicians were not easily distracted.

Chancellor Helmut Kohl, who had reason to be deeply grateful to the Bush Administration for its help over unification, was willing to make a contribution to the multinational force. On 9 August, Hans Stercken, Chairman of the Parliament's Foreign Affairs Committee and a member of the ruling Christian Democratic Party (CDU), said that Germany 'should not say no from the very outset to a request for solidarity in the dispatch of armed forces'. However, later that day the Government decided that action in the Gulf would require a change of law. Instead of dispatching German warships to the region it was decided to send five vessels to the Mediterranean to support the US Sixth Fleet, replacing American ships that had left for the Gulf. A similar move had been taken in 1987–8, during the international naval build-up in the Gulf, so there was a precedent.

But even such moves required a liberal interpretation of the Federal Republic's Constitution. According to Articles 2 and 24, the use of German forces was confined to self-defence, including participation in alliances aimed at 'bringing about a peaceful and lasting order in Europe and among the nations of the world'. A narrow interpretation argued that participation in alliances covered only the NATO area, but a broader interpretation saw possible support for wider collective security arrangements, including the Western European Union (WEU) which – unlike NATO – did allow for operations outside the European area.[19]

These limitations reflected the post-war revulsion against militarism. Germany was the only nation whose forces were wholly integrated in

NATO. They were configured for central front operations and did not have much of a capability (such as a bluewater Navy) for overseas activities. As far as the Middle East was concerned, these constraints were significantly heightened by German sensitivity over the security of Israel because of the Nazi genocide against the Jews.

For the Government the question was how to handle such a divisive issue in the run-up to unification and the first all-German elections in half a century. Any move to send forces into the Gulf would undoubtedly trigger a political row, with the Greens and the Social Democrats calling for continued restraint. By mid August there were reports that Germany was considering sending minesweepers to the Gulf as part of the West European task force to be set up under the auspices of the WEU. To the irritation of Chancellor Kohl, Foreign Minister de Michelis of Italy quoted him as saying to Prime Minister Andreotti that 'West Germany will take part within the framework of its legal and practical means' in any WEU action, and it was suggested that Bonn was encouraging Belgium and the Netherlands to take the initiative with the WEU so that the Federal Republic could join in. As expected, once this inclination was leaked a political row broke. Despite Christian Democrat demands for support for a European cause, a Green spokesman, Alfred Mechtershelmer, claimed that it would be 'superfluous and dangerous' if Germany took part 'in any sabre-rattling in the crisis region', while the Social Democrats promised to use all parliamentary and constitutional methods to prevent German forces from operating outside NATO territory.[20]

All this confirmed that the question of interpretation of the Constitution was itself highly political. The Foreign Minister, Hans-Dietrich Genscher, wished to avoid a constitutional argument with the opposition, whom he felt to be supported by public opinion. While he was prepared to see a change in the Constitution to allow support of a UN peace-keeping force, he doubted whether the Government could find the necessary two-thirds majority in Parliament to go beyond that – and it would be disastrous to try and to fail. Kohl was reluctantly persuaded by Genscher, and Defence Minister Stoltenberg, that without changes in the Constitution no forces could be sent. In a sense the problem was, as one astute observer noted, that modern Germany lacked a concept of power politics to cope with such situations. Power politics was rejected because of its grim associations with Hitler, but the alternative language of affability and peaceableness provided no policy guidance.[21]

All Kohl could do to demonstrate German solidarity, therefore, was to offer a promise that he would seek to revise the Constitution after the

December elections. In an interview on 9 September he noted the harm that would be done to Germany's reputation 'if the judgement around the world was that if there is money to be made they're here, but if the issue is taking responsibility they evade it'. He stressed, however, that he was only talking about missions in support of UN decisions:

> As a member of the United Nations we cannot stand aside when the United Nations calls on us to take responsibility.[22]

For now he offered indirect support: permission for US forces to use American bases in West Germany to transport troops and material to the Gulf; a loan of ten wheeled light armoured vehicles able to detect poison gas; civilian aircraft and commercial ships to help transport US troops and equipment from Germany to the Gulf; financial support, as part of the European Community's package, to ease the impact of the embargo on Jordan, Turkey and Egypt. Germany's best way to calm its allies in these circumstances was by reaching into its wallet.

This became the response to American demands for more action, consolidated during a visit by James Baker on 16 September. By now American congressmen were contrasting the $8 billion found by Bonn to support Soviet troops in East Germany until they could be repatriated as part of the deal with Moscow, with the lack of contribution to US operations in the Gulf. Having used German economic strength to sort out the numerous problems of unification, it was not surprising to find this same strength being looked to for the solution to other problems, even though unification itself was proving to be more expensive than expected. Nonetheless, the Germans managed – with some creative accounting – to come up with a package worth DM3.3 billion, combining its military support to the US with economic assistance to those states in the economic front line.[23]

Japan

The situation in Japan was comparable to that of Germany in terms of a post-Second World War Constitution appearing as a brake on any activity that could be remotely described as being 'military' beyond its own borders, and the inclination to use national wealth as an alternative to more direct participation. The Japanese response was further clouded by its keen sense of dependence upon the Middle East for 70 per cent of its oil imports and structural limitations in national decision-making, resulting from the faction-ridden politics of the ruling Liberal Democrat Party (LDP) and the conflicting demands of powerful ministries.[24] These tensions were aggravated in this case by the particular weakness of Prime Minister Toshiki Kaifu, who lacked a power base of his own and had achieved his position due largely to a series of financial scandals which had weakened more senior LDP figures.

Japan was also slow to state support for the US military action, although it did so in fulsome terms when it got round to it. This sense of a readiness to benefit from the efforts of the rest of the international community while avoiding direct responsibility was vividly demonstrated when Prime Minister Kaifu cancelled a trip to Arab states including Saudi Arabia, Egypt and Jordan, previously planned for 16 August. This trip would have given him a unique opportunity to assert Japan's international role, as the first major Western leader to visit the area since the start of the crisis. However, he was inhibited by the fact that he would be unable to convey any agreed policy.

Within the LDP there were also concerns that to ignore Iraq on such a visit would alienate Baghdad even more in the future, and that the soft line adopted up to this point had apparently been successful in getting seventy-three Japanese hostages out of Kuwait. Conversely, it was argued that cancellation of the trip would demonstrate that Japan was unwilling to pull its weight. When it came, the cancellation was presented as a temporary move designed to enable the Japanese Government to 'formulate new measures', and it was promised that the Foreign Minister would go instead to explain this decision.

The Government was searching for ideas other than economic sanctions but appeared reluctant to commit itself to any particular step. Thus, when announcing the cancellation, Foreign Minister Taro Nakayama also said that Japan would not extend financial assistance to those providing military forces – but then the Ministry issued a clarification that this did not mean that such support was ruled out indefinitely.[25]

The most awkward question of all was whether there could be any direct involvement of Japan's Self-Defence Forces (SDF) in the multinational effort. Some senior officers believed this to be a unique opportunity to make a fresh break from the constraints of post-war pacifism.[26] The Defence Ministry raised the possibility of sending some of Japan's forty-six mine-sweepers – more than either the United States or Britain – but then withdrew under pressure from the Foreign Ministry. The prevailing view was that any dispatch of the SDF beyond Japanese borders would be unconstitutional.

Article 9 of the Constitution states that Japan will 'forever renounce force' as a means of settling disputes and that land, sea and air forces will never be maintained. Despite this injunction, the Japanese Army had grown since the

Second World War to a well-equipped 247,000-strong force. However, this had been permitted on the basis of an interpretation that the Constitution would be violated only if these forces left Japanese territory. The Americans, who had actually written the Constitution, now suggested that this interpretation was too narrow, but their arguments had little success.

In this situation it appeared that the Government would find it difficult to go beyond economic aid. This led to severe internal questioning of Japan's whole international posture. As one critic put it:

> The Government is behaving like a rich man whose neighbour's house is on fire. Its attitude is astonishing: here's some money, but please don't ask for any water.[27]

Even with economic aid there were problems. By late August the Government was still putting together an aid package. During his trip to the Middle East, Nakayama had offered financial aid to nations who had suffered as a result of the trade embargo. At the same time President Bush had spoken on the phone with Prime Minister Kaifu to put in a direct request for financial support for US allies in the Middle East as well as for funds and equipment for the military forces gathering in Saudi Arabia. Complaints about Japan's selfish readiness to allow others to shoulder international responsibility while concentrating on building up markets surfaced in Washington, and were limited only by the fact that Congress was in recess. To head off these complaints, officials in Tokyo were told to come up with ideas for expanding assistance beyond financial aid, and for sending Japanese personnel to provide medical, transport or other forms of non-combat assistance in the Gulf. The eventual package that emerged failed to impress. As usual in Japanese political life, it was the result of protracted bureaucratic wrangling, with the Finance Ministry seeking to limit the budgetary impact and top SDF officials excluded from the negotiations for fear that their very presence would spark protests from opposition parties, the public at large, and neighbouring countries which still feared a more assertive Japanese role.

As a result, Kaifu felt unable to offer the direct assistance to the build-up of forces in the Gulf that Washington had sought. Instead of the expected infusion of substantial amounts of cash to meet the urgent needs of the hardest-hit Middle East countries, there were vague mentions of support for Turkey, Egypt and Jordan and other countries hurt by the crisis. Furthermore, apart from $10 million to Jordan, the aid would not be available immediately and would not be going to meet the immediate needs of these countries: like most Japanese aid, it would be tied to large construction projects with the presumption that the contracts would go to Japanese firms.

$1 billion would be spent on sending 100 medical specialists, food, water and medical supplies, such as tents, air conditioners and water carriers, aboard chartered planes and ships to the Middle East. Even here the old constraints proved intense. Because Japan's own Air Force was prohibited from flying abroad it was necessary to charter aircraft from the two largest private airline companies – Japan Air Lines and Nippon Air. They were reluctant to be seen as a surrogate Air Force, and Japan Air Lines had an additional concern, with twenty-three of its flight crew held as hostages by Iraq. After extensive arm-twisting they agreed to a few flights to the Gulf but with extremely strict conditions: no explosives, weapons or vehicles, only food, water or medical equipment; no military personnel; a guarantee of safety for crew (although this was meaningless, as the self-defence forces could not accompany aircraft); and finally, no cargo picked up outside of Tokyo.[28]

This initiative had failed to impress the anti-Iraq coalition. Against a background of critical comment in Congress – the House passed a bill threatening to remove US troops from Japan – and on the eve of his visit to Washington and the Middle East, Kaifu received an American team charged with obtaining contributions from allies not participating in the military effort. They were told that the $1 billion already announced was 'acceptable'. The Japanese did not expect to be asked for more. One of the team, Lawrence Eagleburger, later recalled enumerating all the costs, including potential loss of life, that the United States was accepting. The contribution was raised to a level beyond the American expectations.[29]

Kaifu announced the new package on 14 September, adding another $3 billion to the $1 billion already committed. Of the total $4 billion, half was to assist military mobilization in the Gulf[30] and the other half to provide economic assistance for Jordan, Turkey and Egypt. This assistance did not convey a sense of urgency, in that it would still take months before the money was spent and it was still geared to development projects such as factories and roads. Coming three days after Congressional expressions of displeasure, it tended to confirm the impression that Japanese contributions were geared to keeping the United States quiet as much as an assessment of need.[31]

Most dramatically, Kaifu announced that he would be seeking legislation in the Diet (the Japanese Parliament) in October to enable thousands of Japanese to serve in non-combat roles in the Gulf. The objective was to finish work on the bill before the November inauguration of Emperor Akihito. Almost immediately the Socialist Party said it was opposed. This was sufficient to doom the measure, because the Socialists led a majority opposition coalition in the upper house, where the LDP had only 113 out of 252 seats compared with its majority in the lower house of 285 out of 512 seats. No leading politicians picked up the idea with any enthusiasm, and certainly none went so far as actually to advocate sending troops. The public seemed ready to support the anti-Iraq coalition but only at a distance.

Nonetheless, at least to show willing, the Government decided to press on with the measure. At a press conference on 27 September Kaifu said that it was important for Japan to 'co-operate with sweat' in addition to money. Yet at the same time he insisted that the proposed 'United Nations Peace Co-operation Corps' would not 'let them go where danger may follow'. On the one hand, the Gulf crisis had thrown into relief the lack of a 'system' whereby Japan 'could co-operate with the United Nations to contribute to peace'; on the other, 'Japan will never become a military power'. The Government insisted that:

> The dispatch of the corps will not be aimed at the use of force or even the threat of the use of force.[32]

These assurances did not satisfy members of the Opposition, who accused the Government of simply surrendering to American pressure. Miss Takako Doi, the Socialist leader, claimed that unarmed soldiers would be followed by armed soldiers 'as surely as night follows day'. When in mid-October Kaifu introduced the bill into the Diet she asked him if he was 'not asking the youth of Japan to shed blood on the battlefield'. The entry of the bill had itself been delayed because of further arguments within the LDP over its main clauses. The basic idea was to send 1,000–2,000 personnel to the Gulf. These could be on loan from Government agencies or volunteers. As it would not be possible to find many volunteers, some members of the SDF would have to be involved, but only in a very circumscribed manner.

In the inevitable working of details, questions of principle lurked. Would the members of the SDF be armed? Would the ships or aircraft carrying them be allowed to defend themselves? As the LDP leaders struggled with these issues, the initial inclination was to require any SDF recruits to leave the force, not wear uniforms or carry weapons, and not engage in combat-related activity. Some of the younger members of the party toughened the language, although here it was suggested that the motive might have been to ensure its defeat and the consequential humiliation of Kaifu.

It soon became apparent that the proposed bill was a still-born idea. The Socialists remained strongly anti-militarist and the second opposition party, Komeito, would only support a much weaker concept. Meanwhile there were mutterings of discontent from Japan's Asian neighbours, who saw a precedent for Japanese intervention in regional affairs in the making, and this rekindled the unhappy memories of the 1940s. Officials were saying that the only threat to the Government would come if the bill failed in the lower house, but it would not be their fault if it was defeated in the upper house. By the end of October there was no hope for the bill. With opinion polls showing a majority against the Corps,[33] some LDP leaders began to voice open criticism of the idea and in November it was withdrawn. Long after the Gulf conflict was over the argument was still going on.

The Soviet Union

Following the Baker–Shevardnadze joint statement, the Soviet Union had been committed to working closely with the Americans. Any solution short of an unconditional Iraqi withdrawal would be detrimental to the evolving international order and, in consequence, to the already shaky *perestroika*. On the other hand, Soviet spokesmen did not wish to play down the significance of the difficulties Moscow was facing in jettisoning one of its few allies in the Middle East. Voting for sanctions against Iraq 'bears on the living tissue of the comprehensive Soviet–Iraqi economic, scientific and technological relations, built over the years'.[34] There was anxiety not only with regard to the fate of the Soviet advisers but also that Iraq might cancel its debt.

The outcome of these contradictory urges was a policy of official support for the international demand for Iraq's unconditional withdrawal, punctuated by occasional dissent and later diplomatic detours. A natural way for Moscow to overcome these tensions was to work for the United Nations to become the focal point of international action against Iraq. Thus almost as soon as Desert Shield was announced, the Foreign Ministry spokesman, Yuri Gremitskikh, observed that:

> The experience of many years shows that the most correct and sensible way of acting in conflict situations is through collective efforts and the utmost use of UN mechanisms ... We are for the Security Council to tackle this most urgent issue [of the Iraqi invasion of Kuwait] now ... We are also prepared for immediate consultations within the framework of the UN Security Council's Military Staff Committee.[35]

The theme that the Military Staff Committee could have a useful role, especially in the context of the enforcement of the embargo, was picked up by Soviet commentators over the following days. On 9 August, in response to Iraq's official annexation of Kuwait, the Soviet news agency, Tass, stated the USSR's readiness 'to begin immediate consultations within the Security

Council military staff committee which can fulfil very important functions in compliance with the UN Charter'. A day later a firm proposal on the revitalization of the Committee was actually made at the UN. This theme, however, carried with it the divisive implication that if the UN was organizing a military response to Iraqi aggression, in part at the urging of Moscow, then would not Moscow also be obligated to contribute its own forces? This is why in the end there was little dissent from the American view that if there was to be any role for the Military Staff Committee this need not extend much beyond the extension of national actions to enforce the embargo.

The final factor governing Soviet actions was concern for the fate of its own nationals in Iraq and Kuwait. On 11 August, President Gorbachev established a Government commission to plan for their evacuation. Soon it was announced that 880 Soviet citizens in Kuwait (including fifty military advisers) would be allowed to leave. There were, however, an additional 7,791 Soviet citizens in Iraq.[36] Permission was obtained for 2,000 family members to leave – but not for the men. Of these, 193 were military specialists, distinguished by a Soviet General from military advisers in that the latter would assist in the organization of Iraqi armed forces, and even combat operations, while specialists would assist only in familiarization with hardware delivered under contract.[37]

As with France, the Soviet Union gradually found itself more committed to the anti-Saddam cause. In late September Eduard Shevardnadze told the United Nations that the international community had the 'right' to use force against Iraq if it continued with its occupation and even suggested that Moscow might be willing to contribute forces of its own – provided that they were there as part of a collective UN effort under the direction of the Military Staff Committee. Baker even cleared the way with King Fahd for Soviet troops to arrive in Saudi Arabia.[38] Shevardnadze later told correspondents that 'the Iraqis should not bring things to a point where extreme measures might be required ... there is just one way out and that is for Iraq to withdraw from Kuwait'.[39] This in turn led to a reaction in Moscow where hardliners took issue with Shevardnadze's apparent willingness to commit Soviet forces to the conflict. The Soviet Parliament – which believed that it now had a right to be consulted on such matters – asked the Foreign Minister to explain himself. Shevardnadze answered that he was raising a possibility 'in principle' because as a permanent member of the Security Council the Soviet Union would have a special responsibility for any operation carried out under UN auspices. He was clear that the situation was not akin to that of Afghanistan and stressed that 'the Soviet leadership has no plans or intentions to get involved in military operations'.[40]

It is doubtful if Soviet forces would have been in any position to assume a major military role. Whatever their disagreements, both 'old and new thinkers' within the Soviet leadership shared unease regarding a military move against Iraq. The former feared war mainly because it was bound to introduce Western power into the Gulf; the latter because physical force had been discredited as a foreign policy instrument. Both were mindful of the Afghanistan fiasco and could not envisage the Soviet Union fighting a war under the leadership of the United States. With the chaos in the country growing by the day, and morale at rock-bottom after Afghanistan, it was hard to imagine the units being motivated to take on a former ally at the side of the former enemy. One Soviet correspondent, comparing the support given to American troops in the Gulf from home, imagined the letters that Soviet soldiers in the desert would be receiving: 'The mother cannot buy potatoes in Moscow, the brother was killed in Armenia, the bride became a whore in Odessa. And the next day is the attack, the struggle to liberate Kuwait from Iraqi aggressors.'[41]

PART THREE
Sanctions, Hostages and Diplomacy

CHAPTER 8
Saddam's Unwilling Guests

As the battle-lines were drawn in the first half of August the instruments of pressure available to the two sides were identified. For the moment the coalition would depend on economic sanctions. Saddam's most effective bargaining counter appeared to be the fate of the foreigners caught in Iraq and Kuwait by the crisis. In addition to the hundreds of thousands of people from the Arab world and South Asia, who were soon put in a desperate position, there were thousands of Westerners whose fate would be of intense interest to their governments.

Foreigners became caught up in two distinctive types of predicaments: there were those who were allowed by the Iraqis to leave but lacked the means to do so, and those (Westerners and Soviet nationals) who had the means but were denied the permission, thus becoming Baghdad's hostages. The first group involved many more people but the second had far greater political significance for the evolution of the crisis. The hostage issue touched a sensitive nerve in the West due to the numbers and diversity of those involved, the varying conditions in which they were allowed to live, and the cynical manner in which their fate was manipulated. In both cases the plight of the ordinary people caught up in the great imbroglio turned opinion against Saddam. In the end, he was not even able to use his control over the hostages to any strategic advantage.

Refugees

When Iraq occupied Kuwait it took over a country full of foreigners brought in to support all sectors of the economy. An estimated 83 per cent of the Kuwaiti workforce was made up of expatriates from 108 countries, bringing the number of foreigners in the emirate to nearly 1 million out of a total population of 2 million. The expatriate community in Iraq was as substantial, if not so disproportionate to the rest of the population. Those caught in Kuwait were soon anxious to escape the rapidly deteriorating conditions. For those in Iraq the urge to leave had less to do with fear than with the loss of work, as projects were closed and hard currency became scarce.

Immediately after the invasion a number of Kuwaitis and Westerners crossed the border into Saudi Arabia, but the decisive majority of expatriates were trapped in Kuwait, whose borders with Saudi Arabia were quickly sealed by the Iraqis. However, it soon transpired that Baghdad had no intention of keeping all of this large community under its control, particularly since the release of many of these people served its political ends.

It was not so much expatriates but Kuwaitis whom Iraq was happiest to see departing. In the middle of September 1990 the Saudi border was suddenly reopened by Iraq and up to 9,000 Kuwaitis poured over. While some of these refugees were believed to be Iraqi agents infiltrated into Saudi Arabia, this flow of Kuwaitis reflected a wider Iraqi design to change the demographic balance in Kuwait, so that when the Kuwaiti question was put on the international agenda, the 'wishes' of the Kuwaiti people would be a foregone conclusion. Indeed, according to a report published on 19 December 1990 by the human rights organization Amnesty International, some 300,000 Kuwaitis, a third of Kuwait's indigenous population, had fled the country since the invasion.[1] The exiled Kuwaiti Government had access to sufficient wealth to care for all its people outside Kuwait.

As for the expatriates, in the first instance, diplomats could leave but not ordinary citizens. Some of those on visitor's visas were able to depart, but not the longer-term residents who needed exit visas, none of which were being issued. Then on 11 August the Iraqi Government decided to allow those from Arab states and Third World countries – but not Western nationals – to get exit visas.

This differential treatment of Third World and Western countries was fully in line with Saddam Hussein's tried strategy of divide and rule. He wanted to portray Iraq as the aggrieved party, the hapless victim of a 'neo-colonialist, imperialist plot' to subdue an independent, strongly willed Third World state. Hence, within a couple of weeks of the invasion the exodus of Third World nationals began in earnest, with all of Iraq's neighbours – Jordan, Syria, Iran and Turkey – grudgingly accepting refugees. The most reluctant host among these was Turkey which, having absorbed dozens of thousands of Kurds fleeing Iraq in 1988 and some 300,000 ethnic Turks from Bulgaria in 1989, had no inclination to take in additional large numbers of foreigners. Instead it preferred to serve as a transit station for refugees rather than a terminal stop: by early September 1990 some 26,000 refugees had arrived in Turkey but only 10,000 were placed in camps. Iran served a similar purpose, particularly for those Pakistani refugees on their way home.

The main refugee problem was thus concentrated in Jordan. Immediately after Iraq's announcement that foreigners could leave the country, some 20,000 refugees a day were flowing across the Iraqi–Jordanian desert frontier. To stem this haemorrhage Jordan closed its borders, but they had to be reopened as columns of packed cars with some 50,000 people edged towards the border post. People were arriving after long, arduous journeys of often more than 1,000 miles from Baghdad, having lost their livelihoods and their belongings. Many were unlikely refugees, having led comfortable existences in Kuwait or Iraq and being not at all accustomed to a life at subsistence level, and they would arrive at a desert camp with minimum shelter in intense heat with a chronic lack of water and a risk of epidemic. There was therefore a need to organize supplies, cope with the sick and evacuate the largest number of people in the fastest possible way.

Around 70 per cent of those who came through Jordan were Egyptians, who posed few long-term problems. Cairo organized airlift and also sealift from the port of Aqaba, and by the end of August some 85,000 were already home and others were leaving at the rate of over 5,000 a day.[2] Jordanian and Palestinian refugees could go home or to relations and friends in the country. The main problem was with those from the Indian sub-continent who had no easy route to follow home. Of these the Indians were the most fortunate, as their Government organized special flights and, eventually, ships, and was soon getting out some 3,000 people a day. The Bangladeshis and Sri Lankans were most desperate. Due to the meagre means of their Governments, they were dependent upon the International Organization for Migration (IOM) to organize special flights to move them out.

As the numbers entering the country exceeded those being repatriated the crisis intensified. On 23 August King Hussein said that 185,000 refugees had arrived in Jordan since the invasion and only 67,000 had been moved on. To ease the situation it was necessary both to improve the conditions of the camps and to speed the flow of flights out of Jordan. This was by no means an easy task, since Amman airport was not geared to such traffic and this created bottlenecks. Gradually the IOM got on top of the problem, having obtained sufficient funds to charter the necessary aircraft. By the middle of September the organization had repatriated more than 31,500 people with 107 flights.

Sufficient aid gradually began to arrive at the camps, though there remained problems with distribution of food, water and medical assistance. There were also a number of complaints over the quality of the co-ordination among the aid agencies and the Jordanian Government.[3] Part of the problem was that the Jordanians themselves initially failed to appreciate the severity of the problem, and it was not until 22 August, eleven days after the border had been opened, that they first appealed to the United Nations for help. It was only on 12 September that a full-time official, Prince Sadruddin Aga Khan, began to help co-ordinate the refugee crisis. The Jordanians made little secret of their frustration with the UN and with the West in general, feeling that they were being allowed to suffer because of their sympathetic stance towards Saddam Hussein. In the words of Crown Prince Hassan,

> the plight of these persons . . . has evoked only the faintest of responses from the world community, and from a world press more interested in war scenarios than in humanitarian relief.[4]

By the middle of September the estimates of those stranded in Jordan varied from 70,000 to 105,000, with around 7,000 entering the country each day. Their conditions were at least improving, as water supplies were slowly organized and new camps were built to get people out of the desert camp at Sha'lan, where they were initially hosted. There were fears that the 600,000 foreign workers who still remained in Iraq and Kuwait might create a new surge of refugees, especially since more than half of these people were estimated to be Asians. In October Jordan appealed to Iraq to limit the number of refugees to 14,000 per day should a new exodus begin. In practice, however, by this time the first refugee crisis was virtually over. The reception camps and the transit to home countries were now organized. Those who had passed through the system had often been completely impoverished and suffered considerable privations, but, despite the fears in this respect, deaths were few and disease did not take hold.

All of this meant that the release of the non-European nationals, with its attendant refugee problem, failed to rally the Third World behind Baghdad. Quite the reverse. Despite the anxiety in many countries over the safety of their nationals, and despite the irritation of the victims themselves with what was perceived as international, mainly Western, indifference to their plight, these sentiments were not translated into practical measures against the anti-Iraq coalition. Rather, most refugees tended to blame Saddam Hussein for their predicament, and as they went home they were instrumental in turning popular opinion against Iraq.[5]

Hostages

Western nationals appeared more promising as a political instrument. For President Bush there were inevitably powerful memories of how the hostage crisis with Iran helped finish Jimmy Carter's presidency. Later on, during the Reagan years, the fate of a few Americans held in Beirut by Islamic militants led the Administration into one of its most foolish escapades, with the attempt to secure their release by supplying arms to Iran (and then using the money to fund the Contra rebels opposing the Sandinista Government in Nicaragua).

This sensitivity to the safety of Western nationals was significantly exacerbated by the grim realization that any hostage problem during the Kuwaiti crisis would assume a far greater magnitude than any of the previous ones. Consequently, the initial policy of the major Western Governments to the Iraqi occupation of Kuwait was to attempt to uncouple their response to this from the position of foreigners caught in Kuwait, by going out of their way to deny that the foreign nationals were hostages. The nationals were advised by their respective embassies to stay indoors and keep their heads down.

Bush decided on 3 August to be forceful and direct on the issue with the Iraqis, but only in private. He did not want to overplay the issue and so refused in public to utter what American officials called the 'H-word' for 'hostages'. No demands had been made by the Iraqis, it was pointed out, and there was no reason to doubt that the foreign nationals would be released. Meanwhile, the Iraqis were informed of their responsibility for the foreigners' safety, and warned that holding on to them would have no effect whatsoever on the coalition's policy. 'We are not calling them hostages,' explained Secretary of State Baker on 12 August, 'because discussions are ongoing . . . about obtaining permission for them to leave'.[6]

Yet the signs that the Iraqis were aware of the potential bargaining value of foreigners had been there since 3 August, when it became known that thirty-four British servicemen of a military liaison training team had been seized from their homes at a training base near Kuwait City, taken to Baghdad and put in a hotel (the team in total was sixty-six strong with fifty-five dependants). A couple of days later they were joined by fifty-eight British passengers of the 367 passengers and crew on board a British Airways jumbo jet, landing for a stopover in Kuwait *en route* to Kuala Lumpur just as the Iraqi invasion got under way.

At this stage of the crisis the Iraqis still refrained from an overt and straightforward manipulation of the foreigners' presence. When US Chargé d'Affaires Joseph Wilson, with instructions to press for the free movement of all foreigners, met Saddam on 6 August, he was told that the President had yet to make a decision, as he was presumably waiting for the outcome of Cheney's mission to Riyadh. He was suspicious that the Americans only wanted their people out to facilitate an air strike. Foreign Minister Aziz, for his part, mocked the idea that the foreigners were hostages, for such people normally 'do not stay at hotels, drink beer and enjoy their lives'. On 10 August Aziz described the restrictions on foreigners as a 'technical' matter, and two days later as 'temporary precautionary measures'.[7] This theme was reiterated by Iraq's representatives in the West, who argued that there were no limitations on foreigners' freedom of movement within Iraq, and that the delay in issuing exit visas for these people was due to the 'authorities' overwhelming preoccupation with the struggle against the American starvation campaign against Iraq', which leaves them no time 'to make the necessary travel arrangement for the foreigners'.[8]

This official evasiveness notwithstanding, Baghdad had other indirect channels to air its thoughts regarding the status of those Western foreigners under its control. On 6 August, the day that Saddam met Wilson, a formal link between the position of the foreign nationals and the imposition of economic sanctions was being made by Lt.-Colonel Walid Saud Muammad Abdallah, the Foreign Minister of the puppet regime installed by Iraq in Kuwait following the invasion. 'Those conspiring against us and other brothers in Iraq,' threatened Abdallah, 'should not expect us to act honourably.' He continued:

> Countries that resort to punitive measures against the provisional free Kuwaiti Government and fraternal Iraq ... should remember that they have interests and nationals in Kuwait. If these countries insist on aggression against Kuwait and Iraq ... the Kuwaiti Government will then reconsider the method for dealing with these countries.[9]

By this time Britain and other European countries were becoming more outspoken in their doubts as to Iraqi motives. The British Foreign Minister, Douglas Hurd, sought to disabuse the Iraqis of any idea that the foreign community could be used as a weapon in the developing confrontation. 'I do not think it can possibly deter us,' he said, 'with the rest of the international community, from taking the steps that we have already taken and the steps now being discussed at this moment in the Security Council for a full trade embargo.'[10]

The seriousness of Hurd's warning, which was reflected in the passing of two additional Security Council resolutions on 6 and 9 August respectively – implementing economic sanctions and condemning the annexation of Kuwait – left no visible impact on Baghdad. In a radio interview on 14 August, the Iraqi Ambassador to Paris, Abd al-Razzaq al-Hashimi, Baghdad's most senior representative in Western Europe, implied that the fate of the foreign nationals in Iraq and Kuwait would depend on the behaviour of their respective Governments, and expressed the hope that the militancy of the Western powers would be curbed by their concern for the safety of their nationals.[11]

With Iraq's intentions regarding the foreign nationals now evident, Italy, acting on behalf of the European Community, requested that the Security Council consider the matter. Resolution 664, unanimously adopted on 18 August, expressed 'deep concern' for the 'safety and well-being of third state nationals in Iraq and Kuwait', and demanded that Iraq accept its obligations under international law for their safety, security and health and also permission and facilities for their immediate departure. The UN Secretary-General was to consult the Iraqis to secure the release of the foreign nationals.

As so often in the crisis, a tough line from the international community prompted Iraq to harden its own stance. Anxious to avoid any public loss of face, Saddam responded to the UN resolutions by personally unravelling his plans concerning the foreign nationals. In an 'open letter' to the families of foreigners in Iraq, broadcast by Baghdad Radio on 19 August, he expressed his 'pain' at having to confine their beloved ones to Iraq and blamed the United States and Britain for their predicament. However, he argued that this move, particularly in the case of those 'whose Governments have a hostile position and are taking part in the preparations for aggression and the economic embargo against Iraq', was designed to open 'a deep dialogue' for a peaceful resolution of the crisis and the aversion of war. Should the West pull out of the Gulf on a fixed timetable and undertake not to attack Iraq, these people would be immediately released. For the time being, 'their presence with the Iraqi families working in the vital targets may prevent military aggression'. And to underscore his determination to host 'the foreign guests', as he preferred to call them, Saddam decreed that 'every citizen, regardless of nationality, harbouring foreigners – who are forbidden to leave the country – would be sentenced to death'.[12]

In adopting his hostage policy Saddam had several interconnected objectives: to generate public pressure on the Western governments to forgo a military action against Iraq, or at least by using the hostages as a 'human shield' to deter military strikes against Iraq's strategic locations, particularly its non-conventional arms industry, and to keep a war limited to Kuwait. These expectations, already visible in Saddam's 'open letter' to the hostages' families, was persistently echoed by senior military officials. 'The people of Iraq have decided to play host to the citizens of these aggressive nations as long as Iraq remains threatened with war,' argued the Speaker of the Iraqi Parliament, Sa'di Mehdi Saleh. 'This measure will remain in force until such time when sufficient guarantees are presented to the people of Iraq that the danger of oppressive aggression has been eliminated.'[13] The Iraqi Ambassador to the United Nations, Abd al-Amir al-Anbari, told the Security Council that the foreign nationals would suffer whatever fate the Americans had in store for the whole of Iraq:

> ... the Iraqi people as a whole is the hostage of American terrorism and is the victim of the food and medicine blockade ...
> ... The security and safety of foreign nationals is guaranteed if the United States and its allies guarantee that they will not attack Iraq. However, if the United States of America and its allies should persist in their policy of aggression and attack Iraq with their military force ... making Iraqi women, children and old men victims, then whatever the Iraqi people would be subjected to would also be applied to its foreign guests.[14]

In addition to warding off an American attack, the Iraqis used the Western hostages to undermine the economic blockade by reinforcing the warning that foreigners must share the deprivations inflicted by sanctions on the Iraqi people with a specific mention of the risk to foreign babies resulting from a blockade. 'Since the children of the world – whatever their nationality – are the favourites of God and the leader Saddam Hussein,' ran an official statement of Iraq's Ministry of Labour and Social Affairs on 18 August,

> and in keeping with our humanitarian principles, we have decided to give equal attention to the needs of the children of the foreign families as to those of the children of Iraq. If the boycott leads to shortages in children's milk, medicine, and other goods, the resultant scarcities affecting the Iraqi children in terms of food, medicine, clothing and otherwise, will equally affect the other children.[15]

A further purpose was to divide the coalition by rewarding those who hinted at a more flexible and accommodating attitude. By conditioning the hostages' release on the behaviour of their respective Governments, Saddam hoped to drive a wedge between the Governments and their constituents, and among the various members of the anti-Iraq coalition. Already in his 'open letter' of 19 August he tried to prove to the hostages' families that his quarrel was not with them but rather with their aggressive leaders. While addressing those families as 'beloved children of God, dear and beloved children in Europe and the United States', he simultaneously invoked curses on their respective governments for 'starving the Iraqi people to death'.[16] Speaker Saleh carried this theme a step further by intimating on 19 August that 'as a gesture of goodwill, the National Assembly had decided to allow a number of the nationals of Austria, Sweden, Switzerland, Finland and Portugal to travel outside Iraq because their states have not dispatched forces or weapons to the region'. The fate of other Westerners, he said, 'will be examined in light of their governments' position in not preventing exports of foodstuffs, medicines, and other material to Iraq'.[17]

A similar attempt to split the coalition was made in late August when, following the statement by the European Community condemning the use of hostages, the Iraqis implied their readiness to release 600 nationals of seven EC countries – Italy, Greece, Belgium, the Netherlands, Spain, Denmark and Ireland. In early September, Iraq offered to release all the Japanese hostages if Tokyo agreed to partly lift its economic sanctions.[18]

Although all these Iraqi initiatives came to naught, it soon transpired that the graduated release of hostages had become Saddam's main instrument of courting, or 'punishing', certain governments for their behaviour. The coalition had thus little choice but to recognize that a major new dimension had been added to the crisis. As Thomas Pickering, US delegate to the UN, put it, with the announcement of the human shield policy Iraq had effectively 'crossed the Rubicon'.[19] On 20 August Bush used the 'H-word' for the first time at an ex-servicemen's convention.

Table 1: Foreign nationals in Kuwait and Iraq (early August 1990)

COUNTRY	IN KUWAIT	IN IRAQ
Argentina	51	In both
Australia	90	69
Austria	70	70
Bangladesh	59,800	15,000
Belgium	21	38
Brazil	?	450
Canada	500	200
Chile	7	In both
China	3,000	5,000
Cyprus	30	10
Czechoslovakia	26	366
Denmark	83	17
Egypt	120,000	1,200,000
Finland	23	23
France	290	270
Germany	290	450
Greece	180	47
Hong Kong	19	–
Hungary	5	182
India	172,000	10,000
Indonesia	709	?
Iran	40,000	–
Ireland	50	300
Italy	152	350
Japan	278	230
Luxembourg	2	4
Malaysia	10	10
Mexico	17	In both
Morocco	6,000	30,000
Netherlands	83	150
New Zealand	11	24
Norway	17	35

COUNTRY	IN KUWAIT	IN IRAQ
Pakistan	30,000	15,000
Palestinians	300,000	170,000
Philippines	45,000	5,000
Poland	40	2,700
Portugal	50	50
South Korea	96	612
Soviet Union	534	7,830
Spain	106	34
Sri Lanka	85,000	?
Sweden	120	40
Switzerland	71	69
Syria	30,000	n.a.
Taiwan	141	?
Thailand	5,600	6,200
Tunisia	1,565	2,000
Turkey	2,480	4,000
UK	4,000	640
USA	2,500	600
Yugoslavia	300	7,000
TOTAL	910,000	1,485,000

Source: Various.

Table 2: Position of refugees in Jordan (early September 1990)

COUNTRY OF ORIGIN	JORDAN	NO MAN'S LAND	REPATRIATED	STILL IN KUWAIT
Bangaldesh	12,000 +	12–15,000	1,200	35–40,000
India	3–5,000	15,000 +	13,467	120,000
Pakistan	3,000	10,000 +	6,000	50,000 +
Sri Lanka	3,000	'many thousands'	182	95,000
Thailand	1,500	nil	4,500	nil
Philippines	2,200	3,000	3,132	40,000

Source: *Independent*, 5 September 1990.

Table 3: Refugees in Jordan

DATE	TOTAL ENTERED	NUMBER IN CAMPS
22 August	185,000	118,000
30 August	330,000	114,000
5 September	420,000	105,000
14 September	470,000	45,000
27 September	510,000	33,000
1 October	530,000	43,000

Source: Various.

CHAPTER 9
From Embargo to Blockade

While the taking of hostages at the very least complicated plans for military action, it made little difference to the strategy of economic pressure. For the United States, part of the advantage of bolstering up Saudi Arabia was that it had become better placed to stand up to Iraq in implementing the embargo. Nonetheless, the enforcement of sanctions also demonstrated that there was no clear dividing line between economic and military measures, for it was through this means that the precedents were set for gaining international authority for the use of military force.

Following the passage of Resolution 661, most nations fell in line on the imposition of sanctions. Even doubters like Brazil suspended all trade along with traditional neutrals such as Switzerland. An Iraqi attempt to convince Syria that it should forget old enmities and reopen the pipeline passing through its territory in the face of 'imperialist' pressure met with no response. The only obvious weak link in the sanctions regime was Jordan, whose tottering economy was dependent on oil supplies from Iraq and which could ill afford to lose the $500 million of trade now at risk. Also, Saddam was very popular among Palestinians in Jordan (who account for some 60 per cent of the country's total population) and King Hussein had no desire to alienate the majority of his subjects. Finally, being fully aware of Jordan's position as a buffer state between Iraq and Israel, the King feared that an excessive pressure on Iraq might drive Saddam into an impetuous move which, in turn, could trigger a tough Israeli response against Jordan.

Hence the continuation of the traffic across the Jordanian–Iraqi border despite the sanctions resolutions, and hence the King's desperate attempts to manufacture a peace settlement on terms favourable to Saddam. When he went to Washington on 16 August he still hoped to be accepted as a mediator, but instead found himself subjected to pressure to comply with the sanctions, with a promise of economic assistance if he did so. In practice by this time the threat of a naval blockade of the Red Sea port of Aqaba, through which Iraq received much of its supplies, was already reducing traffic. In a way King Hussein was helped out of his dilemma by having the choice made for him by the international community. Britain, with its close relationship with Jordan, was anxious to help the King in his predicament and so called for help to meet the $2 billion loss of revenue claimed by Jordan.

The determination to ensure strict enforcement of the embargo was most important, however, not for its impact on individual countries but because the decision to turn the embargo into an effective blockade (although it was not described as such) both set the precedent for international support for the use of force and, in so doing, shaped future American decision-making.

The initial American intention was not to seek further authority from the United Nations to enforce the embargo. As noted earlier, sufficient authority was judged to come from Article 51 of the UN Charter, which affirms 'the inherent right of individual or collective self-defence'. Thus on 11 August Bush insisted that he had the authority to stop Iraqi ships if they tried to break the embargo. Iraq quickly rejected this interpretation, and Tariq Aziz warned that any attempt by the US to intercept oil tankers (of which Iraq had twenty) would be an 'act of aggression against Iraq' that would go beyond the mandate of Resolution 661. The next day this position was countered by Secretary of State Baker. The Administration had just received a letter from the Emir of Kuwait requesting 'of us and of other nations support for enforcement of the UN economic sanctions'. He added: 'We now have the ability, the legal basis, for interdicting those kinds of shipments.'[1] This rigorous enforcement of the embargo could begin 'almost immediately'.

Baker's reference to interdiction here is as relevant as that to Article 51. It was used to avoid describing the enforcement of the sanctions as a blockade. In international law a blockade has been defined as a naval operation undertaken in time of war to prevent vessels of any or all states from entering or leaving specific coastal areas. Establishing a blockade means recognizing the 'belligerency' of the blockaded party. It requires this to be formally notified and declared, thereby creating the right to stop and seize neutral shipping that may be contravening the blockade. An embargo, which is usually seen as an act of economic reprisal and a peacetime action, does not have the same connotations of belligerency. A formal blockade, whether or not organized by the UN, would technically be an act of war and as such would have required Congressional support. By talking of 'interdiction', which does not have a proper definition in international law but was used by the United States as being synonymous with 'interception', the Americans hoped to describe a specific action that was not quite a formal blockade.[2] Even so, it would permit the essential feature of a blockade – the readiness to warn a suspect ship, fire a shot across the bow if it refuses inspection and then, if necessary, fire at the ship to disable it.

This policy created a stir in the Security Council when the American Ambassador discussed it with his fellow members on Monday 13 August. It soon became clear that the general view was that if the action against Iraq had to be stepped up this must come through another UN resolution and not unilateral American action. Secretary-General Perez de Cuellar observed that 'only the UN, through Security Council resolutions, can really bring about a blockade'. His view was shared by France and the Soviet Union which expressed outright opposition to the American position. In Britain, Mrs Thatcher was convinced that no UN vote was necessary,[3] but her Ambassador in New York, Sir Crispin Tickell, was sensitive to the feeling in the Security Council. He attempted to give the British position a more moderate gloss by arguing that the Royal Navy would be essentially monitoring the observance of sanctions. It would, if necessary, board ships to do this but would then report back to the UN if it discovered anything untoward.

The British and American Ambassadors argued back to their national capitals that the good work of the previous two weeks in building a formidable consensus in the United Nations would be undone if further actions were taken outside the international organization. The Pentagon was nervous about delays in getting an agreement and the problems of sorting out rules of engagement with a multilateral force. On Thursday 16 August it sent out rules of engagement to two dozen warships in the Gulf, the Gulf of Oman and the northern end of the Red Sea. These instructed US warships to stop, board and search suspect vessels. If they failed to respond to signals then the US captains would be permitted to use 'minimum force' to stop them. The rules were to come into effect from 03.00 the next morning.

Having underscored its readiness 'to go it alone', the Administration was persuaded to try the Security Council route. Its evident readiness to push forward with a blockade provided a spur to those Council members who might otherwise prefer to wait to see how the sanctions were working before moving on to this next step. This was the context in which Moscow suggested that the Military Staff Committee of the UN should be resurrected, indicating that so long as the blockade was undertaken under UN auspices it might even be prepared to join in. Both France and China appeared to accept the argument that a formal UN resolution was the best way to impose limits on American military action.

On the Sunday two Iraqi oil tankers, under orders not to obey Western vessels, defied warning shots across their bow from US warships. These were in fact the first shots fired by American forces during the crisis. They failed to influence the Iraqis. Tariq Aziz spoke of an 'act of piracy'. Although authorization had been given to use disabling fire, the shots were not followed up other than by surveillance of the tankers. Despite making the case for unilateral action, Washington wanted authority to disable them if they appeared to be attempting to break the embargo before they entered the Yemeni port of Aden during the coming couple of days.

With this test developing, the Americans pressed for an early decision. At a midnight Security Council meeting the Yemenis, as members of the Council, were pressed for assurances that they would not unload oil. When these were received Pickering was able to tell the State Department that there was now a breathing space to get a resolution. He pointed to the large majority in the Security Council clearly in favour of getting a new resolution: if this were achieved there would be an additional sense of legitimacy with collective support for the use of force. He was optimistic about getting a resolution through the Council.

Among the five permanent members of the Security Council the Americans began to sound out opinion on a clear UN authorization to enforce the embargo, but without the encumbrance of a United Nations force with a United Nations command, which was judged unwieldy and impractical. Thus, rather than making a blockade mandatory with all the implications this would have in terms of both domestic American and international law, the Administration wanted the resolution to be confined to a request for assistance from member states to 'do their utmost' to enforce the embargo.

Since this would essentially mean a UN umbrella for national actions, the American initiative soon ran into difficulties. China was unhappy with this formula, which seemed designed to give the Americans *carte blanche* to take whatever military action they chose. If the Administration wanted to avoid a Chinese veto – or even abstention – then some limits on its freedom of action were to be accepted. The Soviets were still pressing for the activation of the UN Military Staff Committee and were reluctant to support such a step without a clear instance of sanctions-busting. Both China and the USSR warned that they would veto any draft American resolution pushed forward simply on the basis of the ships *en route* to the Yemen, about which information was still vague.

These reservations notwithstanding, neither Moscow nor Beijing was willing to close the door on the American initiative, particularly in the light of Iraq's intensified efforts to break the embargo. They accepted that the Iraqis did appear to be setting a test, with up to five Iraqi tankers and four cargo ships reported to be heading for Gulf ports. The British passed around photographs of sanctions-busting activities.[4] Indications came from the

Soviets, the Chinese and the French that they were prepared to support some enforcement of the embargo (or at least in the Chinese case not impose a veto).

The key country in all of this was the Soviet Union. Saddam wanted Moscow to use its influence to block the American attempts in the Security Council. To this end he sent his Deputy Prime Minister, Sa'dun Hammadi, to the Soviet capital on 20 August. Eduard Shevardnadze said that there still had to be unconditional withdrawal and the release of all hostages. He hoped that this demand, coming from an erstwhile friend and reinforced by the threat of another hostile UN resolution, might bring the Iraqis back to their senses. In Hammadi's response he thought he detected some wavering.[5] Later that day Shevardnadze called Baker and asked the Americans not to rush into a resolution but to allow Baghdad at least some time to contemplate its position.

While the Administration considered the matter the embargo could not be enforced. In Washington the Deputies Committee debated whether there was anything they could do short of the use of force to stop one tanker (the other was now going back to Iraq) from reaching port. One possibility was to offer asylum to the Iraqi pilot and captain, because Saddam had threatened with execution any captain who allowed his ship to be boarded. However, the tanker docked at Aden that day. The British claimed that oil was discharged, although the Yemeni authorities insisted that the ship had been prevented from unloading.[6]

On Wednesday 22 August, at his holiday home at Kennebunkport in Maine, the President was joined by top advisers – apart from Baker, who was in Wyoming.[7] Powell briefed the group on the military situation. His main concern that day was to get authorization to call up the reserves. The discussion then focused on whether the US Navy should 'interdict' Iraqi ships or wait until a UN resolution was passed, and if there was to be a wait how long should it be? All this depended upon the Soviet Union. If the Administration waited, would Moscow desist from vetoing the resolution?

The arguments in favour of immediate interdiction noted that Saddam was posing a determined challenge to the embargo. Washington's credibility was at stake. Here was the first potential use of force and the United States dare not back down lest it appear a 'paper tiger'. If it hesitated, inevitable questions would be raised about its readiness to stay the course. Moreover, if the Administration went for a UN resolution and then failed to get it – perhaps because of China rather than the Soviet Union – that would be the worst result of all. Both its rights under Article 51 and its leadership of the anti-Iraq coalition would have been damaged. There was concern that the

Soviet Foreign Ministry was playing games. Shevardnadze had warned that he was under pressure from his military, who were claiming that the American rush to enforce the embargo was merely a harbinger of things to come. There was some evidence that Soviet military specialists in Iraq might be playing a less marginal role than claimed by their Government.[8] Even if Gorbachev's intentions were honourable, he might be being used by the Iraqis to stay the American hand while the embargo was being breached in a conspicuous manner.

Against these arguments were the merits of maintaining as broad a coalition as possible – especially if the crisis was going to be protracted. A successful UN resolution would strengthen international support and show that the United States was not acting in isolation. This would also help with domestic opinion. Just because Saddam had set a test it did not mean that the US had to accept – there would be other opportunities to prove American resolution. General Powell was relaxed that enforcement could begin later if necessary.[9] Baker from Wyoming argued that with time Gorbachev could be persuaded to support the resolution. He first needed to be convinced that he could not get Saddam to admit defeat on Kuwait.

Of the President's advisers, Scowcroft was the most convinced of the need to press ahead without waiting for further UN authorization. However, the most intense pressure for this position came from London. Mrs Thatcher was alarmed that the tanker had been allowed to get through to the Yemen and argued that it was unwise to go on warning and then doing nothing. According to her top adviser:

> This was probably the first real test of the arrangements we had put in place, and if we let Iraqis circumvent them in any way that would be taken as a signal of weakness. It wouldn't be seen just by the Iraqis in that sense . . . but by the rest of the world.[10]

Having been persuaded two weeks earlier by the Administration that Article 51 was sufficient authority for military action, she was now worried that this was being undermined by the readiness to seek new authority. In this she was already thinking ahead to an eventual need to take offensive military action to liberate Kuwait. There were also fears about being 'led up the garden path by the Russians', who might just be stalling to help Saddam.

These views were expressed in conversations between Scowcroft and Charles Powell in Downing Street. During the day Bush spoke regularly to Baker who was in turn in touch with Shevardnadze in Moscow. Bush also spoke to Gorbachev. In the end the President decided that he had least to lose by following the diplomatic route and giving Gorbachev a few days. The

President rang Mrs Thatcher to convince her that this was the right course. She said, 'All right George, all right. But this is not the time to go wobbly.' Scowcroft recalls Bush's amusement – 'We used the phrase almost daily' after that.[11]

In conveying the decision, Baker told Shevardnadze of the American suspicion that the Iraqis were trying to use Moscow's good will to split the Security Council. This was therefore a crucial test of US–Soviet co-operation. While he hoped the two could work together, if necessary the United States would act alone. The Foreign Minister had asked for five days' grace. He was only given three. Any later, and the other ships which were challenging the embargo would have progressed too far.

With this tight deadline Shevardnadze persuaded Gorbachev to write a tough letter to Saddam on 23 August. According to the Soviet news agency, Tass, this 'urgent' message warned the Iraqis that the situation in the Gulf was 'extraordinary and extremely dangerous' and that Baghdad should begin implementing 'without delay' UN resolutions concerning both the illegal occupation of Kuwait and the holding of hostages. Failure to do so would 'inevitably compel the Security Council to adopt corresponding extra measures'.[12] Gorbachev demanded a reply by the evening of the following day, when the Security Council vote would be taken. The Iraqi reply was unyielding[13] – Shevardnadze told the Americans that it was not even worth commenting upon. The vote was passed on the morning of Saturday 25 August.

Resolution 665 gave the Americans – and others who chose to be involved in enforcing the embargo – the right to disable ships which refused to stop and have their cargoes inspected. To allay fears among the non-aligned countries that the Americans were attempting to hijack the Security Council to allow them to go ahead with all guns blazing, the Chinese and the Soviets refused to accept a reference to the 'minimum use of force' which could be a matter for interpretation (nobody ever admits to using anything other than the minimum). Instead, they preferred to spell out precisely the nature of the authority given by the UN. The resolution thus called upon member states deploying maritime forces in the area

> to use such measures commensurate to the specific circumstances as may be necessary under the authority of the Security Council to halt all inward and outward maritime shipping in order to inspect and verify their cargoes and destinations and to insure strict implement-ation of the provisions related to such shipping laid down in Resolu-tion 661 (1990).

It also required the states concerned to co-ordinate their action 'using as appropriate mechanisms of the Military Staff Committee'. There was no obligation here. The Americans had agreed only to have political discussions with both political and military representatives. There would be no discussion of operational matters.[14] If the Soviet Union had decided to participate in the blockade then the use of the Military Staff Committee might have been deemed 'appropriate' – otherwise the Western countries had alternative means of co-ordination. However, meeting with the French Foreign Minister, Roland Dumas, after the vote had been taken, Shevardnadze stressed that 'We have no intention of using force ourselves', or of joining in any 'operations of force'.[15]

After being sent round other members of the Security Council for comment, the resolution was adopted by a 13–0 vote, with Cuba and Yemen abstaining. The fact of Chinese support was influential in reassuring the non-aligned members of the Council that the Americans understood the need to work within the agreed UN guidelines. Thus, after a false start, the Americans had accepted that they had to keep working within an international consensus in a manner that would have been inconceivable just a few years earlier. Iraq was forced again to recognize that the international community was unimpressed by its bluster, and that it had little choice but to respect the naval embargo. With diplomatic efforts to resolve the crisis resumed and Perez de Cuellar due to meet Tariq Aziz at the end of the month, Saddam retreated. The orders to Iraqi ships not to allow themselves to be searched were overturned.[16]

Air embargo

The United States and its allies were now able to stop anything from getting through to Iraq by sea, but there were regular reports of air shipments to Baghdad from Jordan, Libya, Sudan, Tunisia and Yemen. Although this was sufficient to push through spare parts of critical pieces of machinery and other high-value items, initially it was not considered such a dramatic loophole that it required immediate action. When Iraqi troops violated French diplomatic property in Kuwait in mid September, part of France's response was to press for an air embargo.

This would be the first of its kind ever to be implemented, and had a number of features which distinguished it from a naval embargo. The requirement would be for all countries to close their airspace to planes flying to and from Iraq and Kuwait unless the aircraft had been inspected to ensure that they were not violating sanctions. The UN could not be allowed to authorize the shooting down of planes, as that is banned by the 1944 Chicago Convention. This was reflected in the draft resolution which said that states would not permit measures that would 'endanger the lives of persons on board or the safety of the aircraft'. However, as Washington did not want obligations to be spelled out so clearly, the final draft merely mentioned the Chicago Convention.

Though it could not be shot down, an aircraft attempting to breach the blockade would face severe difficulties – it would have to navigate without the assistance of air traffic controllers (who would in effect be responsible for implementing the blockade) and could not expect to be granted insurance. An aircraft breaking the air embargo would need to file an incorrect plan with the controllers. It would then need to avoid detection in an area in which all aircraft were being carefully monitored. If caught it could face fighter aircraft employing international guidelines on the use of tracer bullets to warn civil aircraft to land, as well as agreed wing signals.

On 25 September Resolution 670 was passed, with only Cuba voting against. The ease with which the resolution was passed was itself an indication of how much the international mood had shifted over the weeks since the maritime blockade resolution had been passed. States were now obliged not to allow aircraft to fly from or to overfly their territory to Iraq or Kuwait unless the cargoes had been inspected to show that they were allowed under the humanitarian exemption. Passenger flights were not included – especially as there were still efforts under way to extract foreign nationals – although this was only implicit in the resolution and had to be clarified later.

The resolution also obliged states to detain Iraqi ships, reminded Governments of their obligations to freeze Iraqi assets and protect those of the legitimate Government of Kuwait, and threatened actions against any state evading these measures. With this move the United Nations had exhausted virtually all options short of direct military action. The only other possibility to isolate Iraq would have been to sever all diplomatic links and ban postal and telecommunications services, jam radio and television broadcasts and so forth. The general view was that such measures would if anything be counterproductive, and could drive Saddam Hussein, whom the coalition still hoped would back down, into a precipitous move.

Enforcing the embargo

A UN resolution had a number of advantages in easing co-operation among the many states which were prepared to show solidarity by sending naval forces. The hardening of attitudes around 20 August, just before Resolution

665, led the various navies congregating in the Gulf to work out how to co-ordinate their efforts. There had been an initial meeting in Bahrain of naval commanders on 9 and 10 August but co-ordination still left a lot to be desired. The more cautious were unwilling to venture closer to the Gulf than the Red Sea or to go further than warning shots; others were ready to board suspicious vessels in the Gulf.

Even the British and American navies, with their close relations, found agreement on rules of engagement difficult – for example, the British were worried that the Americans would be too hasty in firing on the basis of electronic data picked up from approaching aircraft, and too ready to use force against ships suspected of breaking the embargo.[17] One British official was made nervous by being told that the Americans would rather risk a '*Vincennes*' than a '*Stark*', namely, that they would prefer to shoot down an innocent aircraft rather than run the risk of becoming the victims of others' mistakes.

There was a particular question for the European navies – of which a number were arriving in dribs and drabs – for the political mood of the times expected them to work closely together. The British would have liked to use the opportunity to extend NATO's boundaries but the Gulf was judged 'out of area', so the obvious co-ordinating mechanism was the Western European Union (WEU). The fact that this was chaired by France at the time meant that at least Paris would be more inclined to accept a multilateral approach. Belgium and Italy would not have contributed outside such a European framework. The British also found that the forum was useful in convincing less robust allies that if they enforced an embargo effectively they might be able to put off a land war, and in asking for particular capabilities, such as more tankers. However, as the WEU lacked its own command system and had no standard operating procedures, working out rules of engagement and sharing responsibilities came to involve time-consuming negotiations. In Paris on 21 August the WEU decided to arrange a meeting in the Gulf, on board a French ship on the 24th, to agree co-ordination and arrange a division of responsibilities with the United States. The European ships were divided into three zones – in the Gulf of Oman, and one each to the north and south of the Straits of Hormuz.[18]

With the UN resolution in place, and the Iraqi Navy clearly not disposed to challenge the embargo, enforcement settled down into a largely routine set of operations. The first boarding of an Iraqi merchant vessel took place on 31 August, though the *Al Karamah* was discovered to be empty. On 4 September, the *Zanoobia* was found full of tea for Iraq and diverted back to Sri Lanka. Ten days later the *Al Fao*, despite also being empty, ignored warning shots and was boarded in a joint US–Australian operation. Eventually twenty-three navies came to be involved. Until the end of the war, together they made over 7,500 challenges to ships in the Arabian and Red Seas, boarded 964 and diverted fifty-one – largely without incident. Eleven warning shots were fired, but none to disable. The bulk of the challenges were in the Gulf; however, 90 per cent of the diversions and boardings were in the Red Sea, as the Iraqis tried to slip cargoes into the Jordanian port of Aqaba.

CHAPTER 10
Poor Communications

In late August there were reports of secret approaches from Iraq to the United States, involving an exchange of hostages in return for the lifting of UN sanctions and guaranteed access to the Rumaila oilfield. These seem to have been based on over-interpretations of Iraqi contacts with a former US official conveyed to Brent Scowcroft. Scowcroft reaffirmed that the United States was 'prepared to talk about anything after a pullout from Kuwait'. There could only be talks 'within the context of compliance with United Nations resolutions'. The Iraqi denial was as swift: 'Kuwait is part of Iraq. We have said this and the legislative bodies in Iraq have issued a clear decree.'[1] The Iraqi line was, as Tariq Aziz promised, that the 'whole situation in the region could be discussed', though the particular situation involving Kuwait was an 'Arab question'.[2] There did not appear to be much room for direct diplomacy.

Nor was there seen to be much need. There was general optimism in the coalition that the political pressure on an increasingly isolated Saddam would oblige him to offer more concessions as time went on. Arab leaders no longer trusted Saddam to honour any agreements. There was a widespread determination that it was better not to have a deal if that could be interpreted as an Iraqi reward for the seizure of Kuwait: the crime should not pay dividends. The Iraqis, too, had a long-term strategy, exploring the weakness in the coalition, especially its Arab component.

The hostages: a bargaining chip?

However, in addition to the initial issues of the seizure of Kuwait and the threat to Saudi Arabia there was now the matter of the hostages, and this required more immediate consideration. This was an unusual hostage crisis. It was but one part of a much larger crisis with many political, economic and military dimensions. The treatment of the hostages in Iraq was in contrast to that of Westerners held by militant factions in Lebanon, kept in isolation and in dire physical conditions. Accommodation in Baghdad was in comfortable hotels and the hostages' physical condition was open to media scrutiny. In fact the Iraqis took pains to keep them on television screens worldwide and so distort the Western debate regarding the strategy against Iraq. For the same reason, the US Government kept the names of hostages from the press to play down the publicity.

The Iraqi attempts to manipulate public opinion were a mixed success. They kept the whole crisis to the fore at a time when interest might have subsided during the wait for sanctions to take effect. Public anxiety was dulled precisely because those individuals seen were not those whose position was most dire – that is, those in hiding in Kuwait or held at 'strategic sites' – and because there were so many of them that the issue could not be readily personalized. Nevertheless, Saddam's crude handling of the hostage issue often backfired, arousing Western public opinion against Iraq. Particularly galling was a television spectacle showing Saddam paying a 'goodwill visit' to a group of British hostages. Having explained to his captive 'guests' why their stay in Iraq served the cause of peace, Saddam took seeming personal interest in the wellbeing of a seven-year-old boy, Stuart Lockwood. 'Did Stuart have his milk today?' he asked in Arabic, patting the boy's head. Stuart's expression was eloquent and chilled spectators throughout the world. Douglas Hurd called this 'shameful theatricals'. Prime Minister Thatcher was far more sardonic, ridiculing Saddam as 'hiding behind women's skirts' – a considerable insult to an Arab leader.

When a week later Saddam met another group of hostages, he was lost for words when an English woman asked him why he was using children in a political game which they could not understand. He rambled along familiar lines about helping to prevent war, but the point was well taken. Soon afterwards, on 28 August, an official statement said that Saddam had been 'deeply affected' by meeting Western families prevented from leaving Iraq and had ordered that 'all women and children . . . be free to stay or leave'.[3] This was judged to be a response to pressure from Iraq's Arab allies, and possibly a gesture before the scheduled meeting of the UN Secretary-General, Javier Perez de Cuellar, with Tariq Aziz on 30 August. A simpler explanation may be that Saddam fully recognized the embarrassing and damaging aspects of his reliance on threats to women and children.

In the coming months he would show greater skill in manipulating the hostages for his political ends, making simultaneous use of the 'stick' and the 'carrot' in his dealings with the coalition confronting Iraq. Thus, while allowing the women and children to leave Iraq, Saddam was hardening his grip over the male hostages. Those that had been detained already were being sent to 'vital installations', while more men were systematically detained. When some of the women who had been hiding with their husbands in Kuwait emerged in order to leave the emirate, their husbands were rounded up. In the ensuing days there were regular reports of British, American, French, German and Japanese nationals being arrested. On 6 September Iraq's Justice Minister, Akram Abd al-Qader Ali, proposed stiff penalties for foreigners attempting to escape from Iraq and reiterated the warnings to Iraqis and Kuwaitis against hiding foreigners. The next day the Information Minister, Latif Nusseif Jasim, said that Westerners in Kuwait who gave themselves up would not be taken to military or civilian installations, but warned that it would be dangerous for them to remain in hiding in Kuwait. By the start of October well over 600 foreigners were being held at strategic sites – including 103 Americans, 260 British, seventy-seven Germans, 141 Japanese and eighty French. There was no obvious logic to these numbers: the British were more numerous because they were the largest group. The numbers of Japanese were quite disproportionate, but perhaps reflected the perceived potential of Japan as 'sanctions-buster'.

Had Saddam treated the hostages with sufficient brutality, the crisis might have been brought to a head at a time when the coalition had not been properly forged. However, Saddam felt unable to be completely ruthless. A number of Arab states (including potential allies like the eccentric Libyan leader, Mu'amar Gaddafi) criticized his hostage policy. He lost the sympathy of important states which might have followed a more conciliatory line, such as the Soviet Union.[4] He probably knew that if he moved too hard against civilians he risked prompting the West into action (even though there was clearly no opportunity for a rescue operation). In addition he was able to make a symbolic political point by demonstrating his power over the lives of individuals, for good as well as for ill.

This last point was, perhaps, best illustrated by the long procession of foreign dignitaries making a pilgrimage to Baghdad to plead for the release of the hostages. The first such pilgrim was the Austrian President and former UN Secretary-General Kurt Waldheim, who arrived in Baghdad on 25 August 1990 to secure the release of the Austrian nationals. Waldheim's lack of candour about his wartime activities with the German Army had led to his becoming effectively a *persona non grata* in the West. By contrast he was well regarded in the Arab world, where there was less concern with his past. Waldheim was judged to have been relatively sympathetic on the dispute with Israel. As a result most of his contacts as head of state had been with Arabs.[5] The only Western head of state to visit Iraq during the crisis, Waldheim's visit to Baghdad gave Saddam an ample opportunity to present the case for his 'hostages policy' in a well-attended press conference. Although Waldheim claimed that he had given Saddam no promises on the embargo, he was rewarded with all the 140 Austrian hostages.[6]

The former Democratic presidential candidate in the United States, the Reverend Jesse Jackson, who had made something of a career of visiting the Middle East to seek the freedom of hostages and prisoners, arrived at the heels of Waldheim with the ostensible purpose of making a television programme. On 2 September he left Baghdad with four elderly and sick male hostages on an aircraft already taking a large group of women and children. In the following months Waldheim and Jackson were to be followed by a string of foreign visitors, from the veteran boxer Muhammad Ali to Yusuf Islam (the former pop singer Cat Stevens), to the former premiers Willy Brandt, Edward Heath, and Yasuhiro Nakasone. Most of these returned with a batch of hostages, whose size reflected each visitor's relative importance for the Iraqi propaganda campaign.

France avoids a deal

The main target of the Iraqi hostage policy was France, which had been identified by Saddam as the weakest Western link in the coalition. France had a reputation of doing deals to get its nationals freed, never liked to be seen to be slavishly following an American lead, and had also been Iraq's closest Western friend. In the early days of the crisis President Mitterrand had been reluctant to implement a full blockade and had made the release of French citizens an immediate priority. He had not minded if Saddam got the idea that the release of the hostages would reduce the general level of tension.

The first contact between Paris and Baghdad was established on 14 August, when Claude Cheysson, the former Minister of Foreign Affairs, went to Tunis as one of Mitterrand's special emissaries and met Yasser Arafat, the PLO chairman and, perhaps, Saddam's staunchest Arab ally. In the meeting Cheysson lectured Arafat on the unacceptability of hostage-taking, yet requested his intercession on behalf of the French citizens, asking the Palestinian leader to tell Saddam that France was a special case and worth cultivating through the release of its nationals. Recognizing the opportunity to boost the PLO's standing in a major Western capital, Arafat promised to use his good offices in Baghdad.[7]

On 18 August the PLO announced that Baghdad did intend to treat French citizens as 'friends', and that Iraq had promised to give France special consideration. However, if this statement implied that a bilateral deal was in the making, it was soon overtaken by events. This was the day of the UN vote on hostages (backed by France), followed by the Iraqi announcement of the human shield policy involving 'nationals of aggressive nations'. There were also allegations in the French media that the Government was covering up the plight of French people in Kuwait and Iraq so as not to jeopardize secret negotiations. Until that time, the Government was still distancing itself from the US efforts to orchestrate a blockade, and publicly denying that French citizens were being detained by Iraq. Faced with mounting domestic criticism, the French authorities were forced to admit, on 20 August, that twenty-seven people had been picked up by the Iraqis and taken to undisclosed locations.

The Foreign Ministry also had to deny press reports referring to Cheysson's discussions with Arafat. In an attempt to demonstrate its positive role in the international efforts to defuse the crisis, the PLO leaked details of the Tunis meeting, to the embarrassment of the Government. Most damaging was the suggestion that France might use its special links with the Arab world to obtain the freedom of French hostages independently of those of other nations.

With public opinion hardening and the allies needing reassurance, Mitterrand began to take the American position on the need to enforce the embargo more seriously. On 20 August a French Foreign Ministry spokesman accepted that 'for an embargo to be useful it must be observed, hence the need for the rigorous application of such measures'. The next day a tough statement of the formal French position was delivered by the President himself, after the meeting of the Select Council at the Elysée Palace.[8] It supported the idea of enforcing the embargo, and took a sombre line on the possibility of an 'Arab solution' and the need to 'stand together'. 'The fate of all foreign nationals in Iraq, who are the victims of this intolerable act, confronts us with a global humanitarian problem which does not allow for separate actions.'

Saddam responded angrily. 'We do not blame the United States or Britain so much for the crisis,' he said in an interview on 29 August with French Television, 'because they have never pretended to be friendly to us. But I cannot understand the position of France. France is the only country that we find fault with.'[9] The ensuing deterioration in Franco–Iraqi relations led to signs of tension within the French Government. When on 5 September Foreign Minister Dumas warned Iraq that it might have 'only a few days' left to settle the conflict peacefully, and questioned the possibility of an Arab solution 'when the Arabs themselves are divided', Defence Minister Chevènement responded by warning against 'getting carried away by irresponsible ideas ... no legal basis exists today for armed intervention against Iraq or even to liberate Kuwait'. Any war, he said, 'would cost 100,000 lives and would engulf the entire Middle East'.[10]

This division within the Government was further exacerbated by Mitterrand's readiness to authorize various people with some sort of standing in the Arab world to act as informal emissaries, with their role deniable if it became embarrassing but sufficiently credible for them to be able to develop any promising openings. During the autumn of 1990 a surprising number of such emissaries were at work, often in ignorance of each other's efforts. This meant that the French Foreign Ministry at the Quai D'Orsay was often unclear about the exact policy being conducted by the President from the Elysée Palace, although Foreign Minister Roland Dumas remained the President's most influential adviser. Such diplomacy lent itself to probes from the PLO and other self-styled Arab mediators.

Perhaps drawing hope from these evident divisions and despite having embarrassed the Government, the PLO continued to pursue the French connection. Yasser Arafat visited Paris in late August for an informal meeting with Prime Minister Michel Rocard and his advisers, where he emphasized Kuwait's responsibility for the crisis and the consequent need to push for 'a political settlement of the crisis in an Arab context', even at the price of distancing France from the 'aggressive posture of the United States'. For his part Rocard was uncompromising. Seizing Kuwait and then taking the hostages were both illegal. 'We will not compromise the law,' he said, 'the withdrawal must be total and unconditional.' Nor would he accept a separate deal involving only the French hostages: 'We don't want, under any circumstances, to appear as if we are acting alone in this matter. We demand the liberation of all the hostages, or nothing.'[11]

Saddam's interest in the French channel was shown in his release of a number of French nationals, and expressions of hope that France 'would refrain from linking its interests to the aggressive US policies in the world'.[12] In mid September, when Iraqi troops forcefully entered the residence of the French Ambassador in Kuwait, seizing several people, Saddam quickly apologized and released the sick and the elderly among the French hostages.[13] Mitterrand, however, remained unimpressed. Announcing his decision to send ground forces to the Gulf and calling upon the Security Council to extend the economic embargo to cover air transport, he said:

> There is no sign visible from Iraq which would indicate that we shall escape an armed conflict. To judge by the course of Iraqi actions

there seems to be a bellicose spirit which does not appear to have weighed the risks.[14]

Perez de Cuellar

The only direct talks to take place in the early months at an official level, once 'the Arab solution' had failed, involved United Nations Secretary-General Javier Perez de Cuellar. They did not get very far. The Secretary-General could speak with both the backing of an unprecedented series of Security Council Resolutions and the apparent advantage of being a man of the Third World. The Security Council was pleased to endorse any contacts he might be able to make with Baghdad, just so long as he stayed within the confines of the resolutions.

Perez de Cuellar had indicated some unease at the trend of events up to this point. Although the UN played an unusually prominent role, this was solely in the context of pressure on Iraq and not in terms of seeking a settlement. He had kept in the background (even spending time on pre-arranged visits to Central America), avoiding comment on the resolutions, in the hope that a lack of exposure would enable him to be acceptable as a mediator. When the vote was taken to enforce the embargo, his own chair was conspicuously empty. Afterwards he wrote on his own initiative to Baghdad, offering talks either in Geneva or New York. Explaining his action, he observed that after the unprecedented measures of the past few weeks 'it is my turn to initiate diplomatic negotiations to find a resolution'. It was soon agreed that he would go to Amman to meet Iraq's Foreign Minister, Tariq Aziz.

He further hoped that the backing of Cuba and Yemen as well as of the Western states would make it difficult for Saddam to send him away empty-handed. Presumably the Iraqis would also understand that complete intransigence would strengthen the case for military action to liberate Kuwait. His aides claimed that this role was understood and accepted by the Ambassadors of the permanent five.[15]

Perez de Cuellar knew Aziz well from the negotiations that had brought an end to the Iran–Iraq War. His impression was not wholly favourable. Aziz, for his part, shared the general Iraqi suspicion that the Secretary-General favoured Iran. Any hope that these personal differences might be overcome by the determination to find a solution did not last long. Just as he left for Amman, Perez de Cuellar asked for maximum restraint by all concerned. Saddam responded by confirming his annexation of Kuwait and declaring it Iraq's nineteenth province. This did not suggest that Kuwait was negotiable.

Perez de Cuellar's final stop before Amman was in Paris, the Western capital seemingly most interested in a deal. With Saddam's announcement he was now obliged to scale down expectations. The UN resolutions, he observed, were not his. 'I cannot make concessions on what does not belong to me. I'm not a merchant. I can discuss without negotiating. I rely on the political will of all concerned.'[16] The ideas he took with him revolved around the possibility of a UN peace-keeping force to monitor and police withdrawals, setting up a mechanism for serious negotiations between Iraq and Kuwait, and, if it seemed worthwhile, a personal visit to Baghdad. He could only negotiate the smooth return to the status quo ante. The Iraqi agenda by contrast bypassed the position of Kuwait and attempted to relate the hostages to the economic and military pressures it was facing.

After two days of talks, Perez de Cuellar reported failure. He had been looking for some 'flexibility, a readiness to begin the process' of discussion. He had found none. Aziz's statement proceeded along familiar lines, adding only that the Iraqis 'would like to continue our contacts in the future, in order to seek and to explore the ways and means to bring about peace, justice and stability to the region as a whole'. He stressed once again that Arab problems needed an 'Arab solution', ignoring Perez's blunt observation that the Arabs were divided and that the Security Council had every right to be involved. Given this wide gap, the disappointed Secretary-General was left to conclude that Saddam was simply trying to gain time to consolidate his annexation of Kuwait.[17]

Saddam's Arab allies seek a 'face-saving' formula

The fact that these futile talks took place in the Jordanian capital was a source of regret to King Hussein, the person with the greatest stake in an early settlement. He was caught between his old friends in the United States and Britain, from whom he was becoming increasingly estranged, and his new friends in Baghdad, whose embrace he abhorred but whose policies were popular in Jordan, where the rich and unsympathetic Kuwaitis were unpopular and the Palestinian cause was to the fore. The King had for years survived through his ability to find a middle ground in Arab politics, but this crisis was so polarized that there was no middle ground to be found.[18] The sudden surge of Third World refugees into Jordan and the enforced collapse of legal trade with Iraq further afflicted Jordan's chronically weakened economy. When he had met with President Bush on 16 August in Washington, Hussein had been pressed on adherence to sanctions; for his own part, the King was desperate to find some possibility of an American readiness to compromise. On 27 August he set off again to visit Libya and Algeria, and then rushed to Washington and London. His lack of contact with the most important Arab leaders in this crisis, who resented his association with Saddam, underscored his isolation and limited room for manoeuvre.

The plan he developed at this point drew on one that had been announced by the PLO, if anything politically closer to Iraq than Jordan, on the day of his departure. The PLO plan involved freezing the military build-up in the Gulf, withdrawal of Iraqi troops from Kuwait and US forces from Saudi Arabia, and the replacement of both by UN or Arab peace-keeping forces, with a committee set up by the Arab League to discuss the territorial dispute. This was absorbed into a joint plan with Jordan, which envisaged modelling Kuwait on Monaco's relation with France, with a constitutional monarchy conceding certain functions to Iraq. At the start of September, Abu Iyad, Arafat's deputy in al-Fatah, the PLO's largest constituent organization, floated the idea of US guarantees not to launch a military strike against Iraq, in return for the departure of all foreign hostages and Iraq's withdrawal from Kuwait, except for the island of Bubiyan, which would improve Iraq's access to the Gulf, and a border strip including the al-Rumaila oilfield. The people of Kuwait would decide their own future but the Emir would not return to the throne.[19]

There was no sign that Saddam had any interest in these moves. When on 5 September King Hussein had more talks with the Iraqi leader he allegedly tried unsuccessfully to persuade him to change his mind 'to make Kuwait negotiable'. Saddam would not budge. He called a staff officer to the room and asked him what would be the feeling of the military to a possible withdrawal from Kuwait. 'Oh, God forbid, sir, please don't utter these words,' came the reply. The King did not press the matter further. A few days later the Ba'th Party issued a brief to its members, making any public discussion of withdrawal punishable by death, for this would be defeatist.[20]

Mixed signals from Moscow

Moscow had been one of Saddam's foremost disappointments. The Gulf crisis had begun as President Gorbachev still appeared strong domestically, with 'new thinking', best represented by Foreign Minister Shevardnadze, on the ascendant. This had enabled these two men to forge a policy based on condemnation of Iraq for violating the principles of international law and the use of the United Nations to reverse the Iraqi aggression. However, at the same time, Gorbachev was aware of growing criticism of his foreign policy from conservative circles alarmed at the unification of Germany, the collapse of the Warsaw Pact, arms control treaties on unfavourable terms, and now the abandonment of an old (if problematic) Soviet ally and connivance at the creation of what they suspected would turn out to be a permanent American military presence in the Middle East.

At the end of August, General Vladimir Lobov, the Warsaw Pact's Chief of Staff, suggested that part of the American objective was to replace their foothold in Europe, which might be lost as a result of German unification, from where they had in the past controlled Middle Eastern oil. Now the build-up in Saudi Arabia would drastically change the strategic balance in the region. This was all the more worrying from the Soviet perspective, as Iraq was only 200 kilometres from the borders of Georgia, Armenia and Azerbaijan and the United States might get in a position to exert pressure on events in this region.[21]

Such sniping from hard-liners in both the military and the Supreme Soviet led to official refutations of the suggestion that the whole affair was being manipulated by Washington to strengthen its overall strategic position. On 3 September the Foreign Ministry spokesman, Gennadi Gerasimov, noted that the Americans did not enter Saudi Arabia on 'their own initiative' but had been 'provoked' by Iraqi actions.[22] Another argument was over the role of the Soviet military 'specialists' still in Iraq. The Foreign Ministry wanted them to leave. The Defence Ministry believed that they should stay until their contracts expired.

Since Gorbachev's 'new political thinking' assumed the supremacy of global considerations over regional issues, it was natural for him to subordinate his old (and uneasy) links with Iraq to the newly forged collaboration with the United States. In early September it was announced that he and President Bush would have an emergency meeting in Helsinki to discuss the crisis. There was soon a request from Saddam, unnerved by the speed of the Soviet slide from countering to reinforcing American policy, for Tariq Aziz to be received in Moscow. Gorbachev agreed, less because he sought to take an initiative himself than to keep his lines to Iraq open. Aziz did not find the meeting on 5 September fruitful. While he expressed his satisfaction at having discovered in Moscow that the Soviet Union was still a friend, and welcomed a more active Soviet role in the crisis, the message he got from Gorbachev was unequivocal. 'What you did was an act of aggression,' he was told, 'and we cannot and will not back you in any way. We are ready to help ... on the basis of complete withdrawal.'[23] This chilly message was well reflected in the official Soviet report, which simply described the encounter as 'frank' – traditional diplomatese for acrimonious. Even Shevardnadze's comment, prior to the meeting, on the positive influence of a Middle East peace conference was qualified by Gennadi Gerasimov, who took care to reject formal linkage, saying that this would 'put off solution of the conflict in question indefinitely'.[24]

Alarmed by the intensifying Soviet–American co-operation, on the eve of the Helsinki summit Saddam dispatched a personal message to Presidents Bush and Gorbachev urging them to review their policies on the crisis, to withdraw all foreign troops from the Gulf, and to stop harassing Iraq. 'Iraq has not invaded any of your countries,' he wrote, 'and has never had any premeditated intention to cause harm to anyone at all.' Nor had it committed any aggression against Kuwait, which 'has been part of Iraq in the not-so-remote past'. On the contrary, the restoration of Kuwait to the 'motherland', Iraq, was a historically just move whose particular timing had been determined by the vile activities of 'the corrupt former Kuwaiti rulers who conspired against Iraq and their greater people', thus driving the region to the verge of a 'deep abyss'. Therefore, the foreign powers had no business to do in the Gulf. The Kuwaiti question was an internal Arab affair and external military presence in Saudi Arabia was tantamount to an 'invasion' of Islam's holy sites and was bound to fail shamefully.

'While you will be in a position to make decisions that may affect humanity,' he cautioned, 'you will be flanked by angels on one side and by devils on the other, each arguing his case.' Failure to heed the voice of reason would entail catastrophic consequences for the entire world, but primarily for the Soviet Union and the United States:

> He who represents the Soviet Union must remember that worries and suspicions about the superpower status assumed by the Soviet Union have been crossing the minds of all politicians in the world for some time . . . Those concerned must choose this critical time and this critical case in order to restore to the Soviet Union its status through adopting a position that is in harmony with all that is just and fair . . .
>
> President Bush must not bring his country and its status down to a lower level, because we are certain that its position will drop on the scale of appreciation and effectiveness if it falls in the abyss of war.[25]

This emotive plea left no visible impact on the two men. Neither was willing to allow Saddam to retain his loot, as evident from their joint call to Iraq to 'withdraw unconditionally from Kuwait, to allow the restoration of Kuwait's legitimate government, and to free all hostages held in Kuwait and Iraq'. The two had managed to work out a general approach to the crisis: there would be no rush to war and the efforts for a peaceful resolution of the crisis through the United Nations would continue. However, Iraq should not underestimate the extent of international resolve to reverse its aggression: 'If all the steps now being pursued fail, we are ready to consider other measures in accordance with the Charter of the United Nations.'[26]

CHAPTER 11
Enter Linkage

The source of the diplomatic deadlock was that fundamental difference over the status of Kuwait. The logic behind proposals to ease Saddam out of Kuwait by allowing him to 'save face' was that he could be mollified by a little something which he could claim as a direct gain from the adventure: a spare island, debts written off, privileged access to Kuwaiti facilities or the sort of special regard for a big neighbour's sensitivities that the East European states used to show the Soviet Union. But if Saddam were able to secure sufficient concessions to relieve his chronic predicament and make the Kuwaiti adventure worthwhile – and such concessions would have had to be vastly greater than even the formulas offered by Iraq's Arab allies – then the fundamental principle that aggression must not pay would have been undermined. On the other hand, if the concessions were trivial then they would neither prevent Saddam's humiliation nor alleviate the economic plight which had driven him into Kuwait in the first place. There was also the question of the West's face – of being seen to acquiesce in something condemned as contrary to the most elementary principles of international law, and for the invited American presence in Saudi Arabia to be treated as equivalent to the uninvited Iraqi presence in Kuwait.

France offers linkage

The Anglo-American presumption therefore continued to be that Iraqi withdrawal could be triggered only by the large sticks of blockade and the threat of war rather than by the promise of little carrots. The French, however, had always been proud of their penchant for creative diplomacy. With Bush and Gorbachev in accord, the Iraqis looked again to Paris to take an initiative. In early September Iraq's Ambassador to Paris, Abd al-Razzaq al-Hashimi, used intermediaries to pass word to the French Government that some overt gesture, such as a direct approach from the President, might provide Saddam with an opportunity to extricate himself from the impasse in which he now found himself. Saddam still considered France a friendly nation although 'he does not understand its present attitude'.[1] A demand for a senior minister to visit Baghdad was picked up by all French emissaries to the region. Apparently by this means Saddam hoped to demonstrate that he was still a substantial international figure.

These hints were received by the Government as a trap intended to divide the coalition and identify France as its weakest link. It was inconceivable that President Mitterrand would give Saddam a blank cheque by making the suggested gesture. This did not mean that the French were disinterested in exploring the possibilities of a settlement. Having proved his commitment to the liberation of Kuwait, the United Nations and the rule of international law by supporting the embargo and dispatching troops, Mitterrand was not averse to a diplomatic initiative, especially if in the process he could involve some concrete gains for France. His opportunity came with a scheduled speech to the UN General Assembly on 24 September.

He did not consult the United States (although prior to the speech he spoke to Bush on the phone), his European partners, the Arab members of the coalition, or even his own diplomats. Until the last moment he was amending it. The speech claimed to set a 'logic of peace' against the prevailing 'logic of war', for which he blamed Saddam. While demanding that Iraq comply with the UN resolutions by withdrawing unconditionally from Kuwait, he appeared to recognize the legitimacy of some of Iraq's territorial claims on Kuwait, and, no less importantly, suggested that the resolution of the Kuwaiti crisis would be followed up by a comprehensive peace conference on the Middle East. 'Everything is possible' if Iraq announced its readiness to withdraw from Kuwait and free the foreign hostages. Then the UN could be brought in to guarantee the withdrawal and 'the restoration of Kuwait's sovereignty and of the democratic will of the Kuwaiti people'. Here there was no mention of the unconditional restoration of the al-Sabah family. There could be 'direct dialogue' on all outstanding regional issues, including the presence of foreign troops in Lebanon, the aspirations of the Palestinian people for an independent state, and regional arms cuts.[2]

The speech was received with considerable concern by France's partners. James Baker is said to have described it as 'an appeasement speech, like those heard in Europe in the 1930s'.[3] It reinforced fears that France had its own agenda and was trying to strike a separate path. The Saudis for their part were alarmed by talk of the democratic will of the Kuwaiti people and the apparent readiness to ditch the al-Sabahs (with whose fate the Saudi ruling family could readily identify). Like other Arab members of the coalition, they were hurt by being portrayed by Mitterrand as indifferent towards the Palestinian problem. Soon French diplomats were explaining that the President's remarks had been over-interpreted and that he was not deviating from UN resolutions. Nevertheless, in practice Mitterrand had given a boost to the idea contained in Saddam's 12 August statement linking the resolution of the problem of Kuwait to other regional problems.

The link was in some ways unavoidable. The Arab members of the coalition could not allow Saddam to monopolize the Palestinian cause. Without dropping their public opposition to Iraq's linkage policy, they indicated to their international partners that a positive response to a settlement of the Palestinian problem was desirable, though not in the context of a compromise with Iraq. This, in turn, put President Bush in an uneasy position. Despite his dismay with Mitterrand's speech, he was also obliged to recognize the force of the allegation that the West was applying double standards when it came to acting against an illegal occupation of territories, even though the circumstances between the Kuwaiti and the Palestinian cases were quite different. In his speech to the General Assembly, after reiterating the call for an unconditional Iraqi withdrawal from Kuwait, and criticizing in strong words the destruction wrought by Iraq in Kuwait, Bush took many in his audience by surprise, by arguing that an Iraqi withdrawal would pave the way 'for Iraq and Kuwait to settle their differences permanently, for the Gulf states to build new arrangements for stability; and for all the states and peoples of the region to settle the conflict that divides the Arabs from Israel'.[4] A similar position was taken a couple of days later by Douglas Hurd, who argued that the five permanent members of the Security Council should start preparing a Middle Eastern peace conference once Iraq had withdrawn from Kuwait.

These declarations were still a far cry from Saddam's aspirations. They neither called for a simultaneous resolution of all regional conflicts, nor agreed to leave the Kuwaiti issue at the bottom of the agenda. Instead they predicated any progress on the Arab–Israeli conflict on Iraq's unconditional withdrawal from Kuwait. The United States and Britain remained as adamant as ever that one way or another Iraq would have to leave Kuwait. Nonetheless, these public allusions to the Arab–Israeli conflict were viewed by Saddam as an important breach in the wall of Western hostility, which he was determined to expand. His strategy of shifting the onus of responsibility for the stalemate from his own aggression to the longstanding Palestinian issue was beginning to bear fruit.

To this end he was helped by an incident on Monday 8 October, in which Israeli security forces killed twenty-two Palestinians in a clash on Temple

Mount in Jerusalem. Saddam immediately connected the tragic incident to the American presence in Saudi Arabia:

> After the Zionists thought that the American occupation of the sanctities in Najd and Hijaz and the desecration of Mecca and the tomb of the Prophet, may God's peace and blessing be upon him, provide them with a golden opportunity to entrench their occupation of Jerusalem ... they attempted to destroy the al-Aqsa mosque after they failed to burn it and to destroy it through excavations.[5]

Immediately the issue was internationalized, as a readiness to condemn Israel came to be seen as a test of the Security Council's even-handedness. The Americans were put in a considerable dilemma, for there were powerful counter-pressures. Washington was suspicious of the ease with which the UN would rush to criticize Israel even while ignoring the excesses committed elsewhere in the Middle East. Yet if Washington vetoed a resolution now it would embarrass those Arab members of the coalition whose support it was so anxious to sustain.

The PLO had been trying since September to get a resolution on the occupied territories through the Security Council. Up until Temple Mount it had appeared moribund. Now it had a new lease of life. The text which was tabled was the sort on which the Americans could normally expect isolation. Ambassador Pickering sought to find a way to 'persuade the other members of the Council that we were prepared to negotiate in good faith but not to change our basic policy'. If an agreed statement could be found then that would be much more positive than dividing the Council with a potential US veto, thereby jeopardizing the cohesion achieved over Kuwait.[6]

The new British Ambassador to the UN, Sir David Hannay, acting as President of the Council for October, was tasked to negotiate a compromise resolution. This involved intensive discussions with the American delegation on the one hand and the Yemeni on the other, who in turn were talking to the PLO. The initial Yemeni draft, introduced on the Monday in the immediate aftermath of the killings, demanded a three-nation Security Council commission which would mean in practice telling Israel how it must manage the occupied territories and also calling for Israel, as an occupying power, to protect the civilian Palestinian population, using language very similar to that used in connection with the Iraqi occupation of Kuwait. All this was unacceptable to the Americans, who circulated – but did not table – their own draft which condemned Israel for the killings (in fact in stronger language than was eventually adopted) but did not suggest any concrete action.

The PLO would not go along with this, although by Wednesday they had dropped the demand for a Council-mandated Commission and settled for a less controversial mission under the auspices of the UN Secretary-General, with the proviso that the aim of such a mission must be a recommendation that Israel protect the Palestinian population in the territories. The British then reworked the text to make this recommendation an option rather than a stated objective, only to be told by Yasser Arafat (who met the British Ambassador in Tunis) that the mission would not now have sufficient powers. Britain doubted whether any more could be obtained from the Americans and worked to convince the PLO that the current draft was the best available. By way of doing so they had to persuade the French, who had been prepared to vote for a PLO-backed resolution, to soften their stance. This was achieved on Thursday by a call to President Mitterrand from President Bush. Thus the text eventually adopted on Friday 12 October required the mission to report back its 'conclusions' on the question of a recommendation.[7]

France's reward

France's support for a strong anti-Israeli resolution seemed to have reinforced the Iraqi belief that the French could be lured away from the coalition. Mitterrand's UN speech of 24 September had led to nine French hostages being allowed to leave Iraq. Their release was organized by M. Gilles Munier, a left-wing Gaullist and President of the Franco-Iraqi friendship society. Having spent two weeks in Iraq, he reported indications that Saddam would consider the release of all French hostages in exchange for the visit of a senior figure from the French Government or opposition 'in order to give a precise explanation of the Iraqi viewpoint'.[8] This proposed visit remained a constant Iraqi theme though there was no hint of what might be discovered on arrival. Full explanations of the Iraqi viewpoint were already plentiful.

After the Temple Mount vote, Foreign Minister Roland Dumas was told that if he made a detour to Tunis he would get an important message from Saddam delivered by Yasser Arafat. All the PLO leader had on offer was a plea for a face-saving device and a repetition of the call for Dumas or another senior minister to visit Baghdad. Dumas indicated that he would be prepared to do so if he received just one 'concrete signal' from Iraq. Mitterrand's UN speech, however, was as far as France could go. There could be no extra initiatives.

Not long after Dumas had left Tunis, Claude Cheysson arrived, as a member of a European delegation. On 16 October, with Arafat acting as an intermediary, he had dinner with Tariq Aziz, who was also in town. After they had discussed the attack on the French diplomatic residence in Kuwait City and its aftermath, Aziz admitted that the invasion of Kuwait was a 'mistake', and asked how Iraq could extricate itself. Cheysson responded by stressing the liberation of all hostages if Iraq were to have any chance of being 'considered as a respectable partner.' He then returned to the familiar territory of the evacuation of Kuwait followed by an 'Arab peace' plan involving the countries of the region. Aziz appeared interested but stressed the need for an official French negotiator. All Cheysson could do was remind Aziz of the official position that there could be no negotiations or official contacts until Iraq had at least announced its intention of withdrawing from Kuwait. Pressed by Aziz, he agreed to convey the request to the French authorities. He also took the opportunity to ask for the liberation of the hostages. Aziz in turn promised to convey this request to Saddam. He indicated that Iraq was looking to France not only to lead the way out of the diplomatic impasse but also to stay the American hand if there was any move to launch an attack. He even claimed that he had persuaded Saddam that the entry of French troops into Saudi Arabia was helpful as they would prevent the United States from starting war against Iraq.

Before he left Tunis, Cheysson once again met Arafat, who promised to 'take care of the hostages'. Arafat's French contacts then continued with yet a further visit to Tunis, this time by Edgar Pisani, an old Gaullist minister and another emissary of Mitterrand, who also stressed the plight of the hostages and the extent to which Saddam's policy in this regard was counterproductive. After three French contacts in the space of a few days, Arafat was now convinced both that the French were engaged in a serious diplomatic effort and that their main priority was the hostages. He promised Pisani that he would make the point to Saddam.[9]

On 20 October Arafat continued his own shuttle diplomacy to Baghdad. Two days later he was able to report back to Pisani that the French hostages would be liberated. When Pisani reminded him that he had been talking about all the hostages, Arafat replied: 'Take this for now. It is only a beginning, the rest will come later.' That same day, Saddam Hussein proposed to Iraq's National Assembly to approve the release of all 327 French 'guests' held in Iraq and Kuwait. According to Saddam, his decision was a gesture of goodwill to the French people, who 'have rejected Bush's aggressive methods . . . and have proven that they are a people who understand the meaning of the required correct stand towards events'.[10] Tariq Aziz was more elaborate than his master. In a speech at the National Assembly following its approval of

Saddam's recommendation, he hailed the long record of Franco-Iraqi friendship and expressed his hope that the moderate thrust of French policy would affect the other European states, since 'France plays a key role in Europe and the French stand always reflects on the European stands in one way or another.' He then went on to argue that there was an 'undeclared' facet to French diplomacy in addition to the declared part, which precluded the possibility of French participation in a military action against Iraq. 'Yes,' he admitted, 'the French forces are still there, but we have heard reassurances that these forces will not be used in a military operation against Iraq.'[11]

Not surprisingly, the unexpected Iraqi decision to release the French hostages generated a windmill of speculations about a bilateral deal. Commentators were particularly keen to underscore a redeployment by the French military contingent in Saudi Arabia, thirty kilometres away from Iraq, on 20 October. These speculations were vehemently denied by the French, who argued that there had been 'nothing between France and Iraq which could be described as negotiations', merely 'normal diplomatic contacts between officials concerning the hostages'.

Initially the Iraqis confirmed the French denials;[12] however, on 10 November they changed their version and argued that the release of the hostages had been agreed upon a month earlier during Aziz's secret meeting in Tunis with Claude Cheysson. In the Iraqi account this meeting had been mediated by the PLO and had taken place with the full approval of the French Foreign Minister, Roland Dumas. Although Dumas hurried to deny such a deal, Cheysson, when pressed by the media, notably failed to disavow his meeting with Aziz.[13]

The Iraqi revelations were not accidental. Rather, they reflected Saddam's irritation with what he perceived as French ingratitude for his generous gesture. He had assumed that the release of the hostages would constitute the significant gesture necessary to get the much sought-after visit from a senior French politician, only to realize later that the only person Mitterrand was willing to send to Baghdad was an 'administrative figure' charged with arranging the departure of the hostages. More importantly, the Iraqi revelations were a deliberate spoiling tactic, aimed at driving a wedge between the United States and France on the eve of James Baker's arrival in Paris to co-ordinate the coalition's Gulf strategy.

The hostages lottery continues

By then, Saddam had already expanded his attempts to divide Western public opinion through the hostages problem well beyond France. At the time that the French release was announced the former British Prime Minister, Edward Heath, was in Baghdad on a 'private humanitarian visit'. Arriving with a long list of the elderly and sick who deserved release, the former Premier entered into a protracted haggle with the Iraqis, eventually returning with thirty-eight grateful people, a far cry from his original expectations. Because of Heath's status the visit aroused considerable political interest. The British Government was unenthusiastic about the visit but did not try to stop him. Heath told Saddam that holding hostages caused offence, including to his Arab friends. Saddam acknowledged this but insisted that he was looking after his country's defence, although Heath also told him that putting hostages in strategic sites would not stop Mrs Thatcher authorizing bombing. Although Saddam told him that it would be 'difficult' to leave Kuwait and that even then he would still fear Western strikes, Heath judged that Saddam was interested in a settlement, that he was not 'mad' or unaware of the pressures upon him, and that insufficient was being done to help him save his face.[14]

The Heath visit, the special favour accorded France and the general sense that the hostage issue was getting out of hand drove the leaders of the European Community, who insisted from the outset of the crisis that they would make no concessions as a result of the seizure of the hostages, to try to establish a common policy. On 28 October the member states affirmed

> their determination not to send representatives of their governments in any capacity to negotiate with Iraq the release of foreign hostages and to discourage others from doing so. They ask the Security Council to continue its efforts to achieve the immediate departure of all hostages and they encourage the Secretary-General to send a special representative to Iraq to this end.[15]

Unfortunately the credibility of this policy was undermined almost immediately by a proposed visit by the former German Chancellor, Willy Brandt, to Baghdad. With Germany, as with France, there were reasons to suspect a degree of softness in the overall stance on the crisis. On 26 October the German Foreign Minister, Hans-Dietrich Genscher, revealed that Iraq had offered to set free all the 400 German nationals if he would travel to Baghdad to collect them. He refused to do so because Germany would not break ranks with other Western Governments in this manner.

Brandt, nevertheless, decided to make the visit, having been inspired by Heath (the two had worked closely together in the 1970s on the Independent Commission on Development).[16] Just after Heath's visit, Brandt met with 400 relatives of German hostages asking him to go on a similar mission, but he indicated that he could not because of the wishes of the German Government. At this point Chancellor Kohl and Foreign Minister Genscher relented, as they became nervous about popular concern over the German hostages in the period up to the impending December elections. Hence, having supported Brandt, the Government came up against the EC's determination to put an end to such visits. The German Government was supposedly in favour of a common Community foreign policy.

By way of squaring this circle, Genscher and Kohl sought to give the mission a higher status. The Chancellor contacted his Italian counterpart, Giulio Andreotti, who served at the time as President of the European Council of Ministers, suggesting that the Community should offer to send three senior figures to Baghdad as emissaries of the United Nations. He suggested a trio of Community figures, with Social Democrat Brandt complemented by Christian Democrat Emilio Colombo of Italy (former Prime Minister) and Liberal Democrat Willy de Clerq (former European External Affairs Commissioner). The Italians were prepared to go along with the idea but the plan failed when Perez de Cuellar refused to give such a trip UN authority.

The German initiative was met by strong criticism from a number of European capitals, with Britain complaining bitterly at this disregard of the Community's own guidelines. This criticism was muted only by the desire not to harm Kohl just before the elections. In the meantime, while the German Government was trying to put its act together, it was faced on 1 November with a *fait accompli* when Brandt announced that he was going anyway. Reluctant to let a Social Democrat have all the credit for hostage release just before the elections, and unable to give Brandt their formal blessing, Kohl and Genscher rejected the British criticism and offered their 'good wishes'.[17] They provided a Lufthansa jet to bring home the Germans whose release they hoped Brandt would secure.

On the eve of Brandt's arrival, and with former Japanese Prime Minister Yasuhiro Nakasone in town, Saddam drew another card from his sleeve by announcing, on 4 November, that all hostages would be freed if either Japan or Germany plus one permanent member of the Security Council were to say that they opposed military action against Iraq.[18] The Japanese Government denied that Nakasone negotiated the release of hostages or that he offered any link with the Middle East crisis. However, one of those closely involved with Nakasone's trip has described how it was decided to let the Liberal-Democratic Party parliamentarians travelling with him concentrate on the Japanese hostages, so as to allow Nakasone to speak for all hostages. He took with him a peace proposal offering, in return for withdrawal, linkage, the administration of Kuwait by the UN and its oil policy by OPEC, rather than a return to the al-Sabahs, and bilateral negotiations on territorial issues. Nakasone concluded that Saddam simply did not understand his international isolation.[19] He returned home with seventy-four Japanese hostages. Brandt's haul, on 9 November, was some 180 people.

As Baghdad would not talk to the UN about the hostages, as the EC had hoped, there was no obvious form of communication if the elder statesmen were to be reined in. The Community decided in November to ask the Mahgreb states to help and this appears to have become a significant source of pressure on Saddam, who could not readily ignore this group of states.

For three months the hostage question had provided a substantial distraction but had not in itself altered the main features of the confrontation. It had brought senior political figures to visit Baghdad where, despite all their protestations, each seems to have explored the possibility of a peaceful settlement with Saddam. Heath remarked on how calm Saddam appeared, while Brandt spoke of 'the intensity of his engagement'. They encouraged the view that the problem lay with Western inflexibility, without being able to be precise as to Saddam's potential flexibility.

The Soviet initiative

It was the Soviets, rather than the French, who at this stage sought to offer Saddam a dignified climbdown by sending a senior figure to Baghdad to negotiate directly with the Iraqi leader. The response to Mitterrand's United Nations speech indicated that the idea of a peace conference on the Middle East was attracting considerable interest and was being pushed, not surprisingly, by the PLO. As the Soviets could claim paternity for the idea of a Middle East peace conference, which they had been mooting ever since the 1973 October War, it was tempting to see whether some sort of formula for ending the crisis could be built around it.[20] It also offered an opportunity for Moscow to reassert some of its old influence in the Middle East, from which some in the Soviet leadership felt it had been excluded by the United States. Part of the same effort was the groundwork for re-establishing diplomatic relations with Israel.

Gorbachev had been considering an initiative along these lines before Mitterrand. On 4 September, Shevardnadze explicitly linked the Gulf crisis to the Arab–Israeli conflict, arguing that Israel's agreement to participate in an international conference on the Middle East could exert a 'positive influence' on the events in the Gulf.[21] Four days later, on the eve of the Helsinki summit, Gorbachev discussed the possibility of using the

Palestinian issue in getting Iraq out of Kuwait. He was anxious to find some political solution because of the consequences of war. He appears to have been influenced by the analysis of his chief military adviser, Marshal Sergei Akhromeyev, whom he took with him to the meeting with Bush. Akhromeyev warned that war would bring terrible losses and destruction, which the Iraqis might not be able to withstand. On this basis, he argued to Bush, and with international support now solid, it was time to explore a political solution.[22] In order to keep Gorbachev's support, Bush did not object.

The explorer was to be Yevgeny Primakov, a noted Arabist and a member of the Presidential Council, who had known Saddam Hussein for many years. He arrived in Baghdad on 4 October and first met Aziz, who treated him to an extended proof of Iraq's right to Kuwait. The next day he met Saddam.

He did make some progress on the question of Soviet nationals. The issue with Soviet citizens in Iraq had been somewhat different from that of other foreign nationals. From the outbreak of the crisis to the start of October, 2,617 Soviet nationals had been brought out of Iraq but that still left 5,174 stranded.[23] Many encountered severe difficulties in getting exit visas, largely because they were judged to be under contract (mainly in the oil industry). Increasingly irritated statements from Moscow had made Saddam aware that any hope of a softer line from his erstwhile allies would be jeopardized even more if their citizens were not allowed to go. Primakov's visit provided a useful opportunity to make a gesture in this respect.[24]

However, on leaving Primakov also said that he was 'no longer pessimistic' on the prospects for a peaceful solution. His own description of the meeting has Saddam describing the conspiracy against Iraq, agreeing that he had a 'Masada complex' (that is, would commit suicide rather than surrender), and exhibiting over-optimism with regard to support in the Arab world and anti-war protest in the West. The basis of Primakov's optimism appears to have been no more than a statement from Saddam indicating that while he stood by his 12 August statement, 'the time linkage and the process leading to a solution of the Palestinian problem are to be discussed at negotiations' – a hint but no more that the Kuwait problem might not be the last on the agenda.[25]

The plan designed by Primakov at this point was ventilated in Soviet commentaries, placing particular weight on the possible convocation of an international conference following Iraq's withdrawal from Kuwait, and it was even suggested that some movement in this direction might be taken after the first Iraqi public commitment to withdrawal. It was also speculated in Moscow that Saddam had agreed to withdraw in return for access to the two contested islands.[26] This was doing no more than anticipating the results of talks with Kuwait which, Primakov proposed, Saddam should know would begin after his withdrawal. As often happened in the crisis, whenever rumours of Iraqi concessions started to circulate, they were immediately denied by Baghdad: on 14 October the Iraqi News Agency categorically stated that 'Kuwait was and will continue to be Iraqi land for ever.'

Primakov was then dispatched by Gorbachev to talk to key leaders about his plan. When he went to Washington on 18 October the reception was cool. The Americans were aware that Primakov's mission was controversial with the other key Soviet players – Eduard Shevardnadze and UN Ambassador Vitaly Vorontsov – so that co-operation with Moscow was not dependent upon a positive response. While Baker and Scowcroft, and then Bush, listened to what he had to say, they were not convinced. They saw no reason to make any concessions on substance to Saddam and did not accept his analysis of the inevitable disaster of war or the importance of the views of the Arab masses even if they were, which they doubted, as radical as he described them. The Primakov plan appeared as the repackaging of old ideas. Bush did not object to him returning to Baghdad, but only saw point if an 'uncompromising position' was transmitted. He did, however, promise that the US would listen to any 'positive signal'. A trip at Gorbachev's request to see Margaret Thatcher (who had been excluded from his original itinerary) produced, by Primakov's account, a diatribe on the inevitability of war.[27] Afterwards James Baker made it clear that the United States was 'unwilling to engage in a search for partial solutions', nor accept 'a negotiated arrangement that would enable Saddam Hussein to claim benefits from his unprovoked aggression against a small neighbour'.

When Primakov arrived back in Baghdad at the end of October, there was little expectation of a breakthrough. He urged the coalition to postpone another pending Security Council vote – this time on Iraqi compensation for all the losses suffered as a result of its action – so as not to poison the atmosphere for his talks. To make life easier for the Russians, the Americans agreed – although only for thirty-six hours.[28] Gorbachev spoke of 'indications that the High Command in Iraq has realized that problems cannot be solved through ultimatums'.[29] Primakov had met the High Command, who had been gathered together for his benefit when he met Saddam again on 28 October. Saddam, in his account, seemed more sober and did not spend time on rightful ownership of Kuwait. When Primakov broached the question of withdrawal and conveyed the signals he had picked up of a greater readiness to contemplate war, Saddam responded:

How can I announce the withdrawal of troops if I am not informed how the question of the removal of the US forces from Saudi Arabia will be resolved? Will the UN sanctions against Iraq be lifted, or will they remain in force? How will my country's interest concerning an outlet to the sea be ensured? Will there be some form of linkage between the Iraqi troop pullout from Kuwait and a solution to the Palestinian problem?

Without unequivocal answers to these questions, Saddam argued, nothing could be done. 'You must understand one thing,' he told Primakov, 'on 15 August I gave away all the fruits of the eight-year war against Iran and returned to the previous situation. The Iraqi people will not forgive me for [another] unconditional withdrawal from Kuwait. They will ask me: "And what about the outlet to the sea?"' The value of continued contacts, Saddam therefore suggested, was to get answers to these questions.[30] If this was flexibility it was very meagre, for Saddam could not be given a positive answer to any one of those questions prior to a pull-out from Kuwait.

Neither Primakov nor Saddam was interested in giving the impression of a total fiasco. Saddam described the talks as 'profound and very useful'.[31] Primakov went from Baghdad to Cairo where he optimistically asserted that he was 'convinced that the Gulf crisis can be solved without recourse to military force'. In an interview on the Soviet television upon his return to Moscow, he elaborated on the source of his optimism:

> During the first meeting, Saddam simply said that Kuwait is part of Iraqi territory and adduced some arguments to substantiate this view and so on. This time he did not raise either the issue or the arguments. It seems to me that he is now more in favour of a political solution.[32]

On the basis of a telegram from Primakov, Gorbachev claimed that Saddam's 'position is no longer the same which he held some time ago', described a military solution to the crisis as being 'unacceptable', and encouraged the idea of a solution in the 'framework of an inter-Arab conference since these events are happening in Arab lands'.[33]

Not everyone in Moscow shared this optimistic judgement. Foreign Minister Shevardnadze, hardly disguising his irritation with the attempts to appease Baghdad, responded to Primakov's assessment that a peaceful resolution of the crisis was in the offing by emphatically stating that it was 'difficult to say what the concrete ways for a political settlement might be' and that, in any event, 'Primakov's mission was not the last hope'. *Izvestiya* was more outspoken of Primakov's mission, defining it bluntly as a failure.[34]

As the two best-placed members of the Security Council to explore a negotiated solution, it was fitting for the diplomatic efforts of September and October to be concluded with a Franco-Soviet meeting at the highest level. Both Gorbachev and Mitterrand were now acutely aware of the danger of being seen to be offering diplomatic favours to Baghdad in return for the release of their own nationals.[35] Despite having received preferential treatment from Baghdad, they took care to end their meeting in Paris with a joint statement calling for all hostages to be released. Another field of unanimity was their mutual conviction in the virtues of a Middle East peace conference for its own sake and their lingering hope that this might be used as a carrot to get Saddam out of Kuwait. Finally, both Mitterrand and Gorbachev sought to use whatever credibility they might have in Baghdad to reassure Saddam that if he did withdraw then he would not be attacked. By this time both also recognized that if a diplomatic solution were not found soon, some sort of military action was inevitable.

Gorbachev said that there would only be a case for war if all 'political means have been exhausted' – a point quickly picked up by Valentin Falin, Head of the Central Committee's International Department, who insisted that 'sanctions are sure to prove effective'.[36] This backtracking unnerved those in Washington who had been pleased by the robust support for stronger means, should they prove necessary, shown by Gorbachev at Helsinki and by Shevardnadze at the United Nations. Talk of peaceful solutions and sanctions providing sufficient pressure was coming to be seen in Washington as so much wishful thinking.

CHAPTER 12
The Oil Weapon

The Bush Administration's first concern had been that Iraq would not stop at getting 20 per cent of the world's oil reserves, but would attempt to double that stake by taking Saudi Arabia and thereby exercise critical influence on the world's most important single commodity. The seizure of one state by another is always reprehensible. However, it was often remarked through the crisis and afterwards that it excited the major powers only because it took place in the region which contains 65 per cent of the world's known oil reserves and 25 per cent of current oil production. This is too simplistic.

If Saddam were allowed to shape the Middle East to his own designs that would create a global oil crisis. On the other hand, the action needed to stop him must also create a crisis. While it was never the case that the Gulf crisis was solely about oil, oil infused every aspect. It created a stake for all concerned in its speedy resolution and constituted some of the most serious costs. Initially, it was oil that provided each side with one of its most effective weapons: for Saddam the hope that the impact of an oil shock on the world economy would undermine the will of his opponents, who in turn hoped that the loss of Iraq's oil revenues would oblige it to abide by the Security Council's resolutions.

The oil price

As the crisis broke, memories inevitably went back to the First Oil Shock, attending the October 1973 Arab–Israeli War when oil prices quintupled, and the Second Oil Shock after the fall of the Shah of Iran in January 1979, when the price doubled. Was this going to be the Third Oil Shock?

The initial rise in oil prices suggested that it was. In July the Organization of Petroleum Exporting Countries (OPEC) had agreed to a move from $18 to $21 per barrel. The new price was almost reached on the first rumours that an invasion was under way: by the time the seizure of Kuwait was an established fact it had gone up to $23, the highest level since 1985. Fear that

Saudi Arabia was Saddam's next stop soon pushed it up to $27. The consequences of a continuing rise in prices were plain: fearing a recession, stock markets in the world's capitals took a dive.

Nonetheless, there were good reasons to be more sanguine over the impact of the Third Oil Shock compared with the First and Second. Oil had become a less important cost component for countries of the Organization of Economic Co-operation and Development (OECD) than before: there had been a decline in energy consumption as a result of a drive for greater efficiency, and they had also reduced their dependence upon Middle Eastern oil. Another source of comfort was that official oil storage facilities were full. As the crisis broke the International Energy Agency (IEA) announced that stocks held on land in industrialized countries were sufficient to last for ninety-nine days (468.4 million tonnes). In the oil-importing countries stocks were sufficient for five months' supply without further imports. The American strategic reserve itself approached 600 million barrels, and this could be supplied to the market at a rate of 2 million barrels per day (bpd).[1] This substantial American reserve accounted for 60 per cent of the total, with Japan and West Germany the other major holders of reserves.

This more optimistic picture had to be qualified by evidence that the oil companies held lower stocks than in previous crises. These were only seventy days, of which some sixty-five days represented the minimum needed for legal and working balances. After the supply glut in the mid 1980s companies had judged that they no longer needed to keep the level of stocks held previously, enough for some three months. There were also some practical questions as to whether, if put to the test, the US strategic reserve could cope with a major crisis.[2]

OPEC was not the power it had been in the 1970s. The measures it had taken then to force up prices had resulted in a backlash, with extra reserves being found and mobilized, thus generating a glut in the 1980s and even making it possible to cope with a war between two oil-rich countries. In these conditions OPEC had found it difficult to function as an effective cartel in setting quotas and prices, which had been one of the main stimulants to the Iraqi–Kuwaiti dispute. The crisis itself had exacerbated the sense of disarray in OPEC. The organization's Geneva meeting before the invasion had provided an unwitting setting for the conflict between Iraq and Kuwait to come to a head and was followed by one of its members swallowing another.

The crisis posed a serious challenge to the world oil market because two oil producers – equivalent to at least 4 million barrels a day (or about 7 per cent of world demand) – had been extracted. However, a number of countries were in a position to increase their production to make up for the lost supply in order to stop prices rising. Saudi Arabia itself could pick up around two-thirds of this, so long as its security was guaranteed. Unlike the 1970s, the key producers were well aware of the dangers of an excessively rapid price rise. They might obtain a short-term windfall but past experience warned that the main result of excessively high prices was to encourage a global recession, which would have a negative impact on their economic health, and also stimulate a search for both extra oil and energy alternatives, both of which would depress the long-term value of their reserves. Their interest was therefore to prevent prices from rising too strongly.

Despite this logic, by the middle of August there was no evidence of any oil producers preparing to meet the gap left by the embargoes on Iraqi and Kuwaiti oil. By this time prices had hit $30 a barrel and Saudi Arabia was expressing concern that in adhering to the official OPEC quotas the coalition, of which it was now a critical member, would be weakened. On 19 August the Saudi Oil Minister, Hisham Nazar, announced that his country would increase production by 2 million bpd with or without the blessing of OPEC, if the organization did not agree within two days on an emergency meeting to authorize increases in output. As the Saudis were then producing 5.38 million bpd, they were threatening to increase production by well over a third.

Iraq, still hoping that economic pressures would undermine the cohesion of the coalition, quickly declared that any such increase would constitute an 'act of aggression'. This made the Saudis all the more determined to obtain approval for increases in output through OPEC. Eventually, on 26 August, OPEC ministers met – just a month after the ill-fated gathering in July when Iraq had been pressing for suppressed output in order to raise prices. The August meeting was at first described as an informal consultation – at least until a majority of the members present agreed to turn it into a formal meeting to set new quotas.

Iraq was not alone in opposing the Saudi initiative. Its former enemy, Iran, was also a price hawk and pleased at the price's general direction. In addition, it was politically important in Tehran to be seen to be acting independently of Riyadh. Libya was also sympathetic to Iraq. These three countries argued that there was already enough oil around to meet demand without new measures. Others, including Indonesia, Algeria and Nigeria, supported a modest increase, but not quite enough to meet the shortfall as they wanted to see the markets strengthened anyway. They did not see it as being the cartel's mission to save the West from its economic crisis. If matters were that serious then the West should release some of its strategic reserves. The largest group, however, was composed of Saudi Arabia, Venezuela, Kuwait, the UAE and Qatar, who warned of the adverse consequences that might flow from excessively high prices.

Within OPEC these were well-rehearsed arguments. The new element came from the shifting power balance within the organization. Iraq (because of the presence of a representative of the Kuwaiti Government-in-exile) and Libya failed to show up for the informal consultations called by Sadek Doussena, the Algerian minister who was also OPEC President. This left Iran as the sole speaker for the price hawks at the meeting. There may have been resentment at the lobbying by the Saudi and Kuwaiti delegations and the threat from Saudi Arabia, as well as Venezuela, to act regardless of any decision, or at the sense of being asked to line up with Washington in a conflict with one of OPEC's key member states. In the end the majority were still persuaded that Saudi views had to be accommodated if the organization itself was to have any hope of surviving this crisis. The sense that the embargo might be in place for a long time and that winter was coming also encouraged a decision.

On 28 August an agreement was reached which called for the suspension of quotas to provide for higher production, according to capacity. It allowed for the return to quotas when 'the present crisis is deemed to be over'. To give this decision authority the ministers went into formal session, issuing invitations to the Iraqis and Libyans to attend before they did so. The two did not come, but with ten of the organization's thirteen members supporting the suspension of quotas, the decision was passed.

As a result it was assumed that there would be little trouble in making up at least 80 per cent of the lost Iraqi and Kuwaiti oil, and this was soon achieved. The bulk came from Saudi Arabia, Venezuela, the UAE and to a lesser extent Nigeria. By the time OPEC met again in December, with prices now falling back towards the $20 mark, the concern revolved around a return to quotas when the crisis was over.

Yet before the market kept up with the new supply the initial impact of the August OPEC decision was barely perceptible. Not surprisingly this led to complaints about oil companies pocketing their windfall profits at the expense of the consumer. Ever sensitive to American public opinion, President Bush asked the oil companies to show restraint in their pricing policy, as did the British Government.

In practice, the price was linked as much to fears of war as to actual output. Along with share prices, the oil price rose and fell in accordance with the latest news from the diplomatic front. Thus, even after the OPEC agreement, prices rose from $27 to $29 as a result of dispiriting news on the crisis, and on 21 September they reached $35 after a particularly bellicose statement by Saddam Hussein. Discussion of an oil price of $40–$50 per barrel in the case of an outbreak of hostilities was already being mooted, and some, noting the reports of the mining of Kuwaiti oilwells and possible attacks on Saudi oil installations, put it even higher. A much quoted estimate from Sheikh Ahmad Zaki Yamani, the former Saudi Oil Minister, predicted that prices might go as high as $100.[3]

The strategic reserve

With oil producers playing their part, the focus of attention shifted to the oil companies and the strategic petroleum reserve. There had been a long-standing argument between the Congress and the Reagan Administration over whether the strategic reserve was geared to shortages or to stabilize prices, with the Congress arguing for the latter purpose. In 1984 the Administration had agreed on 'early use' in the event of a disruption.[4] The Gulf crisis felt like a major disruption but the Administration, encouraged by the West Germans and the Japanese, argued that the emergency was not yet serious enough to warrant the release of stocks. There was a clear presumption that the major emergency was yet to come.

If the International Energy Agency was saying that it did not believe that the moment was right for the release of stocks because such a measure should be left for a major disruption following the outbreak of hostilities, then it was not surprising that this possibility became part of the oil industry's calculations and they kept up their stocks for a 'real emergency'. As noted earlier, companies' stocks in the autumn of 1990 were at an historic low and reducing them further would leave no scope to cope with accidents, unusual bad weather conditions, and equipment breakdowns – as well as war. Consequently pressure did grow on the Administration to use its reserves to dampen prices and on 26 September it did allow for 5 million barrels to be sold off from the strategic reserve. This was presented more as a signal to speculators that if necessary the United States would draw down reserves and so depress prices, rather than as an indication of a real emergency.

With the increased output and the depressed demand (due to higher prices and the lack of major accidents or unusually severe winter), oil prices began to fall back to pre-crisis levels. The much feared Third Oil Shock had proved to be manageable. In retrospect, it is hard to avoid the conclusion that if this release had been made earlier the economic damage caused by the crisis might have been reduced.

Economic shocks

By the time the price began to subside the boost to inflation resulting from the period of high prices had already had its effect. Prior to the crisis the American and British economies were already in trouble: the combination of the oil prices, the extra projected expenditure on military operations in the Gulf and the consequentially high interest rates tipped them in the direction of recession.

They were by no means the worst afflicted. The world's poorer nations were much more vulnerable. The critique of the coalition campaign to the effect that it was merely a battle for cheap oil prices suggested that this was solely a Western interest. In practice the burden of oil prices relative to the rest of the economy was much greater in the post-communist and the developing countries.

The crisis came at a particularly cruel moment for the economies of Central and Eastern Europe, which were beginning their slow reconstruction following years of communist mismanagement. The Soviet Union had already decided to reduce the flow of oil to its old allies and charge market prices. Now they had to cope with loss of trade with the Gulf states and the probability that they would not be able to recoup loans to Iraq – often made by the old regime to finance its arms sales. Hungary, Poland and Czechoslovakia had been receiving oil in lieu of large loans to Iraq. In September, Poland estimated that its losses from the crisis were $500 million and that they were likely to rise to $1.5 billion. Some estimates put the cost to the countries of Eastern Europe of the Soviet decision to charge for its oil at market rates at between $8 and $10 billion. When oil prices were raised to $25 a barrel, the additional bill was doubled again. The World Bank estimated that the dual crisis would cost the post-communist countries $15 billion a year or 5 per cent of their GDP.

Even the Soviet Union did not do as well as might have been expected from the surge in oil prices, although exports of oil and gas furnish 80 per cent of its hard currency earnings. While some Western estimates suggested a windfall of $10 billion from the increase in oil prices in 1990, with another $27 billion in 1991, this had to be set against a decline in oil production and shortages inside the country, as well as the fact that other producers such as Saudi Arabia and Venezuela were better placed to exploit the situation.[5] Soviet oil production was only 11.4 million bpd in 1990, barely 0.5 million bpd up on 1989 which had not by any means been a peak, and exports were down by 250,000 bpd.[6] In addition there were the problems of the consequent rise in inflation and the losses resulting from the disruption of trade with both Iraq and Kuwait. Losses from the imposition of sanctions in 1990 were put at $800 million, including $525 million resulting from a failure to deliver Iraqi oil to India, Bulgaria, Romania and other countries for re-export, and $290 million worth of goods and services not delivered to the Soviet Union. Goods and finances not delivered from Kuwait reached $115 million.[7]

Even harder hit were some developing countries. Since the first shock of 1973 their share of world consumption had risen from 18 per cent to 28 per cent, and for many poor countries this remained the largest single item on the import bill. $40 a barrel could cost the Third World $120 billion over a full year. This was in addition to the economic damage caused by loss of trade with Iraq and workers' remittances. One calculation was that if oil prices remained $10 and more higher than the OPEC benchmark of $21, the price difference would mean a monthly transfer of $20 billion to oil exporters, of which $1.5 billion would be paid by the world's poorest countries.

A belt of Asian countries – Pakistan, India, Bangladesh, Sri Lanka and the Philippines – relied on remittances from the Gulf to meet the cost of their energy imports. Thus India got 40 per cent of its energy imports from Iraq and had more expatriates in Kuwait and Iraq than any other non-Arab nation (172,000). Sri Lanka, selling $100 million worth of tea to Iraq each year, refused to comply with the sanctions. Remittances of $100 million from Kuwait alone accounted for 0.6 per cent of Bangladesh's GNP. Bangladesh and Pakistan were the only two Muslim countries in Asia to agree to a request from Saudi Arabia to send forces – in the hope of receiving more generous treatment. Indonesia and Malaysia declined. Pakistan asked Riyadh to compensate its economy for $1 billion losses.

In September 1990 the World Bank described ten countries as most immediately affected: Egypt, Jordan, Morocco, Pakistan, Turkey, Sudan, Bangladesh, India, the Philippines and Sri Lanka. At least sixty countries were seriously affected through their balance of payments. Jordan was judged the worst hit. The bank estimated losses of 30 per cent of Jordan's national income and 4 per cent of Egypt's. Turkey estimated a loss of nearly $2 billion.

In response to these mounting problems, in late September President Bush launched the Gulf Crisis Financial Co-ordination Group, involving twenty-four nations – the OECD states and the larger Gulf states. By its second meeting in mid October, agreement had been reached on the size of the problem. Bush agreed to work for $5 billion worth of loans to Eastern Europe, which was now expected to lose $12 billion in 1990–91.

On 6 November the group agreed on an aid package of $13 billion. This would go largely to Turkey, Egypt and Jordan, who would share $10.5 billion by the end of 1991, with the other $2.5 billion to other countries such as Morocco, Pakistan, and the Philippines. By mid November, nineteen states had asked for assistance from the UN, but nothing had been arranged for the poorest countries.[8] The money was to be raised largely from Saudi Arabia and other Gulf states which had experienced windfall profits. Japan committed $2 billion for the current fiscal year, while the European Commission found $700 million out of the $2.2 billion contributed by the Community as a whole. There was concern that Jordan was not getting sufficient help because of the continuing irritation of conservative Gulf states with its stance during the crisis.[9]

Even then, the implementation of these promises was less than straight-forward. Take, for example, the efforts of the European Community. One of the few roles that the Community could accept for itself was to provide help for the more hard-pressed front-line states. The Commission and member states thus paid out Ecu 100 million to help 144,000 expatriate workers leave Iraq and Kuwait. The difficulties in agreeing aid packages as a matter of urgency were illustrated by the problems encountered with an agreement to organize help for Jordan, Turkey and Egypt.[10] Although other countries had presented claims, these were the three that had made direct approaches to the Community. Of these Jordan was the most needy, but Egypt and Turkey were deemed more worthy politically.

By early September 1990 a financial aid package for these three countries had been devised, involving immediate assistance of around $500 million by the end of the year in the form of both loan support and guarantees and direct grant aid, with the acceleration of some existing programmes. As with all such schemes, there were debates over the mix of loans and grants and the mix between contributions from the Community's own budget and from individual states. There was a further problem arising from Greek hostility to Turkey and its contention that the latter's 1974 invasion of Cyprus was a comparable act of aggression to that of Iraq's against Kuwait. In the event it was agreed to commit $2 billion (Ecu 1.5 billion) in aid until the end of 1991 to the three states.

This was then followed by indecision over where the money should come from. The original Commission proposal was that half should come from the Community budget to lessen divisions over national contributions. This was then cut down to a third (Ecu 500 million) in grants and loans from the EC budget with the rest from individual members. Britain, France and Germany all argued that they should pay less, as they were contributing to the international effort in other ways. It took more than two months before the member states agreed on the allocation of their shares and then the Community's own contribution was held up in a dispute between the European Parliament and the Council of Ministers and was delayed until 1991.

By the end of January 1991, the Commission decided that it must speed up the aid. It decided to share out aid from the Community's 1991 budget, giving Egypt and Jordan grants worth Ecu 175 million and Ecu 150 million respectively, and Turkey Ecu 175 million in interest-free loans, with the objective of 80 per cent of the aid arriving by the end of February. The Commission had been left to sort out the distribution after the Foreign Ministers of the twelve had failed to agree on the issue. This was largely because of a Greek bid, which was voted down, to get Turkey to pay interest on loans. The performance by the individual states was even less impressive: by the end of January 1991, only one third of the Ecu 1 billion pledged by individual members had reached the three states.

As with the foreign nationals caught in Kuwait and Iraq, the worst hit by the Third Oil Shock were those with not only the weakest economies but the weakest political voices. If Saddam hoped that the economic dislocation would put unbearable pressure on his main opponents he was to be bitterly disappointed. The worst consequences were felt elsewhere. The coalition had a similar problem: those who were most likely to suffer from the sanctions imposed on Iraq were not its political élite.

Table 4: Oil Exports of Kuwait and Iraq

1,000s of barrels per day		
	KUWAIT	IRAQ
USA	100	580
EC	150	620
Turkey	–	335
Japan	250	230
Korea	50	–
Taiwan	100	–
Refined products	750	–
Far East	–	400
Brazil	–	160
Other	100	500
TOTAL	1,500	2,825

CHAPTER 13

The Food Weapon

In a speech to the United Nation's Security Council on 25 September, when the air blockade was being discussed, Secretary of State James Baker stated that:

> the international community . . . has set a high and rising penalty upon Iraq for each passing day that it fails to abandon its aggression.
>
> These penalties are beginning to take effect, and bellicose language from Baghdad cannot compensate for the perils of isolation. Threats only prolong the needless suffering of the Iraqi people.[1]

But this statement begged the question of how long the international community was willing to wait for the penalties to take effect and the extent to which it was prepared to accept any responsibility for the suffering of the Iraqi people.

There was no doubt that the sanctions were a remarkable technical success and exacerbated Iraq's economic problems. Saddam had seen the seizure of Kuwait as an opportunity to escape with one bound from these problems, but all that had happened was that they had become aggravated. He was in control of 20 per cent of the world's oil reserves but unable to sell any of it. He could not even give it away – as he offered to do at one point to any Third World consumer able to come and collect[2] – because of the embargo. The cash squeeze was complete. Some 95 per cent of Iraq's income had come from oil or oil-related products. It was also fully in debt, so those who might have been tempted to keep it supplied by charging black market prices were doubtful if they would see their reward.

With direct sea and air routes to Iraq cut off, all goods had to travel by land and this too was illegal. Even in Jordan, where the population was most sympathetic to Saddam, the Government dared not be seen to be helping Iraq break the embargo, and officials from the UN and Western embassies were watching out for major breaches.[3] There was a long history of smuggling in the region. There were many ways to move goods into Iraq through its porous borders with Turkey, Iran, Syria and Jordan. But this illicit traffic was trivial compared with Iraq's overwhelming needs.

Iraq could earn no money and it could buy few goods. It could not benefit from its seizure of Kuwait, except through plunder. The question was whether it could be persuaded through economic pressure to abandon its newly gained nineteenth province. Studies on the efficacy of economic sanctions do not leave much room for optimism.[4] They warn of low success rates as the supposed victim finds ways of getting round the sanctions. The effort may be expensive, but so long as the country can sustain itself then it has no need to allow those imposing the sanctions to force a change in its fundamental policy. The question of sanctions against Iraq followed months of argument concerning the value of economic sanctions in forcing South Africa to abandon apartheid, in which both President Bush and Prime Minister Thatcher had taken notably sceptical views.

The Iraqi case was clearly different from others. On the one hand, Baghdad had only oil to sell to the outside world, and this simplified the task for the blockaders. But on the other this meant that Iraq had plentiful supplies of the exact commodity that had been the target of embargoes in the past. An oil-producing country that could not sell oil had little long-term future, but the battle of wits between Saddam and the rest of the world was about short-term survival. If Iraq could keep going under siege for long enough then, Saddam might hope, he could eventually obtain a settlement on tolerable terms.

As he was not getting any new lines of credit, Saddam felt himself to be under no compunction to meet his debts. If he could extricate himself from this situation and still hold on to Kuwait then it might all be worthwhile. With such a share of world oil reserves, observed Tariq Aziz, Iraq had established itself 'as a regional power that is worth taking into considertion'. Deputy Prime Minister Sa'dun Hammadi reminded the Iraqis that they now owned 194 billion barrels of oil reserves and could expect revenues reaching $46 billion a year.[5] Until this happy day, however, the prospect for the Iraqi economy was one of a slide into destitution. It was now losing approximately $1.5 billion of foreign exchange earnings monthly, a figure equivalent to more than a third of its total national product. The collapse of many major projects set back the various industrialization programmes. Over time this, plus the general isolation of the country, would have had an effect. However, the use of sanctions as a coercive weapon depended upon economic pain turning into popular discontent, or at least upon Saddam recognizing this as a possibility and acting before it became a reality. That in turn depended on finding the limits of his repressive apparatus, though this was well able to stifle expressions of dissent, and hurting the population.

The food weapon

In this regard food was an area of real vulnerability. Iraq was notable for imports of some 75 per cent of its food requirements.[6] Now it had to feed not only 17 million of its own people, but also the 1.5 million in Kuwait. But to exploit this vulnerability raised questions of both practice and principle. The former related to the various methods by which Iraq might survive the embargo, such as stockpiles, rationing, home production and smuggling. The question of principle was whether it was morally right to deny food to a population in order to put pressure on its leadership.

To complicate things further, Protocol 1 of the 1949 Geneva Convention prohibits the 'starvation of civilians as a method of warfare'. While neither the United States nor Iraq had adopted this protocol formally, both acknowledged its moral force. This tension between denying use of the 'food weapon' while at the same time relying on a degree of civilian suffering in order to put pressure on Saddam had been evident from the first UN debate on economic sanctions. As is always the case, there was a general preference for punitive economic measures if the alternative was direct military action, but there was still anxiety that the food weapon should not be pushed too far. As a diplomat at the UN succinctly observed:

> The sanctions weapon when applied to food is a double-edged sword. We want Iraq to hurt, but cannot be seen to use famine to bring the country down.[7]

Hence the clause in Resolution 661 allowing 'supplies intended strictly for medical purposes, and, in humanitarian circumstances, foodstuffs'. In an earlier draft the word 'special' had appeared before 'humanitarian', but Ethiopia, with its own bitter experience of famine, had refused to accept any suggestion that starvation could be used as a weapon. The word was therefore removed. Similarly, in opposing Resolutions 661 and 664 on the embargo, Yemen and Cuba complained that despite disclaimers the objective was to starve Iraq into submission. The determination of Washington to prevent anything getting through into Iraq appeared to support that interpretation. Over the months of the crisis this question of food and humanitarian supplies dominated the deliberations of the UN's Sanctions Committee.[8]

The issue was difficult for the United States and its allies, as they insisted on an absence of hostility to the Iraqi people, presented as much as victims of

Saddam's regime as the Kuwaitis. If the embargo was seen to be causing real distress then it would prove harder to sustain: but if there was no distress then it was evidently ineffectual.

There was also a tension here for Saddam in that if he overdid the allegations of distress caused by the sanctions then that could encourage the view that they were biting. This was where the hostages came in. Saddam pointed out that if there was to be general suffering in Iraq then it would be shared by all those foreign nationals whom he had trapped. If Iraqi babies were to starve, then so would Western babies. However, the propaganda was more subtle than this. The images coming out of Iraq were divisive in showing Western hostages living in comparative comfort in five-star hotels while Third World nationals were expected to fend for themselves, having been denied ration cards. By this method Iraq hoped that it would be Third World Governments who became most anxious to get food into Iraq if only for their own nationals, and if they were to be allowed to do that then it would insist that supplies were also imported for the general population.

This approach soon appeared to be working. At the end of August, India, which had taken a cautious line on the conflict from the start, told Western Governments that it planned to send a ship to Kuwait with 10,000 tonnes of food and medicine to help the nearly 200,000 Indians still stranded in Kuwait and Iraq. Others, including the Philippines and Yugoslavia, were also anxious to get food to their nationals. During the first week of September, two Bulgarian ships laden with twenty-six containers of baby food for Iraq were barred from leaving Hamburg.

On 6 September, the Sanctions Committee of the Security Council met to consider the criteria for humanitarian assistance. The Western members did not want to provide Iraq with a general opportunity to break sanctions. If the distribution of food was left to the Iraqis then there was no reason to suppose that it would not go to Iraq's political élite and military. Indeed, Saddam had made it clear that because of the threat of American military action, Iraq's armed forces had the first call on supplies of all commodities. Furthermore, as there was no evidence of real distress being caused by the sanctions there was no need to rush into concessions: better to spend the time developing clear guidelines should some humanitarian assistance eventually become necessary. Yemen, along with Cuba and Colombia, was much more keen on getting food into Iraq than worrying about the manner of its distribution. Others, including China, saw no harm in supplies for humanitarian purposes and were uncomfortable with the thought that the first victims of the UN would be foreign nationals along with young, elderly and ailing Iraqis.

Although the Sanctions Committee did not come to any firm conclusions, it decided to ask the UN staff and humanitarian agencies to explore the position of 'persons who might be specially suffering, such as small children'. If, as Saddam claimed, baby food was found to be in short supply, then shipments might be made so long as the Iraqi authorities allowed the UN to organize distribution. This approach then put Iraq in a difficult position because it meant allowing UN inspectors or the International Committee of the Red Cross into Kuwait (which, in the Iraqi view, no longer existed) as well as Iraq on a fact-finding mission. Baghdad refused to allow the UN such access. The Americans were of course not unhappy that it was the Iraqis who were holding up relief operations as this shifted the blame to Saddam.

A breakthrough on the issue within the UN came during the Bush–Gorbachev summit on 11 September in Helsinki, which confirmed the trend towards permitting humanitarian assistance under proper controls. It was agreed that any exemptions for food

> must be strictly monitored by the appropriate international agencies to ensure that food reaches only those for whom it is intended, with special priority being given to meeting the needs of children.

At a news conference after the meeting Bush explained that:

> I hope that nobody around the world interprets this as our view that now there should be wholesale food shipments to Iraq . . . So this should not be interpreted from the US standpoint as a wholesale big hole in the embargo.[9]

Not surprisingly, Baghdad's response was uncompromising. 'We are not going to allow food supplies to be managed by foreigners or outsiders,' said the Iraqi Ambassador to the UN, Abd al-Amir al-Anbari, 'that is for the Iraqi people and the Iraqi Government alone.'[10]

The issue, therefore, remained unresolved. For the Indians this was unacceptable. If the Iraqis would not allow international agencies to distribute food, would they object if India used its embassies and consulates and the offices of Indian companies to distribute food to its stranded nationals? Aware of India's predicament, the Sanctions Committee decided to allow an Indian ship to set sail, on the assumption that the rules governing the distribution of its cargo would be worked out by the time of its arrival. In this way the propaganda advantage might be turned on Iraq. The Chairman of the UN Sanctions Committee, Mrs Marjatta Rasi of Finland, accused Iraq of 'using food as a weapon' by denying aid to foreign workers in Iraq and Kuwait when there was no evidence of a serious food shortage in Iraq.[11]

On 13 September Security Council Resolution 666 was adopted, with

Cuba and Yemen again voting against. It stressed that only the Security Council could determine what would constitute humanitarian circumstances, and that they would keep the matter under constant review; it reminded Iraq of its obligations to foreign nationals, requested information from the UN and other humanitarian organizations on the availability of food, especially those most at risk – children, expectant mothers, the sick and the elderly. Any foodstuffs should be distributed:

> in co-operation with the International Committee of the Red Cross or other appropriate humanitarian agencies and distributed by them or under their supervision to ensure that they reach the intended beneficiaries.

Living with sanctions

Saddam was extremely sensitive to signs of popular discontent. He must have had serious doubts about his ability to resist the sanctions indefinitely, given that his success in the Iran–Iraq War depended on the financial help of Saudi Arabia and Kuwait, which had enabled him, by and large, to isolate the Iraqi public from the economic effects of the war. In the short run, however, the emergence of a new enemy at the gates gave him a crucial respite. Prior to the invasion of Kuwait, he had to deliver the promised economic reconstruction without delay. Once Iraq had been thrown again into a state of emergency, he could resort to his favourite technique of putting the blame for the consequences of his blunder on the victim, and asking his subjects to trade the hazardous present for a rosy picture of the future. As he put it: 'the large wealth and the future which will be secured after the victory is achieved, are contingent on the success of [your present sacrifices]'.[12]

He accompanied his rhetoric by nationwide measures aimed at strengthening the Iraqi morale and at demonstrating the intensity of Baghdad's resolve to resist the international sanctions. 'The Iraqis are ready to eat the soil and not to bow their heads to the aggressive invaders,' Saddam declared emphatically.[13] Yet he did everything within his power to prevent his subjects from having to resort to such desperate means. In a personal call to the Iraqi women 'to reorganize the family's economic life', Saddam pleaded that they spend only on the necessary victuals and see that 'the quantities of food placed in cooking pots and on the table would only meet the needs of our new life'.[14] In October, when his decision to ration gasoline and motor oil supplies aroused widespread discontent, he backtracked within days, sacking his Oil Minister on grounds of providing him with false information.[15]

To ensure an orderly supply of basic foodstuffs, Saddam resorted to his tried technique of the 'stick and the carrot'. On 11 August he decreed that hoarding of foodstuffs for commercial reasons would be considered 'a crime and an act of subversion that affected national and pan-Arab security' and would, therefore, be punishable by death. A month later the Revolutionary Command Council ordered the expropriation of private agricultural lands which were not cultivated 'in accordance with the scheduled agricultural density'. At the same time, the authorities began to issue the population ration cards for the purchase of basic foodstuffs.

Alongside these measures, Iraqi farmers were offered a series of incentives designed to induce them to increase their production. These included exemption of peasants from military reserve service and duties of the Popular Army, permission to cultivate certain state-owned lands, reduction in the prices of seeds and fertilizers, and higher financial returns for wheat, rice, and barley bought from farmers. Campaigns were launched to encourage conservation and higher production, and competitions were held to develop indigenous substitutes for food products. Within this framework, farmers and herdsmen were advised to substitute local fodder for imported feed-grains for cattle, while ordinary Iraqis were encouraged to take up fishing, start vegetable gardens and raise chickens.

The rationing system appeared efficient after it was introduced from 1 September. By this time Baghdad residents were already reporting long queues at bakeries and acute shortages of meat, flour, rice and powdered milk. Pastry shops were closing because of the lack of sugar while the prices of particular commodities, such as cooking oil, were skyrocketing. On the other hand, fresh fruit and vegetables remained plentiful.

A lot depended on whether, in combination with rationing, supplies were sufficient to maintain an acceptable standard of living for some time. When sanctions were first imposed the initial assumption was that they could bite deep in a matter of months because supplies were limited. As the import bill had been steady for a number of years there was no evidence of conscious preparation for a siege and so it was thought that there would be no more than two to four months of staple food supplies in store,[16] most of which would have come from the United States under its agricultural credit scheme. The OECD estimated that, with the harvest, supplies might be extended for eight months for wheat, two months for rice and less than a month for sugar; American estimates were four to five months for both wheat and rice.[17]

Given that the alternatives to sanctions appeared to be either appeasement or war, this sort of time-frame seemed to offer a reasonable hope of a satisfactory conclusion. Thus Mrs Thatcher observed that 'it will take time for sanctions to work ... it's just becoming obvious that some of them are beginning to work. I would think you need to have a look at it over a few months.'[18]

However, soon the estimates moved up. In the context of the debate in the United Nations over Iraq's requirement for 'humanitarian' food relief, Marjatta Rasi suggested that Iraq's supplies were 'plentiful, with enough to last anywhere from two months to more than six months'. The Americans gave an estimate of a year's stocks.[19] It was hard to judge private stocks of food but there was evidence that people had learned to keep their larders full during the war with Iran. It was also apparent that Iraq's readiness to plunder Kuwait, emptying its food warehouses and supermarkets was extending the stocks, as well as producing the paradoxical sight of stores in Baghdad offering luxury items rarely even seen before, while basic items were becoming scarce.

The main cause of this reassessment was Iraq's own food supply. The grain harvest had been assumed to suffice for between six weeks and two months in normal times, lasting possibly twice as long under rationing. However, as a result of earlier efforts to reduce the import bill, Iraq achieved a bumper wheat harvest in 1990 of 400,000 tonnes compared with only 100,000 in 1989. Moreover, it could well increase agricultural production further in 1991 as there was no shortage of water. The only limiting factor might be manpower shortages, resulting from the flight of foreigners and military conscription, when it came to constructing the irrigation works necessary to cope with soil salination.[20]

In late September the CIA concluded that 'in the short or medium term' sanctions would not drive Iraq from Kuwait. At about the same time the British Joint Intelligence Committee concluded that while 'weak spots' were developing, none was likely to bring down Saddam's regime.[21] The CIA estimate was later developed further in Congressional testimony in early December by William Webster, the CIA Director. He described the remarkable efficiency of the sanctions in technical terms. More than 90 per cent of imports and 97 per cent of exports had been shut off. Baghdad's financial resources had been 'choked off'. The loss of imports was severely affecting industrial production. Ordinary Iraqis were having to pay black market prices for staple foods or spend long hours in queues.

Despite all of this, the most vital industries, including electrical power generation and refining, did not yet appear to be threatened. New food coming into the shops from the harvest was providing a psychological boost as well as extending the longevity of the stockpiles. By the spring, foreign exchange reserves would be virtually exhausted so there would be little cash with which to entice smugglers. It would also become harder to keep basic services running, and this would only become possible if lower priority activities were shut down. Still, at reduced levels of consumption Iraq's food stocks could keep going until the spring, when the next harvest would become available. Depending on such factors as available seed stock and weather conditions, it could continue to expand production, even though it could never become self-sufficient.

This mixed picture meant that the political utility of sanctions did not appear to be matching the technical efficiency. Webster's summation gave little ground for optimism that the crisis could move to an early resolution solely through economic pressure:

> Despite mounting disruptions and hardships resulting from sanctions, Saddam apparently believes that he can outlast international resolve to maintain those sanctions. We see no indication that Saddam is concerned at this point that domestic discontent is growing to levels that may threaten his regime or that problems resulting from the sanctions are causing him to rethink his policy on Kuwait. The Iraqi people have experienced considerable deprivation in the past. Given the brutal nature of the Iraqi security services, the population is not likely to oppose Saddam openly.
>
> Our judgement has been and continues to be that there is no assurance or guarantee that economic hardships will compel Saddam to change his policies or lead to internal unrest that would threaten his regime.[22]

The question was one of time-span. Some specialists on sanctions judged the Iraqi case to be the most promising opportunity to demonstrate their efficacy in the twentieth century. Three Americans, who had undertaken pioneering and largely sceptical research in this area in the past, observed that:

> Historically, when the sanctioning country or group accounted for half or more of the target's trade, the sanctioners had a 50 per cent chance of achieving their goals. In the average successful sanctions case, the boycotters accounted for 28 per cent of the target's trade, far below the Iraqi situation.[23]

But they also noted that it all depended on what one was trying to achieve with the sanctions, and when the stakes were high so would be the resistance of the targeted country. This, they recognized, might be sustained for up to two years.

In practice, therefore, the economic weapon by itself seemed unlikely to bring Saddam to heel, at least during the time-frame in which it would also be possible to sustain the complementary political and military pressures, without which the sanctions themselves could not be maintained.

Economic measures were not a complete alternative to military action because they depended on military moves to enforce them. The American deployment into Saudi Arabia, while prompted by the fear of a second Iraqi aggression, was also motivated by the need to bolster up the kingdom so that it would dare to stand up to Iraq in implementing the embargo. Thus, rather than helping to avoid resort to a military option, sanctions helped make a military option more feasible.

It was the stark nature of the Iraqi challenge which made it possible to organize such a tight sanctions regime – but because it was so stark the resultant pressure was insufficient to sway the Iraqi leader. For their greatest influence, sanctions need to be linked to either a significant local opposition in Iraq, which could build on any discontent, or else a promising diplomacy which Saddam could use to extract his country from the distress his actions had caused it. Neither condition seemed to be available.

PART FOUR

All Necessary Means

CHAPTER 14
The Offensive Option

The first weeks of the crisis were taken up with reacting to the shock of the seizure of Kuwait, moving forces to the Gulf, organizing the sanctions regime, orchestrating diplomatic activity through the United Nations and coming to terms with the hostage crisis. Once Iraq had been isolated, economically and politically, thoughts began to turn to the next possible stage – war.

The President had received broad political support. There had been early questions about the readiness to accept either casualties or a protracted crisis,[1] but gradually confidence grew that as Saddam had not struck when he had the opportunity, then he would probably not do so at all. With many commentators not appreciating the enormous logistical challenge involved in Desert Shield, as early as the third week of the crisis an imminent war was widely touted. This expectation grew around three developments. The first was the question of enforcing the UN embargo, and the action to be taken to stop Iraqi tankers. When asked about this, and before he had agreed to a new UN resolution, Bush responded purposefully to press queries: 'You just watch. You just watch and see.' The second tension-raising development was Iraq's demand to all countries that they close their embassies in Kuwait City by 24 August. Most refused, and some, such as the United States, Britain and France, also refused to remove their personnel. If the Iraqis had stormed the embassies some response would have been necessary: in fact they chose to lay siege. Finally, there was the anger at the seizure of hostages, very much reflected at the time in Bush's pronouncements. A *Wall Street Journal*/NBC poll showed 70 per cent of Americans prepared to attack Iraq if it mistreated or imprisoned American hostages, with only slightly fewer (67 per cent) ready to attack in response to Iraqi sponsorship of terrorism.[2]

However, the Administration was in no position to launch a full offensive and had no intention of doing so. It was not until the start of September that the basic defensive force of 40,000 men was in place. The pre-positioned ships based in the Indian Ocean were able to get to Saudi Arabia and unload basic stores for the Army and Air Force within days of Desert Shield having been set in motion, but the sheer scale of the proposed deployment required stretching air and sea lift capabilities to the limit, drawing in civilian aircraft and ships, including some of Second World War vintage.[3] The bulk of the personnel could be carried by air but only 5 per cent of the cargo. The sea lift was hampered by delays in ready reserve ships being activated and by greater demands than expected as a result of units taking extra equipment and stores. Further pressure resulted from the decision to concentrate on combat rather than support capabilities in the first days, and then by a doubling of the local supply requirements from thirty to sixty days. If it had not been for the quality of Saudi ports and airfields the delays could have been extremely severe.

In late August, in an effort to calm the war speculation, Scowcroft stressed sanctions as a 'clear policy with clear objectives' which would need time to take effect. 'We have our strategy in place. Let's see if it works.'[4] Bush's belligerent rhetoric was toned down and there was more talk about giving diplomacy a chance and completing the original build-up. When the President was asked at the end of August whether Saddam should be overthrown, he insisted on the need to 'get on with the business at hand, the shorter-run business . . . of making right the situation in Kuwait'. Scowcroft underlined the point: 'We can't necessarily solve all of the problems relevant to Saddam Hussein, some of which go back a number of years, like his possession of chemical weapons and so forth.'[5] In Saudi Arabia General Schwarzkopf called the Iraqi generals 'a bunch of thugs' but also said 'there's not going to be any war unless the Iraqis attack'.[6]

'I can't sort of dice with weeks and months,' observed British Foreign Secretary Douglas Hurd, lauding the virtues of patience and firmness. No member of the Western–Arab coalition was in 'an unreasonable rush', for 'everybody knows the military option is a destructive option'. Saddam needed time to appreciate the parlousness of his position: 'The stranglehold, the noose, will gradually tighten until they have withdrawn from Kuwait.'[7] Thus, although Thatcher's rebukes to her European allies for their feeble response to the Iraqi aggression resulted in some counter-accusations (such as that from Spanish Premier Felipe Gonzalez – 'We don't have the same warmongering ardour she is capable of at times'), in practice there was 'no sign of a war party in the British Government'.[8]

In Kuwait the Iraqis also seemed to be preparing for a long haul. The Revolutionary Guard divisions had been pulled back behind a defensive belt manned primarily by infantry and artillery. By the middle of August there were 150,000 Iraqis in Kuwait with an estimated two divisions of 30,000 men in Kuwait City itself. A crescent-shaped defensive line facing the Gulf indicated that their main concern was an amphibious assault. Forces on the western border were more thinly spread. In late August, when General Powell was asked to characterize the Iraqi deployment in Kuwait as offensive or defensive, he described it as 'ambiguous'. With tanks and artillery, it was 'a very capable force that does have the capability to go on the offence'.[9] However, in reality Saddam's offensive option was rapidly declining.

By the middle of September the American troop numbers were reaching 150,000 and there was a formidable array of air power in place. The *New York Times* reported that 'at the Pentagon they talk about October 15'.[10] After that point President Bush would have the makings of an offensive option. A cursory reading of the American trade press would have revealed growing confidence with regard to the ability to mount devastating strikes against strategic targets in Iraq. Saddam felt sufficiently disturbed to convene a meeting of the Revolutionary Command Council to discuss a war strategy, including an extension of the conflict to Israel and the Saudi oilfields. There were public warnings as to the dire consequences for the coalition of any attempt to liberate Kuwait. It was at this point that his chieftains began threatening the coalition with the 'mother of all battles'.[11] In addition, forces were pouring into Kuwait and southern Iraq, and soon troop levels were reported to have reached 430,000, and they were digging in.[12]

Despite all the speculation, the Administration was only just beginning to think about an offensive war plan: none was yet available for execution, apart from a strategic air campaign in the event of an early emergency. On 25 August, Schwarzkopf had briefed Cheney and Powell on an outline offensive operation which involved the obvious principle of achieving air superiority and then isolating Iraqi ground forces in Kuwait. However, it was assumed that it would take another eight months before this operation would be ready to go. More serious planning was prompted by the need to think beyond the first stage of the Desert Shield deployments which would be completed by 1 December. In early October Powell asked that a decision be taken as to whether there would be continued deployments thereafter. Along with James Baker, he was certainly not over-enthusiastic with regard to direct military action, at least not before it was clear that the economic strategy was failing. His main concern was that if the President did wish to go further he should be fully aware of the risks involved and the need for sufficient forces to do the job properly. It was evident that Bush, reinforced by Scowcroft, was becoming impatient and increasingly pessimistic with regard to the effectiveness of sanctions. On 9 October he aired his doubts publicly:

Sanctions will take time to have their full intended effect. We shall continue to review all options with our allies, but let it be clear, we will not let this aggression stand. Iraq will not be permitted to annex Kuwait. And that's not a threat, it's not a boast, it's just the way it's going to be.[13]

The offensive option

Though Bush now wanted a briefing on an offensive option, none was available. On 6–8 October, Army Chief Carl Vuono flew to Saudi Arabia to see Schwarzkopf, who, having read the press speculations, was becoming anxious; he thought he had explained that the planned defensive deployment – which was still far from complete – was not suited to an offensive operation. Schwarzkopf spelled out his misgivings in a press interview:

Now we are starting to see evidence that the sanctions are pinching. So why should we say, 'Okay, gave 'em two months, didn't work. Let's get on with it and kill a whole bunch of people?' That's crazy. That's crazy . . .[14]

When Schwarzkopf's Chief-of-Staff, Marines Major-General Robert B. Johnston, presented the first ideas for an offensive option, on 10 October, he took care to emphasize that there had been little time for a serious staff effort.

The plan was in four overlapping phases. Phase One was a series of air attacks against Iraqi command, control and communications, the Iraqi air force and air defence system, and chemical, biological and nuclear weapons facilities. Phase Two would be intensive bombardment of the infrastructure, such as supply lines and stores, supporting Iraqi ground forces. In the third phase, the air attack would move on to Iraqi ground force positions. These phases would overlap somewhat. As early as a week after Phase One, the fourth, and last, phase would begin – a ground assault against the Iraqi forces in Kuwait.[15]

The airpower aspects of the campaign, which were natural extensions of the plans developed for defensive operations, raised few problems. This, after all, was the area of greatest American strength. The problems arose with the ground attack, which involved a single corps attack at night, overwhelming Iraqi defences to reach the high ground north of the Mutla Pass and Ridge. Paul Wolfowitz recalls feeling that 'this looks a bit like the charge of the Light Brigade'.[16] To have any chance of working, all units would have to be at the right place at the right time. If anything went wrong nothing could be done to defend Saudi Arabia because all the reserves would have been used up.

In response to a series of queries concerning the directness of the assault against the enemy's strongest positions and the lack of any use of mobility to move west and outflank Iraqi forces, Johnston explained the limitations imposed by the planned size of the American force and the initial terrain analysis, which suggested that the Iraqi desert was 'too soft and wet for the support vehicles to carry the necessary supplies'. Schwarzkopf had not intended the plan to be convincing. His message was clear: ground forces were insufficient to guarantee success.

The next day Johnston briefed Bush and his top advisers. The response was exactly the same as the previous day. Why, asked Scowcroft, go 'force-on-force'? Why not 'go around and come in from the side'? Johnston again stressed the problem. More forces were needed, and if they were going to be suitable for offensive operations, bringing them just from Europe would take at least a couple of months.[17] The period to aim for, he suggested, was between 1 January and 15 February. After that point operations could be hampered by the weather – first rains and then intense heat – and the Islamic religious holidays. On 17 March the holy month of Ramadan would begin and then in June there was the annual pilgrimage to Mecca. Johnston took care not to argue that the timing of war should simply be determined by the weather.

After this meeting the Pentagon began its own analyses of the flanking option. At Riyadh, Schwarzkopf had already briefed his planning cell to work up ideas along those lines. In the joint planning on the defence of Saudi Arabia, which had only begun in earnest on 13 September, Schwarzkopf had argued the need for a mobile defence rather than the Saudi preference for a more static defence based on strong-points.[18] The American debates on manoeuvre warfare over the previous decade, embodied in 1986 in the Field Manual FM-100-5 Operations (Air-Land Battle), and the evident desire to avoid the casualties that would follow from a head-on confrontation, meant that it was natural for the coalition's operational plan to turn on what came to be known as the 'left hook'. The basic issue was feasibility. Could the necessary forces be made available, would the terrain support such a wide encirclement and would Saddam realize what was up in time to redeploy his forces? Schwarzkopf hoped that he could keep the attention of the Iraqi commanders focused firmly on the sea by ordering rehearsals of major amphibious landings, but he never had any serious intention of mounting a landing because of the high casualties that would inevitably result. The potential of strikes launched from Turkey or Syria, or through Jordan, were examined seriously in the Pentagon but were never runners because of their obvious political problems.[19]

The immediate assessment in Washington, after Bush had received the briefing on 11 October, was that the basic concept for a ground attack must be a wide envelopment of Iraqi forces to the west. The next step was to explore the extra strength needed to realize the offensive option. On 21 October Powell visited Schwarzkopf to inform him of the decision and to assess his requirements. These, he was told, involved a doubling of all his planned air, sea and ground forces. The key shift was to move from a one- to a two-corps attack. Against the higher logistics and planning demands there was the fundamental advantage of the prospect of a decisive defeat for the Iraqis. To bolster his offensive capability he wanted the VII Corps based in Europe, with its two heavy tank and one mechanized divisions.

While this was going on Bush had to return to his domestic responsibilities. For much of October he was preoccupied with the poor state of the economy and protracted budget negotiations (which included the President reneging on his election pledge not to raise taxes). With uncertainty over Gulf policy his standing in the polls was in decline. His approval rating, which had jumped almost twenty points to 76 per cent in the first few weeks of the crisis, was down to 60 per cent, and support on Gulf policy had also slipped from 76 per cent to 57 per cent.[20] It was not until late October that Bush was able to concentrate again on the Gulf. By this time the campaign for the Congressional elections on 6 November was well under way and he did not feel able to introduce a controversial question of extra forces.

The main concern up to this point, prompted by reports of boredom and low morale in the desert, was over the rotation of troops so that units could be relieved. Training requirements meant that this would be problematic if moving to an offensive strategy.

Nonetheless, even before Powell had reported back from his Saudi visit, Cheney began to prepare the political ground. On 25 October he told ABC that 'we are not at the point yet where we want to stop adding forces'. When then asked on CBS if the Pentagon was getting ready to send another 100,000 troops, he agreed that 'it's conceivable that we'll end up with that big an increase'.[21] An inquiry from the Senate Armed Services Committee, to whom Cheney had testified the day before, produced the observation that there had never been a formal cap on troop numbers.

On 30 October Bush met with Baker, Cheney, Quayle, Sununu, Scowcroft and Powell to decide on whether to switch to the offensive option. For the first time he was briefed on the concept of holding Saddam's forces with an initial attack while they were being cut off by a flanking attack to the west. To achieve this, the planned forces would need to be doubled. If he wished to avoid casualties, then flanking attacks would be necessary and this would require a strong armoured force, which would take up to three months to get in place and would be expensive, with the transportation system acting as the major constraint. As can be seen from Table 5, the extra elements, in addition to those originally scheduled to be deployed under Desert Shield, were in the key offensive forces – strike aircraft, heavy armoured brigades, aircraft carriers.

Table 5: Planned force levels for defensive and offensive options

FORCES	DEFENSIVE 5 DECEMBER 1990	OFFENSIVE 15 JANUARY 1991
USAF		
Air-to-air	111	195
Dual role	240	426
Air-to-ground	339	477
Attack helicopters	272	383
GROUND FORCES		
Heavy brigades	7	17
Light infantry brigades	6	6
Mobile expeditionary force elements	1	3
Marine amphibious brigades	1	2
US NAVAL FORCES		
Aircraft carriers	3	6
Battleships	1	2
Cruisers	7	13
Destroyers, frigates	11	20
Amphibious ships	13	31

Source: CENTCOM.

Powell told Bush that he did not 'do marginal economic analysis looking for crossover points. I go in with enough to make sure ... we're not operating in the margin.' He intended to 'win decisively'.[22] Cheney also opposed incrementalism. He wanted to get the build-up over with and not return regularly with requests for extra forces. Bush reportedly concurred: 'If that's what you need, we'll do it.'[23]

Decision-making

This critical decision, like so many others during the crisis, was taken by a relatively small number of people. By this time the Bush Administration's decision-making had matured into a four-layered process. The first layer was the Deputies Committee, the routine crisis management group, which was chaired by Scowcroft's Deputy, Robert Gates. This included not only the core agencies of State, Defence, Chiefs-of-Staff, the Security Council staff and the CIA, but also the Attorney-General, representatives from the Treasury and occasionally from Commerce and other agencies. Admiral David Jeremiah was Colin Powell's representative. The next layer was a small group, taken from the Deputies Committee, but involving only the core agencies plus Richard Haass of the NSC staff. This group framed many of the key papers and issues for the inner Cabinet. There was also a separate economic steering group led by Lawrence Eagleburger of the State Department, which included John Robinson of the Treasury and Don Atwood of Defence, and which concentrated on the burden sharing issue. The Deputies Committee met daily and sometimes twice or three times a day. Richard Haass drafted most of the papers for this committee. They would often go through two or three versions before being sent up to the principals in the so-called 'gang of eight'.

This was the third layer. The 'gang' consisted of the President plus his closest advisers – Vice-President Dan Quayle, White House Chief-of-Staff John Sununu, National Security Adviser Brent Scowcroft, Secretary of State James Baker, Secretary of Defense Richard Cheney, Chairman of the Joint Chiefs-of-Staff Colin Powell, and Robert Gates, who acted as the link with the Deputies Committee. The fourth layer was the President himself, who brought to bear his own particular combination of restlessness, uncertainty and determination when it came to pushing the process along or taking initiatives.

At the Deputies level there was a close understanding of the nature of the international coalition that had been put together and the requirements for sustaining it. The requirements of American domestic politics were less well understood. Here the 'gang' were more competent, especially Quayle, Sununu and the President himself. When the first key decisions were taken in early August, there had been little opportunity for serious discussion with Congress. However, the nature of both Saddam's aggression and the

American deployment meant that Bush's actions were widely supported and there was comparatively little dissent. Now Bush was proposing to double the US deployment and move from a defensive to an offensive mode. The implications for the United States were startling, yet little attempt had been made to develop a political consensus. As the key Administration players had been working through their own personal odyssey, the wider political community had been preoccupied first with the complex executive-legislative budget negotiations and then with the Congressional election campaign.

The actual announcement had to be delayed until Baker could consult with King Fahd and get his permission for the extra troops on Saudi soil. The Saudis, by and large, preferred a strike to come earlier rather than later, but they were nervous about the domestic consequences of continuing to host such a large Western presence on their soil. This decision meant that the American stay might be shorter but the immediate impact would be larger. There had also been public statements to the effect that US forces would not be allowed to invade Iraq to rescue hostages or to drive Iraq out of Kuwait. The Defence Minister, Prince Sultan (who had been opposed to the American deployment in Saudi Arabia and who later in October made more dovish statements), insisted that the kingdom was 'not a theatre for any action that is not defensive for Saudi Arabia'.[24]

Other Governments also needed to be consulted. Even the British, who were generally kept well informed about trends in Administration thinking, were surprised. They had been having a parallel debate about the feasibility of sanctions and the force levels required, but this had not yet come to a head.[25] The British had indeed assumed that the most likely time for the use of armed force was mid-November. Air Chief Marshal Sir Patrick Hine, in overall charge of Britain's Gulf forces, though based in Britain, had ordered his own studies when the Government had decided to send the 7th Armoured Brigade in September and concluded that an enveloping manoeuvre would make most sense,[26] but at the time detailed planning in the Brigade still assumed a direct breaching attack. Hine had met with Schwarzkopf and was aware of the latter's determination to get reinforcements, but he could not have been given details on the scale of these reinforcements, for this was just before Powell's visit, and he did not know what he would get. The initial reaction in Britain to the news of the doubling of forces was that getting the extra units to the front risked excessive delay to the start of the operation. When Baker reached Moscow on 8 November he heard that Bush was about to announce the new strategy. He tried to get a delay so as to allow more time for domestic and international opinion to be prepared, but the White House wanted to end the speculation.

An announcement during the last stages of the election campaign would have undermined what prospects there might have been for a bipartisan approach but so did a lack of consultation. The first that the most important members of Congress knew about the shift in policy was a phone call just before the formal announcement – in Senator Nunn's case, in a restaurant. Bush announced the doubling of forces to create an 'offensive military option' on the basis that Iraq had not responded to a succession of UN resolutions, that Kuwait was struggling for survival and because 'Iraq's aggression is not just a challenge to the security of Kuwait and other Gulf nations, but to the better world that we all have hoped to build in the wake of the Cold War.'[27] The crisis had moved to a higher and more dangerous stage.

CHAPTER 15

The Great Debate

The announcement on the doubling of US forces in the Gulf came as a surprise. Apart from Richard Cheney's one signal, there had been little preparation of public opinion for the dramatic switch in strategy conveyed in the President's short statement. Bush did not like making speeches – he was not a 'great communicator' like Reagan. No effort was made to turn the announcement into a big occasion, with advance briefings and an opportunity to provide a thorough rationale for the new strategy. Those who might have been brought round to an appreciation of its logic had not been consulted and felt themselves therefore to be under no obligation to give support. Particularly annoyed was Senator Sam Nunn of Georgia, Chairman of the Senate Armed Services Committee, one of the most respected Congressional voices on defence issues and no dove. He immediately called a series of hearings which provided a forum for a sustained challenge to Administration policy.

The bipartisan basis of policy was lost. That weekend saw a series of intensive reactions from Democrat politicians alarmed at what they judged to be the President's sudden lurch to war. An opinion poll just after Bush's press conference of 8 November showed that only 41 per cent felt that they had been given a satisfactory explanation of why extra troops were being sent to the Gulf, compared with 60 per cent satisfaction with the explanations for the original deployment in August. There was declining confidence in resolving the crisis without fighting, but the Administration was judged too hasty in its move to an offensive option. There was still a clear, though declining, majority for troops in Saudi Arabia, but a slight majority opposed the latest increases. For Bush the poll was also troubling as it showed a decline in his approval rating for the handling of the crisis. In August it had reached 75 per cent. By October it was already down to 59 per cent. Now it just touched 50 per cent.[1]

The next two months were taken up with a great debate over whether the issues at stake in the Gulf were worth war.[2] The politics of the question concerned whether or not Bush would be forced to seek a compromise because of a lack of domestic support, and the impact of this possibility on the calculations of the rest of the coalition as well as on Saddam. The concern that the President might well 'wobble' in these circumstances meant that he was put under pressure by hawks as well as doves. As we shall see in the next chapter, throughout this period Bush's diplomacy was influenced by the need to demonstrate reasonableness. In the end, however, Saddam's intransigence meant that Bush was not faced with any awkward compromises and was able to obtain just enough Congressional support.

The problem facing Bush stemmed not only from poor presentation of policy but also from its internal contradictions. In part these reflected the basic tension between the 'Kuwait problem' and the 'Saddam problem', but they were also due to the unwillingness to rely solely on Bush's own geopolitical rationale for reversing the Iraqi occupation of Kuwait and a search for an additional rationale that would prove persuasive to the American people.

Opposing aggression

There seems little doubt that Bush was influenced most of all by the need to uphold the principle of non-aggression and the analogy with the failure of appeasement in the 1930s. This remained a seminal experience for Bush's generation (and for that matter Margaret Thatcher's and François Mitterrand's). The President himself tended to describe the crisis in these terms. When he spoke to Congressmen the day he took his decision on doubling forces, he reported that he had been reading Martin Gilbert's lengthy history of the Second World War.

The rule that the stronger should not devour their weaker neighbours, and that borders between states should not be changed through armed force, was why Iraq was so clearly isolated in the United Nations. It was part of Saddam's case that Kuwait had been an artificial entity and, in consequence, that its boundary with Iraq was illogical and lacked historical justification. This contention was in itself dubious, but even if valid to act upon it would produce an awkward precedent, for around the world there are numerous comparable disputes.

Only the most diehard supporters of Saddam argued in favour of one state being allowed to take over another by force. Even Cuba and Yemen voted in the Security Council against the annexation of Kuwait. So there was little doubt that an important principle of international relations was at stake. As it was affirmed in a series of United Nations resolutions, this was also of some significance to those who have criticized Western policy in the past for its neglect of the UN. Resisting aggression provided the classic basis for a 'just war'.

Nonetheless, there were a number of arguments used to question the firm application of the principle in this case. One was that the Kuwaiti regime lacked legitimacy and had brought the crisis upon itself through its provocative behaviour during the first half of 1990. Examination of the al-Sabah regime made it clear that this was no paragon of democracy, and that the Kuwaitis themselves had shown greed and insensitivity in the past. In this they were not unusual in the Middle East. It was also pointed out that a number of the Arab members of the coalition scored badly on human rights.[3] However, it had never been claimed by the Bush Administration that democracy was at stake in the Gulf, and in fact the Kuwaiti regime in many ways had been comparatively mild and generous when compared with some of its neighbours.[4] Nor was a principle very impressive if there was only going to be a response when the victims were nice, inoffensive souls. As the philosopher Michael Walzer observed, 'aggression is always an attack on the status quo'. Resisting it does not endorse the status quo – all that is required is that 'it be changed by other means and by different people'.[5]

Another dubious precept was that rules which cannot be enforced completely should not be enforced at all. However, the accusation that opposition to aggression tended to be extremely selective was damaging, especially in the Middle East. The response to Saddam's aggression was 'unprecedented', thundered Noam Chomsky, only 'because he stepped on the wrong toes'. A number of examples of double standards could be cited, including Syria's involvement in Lebanon, the 1974 Turkish partition of Cyprus and, from outside the region, the Indian takeover of Goa and the Indonesian of East Timor.[6] Another two examples revolved around the failure to act against Iraq's attack on Iran in 1980, compounded by the courting of Saddam since the early 1980s,[7] and Israel's occupation of Arab territories since 1967. Israel, complained one critic, had been violating the UN Charter 'every month and every day and every week'.[8]

As shown earlier, the comparison with Israel was particularly sensitive in the Middle East, but not so much in the United States where there was sympathy for Israel's security predicament. The comparison at any rate was not exact.[9] The case of the Iraqi invasion of Iran in 1980 was different in that it was used to suggest that Iraqi misbehaviour was condemned only when it suited the West to do so. Unlike the invasion of Kuwait, there were mitigating circumstances in 1980. Revolutionary Iran was generally considered to be a dangerous state and was attempting to subvert the regime in Iraq.

Nonetheless, the muted objections to what was still overt aggression, and the general attempt by Western countries to ingratiate themselves with Baghdad in the search for large contracts, did not provide an impressive backdrop to a principled stand in 1990. Yet, as in the 1930s, past appeasement provided no grounds against taking on a dictator when the nature of his regime became impossible to ignore – it only made the task more difficult. The West was paying for past over-indulgence of Saddam Hussein, but that in itself was no reason to continue the practice.

The final type of qualification to the principle of non-aggression was that it was being applied in the Kuwait case only as a cover for less elevated motives. Even if justified, this charge would not invalidate the principle. Virtuous acts do not cease to be so even when prompted by non-virtuous purposes. Slogans such as that used by the anti-war protest movement in the United States of 'no blood for oil' neatly side-stepped the whole question of aggression. A number of hawks, as well as doves, also felt more comfortable with the hard realism implied by an economic rationale. They judged it entirely proper to contemplate war for the sake of energy supplies. They agreed with the doves only that the simple principle of opposing aggression served as an inadequate justification and an unconvincing explanation.

Oil was obviously an extremely relevant factor in the crisis. If it were not for oil, Kuwait would not have been invaded in the first place, nor would the Americans have moved so resolutely to defend Saudi Arabia. Given America's dependence on foreign oil, it was not a complete caricature to suggest that troops were sent initially to the desert 'to retain control of oil in the hands of a pro-American Saudi Arabia, so prices will remain low', although it is doubtful that many of those involved in the decision considered their own motives to be primarily economic.[10]

How important oil was in influencing the decision to liberate Kuwait was less clear. The Iraqis were happy to stress their readiness to sell oil to the United States. They were price hawks, but if they were not controlling Saudi reserves then their ability to push the price up would be limited. Moreover, the prospect of war amid the oilfields had made markets jittery, and many warned that the oil price would reach historic highs in the event of a war which, for example, could see serious damage inflicted on the Saudi oilfields. Nonetheless, the importance of secure oil supplies was stressed by the Administration and its supporters, although they also oscillated with regard to the importance it deserved. Thus one week (16 October) Bush insisted that there was no concern about oil, only aggression, while the next (22 October) he warned how 'our jobs, our way of life, our own freedom, would all suffer if control of the world's great oil reserves fell into the hands of that one man, Saddam Hussein'.

The 'Saddam problem' and the new world order

One of the reasons why Bush could claim that a stronger stand could now be taken on the principle of non-aggression was the fundamental change that had taken place in the international system, most notably the end of the cold war. Now that it was possible to co-operate with Moscow, there was no need to judge every regional issue in terms of its relevance for the superpower confrontation and the United Nations could be made to work as originally intended. When Bush announced the Desert Shield deployment of 8 August he spoke of a 'new era', which could be 'full of promise, an age of freedom, a time of peace for all peoples', and which would be put at risk if there was a failure to resist aggression.[11] Over that month his ideas started to crystallize, especially as he became more trusting of Soviet policy and confident in the United Nations. On 23 August, the day after it had been decided to go for a UN vote on the enforcement of the embargo and not push ahead uni-laterally, Bush had a long discussion with Scowcroft during a not very fruitful fishing expedition off Kennebunkport, on the implications of Third World crises not invariably becoming a 'test of wills' between Washington and Moscow.[12] His ideas were then given public expression in an address to Congress on 12 September, when he added an extra objective – a 'new world order' – to American policy in the Gulf. This was 'a unique and extra-ordinary moment'. Though 'grave', the crisis offered 'a rare opportunity to move toward an historic period of co-operation'.[13]

If the exuberant language was taken at face value Bush was promising an impossibly complete transformation in international politics. It was easy to point out that much of the old political game would go on as before. To get the necessary votes in the United Nations and hold together the anti-Iraq coalition, it was imperative to help sustain Gorbachev in power even as the bases of communist rule crumbled beneath him, to forget the Chinese massacre in Tiananmen Square and to find common cause with Asad of Syria.[14]

Americans might feel that they had reason to wonder whether theirs was the only country actually interested in this new world order. As evidence of growing domestic problems mounted, the lack of effort of other richer nations, such as Japan and Germany, was used to suggest that the United States was being taken for a ride. This charge was eased by the Administra-tion's efforts to draw as many nations as possible into the coalition, obliging those who were unwilling to send forces at least to contribute funds. Bush was himself concerned about the rising cost of Desert Shield, which was running at an average of $28.9 million a day by the end of August. In September a high-level group was sent to get the Japanese, Germans and others to contribute funds. Despite some success, the grumbling did not cease. In November, Representative Les Aspin, Chairman of the House Armed Services Committee, rated the contributions made by other nations to the action against Iraq. Only Turkey and Egypt got A while Germany and Japan got C.

> If Americans are critical today of the relative unwillingness of others – chiefly Europeans and Japanese – to share the burden of this confrontation, imagine how critical – even furious – they are likely to be when they see few others paying the bloodprice.[15]

Particular irritation was generated by a feeling that the Gulf kingdoms, including Kuwait, were taking American military support for granted. The noted liberal historian Arthur Schlesinger Jr took up in the *Wall Street Journal* a quote from a Gulf diplomat chuckling that his teenage son would not have to die for Kuwait – 'We have our white slaves from America to do that' – to conclude that the involvement in the Gulf was 'increasing Arab contempt for the US'.[16] The idea that the United States had been reduced to providing mercenaries for feudal Gulf rulers, reinforced by the 'tin-cup exercise', could be presented as being degrading rather than the pursuit of a noble idea of world order.

William Pfaff warned of the characteristic American errors of 'moralization of the war and demonization of the enemy', being unwilling 'to accept conflicts on their own terms', so that each is 'held to be of vast significance, and any failure or compromise is said to threaten disaster in series'.[17] By putting the future of the world at stake in this particular instance, Bush could be criticized for setting himself impossible standards. This criticism grew in force with each additional requirement for the 'new world'. For example, if 'just treatment for all peoples' was to be a central value, then this would require an unprecedented degree of intervention in the internal affairs of other states which could give the impression of an attempt to refashion the world according to Western values.

However, this was not Bush's intention. Indeed, his political instincts warned him against getting too involved in Third World disputes. The Panama experience, in which the drug-trafficking and corruption he had sought to eradicate through the intervention and seizure of General Manuel Noriega had soon resurfaced, warned against any attempt to impose change on very different societies. The new world order was less a charter for universal human rights than a belief that traditional rights of states could now be protected if the world's great powers could both show respect themselves and demand it from others.

Understanding Bush's concept helps make sense of his approach to the 'Saddam problem'. Just as had been the case before the crisis broke, he showed little interest in the effect of Saddam's regime on the Iraqi people. He would have been prepared to continue to turn a blind eye to the internal repression and the persecution of the Kurds if Saddam had been prepared to play a more responsible role in regional affairs. There was no attempt to cultivate an alternative Iraqi leadership or show support for Kurdish aspirations. Bush and his advisers could see problems flowing from a close association with the Kurds because of the implications of Kurdish autonomy for Turkey, or with the Shi'ite community because the Saudis still felt more comfortable with the minority Sunni élite, and there was also no desire to encourage the sort of Islamic fundamentalism that had caused so much grief in Iran.

The problem with Saddam was that he was aggressive. Bush showed himself to be enormously moved by the reports of Iraqi atrocities within Kuwait because this illustrated precisely why aggression was so terrible and had to be opposed. On 21 September he was shown intelligence material demonstrating the extent to which Iraq was systematically plundering and dismantling Kuwait. A week later the President and his advisers met the Emir of Kuwait in the Oval Office, in a meeting intended to demonstrate that there could be no compromise over the position of the al-Sabah regime in Kuwait. It seems, however, to have had a more significant impact. The Emir described, in 'quiet, almost under-stated terms', how Kuwait was being steadily dismantled and depopulated, through murder and forced emigration. He told of Kuwait being raped, of people being pulled from their homes, tortured and killed.

The effect was quite emotional. For Bush and his officials this came as a timely reminder that at stake was more than just 'abstractions and principles' but also the fate of thousands of people. When Bush discussed the visit with Mrs Thatcher, the Prime Minister's adviser noted that he had 'rarely seen a man so moved to suppressed fury and disgust by what he had heard, and I think it became a very important part of his overall approach to resolving this problem'. According to Scowcroft, it reinforced rather than created a tendency in the President's thinking by bringing home Kuwait's fate in personal terms.[18] It emphasized that the process could reach a point where Kuwait could not be put back together again. There was thereafter an increased sense of a time limit: the longer the liberation took the less would be left of Kuwait.

Briefing reporters after the meeting, Scowcroft warned that Iraq's 'systematic destruction' of occupied Kuwait was hastening the possibility of war. 'There is no question that what is happening inside Kuwait affects the timetable.' As the Emir departed, Bush said that

> we must keep all our options open to ensure Iraq's unlawful occupation of Kuwait is ended, and Kuwait's legitimate government secured.

Iraq had 'ransacked and pillaged a once-peaceful and secure country, its population assaulted, incarcerated, intimidated and even murdered'. All this made it more difficult for Bush to accept the argument that he must wait for sanctions.[19]

Inevitably a number of the stories were exaggerated, including one about babies being thrown out of incubators which were to be sent back to Iraq. It seems to have started when a hospital hid their incubators to keep them from the Iraqis, combined with the burial of a backlog of thirty foetuses and babies who had died from natural causes. Suspicion later grew when the Kuwaiti witness turned out to be the daughter of the Ambassador to the United States, coaxed by a public relations firm.[20]

Even though this story was embellished for public relations purposes, there was no reason to doubt that life in Kuwait was grim. In December, Amnesty International published a detailed report on 'the arbitrary arrest and detention without trial of thousands of civilians and military personnel; the widespread torture of such persons in custody; the imposition of the death penalty and the extrajudicial execution of hundreds of unarmed civilians, including children'.[21] The report's devastating account of abuses was made all the more credible because of the internal Iraqi record, and also because Iraq had rebuffed the efforts of a number of organizations, including Amnesty and the International Committee of the Red Cross, to investigate the charges. Bush appears to have been an avid reader and became even more convinced that this was a question of good versus evil.

There had been many similar reports before, from Amnesty and other authorities such as the UN Human Rights Commission, on Iraq and also on other Middle Eastern countries now working closely with the United States. Most had passed unnoticed. Bush obviously welcomed this report because it supported his case. This was not, however, purely cynical. It reflected a moral distinction between the abuses that a people might suffer from their own Government and those consequential on their occupation by a foreign Government. There were limits as to what the international community

1. Arab leaders meet in Baghdad in May 1990. Saddam Hussein sits between his foreign minister Tariq Aziz (right) and the Secretary-General of the Arab League, Chadli Klibi.

2. As Kuwait is annexed, PLO chairman Yasser Arafat jokes with Saddam Hussein, 9 August 1990.

3. 'Have you had your milk today?' Saddam with British hostage Stuart Lockwood.

4. The UN votes for 'all necessary means': Resolution 678 is passed by the Security Council, 29 November 1990.

5. Tariq Aziz smiles while James Baker keeps a straight face as they meet in Geneva, 9 January 1991.

6. UN Secretary-General Perez de Cuellar seeks a way out of the impasse. Baghdad, 13 January 1991.

7. Prime Minister John Major meets with President François Mitterrand,
14 January 1991.

8. As the war starts President Bush works the phone with his national security adviser
Brent Scowcroft and White House Chief of Staff John Sununu (left).

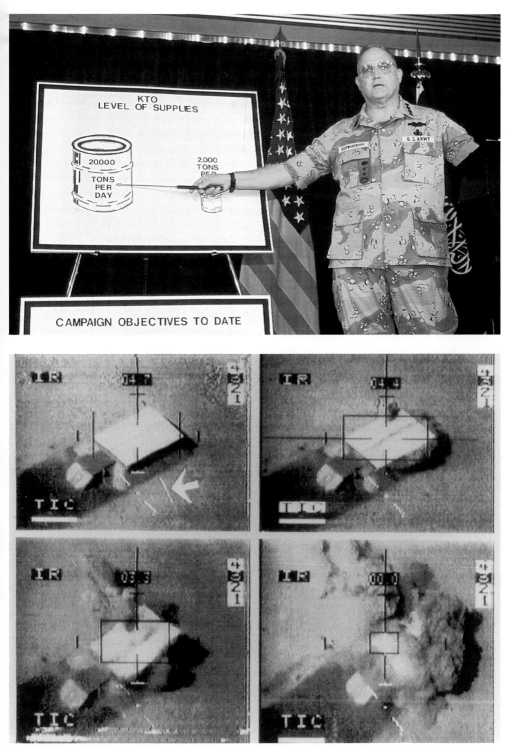

9. General Norman Schwarzkopf briefs reporters on the cutting of Iraqi supply lines.
Riyadh, 1 January 1991.

10. Target destroyed: the use of precision weapons in the air war.

13. Kuwait City is liberated with the oil wells burning in the background.

Opposite
11. Discussing the start of the ground campaign: Secretary of Defense
Richard Cheney meets with King Fahd of Saudi Arabia, 10 February 1991.

12. Chairman of the Joint Chiefs of Staff General Colin Powell faces Israeli pressure
from defence minister Moshe Arens for more action against the Scuds.

14. Schwarzkopf salutes Iraqi General Sultan Hashim Ahmad at the cease-fire talks at Safwan airbase, occupied Iraq, 3 March 1991.

could do about the former; it was basic to world order that every effort was made to prevent the latter.

This moral framework also helps explain Bush's regular comparisons between Saddam and Hitler, which began in August. At one point he even suggested that Saddam was the worse of the two.[22] Yet Bush was unwilling to solve the 'Saddam problem' in the way that the 'Hitler problem' had been solved in 1945, because he did not want to get involved in the restructuring of the Iraqi state. It was also clear that any attempt to 'get Saddam' in person would impose extra demands on any military operation. Far greater force would be required, as it would be necessary to take Baghdad.[23] The Iraqi leader had spent most of the 1980s fighting a war against an enemy which was quite explicitly pursuing his elimination, and it was evident that if stakes were raised too high then any concessions became impossible, for it would mean the end of Saddam's personal rule. So although Bush's rhetoric created the strong impression that Saddam was his target, at no point did he ever suggest that this was a formal objective. It was more that the descriptions of Saddam encouraged the view that this *should* be the objective or that, despite disclaimers, it actually was. Thus, when in mid-September the Chief-of-Staff of the US Air Force, General Michael Dugan, made some incautious remarks about plans to wage war against Saddam Hussein himself he was promptly sacked by Cheney.[24]

But if Saddam's regime was naturally aggressive, could the coalition afford to leave him in place even if, this time, he acceded to UN resolutions? The proposition that any outcome, including a pre-emptive Iraqi withdrawal, which left Saddam's regime wounded rather than eliminated would be harmful was promoted by Israel, but shared by most other countries in the region who, even if they could not say so directly, were finding it harder to imagine feeling secure so long as Saddam was in any position to cause trouble.

James Baker was pressed on the question of Iraq's post-withdrawal military potential by Congressman Stephen Solarz in early September. Baker agreed that this was very important and would need to be addressed as part of a new 'security structure' in the region. Solarz, dissatisfied, became more blunt: 'is it possible to eliminate the Iraqi nuclear, chemical and biological weapons programmes without physically destroying them?'[25] The Administration, however, could not argue against a settlement involving the evacuation of Kuwait on these grounds, but did begin to argue that Iraq's 'capacity for future aggression' must be part of any settlement with Iraq.[26]

How high a priority this could be was doubted. From October 1990 any solution which left Saddam's power intact habitually came to be described as the 'nightmare scenario'.[27] If the international community would find it hard to avoid giving Saddam diplomatic 'sweeteners' to ease his withdrawal from Kuwait, it was unlikely to insist on extra demands. This point was made forcefully by former Pentagon official Richard Perle:

> If Iraqi military power survives the current crisis, Iraq will dominate the Gulf. Saddam Hussein will press his thumb on the Western world's jugular whenever the spirit moves him. Every day that the West waits for the sanctions to take effect is a day in which it is exposed to the risk of a sudden diplomatic shift that enables Saddam Hussein's military to escape the noose.[28]

One of the most controversial elements of this potential was Saddam's nuclear programme. When questioned by Congress in September, Cheney claimed that the removal of Iraq's incipient nuclear capability was a long established objective of US policy.[29] However, before the invasion the best estimate was that Iraq would not acquire nuclear weapons for five to ten years, although there had been some stirrings in Congress to the effect that this estimate was too optimistic and had been toned down so as not to disrupt the policy of good relations with Iraq.[30] In July Israel had given Cheney some hard evidence of the faster than expected progress of Iraqi work on high-speed centrifuges designed to enrich uranium, and this had reinforced internal pressure for a new estimate.[31] A special intelligence estimate prepared for Bush in the autumn of 1990 reportedly concluded that it would take 'six months to a year, and probably longer'.[32] By the end of October, Iraq's nuclear programme had been clearly established as an objective. CIA Director William Webster observed that the Administration would have 'no real confidence that the area will ever be secure again' unless Saddam were 'disassociated from his weapons of mass destruction'.[33]

The case could therefore be made for denuding Iraq of its ability to make aggressive war, but there was still reluctance to make a case to remove the man whose ambitions and fears seemed likely to prompt this aggression. One route, consistent with a stress on international law, was suggested by Mrs Thatcher, but it ran up against the unwillingness, found as much in the British Foreign Office as the American State Department, to make commitments that could involve the occupation of Baghdad. The Prime Minister's approach was, if anything, more legalistic than President Bush's. Her tendency to boil issues down to a fundamental principle led her to describe objectives solely in terms of reversing the Iraqi occupation of Kuwait. This approach was widely supported in Britain, including the main opposition parties. Fighting aggressors can appear as almost a national calling in Britain.

Mrs Thatcher was nervous about too great a stress on oil supplies as a rationale, because this tended to cloud the basic issue of aggression and would not be sufficient to obtain public support for a long campaign, let alone direct military action. Talk of a 'new world order' was described as 'vague',[34] while even the attention to weapons of mass destruction was seen as 'clouding' the issue,[35] although she later changed her mind on this score. She also agreed that to make Saddam's regime the policy object rather than Kuwait risked alienating Arab support and setting unrealizable goals.[36]

The complication to this simple setting of objectives came with the hostage issue. This was a new crime, additional to the basic crime of aggression. Britain had more of its citizens held than any other Western country. Yet, as had been the case over British hostages in Lebanon, the Prime Minister stuck robustly to the principle that deals with 'criminals' should never be struck since they could only encourage 'criminality'. She felt confident enough to tell David Frost in early September[37] that holding hostages would be no bar to military action if this was judged necessary:

> If you allow the taking of hostages, terrible as it is, to determine your own action against a dictator, he has won, and all he will ever do, or anyone else with similar ambitions will ever do, is to take hostages knowing that other people will never take the requisite action to stop such a dictator.

Again reflecting her own legalistic inclinations, though not her legal advice, she sought to guarantee the safety of the hostages through deterrence – threatening retribution if they were harmed: 'We could do what we did at Nuremberg and prosecute the requisite people for their totally uncivilized and brutal behaviour . . . I don't want them to think they are going to get away with it, because they won't.' This idea struck a responsive chord with President Bush although the State Department also thought this a bad idea, if for no other reason than that it implied that the allies would have Saddam in their jurisdiction. In the end, the net result of this issue was a reference in Resolution 674 of 29 October, which dealt with Iraq's general responsibilities under international law, to the Fourth Geneva Convention and the liability of 'individuals who commit or order the commission of grave breaches'. This still avoided making Saddam himself the focus of coalition efforts. When Mrs Thatcher stated the essential objectives of policy towards Saddam at the Conservative Party Conference in October, the focus was on criminal acts rather than the criminal: 'you get him out, make him pay, and see that he is never in a position to do these things again'.[38]

Selling the threat

Bush did not have Thatcher's advantage in terms of public opinion. Britain might be doing more than most but its contribution to the management of the crisis was dwarfed by that of the United States. He was pushing the American people to accept unwelcome commitments and sacrifices without great presentational skills. His Secretary of State was also a man with a keen sense of domestic politics, whose technique was to accumulate persuasive arguments rather than stick to a single theme.

This difficulty was aggravated rather than eased by Bush's public opinion advisers. In October Robert Teeter, Bush's chief pollster, had warned that there were too many competing explanations around, but he and his staff were inclined to look for the explanations which attracted the highest public ratings. In terms of overall approach they noted that Bush seemed to be at his most natural when personalizing politics, whether in a positive sense in constructing the coalition, or negatively as in the 1988 campaign against Governor Dukakis; hence, his public relations advisers saw it as natural for Bush to make his case by picking on Saddam. The personal dimension was already well established, given Saddam's dominance of Iraqi politics. One working paper reportedly observed that, in contrast to President Reagan's unconvincing attempts to demonize Noriega and Gaddafi, the American public took Saddam Hussein a lot more seriously, not only because for them he was 'a bad guy', but because they saw him as a threat. Better still, Saddam did not even seem to care about his dark image in the United States. On the other hand, poll evidence suggested that the Hitler analogy for Saddam had not rung true because 'in the eyes of a majority of people, there couldn't be somebody more harmful than Hitler'.[39]

To Bush the point of the analogy with Hitler was as much about recalling the dangers of appeasing aggression as to make Saddam look evil. In agreeing to tone down this comparison, he was losing the one aspect of the personalizing approach that was relevant to his broad agenda while encouraging the view that the objective of policy was to deal with this particular individual. It accentuated the 'Saddam problem', for which Bush lacked a solution, at the expense of the 'Kuwait problem', for which he did. Teeter had observed that one of the arguments with the strongest appeal was fighting aggression, but he also noted that protecting the lives of Americans, and in particular the hostages, scored highly.[40]

The hostage issue certainly struck an emotive chord. However, the families of hostages were not arguing for the use of force, which they saw as putting their beloved ones at risk. Furthermore, this was essentially a secondary issue where Saddam could be conciliatory without compromising on the fundamentals, which is what he did in December. If the hostages had been used as the main argument to justify the potential use of force then this would have then been removed.

By apparently foraging for a compelling rationale, oscillating between a calculated act of self-interest or a moral crusade, the administration sowed confusion and obscured the central case of opposing aggression. Multiple rationales, each expounded with a different domestic constituency in mind, contributed to the aura of uncertainty which came to surround American policy. The advantage of sticking to a simple and basic objective was that there would be no doubt when it had been met. With multiple objectives, success could never be complete. A highly political approach to the setting of strategic objectives risked opening up a gap between ends and means.

In a speech on 29 October, stating that the Administration would 'not rule out a possible use of force if Iraq continues to occupy Kuwait', James Baker stressed that aggression must not be appeased. Saddam's version married contempt for civilized rules of behaviour with modern destructive methods, and if it was not opposed now there would be more aggression in the future. He pointed to 'what Saddam Hussein is doing to the people of Kuwait' – a story not told 'frequently enough' because Saddam 'controls access to the true story of Kuwait'. He also added points on stability and the Middle East, and then made a strong pitch on the question of hostages. Saddam was 'making political and economic war on our citizens still in Iraq and Kuwait', adding that 'the very idea of Americans being used as human shields is simply unconscionable'.[41]

Baker stressed the hostage issue the next day when he and Bush met with some fifteen Congressional leaders. This was just before the President made the decision on doubling forces. The legislators noted that Bush was more tense than they had seen him recently. They got the message that he was moving towards the use of military force but they were unclear as to why this was so. It was agreed that sanctions would take more time to work, but why not be patient? Even if it took another year this would still be preferable to force. The point about the destruction of Kuwait got lost in an argument about hostages instigated by Baker. The Congressmen were surprised. The hostages did not seem to be being maltreated. Was not deprivation of liberty maltreatment? responded Baker. Yes, they agreed, but so it was three months ago. What had changed in the condition of the hostages to justify this new tough attitude? Speaker Tom Foley remembers the meeting as 'the most contentious' of those that took place at the White House. He concluded: 'Mr President, be cautious before you lead the country to war,' and left aware of a new mood but without a hint that a decision had been taken to double forces.[42]

Baker then turned back to the economic argument, but this merely highlighted the confusion. On 13 November he observed that:

> The economic lifeline of the industrial world runs from the Gulf, and we cannot permit a dictator such as this to sit astride that economic lifeline. To bring it down to the level of the average American citizen, let me say that means jobs. If you want to sum it up in one word: it's jobs.

The polls which showed the fall in confidence over the President's handling of the crisis also indicated that many more people assumed that the troops were supposed to be defending oilfields rather than America's friends. The answers with regard to what might be a good enough reason were instructive. They suggested that the American people were unimpressed by arguments of economics and principle, but they could well understand an argument based on the threat of an Iraqi nuclear capability, which could be translated into a threat to their safety.[43]

Not surprisingly, this revelation was soon followed by an Administration campaign to highlight the nuclear risk. In a statement to US forces in Dharhan on 22 November Bush said:

> Those who would measure the timetable for Saddam Hussein's atomic weapons program in years may be seriously underestimating the reality of the situation and the gravity of the threat . . . No one knows precisely when this dictator may acquire atomic weapons or who they may be aimed at down the road. But we do know this for sure: He has never possessed a weapon that he hasn't used.[44]

Scowcroft made the point that this was one reason not to rely solely on an economic embargo to force Iraq's withdrawal from Kuwait: that could mean ultimately facing an Iraq armed with nuclear weapons.[45] The convenience of an alarmist estimate did not escape observers. In evidence to Congress, a variety of experts questioned whether an Iraqi nuclear weapon would be available quite as quickly as the Administration was suggesting. There was insufficient evidence to believe that 'a crude, non-deliverable nuclear device in six months should define the boundary of the soonest or the best effort the Iraqis could mount'.[46] The 'fastest example of weapons acquisition in human history', mocked Richard Falk.[47] However, post-war evidence suggested that the Administration was closer to the mark than many of its critics. Thus David Albright and Mark Hibbs, having suggested that the Iraqi nuclear threat was being hyped and that Baghdad needed between five and ten years 'to produce weapon grade uranium', concluded after a thorough examination of the evidence secured by the post-war UN Special Commission that 'by the mid-1990s Iraq could well have emerged with a small nuclear arsenal that would have fundamentally changed the Middle East'.[48]

The case for caution

The basic case that the Administration had to make in November 1990 was for bringing the issue to a head sooner rather than later. The Administration had its reasons – the destruction of Kuwait and Iraq's nuclear potential, doubts over the impact of sanctions and the difficulties in managing the coalition, reinforced by the Temple Mount incident. This still assumed that the higher risks involved in resolving the crisis by force would be worth the consequent gains.

If the whole affair was at root only related to what Senator Daniel Patrick Moynihan called 'a small disturbance in a distant part of the world',[49] then the costs of an embargo and defensive deployment might be appropriate but those of war would be quite unacceptable. Even if the larger stakes claimed by the Administration were accepted, these still had to be shown to be proportionate. Thus, as James Schlesinger observed, there was little doubt that the United States and its allies could inflict a crippling military defeat on Iraq. 'The question is, at what cost, and whether it is wise to incur that cost.'[50]

The prudent course in August had seemed to contain Saddam and wait for sanctions to have their effect. Reflecting widely held views at that time, the military historian, Sir Michael Howard, warned of how a military confrontation 'would precipitate a conflict as prolonged as that of Korea and probably as unwinnable as that of Vietnam'. He underlined the basic fears – of the original *casus belli* being forgotten, of the Islamic world forgetting the Iraqi aggression and the allies becoming divided, of the unity of the UN shattered, and Saddam becoming a martyr – that were repeated by those wary of a military confrontation.[51] By early September he had become confident that the argument for waiting patiently until Iraq either capitulated or initiated military action was prevailing. The American people knew that waiting involved no hardship.

They learned from Vietnam that wars go on for an unpredictable length of time and involve an unpredictable number of people – and not always the right people – being killed. This time, moreover, many American civilians will be at risk. Under these circumstances they are likely to be as patient for as long as it takes.[52]

A *Washington Post*–ABC poll found that while three-quarters of the American people would support going to war against Iraq, they had air strikes largely in mind, for four out of ten said that the United States 'should not get involved in a land war in the Middle East even if Iraq's invasion means that Iraq permanently controls Kuwait'.[53] James Webb, former Secretary of the Navy, asserted that war could 'galvanize the Arab world, invite chemical retaliation and expand hostilities, and encourage worldwide terrorism – in short, open up a Pandora's box'.[54]

In the European press it was widely presumed that the Americans were out of their depth in the Middle East, with the presumption that Saddam understood the Arab political mind much better.[55] In the Congressional hearings of late 1990 there were regular warnings that a bellicose American policy risked stirring up anti-Americanism, turning Saddam into a great hero and complicating attempts to resolve the Arab–Israeli dispute. When, on 4 September, Baker had suggested a new security structure for the Middle East designed to block Saddam, modelled on NATO, he had been forced to back down because of Arab reaction to the implication of a long-term American presence. Many specialists in Arab affairs attached great weight to evidence of pro-Saddam and pro-Palestinian sentiment and concluded that this could render pro-American regimes highly vulnerable and lead to a radicalization of the region and further 'disorder'. More cautious voices warned against exaggerating pan-Arabist fervour and discounting the influences of personalities and calculations of interest.[56]

In some ways, however, the most damaging criticism was that the Administration had boxed itself in. This was the position taken by Sam Nunn and the former senior officers who spoke at the hearings. There was no need to take matters to the brink so hastily. The deployment of 8 November might force the United States to fight 'prematurely and unnecessarily'. The very presence of the extra troops could 'narrow our options and our ability to act with patient resolve'.[57] By doubling the troops, the critics contended, George Bush had become locked into a military logic at the expense of diplomacy and less violent forms of pressure. They argued that he should have stuck to a combination of defence of Saudi territory and rigorous enforcement of sanctions. When he allowed himself to be convinced in the autumn that he must create an offensive capacity by raising substantially the level of forces deployed in the Gulf, he made it much more difficult to settle down for a long haul. His proliferation of war aims, bringing in everything from nuclear programmes to Saddam's criminality, confused diplomatic efforts at a solution. In the process of making the case for military action he was obliged to play down the impact of economic sanctions.

In August the former Secretary of State Henry Kissinger had observed that

> Time is not on the American side. American staying power in the face of public, regional and allied pressures is usually inversely proportional to the scale of deployments.[58]

The reaction to Bush's announcement seemed to confirm Kissinger's prediction. For the Administration to justify the extra troop deployments it was going to have to demonstrate that it raised the chances for a peaceful settlement by warning Saddam of the consequences of continued intransigence. If Saddam remained intransigent then at least this would have been proved by a serious diplomatic effort and the case for force would have been reinforced. The Administration was obliged to rely on the old Roman nostrum: 'If you want peace, prepare for war.'

Table 6: Justifications for an attack on Iraq

	GOOD ENOUGH	NOT GOOD ENOUGH	DON'T KNOW
To restore the Government of Kuwait and defend Saudi Arabia against aggression	35	56	9
To stop Saddam developing nuclear weapons	54	39	7
To protect the source of much of the world's oil	31	62	7

Source: CBS News, 19 November 1990.

CHAPTER 16

Two Miles Forward, One Mile Back

The UN vote

Margaret Thatcher remained concerned that the Americans might still 'wobble'. The doubling of troop numbers had made her nervous largely because of the time that it would take to get them in place and the diplomatic mischief that could be done in the meantime. She remained concerned that the Americans had over-committed themselves to obtaining an extra UN resolution for each new turn of the screw. A resolution on force, she feared, might be just too much for the Russians and Chinese to swallow, and to try and fail would be worse than not having tried at all. Why take the risk when sufficient authority could be derived from Article 51 of the UN Charter, allowing for the inherent right of self-defence?

She had set her case as early as 6 September, during an emergency Parliamentary debate:

> To undertake now to use no military force without the further authority of the Security Council would be to deprive ourselves of a right in international law expressly affirmed by Security Council Resolution 661; to do injustice to the people of Kuwait, who are unable to use effective force themselves; to hand an advantage to Saddam Hussein; and it could put our own forces in greater peril.

The opposition leader, Neil Kinnock, said that his party was not opposed to the use of force without further UN support – it would just be better to have this wide support:

> If military action was taken when sanctions had been in force for a matter of weeks or months, or when there had been no further provocation, and when there had been no further effort to achieve agreement to a mandate to attack, either in the Security Council or the UN military staff committee, the military action could shatter the consensus that has been developed.[1]

Thatcher's position was wholly unrealistic if there was to be any hope of sustaining a broad coalition. Not surprisingly France took the view that another resolution was needed, and, even less surprisingly, so did the UN Secretary-General, Perez de Cuellar. More important, though, was the fact that James Baker was more inclined to go back to the UN. When he addressed the issue in September, insisting at the time that the coalition was not 'running out of non-military options', Baker suggested that if the President decided to use force, 'I think he would want to move in a manner that would seek to preserve as much of the international consensus as we could – and, hopefully, all of it.'[2]

The Administration accepted that in strict legal terms Article 51 authority would be sufficient, but it was worried about the politics. Bush did not have the domestic backing on the crisis enjoyed by Thatcher. The need to go to the UN had been a prominent theme of Congressional attitudes on intervention in the past. If a vote was going to be needed it was tempting to pose it in terms of 'whether we could live up to a UN obligation'.[3]

In October, Baker asked the Deputies Committee to start to draw up the outlines of a UN resolution. Apart from the 1950 Korean resolution there was little to go on.[4] In preparing a draft, they assumed that there was no point in demanding immediate action because their forces would not be ready for some time and the Iraqis should be given a chance to get out peacefully. The word 'ultimatum' should not be used. They did not want the resolution to be too specific, or to be put under Articles 42 and 46 of the UN Charter, because this could encourage the Military Staff Committee of the UN or the Security Council itself to become involved in setting limits and interfering with the conduct of the war. Article 42 would also require that force be used only when the Security Council determined that sanctions 'would be inadequate or have proved to be inadequate'. This was clearly implied but no formal determination was to be made. The only nod in the direction of Article 42 was that some of its language, including the need to 'restore international peace and security', was incorporated.

The central idea was to authorize the use of force, but not to mandate it. Baker suggested the phrase 'all necessary means, including military force'. The State Department lawyers raised no objection. There had been no problems with the ambiguous language of Resolution 665, enforcing the embargo, which had spoken of measures 'which may be necessary' and had been understood to be referring to force.

After some consultations with the British, who had little choice but to go along, the basic form was agreed by the end of the month. The Americans had a deadline in mind for the end of November if for no other reason than that they held the presidency of the Security Council for that month, while Yemen was due to take over in December. To achieve this, Baker set out in early November on a global trip to meet major members of the coalition and the Security Council.

He arrived in Moscow on 8 November 1990. His first task was to justify the planned increase in forces and explain that, while no decision had yet been taken, it might be necessary to resort to war. With this in mind he needed to know if a UN resolution to support the use of force would get a sympathetic response. At the Helsinki Summit on 9 September, Bush and Gorbachev had issued a statement to the effect that if the current steps failed they were 'prepared to take additional ones consistent with the UN Charter'. Shevardnadze had agreed this without Gorbachev but the President, who was more cautious, went along. On 7 November warning notes had been sounded both by Primakov, continuing to stress the need for a peaceful settlement, and Defence Minister Yazov, noting that 'the US is ten times stronger than Iraq, but if war starts they will also suffer'.[5] There was clearly a fierce debate raging in Moscow between the Arabists led by Primakov, and the pro-American Shevardnadze, which was in itself complicated by the growing hard-line pressure on President Gorbachev to slow down the pace of domestic reform and of concessions to the West in the security sphere.

First Baker and his team met with Shevardnadze for a series of discussions lasting some ten hours. The Soviet Foreign Minister's initial reaction was that increased pressure on Saddam might be needed, but was not talk of using force premature? It would be better to find ways first of adding to the economic squeeze. Baker sought to convince him that, even if there had been no leakage at all, sanctions, by themselves, would not work since Saddam was prepared to sacrifice the Iraqi population. He went on to explain the difficulties the Americans faced with their forces if they were asked to wait. If they were not ready to move by early next year, then a combination of Ramadan and the deteriorating climate could postpone any military action for another year. Meanwhile it would become progressively harder to hold together the anti-Iraq coalition. Baker stressed that the need was to get in a position to use force; if Saddam saw sense it would not be necessary actually to do so.

Shevardnadze allowed himself to be persuaded and he did not return to the issue of principle. Instead, his questions took a different line. Have you really thought about what it means to use force? Have you asked all the right questions? He had his own memories of Afghanistan, and what the Politburo had been told by the Soviet military. The worst outcome would be for force to be used without it being decisive. In order to convince Shevardnadze that the United States was 'not doing this in a fly-by-night way, that we knew what we were doing', the Soviet Foreign Minister was given a full briefing on American military plans, something that would have been unthinkable just months before.

Baker then suggested the 'all necessary means, including force' clause to Shevardnadze, who proposed an amendment 'but not including nuclear force'. Baker could see the potential for a complicated and unhelpful debate about what was and was not permitted. This was finally settled by deleting 'including force' and just having 'all necessary means' as sufficient authority. Meeting with the press, Shevardnadze announced his conversion. Force, he said, 'could not be ruled out and a situation may emerge which effectively requires such a move'.[6]

Then Baker's team went to Gorbachev's dacha outside Moscow, where they met for about two hours. Baker made his basic pitch again, though Gorbachev had already been briefed by Shevardnadze. Gorbachev first described the Soviet domestic situation, thereby giving Baker another reason for bringing the Gulf crisis to a head while there was still a Soviet leadership with which he could co-operate. He agreed that they could not let Saddam get away with his seizure of Kuwait. It contradicted all his own ideas of 'new thinking'. Baker recalled being told by Gorbachev that 'what is really impor-tant is that we stick together', intertwining his fingers to emphasize the point, but also that his request created real difficulties. 'You are asking the Soviet Union to approve the use of American force against a long-time ally of the Soviet Union,' he said.[7]

Why not two resolutions, Gorbachev asked, one to authorize the use of force and a second on implementation. Baker demurred. He did not relish the idea of getting over the same hump twice, with the possibility of some tricks from Saddam in between. He was prepared to agree a deadline, so that there was some time before the resolution became operative. While he promised to find some way to work with the Americans, Gorbachev avoided committing himself straight away. All he promised was to give President Bush an answer when the two men were scheduled to meet in Paris on 19 November at the summit of the Conference on Security and Co-operation in Europe (CSCE).

When the two Presidents met, Gorbachev did confirm his general sup-port. However, he did not want it announced immediately lest it look too much like a *fait accompli*. He wanted one more try with Saddam and he also had his own views on what the resolution should contain. A few days later he had yet another fruitless meeting with Tariq Aziz, in which he warned that he would have no choice but to support a UN resolution if there was no sign of an Iraqi climbdown. Whether Gorbachev had ever expected these regular showdowns with the Iraqis, now almost *de rigueur* before consenting to each tightening of the screw, to produce any results is hard to guess. The main advantage was probably to demonstrate to domestic critics the depths of Iraq's intransigence.

Of the other Security Council permanent members, the only problem with Britain was that it was taking an even tougher line, while for France Mitterrand gave his assent when he met with Bush at the CSCE summit which he was hosting. That left China. Before going to Moscow, Baker had managed an opportunistic meeting with the Chinese Minister of Foreign Affairs, Qian Qichen, in Cairo on 6 November where he managed to secure an abstention. Later, Shevardnadze visited Beijing, as Gorbachev was anxious to be sure that he would not be embarrassed by a Chinese veto.

Beijing's pre-crisis relations with Kuwait had been good but with Iraq they had been even better, for this was one of China's largest markets for the export of goods and labour. $4.16 billion of arms were sold to Baghdad during the 1980s. Beijing's initial response to the occupation of Kuwait had been cautious, stressing the need for an Arab solution. However, the crisis came gradually to be seen as a way of ending China's ostracization by the major powers which had followed the 1989 massacre in Tiananmen Square. As a veto-wielding permanent member of the Security Council it realized that it had a card to play so long as the crisis was being managed through the United Nations. Nonetheless, because of its self-image as a member of the Third World and an opponent of 'imperialist' interference, China was not able to take full advantage of the situation, and described the crisis in terms of a clash between a 'little hegemonist' (Iraq) and a 'big hegemonist' (United States). For Beijing, an abstention was the best way to manage the tension between a commitment to a peaceful settlement and an unwillingness to alienate the Americans.[8] Recognizing these facts, Baker worked to make a veto even more difficult by inviting the Foreign Minister to Washington after the Security Council meeting.

Baker had contact with all the other ten Security Council members. Of these Canada, Finland and Romania were sure, but with China abstaining he still needed another two Third World votes to have a sufficient majority, and he wanted as few negative votes as possible. Zaïre and the Ivory Coast remained solid. Baker travelled to Bogota to get the Colombian vote, while Britain helped put pressure on a doubtful Islamic Malaysia. Despite its radical nature, Ethiopia had remained impressed by historical allusions to Mussolini's aggression of the 1930s against the then Abyssinia. In New York, just before the actual vote, Baker even met the Cuban Foreign

Minister, Isidoro Malmierca. This was hardly normal practice for an American Secretary of State; yet this gesture in the direction of the legitimacy of the Castro regime was to no avail. Cuba would not support the resolution. Nor would Yemen, where Baker and his team arrived on 22 November, Thanksgiving Day,[9] in an effort to persuade President Saleh to vote with them. They left him apparently undecided, with a parting observation from one official that 'everything has its price'.

The draft resolution began to circulate on 24 November, and informal discussions began among the 'permanent five' two days later. That day the Kuwaitis briefed the Council on Iraqi atrocities. This helped the Americans convey a sense of urgency and also led to the passage of another resolution – SC 677 – on 28 November, designed to prevent Iraq from making permanent changes to Kuwait's demographic structure.

The draft contained a deadline of 1 January 1991.[10] The Kuwaitis had lobbied against a pause. The British, too, had not wanted any date mentioned at all because it could tie the coalition's hands, create a temptation for Saddam to launch a pre-emptive strike and also risk the appearance of vacillation if force was not used after the relevant date had passed. However, the British influence was now in decline, because Margaret Thatcher was being replaced by John Major as Prime Minister during the course of these negotiations, and other members of the Government were not as wary of the UN route as she was. At any rate, Baker had persuaded Bush that he would not get the resolution if he was not prepared to insert a date before which force would not be used, and the British were not going actively to veto such a resolution.

Gorbachev was attached to the idea of a 'period of goodwill', a phrase which Moscow inserted into the final resolution. He still clung to the hope that at some point he would be able to persuade Saddam to see sense and so wanted 31 January as the conclusion of this pause. The Americans were unhappy about such a long delay. At France's urging it was agreed to split the difference on 15 January. As Foreign Minister Dumas explained, the 15 January formula meant that it would be seen as the 'last appeal and indeed an ultimatum'.

Yemeni indecision continued up to forty-five minutes before the vote was taken on 29 November. The session began with the Yemeni Ambassador on the phone to San'a, where a meeting was in progress on how Yemen would vote. The result was a 'no' vote. When the Americans were informed of this, they sent a message back to President Saleh that such a vote would be a grievous mistake and probably costly, as the United States would deny an aid programme for Yemen. After the Yemeni Ambassador concluded his speech by saying that peace should be given a chance, Baker observed that this had been the most expensive vote he had ever made.

With Cuba joining Yemen, that meant two votes against plus the Chinese abstention. The other twelve members supported Resolution 678. It allowed Iraq 'one final opportunity, as a pause of goodwill' to comply fully with all eleven resolutions on the conflict already passed. If this had not been done by 15 January, member states, co-operating with the Government of Kuwait, were authorized 'to use all necessary means to uphold and implement' these resolutions and to 'restore international peace and security in the area'. All states were requested to provide 'appropriate support' for any actions taken. In a later unilateral statement Baker made it clear that 'necessary means' was synonymous with force. The line between war and peace had been drawn.

The extra mile

The passing of Security Council Resolution 678 was disconcerting for Saddam. Wherever he looked, the choices seemed bleak. Unconditional withdrawal would most probably damage his position beyond repair. The economic plight which pushed him to occupy Kuwait had not only remained but had been significantly aggravated by the sanctions. Iraq's political system had not become kinder, and the nation's patience with its leader would soon be running thin. Plots were certain to lurk around the corner.

The alternative boded equally ill. Once the full impact of the economic sanctions had sunk in, public discontent could well force him into a hasty withdrawal. An all-out war which would destroy Iraq's military machinery and strategic infrastructure was a recipe for his personal destruction. Saddam's only hope, therefore, lay in the collapse of the international coalition before sanctions had been given sufficient time to bite, or full-scale hostilities had broken out. But how realistic was this prospect after the passing of Resolution 678?

At this moment of great anxiety a rope was offered from an unexpected direction. On 30 November, the day after the diplomatic triumph at the United Nations, Bush made a dramatic move: he announced his readiness to go an 'extra mile for peace' and offered direct talks between the United States and Iraq on a peaceful resolution to the Gulf crisis. He was willing to send Secretary Baker to Baghdad and to receive Foreign Minister Aziz in Washington, to meet himself and representatives of the international coalition. The savvy judgement in Washington was that the whole exercise was designed largely to reassure the American people that no avenues were being left unexplored, and to draw the sting out of the Congressional charge that the Administration was in a headlong rush to war. As Baker himself was to admit later: 'If force ends up being used we owe it to the American people and to others to show that we left no stone unturned in the search for peace.'[11]

At the same time, to counter charges from the opposite direction that domestic pressures were panicking him into concessions, Bush took care to emphasize that his offer should not be construed as the initiation of negotiations, but rather as a last attempt to drive home to Saddam the seriousness of his situation, so as to bring about Iraq's unconditional withdrawal from Kuwait and the full release of foreign hostages. The value of the exercise would be to ensure that Saddam was left in no doubt of the seriousness of his position. 'I am not hopeful we are going to get a lot out of this,' he warned, 'we are just going the extra mile . . .'[12]

In practice, it was probably at least half a mile too far. Bush and Baker had been planning a diplomatic initiative of sorts for quite some time. Baker had discussed an offer of direct talks with Iraq in his pre-UN vote globe-trotting, as the Soviets had made some such offer almost a condition of their support in the Security Council. A day after the vote, Baker brought up the issue once more in a meeting with the other foreign ministers of the permanent five. He then reported back to Bush that there was general support for a gesture of goodwill. Meanwhile, the President had been watching the Congressional hearings with growing alarm and decided to accelerate the initiative in the face of the barrage of criticisms being generated. While he was gratified with the UN vote, that week had started with two former Chairmen of the Joint Chiefs-of-Staff in the Senate hearings making a plea for more time.

However, while the principle of approaching Iraq was widely accepted, few of those consulted on the issue expected an American offer of a visit at the proposed level. Previous discussions had only really revolved around the extension of an invitation to Aziz. The offer to send Baker was virtually an ad lib, inserted by Bush with barely any discussion among his professional advisers as to its likely impact on Iraqi perceptions. The idea was developed a few days earlier at the house of the Mexican President, Carlos Salinas, as Bush mused on the problems of convincing the American people that everything had been done to avoid war. One source says that the idea was Sununu's.[13] Bush was tempted, especially as he saw his domestic base crumbling. With Baker, he was obsessed with the thought that Saddam simply did not understand his predicament because nobody dared tell him – his ministers had to be sycophants in order to survive. Talking directly to Baker, he could not fail to get the message. Only Cheney and Scowcroft were consulted. Cheney did not mind. Scowcroft was less than pleased because of the signals that it would send to the Arabs with regard to Bush's resolve, as well as a nagging suspicion that Baker would not be able to resist the temptation to negotiate a deal. So rushed was the announcement that Bush had not thought through the implications of being less than precise as to the date of the Baker visit, except that it would be before 15 January. As he later acknowledged, this turned out to be a mistake.[14]

Up to this point Bush had shown a sensitivity to his coalition partners while underestimating Congress. Now, as he took a move that would be welcomed by Congress, he was underestimating his partners, most of whom were alarmed at this sudden announcement. At least domestically the move paid off. An opinion poll showed overwhelming support and a rise in the President's approval rating.

Saddam was ecstatic. From the beginning of the crisis he had pressed for direct negotiations with the United States. The line was that nothing would be conceded prior to negotiations, but all manner of possibilities opened up if the Americans would only sit down with the Iraqis. In the past all such proposals had been rebuffed. They had even invited Bush himself to come to Baghdad for talks and then expressed their irritation at the rejection of this offer. Still seeking to establish themselves as equal partners of the United States in crisis management, the Iraqis had proposed a meeting of experts to prevent accidental air and naval clashes that might escalate to war.[15] A few weeks before the passing of Resolution 678, the Iraqi Information Minister, Latif Nusseif Jasim, insisted that his country was prepared to discuss 'every aspect of the crisis in the Gulf, without exception', so long as the Americans were prepared to negotiate without any preconditions. Then the White House response had been that there was 'no reason for any special envoy'.[16]

Now, when Saddam's position was at its lowest, the Americans were suddenly willing to negotiate. This, in turn, led him to interpret Bush's announcement, in the context of his evident troubles at home, as the start of a climb-down. Perhaps he had been right, after all, in telling Ambassador Glaspie, during their conversation in July, that the United States did not have 'the stomach' for a costly war. Perhaps the Americans would be willing to reach a compromise that would allow him to emerge from the crisis with a real gain that would thrust him into regional prominence and ensure his political survival. 'The enemy of God, the arrogant President of the United States, George Bush, had consistently opposed dialogue ... His initiative is [therefore] a submission to Iraq's demand, on which it has insisted and is still insisting,' rejoiced the Iraqi mass media, 'namely, the need to open a serious dialogue on the region's issues. This is because the Gulf crisis, as they call it, is in fact a reflection of a chronic crisis, the Palestine crisis.'[17] The BBC's John Simpson reported from Baghdad: 'There's no mistaking the feeling here that President Saddam Hussein has got the Americans on the run.'[18]

On 2 December Saddam went on television. Guardedly optimistic, he assessed that the chances of a peaceful solution to the crisis were fifty-fifty, arguing that this would depend on whether the US–Iraqi encounter was to be 'a real dialogue' or only

> a formal session to give the American Congress, the American people, and international public opinion a good conscience and to allow them to say they tried to talk with Iraq and that Iraq refused to give up its position, then in that case we are closer to war.'[19]

CHAPTER 17

Making a Date

Releasing the hostages

Saddam's surge of optimism following Bush's extra-mile offer was further fuelled by a series of encouraging developments. In early December, Defence Minister Pierre Chevènement, the strongest sympathizer of Iraq in the French Cabinet, indicated the possibility of redrawing Kuwait's borders if Iraq withdrew from the principality, and called for an international conference on the Middle East after the Iraqi pull-out. This call was echoed by Foreign Minister Dumas, who also implied that he might follow Secretary Baker's footsteps and visit Baghdad.[1] Most importantly, in an about-face in American longstanding opposition to an international conference on the Middle East, on 5 December the US Ambassador to the United Nations, Thomas Pickering, implied his Government's readiness to consider such an idea.[2]

Whatever his original intentions, perhaps President Bush had unleashed forces that might prove beyond his ability to control. The drive towards war appeared to have slowed down. The 'peace camp' was capitalizing on the unexpected gesture to push the demand for a political resolution of the crisis with greater vigour. A public controversy as to whether the President had the constitutional powers to move the nation towards war, without clear authorization from the Congress, was under way. Senior Democrats like Edward Kennedy and Sam Nunn, as well as senior military figures, were questioning the prudence of a military action and demanding that sanctions be given more time. In Britain, Saddam's most stern opponent, Margaret Thatcher, had been unceremoniously bundled from office.

What was needed at this critical juncture, Saddam seemed to believe, was a dramatic move that would tip the scales in favour of the 'peace camp'. And what could be more dramatic than the release of all foreign hostages in Iraq and Kuwait? Such a move was bound to be seen as a major show of goodwill and was likely, therefore, to set in train a political momentum that would be difficult to contain. If handled skilfully enough, this move might enable him to retain some of his newly acquired possessions and might even lead to the convocation of an international conference, thereby diverting world attention from Kuwait to the Palestine problem.

At any rate the hostages had outlived their usefulness. Given the clear UN mandate for the use of force against Iraq after 15 January, they could hardly shield him from the American wrath as they had done before. For three months the hostage question had provided a substantial distraction but had not in itself altered the main features of the confrontation. The processes by which individual hostages were released were rapidly becoming farcical. There were hints of concessions but nothing firm. There were some indications that medical supplies (which were allowed under the embargo) were being delivered in an effort to get hostages released quicker, but that was all.[3] Their value as human shields was also becoming dubious – at least in Kuwait. It was reported in late November that few were now being kept in the emirate and that a number had been redeployed to Iraq to make up numbers depleted through various releases. It was becoming hard to avoid the conclusion that the hostages themselves were becoming parting gifts to people who had bothered to make a pilgrimage to Baghdad, with few obvious criteria determining who was released and when. Finnish envoys were told that they could take only five out of fourteen, so they selected three sick and drew lots for the other two. An American-Iraqi, Salim Mansour, insisted that the fourteen Americans identified by diplomats for release on humanitarian grounds should travel to New York with him for a news conference. If they refused, he threatened to select a different fourteen.[4] One journalist observed how in one morning in November in the al-Rashid Hotel, 'a distraught Australian poetess was in tears at the reception desk because she had secured the freedom of only two Australians while in the lobby the leader of Sweden's Muslims, whose efforts had been more successful, was accepting congratulations'.[5]

As the CSCE summit convened in Paris on 18 November Saddam had attempted one last use of the sanctions card. Aware that March was seen as a practical deadline for the use of force, he offered to release all hostages, in batches, over a three-month period starting from Christmas and concluding on 25 March 1991, unless something 'mars the atmosphere of peace'.[6] 'If after that date [President Bush] still has the devil in his head,' he said, 'and if he decides to attack us, we shall then count on God to meet any eventuality.'[7]

Yet again he did not have the conviction to carry this policy through. On 20 November he announced his decision to release all remaining German 'guests' (180, including forty-four held at strategic sites), apparently in appreciation of a positive anti-war remark Chancellor Kohl was judged to have made during a meeting with President Bush. Then news broke out that 215 foreign workers who had been working for Dutch dredging companies would be released. 24 November saw the ordering of the release of most of the 300 Italians left in Iraq, as well as thirty Irish nurses and ten British men whose wives had come to seek their release. Two days later out came ten Greeks, and the Swedish Foreign Ministry reported freedom for all the remaining Swedish hostages, numbering around fifty-six. On 28 November Saddam asked his Parliament to allow all Belgian nationals to leave. More importantly, in an effort to forestall Soviet support of Resolution 678, he promised Moscow that he would carry out his pledge, which he had broken before, and allow 1,000 Soviet workers to leave Iraq.[8]

Increasingly it seemed as if Saddam's hostage policy was concentrating on the British and Americans, some of whom were still being moved to strategic sites. At the start of December Saddam met with his main regional allies – King Hussein of Jordan, the PLO's Chairman Yasser Arafat, and the Yemenite Vice-President, Ali Salim al-Bid. While endorsing his overall strategy, they confirmed his own impression and the general argument that he had been hearing from a number of visitors that the chances of a settlement would be immeasurably improved if the hostage issue could be brought to a close. This convinced him that a unique opportunity to ride out the storm was at hand, and that he had an irreversible chance, albeit by no means without risk, to rebound, to emerge from his confrontation with a real achievement. Not only might he survive with dignity, but he might attain new international power. Given this balance of risks and opportunities, Saddam decided to strike. Immediately after Bush's 'extra mile' speech, he allowed deliveries of food and drink to the besieged American embassy in Kuwait. A week later, on 6 December, he announced the release of all foreign hostages. In doing so he mentioned the readiness of the European Community to talk to Iraq and the evidence of strong anti-war sentiments inside the United States. At this time 3,400 foreign nationals were still trapped. This included 584 hostages at strategic sites and 1,200 Britons and Americans in Kuwait hiding from Iraqi forces. As they finally got out of the country, Bush observed that he now had one less thing to worry about.

Nightmares

The fact that the reaction to Bush's 'extra mile' initiative was far warmer among Saddam's allies and the non-aligned than it was among members of the coalition indicated the widespread suspicion that the exchange of visits would be a prelude to a sell-out. This impression was reinforced by a series of rumours concerning pressure on Kuwait to concede on the disputed islands and oilfields, and of secret Saudi soundings of Iraqi readiness for a settlement involving the standard Kuwaiti concessions.[9] Even if there was no intention to go quite that far, it was hard to avoid the impression that some deal was in the offing, some reward in return for a withdrawal from Kuwait. If there was nothing to discuss with Saddam, why was Bush willing to send his Secretary of State to Baghdad? Could his expressed readiness 'to discuss all aspects of the Gulf crisis within the mandate of the UN resolutions' imply a softer stance on the Arab–Israeli dispute?

For reasons such as this, leading hawks began publicly to voice their concern. Henry Kissinger observed that Baker's proposed trip filled him with foreboding: 'I have not been this worried in decades.' If a compromise were struck, he warned, then

> not only is aggression rewarded but 400,000 Americans have appeared in an area and left again without having achieved something that might have been achieved without such a huge display of military force.

Richard Perle suggested that Saddam was 'observing Bush's tendency to buckle under pressure' and his consequent hopes would make the crisis harder to resolve.

The Arab members of the coalition took a similar view. They had not been consulted beforehand. While putting on a brave face in public and praising Bush's initiative as 'characterized with wisdom, far-sightedness, and audacity',[10] they were taken aback. Saudi Ambassador Bandar was livid. 'To you sending Baker is goodwill,' he warned Scowcroft. 'To Saddam it suggests you're chicken.' Saddam would naturally agree to see Baker just before the UN deadline. He also pointed out the unacceptability of making major changes of policy without consulting key allies.[11] When the polls showed a positive response, Administration officials were quick to point out that the tactic had worked, again reflecting their concern with the domestic rather than the international political impact.

Before long the Arab heads of state were engaged in hectic consultations. Having spoken on the phone to President Mubarak and the Kuwaiti Emir, King Fahd publicly urged Saddam to withdraw unconditionally from Kuwait and to restore the legitimate Kuwaiti Government. The world was determined to reverse the Iraqi aggression, he said, and Saddam should not delude himself that Bush's initiative implied readiness for a compromise.[12] This position was echoed by the Syrian Minister of Defence, Mustafa Tlas, who announced on 1 December that his country would soon increase its military presence in the Gulf; a similar statement came from Egypt a few days later.[13]

On 3 December, the Saudi Foreign Minister, Prince Saud al-Faisal, arrived in Cairo for a tripartite meeting with his Egyptian and Syrian counterparts, the third of its kind since the beginning of the crisis. In the joint communiqué concluding the summit, the three condemned the occupation of Kuwait in strong words and expressed their hope that Resolution 678 would drive Iraq to comply with the rest of the UN resolutions. 'Bush's initiative creates the last chance for removing the danger of war from the region,' they cautioned, and Saddam had better seize this opportune moment to withdraw from Kuwait, rather than embroil the region in a bloody and futile war.[14]

But how real were the chances for a peaceful Iraqi withdrawal from Kuwait? The consensus in the American intelligence community was still that Saddam would probably withdraw when faced with the reality of coalition power. However, to judge from the Egyptian, Syrian and Saudi mass media, this was too optimistic. 'Saddam's sick imagination and insane dreams have reached the point where he thinks that he can intimidate all the countries that have extensive ground, naval, and air forces deployed around Iraq,' argued the Egyptian daily, *al-Akhbar*, 'if this is actually what is on his mind right now . . . Saddam may commit his worst and most reckless mistake yet and reject the lifejacket Bush has thrown to him.'[15]

This assessment was not shared by the Israelis. To the contrary, the main fear in Jerusalem was that the Administration was laying the ground for a compromise that would allow Saddam to retain parts of Kuwait and, in consequence, to emerge victorious from the crisis. Right-wing ministers Ariel Sharon and Yuval Ne'eman compared the impending US–Iraqi meetings to the 1938 Munich summit, where the Western democracies surrendered parts of Czechoslovakia to Nazi domination.[16] The leading troika – Premier Shamir, Defence Minister Arens, and Foreign Minister Levy – remained cool-headed. Arens expressed his confidence that the Bush initiative would yield positive results and Shamir, though admitting that Israel had not been consulted in advance, promised to take up the subject during his scheduled meeting with George Bush later that month.[17]

In these circumstances, Washington had to move quickly to regain control. There should be no bandwagon with a series of states opening up separate negotiations with Iraq. Baghdad must not be allowed to use the exercise simply to procrastinate. In a phone conversation with King Fahd, President Bush promised that there would be no concessions to Saddam, and the same message was relayed to Israel in a presidential message to

Foreign Minister Levy.[18] All that Baker wished to do, the President argued, was deliver an ultimatum. The only assurance Saddam would get was that compliance with UN resolutions would be rewarded with an American promise not to attack. The Americans would still expect to retain a sizeable military presence in Kuwait until the legitimate Government was fully restored, and territorial disputes had been settled. They also intended to sustain the economic sanctions until Iraq had given up its chemical weapons and demonstrated an honest intention to abide by the Non-Proliferation Treaty. Even then, there would be a continued embargo on high-technology and military equipment.

Still the concept of a diplomatic solution was infectious. On 5 December European Community ministers decided to ask Aziz to meet them in Rome after he had met Bush. The idea of an international conference to discuss the Arab–Israeli dispute had already been widely mooted as a building block in a settlement, and was soon under discussion at the United Nations. In this developing mood it was not hard to imagine the difficulties confronting the American Administration if Saddam began to show just the slightest interest in a compromise. The London *Economist* aptly described this widely canvassed scenario:

> Mr Baker flies into Baghdad saying he is not there to negotiate. Mr Hussein promptly offers to withdraw from Kuwait, minus a few details – harbour rights on Bubiyan island, say, or small border changes. Mr Baker sticks to his brief and flies home announcing that diplomacy has failed. America, however, is agog with excitement and relief. It was reluctant enough to fight for Kuwait-without-strings. Why risk war for the extra few trifles?

Unfortunately, it warned, these would not be trifles. However unimportant an individual concession might be,

> in Baghdad, and throughout the Middle East, any one of them would be amplified many times, enhancing the prestige of the Saladin who took on America and made it shrink away. A peace at that price would not be peace, merely a pause before bloodier conflict in the future. The result would be a diminished America, and a more dangerous world.[19]

No extra mile

If this was Saddam's opportunity, true to form he failed to seize it, preferring instead to attempt to make his point in the discussions over the substantive negotiations. In Baghdad, Chargé d'Affaires Wilson entered into a procedural haggling. The Iraqis wanted to base the talks on Saddam's 'peace initiative' of 12 August, though the Americans had no intention of discussing the Palestinian question. The Iraqis noted that Bush had indicated a desire to invite a number of coalition ambassadors to Washington to attend the talks with Aziz. Who would be invited? They would be happy to see at the meetings 'representatives of countries and parties that are connected with unresolved disputes and issues', such as their French friends, but the presence of the Kuwaiti Ambassador would be quite unacceptable. When Saddam suggested that he might have his friends with him when Baker visited, such as Yasser Arafat, the Americans quickly dropped the point. Aziz also wanted to meet Congressional leaders and to take full advantage of his stay in Washington by hanging around for five days: he was told it was limited to two days and one night.

The week beginning 12 December was suggested as the best time for Aziz's visit; soon the date of 17 December was pencilled in. However, apprehensive of Iraqi prevarication, the United States would not go firm on that date until Baker's visit had been scheduled as well. This visit was now making the Americans nervous. They wanted to keep it as short as possible to reduce the potential for Saddam to exploit it. Having been embarrassed by the release of the transcript of April Glaspie's conversation with Saddam, they were even wondering whether Baker should be wired for sound. (When he eventually met Aziz they were recorded.) In particular the Americans were concerned that Saddam would set a date to cause maximum delay. Any day between 20 December and 3 January would be acceptable to the United States, but it would not agree to any dates just before the UN deadline 'because Iraq is not going to be able to leave Kuwait in just a couple of days'. If the Iraqis insisted on such dates then that would prove that their only objective was to evade implementing the UN resolutions.[20]

This was indeed what Saddam was trying to achieve. Realizing that despite the deep relief worldwide over the hostages' release, the US Administration would not budge from the demand for unconditional withdrawal, he calculated that his only hope of avoiding war was to try to circumvent the 15 January deadline by postponing his meeting with Secretary of State Baker to the last possible moment. He therefore accepted the American request to dispatch Aziz to Washington on 17 December, but refused to meet Baker before 12 January. To justify this decision, Iraq's Ambassador to the United Nations, Abd al-Amir al-Anbari, argued that this date had been chosen to give Aziz ample time to stop in Rome to see European Community leaders, and to hold meetings with Iraqi officials

244

before Baker's visit.[21] Later it was suggested, even less credibly, that Saddam was simply too busy to meet Baker before that date.

After almost two weeks of haggling, the two sides could still not agree dates. Baghdad was making the date a matter of principle. 'It is up to Iraq to set appropriate dates for visits to its capital and talks with its President.' It was inconceivable that the Americans should 'dictate dates', while giving the Iraqis only one option. The American preoccupation with the 15 January deadline was also unacceptable. Iraq refused to 'link the time of the meeting with the American resolution which was issued by the UN Security Council – that resolution which was passed through bribery and blatant pressures.'[22]

George Bush was worried that Saddam was trying to use the question of dates to impose further strains on the coalition. Recognizing that the European Community represented an obvious target, he wrote to the Italian Prime Minister, Guilio Andreotti, as President of the European Council, that this attempt to postpone the meeting was 'just the latest example of Saddam's desire to use diplomacy to weaken the coalition formed against him and to push further back the potential use of force, thus rendering it less probable'. Bush judged it important not to show any further flexibility lest he appear desperate for a meeting. As a result, on 15 December Saddam made a significant step towards the brink, threatening to call the talks off. 'We will not go to the United States to receive orders,' he said; 'if the US President George Bush insists on repeating the UN resolutions, then there will be no reason for us to go.'[23]

This move was found depressing in the Western capitals. In his earlier dealings with the French, Saddam had appeared to place great store on a visit by a senior Western statesman to Baghdad which could afford him the recognition he craved and an opportunity to display both his power and his reasonableness. Now the opportunity had been handed to him on a plate and he failed to take advantage. The Europeans felt that they had little choice but to cancel their own proposals for a meeting. The hawks had to conclude (as the CIA was said to advise) that Saddam was still unconvinced that the Americans would dare attack, and that Bush's original gesture may have helped convince him that the Americans had no stomach for war. The doves, for their part, now had no diplomatic process upon which to pin their hopes. Perhaps, as the official Iraqi commentary suggested, Saddam's self-importance was such that it was not enough that Baker should come to Baghdad: Saddam should also set the date.

No Arab solutions

Saddam's own diplomatic offensive depended upon a supposed appeal to Arab sentiment. Part of this revolved around the claim that it was improper for non-Arabs to expect a say in decisions on Arab disputes. Another obvious part was to stress Iraq's role in championing the Palestinian cause. A third element was to highlight the importance of safeguarding Iraq's military power as an all-Arab asset and to ensure that it was guaranteed as part of any settlement. While the Arab members of the coalition might be undermined by this set of propositions, others would find it persuasive while the Europeans, especially France, were judged to be so anxious for a diplomatic settlement that they would use Iraqi prevarication as a reason for pressing for a more conciliatory approach in Washington – where there was an expectation of further cracks in domestic support.

This was part of the strategy worked out in Baghdad in early December by the heads of Jordan, the PLO and Yemen when they met with Saddam. If any peaceful solution were to be found, Saddam would have to be given a substantial *quid pro quo* in return for relinquishing his hold on (most of) Kuwait. King Hussein, still the most desperate for a compromise and still seen as the most promising salesman to the West, believed that Bush's initiative placed him in an ideal position to mediate a peaceful settlement. Like Saddam's other sympathizers, he took comfort from the mini-summit in Baghdad on 4 December, in the first rush of optimism after the 'mile for peace' initiative, where Saddam allegedly implied that he might compromise on Kuwait if there were progress on the Palestinian issue. What was required to break the diplomatic stalemate, the King argued, was to convene an international peace conference on the Middle East on the basis of Saddam's 12 August initiative, simultaneously with the beginning of an Iraqi withdrawal from Kuwait, with some concessions from Kuwait, along familiar lines, to satisfy Iraq's economic and security concerns. The need for Kuwaiti concessions, he emphasized, could not be overstated: the crisis began as an Iraqi–Kuwaiti rather than an Iraqi–American dispute, and had to be resolved within this framework.[24]

The Jordanian media were even more outspoken than their monarch in underlining the merits of international concessions to Iraq:

> Fraternal Iraq has long expressed its readiness to enter into negotiations with the US Administration for a peaceful settlement. They have never abandoned the peaceful approach, even during the most difficult times when the drums of war were being beaten in an unprecedented manner... The Administration should therefore understand that any negotiated

settlement requires substantial American concessions including, first and foremost, cessation of the calls for unconditional withdrawal.[25]

Saddam, however, was not making life easy for his Arab allies. In a 15 November interview with ABC News, when asked directly whether he would be prepared to negotiate about withdrawal from Kuwait if the United States dealt decisively with Israel over the occupation of Arab territories, he answered: 'Yes, in the same spirit, we are ready to discuss and implement a comprehensive and full peace for the region as a whole, provided each issue is discussed in accordance with its own background and by the same standards.' This could be read as simply a more positive gloss on his previous statements, for it contained no promises. He then went on, putting words in the mouth of Edward Heath, to indicate that the question of where he might be expected to withdraw to was complex. This could be taken as an indication of a readiness to negotiate a partial withdrawal or that the issue of the ownership of Kuwait was not well understood in the West.[26]

Now, a month later, interviewed by Turkish Television on 16 December, he argued that 'the Kuwait question must be forgotten until a complete solution of the Palestine problem'. Only then might he be ready to discuss 'its nineteenth province, Kuwait . . . and show self-sacrifice as far as others had done'.[27] In practice this was the same as the 12 August initiative: a firm statement that the Palestinian problem must be settled (not merely discussed) before anything else could be addressed, and then only a vague commitment to discuss (but not settle) the Kuwaiti question. Even with an Arab–Israeli conference convened with the best will in the world, negotiations towards a settlement would take months, if not years, by which time Saddam's hold over Kuwait would be irreversible. And as if to dispel any remaining hopes that Iraq would be willing to leave Kuwait in return for an Israeli withdrawal from the territories, the Revolutionary Command Council issued a special communiqué stating the nature of Iraq's perception of a linkage:

> When we stand for linkage as stated in the 12 August initiative, the belief that Kuwait is part of Iraq is unshakable, and that it is the nineteenth province is a fact treated by our people and their Armed Forces as a great gain . . .
>
> It has become a symbol of honour and virtue in this major battle – the mother of battles. We have wanted to establish a link between any gain for the [Arab] nation and any [Iraqi] national gain.[28]

Sensitive to the possible impact of Saddam's claim on their Arab members, the coalition leaders were doing everything possible to demonstrate their commitment to the Palestinian cause, without actually crediting Saddam Hussein. In early December discussions were under way of a draft UN resolution proposing a conference at an 'appropriate time'. Eventually, on 20 December, a resolution was passed on the dispute and a call, separate from a firm resolution, was made by the Security Council for convening an international conference. This was as far as the Americans could go without using their veto.[29]

Since King Hussein was no longer seen as impartial enough to be a credible mediator, Algeria's President Chadli Benjedid stepped forward as an alternative, capitalizing on what was widely assumed to be (on the basis of only flimsy evidence) his country's fine record in mediating within the Arab world.[30] Following King Hussein's observation that if the United States could talk to the Iraqis then so could other Arabs, Chadli set himself a hectic schedule of talks with the Jordanians, the Iraqis, the Saudis and the Kuwaitis.

The key to this effort was the Saudis. There appears to have been some suspicion among Arabs that there was a schism within the Saudi royal family, which had been exacerbated by dire warnings from Iraq and its friends that the desert kingdom would not be forgiven for supporting the United States in the shedding of Arab blood. The basis for Benjedid's plan, therefore, was to work on any inner Saudi doubts, so that they in turn could influence the Kuwaitis, thereby cutting the Americans out of the deal. The Algerians worked carefully on the Saudis. Benjedid had a number of meetings with a representative of King Fahd, from which he believed he had received assurances of a welcome in Riyadh, and a sense that the King was anxious for a peaceful solution and might even be ready to consider the position of US troops in Saudi Arabia and sit down with the Iraqis. It was understood that the Saudis would not do this unless Iraq at least began to withdraw.[31]

Benjedid arrived in Baghdad as the Revolutionary Command Council was announcing that it had given up on the talks with the Americans, armed with the not-too-novel ideas for the simultaneous withdrawal of Iraqi troops from Kuwait and American forces from Saudi Arabia, with a pan-Arab contingent assuming responsibilities for security in a transitional phase.[32] He found the Iraqis in an intransigent mood, unwilling to budge on the question of Kuwait. When the first news of Algerian ideas appeared, Minister of Information Jasim had moved quickly to squash any ideas of Iraqi concessions: 'Kuwait is Iraqi – past, present and future – and not an inch of it will be given up.' In Jordan, Oman and Iran the Algerian ideas were warmly received, but there was little enthusiasm in either Syria or Egypt – and Benjedid never made it to Saudi Arabia.

A date agreed

While Saddam's allies were seeking to get him off the hook, contacts between the Americans and the Iraqis were resumed just after Christmas. At the American Embassy in Baghdad, Joseph Wilson told reporters that he had 'not given up on the diplomatic process'. His Government was now prepared to consider dates after 3 January. One report identified 9 January as the last date which could allow Iraq time to withdraw before the expiry of the UN deadline, and thus the last possible date for talks.[33] Alongside the critical voices from Europe, pressure was building up within the United States. The opinion polls still gave an uncomfortable message.

Key Congressmen – Robert Dole, Les Aspin and Lee Hamilton – all called for one last effort. Dole, one of the President's supporters, observed that

> I have sort of a gut feeling the American people are not yet committed to war, and they want to make certain that President Bush has done everything, pursued every avenue for peace, before the fighting starts.[34]

The Kansas senator, who had been used as an intermediary to Baghdad in April 1990, was told by the Iraqi Ambassador to the United States, Muhammad al-Mashat, that contrary to other statements the date for the Baker–Aziz meeting did not have to be 12 January. President Bush himself indicated that he had not quite given up on diplomacy when he reported in an end of year interview with *Time* magazine that he had a 'gut feeling' that Saddam would withdraw.[35] This optimistic notion was repeated by White House spokesman Marlin Fitzwater who, while observing no visible change in the Iraqi (or American) position, adopted a conciliatory tone. When asked if talks could start he said: 'Well, we will have to wait and see what we hear from them.'[36]

Then, on 3 January, once again the US took an initiative. Bush proposed a meeting between Baker and Aziz in Geneva between Monday and Wednesday, 7 and 9 January. This carried neither the symbolism of a visit to Baghdad nor the level of contact. The conditions set were also stark: 'No negotiations, no compromises, no attempts at face saving, no rewards for aggression.'

This decision originated in a meeting held by Bush on New Year's Day with Scowcroft, Gates, Cheney and Powell. The next Thursday, on 3 January, when his own deadline for a Baker visit to Baghdad was to expire, Congress would be returning from its Christmas break with demands for a Congressional resolution before Bush could go to war. A day later the

European Foreign Ministers would be meeting with proposals for a separate initiative on the table. Bush decided that he had better have one last go. On the evening of 2 January, Wilson was briefed and John Major and François Mitterrand were contacted. Bush then held an unusually early press conference the next morning to the first news bulletins, so that Congressmen would know of the development. Then he briefed Congressional leaders, telling them that this was the last set of proposals he would make. In turn they agreed that no resolution would be put to Congress before the Baker–Aziz meeting. The ground was thus set for what seemed to be the last American peaceful effort to dislodge Iraq from Kuwait.

Table 7: Number of Westerners in Kuwait and Iraq

COUNTRY	EARLY AUGUST	LATE SEPTEMBER	6 DECEMBER 1990
Australia	159	124	21
Austria	140	0	0
Belgium	62	46	10
Canada	325		88
Denmark	97		51
Finland	48		12
France	530	350 (260)	38
Greece	247		17
Ireland	350	320	253
Italy	402	331	194
Japan	508	352	239
Netherlands	233	177	133
New Zealand	35		0
Norway	52		22
Portugal	100		16
Spain	140		1
Sweden	160		58
Switzerland	122		86
UK	4,640	1,430	1,168
USA	3,580	1,130	700
West Germany	740	444	15

Sources: Various.

Table 8: Visitors to Baghdad and the release of hostages

DATE	INDIVIDUAL	NATIONALITIES
25 August	President Waldheim of Austria	95 Austrians
2 September	Jesse Jackson	43 women and children and 4 sick American men
15 September	Ahmad Ben-Bella, former President of Algeria	a few elderly and sick French
1 October	Gilles Munier of Franco-Iraqi Friendship Group	9 French
5 October	Brigitta Kohler (former member of GDR Parliament)	4 Germans
14 October	Yusuf Islam (Cat Stevens)	4 British Muslims
15 October	Spanish Parliamentary delegation	15 Spanish
23 October	Salim Mansour, American–Iraqi Foundation	14 Americans
24 October	Edward Heath (former British Prime Minister)	33 sick and elderly Britons
7 November	Yasuhiro Nakasone (former Japanese Prime Minister)	74 Japanese
7 November	Swedish Islamic Group	5 Swedes
7 November	Australian poetess	2 Australians
7 November	Italian Parliamentary delegation	20 Italians
7 November	International Trade Union Federation	2 Germans and 2 Portuguese
9 November	Willy Brandt (former West German Chancellor)	140 Germans, 15 Italians, 10 Dutch and 5 Britons
17 November	Anker Jorgensen (former Danish Prime Minister)	16 Danes
10 November	David Lange (former New Zealand Prime Minister)	17 New Zealanders
16 November	Arab-Australians	2 Australians
17 November	Three Canadian politicians	Canadians
22 November	Edgar Oehler, Swiss Parliamentary Group	36 Swiss
22 November	Delegation of European politicians led by Jean-Marie le Pen	35 Britons, 15 Italians, 15 Germans, 6 Irish, 5 Dutch, 3 Danes, 2 Belgians, 1 Portuguese, 1 Greek

DATE	INDIVIDUAL	NATIONALITIES
22 November	Swiss Parliamentary delegation	16 Swiss, 4 Irish, 4 Swedes, 4 Germans, 4 Dutch, 4 Belgians, 2 Britons
24 November	British wives	10 husbands
25 November	Ron Brown (British MP)	5 Britons
26 November	Greek Pacifist Group	10 Greeks
26 November	American families	3 Americans
29 November	Archbishop Hilarion Capucci, former Greek Catholic Patriarch of Jerusalem	68 Italians
29 November	Canadian Parliamentary delegation	6 Canadians
2 December	Tony Benn (British MP)	15 Britons
2 December	Muhammad Ali (former boxer)	15 Americans
4 December	General Miroslav Vacek (former Czech Defence Minister)	40 Czechs
6 December	Antonio Anoki (Japanese MP)	36 Japanese

CHAPTER 18

Showdown in Geneva

As with the initial announcement of the 'extra mile', President Bush's latest announcement rekindled fears among America's regional allies, and hopes among Saddam's sympathizers, of last-minute wobbling. The Palestinian leadership chose the moment to underscore its alignment with Iraq. Addressing a popular rally in Baghdad, Yasser Arafat said that should war break out, the Palestinians would be 'in the same trench with the Iraqi people to confront the US–Zionist–Atlantic build-up of invading forces, which are desecrating Arab lands'.[1] His deputy, Salah Khalaf (alias Abu Iyad), resorted to even more fiery rhetoric. 'The Palestinian and Jordanian people will stand by fraternal Iraq in any aggression against it,' he announced at a public gathering in Amman. 'We shall not abandon Palestine. We renew the pledge to liberate all of Palestine inch by inch from the sea to the river.'[2]

In private, however, Abu Iyad was apparently far more sceptical about the chances of achieving this goal, officially renounced by the PLO when it recognized the existence of the State of Israel in December 1988. During a meeting with Saddam in mid November 1990, he reportedly outraged the Iraqi leader, as well as his own boss, Yasser Arafat, by bluntly criticizing the damage caused by the Gulf crisis to the Palestinian cause. Abu Iyad was murdered on 15 January by a member of the Abu-Nidal group, who had managed to infiltrate the PLO. It is not entirely clear whether the murder was Abu Nidal's private initiative (the two had been trying to kill each other for a long time), or was ordered by Saddam, as revenge for Abu Iyad's alleged defiance.[3] Whatever the truth of Abu Iyad's encounter with Saddam, the PLO was already paying a price in terms of its estrangement from mainstream Arab governments. One consequence of this was that Arafat hurried back to Tunis and was unable to advise Saddam – for better or worse – during the war.

The response of the Arab members of the coalition to Bush's announcement was to convene quickly yet another meeting of their foreign ministers in Riyadh. While paying obligatory lip service to the forthcoming meeting in

Geneva, they warned the Administration against reaching 'any settlement based on a partial withdrawal from Kuwait or on rewarding an aggressor'.[4] Bush was equally quick in reassuring them that he had no intention of letting Saddam off the hook at such a crucial stage in the crisis. The only purpose of the Geneva meeting, he asserted, was to ensure that the Iraqis appreciated the seriousness of their situation, that force would be used against them if necessary. As Saddam approached the brink, when he might just back off as he had done in the past, then the wisdom of such a course should be underscored. The meeting was Saddam's last chance to save his skin. It was up to him to decide whether or not to avert war.

The Administration examined a number of possibilities for the meeting prior to James Baker's departure for his European trip. One was that the Iraqis would walk out almost immediately, another that some token concession would be offered by Baghdad to string the Americans along. Another would be an invitation for Baker to visit Baghdad. A positive response was publicly ruled out prior to the meeting.

In these discussions the Americans came up with a series of tests which they would have been prepared to outline, in public, if there was even a hint of Iraqi compliance with the UN resolutions, involving practical demonstrations of its readiness to implement a full, unconditional withdrawal. This was to forestall any tactical device designed to get something out of the Kuwaiti adventure and divide the coalition. In order to avoid accusations of shutting the door on peace if the meeting came to naught, it was agreed that the Administration would encourage the UN Secretary-General, Javier Perez de Cuellar, to prepare to visit Iraq for a last minute 'rescue mission'.

Because of doubts as to whether Saddam was ever given the unvarnished truth from his necessarily sycophantic aides, it was decided to send him a direct letter from the President. The idea was to convey a stern but not hostile message, in plain and simple language sufficient to eliminate any doubts that the Americans were not serious. The general line of argumentation followed a familiar pattern: the only way to avoid war was to comply with Resolution 678, and this reflected the view of the entire international community and not just that of the United States. Any war resulting from Iraq's obstinacy would be a calamity for that country, and if President Saddam failed to understand this and how isolated he was, then hopefully the letter would 'eliminate any uncertainty or ambiguity'. There could be no reward for aggression nor negotiations over possible withdrawal. The advantages to Iraq after compliance with UN resolutions were an 'opportunity to rejoin the international community' and for 'the Iraqi military establishment' to escape destruction; the disadvantages attending rejection would involve much more than the loss of Kuwait. Saddam should not misconstrue the 'diversity of opinion that is American democracy' for the lack of American resolve. The penultimate paragraph contained a stark warning:

> the United States will not tolerate the use of chemical or biological weapons, support of any kind of terrorist actions, or the destruction of Kuwait's oilfields and installations. The American people would demand the strongest possible response. You and your country will pay a terrible price if you order unconscionable action of this sort.

The President concluded by asserting that he was writing 'not to threaten, but to inform'. Whether there would be further violence was in Saddam's hands. 'I hope you weigh your choice carefully and choose wisely, for much will depend on it.' It was a warning to be underlined by Baker in the meeting.

Baker arrived in Geneva in the morning of 9 January, at the end of an exhausting schedule which included visits to five European countries. Preliminary talks between advance parties to arrange the encounter at the Salon des Nations in the Geneva Intercontinental Hotel had not been encouraging. There had been intense debate over every possible aspect of procedure. The Iraqis, for example, insisted that the two delegations walk into the room and sit down at exactly the same time.

This the two men did. Then the cameraman came in for a photo and Baker and Aziz were asked for a handshake. Baker complied, carefully avoiding a smile as he did so. Aziz smiled. When the media were out of the way, the two delegations got down to business. Baker had with him three of his officials: Robert Kimmitt, Under Secretary of State for Political Affairs, Dennis Ross, Director of the State Department Policy Planning Staff, and John Kelly, Assistant Secretary of State for Near Eastern and South Asian Affairs. Aziz was flanked by Iraq's Ambassador to the UN in Geneva and Saddam's half-brother, Barzan al-Takriti, and by Saddam's personal interpreter.

Lasting for nearly seven hours, the meeting was conducted throughout in a calm and polite manner, without raised voices. The American members of the delegation were impressed by Aziz's professionalism: Baker later remarked that Aziz did not have 'a great deal of latitude', but 'did a very good job with an extraordinarily bad brief'.[5] Although Aziz knows English, he spoke Arabic, using English only on occasion to make himself clear. This may have been to ensure that his language was correct, or simply for the benefit of his handlers, and in particular Ambassador al-Takriti. This was one reason for the prolongation of the encounter. As the Americans expected it might be, the meeting was taped, although this time the transcript was not released until a full year after that event.[6] Unless otherwise stated, quotations are from this text.

The first key item of business was Bush's letter, which Baker wished to deliver to Saddam. It was in a sealed 8 × 10 manilla envelope but with a copy in English outside it. Aziz took the copy and read it, for what seemed to the American delegation an inordinately long time, underlining the passages about the use of force, but not saying a word. One member of the American delegation noticed him beginning to perspire and a slight tremble in his hand and judged him to be under considerable strain. When he finished, he did not consult with his colleagues but simply looked at Baker and said that he could not accept it. He explained that it was 'full of threats and it has a language which is not normally used in dialogue between heads of state', adding sardonically that the Americans could publish it in their media. He then put the letter back on the table. Baker commented on the responsibility accepted by Aziz: as his colleagues had not seen the letter and as the Americans might decide not to publish it, he would be the only Iraqi aware of its contents.

There were three aspects of the debate between the two men which then followed: the nature of the American threats to Iraq and the Iraqi counter-threats; the exploration of the origins of the dispute; the search for a negotiated settlement. The last of these was scant. Baker did not move beyond the UN resolutions and Aziz beyond the vagaries of the 12 August statement by Saddam. The history of the dispute took up a considerable amount of time but went over familiar ground, and was interesting only in incidental detail. The trading of threats, albeit undertaken in a measured way, provides the most striking feature of the exchanges.

This got under way immediately after the episode with the letter, and had become even more important to Baker because the letter had not been taken. He sought to impress upon Aziz the reality of American power, helped by permission from the military to be quite explicit. He hoped to convince the Iraqis that they were not going to be able to 'set the terms of this engage-ment, as you might have done in the Iran–Iraq War'. If they realized the 'scope and magnitude of the technology' they were about to face then they would be well advised to follow all the 'Security Council's resolutions' and leave unconditionally. The midnight deadline on 15 January was real.[7]

The only question was whether or not Iraq would leave Kuwait peacefully or through force:

> It is obvious that if there is a peaceful settlement of the crisis and you
> withdraw, those who are living in Iraq now will have a say in the future

of Iraq. But if the withdrawal happens as a result of the use of force, others will decide that future.

Baker insisted that he was communicating rather than threatening, because it was up to the Iraqis what they did with the information. He told Aziz of the 'absolute technological superiority', as well as superiority in 'overall weight' of the international forces deployed in the region, and their 'smashing destructive powers'. He stated specifically that as a result 'your ability to command your forces' would be destroyed, but also that 'we will give your troops in Kuwait the opportunity to save themselves. It is not part of our plans to destroy these forces immediately and swiftly.' There would be 'no UN truce creating a breathing space or negotiations'. The war would be fought for 'a quick and decisive end'. He then moved on to an explicit and critical threat:

> [I]f the conflict starts, God forbid, and chemical or biological weapons are used against our forces, the American people would demand revenge, and we have the means to implement this. This is not a threat, but a pledge that if there is any use of such weapons, our objective would not be only the liberation of Kuwait, but also the toppling of the present regime. Any person who is responsible for the use of these weapons would be held accountable in the future.
>
> ... we will not permit terrorism to be directed against Americans or against their partners in the coalition, and also we will not allow any attempt to destroy Kuwaiti oilfields.

Even if these things were avoided the Iraqi state was at risk. As a result of a war it would be transformed into something 'weak and backward'.

As the Iraqi leadership studied these warnings later, they could have drawn three conclusions. First, the Americans believed that its grip on power would be weakened by any war, as a result of its destructiveness and the specific attacks on the command structure; second, any use of chemical or biological weapons would lead to a dangerous escalation of allied war aims; and finally, this escalation might also be true for terrorism and the destruction of the Kuwaiti oilfields, but there was some ambiguity here.

Tariq Aziz for his part sought to disabuse the Americans of their belief that the Iraqis were ignorant of American power – 'We are an active government that works a great deal, reads, analyses and follows up.' There were 'no illusions' about US intentions, nor about war itself, having just been through an exceptionally long and painful one and emerged victorious. He then continued to make his own confident assertions:

> I tell you that the current leadership will continue to rule Iraq now and in the future, and that those who will disappear from the political theatre are not the Iraqi leadership but some of your allies in the region.

If war 'erupts', he stated, 'we will win'. There was no fear in Baghdad of the impending war. Iraq, he observed, came out of the war with Iran 'with huge military power'. With regard to the specific threats made by Baker, Aziz said little, though later, during a discussion of allegations of past chemical weapons use, he said: 'Yes, we have weapons. But we will not use them irresponsibly. We will use them to defend our country, if the need arises.' Much later in the discussion, when the two returned to the likely outcome of a war, Aziz stressed over again that while the next war might be different, the past one had told the Iraqis much about combat and endurance. They would be fighting 'on our own soil'. Unlike the Americans, who wanted a short war, 'we are determined and confident that it will be long'.

He dismissed Baker's observations on the broad nature of the coalition. The war would be America versus Iraq. British forces were few and French were fewer. He was utterly dismissive of the possibility that Iraq would confront Arab forces on the battlefield. 'Their leaders might tell you that they would fight on your side,' he said,

> but when a war breaks out between an Arab and Muslim country on the one hand, and foreign powers such as the United States, Britain, and other foreign nations, on the other, combatants will not keep in mind that they will be fighting to vindicate UN resolutions ... The soldier in our region does not fight only when ordered to do so. Indeed he fights out of convictions ... Against the backdrop of your ties with Israel, I would like to tell you in all sincerity that if you initiate military action against an Arab country, you will be faced with hostile sentiment in the region, and in many Muslim states as well.

Citing Nasser as an example, he also observed that 'never has an Arab regime entered into a war with Israel or the United States and lost politically'.

It is remarkable how little discussion there was during the meeting of any way out of the crisis. After issuing his warnings in the opening statement, Baker promised that Iraq would not be attacked if there was a positive response to the Security Council resolutions. The United States had no intention of sustaining its current level of military force once Iraqi forces had withdrawn, he said, especially those equipped with offensive capabilities, and it supported 'the idea of settling differences between Iraq and Kuwait peacefully as provided for by Resolution 660'.

This latter offer might have been intriguing for Aziz to explore. He never picked it up nor contemplated any change in the new status of Kuwait. The only specific offer he made was to invite Baker to visit Baghdad, an impossibility given both the past wrangling about dates (which was gone over again at great length) and the lack of any movement on the Iraqi part. He denied the validity of the UN resolutions orchestrated by the United States, observing the double standards illustrated by the pressure they were prepared to put on Iraq on the one hand, and Israel on the other, when it came to implementing UN resolutions. Throughout he reiterated the linkage between the invasion of Kuwait and the Palestinian problem and the centrality of this issue for the Iraqi leadership. 'We truly believe,' he said, 'that the failure to resolve [the Palestinian question] will pose threats to Iraq's security.' He then offered his own vision of a settlement:

> I would like to tell you in all sincerity and seriousness that we would have no problems implementing legitimacy and the rules of justice and fairness if these principles were to be honoured with regard to all regional conflicts. Such a thing would promote our interests and realize our aspirations ... However, we do not want to see these principles implemented with regard to a single issue ... this would mean that double standards were at work ... If you are willing to work to achieve peace, justice, stability, and security in the whole region, then you would find us at the forefront of those willing to co-operate with you in this regard.

What this co-operative approach might mean Aziz would not say. He gave no indication of accepting the implications of his statement – that somehow Iraq's occupation of Kuwait was on a par with Israel's occupation of the Golan Heights and the West Bank. Baker was more concerned with denying the validity of linkage, in that Kuwait had not been invaded because of Palestine, than probing into how it might work in practice. In the press conference after the meeting, Aziz was less evasive. When asked whether Iraq would be willing to leave Kuwait if promised an international conference on the Palestinian problem, he answered with a categorical no, insisting that he had not alluded to such an option during the talks, nor indeed to any readiness to withdraw. All he had promised Baker, he said, was that if the United States would respect 'international legality', it would find Iraq 'very co-operative'.[8]

As they were talking, Bush's letter remained on the table. When breaks were taken, the US security staff kept a vigilant eye on it. As the meeting came to a close, Baker asked Aziz once more if he would take the letter and

Aziz said he could not do so. Baker instead picked up the copy with Aziz's underlinings. State Department officials took the sealed envelope back for the White House. The two men left for their respective press conferences.

By the time that President Bush got up that morning the meeting was already a number of hours old in Geneva. Together with Cheney, Scowcroft and Quayle, he watched the reporting on CNN in a small office off the Oval Office. Unlike other viewers who, due to the unexpected prolongation of the meeting, were speculating a possible diplomatic breakthrough, the four were aware that there had been none. At the first break – for lunch – Baker reported back on the lack of progress and Iraq's refusal to accept the letter. As the Geneva meeting concluded, the President and some of his top advisers, including Cheney and Powell, were meeting with members of the Congressional leadership. They broke away to watch Baker's press conference, needing only to look at the Secretary of State's face to confirm the result.

Emerging from the conference hall in an evidently sombre mood, James Baker pointed an accusing finger to Baghdad. 'I heard nothing which showed any Iraqi flexibility whatsoever,' he told a press conference. To the contrary, during the talks Aziz gave the impression of a

> man who thought that fate had sort of decreed that this was the way it was going to be, and if they were going to have to take this sort of punishment, so be it, that was what was going to happen.[9]

'The conclusion is clear,' he said. 'Saddam Hussein continues to reject a diplomatic solution.'[10]

After Baker's press conference Aziz sent an aide to the CNN control room to check whether Bush was also going to talk to the press, which would have upstaged him. Having discovered that the President was waiting to hear him, he gave his own account. Iraq was interested in 'a genuine, constructive dialogue between the two nations in order to make peace in the region', he argued, but the Americans had no intention to conduct such a dialogue. All they wanted was to impose their terms on Iraq, forgetting that this proud nation 'would never yield to threats'.[11] Neither Saddam nor Aziz appeared to have expected anything concrete in Geneva: the two did not even talk to each other during the course of the day.[12]

CHAPTER 19
Deadline Diplomacy

With the conclusion of the Baker–Aziz meeting American diplomacy had run its course. In Europe the issue was whether the Community should try and take over the running. The problem with a separate and ostentatious diplomatic effort was that it must either convey the agreed coalition message, which would be pointless, or convey a different message, which risked a split in the coalition. Nonetheless, sentiment for a distinctive European initiative had been running strong since December.

The European Community followed the 'mile for peace' proposal by offering direct talks of their own with Aziz. When Iraq rejected the American proposals for the Baker visit, the EC was told that a European visit would still be welcome. Having been kept in the dark about Bush's original initiative, the European ministers – meeting in Rome in mid-December – felt themselves under no obligation to leave all the diplomatic activity up to Washington. The Italians, with the other Mediterranean states of Spain, Greece and France, wanted 1 January to be set as a deadline for a European initiative if the American talks had stalled completely. The majority saw no purpose in creating the impression of a split with the United States. They stuck to the original position that Aziz could only be seen on his return from talks in Washington.

France was still hinting that if nothing came of an Iraqi–American dialogue it might well take up the challenge and send Foreign Minister Dumas to Baghdad, 'even if there is a partial proposal from the Iraqis that merits discussion'. The relevant date here was 3 January 1991 – the last date set by Washington for Baker's visit to Baghdad. With German support, President Mitterrand wanted the Community to meet the next day. Though still sticking close to UN resolutions, he hinted that there might be some extra time for an Iraqi withdrawal so long as there was a definite timetable.[1]

In general, the Germans contented themselves with support for French initiatives in the EC. France's military commitment and position on the Security Council gave it more standing in crisis diplomacy. Nonetheless, the

Foreign Minister, Hans-Dietrich Genscher, felt a vocation as a crisis manager and spent his Christmas vacation in a series of discussions with key participants. Contacts with Iraq's Ambassador to Bonn led to proposals for a 'democratic' form of government in Kuwait that would allow for the removal of the al-Sabah family from office. It was hard to see how the 'democratization' argument would impress the Iraqi dictator – except to the extent that he had altered the demographic structure of Kuwait (a move to which the UN had been adamantly opposed).

Genscher appears to have identified the Yugoslavs, who had good contacts with Iraq and a claim to be representing the non-aligned movement in the search for peace, as a potential intermediary between the EC and Iraq. On 28 December, the Yugoslav Foreign Minister, Budimir Loncar, arrived in Baghdad to be met by Aziz wearing a military uniform. That evening and the next day the two had intensive discussions. Aziz was in a tough mood. On 30 December Loncar got to see Saddam, who was equally unyielding. 'The people of Iraq are ready to pay the price of their dignity.' At one point he said that he would make a concession if one was forthcoming from the other side. Following this up, Loncar put forward the idea that he had presumably been developing with Genscher. That day the Community had announced a meeting planned for 4 January. Why not negotiate with the Europeans? A gesture from Iraq and then the EC could issue a forceful statement urging a peaceful settlement. When pressed by Saddam, Loncar had to admit that the EC would side with the United States in the event of war. The Iraqi leader showed no interest in discussing the matter further.[2]

The idea of using states sympathetic to Iraq as intermediaries was also reflected in a proposal to send an EC mission to Tunisia, Algeria and Jordan. The doubtful nature of such efforts meant that those most anxious for progress returned again to the possibility of the Europeans arranging a direct meeting of their own. The new President of the Council of Ministers, Luxembourg, supported this idea: Foreign Minister Jacques Poos expressed his readiness to visit Baghdad.

One reason why President Bush revived the idea of a Baker–Aziz meeting on 3 January, the day before the Community was due to meet, was to head off such an initiative. When the EC Foreign Ministers gathered the next day, they did not know whether Iraq would respond positively and so they set about discussing among themselves whether they should send the troika of the Italian, Luxembourg and Dutch foreign ministers to Baghdad even if the Americans were rebuffed. Luxembourg, France, Germany and Italy believed it imperative that this should be tried if all other diplomatic communications failed. Due to their presumed greater experience of dealing with the Arab

World, European countries might somehow succeed where the United States had not.

As the Community was bound to insist on the full implementation of UN resolutions, the only likely room for manoeuvre was over the possible linkage with the Palestinian dispute. In all the agitation for a political settlement at this time, this was clung to as the last best hope.[3] The French (along with the Russians) believed there were signs of an Iraqi willingness to withdraw in the event of major concessions on the Palestinian problem, although there had never been anything firm on this and certainly no evidence that Saddam would be satisfied with a promise to convene an international conference already agreed in principle at the UN. Nor was the benefit to Saddam evident in other ideas, such as tolerating a public Iraqi pledge of withdrawal without physically leaving Kuwait by 15 January, rather than demanding actual withdrawal by that date.

Britain and Holland made it clear that they would not support linkage. Direct talks with Iraq were acceptable only if, as proposed before, they followed direct US–Iraqi talks. The British were highly sceptical anyway regarding the chances of a negotiated compromise. They had agreed to the proposed meeting with the Iraqis in December largely to ensure collective action and pre-empt others from 'making individual pilgrimages to Baghdad'. In the Anglo-Dutch view, the best hope of persuading the Iraqi leader to withdraw still involved leaving him in no doubts regarding the seriousness of his situation, sweetened only by assurances that there would be no military action if Iraq did withdraw.

The debate eased as news came through that Iraq had accepted the American invitation. The Community could now offer to meet Iraq in a follow-on meeting. There was no longer any need to worry about the Iraqis saying 'no' to the US and 'yes' to Europe, thereby suggesting that the Community was a soft option. To the chagrin of the most enthusiastic promoters of the European option, Iraq said 'yes' to the US and 'no' to Europe, on the grounds that in the past Europe had provided nothing more than an echo of American policy and had demonstrated its subservience by backing away when the initial attempt to set up the Baker–Aziz talks faltered. Aziz made clear in his press conference following the Geneva meeting that Iraq would only be interested in talks if the Community visibly exceeded American limits by agreeing that the 'troika' should visit Baghdad. Even the Euro-doves recognized that this would be humiliating.[4] Saddam was now dubious about any initiatives from Europe. The fact that the release of hostages had brought about no reciprocal concession, but rather an expression of relief from Bush that his hands were less tied, even raised questions with regard to French complicity in a plot with the US, as Paris had made the boldest claims for the positive consequences of such a move.[5]

Mitterrand tries his hand

Paris was unaware of such suspicions. A unilateral French effort had been under consideration for some time. Unlike the open diplomacy of the Americans, designed to demonstrate to Saddam the cohesion of the coalition, French diplomacy was concerned with finding a way out of the impasse without attracting accusations of seeking a self-serving deal. President Mitterrand was inhibited by widespread suspicions that he was doing precisely that. His backdoor diplomacy was also confused by a number of potential emissaries whose actual status was uncertain to themselves as well as to the Iraqis.

One such person was Edgar Pisani, director of the Institute of the Arab World in Paris and a key figure in Franco-Arab contacts. In late September he met the former Algerian leader Ahmad Ben-Bella in Madrid, where the two decided to explore ways of avoiding the drive to war. Ben-Bella wanted to convince Saddam to talk to Mitterrand, with Pisani acting as an authorized French emissary and Saddam's half-brother, Barzan al-Takriti, speaking for the Iraqi President. For the contact to succeed some sort of plan was needed: Pisani and Ben-Bella met in mid-November to identify the basis of a settlement, which somehow had to see Kuwait liberated without Saddam being discredited. They looked back to the last Saudi proposals prior to the Iraqi occupation of Kuwait, namely, Kuwaiti concessions on Iraqi debts, the Rumaila oilfields, and a lease of the Bubiyan and Warba islands to provide access to the sea. To this they now added the Palestinian question. Pisani recognized that this was rather generous to Saddam who had, after all, been the aggressor. When he discussed this with Mitterrand he got authority to meet with Barzan but not to visit Baghdad.

They met on 5 December in Geneva. Pisani explained that he was not empowered to negotiate, but was anxious to reassure his suspicious counterpart (who had gained notoriety as head of the main Iraqi security service, the Mukhabarat, between 1974 and 1983) that there was no plot against Saddam, only concern at the upset to an emerging regional and international balance caused by his invasion of Kuwait. Pisani also stressed the hostility against Iraq generated by the holding of the hostages, suggesting that their liberation would turn international public opinion. War would then be impossible because nobody in France and America would want to die for the Emir of Kuwait. It was a message which fitted in with Barzan's own assessments. He promised to take it to Baghdad.[6]

By Christmas 1990 Pisani had tried again with Barzan.[7] Beforehand he developed a plan of his own, which had even scripted the dialogue for the main participants, based on Saddam using the various gestures made on the Palestine problem in recent months to assert his desire to avoid war and readiness to withdraw from Kuwait if foreign troops left the Gulf states. The conclusion of the mini-drama involved four 'calendars': for withdrawal from Kuwait, the progressive withdrawal of foreign troops, an international conference on Palestine, and measures to deal with regional security, oil and Lebanon, as requested by Saddam. Again Barzan promised to transmit this 'very interesting' plan to Baghdad. Encouraged, Pisani reported back to Mitterrand, who seemed satisfied, but would still not let him visit Baghdad.

The reason was that Mitterrand, not content with one intermediary, had chosen Michel Vauzelle, Chairman of the National Assembly's Foreign Affairs Committee, as emissary to Saddam. Mitterrand had been considering Vauzelle since November, when Primakov had argued that his conversations with Saddam had suggested that the Iraqis might be more forthcoming if there were clearer signs with regard to the more positive consequences of withdrawal from Kuwait. Vauzelle combined a good personal relationship with the President (he had served as his spokesman from 1981 to 1986) with a national position as a leading parliamentarian unencumbered by the constraints faced by a Minister or an Ambassador.[8]

Vauzelle still had to go through the normal preliminaries with Yasser Arafat, who seemed to have become Saddam's doorman, checking the credentials of would-be visitors to Baghdad. Vauzelle asked the Élysée for permission to meet Arafat in Tunis and this was granted. They met at the end of November, as the Security Council was adopting Resolution 678. Arafat stressed the importance of French arbitration, and as a result Vauzelle asked for permission to visit Baghdad. In late December, with the 'extra mile' initiative in abeyance, Dumas and Mitterrand agreed so long as the visit was seen as unofficial. Vauzelle left on 2 January.

In public, Dumas explained that Vauzelle had 'no mandate for negotiation', but admitted that he was a close friend of Mitterrand and had met the President before embarking on his trip. It was hard to believe that Vauzelle was 'carrying no message' and was 'charged with no mission'.[9] If these emissaries gained concrete evidence that Saddam was prepared to resolve the crisis in a way which loosely accorded with UN resolutions, then Mitterrand was prepared to shift these contacts to official channels. However, even if Saddam offered the requisite hints, the transition from backdoor to frontdoor diplomacy was always going to be difficult because of the need to give credibility to what had hitherto been described as private initiatives without, at the same time, undermining the credibility of the agreed coalition position.

Vauzelle met Saddam on 5 January, the day after the Community meeting. He listened for hours while Saddam developed his familiar conspiracy theory and made little progress. Saddam insisted that he had not rejected all negotiations and appreciated the efforts made by France. 'I understand that President Mitterrand has to adopt a certain attitude,' he told Vauzelle, 'but it would be useful if we could directly talk about this with an official envoy. It is not up to me to decide who should be coming, but Tariq Aziz put all his hopes in a trip by Roland Dumas.' Vauzelle answered that an official trip was inconceivable without a concrete gesture from Iraq.[10] The equation had not changed since the autumn.

Vauzelle returned home on 7 January via Tunis. His message on arrival was that everything was possible 'provided Iraq makes certain gestures', and that the Iraqi price for withdrawal was international movement on Palestine and concessions to meet both economic and political Iraqi grievances in the Gulf. He stressed Saddam's expectations of a French initiative, and when they met urged Dumas and Mitterrand to provide one. It was not so easy. The two were sceptical regarding Saddam's sincerity and saw little point in an official visit at that juncture, when it would be seen as a direct challenge to the Americans. Instead, they decided to continue developing an initiative which could be launched should the Aziz–Baker meeting fail.

Its basis would be a draft resolution to the Security Council. The intermediary was to be Algeria, because of its links with both Baghdad and Paris and President Benjedid's familiarity with the issues following his own recent initiative. After contact was made on 8 January in Algiers with Benjedid, the Algerian Foreign Minister, Ahmed Ghozali, departed for Paris. On arrival he told the familiar story: no joint plan but just a feeling that joint efforts might facilitate a dialogue with Iraq. Dumas had also gained Moroccan support and, apparently, through King Hassan, at least Saudi tolerance so long as the United States was kept informed. Mitterrand planned to send a senior official to Riyadh.

Before doing so, however, it was necessary to await the outcome of the Geneva talks. Mitterrand arranged a press conference for the afternoon of 9 January to launch his initiative immediately after the predicted failure of the Geneva summit. He was wrong-footed by their unexpectedly long duration. The Americans were not displeased. They had promised to keep him informed but the message from Geneva to Paris prior to Mitterrand's press conference was simply that there was as yet no outcome, thus making it difficult for the President to assume either a definitive success or a failure. The grudging Mitterrand could therefore say little other than that France would act 'in the service of peace' right up to the deadline, to which he promised adherence and which could not be extended 'under any pretext whatsoever'. He was in contact with large numbers of countries but denied that he would send an emissary to Iraq: 'The right conditions must be present for such a move and that is not my impression now.' He claimed that the United States now accepted that a firm Iraqi commitment to withdrawal would put off direct action. Significantly, he emphasized the differences on the issue of an international conference on the Arab–Israeli conflict. 'The United States has always been hostile to this idea and now says it could appear an unacceptable concession to Saddam Hussein,' he said. 'I can well understand this position, but it should not lead to a weakening of the French position on the same point.'[11] This was a longstanding French objective: Mitterrand was not 'going to give up at the most important moment'.

The next potential launching pad was a luncheon Dumas had arranged with all Arab Ambassadors to Paris on 10 January. But then Perez de Cuellar announced that he was to go to Baghdad. Frustrated, the Foreign Ministry urged the President to press ahead regardless: any further delay and the opportunity might be lost. Mitterrand refused. He could not undermine the UN Secretary-General. In any event, he did not expect any Iraqi movement until the very last moment. As with many others, he assumed Saddam would wait until the closing minutes of the deadline to obtain the maximum concessions. Furthermore, following Perez de Cuellar's trip, more would be known about Saddam's general attitude which, in turn, might help the French initiative. Last but not least, if Saddam refused the UN and France in turn, then Mitterrand would be able to use this intransigence to justify France's resort to arms.[12]

As they waited for Perez de Cuellar's visit, the French kept their initiative warm. On 11 January, Dumas met Farouq Qaddoumi, the PLO's Foreign Minister. Defence Minister Chevènement claimed that a 'very small gesture' by the US in support of a Middle East conference could provide Saddam Hussein with an opportunity to make a 'very large one' by withdrawing from Kuwait.

> Everyone knows that this conference will be all the more urgently needed after a conflict. So why not make an announcement about it right now, if that would spare us the fighting. That is not the American position, but it is the French position, and my loyalty is only to France.[13]

Meanwhile, Edgar Pisani was still pursuing his now essentially private initiative. He met Barzan in Geneva, the day after the Baker–Aziz talks, and proposed an 'Arab solution' to all the Iraqi–Kuwaiti disputes following an Iraqi withdrawal. Again Barzan claimed interest. He discussed it with Tariq Aziz, who was still in Geneva, and who in turn promised a phone call from Baghdad the next day. Again nothing resulted.[14]

Enter Perez de Cuellar

The Bush Administration had opted for a meeting between Saddam Hussein and the UN Secretary-General as the next diplomatic step. This would emphasize that the pressure on Iraq came from the international community as a whole and not just from the United States. If Saddam really was ready to climb down, he would find it easier to do so to the UN than to the US. This move also had the advantage of making it more difficult for a unilateral French initiative to get off the ground. James Baker's meeting in Paris just before he arrived in Geneva had left him exasperated and suspicious of French intentions, and he wanted to keep them off centre stage for as long as possible. Baker had almost invited Perez de Cuellar to make the trip at his press conference, while Aziz revealed that contacts with the Secretary-General's office had been opened up a few days earlier, when Iraq had indicated its readiness to welcome the Secretary-General to Baghdad. On the evening of 9 January, Perez de Cuellar lost no time in announcing his departure for Baghdad: it was his 'moral duty' to do 'everything to avoid the worst'.

The Secretary-General's handicap as a mediator was that he could not go beyond the mandate of the UN resolutions. All he could suggest was that the Palestinian problem would move higher up the agenda, and that UN troops would help monitor a withdrawal so that the United States would not be in charge of the transition. Like Mitterrand, he had been a longstanding proponent of a Middle Eastern peace conference, and had sundry General Assembly resolutions to back attempts to set one up. He was known to be unhappy with the role of the UN during the crisis, particularly over the deadline and the prospective military action, and had hoped for another Security Council meeting before the deadline expired. The prospect of a meeting with Saddam did not lighten his mood. He viewed his chances of success as virtually nil and saw how his mission might be used as the trigger for military action. Still, he felt that he had to be seen to be making this last effort. Just before departing, he stated publicly that he had 'no proposals to make'. He was travelling to Iraq only 'in order to listen and to be listened to by the Iraqi authorities'.[15]

As with the aborted visit by Baker to Baghdad, the visit of even the Secretary-General of the United Nations had to follow certain proprieties. These were presented by the Iraqis as no more than due protocol but appeared like calculated insults to their would-be interlocutors. Having arrived in Baghdad on the night of 11 January, Perez de Cuellar had to wait nearly two days for his session with Saddam. Meanwhile he was required to endure prolonged meetings with Tariq Aziz and Yasser Arafat. To add insult to injury, this long delay was matched by frustration with the actual meeting with Saddam. When allowed at long last to see him, there were the familiar tales of 'American–Zionist plots' and proposals for Arab solutions, with no promises on withdrawal.

Once again the Iraqis later published a transcript of the meeting.[16] This shows the Secretary-General going out of his way to placate his hosts, and within his extremely limited mandate offering the Iraqi President a ladder to climb down. 'As a man of Hispanic origins,' he told Saddam, 'I feel I am close to the Arab world and to the Palestinian people.' Saddam had 'made a great service to the Palestinian issue because you have placed the fate of the Palestinian people on the agenda'. To offer Saddam some hope, he drew attention to his conversations with George Bush just before he left, when the US President had 'admitted the urgent need' to tackle this problem. There was a promise of taking steps to remove 'weapons of mass destruction in Israel'. He agreed emphatically that Saddam's 'peace plan' of 12 August had not been given due consideration but argued that it could still form a basis for the resolution of the crisis. When the Iraqi leader vehemently attacked the UN resolutions against Iraq, defining them as American and not UN resolutions, Perez de Cuellar agreed. 'I support you as far as the issue concerns me,' he said, 'these are not my decisions, but the resolutions of the Security Council.'

In a marked contrast to the Secretary-General's non-confrontational approach, Saddam remained as intransigent as ever. While expressing Iraq's interest in 'peace with justice', he accused the United States of preventing an Arab solution by internationalizing the crisis from the start. Strikingly, even by Saddam's own account, this much-vaunted Arab solution would not mean relinquishing Iraqi control over Kuwait; rather, it meant that 'the [Iraqi–Kuwaiti] union would have perhaps taken a longer time, allowing everyone to get acquainted with the legalistic steps of the unionist process'. In the wake of a lengthy historical and legal exposition on the artificiality of the Kuwaiti state and its borders, Saddam pointed to a map and posed the rhetorical question: 'When someone says let Iraq withdraw, the question is where to?'

The very fact that Saddam used the words 'Kuwait' and 'withdrawal' in the same breath might have been judged to have been significant. Yet the context was Saddam's insistence that Kuwait lacked firm borders and was followed by reminders that Iraqis 'know that Kuwait is the nineteenth province'. There was no question of withdrawal, particularly under American pressure:

> If we are given all the whole concessions that are in the world, no one will speak the word withdrawal when the Iraqi and American army are face to face and war might erupt in a few hours ... to utter the word withdrawal while there is still a chance for war means that we would be creating the psychological conditions for enemy victory over us.

On this note the meeting ended. Perez de Cuellar left Baghdad in the early morning hours of 14 January. He judged his mission a failure. 'You need two for tango,' he said. 'I wanted to dance but I did not find any nice lady for dancing with. Saddam did not express any desire to withdraw.'[17]

France's last try

The Secretary-General's experience provided few grounds for hope in yet another diplomatic initiative. Aware of this, Yasser Arafat desperately attempted to convince the French that Perez de Cuellar had misread this experience and that there was still a basis for hope. The long wait prior to the audience with Saddam he explained as being due to the difficulties in adjusting the diary of such a busy head of state and the importance of his prior discussions with Mrs Takako Doi, Secretary of the Japanese Socialist Party. This is why he, Arafat, had been asked to keep Perez de Cuellar company while he was waiting, a story which if true conveys something remarkable concerning the relationship between Arafat and Saddam at this time. To calm the Secretary-General down even further, Saddam went so far as to grant him an unusually long audience of six hours as well as to schedule further meetings with Tariq Aziz. Nonetheless, Arafat continued, with this visit Saddam had at last understood that there might actually be a war and was consequently trying to negotiate. As evidence Arafat cited the incident with the map and the rhetorical question about withdrawal from Kuwait. In the PLO leader's view, this was the beginning of a negotiation. When it was not picked up, the Iraqi President was exasperated. What was the UN Secretary-General doing there if he would not negotiate – except as another manifestation of the plot to humiliate him?[18]

Dumas and Mitterrand were more inclined to believe Perez de Cuellar's own version, which they heard from him directly when he stopped in Paris on his way from Baghdad on the morning of Sunday 14 January. Dumas raised again the possibility of France proposing a draft Security Council resolution. The additional possible feature of the initiative – a last-minute trip by Dumas to Baghdad – was ruled out by Mitterrand, having heard of the Secretary-General's humiliation. There would only be point if there was prior assurance that Saddam would accept the French plan.[19]

Dumas and the Secretary-General then flew on to a meeting of the European Foreign Ministers in Geneva which was already in session. In order to travel with the Secretary-General, Dumas had sent a junior in his stead (who also arrived late). Dumas himself did not arrive until the preparatory meeting was breaking up. By this time the European Foreign Ministers, having reviewed recent events and the familiar package of available concessions, had determined that there was little point in a further initiative. Perez de Cuellar's report confirmed this view. Jacques Poos observed that in the light of Saddam's rejections of all proposals, 'the climate does not allow a new peace initiative'. The various ideas of no attack on Iraq in the event of a withdrawal, UN troops to replace American troops, debt relief, and an eventual international conference had all been widely canvassed and Saddam had shown no interest. For some, such as the Italians and the Spanish, the only forlorn hope was that if Baker and Perez de Cuellar had failed to persuade Saddam of the folly of his ways, then perhaps other Arabs might. De Michelis of Italy phoned Yasser Arafat to urge him to impress upon the Iraqi leader the danger of the situation. As Douglas Hurd observed, 'Anyone who suggests that Mr Arafat is going to produce peace out of this problem has a loose grasp on reality.' Arafat gave his normal response: he invited Prime Minister Andreotti to Baghdad.[20]

Arafat himself was still banking on the French. President Mitterrand had not given up on the idea of a solo initiative. He met the Iraqi Ambassador and sent envoys to Saudi Arabia. Dumas was being kept on standby in case a signal came from Baghdad that a trip would be worthwhile. This unilateralism annoyed the smaller European countries, who pointed to the contrast with the staunch French support for a common integrated policy. European Commission President Jacques Delors was reported to have told Prime Minister Rocard and Foreign Minister Dumas that this sort of diplomacy was bad for the Community.

Nonetheless, after the EC had decided not to take further action and in the absence of any encouraging words from Baghdad, Dumas still decided to step forward with the only idea he had left – a proposal for a final Security Council resolution. This had the hallmarks of the classic politician's syllogism: something must be done, this is something, therefore we must do it.

The effort was doomed from the start and served only to cause divisions within the coalition.

All day on 14 January, French diplomats worked on the draft of a UN resolution. It began with an appeal to the Iraqi authorities to 'announce without further delay their intention to withdraw from Kuwait along the lines of a pre-planned schedule, and to begin a rapid and massive withdrawal . . . which is to commence immediately'. This would be controlled and verified by international observers and an Arab peace-keeping force organized through the UN. In return Iraq would get a guarantee of non-aggression and, 'in association with Arab countries, necessary measures to promote all useful negotiations to consolidate the process of a peaceful settlement'. Lastly,

> From the moment this settlement is agreed upon while respecting the Security Council resolutions, the members of this body will provide their active participation to the settlement of other regional problems and, in particular, of the Arab–Israeli conflict and the Palestinian problem by the convening, at the appropriate time, of an international conference, in conformity with the declaration of the President of the Security Council dated 20 December 1990, to ensure the security, stability and development of this part of the world.

This was a 'linkage' but, the French drafters hoped, only vaguely so in that it would come only after the settlement. This was not the only feature likely to be unacceptable to Britain and the Americans. The draft failed to contain any mention of the UN deadline.

While the drafting work was under way, Dumas and Mitterrand had lunch with John Major at the Elysée. The new Prime Minister had made a point of coming over to Paris to meet Mitterrand and show a degree of European solidarity on the eve of a conflict in which they both had forces at risk. Yet, though at that time a version of the plan was being sent out from the Quai d'Orsay to other Foreign Ministries, Major was kept in ignorance. According to the French, Mitterrand did say something to Major at one point about the fact that they were working on a draft for the Security Council, but Major did not react. The President had not pressed the matter because he was waiting for the final text and also for the results of the conversations of his envoy, Jean-Louis Bianco, with King Fahd and Sheikh Jaber in Riyadh and Taif; without their approval, or assurances of their neutrality, nothing could be achieved and the French would not risk an unnecessary row with the Americans. At 15.00 Bianco reported a low-key but not negative response. By this time Major had left.

After the meal Major observed to the press that it was 'hard to see what opportunities could be offered to Baghdad that have not already been offered', on the assumption that his hosts agreed.[21] When he found out later about the draft he could only assume that he had been deliberately misled. It took some time for Mitterrand to restore good relations with Major.

Dumas had spoken to Douglas Hurd, who had expressed polite interest before ringing back to explain that Britain would not give support. The text was unacceptable not only because of linkage but because of the lack of clarity on the modalities of withdrawal, such as monitoring and verification, which could have allowed Saddam opportunities for prevarication if he had chosen to enter into a discussion. Hurd had apparently not discussed it with Major, presumably because he would have had the same reaction.

The same response came from Washington. Baker said the text was 'unacceptable'. It would be opposed if put before the Security Council. He was unconvinced by both the vague linkage and the French timing. Mitterrand remained reluctant to submit the text formally without any sign of interest from Saddam. With assurance of Iraqi compliance the resolution would be a necessary part of the package; without it, there was little point in doing anything other than 'presenting' the text (although this was a distinction lost on casual observers).

That night Mitterrand asked Abd al-Razzaq al-Hashimi, the Iraqi Ambassador to Paris, to meet him. He told him that he was ready to press forward with his initiative if Saddam gave 'one positive signal'. Al-Hashimi had no new instructions: he could only repeat the standard request for a senior French official, preferably the Minister of Foreign Affairs, to come to Baghdad. He had transmitted the French plan to Baghdad and had been told that Saddam was ready to discuss it with Dumas. Mitterrand could not accept the risk of rebuff: he needed something more positive. Dumas received the same message. All the Iraqis would say in response to his prompting was, 'Come, and everything will be possible.' Mindful of Perez de Cuellar's experience, Mitterrand saw only trouble with the Americans and general doubts about France's commitment if he dispatched Dumas. Saddam's obsession with this visit also made the French President wary. He saw 'a trap'. If Saddam really did not want war, he told Dumas, then he 'wouldn't need your trip'.

At 18.00 that evening in New York, the five permanent members of the Security Council met in closed session to discuss the French ideas. China was not opposed, Soviet Ambassador Vorontsov, awaiting instructions, was non-committal. Britain and the United States were opposed, unconvinced by the complex explanation accompanying the French draft, now submitted as a declaration rather than a full resolution. The full Security Council met to be briefed by Perez de Cuellar on his trip to Baghdad before discussing the French plan.

The next day, 15 January, as the deadline loomed for Baghdad, discussion resumed behind closed doors. The British tabled a much tougher counter-text, beginning, 'Even now, on the day of the deadline set by Security Council Resolution 678, the members of the Security Council appeal to Iraq to display wisdom and responsibility and to make the only necessary step, which is to withdraw unconditionally from Kuwait . . .' This was supported by Soviet Ambassador Vorontsov. The Soviet line surprised Paris because it had been assumed that its policy was in line with that of Moscow. Two hours later, Moscow switched to support of the French text. The confusion appears to have resulted from disarray in Moscow. Shevardnadze was on the verge of submitting his final resignation, having dramatically announced his intention to leave the previous month warning of a conservative coup. He was not addressing this particular issue. Vorontsov had followed his own pro-American inclinations until, after Mitterrand had contacted Gorbachev, he was told to vote the other way.

The British and the French squabbled during the morning and into the afternoon in New York, but as Saddam was making no move, they eventually decided this was fruitless. They both withdrew their drafts in favour of an 'appeal to reason' to be made that evening at 18.30 by the Secretary-General. In this he said that:

> with the resolution of the present crisis, every effort will be made to address, in a comprehensive manner, the Arab–Israeli conflict, including the Palestinian question.

This was just tolerable to the British and Americans, as it was the Secretary-General's personal appeal and was based on a recognition of the probability of intensive post-crisis diplomacy rather than firm linkage, and also because it was now patently irrelevant. Iraq had shown no interest in the French or any other initiative, and Saddam had snubbed Mitterrand by announcing that there would be no withdrawal from Kuwait. Prime Minister Michel Rocard was forced to acknowledge that time had now run out and Iraq must be ejected by force:

> The time to act has, alas, come after we did everything we could to avoid it. France's initiatives have not met with the least response from the Iraqi side. No sign, I tell you none, has come from Iraq.[22]

274

CHAPTER 20

Saddam Prepares for War

Deciding on war

For Saddam, all the proposals for a diplomatic solution sweetened a very bitter pill with only a small amount of sugar. The only certain part was Iraq's withdrawal from Kuwait. Western pledges not to attack were firm, but these were the sort of promises he had made himself in the past to others and then ignored. If Saddam withdrew with his military power intact, then other actors in the area – including Kuwait – would want a continued Western presence and he would judge himself to be at continual risk. A partial withdrawal, by which he relinquished all of Kuwait other than, for example, one of the islands, would be of little help. It might help hold off war but was unlikely to see sanctions lifted and so provided no economic relief. If the withdrawal was not part of an agreed deal, then the fortifications from around the perimeter of Kuwait would be abandoned, exposing Iraqi forces in the process. Giving an inch in Kuwait would reveal a lack of confidence in the long-term position and the pressure to complete the withdrawal would be unremitting.

The idea of an international conference on the Arab–Israeli and other disputes, on which so many third parties pinned their hopes, never stood any real chance of enticing Iraq out of Kuwait. Not once did Saddam even imply that it was worth the release of Kuwait, as Aziz admitted after the Geneva meeting. He did not even refer to such a conference. What he meant by linkage was that the Palestinian problem (as well as the Syrian presence in Lebanon) would have to be *resolved*, and not merely addressed, before the Kuwaiti issue could be tackled. Given the complexity of these problems and the lengthy time required for their resolution, the concrete consequence of Saddam's 'linkage' was that he would be given an indefinite respite to 'Iraqize' Kuwait, while at the same time gaining enormous prestige in the Arab world. The vague prospect of a conference after he had been obliged to relinquish Kuwait never interested Saddam. As he could not be seen to be withdrawing simply because of American pressure, he had little choice but to prepare himself for war.

By the start of 1991, Saddam should have been aware that the coalition was more cohesive than expected: calls for popular insurrections against its Arab members had produced a minimal response; the attempt to wean France away through preferential release of hostages had failed; the Soviet Union had supported a series of tough anti-Iraq resolutions in the UN, including Resolution 678. Nonetheless Saddam still apparently hoped that the peace camp in the West, and the variety of would-be intermediaries still visiting him in Baghdad, would help him avert war. It was an almost fatalistic approach, wholly dependent upon political calculations in Washington which he could influence only by making any war seem as terrible as possible.

His residual hope that war might be avoided meant that apparently no serious consideration was given to a pre-emptive attack on coalition forces in Saudi Arabia to disrupt and confuse their preparations. The classic reason against pre-emption is that it makes inevitable what was before merely probable and can be used to justify terrible retribution. In addition it would have required a bold offensive plan at a time when, in military terms, Saddam was in a defensive frame of mind. His land forces were in no position to move forward. Any offensives were going to be essentially political in nature and designed to play on the supposed American intolerance of casualties and the disinclination of Arab members of the coalition to fight another state engaged in a conflict with Israel.

The military requirement was to deter, and if necessary rebuff, the central thrust of the enemy campaign while absorbing the enemy air assault. There was no obvious strategy for war termination other than inflicting such discomfort that the coalition would develop an interest in a cease-fire on terms other than the full implementation of all UN resolutions. Saddam strongly believed that the United States's Achilles' heel was its extreme sensitivity to casualties, and he was determined to exploit this weakness to the full. As he told the American Ambassador to Baghdad, April Glaspie, shortly before the invasion of Kuwait: 'Yours is a society which cannot accept 10,000 dead in one battle,' as if the fact this might be the case with Iraq was some sort of recommendation.[1] A constant theme in the Iraqi media was the evidence of Vietnam that public opinion would resent deaths in the desert and could not cope with the demands of a long war – which, they warned, was much more likely than the few weeks anticipated in the American press.

Saddam's awareness that a war might have to be fought could be seen on 12 December 1990, when the Iraqi Minister of Defence, General Abd al-Jabbar Khalil Shanshal, was replaced by Lieutenant General Sa'di

Tumah Abbas, a seasoned veteran of the Iran–Iraq War. An elderly professional soldier of a rather taciturn personality, Shanshal had assumed his position in mid 1989, following the mysterious death in a helicopter accident of the then Minister of Defence, Adnan Khairallah Talfah, Saddam's cousin. It had been clear from the beginning that Shanshal's appointment was temporary, designed to eliminate mutterings of discontent in the military regarding the cause of Adnan's death. His removal at that particular stage in the crisis, however, was illustrative of Saddam's growing conviction of the imminence of war.

Another indication was the intensification of the regime's hectic efforts to improve Iraq's military and civilian preparedness. Saddam held several well-publicized meetings with the military and the political leadership. Peasants, who at the beginning of the crisis had been exempted from military service as a means to combat the economic sanctions, were ordered to report immediately to their units. The public was given elaborate instructions regarding self-protection against chemical and nuclear attacks, and told to black out homes and to store a medicine cabinet in every apartment. Individuals and institutions were ordered to clear their shelters for immediate use, and to store oil products for an emergency. Civil defence drills were held, including a large-scale exercise of an evacuation of Baghdad, involving hundreds of thousands of people.[2]

The expectations of war were also reflected in the references of the Iraqi mass media to the crisis. Alongside the already standard doomsday scenarios of a 'second Vietnam', and threats to draw Israel into the conflict, a sombre, perhaps even apologetic, tone crept into the official commentaries. The Iraqi people were asked to brace themselves for yet another imposed war which was not of their leadership's choice. 'Iraq has given peace every chance it deserved, and has repeatedly proved that it was seeking peace,' argued the Iraqi press, 'but given the US–Western insistence on war and aggression, Iraq will not hesitate to engage in confrontation and fighting to destroy the invading forces.'[3] And Saddam put his acceptance of the inevitability of war in a somewhat fatalistic fashion: 'If it is God Almighty's will that we fight this battle to cleanse the Arab homeland of all this rottenness, so be it.'[4]

The die had been cast. Saddam's mind seemed to have been made up. War would not have been his first choice. However, caught between the risks of unconditional withdrawal and the risks but also the opportunities of an armed confrontation, the choice seemed self-evident. Were he to succeed in holding on against the coalition for some time, war would offer Saddam the best chance for political survival and even a final victory. The concessions available in pre-war negotiation were inferior to those that might be obtained as a result of battle. In addition, just as the Egyptian President Gamal Abd al-Nasser had managed to turn his country's military defeat in the 1956 Suez campaign, against a Franco-Anglo-Israeli coalition, into a resounding political victory, so Saddam seemingly hoped that the loss of Kuwait in a war with the allies would make him a hero, lauded by the Arab masses as a new Nasser, a leader who defied world imperialism and survived.

Given this apparent state of mind, a last-minute reversal in the Iraqi position was inconceivable. Saddam's readiness to send Tariq Aziz to Geneva and to meet Perez de Cuellar in Baghdad was in each case a propaganda ploy, not unlike his agreement to hold the Jeddah talks with the Kuwaitis prior to the invasion of the emirate. He appeared to have suspected that George Bush had proposed the Geneva meeting only due to Congressional pressures, and that he would offer Iraq nothing except an unconditional withdrawal. It was also an open secret that the UN Secretary-General was constrained by Security Council resolutions. These avenues had to be followed to convince Iraqis that the war they were about to face, merely two years after the end of the prolonged confrontation with Iran, was the result of American intransigence. On 14 January the Iraqi National Assembly endorsed Saddam Hussein's determination to fight. It called on the Iraqi people to 'proceed towards holy jihad', and gave its absolute leader 'full constitutional authority to deal with all that is necessitated by the decisive confrontation to preserve the right and dignity of Iraq and the Arab nation'.[5] Iraq was ready for war.

Iraq's strategy

A strategy of intensive defence, conceding no ground without a hard fight, was Saddam's best hope of achieving his political objective of holding on to as much of Kuwait as possible. The higher the costs imposed, the more the enemy would be prepared to accept a peace on terms that were unobtainable prior to hostilities.

To this end, Iraqi forces barricaded themselves into Kuwait. They constructed a massive defensive line close to the border with Saudi Arabia, a mixture of obstacles designed to stop a tank offensive, with coastal defences prepared for an amphibious assault. The barricade was supplemented by playing on a variety of other fears prevalent in the coalition – of the general destructiveness and uncontrollability of war, of a readiness to resort to chemical warfare or to extend the war to Israel, of an accompanying barrage of terrorist incidents, of ecological horrors consequent on the mining of the wellheads in the Kuwait oilfields. Saddam must bet on his enemy, when faced with all this, breaking before he did. So long as he still controlled part of Kuwait he would be happy to agree to calls for a cease-fire at any time.

Saddam appeared to draw comfort from the war with Iran. However, the persistence of this struggle had not been Saddam's choice, but imposed by a fanatical foe openly demanding his downfall. He survived the war largely by shielding the Iraqi public from its effects. Iran's inability to extend the war to the Iraqi rear, combined with generous financial help from the Gulf states, allowed Saddam to keep it confined to the battlefield and to preserve, by and large, an atmosphere of 'business as usual' for the Iraqi population. Whenever Iran had managed to reach the Iraqi home front during the so-called Wars of the Cities, Saddam had quickly backed down. The Iraqi Air Force had been ineffective in close air support and the pilots were judged to be poor. The chain of command was heavily centralized and unresponsive. With regard to battle experience, Generals who had made their names in the war with Iran were retired, dead or under arrest.[6]

Even Iraq's much celebrated defensive prowess was overstated. Iraqi military operations during the Iran–Iraq War had been conducted under ideal circumstances, with superior firepower and complete mastery of the air. Still defences had been repeatedly breached by the ill-equipped Iranian teenagers, whose advance had been contained with great difficulty and, at times, through the use of chemical weapons. If Iran had not been severed from its main arms suppliers and if Saddam had not enjoyed support from large sections of the international community, he would have lost.[7] The mobilized reservists – now half the total Iraqi force – had shown a readiness to surrender when the opportunity arose.

Saddam could call upon a large number of reserves. Iraq's overall population was not large at 19 million, but he could put together an army of some 1 million men, because the country had been on a war footing for nearly a decade. It was not quite 'the fourth largest army in the world', as the Pentagon described it, but it was nonetheless substantial. The settlement reached with Iran after the invasion of Kuwait allowed the shift of a number of divisions from that border. As the crisis developed, and in particular after Bush's announcement of the US build-up on 8 November, the number of divisions was boosted. On 19 November Saddam announced that he was reinforcing with another 250,000 men (although he was unable actually to achieve this). All young men were called up, to be followed by the middle-aged, and then given extra pay to keep them from grumbling.

There does seem to have been some belief that large numbers of defenders would have a deterrent effect. In mid-November the Iraqi Armed Forces General Command claimed that even without considering the state of morale, the difference in supply sources, and other considerations, all of which are in Iraq's favour – if the battle starts, the wicked US administration would need a ratio of three to one to become technically able to launch an attack against the valiant and faithful God's forces. This would raise the US force requirement to 3 million.[8]

Such reasoning reflected a mechanical belief in the famous three to one ratio, widely held by military strategists to be necessary for an attacking force against an entrenched defence. However, there was plenty of evidence from contemporary conflicts, not least the Arab–Israeli wars, that numerically inferior forces can be victorious if able to exploit qualitative or tactical advantages, such as surprise. If the ratio did have any meaning, it would only be at a local level where part of an attacking force faced well dug-in defenders.

But Saddam could not ensure a heavy concentration of defending forces *all* along the line, for he could have no confidence that the coalition would confine its attentions solely to Kuwait. In addition, significant forces had to remain deployed along Iraq's borders with its Iranian, Turkish, and Syrian neighbours. He was noticeably careful with the Republican Guard, Iraq's best equipped units, which had been expanded from a brigade in 1982 to eight divisions in 1990. With higher pay, better training and access to the best equipment, the Guard was considered to be the most professional of the Iraqi forces and the most loyal to the regime. The Guard divisions straddled the border with Kuwait operating as, at best, a strategic armoured reserve. Some units were regrouped around Baghdad to protect the Ba'th regime should either an external or an internal threat emerge in the course of the war. Saddam was anxious not to hazard the praetorian protectors of his personal rule.

Consequently, there were not enough troops to put along a wide front and so the border defences were manned by less capable troops. The large numbers claimed by Iraq did not arrive in the Kuwait theatre. Despite Western estimates (reinforced by Iraqi statements) of at least 540,000, many divisions were well below strength. Yet even if the high numbers had been reached, the Iraqi forces would probably have been weaker rather than stronger, for the numbers deployed were something of a liability, creating a logistical nightmare. Food, fuel, equipment and ammunition would have been spread even more thinly, with the stretched supply lines from Iraq vulnerable to air strikes.

The most obvious weakness in the Iraqi military structure was the lack of air support. On the face of it, Iraq possessed the world's sixth largest air force. It was credited with some 700 combat aircraft, including the highly advanced types of MiG-29, Su-24 and Mirage-F1. Its air defence system appeared to be particularly formidable. The key role it played during the war with Iran, in breaking enemy morale through sustained campaigns against strategic targets and population centres, underscored the significance of airpower in modern war. The hardened bunkers prepared for the most valuable aircraft, the enormous airfields, and the redundant command and control system all indicated a sensitivity to the dangers of pre-emptive air attack, and presumably the central importance of airpower in Israeli strategy. Israel had, after all, attacked and destroyed Iraq's Osiraq nuclear reactor in 1981. And yet, even during the Iran–Iraq War, Saddam displayed considerable restraint in the employment of airpower, refraining for a long time from carrying Iraq's overwhelming aerial superiority to its logical end. This timidity reflected Saddam's reluctance to put at risk his most effective reserve of military force. This insecure operational concept was extended into the Kuwaiti crisis. He apparently took comfort from the failure of the Americans to win in Vietnam, even with superior airpower.

Another key underestimation was in the area of precision-guided weapons, with which Iraqi defences proved unable to cope. This may not have been wholly unreasonable, given that many of the most modern weapons were unproven and that their effectiveness was widely questioned even in the West, where there were many reports, following the initial Desert Shield deployments, that high-technology systems were suffering in the heat and the dust of the desert environment.[9] In addition, the full significance of electronic warfare was imperfectly understood. Saddam saw missiles as his most reliable means of inflicting a painful blow at the enemy. Iraqi ballistic missile stocks were extensive and, with the benefit of European technology, their range had been extended and some of them were configured with chemical warheads. They represented Saddam's best prospects of taking the war into the enemy camp and so were the instruments of his political offensive, with Israel their primary targets. Missiles could also be used against Saudi population centres and, to a lesser extent, as a threat to the Saudi oil installations. Saddam's first response to Bush's 8 November announcement had been to threaten to turn Saudi Arabia into a battle zone. The fear of missile attacks on Saudi installations, which was given considerable credibility by some analysts, was in part responsible for the expectation that oil prices would rise when the war began.

In a speech a few days before the war began, Saddam told an Islamic gathering in Baghdad that 'thousands of men' at the front were 'underground in strong reinforced positions', ready to 'rise against' the enemy as soon as it attacked. He acknowledged that the coming war would be a testing ground for advanced technology but stressed Iraqi numerical superiority and experience of war. The Americans would 'carry out acrobatics just like a Rambo movie ... they tell you that the Americans have advanced missiles and warplanes, but they ought to rely on their soldiers armed with rifles and grenades'.[10] And it is here that Iraq's numerical superiority and greater dedication would be brought to bear. Saddam sent his own message to President Bush on 16 January. If Bush believed that Iraqi ground forces could be 'neutralized', he warned, 'then you are deluding yourself and this delusion will place you in great trouble'.[11] The coming battle would not just be a 'second Vietnam'. It would be the 'mother of all battles'.

CHAPTER 21

America Prepares for War

In pinpointing an intolerance of casualties as America's greatest potential weakness, Saddam at least here was at one with the Bush Administration. It knew that it had to convince a sceptical public that it could prosecute a war effectively and resolutely to a decisive and not too costly conclusion.

The last major military intervention in the Middle East – in the Lebanon in 1983–4 – had ended in a sullen withdrawal with disproportionate casualties. The lesser escapades in recent American military history – the bombing of Tripoli in 1986 and the interventions in Grenada and Panama – had left lingering doubts as to the professionalism of the American armed forces and their tendency to be muscle-bound, riven by inter-service rivalry and obsessed with technological gimmickry.

Above all, there was the depressing memory of Vietnam, from the escalation of the mid 1960s to the ignominious conclusion in 1974, which was turned to time and time again by commentators and politicians. There was a legacy of unpleasant memories and a lingering anxiety that the United States, despite its great power, was fundamentally strategically incompetent. The members of the coalition dependent upon American military strength, as well as the Iraqis gearing themselves to oppose it, could all look to the Vietnam experience and wonder about the ability of the United States to sustain a commitment when the going got tough. The most important of the supposed political 'lessons' drawn from this experience was that support for a war would wobble once the losses mounted. It was suggested that the United States became unable to prosecute the war in Vietnam because public opinion could not stomach nightly scenes of war on television and the mounting lists of casualties.

For all its potency, the Vietnam analogy was fundamentally misleading. There were no obvious similarities with the situation in the Gulf in political cause, geographic conditions, historical context, and military circumstances. In Vietnam, the United States intervened in a civil war in which its side lacked a popular base. It sought to demonstrate that the war was the result of aggression by one state against another – the north versus the south – but could never do so convincingly. In the Gulf there was no doubt that the United States was seeking to reverse a blatant case of aggression. Consequently, whereas with Vietnam the international community was generally dubious, to say the least, of the way the war was both justified and prosecuted, in the Gulf the United States was part of a remarkable United Nations consensus.

Vietnam's awkward terrain of jungles and paddy-fields, its mysterious and determined enemy, and its confused political situation conspired to show up American power at its worst. The Gulf had created perfect conditions to show it off to full effect: open and relatively uninhabited terrain; an enemy prepared to fight a regular battle instead of shifty guerrilla warfare, yet inferior in the quality of both its manpower and its equipment; an aggressor who manifestly fitted the part.

When US forces pulled out of Vietnam they were demoralized, almost mutinous, and enjoyed minimal respect at home. The fact that the war had been conducted by a conscript army aggravated the discontent, especially as the draft system itself was seen to favour the rich and the well-connected (such as the young Dan Quayle) at the expense of the poor and under-privileged. The men dispatched to fight appeared as innocent victims of a flawed strategy.

The first stage of the recovery from Vietnam lay in the termination of the draft and the move to a volunteer army, as Britain had done a decade earlier. There can be sympathy for volunteer soldiers facing danger on their country's behalf, but it is difficult to argue that it is unreasonable to expect them to fight. Many still worried about the quality of the volunteers who, as with many armies, came disproportionately from the disadvantaged sections of society.

As more money was pushed into defence, the armed forces started to become a more attractive career. Obsolete equipment was replaced and self-confidence grew. The introspection of the 1970s led senior officers to re-examine past practices and doctrine. Many accepted the criticism that they had become intellectually lazy, unable to think strategically in terms other than overwhelming any enemy with massive firepower. As they looked at Soviet doctrine they concluded that US forces, by contrast, had paid too little attention to combined arms operations, integrating land and air power, and to campaigns of manoeuvre rather than attrition. By the late 1970s a new Army field manual had been prepared which embodied these new ideas.

Although designed for a major European war, their principles served as the basis of the Gulf campaign. General Colin Powell was a product of this re-think. At the start of the Gulf crisis he urged the President to take heed of what the military considered to be the major lesson of Vietnam: do not apply military force in a slow, incremental manner but use it to achieve the maximum impact so as to disorientate the enemy and keep him off balance.

President Bush was prepared to go along with this so long as it reduced coalition casualties. On 30 November he promised the American people that any military action would not 'be another Vietnam',[1] and he was determined to keep to his word. Nonetheless, it became a cliché that public support would not withstand the return of the first 'body-bags'. Prior to the war, all the indications were that US public opinion was most brittle on the question of casualties. An opinion poll in the United States in early January showed support for war at 63 per cent, but this declined on the assumption of 1,000 American troops killed – to 44 per cent in favour of war and 53 per cent opposed – and further dropped to only 35 per cent in favour with 61 per cent opposed if 10,000 troops were to be killed.[2]

Any Western Government would seek to keep its losses low in war, but the idea that popular support is dependent upon this, above all other factors, has little basis in practice and was not actually supported by the Vietnam ordeal. Discontent then had not been so much stimulated by the absolute level of casualties nor their depiction on television, but by a faulty strategy. Even then it took a number of years for disillusionment with the Vietnam War to set in. The public and the politicians became disillusioned because casualties were being sustained *to little evident point*. The problem was not the costs of war in themselves but the lack of an attainable political objective worth these costs.[3] The critical variable would not be casualties but rather confidence that the political leadership had reasonable and realistic objectives and was being generally successful in achieving them. Both Vietnam and the British experience in the Falklands suggested the countervailing importance of the 'rally round the flag' factor once war begins.[4]

The most important feature of the impending encounter in the Gulf was that its outcome was not in doubt: the coalition could inflict a crippling military defeat on Iraq and eject it from Kuwait. This point, almost missed because of the overwhelming preoccupation with casualties, meant that the severity of the sacrifice depended on the quality of the coalition strategy. Few were prepared to risk the charge of complacency by claiming that serious losses were unlikely. The military were particularly concerned that the politicians should not harbour any illusions about costs. When Powell and Cheney visited Schwarzkopf to confirm his plans on 19 December they were given a worst case figure of 7,000 killed out of 20,000 casualties.[5]

Brigadier Patrick Cordingley, commander of the British 7th Armoured Brigade, warned journalists in response to a complacent question: 'There are going to be a lot of casualties and inevitably one has to be prepared for unpleasant things to unfold.' The press responded with headlines such as 'Prepare for a Blood Bath'. His superiors were not pleased. The senior British commander expected as many as 500 dead.[6]

An all-out assault on entrenched Iraqi positions could put casualties up to many thousands; skilful use of airpower, mobility, and night-fighting capability could reduce this to a fraction.[7] The published unofficial estimates for deaths[8] tended to be in a range of a few hundred to up to 15,000.[8] For example, Edward Luttwak, one of the most adamant opponents of a land campaign, argued that high casualties were 'almost mathematically certain' even given what he deemed to be extremely optimistic assumptions (which in fact approximated to the actual state of affairs when the land campaign came). High casualties would result from 'the incidentals of war: troops stepping on unmarked mines, short fire-fights with stragglers and hold-outs, mechanical accidents, and the ragged fire of some surviving fraction of the huge number of Iraqi artillery tubes'.[9]

Luttwak argued that the way to avoid such casualties was to avoid a ground war and rely instead on an intensive air campaign. In this he was not alone. In his Congressional testimony, General Colin Powell had vigorously challenged proposals for 'surgical air strikes or perhaps a sustained air strike' and other 'nice, tidy, alleged low-cost incremental, may-work options'. Their 'fundamental flaw', he argued, was to leave the initiative with the Iraqi President: 'He makes the decision as to whether or not he will or will not withdraw. He decides whether he has been punished enough so that it is now necessary for him to reverse his direction and take a new political tack.' Another problem was that such strategies were indecisive and 'not success oriented'. They took no account of Saddam's demonstrable willingness and ability 'to absorb punishment, to callously expend Iraqi lives and to care not a whit about what happens to the citizens of his country'. Also, such strategies would allow Iraq to concentrate on one threat. Powell did not doubt 'the competence and ability of our United States Air Force to inflict terrible punishment.' However:

> One can hunker down. One can dig in. One can disperse to try to ride out such a single dimensioned attack. Recognizing that such attack will do grievous damage to the defenders after such strategy has been executed, the decision is still in the hands of the defender to decide whether or not he has had enough punishment.

He also dismissed any interest in a strategy of 'cannon fodder', in which 'we are just going to run into fortifications without thinking our way through this'.[10]

Powell, along with Schwarzkopf, was worried that a protracted air campaign which failed to produce results would generate demands for a ground campaign for which there had been inadequate preparation. In practice, the real question was not whether a ground campaign would be required but the speed with which it should be entered into. Powell indicated that the conflict would begin with a decisive air campaign and that the ground war would not be simultaneous but would follow the air campaign. When attacked during the House hearings by Representative John Kasich, because he had implied that 'we have to go with all the forces at once', Powell replied, 'I didn't say that, Congressmen ... I never said "at once".'[11] In addition to avoiding casualties there was another reason for delay on the land. While the allied Air Force was ready, the US Army had yet to complete its deployment to the Gulf. The last units were only just arriving and they would not all have become properly equipped and acclimatized until early February. In fact, it was known that the sheer scale of the logistics effort and problems of bad weather in Europe had delayed the arrival of the extra forces ordered in November. As General Calvin Waller observed on 19 December, if he was asked by the President whether he would be ready on 15 January he would say, 'No, I'm not ready to do the job', and advise that hostilities should not be initiated until the full complement had arrived.[12] Bush was less than pleased with this public advice, although Cheney appears to have judged that it would confuse Saddam. As it was, the VII Corps had about 80 per cent of its elements in theatre by the start of hostilities.

The argument for a quick land offensive to follow the first air attack would be to exploit the shock effect. In the initial confusion and panic, the defenders could be expected to be less able to resist a co-ordinated offensive. The late arrivals could be used as a second wave to take over from the tired coalition troops responsible for the first wave assault. However, while the ground forces could find it extremely frustrating waiting for their Air Force colleagues to work their wonders, they were also well aware that their task would be much easier if the enemy lines were softened up through a period of persistent, unrelenting bombardment before they moved forward. If the coalition could hold together for long enough, there were good reasons to wait until superiority on the ground was certain. Powell, though convinced that a ground campaign would be necessary, saw no need to fight the war so as to preclude the possibility of the air campaign doing the trick.[13]

The Bush Administration had a number of advantages that made a decisive application of Western military power feasible. It could bring in all types of capabilities to the requisite levels. The enormous logistical effort would not have been easy to reproduce in other locations also lacking existing garrisons of Western forces. The initial boost in the Gulf was pre-positioned stocks; more important over time were the first-class ports and military airfields put at the coalition's disposal. Saudi Arabia was, in effect, one large petrol station and this eased dramatically what is normally one of war's most pressing supply problems. Further help came from the complete lack of interference and harassment from Iraq. In addition, the difficulties imposed on Iraq as a result of the arms embargo were consider-able. The Iraqi authorities gave the military first priority, but they were still obliged to husband resources and limit training and exercises. Resupply from the Soviet Union, Iraq's main arms supplier, was out of the question.

There was time to gather full intelligence and prepare plans. By the time Desert Storm began, the basic elements of the Iraqi order of battle as well as the essential components of its communications and supply networks were well known; by comparison Iraqi intelligence was minimal. Nor did the coalition have a need to consider a 'second front'. Neither Jordan nor Iran had any interest in taking military action in support of Iraq. Terrorism was a serious risk, but was alleviated by Syria's membership of the coalition and the close attention of the security services to Iraq's diplomatic missions throughout the world. The primary political objective – of expelling Iraqi forces from Kuwait – was clear and had been clarified during the build-up to direct military action.[14] All this meant that coalition planning could follow staff college principles in an almost classic manner.

There were good reasons not to be overawed by Iraq's military capability. One anonymous US intelligence official observed that other than the Republican Guard, and another eight to ten competent divisions, the quality fell off rapidly. But although he judged that 'many of the assessments tend to exaggerate their capability', he still judged that 'the Iraqis would be a very tough nut to crack'.[15]

The major uncertainties surrounded Iraq's readiness and ability to use chemical weapons, and the impact of its ballistic missile force. In general, the Scud threat was played down prior to the war.[16] Fear of an eventual nuclear capability was one reason for defeating Saddam; no one thought that such a capability was already available. Intelligence on the chemical threat was ambiguous: there were occasional signs of preparation, but no systematic effort on the Iraqi side. The threat was taken seriously in terms of delivery of chemical protection suits to the troops. The prospect of Iraqi chemical attacks was, as we have seen, the subject of an explicit deterrent threat from the United States. In late December, Cheney observed that 'were Saddam Hussein foolish enough to use weapons of mass destruction, the US response would be absolutely overwhelming and it would be devastating'. This was interpreted by some as a readiness to use nuclear weapons. However, Cheney said at the same time that the use of chemical or nuclear weapons 'has never been on the table', and Bush had ruled out nuclear use from the start of the crisis. As we have seen, Bush's deterrent threat was based on extending political objectives to include the Iraqi regime rather than extending the destructiveness of weapons. Some officers, wary of the costs of a land war, saw 'tactical' nuclear weapons as a more decisive option. According to a poll, a quarter of Americans would have favoured tactical nuclear use if it would end hostilities quickly and save the lives of American troops. Seventy-two per cent were still opposed even with this positive slant of the question.[17] The overwhelming view was that the political consequences would be wholly negative, with Kuwait being irradiated as it was liberated, the military effects unpredictable, while the potency of modern conventional munitions meant that any specific targets that needed to be destroyed could be destroyed. No effort was made to prepare for nuclear use: some nuclear weapons were removed from warships in order to make room for conventional stores, and Army units with nuclear responsibilities were left behind in Europe.[18]

The United States, Britain and France had all committed themselves in the past, through the UN, not to use nuclear weapons against non-nuclear countries. The United States chose not to repeat this commitment – just to keep Saddam guessing - but Britain and France did. When John Major was questioned on nuclear use in retaliation for Iraqi chemical use while visiting the troops, he replied: 'We have plenty of weapons short of that. We have no plans of the sort you envisage.'[19]

The coalition strategy was hardly a secret. In a variety of unofficial publications the likely targets for the air campaign were outlined and the likely instruments designated. The preference for flanking manoeuvres rather than direct assaults on Iraqi fortifications was made clear.[20] The military options were so fully explored in the weeks before the start of hostilities, in hearings held by the Armed Services Committees of both the US Senate and the House of Representatives, that it was possible for the Chairman of the House Committee, Representative Les Aspin, to produce a detailed and largely accurate forecast of the course of the war.

> The war is likely to begin with an air campaign against strategic and military targets in Iraq and then proceed to a sustained air campaign

against Iraqi military forces in or near Kuwait. The final phase of the campaign would involve the commitment of ground forces. Advocates of airpower will likely get a full opportunity to see if airpower can win by itself. But the US military has made sure that sufficient ground force capability is available to do the job, if airpower does not force Iraq's withdrawal from Kuwait.[21]

The Congress approves war

Since the first rift with the Congress in November 1990 over the doubling of force levels, a debate had been developing over whether the President needed Congressional authorization to launch war against Iraq. In line with his predecessors, Bush resented the War Powers legislation, passed by the Congress in 1975 as a result of a feeling that it had failed to exercise enough control over the drive into the Vietnam War.[22] Bush took the view that the issue at hand was not a constitutional matter and that he did not need Congressional authority. Most Congressmen took the opposite view – even those generally supportive of the Administration's stance. When in mid December Bush met with a number of Congressional supporters, he was told not only that he was obligated to seek Congressional support but also that he would get it. Stephen Solarz warned that if he went to war without constitutional authority he ran the risk of impeachment. 'It would be a hell of a thing,' he observed, 'to have half a million Americans fighting the war in the Gulf to get Saddam Hussein out of Kuwait while a serious effort was being made in Washington to get George Bush out of the White House.'[23]

Since Bush was determined to strike after 15 January if Saddam did not give way, with or without Congressional support, the question – as with the United Nations – was to what extent it was still worthwhile trying to get broader political backing. If he acted without Congress and things went wrong, then he would be in no position to share responsibility. Conversely, it was arguable that to go for support and fail to get it would be even more damaging than not going at all, giving more heart to Saddam. However, as Congress was likely to vote regardless of what Bush did, the President was more likely to be able to influence the outcome as an active participant, and it would be damaging to suggest that he was afraid to do so in case he lost.

If, as some anti-war Congressmen had wanted, the vote had been taken in December, boosted by the Nunn hearings, then the Administration would have had a hard time. However, Senate Majority Leader George Mitchell saw the danger of being accused of undermining the President's diplomatic efforts. By announcing his offer for Baker to meet Aziz on 3 January, just as

Congress was returning from the Christmas break, Bush was able to secure an agreement to delay debate until after the meeting. He had still not committed himself to asking for Congressional authority, but those senior Congressional figures who made the case directly to him that he must took his silent response as an indication that he had not ruled it out. In fact he had been tending in this direction for some time. Three days later the President met with his top advisers for dinner at the White House.[24] Richard Cheney argued against a vote. The President could call on the precedent of Harry Truman dispatching troops in 1950 to South Korea in support of a UN resolution without a Congressional vote. In 1991 the count in Congress was extremely difficult to call. Bush eventually decided, with the unhappy precedent of Lyndon Johnson in mind, that he could not ignore Congressional sentiment. He decided to make a specific request for Congressional authority and this view was conveyed in a letter sent to Congress as the Geneva meeting was under way.

By this time he had reason to feel more confident that public opinion was moving in his direction. A major poll released on 8 January showed that a majority wanted both Bush to consult Congress and Congress to back Bush. The President's approval rating for his handling of the crisis had picked up from its low point in December (from 61 per cent to 67 per cent), and readiness to go to war was up from 55 per cent to 63 per cent. The same message was coming through in other polls, although the anti-war lobby was much more activist.[25]

Many legislators were alarmed at the prospect of finding themselves on the wrong side of such a momentous issue, caught between prudence and patriotism. As the vote had been delayed to the eve of the UN deadline they would have to stand up and be counted, unable to take refuge in ambiguous language susceptible to multiple interpretations. The political balance in Congress was very uncertain, though it was expected from early on that the House would support the President. Republican support was reasonably solid: eventually only two Republican Senators and three Representatives opposed the President. The Democratic leadership opposed the early use of force: Speaker Tom Foley and Majority leader Richard Gephardt in the House, and Majority leader George Mitchell in the Senate. In the Senate the Democrat heavyweights on security issues, Sam Nunn in particular, opposed the Administration. Only Albert Gore was supportive, backed by some of the freshmen Senators such as Joe Lieberman. In the House, on the other hand, key Democrats with strong foreign policy credentials backed the Administration. Dante Fascell, Chairman of the Foreign Affairs Committee, and the liberal Steve Solarz, one of the main Congressional foreign policy experts, ensured that the Foreign Affairs Committee did not oppose the President.[26] Les Aspin, Chairman of the House Armed Services Committee, who was at first sceptical of the Administration's line, produced a number of reasoned analyses of the issues which questioned the view that sanctions would do the trick and that war would lead to high American casualties.[27] The fact that Israel was clearly so anxious to deny Saddam any gain played some role in Congress, with the American–Israel Public Affairs Committee (AIPAC), one of the most formidable lobbies in Washington, supporting the White House. AIPAC reported, however, that Jewish members in both chambers were divided roughly fifty-fifty.[28]

The diplomatic spectacle of the Baker–Aziz meeting helped the Administration. Its length indicated that Baker had not been perfunctory. His reputation as a conciliator and deal-maker added to the credibility of the exercise. When he called the White House to report the negative outcome of his session with Aziz, Bush was meeting with two dozen of his core supporters in Congress. Following that meeting a small working committee was established to draft a resolution.[29]

One House Democrat immediately calculated that Baker's press conference after the Geneva meeting had given the Administration twenty votes; an aide of Senator Nunn concluded that the vote was lost as soon as Baker said 'regrettably'. Aziz's press conference, demonstrating the obduracy faced by Baker, reinforced the pessimism with regard to Iraq's intractability and helped further stimulate the rally-round-the-President effect.

The next day Congress began its deliberations. The opponents had been trying to find language 'to pick up the moderates who don't want to rule out force forever, without losing liberals who don't want force at all'.[30] The most activist were critical of the whole campaign against Saddam. There was no support for the Iraqi occupation, but critics charged that Bush's motives were less than pure, based on oil interests rather than principles, and that the Administration was suffering from a bad case of double standards. Whatever was at stake in the crisis was not worth American lives. The fighting would generate a greater evil than that opposed.

Moderate Congressmen did not feel able to oppose the campaign against Saddam. Most had supported Desert Shield and economic sanctions. Nor, given the strength of pro-Israeli feeling, were they comfortable with suggestions that a little give on the Arab–Israeli dispute would make all the difference. Their argument was that this was not a debate about objectives but means and so there was no need to rush. Thus Sam Nunn based his case on support for the President's original strategy of 'economic sanctions, continued military threat and patience'. At the same time, he felt obliged to warn Saddam that either way he would lose and that if war came, US troops would have the full backing of Congress.[31] Waiting for sanctions to work was admitted to be problematic but preferable to the alternative. Senior Democrats such as Foley were convinced that if Congress authorized force, it would be used, and they were anxious to disabuse their colleagues who hoped that a strong statement would bring Saddam to his senses. 'Do not do it,' he warned in his speech just before the vote, 'under the notion that you merely hand him [the President] another diplomatic tool.'[32]

In his Senate speech, George Mitchell warned against 'a war in which Americans do the fighting and dying while those who benefit from our effort provide token help and urge us on'. He enumerated the risks:

> An unknown number of casualties and deaths, billions of dollars spent, a greatly disrupted oil supply and oil price increases, a war possibly widened to Israel, Turkey or other allies, the possible long-term American occupation of Iraq, increased instability in the Persian Gulf region, long-lasting Arab enmity against the United States, a possible return to isolationism at home.[33]

Mitchell and Nunn sponsored a skilfully drafted resolution in the Senate which authorized the use of force, but only to enforce the embargo, to defend Saudi Arabia and to protect American forces in the Gulf. The use of force to push Iraq out of Kuwait was not ruled out, but only after the exhaustion of further efforts with sanctions and diplomacy.

Their Republican opponents accused them of playing partisan politics with great issues of principle, so risking sending a message of division and equivocation to Saddam. 'The Republican strategy is to get Saddam out of Kuwait,' observed Senate Minority leader Robert Dole. 'Some of the Democrats' strategy appears to be to get Bush out of the White House.' Vice-President Dan Quayle described the preference for continued sanctions as 'wishful thinking masquerading as statesmanship'. To reinforce this position, a letter from the Director of the Central Intelligence Agency, William Webster, in which he was more dismissive of the impact of sanctions than he had been when testifying to Congress in December, was published by Les Aspin. Now Webster said that 'economic sanctions would not force an Iraqi withdrawal from Kuwait for at least a year'. The degradation in combat effectiveness would also be no more than 'marginal', as

> the ability of Iraqi ground forces to defend Kuwait and southern Iraq is unlikely to be substantially eroded over the next six to twelve months even if effective sanctions can be maintained.[34]

This would be especially true if Iraq did not believe that a coalition attack was likely. Another argument supporting a military action was the sentiment among the troops that they wanted the business over and done with and did not wish to hang around in Saudi Arabia indefinitely.

The debate was considered by seasoned observers to be one of the Congress's more mature and reasoned occasions. So many members wanted to speak that both House and Senate had to have overnight sessions on the Friday. There was intensive lobbying, but not the sort of horse-trading on roads and libraries that often characterizes close votes.[35] A key part of the White House strategy, however, involved targeting six Democrat Senators from three key states who, it was assumed, would find it easier to vote for the war if their home-state partner was voting the same way.[36] When the votes came on Saturday 12 January the Administration knew it would win, which it did substantially in the House (which voted first) and narrowly in the Senate. Ten Senate and eighty-six House Democrats were now ready to support the President. The House voted 250 to 183 against the anti-war resolution[37] and in favour of one sponsored by Stephen Solarz and Robert Michel, which authorized the President to use armed force subject to UN Security Council Resolution 678, so long as he made known to the Senate and House his determination that all appropriate means to find a diplomatic solution had been tried without success and were unlikely to succeed in the future.[38] In the Senate the vote was fifty-three to forty-six against the Mitchell–Nunn resolution, and then fifty-two to forty-seven in support of the President.[39]

Loose ends

What was left now for the Administration to do was to tie the few remaining loose ends. After Geneva, Baker flew to Saudi Arabia to brief King Fahd on his abortive meeting with Tariq Aziz, and receive a 'green light' for an American attack. Almost simultaneously a high-ranking delegation, headed by Lawrence Eagleburger, Under Secretary of State, and Paul Wolfowitz, Under Secretary of Defense, arrived in Tel Aviv to 'co-ordinate policy and strategy with Israel in the event that hostilities broke out.'[40] In December, during a meeting with President Bush in Washington, Premier Shamir had indicated that Israel might stay its hand if attacked by Iraq. Since that meeting, however, the Iraqis had been intensifying their threats against Israel and the Administration was anxious to make sure that Shamir would still abide by his pledge.

This was the highest-ever diplomatic mission to Israel since Bush assumed office in January 1989, and its arrival heartened the Israelis. For months they had been expressing their frustration over the lack of strategic co-ordination with the Americans in general, and the delays in receiving US satellite surveillance of Iraqi missile sites in particular.[41] Now, all of a sudden, they were promised Patriot anti-missile missiles (possibly with their American troops) to help intercept Iraqi Scuds and, no less importantly, any intelligence information regarding an Iraqi attack against them. To underline the American commitment, a 'hot line' – code-named 'Hammer Rick' – was established between the Pentagon's crisis centre and the Israeli Ministry of Defence in Tel Aviv.

Shamir reciprocated. While stating in public that Israel's defence 'was always and always will be the sole responsibility of the Government of Israel', and informing Eagleburger that under no circumstances would Israel relinquish its basic right to self-defence, he promised his guests that Israel would not launch a pre-emptive strike against the Iraqi missile sites and that it would, in effect, absorb an Iraqi attack. He also promised to do his best to stay out of the war 'if it is only possible' and to consult the Administration before retaliating.[42]

Elsewhere in the Middle East, Presidents Mubarak and Asad and King Fahd issued last-minute, emotional appeals to Saddam to come back to his senses and make the only move that could prevent war, namely, announce an immediate withdrawal from Kuwait.[43] He did not respond, just as he did not respond to the frantic French efforts to construct a last-minute initiative at the United Nations. An exodus of Western diplomats from Baghdad began. Thousands of peace activists marched in European and American cities to give voice to their fears. At midnight on 15 January the threshold between peace and war was crossed, though the region remained conspicuously tranquil. The following night war came to Iraq.

PART FIVE
War

CHAPTER 22

War by Appointment

War began the day after the deadline lapsed, at 19.00 Washington time on Wednesday 16 January, midnight London time, and 03.00 the next morning, 17 January, Iraq and Kuwait time. It was not a bolt from the blue, a crisis suddenly erupting or a long-simmering dispute bubbling over in an unforeseen manner. The approximate opening date had been known for forty-five days. It was a war by appointment.

Although an attack on that day was not mandatory, the expectations surrounding the deadline created a virtually irresistible logic of their own. The backdrop of heightened military activity, the media arriving *en masse*, peace demonstrations, the evacuation of foreign nationals from vulnerable countries, the suspension of flights by airlines, gyrations in the oil price and jittery stock markets made the actual outbreak of war almost a relief.

On 15 January President Bush signed a national security directive, giving Defense Secretary Cheney in effect a blank cheque, an executive order to start hostilities but with no date attached. The next day the military confirmed that they were ready to go that evening, so the date was filled in. There were last-minute consultations among the coalition partners to confirm the timing. Ambassadors were readied with official letters of explanation for their host governments. In Washington, the Kuwaiti Ambassador was called to the State Department just after 17.00 and told that in two hours the liberation of his country was to begin.[1] Ambassador Bandar rang King Fahd with an agreed message: 'Our old friend Suleiman is coming at 3 a.m.' At the same time, official notifications of the use of force were handed over to the Congressional leadership. Senior Senators gathered for their briefing in Robert Dole's office, attempting to avoid a signal that anything was up. The House leadership was more difficult. First Tom Foley had to be found (he was being fitted for new pyjamas at Brooks Brothers) and then it was necessary for Robert Gates, acting as official messenger, to get to him without giving a clue to the reporters who had staked him out. Gates found a back door.

The British Prime Minister, John Major, had spoken with President Bush on 15 January, just after Parliament had voted on the motion supporting United Nations Resolution 678. Only Major, Hurd and King knew of the timing, as did the Queen. Major had agreed it with Bush during a long car ride to Camp David in the snow on 20 December. On 16 January the Government stuck doggedly to business as usual. Not long before the attack was due to start, senior Cabinet ministers and opposition leaders were rung up. As Downing Street had left the calls till some fifteen minutes before the expected start of hostilities at midnight, those watching television or listening to the radio already knew something was up from Cable News Network (CNN). John Major himself sat in Downing Street flipping between television channels.

The first air strike was geared to a precise timetable, with more than 400 aircraft plus 160 tankers and command aircraft in a carefully synchronized operation. Twelve hours earlier the first B-52s had taken off from their Louisiana base and began their flight across the Atlantic, through the Mediterranean, across North Africa and into the Red Sea. The first actual attacks were by special forces in Apache helicopters which destroyed eight radars at the Iraqi border, designed to protect the two main air defence radars from a low-altitude attack. Alerted by the Apache attacks, the Iraqis activated their air defence system. Iraqi disorientation was reinforced by electronic warfare. Those first CNN pictures which caught international attention, with a background of sirens and a sky full of lights and tracers, were of air defence weapons shooting into the sky. This is why the war appeared to have started early.

Watching CNN, Air Force commanders checked their watches when the raid was in the ninth minute: at the exact moment that the telephone exchange was due to be hit, CNN went temporarily off the air.[2] The main attack was now under way. F-117 'stealth' aircraft, supported by cruise missiles, were striking the three main air defence centres and Baghdad. Targets in Baghdad itself, a city covering some 254 square miles, included the Presidential Palace, Government offices in the centre, and Saddam International Airport to the south-west. Within one hour the forty-five key targets in Baghdad had been struck. There were fifty-six aircraft in the first wave: to the relief of those waiting for news in Washington, fifty-six returned. Soon afterwards the F-15Es went for the Scud sites in Western Iraq. Only one plane was caught on the first night of the war. Despite the intense speculation accompanying the lapse of the United Nations deadline, effective tactical surprise had been achieved.

As the day progressed, allied strikes were extended to cover electrical power, chemical weapons, airfields, headquarters.[3] Thereafter, waves of allied planes systematically pounded military and strategic targets through-out the country. In the first twenty-four hours over 1,300 sorties were flown, of which almost 80 per cent were by the USAF, 13 per cent by the Navy and the Marines, 4 per cent by the RAF and 2 per cent each by France and Saudi Arabia.[4] Thereafter a high sortie rate, averaging between 2,000 and 3,000 per day, was reached.

The plan

The coalition war plan envisaged a 'four phased air, naval, and ground offensive operation' executed over a period of approximately a month. The first phase of Desert Storm, as the campaign was dubbed, was to last between seven and ten days and was intended to achieve air supremacy and incapacitate Iraq's strategic command and control system. The lion's share of this phase was to be executed by the strategic air campaign, but ground forces were also to be involved in the form of covert sabotage and disruption operations by commando units (at times with collaboration with local resist-ance fighters), both along the Iraqi–Saudi border and inside Kuwait and south-eastern Iraq.

With the completion of this stage, the allied air campaign was to shift progressively into the Kuwaiti theatre in order to lay the ground for the final land offensive. A brief phase of twenty-four to forty-eight hours was envisaged to suppress the Iraqi air defence systems in Kuwait, to be followed by intensive debilitation of the Iraqi forces in the Kuwaiti theatre, together with sustained pressure on Iraq's strategic targets.[5] The idea was to reduce the effectiveness of the Iraqi defences; to sever their lines of supply and demolish their command and control and intelligence systems; to destroy the largest number of Iraqi formations (Republican Guard in particular); and to shatter their fighting spirit.

The ground offensive, the culminating point of Desert Storm, was a complex and multi-dimensional operation. Its cornerstone was to be a deep flanking manoeuvre west of the Kuwait border into Iraq which was aimed at destroying Saddam's élite troops, the Republican Guard, and at cutting critical locations and establishing blocking points south of Basra that would channel the withdrawing Iraqi forces from Kuwait into a large killing zone. This attack was to be supported by ground, naval, and air attacks in the Kuwaiti theatre of war to lure the Iraqis into the mistaken belief that the coalition's main effort was in the east.

As the UN deadline loomed, Central Command (CENTCOM) intro-duced a significant revision. Instead of beginning with the strategic air campaign and holding back sustained attacks on ground forces for a late stage, which was already controversial with the Army and the Marines, the considerable air armada that had been gathered made it possible to merge the two phases together and to begin attacks on ground forces from day one. Since the time of the Iraqi invasion of Kuwait in August 1990, when the United States had some 323 fighting aircraft on carriers in the vicinity of the Middle East, it had assembled with its allies a force of 2,430 fixed wing aircraft.[6] The key to victory was complete mastery of the air.

Command of the air

The aerial contest was unequal from the start. Substantial Iraqi resistance, either in the air or on the ground, could have made a significant difference – prolonging the war and causing more losses among the coalition air forces – but none materialized. Saddam's strategy for this stage of the war depended on his extensive air defences absorbing the initial coalition strikes. His own limited offensive air capability would be kept in reserve for use during the land war, while he would extend the war to Israel and Saudi Arabia through Scud missile attacks.

His pre-war confidence was based on the enormous investment Iraq had made in air defence. A remarkable effort had been put into the survivability of the air bases, with some twenty-four very large and heavily fortified main operating bases and a further thirty major dispersal airfields. Some of these bases were huge: Tallil air base in south-east Iraq covered 9,000 acres – twice the area of London Heathrow. To these runways, hardened aircraft shelters were connected by multiple access lines. The protection of the bases was part of the responsibility of a formidable, integrated surface-to-air defence system, employing around 350 interceptor aircraft (of which only the 116 French Mirage F-1s were really capable), up to 7,000 surface-to-air missiles (SAMs) and 6,000 anti-aircraft artillery (AAA) pieces, a system described as 'state of the art'. In addition, the Republican Guard operated their own, apparently independent, system to protect key sites, such as Baghdad (which was guarded by sixty SAM batteries and 3,000 anti-aircraft guns), Tikrit and the nuclear, biological and chemical weapons sites and some airfields,[7] while the Iraqi Army in the field had its own air defence. The national system was integrated, that is, the key components – fighters, missiles and anti-aircraft guns – were centrally controlled to enable them to be used in a complementary fashion, so that the most suitable system would be used, aircraft would not be attacked by their own SAMs, and there could be speedy adaptation to a breach in the outer defence.[8] On the other hand, this centralization also meant that if the principal control centres, located deep in Iraq in hardened shelters,[9] could be neutralized, there would be an immediate loss of effectiveness.

The task for the first strike was therefore to blind the defence and disrupt its nervous system. After the Apache attack on the secondary radars increased the main radars' vulnerability to low altitude air attack, decoys were used to get the radars switched on so that the anti-radar missiles (HARM) could home in on to their emissions. Just in case, cruise missiles were also used. Arriving in Baghdad virtually undetected, the 'stealth' F-117s had as their priority target the air defence control centre. It was hit with laser-guided bombs. According to one account, a computer virus was planted into a printer detected as it was being smuggled to Baghdad for use at the command centre. The result was that as the operators turned on their screens they went blank.[10] Within a couple of hours the integrated air defence system had been rendered ineffective.

By 19 January air defence activity was down to a fraction of its normal level. Surface-to-air missiles barely made an impact. Although some were fired, hits were scarce because they lacked guidance. In the end the anti-aircraft guns, which were easier to operate independently of the central command, hit more allied aircraft.

The Iraqi claims of 150–200 allied losses after a few days were grossly exaggerated but not altogether inconceivable.[11] A number of claims seem to have resulted from SAMs shooting down decoys used to deceive them. In fact twenty-seven US aircraft were lost in combat during the campaign. In most cases the cause was unknown: where it could be ascertained, eleven of the losses were due to anti-aircraft guns and only one to surface-to-air missiles. Of the nine non-US allied aircraft lost, one was attributed to anti-aircraft artillery (AAA) and two to SAMs. Ten American and four allied planes were lost from non-combat causes. These total losses of thirty-six combat aircraft have to be set against the official expectation that as many as this would be lost on the first night alone. However, the Air Force leadership had been convinced from early on that they would have little trouble achieving effective air superiority. General Glosson is said to have told President Bush that he would lose no more than eighty aircraft and probably less than fifty.[12] The actual loss was some 2.5 per cent of the almost 2,500 aircraft on hand, at a rate of barely 0.1 per cent over 49,345 total combat sorties, and an even smaller percentage of the total of 109,876 sorties. The most severe punishment was taken by the low-flying British Tornados, one of which was lost for every eighty sorties as opposed to the American losses of one in every 750.[13]

Neither the long-range radars nor the centralized command centres came back into service. Perhaps because of a lack of spare parts, no attempt was made to repair the damage. It took a while before the allies were confident of this. They knew that the centres had been hit, but not how much damage had been done or whether they could be repaired. On the presumption that they might be brought back into service, CENTCOM pressed forward with attacks on the fighter aircraft bases, so at least they would not be available later.

The attacks on the bases were less decisive. Most aircraft were kept in concrete hangars which required precise attacks using laser-guided bombs, weapons which, in the first instance, were not available because the aircraft which could deliver them – F-117s and F-111s – had to be used against other targets. This meant that the runways had to be attacked, but they were extensive and difficult to put out of action with conventional bombs from a high altitude. The most successful weapon was the British JP-233 airfield denial munition, which dispenses thirty cratering bomblets directly over the runway in a low altitude attack, with 215 delayed action mines that become concealed in the debris.

The allies originally targeted forty-four airfields, sixteen primary airfields and another twenty-eight dispersal airfields. By the end of January, thirty-eight of these had been attacked in over 1,300 sorties. At least nine had been rendered non-operational, indicating the degree of effort that airfield suppression involved. Eight of these appeared to be closed after four nights as a result of the use of the JP-233. The Iraqis moved quickly to repair the runways. This was a complicated business, requiring specially trained crews to spot the craters, clear the anti-personnel mines and the rubble, and then patch the craters with aluminium mats and quick drying cement. They proved to be adept. To confuse the coalition further, they could place mock bomb craters made of painted paper on runways. Matters were not made any easier for the coalition by poor weather, which impeded accurate damage assessment and generally slowed up the campaign.

Consequently, the initial euphoria in the coalition soon gave way to anxiety that not all was well with the air campaign and that Saddam's forces were too well dug in. President Bush was said to be frustrated by the uncertain nature of the damage reports. In a review of the air campaign published in the *Washington Post* on 28 January, apparently reflecting Bob Woodward's sources in the generally cautious CIA, it was suggested that 65 per cent of airfields were still operational.[14] Soon Norman Schwarzkopf, anxious to present a generally more upbeat message of targeting success, stressed that the key test was whether the Iraqi air force had been rendered ineffective, that is, unable to be properly tasked and maintained as well as facing difficulties with its runways, even if it was not possible to put airfields completely out of business.[15]

Because runway denial was proving to be an arduous task, there was little choice but to move to the systematic destruction of Iraq's 594 aircraft shelters. This began in earnest on 23 January. Eventually 375 shelters were destroyed, including 141 aircraft caught inside. Within three days of this campaign, the Iraqis realized that they had a major problem on their hands. Some aircraft were moved to sanctuaries such as residential neighbourhoods or archaeological sites, where they were safe but also unavailable for combat.

Key elements of the Iraqi Air Force began fleeing to Iran. About eighteen support aircraft had left during the first days of the war. Then between the sixth and eighth days of the war another fourteen aircraft fled. On the tenth day the trickle became a flood, with sixty-eight leaving over three days, and now it was the combat aircraft. Eventually 122 combat aircraft sought sanctuary in Iran.[16] After the first surge, the allies set up air patrols to intercept them, with partial success.

The exact reasons for this mass air exodus to a country with which Iraq had just fought a bloody eight-year war were not at first clear. There was concern over Iranian–Iraqi collusion, perhaps to help preserve air assets for the land battle. However, the move does not seem to have been checked with Iranian President Ali Akbar Hashemi-Rafsanjani in advance, and the Iranians appeared reluctant hosts. Western intelligence soon indicated that the Iranians showed no intention of releasing the planes. The flight was therefore recognized as an act of panic on the part of Saddam Hussein, similar to his dispatch of planes to Jordan for safe-keeping at the beginning of the Iran–Iraq War.[17] CENTCOM had been expecting that any flight would this time be to Jordan, but they would have been easily ambushed on this route, while politically it would have implicated the beleaguered King Hussein even more in the Iraqi campaign.

There was one other ruse attempted by Saddam. On the first day of hostilities the Iraqi media asked that prisoners of war should not be killed. 'We will benefit greatly from the pilots being kept alive, as military intelligence may get information from them.'[18] On 20 January, American, British, Italian and Kuwaiti airmen were shown on Iraqi television. Questioned about the nature of their military missions, they gave answers that had been clearly scripted, criticizing the war against 'peaceful Iraq'. Their subdued voices and general appearance indicated considerable psychological pressure and physical violence. 'Our losses were very great,' said one of them, 'and this was one of the main reasons for the fear of American pilots flying against the Iraqi defence. We were talking together and we felt that Iraq had some of the best anti-aircraft systems and the losses to these systems in some aircraft have been very great and were leading to American pilots objecting to being in this conflict.'[19] The treatment of the captured pilots and Saddam's threat to deploy them as 'human shields' at Iraq's strategic sites touched a sensitive nerve in the American public, and generated calls to expand the war aims beyond the liberation of Kuwait to include the removal of the Iraqi leader from power. President Bush pledged to hold Saddam accountable for the consequences of his deeds, and argued that the 'human shield' strategy would not affect allied strategy. John Major said that Iraqi forces would be held responsible for their 'inhuman and illegal' behaviour, implying that Saddam and others responsible could be tried for war crimes after the war.[20] To judge by the decreasing manipulation of war prisoners by Iraq, these warnings seem to have been well taken by Saddam.

Until the flight of the Iraqi aircraft to Iran there was considerable concern that they were managing to stay out of harm's way. So long as they could stay safe in their shelters they were uninterested in combat. Few took to the air to greet the allied offensive; most that did turned and fled as soon as they became vulnerable. There were therefore only limited opportunities for the coalition air forces to take on Iraqi aircraft. By the end of the war barely thirty-five Iraqi aircraft had been destroyed in air-to-air engagements (in which no coalition aircraft were lost). Half these kills were in first few days: most of the rest were of aircraft trying to escape to Iran.[21] All but a few were the victims of the F-15/Sidewinder air-to-air missile combination. Nor did Iraqi aircraft make many attempts to penetrate coalition air space to strike at the enemy, for example against relatively exposed military targets such as battleships, or non-military civilian objectives in Saudi Arabia, such as the oilfields.

It is questionable whether the Iraqi Air Force ever really expected to engage. In the period before the onset of hostilities, at most 200 sorties a day were flown by all types of Iraqi aircraft, less than a quarter of its potential, and on the eve of hostilities hardly any were being flown at all. This may have represented a husbanding of resources, as a result of the embargo, but it ensured that the pilots were poorly trained for such tasks as air-to-air refuelling and night flying. Within twenty-four hours of the outbreak of hostilities, Iraqi sorties had plunged from around 100 (sixty of which were combat sorties) to some 40 a day; by the end of the first week of fighting there were hardly any Iraqi aircraft in the air.[22] On 24 January three Iraqi aircraft attempted to mount an Exocet missile attack against coalition shipping. Two were shot down by a Saudi F-15.[23] From that point the Iraqi Air Force effectively stood down completely and concentrated on escape.

Scuds

The only offensive action taken by Iraq was the launching of Scud missiles against Israel and Saudi Arabia. On 18 January the first modified al-Hussein Scud missiles were fired against the two countries. Alarm was then heightened by reports of eleven trucks leaving the Samarra chemical weapons storage facility. In the event, no chemical warheads were used, but during the war forty missiles were fired at Israeli civilian targets, first and foremost Tel Aviv, while forty-six were fired at Saudi Arabia.[24] They were largely inaccurate and those which were not intercepted caused few fatalities. The total toll in Saudi Arabia was about thirty-one dead and 400 injured, of which twenty-eight dead and ninety injured came in one of the last strikes which hit US personnel in barracks in Dharhran.[25] In Israel two civilians were killed by direct Scud hits while another eighteen died because of heart attacks and gas mask malfunctions. A few hundred civilians were injured. The material damage, though, was more significant than previously anticipated. In Israel approximately 4,000 buildings were damaged at a cost of millions of dollars, with severe disruption to normal life and considerable psychological stress, especially as there were constant fears that chemical warheads might be used. Many civilians left Riyadh and Tel Aviv.

Although these attacks were militarily insignificant, they had a disproportionate impact on allied strategy. The question of Israeli retaliation, which was apparently the main purpose of the Scud attacks, will be discussed in chapter 24. In addition to the political measures designed to forestall an Israeli retaliation, the allies invested considerable effort in finding and destroying Iraq's formidable arsenal of Scud missiles.

The first problem was that estimates of the number of Scuds were poor. After a few days of fighting, General Schwarzkopf reported 'initial estimates' of 'approximately thirty fixed launchers and twenty mobile'. Having expressed confidence that the fixed launchers had been 'neutralized', he added, with evident scepticism, that 'we have estimates that say that we may have killed as many as sixteen of those mobile launchers, but it's very, very difficult to confirm that kind of targeting'.[26] Other sources indicated that only eight of Iraq's fixed Scud launchers had been damaged enough to disable them and that there was 'not one picture of the carcass of a mobile Scud launcher'.[27] Just after this, Schwarzkopf noted the slowdown in the Iraqi launch rate (from thirty-five in the first week to eighteen in the second), claimed that all major production facilities had been destroyed and reported unconfirmed pilot claims of more than fifty kills.[28] Thereafter allied briefers were careful to couch their descriptions of the war against the Scuds in general terms, and for good reason.

The attacks on the fixed launch sites do seem to have been successful: at most they were used as bases for the mobile launchers. These caused substantial difficulties. They operated at night with radio silence, driving into 'boxes' where they would be in range of their main targets, launched and then went out. The liquid-fuelled missiles could be prepared and fired in about an hour. Their rushed procedures may not have made for a precise attack, but against urban targets accuracy was not a high priority. The transporter-erector-launchers (TELs) used by the Iraqis did not look that different from ordinary semi-trailers. To confuse matters further, the Iraqis used fake launchers as decoys and disguised missile launches by firing surface-to-air missiles simultaneously with the Scuds.[29] Not surprisingly, Schwarzkopf compared the problem to one of locating needles in a haystack. Another problem may have been the rigidity of the air tasking order (ATO), the basic co-ordinating mechanism for the various air strikes. This was an extraordinarily complex document, necessary to ensure the optimum use of available strength and to prevent confusion in the air. However, part of the difficulty with the ATO was that it lacked flexibility and was therefore not well suited to the more mobile and unpredictable targets.[30]

These operational constraints notwithstanding, the allies quickly found one method of dealing with Iraq's mobile missile launchers. They maintained permanent combat air patrols (mainly of F-15 aircraft) over the 'Scud launch boxes'. Then, with the aid of satellites and the Joint Surveillance and Target Attack Radar System (JSTARS), a highly advanced airborne radar system still in the process of development, they managed to trace the missile vehicles, either on their way to firing positions or immediately after launching their missiles, and to divert the patrolling aircraft to their targets.[31] The roads in and out of the box were also attacked by A-10 aircraft. The targeting of mobile Scud launchers, and at times their actual destruction, was also carried out by special forces operating in western and eastern Iraq. Schwarzkopf was known to be suspicious of Special Operations, fearing that they would take on glamorous roles, get into trouble, and then need to be rescued in a diversion of mainstream effort. However, Peter de la Billière had worked in special forces and convinced Schwarzkopf that they had their uses. The British Special Air Service (SAS) had worked up a plan to find Scuds, and were soon in western Iraq locating the missiles for aircraft and sometimes attacking them directly. By 26 January they had found all those in their sector. Later an American unit found nine launchers under a bridge on the Baghdad–Jordan highway.[32]

There were hopes, as the land war began, that the Iraqis had exhausted their supply when on 25 February they fired one missile at Saudi Arabia and two at the Israeli Negev in the vague direction of the nuclear facility of Dimona. One of the warheads was filled with concrete, which was some-times used as a ballast in tests, indicating that the crews were having to scrape around for weapons. The next day the last Iraqi missile in the war was fired. However, as the war was about to close, a Special Operations ground team found twenty-nine mobile Scuds in south-west Iraq and immediately called in A-10s to destroy them.[33]

How many mobile missile launchers were actually destroyed by allied forces is difficult to say. After the war, the Iraqis claimed that no mobile Scuds had been destroyed from the air and handed over nineteen to the UN for destruction, along with 138 missiles, implying that around sixty missiles had been caught. Israeli Defence Minister Moshe Arens also claimed that: 'To the best of my knowledge, not a single mobile missile launcher was found and destroyed from the air.'[34] Whether true or not, the 'Great Scud Hunt' had a drastic impact on Iraq's missile campaign, reducing the Iraqi attacks from an average of five missiles per day during the first ten days of the war to a daily average of one missile during the rest of the war.[35] It also pushed the Iraqis out of their 'launch boxes' and forced them to operate from more remote sites, a development which decisively curbed their ability to hit the main population centres in Israel and Saudi Arabia, risked hitting Palestinian homes in the West Bank, and forced them to improvise.[36]

But it also had a drastic impact on the allied air campaign. During the first phase of Operation Desert Storm, some 15 per cent of the strategic air campaign was directed against surface-to-surface missiles. This figure reached 40 per cent after the first week of fighting, as the allies realized to their dismay that Iraq's stockpiles of ballistic missiles were far more exten-sive than previously believed, and that the tracing of mobile surface-to-surface missiles was a significantly more demanding task than originally conceived.[37] In the first two weeks of the war more sorties were flown against Scud sites (1,500) than against Iraqi airfields (1,340) – the other frustrating set of targets.[38]

The significant effort diverted to Scud busting delayed the suppression of the Iraqi air defence systems in the Kuwaiti theatre, disrupted the coalition's operational plans and contributed to the postponement of the ground offen-sive. Faced with a constant shift of targeting priorities due to the Scud hunt, and unable to use its own reconnaissance aircraft to overfly Kuwait, military intelligence had to rely on national imagery for the first three weeks of the war. This, in turn, constrained its ability to provide the military leadership with up-to-date targeting lists and accurate damage assessment.[39]

Patriots

In addition to eliminating surface-to-surface missiles on the ground, they can also be dealt with by interception while *en route* to their targets. As this is normally considered a much more demanding task, the apparent success achieved here by the Patriot air defence missile was surprising, and the Patriot was acclaimed as one of the war's great heroes.

The system involved between eight and sixteen launching stations, each with four missiles in firing boxes, and an engagement control station informed about incoming missiles by a phased-array radar. It was given extra warning time by being attached to the American early warning system. The Patriot had originally been developed as an anti-aircraft missile but was then adapted during the 1980s to defend important targets against incoming missiles. It had never been tested in this role. Although the Patriot was not ready for action in Israel at the start of the war, it was fully deployed in Saudi Arabia. There American sources spoke of remarkable interception rates – forty-five out of forty-seven, while the others were allowed to fall on under-populated areas. In Saudi Arabia the Iraqi aim points were easier to identify.

These assessments, however, were almost certainly exaggerated. Some apparent 'kills' involved no more than a deflection of warheads or attacks on fuel tanks as the biggest part of a fragmenting missile. The poorly construc-ted Scuds would often break up on re-entry into the atmosphere at an altitude of fifteen to twelve kilometres, the height at which the Patriot engages. The breaking up of the missiles also caused confusion. On one occasion, for example, two Patriots apiece were launched against what appeared as fourteen incoming missiles on the radars but was in fact five breaking up in flight. If the Patriot cut the missile in two, then it multiplied damage. There were also instances when the interceptor chased the debris to ground, although there was later a modification so that it became possible to distinguish between the Scud's front and rear end.[40] Most frustrating was the Patriot's failure to fire, because of computer malfunction, on the one instance where major casualties were caused, although the extent of the damage in this case could also be taken as an indication of what might have happened during the war without the Patriots.

Even the sceptical Israelis, who, in the past, had tended to doubt the efficacy of the Patriot against surface-to-surface missiles, were taken in by its performance. 'We are all Patriots' read many a T-shirt throughout the country, demonstrating the deep feeling of relief and gratitude at their arrival in Israel. Yet, as the war progressed the old doubts resurfaced. Not only did the Patriots in Israel have a lower rate of hits than their Saudi counterparts –

probably no more than two hit warheads – but on a few occasions the debris caused by an intercepted Scud was believed to have caused more material damage than would have been otherwise inflicted.

It is true that in retrospect the Patriot was probably a less formidable weapon than it appeared during the war, and that if the Scud had been a more effective missile then the images of this aspect of the war might have been very different. Yet, as with the 'Great Scud Hunt', the psychological impact of the Patriots was more important than their actual combat performance. It meant that those potentially on the receiving end of the missile had reasonable hope that it would be intercepted which, in turn, helped to blunt the edge of the Scud as a terror weapon.

CHAPTER 23

The Strategic Air Campaign

The first days of the air campaign produced some remarkable displays of precision strikes. Astonished journalists watched Tomahawk cruise missiles following a street map and turning corners to get to their targets, while Air Force briefers provided video shots from on-board cameras of smart bombs entering bunkers by the front door. Reports from Baghdad testified to the extraordinary accuracy of strikes which left key buildings standing as shells while those on either side were virtually unscathed.

Although this precision technology had been available for some time prior to 1991, and had been first put to use during the latter years of the Vietnam War, there was general scepticism about its reliability in practice. Even with the most precise weapons, their efficiency depended upon high-quality target information. In the Gulf War such information was obtained to an extent unprecedented in earlier conflicts. It had been gathered in an intensive effort during the months leading up to the war, using everything from satellites to 'special operation groups' to construct a picture of the structure of Iraq, its society and its military machine. European suppliers who had been working in Iraq had been contacted for blueprints of major projects. Academics and journalists with a knowledge of the country were quizzed for relevant details. Nonetheless it was by no means always accurate. One analyst later stated that fifty out of the eventual list of 800 strategic targets had been misidentified.[1]

When General 'Buster' Glosson, in charge of the strategic air campaign, set down his guidance on 12 January 1991 he stated that: 'targets and aimpoints will be selected to minimize collateral damage and limit the impact on the civilian population'.[2] By way of minimizing civilian casualties and collateral damage, as well as vulnerability to the intensive air defences, targets in Iraq's main population centres were largely assigned to the advanced F-117 'stealth' bomber. Never touched by Iraqi air defence, the F-117 was the only aircraft to operate in downtown Baghdad, executing 31 per cent of the first day's strategic raids, despite constituting merely 2.5 per cent of the allied fighting aircraft.[3] The F-117 was a difficult aircraft to prepare for operations, and was vulnerable to bad weather. Only 60 per cent destroyed their targets, although this was a high proportion of those actually launching their weapons. Tomahawk cruise missiles launched from sea also showed extraordinary accuracy and were judged to have hit 85 per cent of their targets, although this estimate was scaled down after the war. Most of the 291 used were launched in the first week of the war against some of the softer targets such as air defence radars, petroleum tanks, and yards for electrical power grids. The smart weapons had to sacrifice some of their punch to make space for precision and this meant that their impact on specific targets was sometimes uncertain. They were also expensive. Nevertheless, because air force planners doubted their reliability, initially several missiles were sent against each target. They gradually became more confident.

The bulk of the available weapons were old-fashioned conventional munitions. The total precision tonnage dropped was 6,250 tons out of 88,500 tons in total – around 7 per cent. So while the scale of the air campaign was awesome – 109,500 total combat sorties flown[4] – much of it was of only moderate accuracy. The 'smart' weapons do appear to have been extraordinarily precise but, as one senior scientific adviser to the military observed, one of the lessons of the war was that 'dumb bombs are just that', with more than half falling outside their designated target circles.[5] However, this does not mean that they were without effect. Continual pounding by B-52s had a psychological effect on Iraqi troops even if comparatively few were killed and little equipment was destroyed.

It is also of note that the bulk of the bombing was well away from Baghdad from where most of the media reporting came. This city of some 4.4 million people contained only forty-five strategic targets and was probably hit by less than 300 F-117 sorties and 150 cruise missiles. John Simpson counted only twenty-nine buildings actually destroyed in the capital.[6] The relatively few strikes against the city were another reason why it appeared surprisingly undamaged.

Another source of confusion in popular attempts to interpret the military briefings lay in the distinction between an 'effective 80 per cent' sortie rate, which meant that 80 per cent of aircraft got to their targets, delivered ordnance and got back, and effective damage, which meant that the target would be rendered inoperable. Furthermore, the daily totals of sorties mounted hid the fact that these included many that were not bombing runs but refuelling flights, defensive patrols and defensive escorts. The hard core of the offensive air campaign was therefore only a moderate portion of the total effort described in the briefings.

More difficult still was the question of what the various strikes were designed to achieve. There was no doubting the ultimate objective of forcing Iraq to leave Kuwait, but there were questions with regard to the relationship of particular targets to this objective. As so often in the past, an opportunity to mount a strategic air campaign was seen by the USAF as a key test of airpower doctrine. Even after the war, claims as to its effectiveness were hotly disputed because of its presumed relevance to the role of airpower in future conflicts. The campaign had objectives independent of the expulsion of Iraqi forces from Kuwait: reducing the long-term ability to exert a regional military influence and weakening the regime's hold on power. Undoubtedly not far from some of the planners' minds was the thought that if these objectives were achieved, Saddam might well be induced to surrender to preserve what he could of his power base prior to the onset of a ground war.

Targeting philosophy

After the First World War, advocates of airpower made far-reaching claims with regard to its ability to decide wars on its own through undermining the will of the enemy population without the bother of a land campaign. This became known as the 'strategic' use of airpower, to be contrasted with mere 'tactical' use in support of ground forces. The logic of strategic airpower culminated in the massive air raids of the Second World War. These raids failed to achieve their intended result. People adjusted to fear and hardship. However miserable they became, unless their distress was taken up at the highest political level they had little option but to suffer in silence, especially in a totalitarian regime.[7]

So the lesson drawn from the Second World War and judged to be validated by most subsequent conflicts was that the morale of a population under aerial bombardment could be extraordinarily resilient. However, rather than concentrate on tactical airpower, a further strategic role was identified, still geared to undermining the capacity of the enemy to prosecute the war on the ground, but by attacking the supporting infrastructure of production, fuel, power and communications as well as front-line forces. The infrastructure had been attacked during the Second World War, but problems of accuracy made it a frustrating process.

The new technologies of precision guidance created options for a modern air force previously unavailable. This further encouraged the shift away from 'mass destruction'. Attacking the enemy's military machine helped reduce casualties to one's own side, while desisting from attacks on enemy civilians was more in line with the Christian 'Just War' tradition which stresses the importance of proportionality of means to ends and of sparing non-combatants. In Vietnam, another idea of limited strikes had been developed by which airpower might be used to send subtle political signals to the enemy capital and be employed in a graduated incremental manner. The Vietnam experience had, however, shown that such signals could be confused and could not contradict the basic message conveyed by the balance of forces on the ground. Meanwhile nuclear strategy also moved to take into account both the accuracy of modern weapons and the utter nihilism of mutual strikes against population centres. The 1980s saw much theorizing about the possibility of targeting nuclear weapons to inhibit economic recovery or to 'decapitate' the enemy by paralysing mechanisms of political and military control. These ideas influenced those who hoped that the considered application of airpower might serve to shorten a war or achieve political objectives separate from the straightforward support of land operations.

This was a challenge which had been taken up in 1990 by those arguing that it made much more sense for the West to base its strategy on its area of comparative advantage in the air rather than the Iraqi advantage on land. There were no serious proposals to undermine Saddam's regime through direct attacks on the civilian population and its morale, and all assumed relatively accurate strikes against military or military-related targets. Beyond that there were significant variations depending on political objectives as well as views about the particular attributes of airpower. Edward Luttwak's objective, for example, was to denude Iraq of its military capacity, thus limiting the potential damage it could do in the future. He claimed that an air offensive directed not against ground forces but against the basis of Saddam's long-term strategic power 'could literally demolish Saddam Hussein's military ambitions within a week or so, and with the loss of not more than a few dozen aircrew at most'.[8] Richard Perle, by contrast, was more concerned with getting Iraq out of Kuwait and so he proposed the use of airpower to support a war of attrition, exploiting Iraq's problem of re-supplying its forces of occupation.[9] Henry Kissinger also wanted to force Iraq out of Kuwait, but he conceived of the use of airpower more along the lines of the traditional concept of coercive diplomacy. It would serve as an adjunct to sanctions, raising 'the cost of occupying Kuwait to unacceptable levels while reducing Iraq's capacity to threaten its neighbours'. Kissinger, declaring himself 'extremely sceptical about a full-scale ground assault', believed that the reduction of Iraq's military power would mean the erosion of the dictatorship's base, thereby encouraging a 'negotiation more compatible with stated US objectives'.[10]

Initial USAF planning was geared largely to the defence of Saudi Arabia, and so had as its first priority any advancing Iraqi tank columns. However, it was natural for the planners to think about strikes against the society supporting the invasion, as well as punitive strikes for deterrence purposes (in case, for example, of an Iraqi strike against Saudi oilfields). As early as mid August a set of eighty-four targets – to be destroyed within a week – had been developed and by the end of the month the Air Force considered itself ready to conduct offensive operations. 'We had no guidance to do that, no mission to do that,' admitted General Charles Horner, CENTCOM's air commander. 'That was just "what if" planning.'[11]

Horner's own approach was to follow the ideas of 'air–land battle' which stressed the integration of air with ground forces. This involved concentrating on the basic elements of Iraqi military power, with a particular stress on the Republican Guard. To the Air Force planners in Washington this was somewhat unimaginative. There the basic concept was that a decisive impact could be achieved by targeting the enemy's 'centre of gravity', an idea developed by Colonel John Warden, deputy director of doctrine, strategy and plans for the USAF, who was in charge of the group developing targeting options in the Pentagon.[12] The debate then turned on what constituted Iraq's 'centre of gravity'. There was no argument that in order to exercise air supremacy Iraq's air defences and Air Force would be the first priority. What came next?

One answer came from the Air Force Chief-of-Staff, General Michael Dugan, in the notorious September 1990 interview which led to his dismissal.[13] The interview came just after Schwarzkopf had declared his strategic air plan ready. It now consisted of 174 targets. Dugan spoke of the 'somewhat conventional list of targets' assembled by the end of August – air defences, airfields and warplanes, missiles, command, control and communications, chemical, nuclear and munitions plants, armoured forces. Secondary targets included Iraqi power systems, roads, railroads and perhaps domestic petroleum production facilities, though not oilfields.[14] He asserted that this was 'a nice list of targets', but they were 'not enough'. He therefore asked planners to interview academics, journalists, ex-military types and Iraqi defectors to determine 'what is unique about Iraqi culture that they put very high value on ... What is it that psychologically would make an impact on the population and the regime in Iraq?' The intent was to find 'centres of gravity, where airpower could make a difference early on'.

The conclusion was that the 'cutting edge would be downtown Baghdad'. The enemy had to be targeted where it hurts – 'at home, not out in the woods someplace'. He had been advised, by the Israelis among others, that 'the best way to hurt Saddam' was to target his family, his personal guard, and his mistress. Because Saddam was a 'one-man show' in Iraq, Dugan said, 'if and when we choose violence he ought to be at the focus of our efforts'. Without him, Iraqi troops 'would all of a sudden lose their legitimacy and they would be back in Iraq in a matter of hours, in disarray'.

There would be a role for ground forces, intimidating Iraqi forces and channelling them into killing zones for aircraft, but Dugan's central proposition was that US airpower could force Iraq out of Kuwait without a bloody land war. This approach stressed the political and economic structure of Iraq, starting with Saddam Hussein, his command and control structure, infrastructure including electricity plants and oil refineries and weapons of mass destruction. This he claimed to be the conclusion of the Joint Chiefs-of-Staff. However, apart from the political sensitivity of describing Saddam as a target in this manner, Dugan's comments suggested more consensus than existed, as was indicated by Cheney's prompt decision to fire him.

To Schwarzkopf's staff at CENTCOM, including Horner, ideas such as this were a deviation from the basic principles of air–land battle.[15] As the year progressed and the decision was taken to increase forces and prepare an offensive option, the Army pushed as hard as possible for a greater portion of the effort to be devoted to attacks on Iraqi ground forces. The Air Force resisted, pointing to the difficulties of taking out individual tanks and artillery tubes, and questioning the stress placed on the Republican Guard as a 'centre of gravity'. The end result was something of a compromise between the USAF's inclination to concentrate on the sources of Saddam's power and the Army desire to see his ground forces cut down to size before it launched its offensive. The Republican Guard was described as a priority 'strategic' target, but attacks on the supply lines and troop concentrations were to come late in the day. Given the amount of airpower available, Schwarzkopf did not think that there was any excuse for excluding more straightforwardly military targets from the start. Nonetheless, in practice, the effort to weaken front-line forces would have to wait.

The Air Force kept control of the planning of the campaign, although this was described as a 'joint' team. The Navy felt that their aircraft and cruise missiles were not always being used to their full effect.[16] General 'Buster' Glosson, in charge of the targeting for the strategic air campaign, and many of his top men, had little experience of air to ground warfare, although they were also sceptical of some of the ideas for 'political' targeting developed in Washington. Despite the number of aircraft available, the allocation of targets followed a tight formula, in part reflecting the sheer complexity of the flight paths and the interdependence of combat, electronic warfare, surveillance, command and refuelling aircraft with each other. While this was clearly successful in terms of managing such a large air armada, and avoiding any strikes against friendly aircraft, it was cumbersome and inflexible. Targets with a high priority were liable to be struck a number of times, even if there might have been reason to change – for example air defence sites and aircraft hangars after full air supremacy had been self-evidently won. When bomb damage assessment proved difficult because of bad weather or the simple ambiguity of the information, the tendency was to strike again just to make sure.

In part because of the experience of Vietnam, the planners had been given considerable latitude when it came to developing the target list. The rejection of concepts of graduated response and civilians picking and excluding targets in the belief that they were sending political messages was underlined by the code-name chosen – 'Instant Thunder' – in stark contrast with the 'Rolling Thunder' campaign in Vietnam. Senior civilian officials were not fully briefed on the target list until 14 January, when Powell took Cheney, Baker and Kimmitt through its main features. President Bush was reportedly not informed of the detailed target set.[17] There had been a more general input on some of the broader political principles that had to be taken into account, such as the need to respect religious sites, primarily the cities of Najaf and Kerbala, which were holy to Shi'ite communities throughout the world. Residential areas were to be avoided, and collateral damage to civilians limited wherever possible. When reviewing the list, Cheney thought it 'gratuitous' to attack the huge statue of Saddam in Baghdad as well as the war memorial and so they were spared. Also spared was the al-Rashid Hotel. Intelligence intercepts and blueprints of the hotel's construction suggested that there was a command-and-control facility in the basement, but since Western journalists made the hotel their base, it was considered prudent to leave it alone.[18]

This in itself indicated the arbitrariness of the political judgements that had gone into the design of the air campaign. As the campaign was not geared solely to military targets there was no reason why the choice of political and economic targets would necessarily be within a military competence. Furthermore, military views differed, with the Army and Navy doubtful as to the effort being put into the strategic campaign compared with the task of 'preparing the battlefield' for the ground offensive, as if the USAF view was that the strategic air campaign had to be given a chance to work before matters were handed over to this second-best form of warfare. The marines eventually began to divert sorties away from pre-planned targets and later withdrew many assets from the ATO.

Inevitably the strategic approach meant attacking structures that were relevant to both civilian and military affairs. This would be true in any society; it was especially true in Iraq. In such a centralized, militarized state, civilian and military facilities could be interchangeable, and the systems of military command and political rule closely interwoven. This, in turn, led to the most controversial moments of the air campaign.

The target set was divided up into twelve areas, as outlined in Table 9 (page 330). By 17 January it added up to 386 targets; ultimately it grew to 723. Every night three or four areas would be chosen for the next day's strikes. The effectiveness of this effort can be assessed by considering some broad areas in turn.

The non-conventional arsenal

Among the most important strategic targets were those relating to Iraq's chemical, biological and nuclear weapons capabilities. Apart from the chemical weapons facilities, the relevance to the immediate hostilities was limited. However, they were seen as the basis of Saddam's ability to intimidate the region in the future, so that their elimination was a war aim in itself. They were given a high priority in case there was an early cease-fire.

The most publicized single episode in the campaign against non-conventional weapons was probably the attack on the so-called baby milk factory, which the Iraqis claimed to have been destroyed on 22 January and later told Peter Arnett of CNN that this was the only source of milk for children under one year. Pictures of the site showed 'Baby Milk Production' signs in Arabic and English. A French contractor who built the plant said that it was designed to produce baby milk and had done so from 1979 to 1980 when French technicians left Baghdad. The Iraqis then had been trying to get it going again with help from a different French company. In May 1990 some New Zealand technicians had observed production in the facility but seen no extraordinary activity.

Not a baby milk factory at all, said CENTCOM, this was a factory for the production of biological weapons. Its dubious purpose was reflected in it being surrounded by a high military fence, with guard posts on all four corners and camouflage paint.[19] According to US official sources, the plant had been converted to biological weapons production in autumn 1990, though it was merely a back-up plant and not in operation when attacked, or alternatively, was not a full plant but used for items relevant to biological weapons production.[20] Schwarzkopf himself indicated that only part of the plant was believed to have a military function, when he claimed that only the relevant part had been attacked.[21] Over time, the Government became noticeably less confident in its assertions, as more evidence of baby milk was found, and it may have been that the intelligence analysts had mistaken the huge milk vats at the factory for devices to mix compounds for military use.[22]

The most important target was the nuclear capability. Intelligence on this was still incomplete, although how incomplete was not realized until after the war. During the intelligence effort connected with the preparation of the target list there was a growing awareness of the scale of the programme, for example a 'fertilizer plant' in al-Qaim in western Iraq had clearly been used in nuclear research and development.[23] Only during the war was the al-Athir complex identified. The USAF managed one strike at this with its last F-117 sortie. The main targets were Iraq's nuclear reactors, and here care had to be taken to ensure that no damage was inflicted upon the fuel rods at the core. The attack had to be geared to causing the structure to collapse without blowing the reactor apart, a matter upon which the British sought regular reassurance.[24]

In Schwarzkopf's end of January report he claimed that thirty-one nuclear, biological and chemical warfare targets had been attacked in over 535 sorties. As a result all known nuclear reactor facilities had been destroyed and Baghdad's nuclear research centre had been reduced to rubble. There was also 'absolute confirmation' that more than eleven chemical and biological storage areas had been destroyed, along with the destruction or at least heavy damage to three chemical and biological production facilities.[25] Immediately after the war, when the US military assessed the likely minimum recovery time for the damaged aspects of Iraqi society, it was assumed that the nuclear programme had been most knocked back. By contrast the chemical weapons capability was believed to have been put back at the very least three years and the biological weapons perhaps no more than a year, although it would take much longer before it could be put in a weapons form.[26]

Shortly after the cease-fire it transpired that Iraq's nuclear programme had been far more advanced and extensive than previously assumed and that it had survived the allied attacks largely intact. The sources of these revelations were defecting Iraqi nuclear scientists. They claimed that the Iraqi objective at the time of the war was to complete a bomb by the end of 1991, and that Saddam was still continuing his nuclear programme apace in the hope of meeting this deadline. They warned that the allies had targeted only three of Iraq's seven nuclear weapons sites, and even there managed to destroy only 60 per cent of the infrastructure, leaving key materials and equipment, as well as scientific personnel, largely unscathed. They identified those nuclear sites that had escaped bombardment during the war.[27] According to one Iraqi defector, one method of enriching uranium, electromagnetic separation, had already yielded forty kilograms of weapons-grade material. In his claim, three sites for operating calutrons, machines based on 1940s technology but capable of enriching uranium, may have been ready at the time of the war to begin manufacturing and testing weapons-grade material. Depleted radioactive isotopes found on the clothing of US hostages suggested that they had been detained at such nuclear facilities.[28]

In January 1992 Iraq first admitted having a production scale uranium enrichment programme dedicated to developing a nuclear bomb. It disclosed that it had bought the components for as many as 10,000 centrifuges, enough for large-scale production of fissile material. If assembled, Iraq would have been able to produce enough uranium for four bombs a year, making its uranium enrichment programme the largest in the world.[29]

Electrical power

A second important area of the strategic campaign concerned Iraq's energy sources, including oil-refining and electrical power. Twenty-eight targets in each of these categories were attacked. Depriving Iraq of its energy sources undoubtedly had an effect on the ability to sustain its army in the field and operate its air defence and military communications.[30] To Air Force planners these attacks took them back to the prominence these targets had had in the Second World War. It was a way of measuring the startling changes in precision since 1945. The USAF calculated that 'two "smart" bombs could function as effectively as 108 Second World War B-17 bombers carrying 648 bombs, and crewed by 1,080 airmen', in attacking generating plants, while all Iraq's refinery capacity was destroyed using less than half the tonnage dropped on a single German refinery during the war.[31] Impressive though these figures are, the strategic relevance of the targets was different in the two cases. They were critical in a prolonged, total war of attrition, but were not necessarily as important in a limited war geared to a decisive land battle.

By late January, eleven of Iraq's major petrochemical plants, including three refineries, had been reported damaged. According to the Air Force, within three days of the strikes refined oil production was down to 50 per cent and in another ten days it was down to zero.[32] It was not yet clear whether Iraq could recover or the extent of damage to electrical power.[33] Schwarzkopf's more positive analysis was that 'one fourth of electrical generating facilities' were completely inoperative, with another 50 per cent suffering degraded operations. However, he suggested that the target plan had sought to achieve a fine balance: 'we never had any intention of destroying 100 per cent of all the Iraqi electrical power, because of our interest in making sure that civilians did not suffer unduly'.[34] The oil industry had suffered more because 'we certainly wanted to make sure they didn't have a lot of gasoline for their military vehicles'.[35] Army Lieutenant-General Thomas Kelly, a frequent Pentagon spokesman during the war, stated that 'if there is an additional effect on the civilian population, it is one that Saddam Hussein has chosen, not one that we did'.[36]

However, by the conclusion of the air campaign, electrical power was the most severely damaged component of the whole Iraqi target system. The post-war assessment of recovery times gave the petroleum industry up to two years; telecommunications, anything from three to twelve years; transportation, three to six years; electric power, five to nine years. These attacks had a deleterious effect on civilian life in Iraq, affecting health and welfare as well as economic activity. The lights went out in Baghdad ten minutes into the war and did not come on again until after the cease-fire. Ironically, this was achieved by massive short circuits as a result of fine carbon fibres. However, subsequently twenty power plants were also bombed.[37]

One particular case was the al-Hartha power plant in Basra. This was attacked early in the campaign, causing the lights to go out and the sewage plant to stop functioning, and was then attacked another twelve times, with the last strike coming half an hour before the cease-fire on 28 February. The Air Force insisted this repeated bombardment was not a mistake: this particular generator would be used to pump oil into fire trenches, to some twenty command and control bunkers and to the environmentally controlled bunkers used to store chemical weapons. One critic, William Arkin, suggested that the facility was unfortunate enough to lie on the standard route used by coalition aircraft, so had been struck if nothing else was available, and that the rules given to pilots for these strikes had been unrealistic. The CENTCOM directive of 12 January had ordered that

> electric targets will be targeted to minimize recuperation time. At electric production/transformer stations the objectives will be the transformers/switching yards and the central building in these yards. Boilers and generators will not be aim points.[38]

Nonetheless, despite this injunction the pilots appeared to have reverted to their standard procedure in training which was to aim for the generators: these were also the largest points to aim for. After the war the Air Force agreed that the strikes might have been more effective than intended.[39]

Command structures

Another critical area of overlap between the civilian and military spheres was command. The Iraqi military organization, essentially modelled on Soviet lines, was hierarchical, with Saddam Hussein at the top of the pyramid. The more the command, control and communications system was degraded, the more ignorant the senior level would be about the real situation on the ground and the less able to issue effective orders to their subordinates. Moreover, as a Pentagon report later put it:

> If rendered unable to command and control their military forces, or to maintain a firm grip on their internal population control mechanisms, they might be compelled to comply with coalition demands.[40]

The plan did not call specifically for the elimination of Saddam himself. There were both legal and practical reasons for this. In legal terms, as Cheney had explained to Dugan the previous September, an Executive Order from the 1970s forbade any agency of the US Government from seeking to assassinate a foreign leader. In practical terms it was well known that Saddam, being sufficiently sensitive to threats against his life, moved constantly from bunker to bunker. There were even reports of 'Saddam clones' – lookalikes who could deceive any agents. It was suspected that Saddam spent much of the war in the residential suburbs, to avoid allied air attacks, keeping in touch with his subordinates through a network of command posts. Some of these were mobile and used remotely placed antennae located some distance away so that his own location could not be pinpointed.

So the position taken by the coalition leadership was that no specific attempt was being made to 'get Saddam' but that if he was 'got', during attacks on the central command structure, then that would be a bonus. There were reports that he was almost caught when travelling back to Baghdad in convoy after visiting commanders in Basra. Only rather late in the campaign did the Air Force actually realize that the State Department would have no objections if this logic was accepted and some effort was made to catch Saddam in one of his command bunkers. According to one account, two special 5,000-lb bombs (Glide Bomb Unit-28) were designed with the objective of destroying highly fortified bunkers. The option was only identified at the start of February, with the go-ahead given on the 14th of that month. On 27 February, the final night of the war, these bombs were dropped on a hardened bunker at al-Taji air base, some fifteen miles north-west of Baghdad, where it was judged Saddam might be hiding. The bunker was destroyed but Saddam had not been there.[41]

The structures of Ba'th Party control, and buildings connected with Saddam's ruling Tikriti clan, were targeted under the heading of 'leadership targets'. There were twenty-six such targets.[42] The political logic of these attacks was not altogether clear – for example, why target Ba'th Party headquarters in Baghdad but not its offices elsewhere in Iraq? Why strike the Ministry of Local Affairs while leaving the Ministry of Culture and Information intact? (Largely, in this case, because one was mistaken for the other.)

A large part of the effort was directed against command, control and communications nodes. Again it was difficult to separate the military from civilian society. The Pentagon estimated that 60 per cent of military communications passed through the civilian telegraph system. However, while that national capability could be destroyed, repairs meant that it was attacked repeatedly. It was more difficult to get at the more dispersed communication facilities, especially when intelligence was so poor. At the end of January it was reported that 75 per cent of Iraq's command, control and communications facilities had been struck and that one third were 'completely destroyed or rendered inoperative'. Twenty 'leadership targets' were also struck and around twelve were 'severely damaged or destroyed'.[43]

At about this time the Iraqis appeared to be taking special measures to restore some military communications which involved calling several standby bunkers into action. Although Saddam moved to these back-up systems, his ability to communicate was put under considerable strain, as these back-ups were both less effective and easier to target. By mid February, it reportedly took Saddam twenty-four hours to get a message to the front.[44] However, the main problem with communications appears to have been less the sending than the receiving. Prior to the start of the war, the Iraqis removed sophisticated communications equipment such as computers and telephone exchanges out of obvious targets so that they could reinstall them later. The field commanders had links with Baghdad but did not use them because they knew they would be traced by coalition signals intelligence and then bombed.[45]

Civilian casualties

Gradually this campaign became interwoven with a developing argument over the extent of the allies' success in avoiding civilian casualties. In his first briefing of the war, Schwarzkopf announced the coalition's determination to reduce civilian casualties. 'We are doing everything we possibly can to avoid injuring or hurting or destroying innocent people,' he said. 'We have said all along that this is not a war against the Iraqi people.'[46]

Despite the intensity of the campaign, the Iraqis did little to contradict this. While there was much vitriolic propaganda with regard to the savagery of the air raids and the suffering caused to the civilian population, Saddam was also wary of alarming his subjects. Instead of exaggerated claims of mass carnage, official figures from Iraq seemed if anything to err on the low side – twenty-three civilians killed and sixty-six wounded after the first day, rising only to forty-one killed and 191 wounded after four days. On 5 February, Tariq Aziz gave figures of 428 killed and 650 wounded.[47]

In some ways Saddam was clearly relying upon coalition restraint. No effort was made to protect the civilian population. There were shelters for less than 1 per cent of civilians. A much publicized civil defence evacuation had been conducted before the air campaign, but none was set in motion once the campaign began. CENTCOM was soon picking up indications that the Iraqis were putting military items in civilian targets.[48] The senior British Commander, General Sir Peter de la Billière, claimed in early February that Saddam was 'transferring his field headquarters into schools where he knows we will not attack him because of our care and concern to avoid areas that are housing civilians'.[49] Later, when targeting policy was becoming more controversial, official spokesmen stressed the lengths to which Saddam was going to use coalition restraint to protect his military equipment: command and control centres on top of schools and public buildings; tanks and artillery beside private homes and small villages; two MiG-21 aircraft parked near the front door of an ancient Babylonian shrine; heavy-duty fuel tankers in the middle of a cemetery; a military headquarters and combat vehicles in and around a hospital.[50]

Saddam, for his part, lost no opportunity to use evidence of human suffering in order to generate political support. The Iraqi people, who no longer could be convinced that their 'valiant eagles' were dealing telling blows at the allied air forces, were asked to translate their anger with Western 'atrocities' into unquestioning support for the war effort. The Arab masses, who took great pride in Iraq's defiant stance, were expected to express their exasperation with their leaders and to pressure the Arab members of the coalition to desist from their 'despicable behaviour'. Finally, the televised scenes of allegedly indiscriminate bombings were designed to strengthen the 'peace camp' in the West and to steer a public debate there about the legitimacy of the strategic air campaign. Having initially pushed out the bulk of the Western media, supposing (correctly) that it was helping the coalition to assess damage,[51] Saddam soon invited them back and sent them on guided tours of civilian damage.

The Iraqis reported attacks on the holy sites of Najaf and Karbala, although after the war the Americans were able to show that they had been untouched, and that refugees, aware of this, had fled to them. The Americans also had a picture of the mosque in Basra with its dome missing. It had obviously simply been taken off, because everything else about the building was intact. Some of the war damage shown was left over from the conflict with Iran.

Saddam's propaganda ploy proved highly effective, at least, in the Arab world. In Morocco some 300,000 people took to the streets, forcing King Hassan into an apologetic explanation of his participation in the anti-Saddam war coalition. King Hussein of Jordan, for his part, responded to Iraq's projected plight by publicly expressing his support for Saddam and blaming the allies for 'committing war crimes under the disguise of UN resolutions'. Even in Damascus, the new yet staunch ally of the United States, there were rumblings of dissatisfaction with the progress of the war. In an interview with the French daily, *Le Figaro*, Defence Minister Tlas expressed a thinly veiled criticism of the United States's slow conduct of the war. 'Had Soviet doctrine been followed,' he said, 'the General Staff would have engaged the ground units after three hours of bombing and with simultaneous air bombardment. The Americans are counting primarily on airpower. I prefer the Soviet doctrine.'[52] Aware of this Syrian unease, Bush made a special phone conversation to Hafiz Asad, in which he reassured the Syrian President that the coalition was doing its best to avoid civilian casualties.

The early claims made by coalition commanders with regard to the success of precision bombing, and the contrast with Saddam's indiscriminate missile attacks that they had stressed, meant that any evidence of substantial civilian damage was highlighted. The concern over damage to Iraqi civilians grew as the attacks moved on to the supply lines, which meant striking roads and bridges. Some 450 sorties were launched against fifty-four rail and road bridges and thirty-two pontoon bridges.[53] Expressions of alarm were heard as three of the six bridges over the Euphrates were hit, and Washington and London urged that the further bridges be spared, though they carried fibre-optic land lines connecting Baghdad with the front. Later special forces cut the lines. This was the first indication that the politicians were getting anxious about the character of the strategic air campaign.

The most controversial attack was on a command bunker/air raid shelter, at the Baghdadi neighbourhood of Amiriya, involving two laser-guided bombs, one of which hit the ventilation shaft. First reports spoke of 500 dead, of which about half were women and children. This was later scaled down to 314.

The Iraqis seized this opportunity to discredit the allied air campaign which, they contended, was aimed at destroying Iraq rather than liberating Kuwait. Foreign journalists were rushed to the scene, and disturbing pictures of bodies retrieved from the wrecked shelter were shown throughout the world. The initial instinct in the Administration was to respond with a curt statement of targeting policy, but Bush's spokesman, Marlin Fitzwater, persuaded the President that it was essential to express compassion for innocent lives,[54] and this led to a massive public relations effort, involving a bombardment of briefings and backgrounders. The bunker was a well-known command and control centre, and the civilians should not have been there in the first place. Was it not remarkable that this was the first such incident? Could it not be that Saddam had been trying to achieve this very effect? General Kelly went a step further, arguing that one could not rule out 'a cold-blooded decision on the part of Saddam Hussein to put civilians without our knowledge into a facility and have them bombed. He had to know we knew this was a military facility.' Awkwardly, Brigadier-General Richard Neal described feeling 'very comfortable' that this 'was a legitimate target'.[55] It was asserted that if it had been known that there were civilians there, the target would not have been attacked.

Though all these claims had some validity, this was not the coalition's finest moment. The intelligence regarding the bunker appears to have been limited and dated, and the target, which had not been of the highest importance earlier, was attacked only because more important targets had already been destroyed. The bunker had been built in the early 1980s as one of about twenty-five civilian air raid shelters for the war with Iran, and was part of a complex including a school, mosque and supermarket, in the new Amiriya suburb, popular with the Iraqi middle class and civil servants. In 1985 it had been rebuilt and strengthened with a 15–16-foot roof of reinforced concrete, and then equipped for use as one of about a dozen emergency headquarters. However, the Iraqi commanders had decided to abandon these shelters as they knew that they were likely to be targeted. They were turned over to the local residents, who were not warned of the risk.[56]

The bunker was initially on the list, but low down, as a 'leadership target'. At the end of January, CENTCOM claimed that it was one of the standby bunkers brought into service to compensate for the destruction of so much of the command and control network. Its roof and surroundings had been camouflaged accordingly. Despite initial claims, it was never seen as a command and control centre. Radar signals had been detected, passing on messages originating elsewhere in Baghdad to front-line troops, which put the bunker higher up the target list but without much additional intelligence as to what was going on at the scene; the view that it was being used by the leadership was further reinforced by some evidence of military trucks and senior government limousines arriving at the centre. The bunker seems to have been attacked largely because of evidence that it was a likely shelter for key military or Ba'th personnel, including Saddam's personal security force, but with some additional indication of its back-up command-and-control function, at a time when it was doing its best to shut down any 'live' network. The USAF also note that four similar targets were attacked that evening: this was the only one with civilians inside.[57]

Senior officers later admitted that the whole affair had been poorly managed, and the result was a growing unease in the allied camp over targeting procedures. A debate was already developing over the priorities in the strategic air campaign. Those who felt that it was important to concentrate on the battlefield were frustrated with what they judged to be the US Air Force's preoccupation with precision weapons attacks and the 'decapitation' of the Iraqi leadership. The conservative approach to bomb damage assessment meant that targets that had probably been destroyed were still being revisited and that other, lesser, targets were being pushed up the list to sustain the momentum of the strategic campaign. If this created the impression that the allies were concerned with pounding Baghdad rather than getting on with the ground campaign, then it could create pressures to start the land offensive before there had been sufficient attrition of Iraqi forces.

For these reasons, even before the bunker was hit, the focus of the bombing was already moving south into the Kuwaiti theatre, largely as the result of the intensifying preparations for the ground invasion but also, perhaps, because of the earlier concerns over the effects of attacking targets where civilian casualties were unavoidable. The experience heightened sensitivity to the issue of civilian casualties. With the sort of air supremacy the allies enjoyed, it was possible to undertake leaflet drops to warn people of an impending raid. A few days after the Amiriya incident, the RAF reported abandoning some missions, and then when one of their smart bombs veered away from the centre of a bridge to hit a civilian area they screened the video to show how things could go wrong. Defence Secretary Cheney reportedly asked Powell to review the remaining 150 targets on the strategic list. Nine similar bunkers to that at Amiriya were taken off the list. Others excluded were largely 'leadership targets' – a regional Ba'th Party headquarters, certain military intelligence buildings, state security buildings and some ministries – ostensibly because of the risk that these too might have been packed with civilians.[58]

While contrary to the coalition's strategic philosophy, the bunker attack may have had an ironic strategic impact. Those occupying it could have been the families of senior officials in the Ba'th Party; if so, the attack may have begun to bring home the costs of war. As acknowledged by Foreign Minister Aziz, the Iraqi leadership had not anticipated the extent of the devastation: 'We were watching the American build-up, and we expected the conflict to be severe. But we did not think the United States would try to destroy all of our telephone exchanges and the rest of our civilian infrastructure.'[59]

Despite such tragic and much publicized incidents, the actual number of civilians killed was remarkably limited when the scale of the bombing is taken into account. The most precise Iraqi figures put the number of civilians killed at 2,278 and the number of wounded at 5,965.[60] When compared to the large number of Iraqis killed in the subsequent civil war and also as a result of the damage consequential on the general post-war breakdown in Iraqi economic and social organization, Iraq's civilian casualties during the war are further dwarfed.

The general dislocation to civilian life caused by the strategic bombing may also have made Saddam concerned about his political base. By the time of the Amiriya attack, civilian life in Iraq was becoming increasingly unbearable. There was no electricity or running water in Baghdad and Iraq's other major cities, and the residents of Baghdad faced the threat of cholera and typhoid epidemics. By early February the Government was forced to announce an indefinite halt to the sale of fuel, thereby leading to the complete collapse of vehicular civilian transportation. Eagleburger later recalled a conversation he had had with the King of Morocco, whom he was visiting when the bunker was hit. King Hassan observed that the incident was 'not going to be viewed in Iraq in the way you in the West view it as the terrible, awful thing it is, but, rather, it is a demonstration . . . to an awful lot of Iraqis as to how vulnerable they really are, and it is probably, in terms of the attitudes in Iraq towards Saddam Hussein, something that will lead to antagonism and criticism of him, not the reverse.'[61]

Table 9: Strategic air targets

TARGET	NUMBER	SORTIES
Electric power	28	215
Naval	20	247
National command authority	26	429
Air defence	29	436
Oil	28	518
Command, control and communications	170	601
Road, rail and bridges	54	712
Nuclear, biological, chemical	31	902
Military support	96	2,756
Short-range ballistic missiles (Scuds)	30	2,767
Airfields	66	3,047
Republican Guard	145	5,646
TOTAL	723	18,276

Sources: Various, including CENTCOM, Greenpeace.

CHAPTER 24
Saddam's 'Israeli Card' Fails

Saddam had long spoken of his missile force as an anti-Israel capability and re-emphasized this on the eve of the war.[1] Striking at the main population centres of the Jewish state would be cheered by the Arab masses, put the Arab members of the coalition in a difficult position, and lay the ground for an Israeli retaliation. To pre-empt the latter, the coalition might move earlier than planned to a ground offensive in Kuwait which, in turn, would enable Iraq to bleed it severely.

Fully aware of all this, the Israelis were torn by their anxiety to deter Saddam through threats on the one hand, and to help the anti-Iraqi coalition maintain its cohesion by keeping a low profile on the other. They ruled out a pre-emptive strike against Iraq and avoided references to *automatic* retaliation,[2] confining themselves instead to rather vague, yet stern cautions against either a direct attack on Israel or an Iraqi entry into Jordan. 'Saddam knows that if he tries to attack Israel we shall strike back,' Prime Minister Shamir told a delegation of US Congressmen in early January, 'our allies are aware of our position and of our state of readiness.' Foreign Minister Levy was even tougher. 'Saddam's threats to attack Israel are a declaration of war,' he said, 'and we do not know whether or not he will actually carry them out. Yet, should he choose to attack Israel, he will face a terrible retribution.'[3]

What did this 'terrible retribution' mean? Could it imply a nuclear response in the most extreme circumstances, such as an Iraqi chemical attack? Some influential Americans certainly tended to believe so. In a press interview on 2 February, Richard Cheney warned that if Iraq were to use chemical weapons against Israel, the latter might retaliate by resorting to weapons of mass destruction.[4] The Israelis themselves, however, were reluctant to let the nuclear skeleton out of the cupboard. 'Nuclear weapons do not have any role in the crisis,' argued the former Minister of Defence, Yitzhak Rabin.[5] The Israeli Chief-of-Staff, Lieutenant-General Dan Shomron, was more explicit. 'Iraq has a limited ability to hit us, and it should take into account a very harsh response,' he said, yet 'we have always declared that *we will not be the first to use nuclear weapons*, and this is our policy today.'[6]

Although this statement could be interpreted as an implicit threat in that it constituted, perhaps for the first time, an official Israeli admission of a nuclear capability, it also reflected a desire to discount the more apocalyptic scenarios of a possible Gulf War. Similarly Defence Minister Arens played down the damage that could be caused to Israel by an Iraqi missile attack, including a chemical one, and expressed his confidence in Israel's 'very great ability to deter Iraq'.[7]

The Iraqis, however, seemed undeterred. In his press conference after the Geneva meeting, Tariq Aziz was asked directly, 'if the war starts . . . will you attack Israel?' His answer had been equally direct: 'Yes, absolutely, yes.'[8] During the first day of the war the Iraqi Ambassador to Belgium revealed that the decision had been taken and that an attack on Israel was imminent.[9] Before long his promise was made good: in the early morning hours of Friday 18 January, five Iraqi ballistic missiles landed in Tel Aviv and three in the northern port town of Haifa.

For a while this ploy seemed to be working. Few fatalities resulted, but the attacks were highly disconcerting for Israelis. For the first time since the establishment of their state, its main population centres had come under an indiscriminate military attack by a regular Arab army.[10] No less frustrating was the painful awareness that they had been 'hijacked' into a war that was not theirs, without being able to do anything about it. Retaliation, one of the main foundations of Israel's strategic thinking over the past four decades, offered no solution. Its underlying logic was to deter attacks against Israel by impressing upon would-be aggressors that their losses were bound to exceed any potential gains. This rationale was completely irrelevant to this particular situation, for Saddam's aggression was designed to trigger a response, not to avoid one.

Furthermore, the low level of casualties both reduced public pressures for retaliation and also made appropriate retribution difficult to design: any attack on civilian targets in Baghdad would almost inevitably be disproportionate. If, as an alternative, the offending missile launchers were to be attacked then Israeli aircraft had no better chance of finding them than the allies, or of causing a greater dent in the Iraqi war machine than was being inflicted on an hourly basis. An attack would also be difficult to execute without American connivance, because of the danger of getting mixed up in allied air activity, while violating Jordanian air space *en route* could lead to escalation on its own.

In these circumstances it made sense to keep the threat of retaliation in reserve just in case a substantial attack was mounted or if a good opportunity arose in the future to punish Iraq. Meanwhile Israel gained political credit for restraint, to cash in at a later date.

If retaliation could only play into Saddam's hands, inaction entailed its own risks. It went against the grain for Israelis to turn the other cheek, and could erode Israel's future deterrent posture. Given the long legacy of acrimony between Arabs and Jews and the fundamental prejudices and misperceptions on both sides, there was no guarantee that the Arabs would take Israel's restraint for what it was, a sign of maturity and strength. Indeed, to judge by the jubilant response in several Arab countries and among the Palestinians in the occupied territories to the Iraqi attack, this move was interpreted as a demonstration of Arab strength and Israeli weakness.

These contradictory considerations faced the Israeli Cabinet as it weighed its response to the first Iraqi attack. The atmosphere was hard. Prior to the meeting Dan Shomron stated that 'an attack on our civilians cannot pass without a response', and his superior, Moshe Arens, observed, 'We have said publicly and to the Americans that if we were attacked we would react; we were attacked, we will react, certainly. We have to defend ourselves.'[11]

In private, however, the political and military mood was far more restrained. 'My instinctive reaction to Iraq's first missile attack was not different from that of any Israeli,' Shomron later recalled, namely, 'a reflex action shaped during a generation of incessant wars: we must retaliate, strike at them, break their bones. It was clear to me that at dawn, after the dust had settled over the first missile attack, we would be called upon to respond. I knew that the Israeli Defence Forces (IDF) were ready for any contingency. The plans were there and what was required was only a "green light".' However,

> a Chief-of-Staff must take into account the overall picture and must make his decisions in a cool-headed, sober, perhaps even cruel fashion. I consulted my colleagues at the General Staff and our unanimous conclusion was that an Israeli response would cause severe damage to the international coalition already on the second day of the war.

Shomron proceeded to the Cabinet meeting, where he recommended restraint. 'An unprecedented coalition of Western and Arab countries has been assembled and all of them are operating against an enemy of ours,' he told the attentive ministers:

> So far the Americans are doing the work for us and are doing it well. Saddam Hussein could exploit an Israeli strike in order to evacuate

Kuwait immediately and direct his forces against us, in the pretext that Israel is his main enemy. What will the Americans do in such circumstances? And what will the Soviets and the Arab states do?[12]

Shomron's recommendation did not pass unchallenged. A small but vociferous group of Cabinet members advocated retaliation. Not surprisingly, this lobby was headed by the two architects of the ill-conceived 1982 Lebanon War – Minister of Housing Ariel Sharon, and Minister of Agriculture Raphael Eitan. They were supported by the ultra-right-wing Minister of Science, Yuval Ne'eman, and the maverick Minister of Finance, Yitzhak Modai. Defence Minister Arens struck a middle path, tending towards retaliation but refraining from pushing his position too far.

Fortunately for Shomron, he found an ally in the person of Yitzhak Shamir. The seventy-five-year-old Prime Minister was as cautious as ever and keenly aware of how the short- and long-term advantages of restraint exceeded the immediate satisfaction of revenge. There was no need to relinquish the right to retaliation at the appropriate moment. He prevailed over the hawks in his Cabinet and ruled against retaliation.

Shamir's decision was also affected by pressures and reassurances from the US Administration and some other members of the coalition. As soon as they heard that Iraqi Scuds were landing in Israel, Scowcroft and Bush agreed that Shamir must be contacted at once to urge him to keep calm and not take precipitate action. The Americans pleaded for restraint and promised 'the darndest search and destroy operation ever in the region [of remaining Iraqi mobile missile launchers]'.[13]

Hardly had the Israelis recovered from their initial shock and resisted the instinctive urge for retaliation when they were hit again by a missile salvo: at 07.00 on Saturday 19 January, three Iraqi Scuds landed in Tel Aviv, causing some damage and injuring a few people.

This time the Israeli response was prompt and resolute. Within minutes of the missiles' landing, fighting aircraft took to the air, both to save time in the event of a political order to retaliate, and to pre-empt a possible Iraqi air strike against Israel. As the planes were hovering along Israel's borders, Defence Minister Arens was consulting his top officers whether or not to retaliate. Opinions were divided. The Minister of Defence and his Air Force commander, Major-General Avihu Bin-Nun, supported a military move against Iraq,[14] while Dan Shomron, his Deputy, Major-General Ehud Barak, and the Head of the Military Intelligence Directorate, Major-General Amnon Shahak, believed that Israel should not make any military move without the prior consent of and co-ordination with the United States.

Such co-ordination, they argued, was all the more important given the considerable political risks of the retaliation plan, and its exceptional operational complexity, even by the standards of the seasoned IDF.

According to the plan, prepared during the previous months, the missile threat from western Iraq was to be suppressed through a combined operation involving air and airborne ground forces. This required overflying Jordanian territory, at the risk of encountering the Jordanian Air Force, as well as maintaining aerial and ground presence on Iraqi territory for a few days with all the attendant operational and logistical difficulties. The plan reflected the Israeli belief that air strikes alone would not deal with the threat, and that pilots more ready to accept the risks of low altitude attacks and trained in attacks on small targets would show greater success. The Americans flew too high to identify their targets and were easy prey to decoys. The missiles had to be identified on the ground. As Arens was to admit a year after the war, nobody in the IDF expected the operation to eliminate missile attacks altogether; yet it was believed that a painful blow at Iraq's missile force would significantly alleviate the pressure on the Israeli public and tarnish Saddam's war strategy.[15]

Heeding his Generals' advice, Arens called Cheney on the Hammer-Rick line. 'Israel's patience is running thin,' he said, 'and it is deeply disappointed with the US failure to stop the missile attacks.' He then informed Cheney that Israel was seriously considering retaliation and requested that the Americans open an air corridor for some four hours for the Israeli Air Force and give Israel the electronic 'friend or foe' identification codes, that would enable it to distinguish between allied and Iraqi aircraft. Cheney declined. 'There is nothing that your Air Force can do that we are not already doing,' he said, 'if there is, tell us and we will do it. We appreciate your restraint but please don't play into Saddam's hands.' The same message was also relayed to Yitzhak Shamir in personal phone calls by Bush and Baker. What Shamir and Arens were not told was that contingency plans had been prepared should Israel ignore the American plea and retaliate; a special air corridor was to be opened for the Israeli Air Force so that no coalition aircraft would also be on their way to Iraq.[16]

In the event the Americans were greatly relieved to find the Israeli Prime Minister far calmer than his Minister of Defence. Israel would agree to hold back for some more time, he said, but it would require clearer indications of America's commitment to its security. Despite Saudi misgivings, the Americans agreed that the Israelis needed better information on the course of the war. Promises were made for more intelligence-sharing regarding the 'Scud hunt' in western Iraq. This was partly to enable Israeli leaders, who might be asked by their constituents why they had left things to the Americans when Israelis could have done the job better, to say that they had made an input, and partly because Israel did have good intelligence on western Iraq and the Iraqi military effort. A planning cell was established in Tel Aviv to get Israeli ideas with regard to potential targets, and Israeli and American photo-interpreters examined the reconnaissance evidence together.

No less important from Shamir's point of view, he was promised real-time early warning of Iraqi missile launches against Israel. This meant that US sensors, connected to its Ballistic Missile Early Warning System (BMEWS), which picked up Iraqi missile launches and transmitted the information virtually instantaneously to Washington, would provide the same information within seconds to Israel, thereby allowing the latter to increase its early warning time from two to approximately seven minutes. Last but not least, he was offered Patriot anti-missile missiles, with their American crews. Shortly after the Iraqi invasion of Kuwait the Israelis had reassessed their previous decision not to buy the Patriot and approached the Administration with a request for the missiles. In September 1990 they were promised two batteries of the advanced version, capable of intercepting surface-to-surface missiles. A month later it was announced that two batteries of the missile were on their way, helped by Congressional agreement that the transfer could count as foreign aid. Unfortunately for Israel, the deal was undermined by senior Pentagon officials who, ignoring three separate White House pledges, insisted on supplying the basic version, which had been designed as an anti-aircraft weapon but was worthless against Scud missiles.[17] During their visit to Israel on the eve of the war, Eagleburger and Wolfowitz offered to provide Patriot missiles with their American troops until the Israelis could train their own crews, but this offer was declined by Shamir. Now, eager to deflect potential public pressure for retaliation and impressed by the performance of the Patriots in Saudi Arabia, the Israeli Cabinet decided to bend the hitherto sacred principle that no foreign forces were ever to defend Israel. Arens raised the issue in his phone conversation with Cheney, as did Shamir with George Bush. An agreement to send two Patriot batteries to Israel, with their American troops, was reached.

Armed with these American pledges, Shamir convened his inner Cabinet for the second emergency meeting in two days. In a replay of the previous session, the hawkish troika, Sharon–Ne'eman–Eitan, pressed again for immediate retaliation, while Defence Minister Arens remained divided and Foreign Minister Levy strongly opposed to such a move. Shamir drew the bottom line. 'I do not think we should react,' he said. 'This is what Saddam wants, to transform the war into one between Arabs and Israel. What do we gain from this, just to have the satisfaction that we retaliated?'[18]

To further reassure the Israelis and to dissuade them from doing anything dangerous by way of retaliation lest it unsettle the coalition, Eagleburger and Wolfowitz were dispatched again to Israel. As Eagleburger described his role:

> When we arrive, we have one set of discussions, as time goes on, Scuds keep landing and we have continuing conversations with the Prime Minister, with the Defence Minister and so forth, and each time there would be a Scud attack, there would be an Israeli reaction, we must do something, and each time we would talk with them and, in the event – they never did retaliate.[19]

Eagleburger never sensed intense pressure to retaliate except at the most senior levels of Government and noted that restraint had popular support. His delegation concluded that it was unlikely though not impossible and that there would be consultation with the US before any action was launched. Indeed, such consultation was to take place on 11 February, in a meeting between Defence Minister Arens and President Bush in Washington.

Arens had been nagging Cheney remorselessly. One account refers to sixty calls from the Israeli Defence Minister to his American counterpart during the war.[20] Now he sought to drive home to the President the alarm with which Israel viewed the continued missile attacks on its territory. He hoped that even if the Administration's opposition to Israeli retaliation did not abate, the increased Israeli pressure and sense of urgency would force the allocation of more resources to the 'Scud hunt'. The mood in the Cabinet, he told Bush, was nearing the point where military action would be considered both feasible and commendable. The Iraqi attacks were increasingly irritating while, in the Israeli judgement, the international stakes of such an action were diminishing by the day. 'The Arab members of the coalition must be aware by now that Saddam is on the verge of defeat,' he said, 'and are unlikely to abandon the coalition as a result of an Israeli retaliation.' Nor did he believe there was any real risk, at this stage of the war, of Jordan being dragged into the conflict should Israel move against Iraq.

During the meeting news came in that another Iraqi missile had landed in an affluent neighbourhood near Tel Aviv, a few blocks from Arens's own residence. Despite this personal demonstration of Israel's vulnerability, Bush would not budge. 'What conceivably can you do that the coalition air forces cannot?' he asked Arens. To that Arens answered that Israel would not limit itself to air attacks but would rather operate against the Iraqi missiles in several other spheres. He then gave the floor to his Deputy Chief-of-Staff, Major-General Barak, who had accompanied him to Washington. Barak, one of Israel's most seasoned officers in commando operations, presented the broad concepts of the Israeli plan for a combined operation in western Iraq without dwelling on its particulars. Bush remained unmoved. This plan was too risky for the cohesion of the coalition even at this advanced stage of the war, he said; there was absolutely no guarantee of its unequivocal success and it could still split the coalition on the eve of the ground offensive. He fully understood the Israeli predicament, but thought it advisable for Israel to continue to hold back.[21]

Bush's reasoning was shared by the majority of the Israeli public and most politicians, who continued to recognize the (albeit painful) merits of restraint. In an impressive demonstration of unity, reserved in Israeli politics only for moments of great external threat, the opposition parties rallied behind the Government. Shimon Peres and Yitzhak Rabin, leaders of the Labour Party, the ruling Likud's main political rival, expressed their support for restraint and called for its continuation. Their call was echoed by the small left-wing parties, which would normally condemn the Likud for its political intransigence and harsh treatment of the Palestinians in the occupied territories.[22]

These small parties were also embarrassed and infuriated by the jubilant reaction to the Scud attacks of the PLO and the Palestinians in the territories, whom they had long considered as potential interlocutors for peace negotiations. Yossi Sarid, a veteran member of Knesset, published a bitter article in which he expressed his deep disappointment with the Palestinian position and called upon them to 'look for him' in case they changed their mind about the Iraqi behaviour. Haim Ramon, one of the Labour Party's leading doves, described the Palestinian 'decision to join Saddam Hussein's bandwagon' as a 'terrible mistake' and cautioned that 'the more Palestinians dance on the roofs, the more remote the prospects of peace become'. Some doves, such as the former ministers and generals Ezer Weizmann and Haim Bar-Lev, took their anger and frustration with the Iraqi attacks a step further by joining the militant minority group advocating retaliation.[23]

That this hawkish view remained a minority did not imply that the policy of restraint could have been sustained indefinitely. A chemical missile attack, or even a large number of fatalities as a result of a conventional strike, could readily fracture the fragile basis of public consensus and trigger a military response. However, the evidence that the allies were dealing with Iraq's mobile missile launchers, as the rate of attacks slackened, helped Israel to stay outside the conflict. Even though the impact of the war had not diminished altogether – the Israeli economy was still losing $25 million per day due to lower productivity,[24] and night-life throughout the country remained paralysed, as people waited indoors for the random missile – life gradually settled into an uneasy, yet bearable routine. Schools were re-opened, hospitals resumed their normal activity, economic life got back to normal, and the special security restrictions in the occupied territories, imposed at the beginning of the war, were gradually eased.

Israel's restraint shuffled Saddam's cards. While gloating that 'Nebu-chadnezzar will feel proud in his grave' and that 'Saladin al-Ayyubi is shouting God is Great', he realized that not only had his ploy to draw Israel into the conflict failed miserably, but it had led to the intensification of US–Israeli relations, with the tacit approval of the Arab members of the coalition. This was illustrated *inter alia* by the deployment of the US-manned Patriot batteries in Israel, and the conclusion of a special bilateral agreement on the 'status of forces', giving American military personnel in Israel and Israeli personnel in the United States a 'privileged status'. Israel also presented the Administration with a request for an additional $13 billion in foreign aid, including $3 billion to cover loss of revenues due to the Gulf War, and $10 billion loan guarantees for the absorption of Soviet Jewish immigrants.[25]

Germany, for its part, anxious to allay Israel's irritation at the substantial involvement of German companies both in Iraq's chemical weapons pro-grammes and in the extension of the Scud missile's range, offered Israel $165 million in 'humanitarian aid' and $700 million in military aid. By February 1991, Israel had already taken the first delivery of German military supplies, including antidotes for countering the effects of chemical and biological weapons, and Patriot missiles.[26]

But the most frustrating reaction from Saddam's point of view must have been that of the Arab members of the coalition. Paradoxically, their position was a mirror image of that of their Iraqi enemy. Like Saddam, they feared that the longer the war dragged on, the more tenuous their position would become. It is virtually impossible to gauge the state of the public mood in tightly controlled systems such as those of the Middle East, and the Arab leaders' fear of their masses is actually smaller than commonly assumed in the West (contrary to the widely held notion, 'the street' has never toppled any regime in the contemporary Arab world). However, fighting alongside the 'infidel' West against a sister Arab country was clearly a source of embarrassment for those regimes. Hence, as Iraqi missiles began landing in Tel Aviv, Arab nervousness grew by the hour.

This was exactly the mood Saddam sought to reinforce. However, instead of translating their anxiety into (public) pressure on the US to revise its war strategy, the Arab members of the coalition restated their commitment to the ejection of Iraq from Kuwait and sought to counteract Saddam's strategy. President Mubarak, head of the only Arab state at peace with Israel, approached Premier Shamir, warned him of the risks and complications attending Israeli retaliation, and urged him to persevere with restraint.[27] At President Bush's request he had also worked on the Syrians to ensure that they would not over-react if Israel did retaliate.

The Syrians, for their part, likely to face the greatest embarrassment in the event of an Israeli–Iraqi clash, went out of their way to castigate and ridicule Saddam's strategy. The missile attacks against Israel, they argued, were extremely detrimental to the Arab cause. They brought no visible gain to the Arabs, as 'every Arab citizen throughout the Arab homeland knows very well that the handful of missiles the Baghdad ruler has fired towards the occupied territories from a distance will neither destroy the Zionist entity, nor liberate any occupied land, nor regain any usurped right'. At the same time the attacks enabled Israel to reap abundant fruits at the very low cost of slight casualties and material damage, including a boost to the Israeli economy through 'many promises for substantial financial assistance from the United States, Germany, and the EC countries', generous American and German military support, and alleviation of Israel's international isolation due to the surge of world sympathy towards the Jewish state. On a broader basis, the war played into Israeli hands, as it would lead to the eradication of Iraq's strategic and military infrastructure, while diverting world public opinion from the Palestinian problem:

> Those committed to the liberation of Palestine do not pull out their forces from the anti-Zionist trench and embroil them in military adventures elsewhere.[28]

All of this meant, in the Syrian analysis, that the war was an exercise in futility on a grand scale and had to be brought to an immediate end through Iraq's unconditional withdrawal from Kuwait. Only such a move could save the Iraqi Army, the Iraqi people, and, indeed, the Arab nation at large from a catastrophe. There was no way for Iraq to win this unnecessary war, and Saddam should relinquish any thoughts of dragging Syria (or for that matter, any other Arab member of the coalition) into war with Israel in order to satisfy his needs. 'You are free to fight the whole world alone,' Mustafa Tlas scorned Saddam, 'but you are not free to claim wisdom and reason. You are especially not free to call on people to join you in this folly.'[29] And the Syrian

Foreign Minister, Farouq al-Shara, reassured foreign ambassadors in Damascus that Syria would not be dragged into war with Israel *even in the case of an Israeli retaliation.*[30]

To underline their determination not to play into Saddam's hands, the Syrians also accelerated their covert activities against the Iraqi regime. Vice President Abd al-Khalim Khaddam, head of a special committee for the removal of Saddam, held hectic consultations with Iraqi opposition factions,[31] and in late January or early February, the Syrian media began openly to call for Saddam's head, arguing that there would never be peace and stability in the Middle East as long as he was alive:

> This new Hitler is a disaster which began when he took control of Iraq's fate and capabilities and the future of our people in Iraq, and the ending of this long suffering requires his removal.[32]

CHAPTER 25
The Coalition Holds

The limited allied losses and the apparent success in containing the war to Iraq and Kuwait, apart from the Scud attacks, made it easier for the coalition to sustain international support. Prior to the start of hostilities there had been many apocalyptic warnings of ecological and economic disasters, terrorism on a global scale, as well as a prolonged and bloody conflict.

The Western fear of casualties was Saddam's main bet, but concern with oil pollution and prices was another.[1] As early as October 1990 Iraq had sent tankers filled with oil to the Kuwaiti port of Mina al-Ahmadi. In December Iraqi experts experimented with explosions on wellheads in the area of the Ahmadi loading complex to perfect the means of their destruction. Through intensive engineering and explosives work all the wellheads in the Kuwaiti oilfields had been wired together. The first limited use of the oil weapon came on 16 January, when Iraqi artillery hit an oil storage tank at the small border town of al-Khafji in Saudi Arabia. A sustained campaign of environmental warfare began on 19 January, when the valves were opened on the Sea Island terminal near Kuwait City, and then the tankers' load was dumped into the Gulf. Flowing at a then estimated pace of 200,000 barrels a day, the oil slick was soon marked as one of the worst-ever oil-related ecological disasters, covering an area of at least 240 square miles. Two days later, the Wafrah oilfields and storage facilities were set on fire, producing large amounts of smoke.[2]

While this action made some military sense by creating a smoke screen that could complicate allied operations, and might also have been in retaliation for coalition attacks on Iraqi oil installations, its main aim was to underline the devastating consequences of a protracted war for the world oil market and the region's ecology. It took until 22 January for the coalition to appreciate what was going on. Then, in another display of precision bombing, which also served to demonstrate allied command of the air, the Sea Island pump was shut down.[3] The coalition was back in control, though this was not to be Saddam's last use of the oil weapon.

The American success in stemming the flow of oil calmed this anxiety until the firing of the Kuwaiti oil wells during the last days of the war. Prior to the war, general scientific opinion had been dubious when it was suggested that burning oil could have a 'nuclear winter' effect.[4] In the event the damage to health and the environment it caused was more local than global.[5] Even most of the estimates produced during the war on the effect of the oil spillage proved to have been exaggerated, as it turned out that no more than 500,000 barrels of oil had been spilled, compared with the worst estimates of up to 11 million.

The economic concerns were eased almost as soon as the war began. Just before, oil was trading at $26 per barrel. Predictions of a speedy rise to $50 on the outbreak of war largely depended upon the emergence of a threat to Saudi oil production. Otherwise, as some commentators were aware, the price was as likely to halve as double.[6] Rather than a shortage of oil, the precautionary measures taken meant that there was a glut. The Saudis had stored huge quantities outside the war zone, while the International Energy Association, in a measure designed to calm the market, had agreed to release 2.5 million barrels per day to meet the worst estimated shortfall in the event of war, and so discourage hoarding. Half the stocks would come from the United States. As the UN deadline grew close, the price edged up to $30. At the same time stock markets were moving down, but only by a few percentage points, reflecting unease rather than panic. As the first news came in on 16 January that war had begun, overnight traders caused oil prices to rise by about $5 in a knee-jerk reaction and stock markets in the Far East fell. However, as soon as it became apparent that the air war was going well, the trend reversed dramatically. There was a net fall of $9 per barrel in the oil price while stock markets rose. The Dow Jones index on Wall Street showed its second highest daily gain. There was little dramatic movement after this point. This does not mean to say that the war did not have a number of adverse economic consequences. Airlines and tourism suffered and the uncertainty meant that investment decisions were delayed. The 'third oil shock', however, had been averted.

The damage to airlines and tourism was the result of fears of terrorist attacks which also turned out to have been exaggerated. This had been a preoccupation of security services around the world since August, when major Palestinian terrorist groups, such as the organization of Abu Nidal, were said to have moved to Baghdad. By September there were further reports of preparations for attacks. Cells of operatives were being put in place, attempts were being made to smuggle in weapons and explosives. Iraqi diplomats as well as terrorist groups were surveying possible targets in

Europe and the Middle East. In a press conference in Baghdad in mid September, Abu Abbas, head of the Palestine Liberation Front, a constituent organization of the PLO which was responsible for the hijacking of the *Achille Lauro* cruise liner and the murder of an American passenger, Leon Klinghoffer, vowed to attack targets in Europe and the Middle East if war broke out. 'If America attacks Iraq, we will fight with our Iraqi brothers,' he said, admitting that he had to confine his operations to Europe due to technical shortcomings. 'We would love to reach the American shore, but it is difficult.'[7] As the UN deadline approached, he escalated further by ordering his supporters to 'open fire on the American enemy everywhere'.[8]

A reported meeting of the Iraqi leadership on 24 December led to orders to cadres in the West to instigate acts of sabotage and terrorism. This intelligence was said to be responsible for a number of expulsions of Iraqi diplomats. Some credibility was given to the story when one of those being expelled, the Press Counsellor at the London Embassy, stated that he was sure that 'if there is any attack on Iraq, a lot of targets in countries in the West will be demolished'. On 7 January Saddam warned that Iraq's battle would cover the 'whole world', relying 'on every struggler and fighter whose hand can reach out to harm . . . aggressors'.[9]

From August to the start of the war little happened, largely, it was assumed, because Saddam did not want to give the Americans a pretext for an attack and to save fire for the war to come.[10] There were a number of options for Saddam to use terrorism – to undermine the Arab members of the coalition through attacks on their diplomats and attempts to foment unrest in their countries, while the West could be shaken by reprisals against airliners.

In practice, Iraq was largely relying on enterprise by sympathizers. Its own missions were ill-suited to terrorist activity, largely as the result of expulsions of suspicious characters, the freezing of its assets so operations could not be funded, and their susceptibility to close monitoring by the security services, who took the threat seriously from the start. It was further hampered because Syria, with its rather full knowledge of the Arab terrorist network, was a member of the coalition and kept a tight lid on those elements of the network it controlled. Iran had no interest in supporting Iraq, so it was keeping its supporters in check while the United States had warned Colonel Gaddafi of Libya not to promote terrorist acts. Lastly, the mainstream PLO was unwilling to add to the political costs already incurred as a result of its support for Saddam by being seen to engage in this sort of activity.

In the war's first few weeks there were a number of low-level attacks against buildings associated with coalition countries, running at about four times the 'normal' level, but nothing to suggest a co-ordinated and well-prepared campaign. In early February Iraq called for the launching of a terrorist offensive. Coded messages coming from Baghdad and addressed to all revolutionary cells were monitored: 'Fight them in all their dens. Strike all the existing interests in the countries of aggression wherever they are,' but nothing much happened as a result of this either.

In the event, the amount of serious terrorist activity was minuscule compared with the intensity of hostilities within the defined combat zone. One report noted that of the terrorist-related incidents over the six weeks of hostilities, most were considered 'minor freelance operations, rather than the major state-sponsored attacks that were feared'. Of the 164 attacks recorded, roughly half were aimed at US business enterprises or installations, overseas. The State Department's final tally was 275. These incidents, it noted, were 'sporadic, unco-ordinated and low-level'. Numerous groups which had sworn allegiance to Saddam 'failed to act'. Others were directed at buildings owned by other prominent members of the coalition. The bulk were in the Mediterranean area, notably Greece, Turkey, Lebanon and the Yemen. There were isolated incidents in Thailand, the Philippines and Tanzania, and also in Peru, where the Iraqi cause was taken up by a local Marxist group.[11] The only time terrorism appeared to hit the United States was when six pipe bombs were found attached to two huge chemical tanks some miles from Norfolk naval base – however, this later appeared to be part of an insurance scam.

Third World views

One area where Iraqi activity outside the Middle East may have had some impact was Asia. In general the tendency in Asia was to view the conflict as a regional matter and to be unimpressed by American descriptions of the issues at stake.[12] When the war began, Iraqi embassies funded pro-Baghdad demonstrations in Pakistan, India, Malaysia and Bangladesh in an effort to exploit Islamic and anti-American sentiment in these countries. Similar attempts in Indonesia appear to have flopped. The demonstrations declined as the money ran out, but they served to highlight the difficulties faced by many governments in a war which could be portrayed as a large Western state bullying a poor Third World country. This tension was very evident in Pakistan and Bangladesh, both of which had sent troops to Saudi Arabia early in the crisis.

The Pakistani Government was unable even to consider using the 11,000 troops it had sent in support of the coalition and was hard pressed not to remove them. It was opposed by Benazir Bhutto who, when in government at the start of the crisis, had refused to agree to sanctions. A widespread attitude among the military was reflected by remarks of the Army Chief-of-Staff at the end of January, describing the war as part of a 'Zionist' strategy.[13] The military's anti-Americanism was opposed by the civilian Government, but it still had to assert that its soldiers had no other purpose in Saudi but to protect Islam's holy places. The civilians, however, observed that Iraq had been more supportive of India in the dispute over Kashmir.

India, for its part, had been modifying its instinctively anti-American line prior to the war, in part in recognition of the changing world order. This was encouraged by discreet American contacts, especially when, in January 1991, India joined the Security Council. The Government allowed US and Australian aircraft to refuel at Bombay *en route* to the Gulf, though this did cause a public outcry.[14]

In Latin America only Argentina took much interest. A destroyer and a frigate were sent to the Gulf. Brazil, which had substantial trade with Iraq, grumbled about the costs but was not in a position to do much about it. By contrast, feeling in North Africa ran very high with large pro-Iraqi demonstrations. Presidents Chadli Benjedid of Algeria and Zine Abidine Ben-Ali of Tunisia both spoke out in support of Iraq, while Mauritania provided shelter for Iraqi civilian jets and, it was rumoured, for Saddam's family. Even the pro-Western King Hassan of Morocco, which had condemned Iraq and sent troops to the Gulf, found himself acquiescing in a general strike in late January called in support of Iraq.

The Anglo-Saxons

A survey of international opinion at the start of the war revealed that those countries where there was wholehearted support were a 'tiny minority'. Even in the industrialized countries, governments were lukewarm – anxious to do enough to show they supported UN resolutions but unable to go further because of a deeply reluctant public opinion.[15] Over time support hardened, largely because the coalition managed to keep the political initiative and contain the effects of the war.

The least ambivalence to the war was found in the Anglo-Saxon countries. Britain, as we have seen, was the most hawkish member of the coalition, seeing its role as stiffening Washington's backbone. Public opinion in Britain accepted the possible use of force by a two-thirds majority almost as soon as the offensive military option came to prominence in November.[16] Although the number ready to use force immediately on the expiry of the UN deadline was 49 per cent, compared with 43 per cent ready to give sanctions more time, it was clear that very few of the latter group were not prepared to support force. It was also of note that the great majority judged that the war aims should include the toppling of Saddam and not just the liberation of Kuwait.[17] Once the war began, it gained 80 per cent support, which rose thereafter to almost 90 per cent.[18]

The British debate on the wisdom of war largely followed the American, with similar arguments and the same spectacle of elder statesmen, in this case Edward Heath and Denis Healey, urging caution. Healey warned of 100,000 civilian casualties, neighbours fighting over the corpse of Iraq, a holy war uniting the Arab peoples, oil at $50 a barrel 'at best' and 'at worse a global ecological disaster'.[19] However, the opposition parties generally supported the Government. The Labour Party officially preferred the continuation of sanctions, but this position became more half-hearted as the war drew closer, so by the time of the Parliamentary debate of 15 January, the line was essentially not to support the use of force until it was used. At the end of that debate the vote was 534 to fifty-seven opposing the use of force. Fifty-five Labour MPs voted against, thirteen more than had done so in the previous December's vote. A further thirty-one abstained. John Major was much more inclined towards a consensus than his predecessor and took care to keep the opposition parties well briefed and sustain bipartisanship. The Churches, after some indications of moral unease, especially among Catholics, eventually concluded that this was a just war. The peace marches were lacklustre affairs. Marjorie Thompson of the Campaign for Nuclear Disarmament (CND), who led the anti-nuclear movement, was apparently relying on things going badly to revive support:

> As casualties start to rise, there will be a groundswell of opinion, and we will be the natural recipients of that concern.[20]

The British commitment of forces to the Gulf was substantial. On 22 November it had been decided to increase the British land forces to an armoured division, with extra ships and aircraft. Almost a quarter of the British Army was thus dedicated to the Gulf, thereby making it possible to demonstrate a substantial commitment to the whole effort.[21] They were fully integrated with US forces – even to the point of having a brigadier change his rank to Lt.-Colonel and wear an American uniform so as to become part of Schwarzkopf's planning cell.

General Peter de la Billière, commanding this force, was determined that it would not take part in a diversionary operation. The previous plan had been to work with the Marines, with whom relations became close, but de la

Billière argued that they should fight with VII Corps, with whom they shared basic NATO procedures, and ensure that British forces played a role in the forward battle against the Republican Guard with the US Army, rather than being held back for more limited holding operations with the Marines. He argued that his forces would have more capability than the Marines needed and they would be operating in a contained area, thus allowing limited scope for manoeuvre. There was another consideration. The Marines were to fight a dangerous battle against the Iraqi barrier defences, in which British combat engineers and armour would inevitably have played a prominent role. Based on his own experiences of forty years earlier, de la Billière may have been anxious with regard to the Marines' direct approach to enemy fire. He later recalled 'an unpleasant experience of a similar situation in Korea'.[22] This determination to be in the thick of things was evident in the services. The Royal Navy continued to press – unsuccessfully – to send one of Britain's three carriers, while the Royal Air Force accepted the highest proportional losses of the war in its low flying raids on Iraqi air bases. This tactic had in part been chosen to avoid contact with Iraqi fighters. After three days with troubling losses and no evidence of Iraqi fighters, the RAF decided to raise their altitude, although later evidence suggested that most of the Tornado losses were not the result of low flying. To keep the RAF active (with the Iraqi Air Force nowhere to be seen there was little to keep the air defence version of the Tornado busy), old Buccaneer aircraft were sent in with modern laser-designators to enable the Tornados to switch to bridges and other hard targets. There was continued pressure for a high sortie rate.

In the other key Anglo-Saxon countries – Canada, Australia and New Zealand – the political reaction was very similar, as was the language used to support military action. Both Australia and Canada made modest military contributions to the war effort: warships from Australia and aircraft from Canada. Australia deployed two frigates (later replaced by two destroyers) and a supply ship. It was the only East Asian/Western Pacific country to do so. It played an active role in enforcing the embargo, and when war came, Prime Minister Bob Hawke immediately ordered this task force to participate in operations against Iraqi forces.[23]

In August Ottawa had also sent two warships – elderly destroyers – and a supply ship to the Gulf. In September, after the Bahrain conference on the organization of the embargo, a squadron of CF-18 fighter aircraft was sent to the Gulf for air defence purposes. With the total of CF-18s eventually reaching twenty-six during the war, and a field hospital arriving just before the start of the ground campaign, this involved the deployment of 2,300 personnel in the Gulf.[24]

As a member of the Security Council, Canada was actively involved in discussions on the various resolutions. Canadian officials later claimed that the country's earlier commitment to Desert Shield had given Prime Minister Brian Mulroney more credibility when he argued with President Bush for a restrained and prudent approach. External Affairs Minister Joe Clark tended towards a more dovish approach than the Prime Minister, reflected in a speech cautioning of war in late October. He warned of thousands of casualties, and did not rule out the possibility that 'young Canadian soldiers will not return to this country for celebration but will stay there for burial'.[25]

By Christmas Canadian public opinion was showing great wariness with regard to a possible war. There was still 60 per cent support for the dispatch of Canadian forces to the Gulf, but it was down from the 69 per cent of September. On 15 January, in the Canadian Parliament, Mulroney argued that the coalition should be supported, largely on the basis of supporting the United Nations. He was challenged by the Liberal Party and the New Democrats, who argued that he was simply following an American lead and that the embargo should have been given more time. After a five-day debate, during which time the war had started and the CF-18s had flown in combat patrols, albeit out of harm's way, the Government was supported by 217 to forty-seven, with most Liberals supporting the Government motion ostensibly because they did not wish to demoralize Canadian forces in the Gulf. By this time public opinion had rallied behind the war to a level of about 75 per cent. On 24 January Canadian aircraft flew their first mission over Iraqi territory. As the air defence role became irrelevant and just a waste of fuel, authority was given on 20 February for the aircraft to be used on strike missions.

France

The readiness of Anglo-Saxon countries to commit themselves to war was not matched by any other substantial group. Hence the importance of France to the coalition – it was a country that could not be accused of being an American puppet and had enjoyed close links with Iraq in the past. This meant that France's partners had to tolerate its diplomatic manoeuvres even when they disapproved.

The need for France to 'buy' its political influence through making a serious military contribution was controversial within the French Government. The most notable dissident was the Defence Minister, Jean-Pierre Chevènement. He persistently attempted to define the limits to the French military role and maximize the distance from the Americans. He located the

French contingent based in Saudi Arabia as far as possible from the Anglo-Saxons, apparently with the aim of being able to dissociate France if necessary from any strikes made by the Americans, and some 150 kilometres behind the front line. He also asserted that the only role of the air contribution of thirty Jaguar, Mirage and transport planes was to protect ground forces. The French commander dealt only with Prince Khaled, the Saudi commander, and not with his American counterpart.

Although President Mitterrand did not endorse this approach, accepting that it would be necessary to work with the Americans if war came, the Defence Minister managed to set the tone for French policy. With French forces organized to avoid participation in war, it was assumed that their purpose was largely to give Paris some standing in the search for a settlement, and this led to discontent within the armed forces as well as among France's allies. The apparent lack of seriousness meant that French officers and officials felt that they were being kept in the dark, with the British far better informed about American intentions.

Following the doubling of US troops and the passing of Resolution 678, Mitterrand realized that his country's position would become untenable unless it worked out some *modus vivendi* with Washington. To stay apart from the Americans would mean working with the Syrians and Egyptians, who were unlikely to be taking a forward, starring role in the campaign. The President wanted a clearly defined French mission at the front rather than the rear, with a specific objective.

To do this the French military contribution would have to be upgraded. The contingent of the Force d'Intervention Rapide sent in September had some desert experience in Africa and a capacity for moving quickly in helicopters and armoured vehicles against limited opposition, but it was lightly armed with little artillery and had a poor logistics tail. Half the 5,000 troops were Foreign Legionnaires. The idea that it could mount a significant independent contribution when it barely represented 1 per cent of American forces was ludicrous.

In late November the President determined that there had to be significant reinforcement. In early December he was presented with three options: keeping forces at 6,000 men; raising the number to 10,000 men to work with the US on flanking operations; and a more substantial increase to 16,000 men in the same role, but perhaps with a more substantial individual mission. Mitterrand opted for the second option: this would be distinctive enough. The extra forces would bring more artillery pieces, tanks and aircraft. The formal decision was taken on 8 December, with the objective of completing the deployment by 11 January.[26]

Defeated in his attempt to prevent French forces fighting under American command, Chevènement submitted his resignation. Mitterrand refused to accept it. The Defence Minister's presence in his Government both calmed the anti-war faction of the Socialist Party and helped with Iraq, with whom he was still hoping to find some diplomatic breakthrough. Chevènement's resignation would thus send the wrong political 'signal'. Chevènement agreed to stay but still wanted to go before any war, so as to avoid responsibility for French troops in a conflict of which he disapproved. So long as he was in government, he qualified the military planning, arguing for a pause after the initial air strikes. On 7 January he tried to resign again. Mitterrand again refused to accept. The timing was still inopportune.

On 16 January the French Parliament met to discuss the war. The Government asked for a resolution of support but not a declaration of war under Article 35 of the Constitution of the Fifth Republic, as this was to be only a UN police action. Prime Minister Michel Rocard told the Deputies that France would place its Gulf troops under US command 'for specific times and missions'. Chevènement's faction voted against, together with the extreme right and left. Mitterrand had gained the support of Valéry Giscard d'Estaing (UDF) and Jacques Chirac of the Gaullists, so the vote was otherwise overwhelming – 523 deputies in favour and only forty-three against, with two abstentions.

Still the Defence Minister attempted to impose limits, even when the war began. Announcing, after some delay, the first French operations, he made no attempt to hide his regret at the start of hostilities. He spoke of a protocol agreed with the American command the previous evening and asserted that 'the objective of the French troops is to attack in Kuwait and in Kuwait only'.

The impression of half-heartedness created by this assertion was not helped by the limited contribution made by French aircraft to the air campaign. They had been based away from Dharhran to demonstrate their separation from the US, and this inevitably created problems of co-ordination. French Mirage aircraft were unable to operate because they were too similar to the Iraqi Mirage, and France's 'Identification of Friend or Foe' (IFF) equipment was incompatible with that of the allies. The old Jaguars able to operate could not fly at night, so their first operations did not begin until the morning of 17 January. Twelve Jaguars struck hardened hangars located on the Kuwaiti al-Jaber base, suspected of containing stocks of Scud and Exocet missiles. Four of the aircraft were hit, although none were downed. By 23 January, six missions had been mounted, of which one had to be aborted because of a sandstorm. The number of French sorties was no more than 0.1 per cent of the coalition's total. Unlike the daring British

Tornado strikes against Iraqi aircraft, the French role was marginal and could be presented as directed against equipment sold to Iraq by France.[27]

Almost immediately after Chevènement's first press conference Mitterrand realized that it would be disastrous to have the Defence Minister explaining the Government's policy. He effectively bypassed his minister by using his own top aide at the Élysée, Admiral Jacques Lanxade, as his direct link with Defence Chief General Maurice Schmitt.[28] On 20 January Mitterrand gave a hastily scheduled broadcast to rebut charges that the prosecution of the war was half-hearted, confirming that France was prepared to attack all relevant military targets, even if they were in Iraq.

However, a political storm had now developed in Paris as Chevènement's position was attacked remorselessly. Former President Giscard d'Estaing queried whether it made sense 'to attack the aggressed and spare the aggressor', as if it would have been best if the allies had targeted only occupied France and not Nazi Germany during the Second World War. Gaullist leader Jacques Chirac described the Ministry of Defence as unreliable. Chevènement defended himself by insisting that he was following the decisions of the President and suggesting that Chirac and Giscard look to their own record of co-operation with Saddam during the 1970s.[29] By now Chevènement was becoming increasingly isolated. Opinion polls showed a sudden surge of support for the war – from 60 per cent being anti-war to 67 per cent approval.[30] On 24 January, the French Air Force made its first strike beyond Kuwait when it attacked Republican Guard positions on Iraqi territory.[31]

By 29 January Chevènement felt that his position had become untenable and he resigned, complaining that the course the war had taken was threatening to distance France from the objectives set by the United Nations.[32] Pierre Joxe was moved from the Interior Ministry to Defence. Thereafter relations with the allies improved, although France still found it difficult to come to terms with the limits, demonstrated by this conflict, to its cherished policy of independence. In early February, for example, when it agreed to set aside a well-established Gaullist policy in order to allow US B-52s to overfly French territory, and even to refuel from bases in France using KC-135 tankers, the news was allowed to seep out only gradually.[33]

Turkey

Turkey was the only NATO member on the front line with Iraq. From the start of the crisis it opposed Iraq and threw its support behind the coalition, accepting a substantial loss (normally put at $7 billion) as a result of the imposition of sanctions. In military terms the key issue revolved around the possible use of the Incirlik base, 500 miles from the Iraqi border, by the US Air Force, which based both F-111 fighter-bombers and F-16s there. By December Turkey itself had 100,000 regular troops backed by 35,000 reservists at the border.

President Turgut Ozal was not only prepared to let the Americans use Incirlik but seemed ready to go further and commit Turkish troops to Saudi Arabia. This became an issue after the UN vote at the end of November, when the Americans requested such a show of solidarity. Authority was gained from Parliament, which was dominated by Ozal's Motherland Party. However, any suggestion that Turkey should go to war against Iraq was deeply unpopular. Ozal faced fierce resistance from the military, leading to the resignation of the Chief of the General Staff, General Necip Toruntay, who had been assumed to be Ozal's man. This followed the departures of the Foreign Minister in October and the Defence Minister in November, demonstrating that Ozal was moving further out on to a limb. Polls indicated that some two-thirds of Turks opposed military action, preferring instead to sustain a policy of rigid neutrality in regional disputes.[34]

For the opposition, Ozal's policies seemed designed to turn Turkey into an agent of American policy and provoke conflict with a neighbour. It was bound up with resentment by both left- and right-wing opposition forces at what was judged to be Ozal's manipulation of the constitution to reinforce his own power. Thus the backdrop to the imminent war was popular unrest, Parliamentary dissent and a divided Government. The sense of being on the front line was increased by the request to NATO to send elements of the mobile force to protect Turkey in the event of an Iraqi retaliatory strike, and the toing and froing within the alliance, especially by Germany, over whether this should be provided. Eventually forty-two German, Belgian and Italian aircraft plus air defence batteries arrived.

Ozal therefore had to tread carefully. The weekend before the war his Cabinet agreed that US pilots would be allowed to use bases for 'humanitarian and limited logistical support', but a decision on offensive air operations was postponed. The credibility of this apparent restraint was somewhat undermined by the arrival of more US F-16s and F-111s into Turkey. As soon as the war began, Parliament was asked to permit the US to use strike aircraft. With Ozal's own party in a commanding position, the vote was 250 to 148. The first American strike from Incirlik took place on 18 January.

With public support still hostile, Ozal took care to deny any intention of picking a direct fight with Iraq:

The Parliamentary authorization to send Turkish troops outside our borders is a precautionary measure. I emphasize that Turkish armed forces will not engage in operations against Iraq unless we are attacked. We do not covet Iraq's, nor any other country's soil, nor is a single inch of our own territory negotiable.[35]

The basic popular mood was jumpy, fearful that Iraq would strike against Turkey in revenge for American strikes. This mood was not helped when a Patriot went off by mistake close to the border on 22 January. Polls showed anything from 70 to 80 per cent of the population opposed to allowing the use of Incirlik. It was not so much that there was sympathy for Saddam, except among some sections of the young and Islamic militants. Two-thirds saw him as a threat. The concern was simply that Turkey would be dragged into an unnecessary war. The polls also suggested, however, that if Iraq attacked, the people would soon swing behind the Government.

Actually Iraq was rather tentative in its condemnation. Tariq Aziz sent the expected protest to Ankara about the US sorties but took five days to do so and was unspecific with regard to the dire consequences that would flow from this unwarranted support to the 'imperialists'. Baghdad basically appears to have been grateful that a second front had not been launched from Turkey. It took time for public opinion to calm down, with the opposition parties still attacking Ozal. There were some pro-Iraqi bomb attacks on Western establishments. However, gradually opinion began to move behind Ozal as it became apparent that Saddam was not about to attack and that, for the first time in 100 years, Turkey might actually have backed the winning side in a war.[36]

Germany

The most substantial European non-participant was Germany. Here events in the Gulf seemed very distant as the Government sought to cope with the unexpectedly heavy demands of unification (which had taken place at the start of October). The Government did not appear to acknowledge the likelihood of actual war until late on. Nor did public opinion – which barely reacted to the invasion of Kuwait but was suddenly deeply moved by the prospect of actual conflict. Germany had the largest anti-war demonstrations in Europe. For those who had sought to create a society cleansed of militarism there was pride at the reluctance to support war. 'I would rather live in a Germany made up of 80 per cent wimps than 80 per cent jingoists,' observed Theo Sommer,[37] as if these were the only alternatives.

The sensitivity of public and political opinion to any involvement in the conflict became evident when in late December Turkey asked for NATO support in case it became a victim of Iraqi aggression, a possibility which grew with the use of Incirlik. Despite attempts by some to argue that NATO was purely an East–West arrangement, Germany eventually agreed to contribute to a small multinational force with eighteen Alpha-jets and about 270 pilots and support workers. These were of limited military value, but even here there were objections that this was putting Germans at unnecessary risk and was exacerbating the dangers of war. It took almost two weeks for Turkey to get a positive response to its request.

Later another 500 men and eleven air defence batteries were also sent to Turkey. The Social Democrats described it as complicity in preparations for war and a provocation to Iraq while the Greens promised to urge service personnel to refuse to serve. Twenty-two thousand German soldiers and reservists did lodge claims to be conscientious objectors,[38] including fifty soldiers from the anti-missile squadrons scheduled to go to Turkey.

As Germany dithered, the Americans reminded the Government that this would not be understood in Congress. Turkey also became furious with the lukewarm German response, pointing out that if attacked by chemical weapons, German companies would be responsible. As the weekend before the UN deadline ran out, there were massive anti-war demonstrations throughout Germany. Kohl sought to bring the public round. He told the Bundestag that while Germans wished to avert a conflict, 'at the same time we know the consequences of appeasement policies'.[39] Nonetheless, his first reaction to the outbreak of war was an expression of 'dismay', while Hans-Jochen Vogel, SPD Chairman, said that he was 'horrified'. Foreign Minister Genscher said nothing until 22 January. Even the commitment to Turkey was qualified – with a promise to come to the Bundestag to obtain permission for Luftwaffe to be involved even if Turkey was attacked.[40] When the war began, Berliners led the way with an anti-war demonstration which was soon followed by one of 200,000 people in Bonn. Some schools sent their children to demonstrations rather than lessons.

Opinion polls showed that Saddam Hussein was blamed overwhelmingly for the outbreak of war – by 85 per cent – with only 3 per cent blaming the Americans, and 79 per cent felt shame at the German material support for Saddam in the past. Opinion was split on the commitment to Turkey. *Der Spiegel* found that 58 per cent supported the sending of the Luftwaffe to Turkey but only 43 per cent were in favour of it actually being used in the event of an Iraqi attack.[41] Gradually senior politicians and some newspapers – such as *Bild Zeitung* – asked for a tougher stand. One analyst has described the debate as being one 'of the most extraordinary intellectual battles within the German media witnessed in recent years'.[42] There was concern that once again Germany was giving the impression that it could only redeem itself with money and proposals of negotiations for their own sake. As a result it did not ever get the full credit for contributing as much as 10 per cent of the total cost of the war.

Another reason for the change of mood was increasing evidence of the involvement of German companies in the upgrading of Scud missiles, the supergun, the chemical weapons plants in Samarra, the artillery and arms construction plant at Taji, and at the Sa'd 16 project researching on chemical and nuclear weapons.[43] These revelations were all the more disturbing given the Scud attacks on Israel, which raised the painful linkage between Germans, gas and Jews. Kohl spoke of a 'special responsibility' when it came to Israel's right to exist. He denounced the attacks as a provocation and promised Jerusalem DM250 million in emergency humanitarian aid. He initially said that he would not send Patriot air defence missiles to Israel, although this position was later reversed following a visit to Israel by Foreign Minister Genscher. Thereafter the German Government became careful to stay in line and not get ahead of its allies who were engaged in combat by calls for a cease-fire or concerns about the course of the war.

The rest of Europe

The general picture from the smaller European countries was that public opinion supported the coalition campaign but preferred to remain outside the actual fighting. Two other European countries were prepared to commit forces. The Dutch were strongly supportive. Foreign Minister Hans Van der Broek worked closely with the British in European diplomacy. The Netherlands put its warships in the area under American control at the start of the war, and in addition sent Patriot missiles to Turkey and Israel. The once formidable Dutch peace movement barely protested.[44]

Italy provided four naval vessels and ten Tornado aircraft (one of which was shot down on the first day). It had no significant ground forces to send even if it had wanted to, as it spent barely 2 per cent of GNP on defence. It had very few volunteers and largely limited-service conscripts.

The Italian Government gained Parliamentary approval for an 'international policing action', out of respect for the constitution's disapproval of force as a means of resolving disputes. Public opinion was less than enthusiastic. A poll on 19 January showed 42.9 per cent in favour, with 52.1

per cent against. By 25 January there had been a slight shift, with figures of 44.1 per cent and 46.9 respectively.[45] At the end of January the head of the Italian Navy resigned after being quoted in a magazine article as saying that war could have been avoided by continuing with the embargo.[46] Another factor in Italy was the apparent opposition of the Pope, causing a rift with the Christian Democrats. He had called war a 'tragic adventure' before it began and then warned of its 'terrible logic'. He said that this was not a just war, and called for a peace conference to resolve the Palestinian question. 'Only war can come from war. I say to all the armed parties: "first of all, stop this war".'[47] This stance caused divisions within the Catholic Church, with some leading figures in the United States and Britain worried about the impact on Catholics serving in the Gulf. Eventually the Pope toned down his language as he acknowledged the argument that pacifism can reward aggression.

Denmark and Norway combined to send a frigate and a supply ship early in the crisis, but announced just before the war that they would be relocated if in danger. Belgium, Spain and Portugal stressed that their ships would not go beyond the enforcement of the embargo. In August Belgium had sent four warships to the Gulf and had responded to Turkey's request for support by sending eighteen aircraft. It had, however, made a point of refraining from sending aircraft to support the embargo and its warships were not allowed to be involved in actions with direct contact with Iraq. It irritated the British by refusing to provide artillery shells requested in November. The later explanation was that this was before the passage of Resolution 678, and the Belgian Government was unconvinced that force would be used.[48] Others suspected that the refusal was out of fear of upsetting an attempt to obtain the release of Belgian hostages in Iraq or of a Belgian family held hostage by the Abu Nidal group (possibly in Baghdad). When the family was released in early January, it seemed as if the price was the release of a Palestinian terrorist jailed for an attack on Jewish youths in 1980, and then an entry visa for Walid Khaled, a spokesman of Nidal's Fatah Revolutionary Council and one of Saddam's strongest supporters. This was an extraordinary time to allow a terrorist leader entry into Europe. He was picked up only after a passer-by recognized him, and was expelled. A number of Belgian officials resigned.[49] Eventually, by way of recompense, Brussels gave Britain 2,800 field beds and a forty-eight-strong medical team in Cyprus. In addition Britain was given a grant of £15 million.

In Spain the most controversial issue was whether B-52s from the United States would be allowed to use the Morón base. Prime Minister Felipe Gonzalez agreed to this plus logistical support, but also took care not to get too close to American policy, for example, by expressing concern over attacks on Iraqi civilians. Public opinion was generally opposed to any involvement.

This kaleidoscope of attitudes and policies became apparent at the European Parliament. Before the war, the Parliament had voted 152 to ninety-six with sixty-three abstentions to reject military action so long as sanctions had a chance of succeeding. When hostilities began, the immediate attempt to hold a meeting of the Parliament was abandoned because the Commission and Council of Ministers refused to attend, saying it would achieve too little too late, then a debate was thwarted (with just hours to go) because the French objected to meeting in Brussels instead of Strasbourg. Eventually a debate commenced on 21 January. Two days into the debate, the members were told by Commission President Jacques Delors that: 'To be brutally frank, public opinion sensed that Europe was rather ineffectual.'[50] That day, after six hours of feuding, members voted out each other's resolutions. Eventually, after a week of wrangling, a compromise resolution was passed by 202 votes in favour, ninety-eight against and twenty-five abstentions, demanding 'explicit' respect by Iraq for UN resolutions, accompanied by 'the start of a full and controlled withdrawal' of Iraqi troops from Kuwait on 'a binding and rapid time-table' which could lead to an end to hostilities.[51]

Burden-sharing

For the most part the United States was not after token military contributions, which would have complicated military planning, but after financial support for its own efforts. This 'tin cup' exercise had begun in September, but once the war began the Administration revived it in order to head off Congressional concern that once again the United States was bearing all the burden of upholding international order. A formula was devised that called for Japan to provide 20 per cent of the cost, the US and its allies another 20 per cent, and the Gulf states the rest. Efforts along these lines proved quite successful: following the start of hostilities Japan pledged $9 billion to the military effort, Saudi and Kuwait $13.5 billion each and Germany $5.5 billion – all in addition to earlier commitments.[52]

Indeed, so successful was this effort that there were suggestions that the cost of the war had to be artificially inflated by including costs that might otherwise have been expected to be incurred, such as purchases of smart weapons, loss of aircraft to accidents (the normal rate of which was not dissimilar to the loss of aircraft in combat during the war). The cost was eventually put at $54 billion, of which most – $48.2 billion - was pledged by allies.[53] After the war there was some grumbling in Germany that the United

States was making a profit out of the war and that Germany should claw back contributions.

Britain did not decide until the war was under way to move to a serious burden-sharing effort.[54] There was initial reluctance, so support was sought in the form of practical assistance - medical facilities, for example, as a means of reducing the pressure on the National Health Service in the event of high casualties, transport (such as a Hercules from New Zealand), and host nation support from Gulf states. Eventually it was judged that both the American campaign for support and the evidence that the coalition was acting on behalf of the rest of the international community warranted some effort. This became reinforced by estimates that the cost of the war might reach £3 billion (it was eventually kept down to £2.5 billion as a result of the short campaign on the ground). France did not mount a campaign to raise funds but did get $1 billion from Kuwait to help cover its costs, and FF 6.5 billion from Germany.

Japan

The burden-sharing debate in Japan proved almost as painful as the debate on a military contribution in the autumn. After the fiasco of the attempt to get a peace corps bill through the Diet, other attempts by Prime Minister Toshiki Kaifu to get his country to contribute more than money to the coalition effort proved to be heavy going. He had not been allowed to send doctors to the Gulf and there was uproar when he proposed at the start of the war to use an administrative order to send five transport aircraft to help UN refugee operations – as opposed to the war effort. The order was issued on 25 January, but the hostility to the move was such that the dispatch of the aircraft risked jeopardizing plans to send more money.

The United States was inevitably going to expect more financial support and Kaifu sought to avoid the spectacle of bargaining with the Americans by moving forward quickly with a generous offer. He proposed a figure of $9 billion. As this was large enough to require special tax increases, it caused consternation and then squabbling in Government and Liberal Democratic Party circles, forcing Kaifu to cancel the press conference in which it was to be proposed. Eventually he did make the announcement, although only after his disgruntled Finance Minister had vetoed a proposal to send another $1 billion to help Egypt, Turkey and Jordan as he had not been consulted on this decision.

The package was immediately attacked by the opposition parties, who were still arguing that anything which implicated Japan in military activity was against the Constitution. Kaifu had the support of the Party and business, who backed aid because of fear of further alienation from the United States. They could see how unfortunate it would be if Japan appeared to be sitting on its hands while American lives were lost, in part to support oil supplies upon which Japan was especially dependent. Nonetheless the public was opposed. There was little tradition in Japan of a resolute defence of a set of values, a widespread feeling that the coalition was using too much force and dislike of the prospective tax increase. One poll at the end of January showed 54 per cent opposed to the aid and only 45 per cent in favour (with the gap widening when it came to the dispatch of transport aircraft).[55] The Social Democrat Party, led by Miss Takako Doi, who had paid a friendly visit to Saddam just before the conflict started, was vigorous in its assertion that the integrity of the Constitution was at stake. To get support, the Government had to make deals with some of the smaller opposition parties, and in particular the Buddhist Komeito 'clean government' party.

The argument was fought out in the Diet throughout February. It turned less on the absolute amount than on the principle itself and on the possibility that there could be restrictions on the use of the funds. Initially James Baker had asserted publicly that the US would expect to put the money into its 'war chest' to buy whatever was needed. However, when the Japanese Government warned that this might mean getting nothing at all, the Americans stated that the proposed amount would just about cover 'transportation, medical supplies, food and logistics support'. The distinction itself was somewhat meaningless, for, as Miss Doi pointed out, 'you can't tell whose money is buying the bread and whose money is buying the bullets'. Even Mr Kaifu at one point appeared not to understand that logistics meant transporting troops and weapons.[56] The vote was not taken until 6 March, after the war was over, by which time a number of Japanese were already suggesting that there was no longer any need for the funds. Nonetheless the bill was passed.[57]

Table 10: Major allied commitments to US costs

(US dollars in millions)

	INITIAL PLEDGE	SECOND PLEDGE	TOTAL PLEDGED
Saudi Arabia	3,339	13,500	16,839
Kuwait	2,506	13,500	16,006
United Arab Emirates	1,000	3,000	4,000
Japan	1,740	9,000	10,740
Germany	1,072	5,500	6,572
Korea	80	305	385
Other	3	17	20
TOTAL	9,740	44,822	54,562

Source: Congressional Research Service.

Table 11: Contributions to British costs

COUNTRY	£ MILLION
Belgium	15
Denmark	8
Germany	275
Hong Kong	15
Japan	183
Kuwait	660
Luxembourg	1
Saudi Arabia	580
South Korea	16
United Arab Emirates	275
TOTAL	2,028

Source: Statement on the Defence
Estimates, 1991.

CHAPTER 26

Preparing the Battlefield

Saddam's dilemma

With Israel holding back and the coalition holding together, and with command of the air and control of the pace of the war, the coalition had no incentive to rush into a land war, which remained Saddam's best hope for a creditable outcome to the conflict. The longer the war dragged on, the dimmer would be his chances of political survival. It was dealing a decisive blow to any hope of economic reconstruction, upon which his political survival would hinge. A sustained conflict would erode national, and in consequence military, morale and force a humiliating withdrawal from Kuwait.

To salvage his strategy Saddam needed to draw the coalition into a premature ground offensive in Kuwait to bring the war to a quick end. This might cost many Iraqi lives but the key political effects would result from the lost Western lives. His hope was that heavy casualties would drive a disillusioned Western public opinion to demand an early cease-fire. He stated this objective at the start of hostilities:

> Not a few drops of blood, but rivers of blood would be shed. And then Bush will have been deceiving America, American public opinion, the American people, the American constitutional institutions.[1]

Even if this was too optimistic (from his point of view), a quick but honourable withdrawal from Kuwait in the course of a bloody encounter could allow him to emerge from the conflict as a 'new Nasser' who had single-handedly fought 'world imperialism' and survived.

Gradually frustration began to tell on Saddam. At first he was as defiant as ever. 'Our ground forces have not entered the battle so far, and only a small part of our air force has been used so far,' he told his subjects on 20 January, in the second personal statement since the beginning of the war (the first being made hours after the outbreak of hostilities):

when the battle becomes a comprehensive one with all types of weapons, the deaths on the allied side will be increased with God's help. When the deaths and dead mount on them, the infidels will leave and the flag of Allahu Akbar will fly over the mother of all battles.[2]

This confidence was reiterated a week later in Saddam's first interview with a Western journalist since the war began. In his meeting with Peter Arnett, a CNN correspondent, Saddam looked rested and relaxed. He was more casual than usual and showed no sign of anxiety. In his view, Iraq had managed to maintain its 'balance' by using only conventional weapons, and would undoubtedly 'win the admiration of the world with its fighting prowess'. When asked whether he had any doubts about obtaining a military victory he unhesitatingly answered: 'Not even one in a million.'[3]

Yet even this remarkable exercise of self-control could hardly disguise the deepening anxiety of the Iraqi President. One did not have to count the number of times he blinked during the interview (as did some diligent psychiatrists) in order to reach this conclusion. In the interview Saddam reported that Iraq had the capability to fix nuclear, chemical, and biological warheads to its missiles and vowed to escalate the conflict if he had to. 'I pray to God I will not be forced to use these weapons,' he said, 'but I will not hesitate to do so should the need arise.' This threat rang familiar and ominous bells from the Iran–Iraq War, when Saddam had often warned the Iranians before resorting to chemical attacks. His use of this weapon against them (as opposed to his gassing of the defenceless Kurds) had always taken place at critical moments, where there had been no other way to check Iranian offensives. Since non-conventional weapons had always been a means of last resort for Saddam when confronted by a formidable foe, the raising of the chemical threat in the CNN interview unintentionally exposed his growing awareness that the moment of truth was nearing.

An equally vivid illustration of Saddam's exasperation was his harsh attack on those 'hypocritical' Western politicians who had promised him that by releasing the foreign hostages he would be able to avert war. Apart from implying his dissatisfaction with the course of the war (had it progressed smoothly, he would presumably have been less troubled by this memory), Saddam's public admission of a mistake was completely out of line with the image of the infallible leader, so carefully nurtured during his twelve-year presidency. He had never publicly expressed self-doubt before, and his slip revealed how disconcerted he really was. Indeed, in an Iraqi television report, showing Saddam conferring with his commanders in a military van, the Iraqi leader looked exhausted and distressed. He sat quietly, nervously clasping his hands and listening anxiously to his generals' explanations. There was nothing in this scene reminiscent of the confident Saddam of the CNN interview. Frustrated with failure of his various ploys, Saddam began to rebuke the coalition for the harm caused by the air campaign, and to taunt it for cowardice in refusing to go ahead with the land campaign.[4]

Khafji

Saddam concluded that he had little choice but to trigger the ground war rather than wait to be attacked. He took a rare military initiative by ordering a limited ground encounter in Saudi Arabia. Such a move entailed grave risks, but the potential advantages were compelling. He would be seen to have seized the initiative from the allies, at least temporarily, so giving the morale of his battered troops in Kuwait a much-needed boost, and it might even create a momentum that would suck the reluctant coalition into a ground offensive. Saddam also apparently thought that the capture of many coalition prisoners would damage Western morale. If he had picked his spot better, attacked at greater strength and executed the attack more effectively, serious disruption could have been caused to coalition plans.

In the event the attack on the Saudi border town of Khafji did not have this impact.[5] A small town, some twelve miles from the border with Kuwait, Khafji had been evacuated early in the conflict because of its vulnerability to Iraqi artillery. The fact that it was abandoned and only lightly defended by Saudi and Qatari troops was advertised on the Western media. There is some evidence that the attack had been under preparation a week earlier. On 22 January, an E-8A JSTARS detected an armoured division's assembly area and a seventy-one-vehicle convoy moving towards Kuwait. Aircraft were called in and fifty-eight of the vehicles were destroyed.[6] On the night of 29–30 January there was another attempt, and this time no early detection. An Iraqi force, comprising two armoured and one mechanized battalion from one of the better Iraqi army divisions, the 5th Mechanized, crossed the Kuwaiti border in the south-eastern front and headed in the direction of Khafji. At the same time an armada of seventeen fast patrol boats, carrying landing parties, began to move down the Kuwaiti coast. Behind them three mechanized divisions with some 240 tanks and 60,000 soldiers were massing near Wafra to follow through.

The patrol boats were detected by RAF Jaguars and then attacked by Sea Skuas from Royal Navy Lynx helicopters, leaving two sunk or damaged and the rest scattered. The central Iraqi armoured battalion met a marine battalion and suffered badly as helicopter gunships and A-10 aircraft were brought in. The Iraqis lost twenty-four tanks and thirteen other vehicles. The mechanized battalion also ran into trouble and was attacked from the air, driving it to a hasty withdrawal northwards. However, the Americans suffered their first casualties in ground fighting when eleven marines were killed (seven of them from friendly fire). Moreover, the last armoured battalion, accompanied by some infantry, did get through in the dark, having forced a Saudi screening force to withdraw.

Taking the small Saudi garrison by surprise, the Iraqis occupied the town. The next day they tried to bring in two additional battalions in support but failed as they were attacked by A-10s. The battalion in occupation, now isolated, was bombed by US aircraft, artillery and helicopters, but resisted attempts to dislodge them for nearly two days. One option was to leave them in the town, which was of no strategic significance. They could not have been reinforced. However, this would have given Iraq a psychological victory and also have left some US marines, who had been on a reconnaissance mission, alone in the town. An Arab force composed of Saudis and Qataris (in fact largely Pakistanis) was sent in to retake the town. On the early morning of 31 January, the counter-attack began. It was initially held, but the attacking force pushed in with intensive fighting. It took another two days to clear up all the remnants of the Iraqi units. The Iraqi losses in men and equipment were high, amounting to dozens dead and hundreds of prisoners. The coalition Arabs lost nineteen killed and thirty-six wounded.

Both parties quickly claimed victory for the first significant ground encounter of the war. The Iraqis described their action as 'a lightning strike into the kingdom of evil'. They argued that it had been planned by Saddam, together with the Revolutionary Command Council and the military leadership, and that the President had visited his troops in Basra a couple of days prior to the battle to personally issue the command for the attack. The coalition, for its part, played down the significance of the battle, and General Schwarzkopf said that it was 'about as significant as a mosquito on an elephant'.[7]

It was far more significant. Despite allied denials, the Iraqis had achieved a measure of tactical surprise, and their ability to hold on for some time was a temporary propaganda gain for Saddam. However, the most important aspect of Khafji was that it failed, with severe casualties and a demonstration of the vulnerability of Iraqi land forces to airpower.[8] Iraq had been prepared to follow up the incursion. The three follow-on mechanized divisions near Wafra, along with a ten-mile-long column making its way through Kuwait, were subjected to ferocious air assaults, which exacted a heavy toll, and were soon in retreat. This limited operation had stretched the command capacity of the Iraqi Army to its limits. During the battle Iraqi units had called haplessly for air support. Now the Iraqi Army knew that command of the air had been conceded completely so that combat on the ground would be a dismal proposition.

'Preparation of the battlefield'

At the start of the war the logic of the coalition's strategy had not been fully appreciated. When there was still a widespread belief that it could all be over within days, the fact that it appeared to be settling down into a prolonged air campaign caused some consternation. So great had been the expectations that this war would be over in a few days or even a few weeks,[9] that political leaders and the military were hard put to dampen down the initial euphoria and warn of a hard slog ahead. The question of whether the public would tolerate weeks of bombing had been recognized prior to the conflict as one of its most uncertain features. This added to the gamble of starting with the strategic air campaign before moving to the battlefield.

After a week, with events apparently failing to reach a decisive conclusion, Colin Powell, Chairman of the Joint Chiefs-of-Staff, felt it necessary to give an upbeat press conference. In a confident performance he described the basic strategy in a striking manner: 'First we are going to cut [the Iraqi Army in Kuwait] off, then we are going to kill it.'[10] Soon it was widely recognized that the coalition need not rush, and the reasons for this were fully appreciated by politicians, anxious to avoid excessive casualties.

Saddam's decision to take his troops into the open at Khafji despite their glaring vulnerability to allied airpower was, correctly, interpreted by the West as an indication of his growing desperation to force the coalition into the decisive ground encounter. This, in turn, reinforced the coalition's conviction not to play this game. At the start of February President Bush pledged to launch the ground offensive only 'if and when the time was right'.[11] He was under little pressure at home to push on with a land war. 'The first danger,' counselled Les Aspin, 'is that we will go to the ground war too soon in order to eject Iraq from Kuwait ... We should understand that there is a conflict between ending the war quickly and keeping casualties down.'[12]

But when would the time be right? Just as Saddam's strategy had been to get the two sides locked into an early ground war, so the coalition depended on patience while the battlefield was under preparation. At the start of the campaign the air forces had been set a standard: in the Kuwaiti Theatre of Operations (KTO), which included Kuwait plus the adjacent area of Iraq up to the Euphrates river, Iraqi armour and artillery were to be reduced by 50 per cent overall, and artillery by 90 per cent in those areas where coalition forces were to be expected to breach Iraqi defences. In addition, Iraqi command and control and intelligence capabilities were to be eliminated and logistics severely restricted. During the initial planning in October it had been assumed that this massive degradation of the Iraqi Army in Kuwait would take about a month.[13]

By way of achieving these objectives, bombardment of the Republican Guard began on the first day of the war. It was discussed in the media in terms of 'carpet-bombing', in contrast to 'surgical strikes'. Neither term was much used by the professional military. Schwarzkopf rejected the term 'carpet-bombing', which 'tends to portray something totally indiscriminate, *en masse* without regard to the target'. He claimed that the allied campaign was much more careful in its organization and choice of weapons.[14] Moreover, the Republican Guard did not really present themselves as a 'carpet'. This estimated 150,000-strong force was dug in over an area of 4,000 square miles (10,000 square kilometres) in generally sandy terrain. In all 5,600 sorties were mounted against the Republican Guard, out of a 35,000 total directed against the Iraqi Army.[15]

Many other key targets were also substantial: a typical ammunition storage site could cover twenty-eight square kilometres. To destroy such a dump could take as many as forty 1,000-pound bombs. There were seven primary and nineteen secondary storage facilities. For some targets only precision attacks made sense, but even here there were problems. Attacks on bridges, of which 54 were eventually hit, carried risks of casualties to anyone, including civilians, unfortunate enough to be using them at the time.[16] Iraqi engineers were also tenacious in seeking to repair bridges and, when that became impossible, to replace them with pontoons. To confuse the attackers, the Iraqis made extensive use of decoys made of wood, cardboard, paper, cloth and fibreglass, including realistic models of tanks bought from an Italian company. The same surveillance problems which hindered damage assessment in the first weeks of the war also hindered target acquisition.

The worst weather in the region for twenty-five years held up many missions and made it extremely difficult to work out just how successful the initial strikes had been. Weather forecasts anticipated low clouds for 18 per cent of the time, but in reality such conditions prevailed for more than twice that amount and so the allies lost 40 per cent of their primary targets during the first ten days of the air campaign. Key targets had to be attacked again just in case they had been missed first time.[17] All this, together with the Scud hunt, delayed the shift to targets in the Kuwaiti theatre of operations.

Bomb damage assessment

One of the reputations that the US military was seeking to overcome was of an institutional optimism which resulted in achievements being grossly inflated, only for credibility to be lost as the contrary evidence mounted. To some extent this had happened with the Scud hunt. Schwarzkopf was anxious that his assessments should be believed. On 27 January he claimed that his command was being 'deliberately conservative'. Therefore, if he announced results, 'you can take it to the bank'.[18]

Discussions of American intelligence capabilities tend to assume almost perfect vision. However, though modern satellite surveillance is remarkable, its coverage is commonly exaggerated. At the time of the Gulf War it was estimated that the US had at most six Keyhole reconnaissance satellites up, each making two passes above the region per day. These are capable of covering between ten and a hundred square kilometres and of resolving objects about fifteen centimetres across and between one and three metres wide. However, they cannot penetrate cloud cover nor see inside buildings, and need to be targeted against areas of special interest. In the Gulf War, the images from the satellites were sent directly to Fort Belvoir just south of Washington, where photo-interpretation was undertaken. Only one space-craft – the Lacrosse radar imaging satellite – was able to penetrate cloud cover. This could produce three-dimensional images of terrain, and was thus very important for the guidance system of cruise missiles, which depended on such information. However, since such detail could not be provided over a wide area, the Lacrosse was not much used for damage assessment. A number of commanders regretted the recent pensioning off of the SR-71 reconnaissance aircraft, which could have provided them with speedy information on particular areas of concern.[19] Key targets were never found: the main ammunition and supply dumps for the Iraqi Army Corps assigned to defend Kuwait went undetected until captured.[20] Without reliable intelligence, aircraft would return to make superfluous attacks against targets already damaged.

Because priority was being given at first to the strategic air campaign and then to the Scud hunt, the satellites were directed against targets in Iraq itself rather than on the front line in Kuwait. Even then only about a third of the previous day's targets could be photographed. Furthermore, the weather was unusually bad – the area was covered in cloud for half the war – and this hindered the gathering of satellite information. Without the most detailed pictures it was difficult to be sufficiently specific on, for example, how deeply armour was dug in or whether tanks that could not be seen from on top were

T-72s or T-55s. More than that, because Iraq's national air defences had been the main priority, the air defences with the troops in Kuwait were still functioning, so threatening any reconnaissance aircraft getting within range. It was not until early February that the first special air patrols were mounted across the lines to assess the state of the Iraqi forces on the ground.

While the accuracy of the intelligence information gradually improved, some basic problems remained. The production of the imagery for the interpreters sometimes 'lagged by days, not hours', during which time the enemy could move or replace his losses. Moreover, as the Iraqi forces were largely static, it was not always clear whether a particular tank was damaged unless there was unequivocal evidence such as a blown-off turret. If the Iraqi approach had not been so static, and had moved Army units and their equipment around instead of keeping them in one place, the developing picture would have been even more confusing.

In these circumstances, calculation of Iraqi losses became as much an art as a science. To handle this, the Army intelligence staff assigned to Schwarzkopf's headquarters developed a formula for bomb damage assessment. They distinguished between armoured vehicles (mainly tanks) and artillery and then brought together information from three different sources. The first source of information was aircraft videos. On the basis of checks from other sources, the interpreters decided that only half the apparent 'kills' they showed should be counted. Reports from A-10 pilots were judged to be more reliable than most as a result of their training in the close air support role, the fact that they normally flew in tandem, and their tendency to loiter longer. Again on the basis of checks from other sources and the fact that flying conditions were often less than perfect, it was decided to include one-third of their reports. Third, all reports of destruction from high-resolution imagery were included.

Not surprisingly, this approach was controversial and sparked heated debates. The Air Force judged it to be far too conservative, arguing that pilots' reports and the sheer amount of effort that had gone into the air campaign must have had a much greater effect. By contrast, the intelligence organs in Washington – the Central Intelligence Agency and the Defense Intelligence Agency – would only trust the satellite pictures and claimed that the damage assessment at Schwarzkopf's headquarters was far too liberal. They 'estimated enemy strengths at the 80–90 percentile a few days before G-Day when we assessed them to be approaching the 50 per cent range'.[21] Schwarzkopf stuck with his own analysts despite intense pressure to push it one way or the other. A few months after the war he observed that 'he would still be over there waiting' if he had relied on the Washington agencies to agree that the Iraqi military had been weakened sufficiently.[22] This argument was in itself symptomatic of a more general tension between a national intelligence geared to the broad needs of the White House and senior commanders, which tended to be competitive and based on a full airing of differences, and the tactical needs of local commanders, who wanted something precise, definite and immediate.

All the early damage assessments more than reinforced the view that the war would take time. The downbeat Washington assesment, two weeks into the air campaign, spoke of little obvious effect on the Republican Guard, no more than scattered, anecdotal reports of ammunition storage dumps exploding and reports of destruction of perhaps three dozen of the Republican Guard's 800 tanks. Most Iraqi supply lines were so far unaffected, thus allowing food and ammunition to reach the front.[23] Schwarzkopf's own assessment of the state of the Iraqi Army did not paint a markedly more optimistic picture. He confirmed the destruction of 178 trucks and fifty-five artillery pieces, and fifty-two tanks destroyed or damaged, along with 125 storage revetments. The one exception was with supply lines. A substantial 790 sorties had been involved in attacks on thirty-three bridges. It was now claimed that there was a 90 per cent degradation in the supply rate. Instead of the 20,000 tons per day required to support troops in Kuwait, only 2,000 tons were now getting through. British estimates considered this to be too optimistic and Western reporters had anecdotal evidence that supply lines were still moving.[24]

However, the rate of attrition did begin to improve. Table 12 shows the bomb damage assessments (not the actual damage) for the key indicators for five-day periods from the start of the war up to 21 February, after which they became daily. The major jump from 27 January to 1 February probably reflects better intelligence on the earlier bombing, rather than a sudden surge in effectiveness. Nonetheless, it can be seen that by early February there was a steady success rate of around fifty tanks and fifty armoured personnel carriers (APCs) per day, with between thirty and forty artillery pieces being destroyed per day.

On 8 February Secretary of Defense Cheney and Chairman of the Joint Chiefs-of-Staff Powell arrived in Saudi Arabia for two days of intensive discussions with the local commanders on the timing of the ground offensive, and to form their own views on the damage assessment controversy. Two days earlier Cheney, defending Schwarzkopf, had clashed with CIA Director William Webster, who was prepared to confirm only a small proportion of CENTCOM's claims. The CIA estimate might have had more influence if Webster himself had more influence. He was not one of the 'inner circle'. Bush tended to trust more the judgement of Robert Gates, a former Deputy Director of the Agency and after the war Bush's choice to succeed Webster.[25]

The practical questions concerned the extent of damage to Iraq's capacity to fight that could be inflicted by the air strikes, and the success of the logistical effort imposed by the need to shift forces westwards. The commanders wanted decent weather on a dark night, so had been looking for nights when there would be the minimum moonlight. Initially 17 February was identified as one of the earliest dates for the ground offensive, but this kept on moving back as the meteorologists watched new weather fronts forming up to the north. Also, the delays caused by the poor weather conditions throughout the campaign and the Scud hunt had pushed the dates back. Cheney and Powell were informed that the air campaign had significantly eroded the might and the morale of the Iraqi armed forces, but not sufficiently to begin a ground war.

In the intelligence briefing they were shown a curve, based on sustained air operations, that led to a cross-over at which the target of 50 per cent attrition for armour and artillery (with 90 per cent artillery destruction at breach areas) would be reached. The cross-over point was 21 February.[26] On this basis, and taking account of the likely weather and moonlight, the window of opportunity had been identified as 21–24 February.

Even if the gloomier Washington damage assessments had been accepted, there were limits as to how long CENTCOM could wait before launching the offensive. There was little point in persisting against well-dug-in troops who might only be vulnerable to air attack when forced to emerge from their shelters by the demands of a land battle. Only then would it be possible to confirm the presumption that Iraqi troops were feeling low and miserable. The actual state of their morale could only be fully revealed when tested in battle.

Furthermore, the land commanders could not wait too long because of the possibility of deteriorating weather conditions and the need to use their forces when they were at peak readiness. Nor was there much sympathy for the view that the bombing campaign could continue without a land campaign until Saddam made the critical concessions. It reinforced the charge of indifference to Iraqi lives and could encourage a myth that the Iraqi Army remained invincible.

When Cheney and Powell flew back on 10 February, they were still dampening down speculation of an imminent attack. Cheney told the press that he had been struck by 'the enormous size of the Iraqi military establishment', of which 'a very significant part' survived. 'Nobody wants to rush prematurely into the next phase of the campaign,' he said, though he admitted that a 'point of diminishing returns' from air bombardments might have been reached. On the next Sunday the US briefer in Saudi Arabia continued in this vein: 'It looks like it's going to be a target-rich environment for a while.' A day later Cheney and Powell met Bush. Again came back the message – more bombing for a while. The following week threw the spotlight on to the continuing air campaign as a result of the tragic bombing of the Amiriya bunker. In Washington there was concern that it was going to be harder to sustain the campaign until the desired rates of attrition had been achieved.

Gradually during that month the reports became more optimistic. On 9 February Brigadier General Neal reported the confirmed destruction of over 750 tanks, 650 artillery pieces and over 600 APCs. Five days later this was up to 1,300 tanks, 800 APCs and 1,100 artillery.[27] This was approaching a third of Iraq's opening inventory. In fact the relevant attrition rate of 50 per cent for front-line forces was reached on 23 February. By this time the second-level Iraqi force were estimated to have suffered some 50 to 75 per cent attrition, although the Republican Guard and some other units were still in reasonable shape. The Guard had been properly targeted only after 15 February when F-16s became available for use. The A-10s employed until that point had been inhibited through their vulnerability to ground fire.[28]

The furore over the civilian casualties in Baghdad almost obscured a series of remarkably upbeat briefings from the US military with the Iraqi position described as 'precarious'.[29] Growing numbers of Iraqis surrendered themselves to the coalition forces. At last Saddam might get the 'mother of battles', but he would have to fight with an army already in a parlous condition. The prolongation of the first stage of the war had left Iraq in no fit state to prosecute the second, where Saddam had once assumed his forces could be employed to their greatest advantage.

Table 12: Equipment degradation in theatre of operations

	TANKS	APCs	ARTILLERY
ORIGINAL	4,550	2,880	3,257
22 January	14	0	77
27 January	65	50	281
1 February	476	243	356
6 February	728	552	535
11 February	862	692	771
16 February	1,439	879	1,271
21 February	1,563	887	1,428
23 February	1,688	929	1,452
24 February	1,772	948	1,474
25 February	1,865 (41%)	992 (34%)	1,462 (45%)
26 February	2,040 (45%)	1,009 (35%)	1,505 (46%)
27 February	3,708 (81%)	1,856 (47%)	2,140 (66%)
1 March	3,847 (85%)	1,450 (50%)	2,917 (90%)

Source: US CENTCOM.

CHAPTER 27
Land War or Cease-Fire?

Sensing that things were moving from bad to worse, Saddam now confronted the need to extricate his forces from Kuwait before their inevitable defeat, without a complete loss of face. France was fully involved in prosecuting the war against him, so the logical intermediary was the Soviet Union.

Moscow's reaction to the outbreak of hostilities had been overly hostile to Baghdad. 'This tragic turn of events,' read an official statement, 'was provoked by the refusal of the Iraqi leadership to meet the demands of the international community, and to withdraw its forces from Kuwait ... by sowing wind, Saddam Hussein is now literally reaping a "desert storm".'[1] Yet care had been taken to promise no military participation, not even symbolic in nature, and two warships were withdrawn from the Gulf.[2] Mikhail Gorbachev had shown himself anxious to broker a cease-fire almost as soon as the fighting had begun. When, following a phone call from James Baker to the new Foreign Minister, Alexander Bessmertnykh, he was informed of the imminent start of hostilities, Gorbachev immediately called George Bush and suggested that direct contact should be established with Saddam Hussein 'to achieve an immediate announcement by him of the withdrawal of his troops from Kuwait'. Simultaneously, he instructed the Soviet Ambassador to Baghdad, Viktor Posuvalyuk, to deliver a personal message to Saddam demanding this 'in the interest of peace in the region'.[3] The Ambassador met Tariq Aziz in the foreign office bunker and delivered the message. The response was typically defiant. The message should have been addressed 'to the house of the oppressor and not to Saddam Hussein and his people'.[4]

Gorbachev then gave support to a surge of diplomatic activity emanating from several non-aligned countries including Algeria and Yugoslavia. At the start of February even the Iranians offered themselves as mediators.[5] They fared no better. The Iraqis remained entrenched in their pre-war position. 'What is currently taking place is unrelated to Kuwait,' explained Sa'dun Hammadi, 'the question is of Zionist and imperialist aggression intended to destroy Iraq and subjugate the whole region.'[6]

Despite this unpromising start Gorbachev persevered. He desperately needed some diplomatic success to revive a reputation that was not only crumbling domestically, because of precipitate economic decline, but also internationally, where it had always been strong before. An attempted clamp-down in the Baltic states had alarmed international opinion and rekindled sour memories of 1956, when Western preoccupation with the Suez crisis had provided Nikita Khrushchev with an opportunity to turn against Hungary. The respected Foreign Minister Eduard Shevardnadze had quit his job in December 1990 after warning in lurid (but prescient) terms of the risk of a coup. His successor, Alexander Bessmertnykh, seemed prepared to continue the same generally pro-Western line, but there were reports that he endorsed internal criticisms that his predecessor had gone too far in supporting US Gulf policy.[7] Bessmertnykh was also overpowered in the special Crisis Committee, established to monitor the events in the Gulf, by die-hard doctrinaires such as Vice-President Gennadiy Yanayev, Defence Minister Dmitri Yazov, Minister of Interior Boris Pugo, and Vladimir Kryuchkov, Head of the KGB – all of whom were to be involved in the August 1991 coup attempt.[8] Outside the Government, conservatives were using Gorbachev's support for the coalition to show just how bad things were getting. Having just lost the Warsaw Pact, now one of the Soviet Union's closest Middle Eastern clients was being spurned, and American forces were operating close to the southern borders and might soon obtain a permanent base there.

Official Moscow reflected all this when, after two weeks of air war, concern began to be expressed that the 'logic of war could be exceeded', that the bombing of Baghdad was excessive and that war-aims were being escalated.[9] With these statements coupled with the loss of Shevardnadze and evidence of a hardline resurgence in Moscow, the State Department became alarmed that they could lose Soviet support. There had been earlier plans for George Bush to visit Moscow in mid February. This was clearly impossible, in the context of both the war and the crisis in the Baltics. However, Bush had agreed with James Baker, despite the scepticism of others, that this was no time for hostile gestures. Hence, when Bessmertnykh arrived in Washington at the end of January for his first trip as Foreign Minister, Baker was anxious to establish a close working relationship with his new counterpart. He attempted to do this via the same method that had worked well with Shevardnadze at the start of the crisis: a joint statement.

When the statement emerged, some eyebrows in Washington and abroad were raised. A cease-fire was on offer in return for 'an unequivocal commitment to withdraw from Kuwait' and there was a promise of 'joint US–Soviet efforts to promote Arab–Israeli peace and stability'. The Israeli Prime Minister, Yitzhak Shamir, was furious that he had not been warned about such an announcement. The State Department was obliged to deny any change of heart. The joint statement, it was argued, merely went over some long-agreed points. This denial was reinforced by White House spokesman Marlin Fitzwater, who also asserted that the Baker–Bessmertnykh statement implied no 'linkage'. Nonetheless, the White House was outraged that Baker had made this move without consultation with the President, with insult added to injury by it being released two hours before the President gave his State of the Union address. Baker was embarrassed. Particularly galling was to be congratulated by the French Ambassador.[10]

This statement may have given Gorbachev hope that at least some in Washington had a serious interest in a cease-fire even if all the formal conditions were not met. On 31 January the Central Committee of the Communist Party demanded in a resolution that Gorbachev engage in further attempts to reach a political solution. On 9 February Gorbachev issued a presidential statement. He expressed his concern that 'events in the Persian Gulf are taking an increasingly alarming and dramatic turn', and called for a 'political settlement on the basis of the Security Council's resolution'. While criticizing Iraq for its 'provocative attempts to extend the framework of the war, to draw Israel and other states into it', he sought to reassure Saddam of Moscow's impartiality by warning the coalition that 'the logic of military operations and the nature of the military actions are threatening to exceed the mandate which is defined in [the UN] resolutions'. He then urged Saddam to 'show a realism that would allow a way out [of the war]', and announced his intention to send a personal emissary to Baghdad to meet with the Iraqi leader.[11] Two days later Yevgeny Primakov was named as Gorbachev's 'personal emissary'.

The announcement of Primakov's mission was accompanied by official promises that he was taking no definite plan to Saddam. These reassurances were received with considerable scepticism not only in the Western and Arab capitals but, according to the independent Soviet news agency Interfax, in the Soviet Foreign Ministry as well.[12] For one thing, it was an open secret that Primakov was the most senior Soviet official with a substantial commitment to the Soviet–Iraqi relationship in general, and to Saddam Hussein in particular. As late as 15 January he argued that Saddam could be convinced to withdraw peacefully from Kuwait, and that a series of conciliatory moves should be taken to induce him to make such a move,[13] and was to argue throughout the war, more forcefully than most, that the gap between Saddam and everyone else could be bridged with a little more time.

Furthermore, the possibility that Primakov was carrying some significant 'face-savers' to Saddam had already been implied in Gorbachev's statement of 9 February, which had actually accepted the Iraqi demand for a 'linkage'. The purpose of the Soviet mediation effort, read the statement, was

> not only to help to bring about the quickest possible solution to the situation of war, but also to set about preparing a stable and equal system of security in the region that is of such importance to the whole world – a system which will, of course, include a settlement of the Arab–Israeli conflict and of the Palestinian problem . . . A worthy place in the post-war arrangements must also belong to Iraq, whose people cannot be held responsible for what has happened.[14]

On 12 February Primakov met Saddam, after being shown bomb damage in Baghdad. He noted that the Iraqi leader had lost some 15–20 kilograms since they had last met in October 1991. Yet Saddam seemed relaxed, perhaps even confident. To underscore his self-confidence, he did not meet Primakov in his bunker but rather in a guest-house in central Baghdad, where he embarked on a virulent attack on the Soviet position. Primakov listened quietly, gaining the impression that this display of defiance was directed towards Saddam's entourage rather than against Moscow.[15] 'Can we be left alone, Mr President?' he asked when the lecture was over. With this request granted, he explained to Saddam the seriousness of his situation.

According to Primakov, he was struck by the practical nature of Saddam's response, which was diametrically opposed to his earlier bravado. 'In the event of withdrawal,' he asked, 'would retreating Iraqis be shot in the back? Would the air strikes stop, would sanctions be lifted? Was it at all possible to effect a change in the Kuwaiti regime?' He then asked Primakov to stay in Baghdad for some more time, so as to allow him to consult his colleagues. Having heard that Primakov had to leave the next morning, he promised to convene his Cabinet immediately and to reach a quick decision.

In his later written account of the visit,[16] Primakov claims to have made no mention of possible concessions to Baghdad; rather, he emphasized America's determination to prosecute the ground offensive, with its devastating consequences for Iraq, and suggested that Saddam immediately announce total and unconditional withdrawal from Kuwait and cease attacks against civilian targets in Israel. Yet at the time, when he returned to Moscow, he did refer to concessions. 'We favour the withdrawal of Iraqi troops from Kuwait, and this must be secured,' he told a press conference. 'At the same time, I want to recall that President Mikhail Gorbachev's statement lists a number of principles, on the basis of which a political solution must be found.'[17]

Whatever he actually told Saddam, Primakov's report left little doubt that he viewed his mission as a success. Commenting on the talks, Gorbachev's spokesman, Vitaly Ignatenko, said that they had 'given rise to hope' and that Tariq Aziz would now arrive in Moscow late on Sunday evening (17 February).[18] The Soviet media were even more euphoric, arguing that during his meeting with Primakov, for the first time since hostilities erupted, Saddam appeared to have offered a qualified peace feeler.[19]

The Iraqi report of the meeting was not so optimistic. No specific promises on withdrawal were mentioned – only a willingness 'to work for attaining a just and honourable solution to all regional problems', particularly that of Palestine. It emphasized Iraq's status as a victim of aggression and accused the Soviet Union of sharing responsibility for this state of affairs, including the strategic bombardments, because of its backing of Resolution 678. It concluded by calling upon Moscow to rectify its previous misconduct by acting

> to stop these crimes, and expressed Iraq's preparedness to extend co-operation to the Soviet Union and other nations and agencies in the interest of finding a peaceful, political, equitable and honourable solution to the region's central issues, including the situation in the Gulf.[20]

The key question of interpretation was how much or little was implied by the phrase 'including the situation in the Gulf'.

The Soviet diplomatic effort was now in full swing. There were meetings for the Kuwaiti and Iranian Foreign Ministers in Moscow and also an invitation to the European Community troika for the weekend. Then on Friday 15 February came the Iraqi bombshell as Baghdad Radio announced that the Revolutionary Command Council was now prepared 'to deal with Security Council Resolution 660, with the aim of reaching an honourable and acceptable solution, including withdrawal [from Kuwait]'.[21]

The Iraqi statement took the world by surprise. This was the first time since 5 August 1990 that the Iraqi President had referred to the possibility of leaving Kuwait, Iraq's nineteenth province. Rays of light seemed to emerge at the end of the tunnel. People in Baghdad were jubilant. 'It is about time we leave Kuwait,' a young Baghdadi told foreign television correspondents with uncharacteristic frankness, 'this war is unbearable. Baghdad is no longer a town. It is a desert.'

Before long, however, disillusionment set in, as it transpired that Saddam's readiness to withdraw from Kuwait was accompanied by a string of conditions which nullified the letter and spirit of Resolution 660. Not only was an Iraqi withdrawal conditional on an Israeli withdrawal 'from Palestine and the Arab territories it is occupying in the Golan and southern Lebanon', and the cancellation of all UN resolutions against Iraq, but it was also predicated on international guarantees for 'Iraq's historical rights on land and at sea', which implied general recognition of Iraq's claim to Kuwait and, possibly, its continued occupation of the emirate in whole or in part. In addition, Saddam compiled a list of demands, including the cancellation of Iraq's $80 billion foreign debt and the economic reconstruction of Iraq by the allied countries and at their expense. Later, aware of the negative impact of these conditions, Iraq's UN Ambassador, Abd al-Amir al-Anbari, sought to mellow them by arguing that they should not be read as such, but just as a series of issues to be tackled – some now and others further down the line.[22] By this time their political damage had been done.

The demands led the Iraqi statement to be dismissed as a 'bogus sham' by John Major and a 'cruel hoax' by George Bush, who also escalated his rhetoric by calling upon 'the Iraqi military and the Iraqi people to take matters into their own hands, to force Saddam Hussein the dictator to step aside'.[23] Saddam's Arab supporters were more sanguine. 'With happiness and joy we received your responsible peace initiative, which is based on your genuine commitment to the supreme Arab interests,' read a personal message from Jordan's King Hussein to Saddam. 'The demands contained in your peace initiative are legitimate pan-Arab and national demands which are in harmony with our Arab hopes and with international legitimacy. We do not believe a single Arab can stand against or reject these demands.'[24]

Other Arabs, however, had no qualms about rejecting the Iraqi demands. 'The Iraqi announcement has torpedoed the bridge to a solution and dashed hopes to save Iraq from the consequences and effects of destruction,' argued the Syrian daily *Tishrin*;

> had the Iraqi leadership been serious about stopping the war, it would have responded in accordance with the Arab and international decisions, hastened to withdraw from Kuwait, and restored the legitimate Kuwaiti Government.[25]

The Saudis went a step further, vilifying not only Saddam's latest move but also ridiculing King Hussein and Yasser Arafat.

> The crocodile tears shed by the lackeys of the Iraqi tyrant are in fact tears of panic ... After they stood by the defeated tyrant and tied their destiny to his successes ... they realized too late that they stood in the

wrong place. [And yet], instead of returning to the right path, declaring their repentance and asking God's forgiveness and the forgiveness of those who they have wronged, these minute and negligible people stagger in the sea of their mistakes, and continue to swim against the current.[26]

Iraq responded by renewing its threat to use chemical weapons. 'If the high-altitude bombings against the Iraqi forces continue,' warned the Iraqi Ambassador to the UN, Abd al-Amir al-Anbari, 'we would have no choice but to resort to weapons of mass destruction.' This statement, with the Iraqi 'peace initiative', was interpreted in Washington as a further indication of Saddam's growing desperation. The air campaign was intensified, preparations for the land war were consequently speeded up, and, although the Administration denied a French assertion that a date for the decisive offensive had already been set, President Bush promised the Kuwaitis that their nightmare was going to end 'very, very soon'.

Moscow was less dismissive than most. Hardline military opposition was building up, with talk of Security Council resolutions being used as a cover for the massacre of Iraqis.[27] Presidential spokesman Ignatenko said that the Iraqi offer had been received 'with satisfaction and hope', while the Foreign Ministry spokesman, Vitaly Churkin, defined it as 'a starting point for peace'.[28] On 18 February Gorbachev received Tariq Aziz and Sa'dun Hammadi in Moscow, where he handed them a four-point plan and looked forward to an early reply. The key points were a guarantee that the threat to Iraq and to Saddam's regime would be removed following withdrawal, an end to sanctions and a loose linkage with the Palestinian question. Unlike previous occasions, according to Primakov, there 'was not the usual rhetoric from Aziz'.[29] The Iraqis left immediately for Baghdad. There were no longer secure communications with Baghdad and so they had to travel back, as they had come, on a special Soviet flight to Tehran and then overland to Baghdad. As they left for home, the plan was transmitted to the Soviet Union's fellow permanent members of the Security Council, as well as Italy and Germany.

This initiative was received with something less than enthusiasm by the allies. The land war was almost ready to be launched. The Bush Administration was coming under pressure to get the whole business over, especially from the Arab members of the coalition, all of whom were aware of the dangers of protracted cease-fire negotiations involving haggling over details, with the allies' military advantage eroding and the weather deteriorating. Saddam could well have hoped that a cease-fire would allow him to extract his army with not only much of its equipment but also its reputation intact. This was reinforced by a number of commentators who still believed that the Iraqi forces were capable of stern resistance in the event of a land war. It may even be that Gorbachev took this view and thought that he was doing Bush a favour by getting a cease-fire on the basis of an Iraqi withdrawal, even if many other key issues were still undecided and Saddam would be in a position to fight another day. Others suspected darker motives, and for a moment in Washington there were divisions reminiscent of the incessant arguments of the Cold War over Moscow's motives. Those who had reaped the benefits of the care taken with Gorbachev over the first eight months of the crisis did not want that to be jeopardized by a rift now. Baker's standing with the White House staff, already damaged by his joint statement with Bessmertnykh of two weeks earlier, was now further weakened by his inclination to put the most positive construction on the Soviet initiative.

On the Monday evening of 18 February the Americans consulted with their allies and agreed a tough line, based on the need to accept all UN resolutions.[30] Gorbachev sent a three-page cable to Bush, but the text was still short on details such as a deadline for withdrawal. No mention was made of prisoners of war and all the other issues, such as compensation, raised in the other UN resolutions. These objections were sent to Moscow almost immediately. Baker spoke twice on the phone to Bessmertnykh, who was pressing for ways in which the United States might be able to accept the proposal. Baker warned that Washington would not hold back to see how this initiative fared and that no linkage would be tolerated. Bush went public with his view that the plan fell 'well short of what would be required'. The Soviet response was that this was a proposal not to the United States but to Iraq.

France, too, showed little enthusiasm with the Soviet initiative. When Gorbachev called Mitterrand, he was told that Saddam was probably simply playing for time.[31] Gorbachev had proposed convening the Security Council, at the earliest possible moment, to register 'Iraq's acceptance'. There was nothing to register, and the Soviet Union's fellow permanent members had not been consulted on the character of this initiative. There was thus no hope of an extraordinary Security Council session. Bush sent Gorbachev a letter containing precise details of conditions that Saddam must meet before there could be a cease-fire.[32]

The momentum appeared to drain further from Gorbachev's initiative as Aziz failed to return to Moscow with the official Iraqi response. Eventually on 21 February it was reported that he was on his way, with a major speech by Saddam scheduled for that afternoon. If this speech were indicative of the substance of Aziz's message, then it was to be one of total rejection. Saddam's tone was uncompromising, with no concessions offered and the standard claim that the allies were not interested in a cease-fire: 'they wanted the word "withdrawal" but they don't care for it now and talk about new things'. Once more portraying the conflict as a battle between the noble forces of Islam and the evil forces of infidelity, he promised to continue the struggle 'irrespective of the nature of the political efforts which we are exerting and the formulation and directions Tariq Aziz carried to Moscow'.[33]

As Aziz arrived in Moscow the presumption there, as elsewhere, was that the answer had already been received. Sergei Tarasenko, head of the planning department in the Soviet Foreign Ministry, was cited describing Saddam's speech as 'the kamikaze message of a man intent on destroying his own people'.[34] However, when Aziz reported back to Gorbachev the message was more conciliatory. Basically Iraq accepted the Soviet proposal; it wanted to add several points, and Aziz had been empowered to negotiate further. After two hours of discussion Gorbachev reckoned that there was enough material to work on. His spokesman told the waiting press that the Iraqi response was 'positive' and that there was agreement on an eight-point plan.

Saddam agreed to a full and unconditional withdrawal from Kuwait in accordance with UN Resolution 660. According to the plan, the Iraqi withdrawal was to begin on the second day after the cease-fire and to be completed within a fixed time-frame. Once two-thirds of Iraq's forces had been withdrawn, all economic sanctions would be lifted and at the conclusion of the withdrawal, all Security Council resolutions would be deemed redundant and cease to be in effect. Prisoners of war would be released immediately after the cease-fire, and the withdrawal of forces would be monitored by countries not directly involved in the conflict under the aegis of the Security Council.[35]

Even though this understanding fell short of the coalition requirements, it doubtless constituted a critical Iraqi concession. In agreeing to the Soviet proposal, Saddam in effect accepted the loss of Kuwait and abandoned his posture as champion of the Palestinian cause. The attempt to link his personal survival to broader aspirations, begun with his 'peace initiative' of 12 August 1990, had come to an abrupt end as he chose to concentrate on the potential threats to his political survival: war crimes trials, reparations to Kuwait, and economic sanctions.

There was, however, no need for the allies to accept any face-savers. Still too many details were unsatisfactory: the release of prisoners of war was mentioned, but rather late in the process and without reference to the thousands of Kuwaitis interned in Iraq; there was no mention of the handing over of Iraqi plans of their minefields; the time-scale was unclear – the allies wanted this to be quick, so as to reduce the numbers of Iraqi tanks, artillery and chemical munitions that could be taken back for later use. Under the Soviet plan sanctions would be removed while Saddam still had forces in Kuwait.

A main concern related to the suggestion that all UN resolutions subsequent to Resolution 660 should be dropped. This would have represented a major victory for Saddam. Not only would it have implied the illegitimacy of these resolutions, but Resolution 660 left too much implicit. In calling for negotiations between Iraq and Kuwait it did not specify, as did later resolutions, that Kuwait must be represented by its legitimate Government or condemn Iraq's attempt to change the demographic structure of the country (the subject of Resolution 677) or insist (as did Resolution 662) that Iraq's annexation of Kuwait be declared null and void and all claims to Kuwait be renounced. Resolution 674 required Iraq to compensate those who had suffered through its occupation of Kuwait, including foreign workers and corporations.[36]

Not long after Ignatenko had finished his press conference, Gorbachev called Bush. The President explained his objections. However, he agreed to talk with the other allies and give a full response the next day. Bush then met with Baker, Quayle and Scowcroft. They all agreed that an immediate response was necessary. At this point Bush left his senior advisers and went to the theatre. He got back to the White House shortly before 10.30 p.m. for another round of consultations. By midnight they had decided that although the Iraqi acceptance of the Gorbachev plan was a step forward, Saddam must be given an ultimatum to comply fully with all UN resolutions. This would both take the diplomatic initiative away from Moscow and prepare the way for the next stage of the war. They did not want Moscow to present the plan to the Security Council as a formal proposal. This could have required a politically awkward veto. As one official observed:

> The Soviet–Iraqi plan wouldn't only have saved Saddam, it would also have let him dictate his own terms for defeat. That was unacceptable. The ultimatum, on the other hand, was a no-lose option for us.[37]

As soon as the meeting broke up after midnight, Scowcroft and Baker began to consult with allies. British officials were worried that the proposed American statement made no mention of reparations or continued sanctions against Saddam, but here the Americans rejected amendment as this would appear too uncompromising. They did agree, at the urging of both Paris and London, to give Iraq more time for withdrawal. The original American suggestion of four days was not long enough: a week was more realistic.

The key debate revolved around the expiry of the ultimatum. A longer deadline would give Gorbachev more of an opportunity to bring Saddam round to the coalition's demands. Baker was still interested in this possibility, and had some support from the Egyptians and the French. Colin Powell, mindful of the fact that there was a risk of moving out of his commanders' preferred period for the launch of the land war, suggested that Saddam be given no more than twenty-four hours. This was Bush's inclination. However, while this issue was being debated, early on the Friday morning of 22 February news came in of the firing of Kuwaiti oil wells by the Iraqis.

Later that day the Pentagon reported that over 149 wells had been put to the torch, and within days as many as 580 wells were either destroyed or burning. Before they fled from Kuwait it was judged that the Iraqis had blown up as many as 800 oil wells, storage tanks, refineries and other oil-related facilities.[38] The timing could not have been accidental. The first plumes were detected at 10.30 in the morning, local time, at the al-Shu'aybah oil processing centre. This was just before Saddam made his speech on 21 February and fourteen hours before Aziz was to arrive at Moscow with a more conciliatory position.[39] Saddam could not have ruled out that Gorbachev's final diplomacy might have produced some results. In the event of war the smoke could – and did – hamper visibility. But as likely as not this was simple vengeance. If he could not have Kuwait's oil wealth then neither could the al-Sabahs.

Accompanied by stories of executions of young Kuwaitis, this made the twenty-four-hour limit unavoidable. In the Deputies meeting the recommendation was soon settled. News of the firing of the oil wells was taken to George Bush just as he was discussing with President Mitterrand the latter's call for a seventy-two-hour delay. The news concluded the discussion.

The next morning Bush had an eighty-three-minute conversation with Gorbachev, described later by Scowcroft as 'very difficult'.[40] Gorbachev argued that the land war would involve enormous bloodshed and expressed confidence in his ability to get Saddam to agree to the necessary terms with a little more time. Aziz had now reluctantly agreed to bring forward the Iraqi withdrawal and accept further delay in the lifting of economic sanctions. Bush thanked the Soviet President for his efforts but made it clear that the new plan did not meet the UN conditions, and that Saddam had ample time to do the right thing. The reports of the destruction and looting of Kuwait meant that it was no longer possible to wait. Gorbachev, for his part, stated his intention to continue negotiations with Aziz to finalize the details of the Soviet–Iraqi plan. Bush came away from the conversation at least convinced that Gorbachev had no sympathy for Saddam and was not trying to protect him: when it came to the crunch the Soviet Union would not break with the United States.[41] Nonetheless, when the ground war started the official Soviet statement observed that the 'instinct for military solution' had 'won through' and an opportunity for a chance to resolve the conflict had been 'missed', and *Pravda* complained that the United States was driving for 'sole leadership in the world'.

'The coalition will give Saddam Hussein until noon Saturday [20.00 Iraqi time, 23 February] to do what he must do – begin his immediate and unconditional withdrawal from Kuwait,' Bush said the next morning. 'We must hear publicly and authoritatively his acceptance of these terms.'[42] Iraq was required to withdraw from Kuwait City by 25 February and allow for the return of Kuwait's legitimate Government, with full withdrawal within a week.

Despite his desperation, Saddam still could not submit to an American ultimatum before his people. He attempted to revive the Soviet peace initiative, which offered his only hope of portraying an Iraqi withdrawal as a morally responsible act, a generous acquiescence to the request of a friendly great power. His emissaries continued to play in Moscow with a new Soviet plan which gave them twenty-one days to get out of Kuwait. Tariq Aziz agreed to a revised six-point plan which was even more flexible, but he needed to check with Baghdad. This might have provided Gorbachev enough time to submit it to the Security Council, but when Saddam's response finally came he wanted it kept confidential until the final details were agreed, so no new momentum could be provided from Moscow.

The American response to Saddam's indifference to the ultimatum was swift. At 04.00 (Gulf time) on Sunday 24 February, President Bush announced that the Commander-in-Chief of the coalition forces in Saudi Arabia, General Norman Schwarzkopf, had been instructed 'to use all forces available, including ground forces, to eject the Iraqi army from Kuwait'. The ground war had begun.

CHAPTER 28
Land War

Iraq's defence

From the start the Iraqi commanders had assumed that there would be a marine landing from the Gulf into Kuwait. By a process of elimination they concluded that this would most likely come to the north of Kuwait City, from where it was possible to get access to the north–south highway to Basra and cut the Iraqi Army in half.[1] To guard against this, two infantry divisions were set into extensive trenchworks backed by anti-air guns for use against the Marines' helicopters, while hundreds of mines were laid to prevent allied ships and landing craft from closing in. Behind them were the regular Army's mechanized and armoured divisions. Even the defence of the city itself presumed that the main attack would come from the sea, perhaps in a second landing in Kuwait harbour to the north. Buildings facing the shore were evacuated and turned into fighting positions, the trench line was extended throughout the city along the beach, and artillery was placed in available sites. An armoured division was based at the airport, ready to move rapidly to counter-attack. In total, four heavy divisions and seven infantry divisions were geared to this threat from the sea.[2]

Later adjustments had to be made to cope with the additional threat of a land attack. The forward obstacle and infantry line was extended from the Kuwaiti coast along the 138-mile border with Saudi Arabia, but only a few kilometres west of Kuwait into Iraq. Minefields sixty to ninety feet deep containing a mixture of anti-tank and anti-personnel mines were followed by anti-tank ditches and barriers, some twelve feet deep and up to nine feet wide, filled with dragon-tooth metal spikes, burned-out vehicles and concrete blocks, as well as fifty-five-gallon drums of napalm that could be detonated by remote control. Infantry brigades were dug into deep trenches, reinforced with concrete-coated steel mesh, wire or reeds – so well dug in, in fact, that they could not withdraw. The two most likely avenues for the coalition offensive had been identified as the coast road and the Wadi al-Batin, a wide valley less than 100 feet deep which formed the border between Kuwait and Iraq. Extra mechanized divisions were put astride these routes. The Iraqis assumed that the allies would be unable to manage without roads to help them navigate. Vast quantities of towed artillery offered cover with indirect fire, along with AAA batteries.

About one heavy armoured or mechanized brigade was available as a mobile operational reserve for every three forward. Light and heavy Republican Guard divisions, with heavy divisions from the regular Army, were held back as a mobile counter-attack force. Two armoured and one mechanized Republican Guard divisions with two regular armoured divisions were placed just north of the Iraq–Kuwait border, where the Wadi opened up into flat desert. If things went really well, they might even be able to move into Saudi Arabia.[3] Their standard equipment was substantial and they had good logistics and engineering support. Of the sixty-three divisions of the Iraqi Army, forty-three were committed to the Kuwaiti theatre; twelve of these were armoured and the rest infantry. The strategy was simple: the front-line forces had been told to stick to their positions and absorb the coalition attack until the counter-attack came.

This strategy had a number of critical flaws. It depended on anticipating the likely thrust of the enemy attack, making it extremely difficult to regain the initiative if the anticipation proved faulty and to shift rapidly from static to mobile warfare. The wide open spaces of the desert did not lend themselves to such static defence. They provided few natural obstacles or opportunities for cover and concealment, while allowing the attacker fast movement. Against an enemy geared to fast-moving warfare and enjoying air supremacy, the Iraqi forces were always going to be hard pressed to control the direction and tempo of the battle.

These problems were compounded by specific features of the Iraqi plan. Because it was heavily weighted to the east, with the focus on either a ground attack up the coastal highway or an amphibious landing, vulnerabilities to the west had not been seriously addressed. There was no serious intelligence operation to assess the enemy's likely strategy. The surveillance aircraft used during the war with Iran were too vulnerable. There was only some monitoring of commercial broadcasts and occasional patrols, rendering the Iraqis a soft touch for deception. Most Iraqi soldiers had little idea of where their own forces were, never mind those of the enemy.

Furthermore, while the Iraqi strategy depended on the strength of its forward defences, the best troops were in the reserve. There were in fact two distinct armies fighting for Iraq. The regular Army, though set out in an appropriate fashion for a static defence, lacked the training and the preparation to execute it effectively. The veterans and civilians who had been mobilized during the crisis were barely trained, poorly supported and weakly led, especially once the coalition had cut the lines to the Iraqi heartland. Some senior Iraqi officers took the precaution of getting home before the battle, issuing their orders by telephone. Those left at the front were unable to cope with the relentless bombardment they suffered or the prospect of combat with a well-equipped and properly trained army. Some had bought white cloth in preparation for surrender in Kuwait City.

By contrast the other army – the Republican Guard – had superior equipment, training and overall support. Seven of the forty-three committed Iraqi divisions were from the Guard. They were in position to mount a counter-attack against any breakthrough by coalition forces, but – as important – they were also in a position to withdraw quickly to be used against either a coalition or internal threat to the Iraqi regime.[4]

The American assessment

In December, the US Army intelligence estimated

> that Iraq had fixed its forces and would not reinforce or redispose them in any significant way; that the Iraqi defence would be positional, with counter-attacks likely by tactical but not operational or Republican Guard forces; that the Iraqi military was fixated on the defence of Kuwait City and Basra and would not improve defensive barriers or move forces westwardly; that the Iraqis intended to use chemicals, possibly as early as the breach areas in the front-line defences but certainly once US forces attacked the Republican Guard.

Two specific defensive actions had also been anticipated: the movement of a few brigades to preplanned blocking positions about twenty to thirty kilometres west of the Wadi al-Batin, and the repositioning of forces to defend Basra. All these estimates, except the prediction of chemical attacks, proved to be accurate.[5]

Close attention was paid to indications that the Iraqis were making any move that might complicate the allied planning: reinforcement in the west; improvement and extension of the barrier system westwardly; shifts in the disposition of the Republican Guard and the operational reserve's heavy divisions; preparations for chemical attack; a readiness to strike to exploit the vulnerability left by the shift of coalition strength westwards – for example down the Wadi al-Batin to Hafir al-Batin, a small city about sixty kilometres into Saudi Arabia.

As the intelligence community watched, the Iraqis appeared to be virtually immobile. They had not spotted the movements of the allied forces nor adjusted their defences, let alone made any attempt to disrupt the considerable logistical effort under way. As the start of the land offensive – 'G-Day' – drew closer, it was evident that even if the Iraqis were aware of what was going on there was little they could do about it, as any movement of their own forces would merely render them vulnerable to air strikes. There was good reason to believe that the flanking movement would be so fast that allied forces would be on top of the Iraqis before they knew what was going on.

Supply lines between Baghdad and the front were now effectively severed: only four out of fifty-four railroad and highway bridges were undamaged, and forty were inoperable. Table 13 shows CENTCOM's assessment of the state of Iraqi forces as the land war began. In total it demonstrates that the 50 per cent attrition mark had not been reached. However, this was largely because the Iraqi forces to the rear had not suffered as much as the front line, where the assessed attrition was 50 per cent or below, especially with regard to artillery. However, this meant that there was still a considerable amount to be done with the Republican Guard.

Table 13: Equipment status at start of land battle (24 February 1991)

RESOURCE	ORIGINAL STRENGTH	DESTROYED/ CAPTURED	PERCENTAGE REMAINING
TOTAL			
Tanks	4,280	1,772	59%
Armoured vehicles	2,870	948	67%
Artillery	3,110	1,474	53%
REPUBLICAN GUARD			
Tanks	986	425	57%
Armoured vehicles	603	145	76%
Artillery	630	129	80%

Source: CINCCENT.

Intelligence was also improving on the state of the Iraqi Army. Khafji had revealed its operational limitations. Command and control had been sluggish. Even after taking the initiative the Iraqi commanders were disorientated by the speed and character of the coalition response and they failed to make the best use of their available troops and fire-power.[6] The equipment captured at Khafji had shown 'a lot of rust and a lack of proper lubrication'.

The overall impression was that both discipline and supervised maintenance were lacking, not surprising for an army under continual aerial attack. The prisoners who were being taken lacked food and water. They knew that medical facilities were poor, so that if they were wounded they were unlikely to survive, and had a keen sense of the coalition's superiority. Again, there still had to be a degree of caution with regard to the state of the Republican Guard. The prisoners and deserters came from the front line, where they were at the farthest reach of the severely attenuated Iraqi supply train. The Republican Guard, closer to home, had more chance of getting some supplies.[7]

In addition, according to Paul Wolfowitz:

> We were beginning to get quite horrible intelligence reports about their treatment of their own people who were trying to escape or desert, execution squads wandering around in the rear area of Iraqi forces, executing people, hanging bodies of people who had tried to escape, and when the commanders of an army turn on their own army like that, you know that it is an army that is in very, very bad shape.[8]

Exactly how many Iraqis were in the theatre was unclear. The figure used publicly at the start of the war was 540,000, and that seemed to accord with Iraqi boasts. British estimates appear if anything to have been higher. The number had apparently been arrived at by identifying the units as they were deployed and checking back with the numbers at which those units operated during the war with Iran. By the end of 1990 there was some awareness in CENTCOM that numbers were probably exaggerated, because many units were often only at 80 per cent of full strength and sometimes as low as 50 per cent. Many conscripts appear not to have joined their units or to have failed to rejoin them after leave. Some bribed their officers to let them go. Estimates of actual numbers at the start of the war now range from 250,000 to 400,000, with no more than two-thirds this number in Kuwait itself. It could well have been at the lower end of this estimate, which put the actual total nearer 250,000, of which 150,000 were in Kuwait. It seems likely that Iraqi forces were down to 200,000 when the ground war was actually launched.[9] The sixty-two B-52s, which flew 1,600 sorties and dropped 30 per cent of all tonnage, may not have produced much by way of precision strikes, but the psychological impact of regular bombardments on Iraqi morale appears to have been considerable. To enhance the effect, leaflets had been dropped warning of impending attacks and also giving advice on how to surrender. Almost all Iraqi prisoners had seen these leaflets.

Although the full extent of this depletion was not appreciated in CENT-COM, there was growing optimism. Early computer predictions had put casualties in a land war as high as 40,000, of which a quarter might be fatalities. As the air campaign began, the predicted cost was 5,000 in a ground war taking at least six weeks. Now the expectation was a week if the Republican Guard was bold enough to come out to fight, a little longer if they kept their heads down.[10] Nonetheless, senior commanders were still thinking in terms of 10–20 per cent losses for their own units.[11] They expected to win, but they did not expect a walkover.

The plan

CENTCOM's plan for the land war reflected the military logic acknow-ledged in many of the pre-war debates, when a campaign based on manoeuvre and envelopment had been anticipated.[12] 'Everyone seems to know that the likely scenario calls for US and British forces to wheel around Kuwait and cut across the southern part of Iraq toward Basra,' observed Leslie Gelb of the *New York Times*, concerned that the advantage of surprise had been lost.[13] Schwarzkopf's 'Hail Mary' play was still remarkably bold.[14]

A rapid move well to the west of the Wadi al-Batin made possible a flanking action far deeper into Iraq than expected, to separate the in-theatre Iraqi forces from their home base and prevent reinforcement or escape up the Euphrates river valley, and then to allow the heavy armoured divisions to mount an attack from the south and west to destroy the Republican Guard divisions deployed along the Iraqi–Kuwaiti border west of Basra. Direct thrusts were aimed at liberating Kuwait City. The Iraqi command was to be disoriented by two diversionary moves – a pretended amphibious landing, and a deception plan to portray the main effort as being an attack from the south mainly along the coast to take Kuwait City.

The Marines wanted to make the landing – which they designated 'Desert Sabre' – real and pressed hard until a week before the actual attack for a change in the plan,[15] but although the Iraqi Navy was not a serious obstacle, the mine-clearing operation would have taken many days to complete and without it casualties could have been substantial. The Iraqis had not planted their mines with particular expertise but the sheer numbers were impressive. They had filled a crescent around the small Kuwaiti coastline with some 1,200 mines concentrated, although this was not fully appreciated at the time, in the centre. On 2 February Schwarzkopf met with the marine and navy commanders who estimated that it would take another ten days of mine-clearing plus naval bombardment to prepare for the landing. The bombardment risked severe damage to Kuwaiti civilians and property – especially as a natural gas plant, among other civilian obstacles, was in the preferred landing site – while the mine-clearing close to shore would be dangerous because it would have to be undertaken within artillery range. The risk did not seem to be worth the potential military gain. Nonetheless, preparations for an amphibious landing were conspicuous through February as the Iraqi Navy, without any obvious hiding place, was gradually eliminated and mines were cleared.[16]

Desert Storm opened with about 120 US and fifty allied ships in the area, including six carrier battle groups. From the start of the war the Navy had been clearing the sea around Kuwait. Aircraft reported being shot at from oil platforms in the al-Dawrah field, forty miles off the coast. SAMs had been placed on the eleven platforms. American frigates and Kuwaiti patrol boats set about clearing them, taking the first Iraqi prisoners. As the Iraqis realized their vulnerability, they began to evacuate the remaining platforms and off-shore islands. A few days later a suspected minelayer was caught near Qaruh island. It was disabled, the island was occupied and the Kuwaiti flag raised once again on Kuwait territory. On 21 January there was a successful attack on the only Iraqi frigate, which was in practice largely a training boat. The Iraqi naval base at Umm Qasr was attacked regularly. With Iraqi aircraft now escaping, surveillance was maintained to see if the Iraqi fleet would attempt to follow this example. The first serious movement came on 29 January when the Royal Navy attacked Iraqi patrol boats apparently involved in the Khafji operation. The next day, after this experience, a large force attempted to escape to Iran. In the 'battle of Bubiyan', twenty patrol boats, tankers and minelayers were chased and harassed. Only two, a patrol boat and an amphibious ship, both of which were damaged, made good their escape.[17]

On 2 February the Iraqi Navy was officially judged incapable of offensive action. The only US naval casualties came when the cruiser *Princeton* and the amphibious assault ship USS *Tripoli* struck mines on 18 February, in an area where none were expected, confirming the problems with an amphibious landing.[18] On 25 February a Silkworm anti-ship missile was intercepted by a Sea Dart air defence missile from HMS *Gloucester*, *en route* to some American ships, although it may have been about to miss.[19] The Iraqi Navy lost 143 out of 165 surface combatants damaged or destroyed.

In the days leading up to the offensive there was a steady preparation for an amphibious landing, including rehearsals. On Saturday 23 February, thirty-one ships swung in the direction of Kuwait City. The battleships

Missouri and *Wisconsin* fired at Iraqi shore defences. The 17,000 Marines, however, stayed on board and did not attempt a landing. The feint was indicative of the resources available to CENTCOM. For most commanders it would have been something of a luxury, in that the resources bound up with the amphibious armada (the largest since the Inchon landings in Korea in 1950) were greater than those being held down.

G-Day

The land campaign involved two distinct pushes: one, led by the Marines, across the Kuwaiti–Saudi border directly towards Kuwait City; the other involving the relatively light XVIII Corps well to the west and the relatively heavy VII Corps, which constituted the 'left hook' designed to envelop Iraqi forces and destroy their most substantial elements.

As the Iraqis were clearly expecting an attack up the Wadi, the 1st Cavalry Division was ordered to keep the Iraqis focused in this direction. On 20 February they conducted a major probing operation, only to discover that the Iraqis had prepared an elaborate ambush. Three men were lost before it was possible to get back behind lines. Then, somewhat to their frustration, they were not to press forward but to maintain themselves as an operational reserve.

The First and Second Marine Divisions, and the Tiger Brigade of the 2nd Armoured Division (taking the place of the redeployed British Army), had the task of crossing the border and breaching the front-line Iraqi defence. They were to move to the south-east of al-Jahra City, where they would establish blocking positions to prevent reinforcements getting through. To their right, two Saudi task forces were to penetrate coastal defences, protecting the Marines' right flank and getting ready to secure Kuwait. To their left the joint Arab forces – Egyptian, Syrian, Qatari, Kuwaiti and Saudi – were to prevent the reinforcement of those Iraqi forces facing the main attack by blocking off lines of communication from north of Kuwait City and then securing the city itself. By keeping the Iraqis preoccupied with events inside Kuwait, they would divert attention from the 'left hook' coming up behind them on the west.

In practice this diversionary ground attack was the most dangerous of all the operations. It required breaching the fortifications, which had gained a reputation over the months as providing Iraqi forces with an extraordinarily effective 'killing ground', not so much to break through but to engage the enemy sufficiently so that he could not react to the main attack on his flank. 'It worried me,' Colin Powell commented later, 'that the secondary attack could cost us far more casualties than the main attack because the main attack, and people flying in helicopters at 100 miles an hour or in tanks moving at twenty or thirty miles an hour, were pretty invulnerable. These were infantrymen who were going right in.' However, a week before the attack Schwarzkopf reported that the Marine reconnaissance units had crawled through the wire and identified the gaps in the defences. Over that week more units went in to mark out avenues bypassing the main fortifications.[20]

During that week special operations groups landed by helicopter to check out the state of the Iraqi defences and, where necessary, to call in air strikes. An effort was made to pinpoint every artillery piece that could be directed against coalition troops. The arguments between the air and ground force commanders had continued up to this point, with the latter unconvinced that enough had been done to degrade the Iraqi force, while the former complained of the difficulty of finding individual pieces in the desert. The ground forces worked on the artillery themselves by enticing it to fire and then using the Multiple Launch Rocket System (MLRS) in counter-attack. Soon the Iraqi artillery learned that it was prudent not to fire.[21]

Bulldozers began to knock down the sand berms erected by the Iraqis as a defensive wall. On the night of G-Day, Iraqi soldiers were subjected to intense bombardment – by everything from B-52s, to multiple-rocket launchers, to helicopter gunships, to naval guns. Iraq's heavy artillery had been one of the most feared weapons in its inventory, especially if used to launch chemical weapons. In the event it was barely noticed.

At 04.00 on the morning of 24 February the coalition ground forces were ready to move. Despite the prediction of good weather, it turned out to be a combination of rain, fog, dust and smog from the oil fires. The smog probably harmed the Iraqis more than the allies because they had fewer aids to visibility. The reconnaissance work done by the marines paid off as their probing attacks pushed them into Kuwait, in some cases even before the deadline. The ditches filled with burning oil had either been dealt with earlier by setting them alight prematurely with napalm, or by dirt being pushed by bulldozers into the trenches. The minefields caused less bother than feared, in part as a result of the shifting desert sand: if it covered the mines too deeply they became inoperable, while if it was blown off by the wind the mines became visible. Since the barriers had been constructed in September and October they had been neglected.

The Iraqis responded as expected, although half-heartedly. The artillery fire was persistent but inaccurate. The First Cavalry's feint up the Wadi led the Tawakalna Division of the Republican Guard to move slowly south. As the Marines broke through, there was a weak attempt at a counter-attack by Saddam's Third Corps but it was pushed back. The Second Marine Division, plus the Tiger Brigade, had a tougher task because in their sector only about 10 per cent of the Iraqi artillery had been silenced. By the next evening they had pushed ahead successfully to positions just west of Kuwait City.

By night on the first day the First Marine Division had reached al-Jaber airport, half the forty-mile distance from the border to Kuwait City. The next day it encountered Iraqi units in the Burgan oilfield, close to the international airport, which they flushed out with a massive artillery barrage into the open where they were caught by tanks and helicopter attacks as well as more artillery. By early Wednesday the airport had been taken after a major tank battle which left all the 100 Iraqi tanks that had been engaged destroyed.

The Arab units moved more slowly. The Saudi-led force to the east attacked the Iraqi 5th Mechanized Division, which had not yet recovered from the attack on Khafji. They were held up by coping with the thousands of prisoners that were being passed into their hands. The Syrians only crossed the border two days into the land war. The Egyptian-led force to the west at least succeeded in getting across the trenches, but they were only a couple of miles into Kuwait and lagging well behind the Marines. The Pentagon Report observes, without comment, that once through the trenches the Egyptians were 'concerned about an Iraqi armoured counter-attack and established blocking positions'.[22] This did reflect the original plan. There was a risk that the Iraqis might be able to cut them off from the Marines. Rather than halt and wait for the Arabs to catch up, which would mean that the current advantages over the Iraqis would be lost, the Marine commander decided to press on. This had an important consequence. It meant that the coalition was closing in on Kuwait City early – before the envelopment forces were in place to cut off any Iraqi retreat.

While the air campaign had been under way, desperate to avoid drawing attention to themselves, the XVIII Corps and VII Corps moved westwards. Some 235,000 troops and all their equipment, 95,000 trucks and other wheeled vehicles, 12,000 tanks and other armoured personnel vehicles and sixty days of stocks were taken along a single highway, the Tapline road, requiring 4,500 trucks moving eighteen a minute past a given spot twenty-four hours a day.[23] In the case of the three and a half divisions of the XVIII Corps this meant covering 800 kilometres in twelve days, leaving behind a deception cell in eastern Saudi Arabia, using such devices as phoney radio traffic to convince the Iraqis that they were all still there. On 16 February, the VII Corps began its own advance to the west, also leaving a deception cell.

The task of the XVIII Corps was to advance to the west of the theatre of operations in order to control the east–west line of communications along Highway 8, the road leading from Kuwait to the Euphrates, thereby isolating Iraqi forces in the theatre. Later they would expect to attack east, in support of the main attack against the Republican Guard. The units of the Corps furthest west were the French 6th Light Armoured Division and the 82nd Airborne Division, who were to drive towards the al-Salman airfield, 105 miles inside Iraq. Just to their east the 101st Airborne Division was being moved by helicopter to establish the Forward Operations Base, Cobra. The VII Corps was to attack west of the Kuwaiti border to destroy Republican Guard forces, cut bridges, roads and rail lines south of Basra so as to block the withdrawal of the Republican Guards, and form a kill zone.

The French-led push to al-Salman began with the rest of the morning attack, as did the 101st Airborne Division's helicopter-borne push to establish the logistics base, from where other forces could be resupplied and refuelled. The French crossed the lines at 05.30. By the evening they were in position to attack al-Salman the next day, defended by the 45th Iraqi Infantry Division. Although it was still at about 75 per cent strength it was unfortunate enough to be facing the wrong way, so as to stop an attack coming out of Kuwait rather than from the south. With the 82nd Airborne, the French mounted an effective artillery and helicopter anti-tank attack followed up by tanks and infantry against soldiers who were mainly interested in surrendering.[24] By mid-afternoon it was over. The French were ordered to set up a defensive position guarding their units to the right against a flanking attack.

The bulk of the 'left hook' was not expected to get on the move until the next day. As the battle was going so well on the Kuwaiti front, Schwarzkopf asked for and was given permission to launch the VII Corps some twelve hours early. The reason was not only the success of the initial attacks, but also a concern about the weather, which was expected to get 'pretty bad the next day', and information of atrocities being committed by Iraqis in Kuwait City, including 'reports that the desalination plant had been destroyed'. All of this argued for getting a move on.[25] The First Infantry Division had breached the minefields for the First British Armoured Division to pass through, soon followed by the remainder of VII Corps. Between eighty and 250 Iraqi troops who had not surrendered were buried alive as their trenches were ploughed over.

The British – charged with protecting the Corps flank by destroying the Iraqi tactical reserve – then turned east to roll up behind the Iraqi front line, while the rest went north before turning east. There the Corps moved as if 'bunched in a big fist' – a 'steel wedge sixty miles wide and 120 miles long with hundreds of trucks carrying the 11.3 million litres of fuel needed to keep the force moving each day'.[26] Their first engagements were with units of the Iraqi Army who were swept aside with devastating results, although the British suffered nine deaths when an American A-10 mistakenly attacked a Warrior Infantry Fighting Vehicle. Using British forces as a pivot, VII Corps turned against the Republican Guard. It approached six divisions, most still at around 75 per cent strength. They were still oriented to an attack coming up through the Wadi and were caught wrong-footed.

The Guard commanders had assumed that the VII Corps was moving towards Kuwait City. Their plan was to use the Iraqi 12th Armoured Division to block this advance while they came down from the north. However, the Republican Guard *was* the target, a fact the commanders realized late in the day. Their task became one of blocking a breakthrough by the VII Corps into the Iraqi rear. By the afternoon of 26 February, three Guard divisions – Tawakalna, Medina and Hammurabi – had established a blocking line by the road which runs parallel to the Iraqi pipeline through Saudi Arabia.[27]

The coalition attacks came with artillery and the multiple launch rocket system, followed by Apache helicopters, before the fighting vehicles came pushing through. By the late afternoon the Tawakalna Division had been overrun. The next morning a brigade of the Medina Division, with a battalion of the Iraqi 14th Mechanized Division, desperately trying to protect a retreat of other forces, were devastated in an attack fought in a sandstorm.

The XVIII Corps also launched its attack towards the Euphrates river valley at 15.00 on 24 February. The commander reported a lack of enemy activity in its attack zone, so the attack was brought forward by fifteen hours. By dusk the next day 101st Airborne Division was cutting Highway 8 to the west, while the 24th Mechanized Infantry Division entered the river valley near al-Nasiriyah. There an Iraqi commando regiment put up a relatively fierce fight for Talil before it was overcome and the division was able to turn east down Highway 8, destroying Iraqi tanks off heavy equipment trailers trying to escape in the opposite direction. By the next day it was established south of the Euphrates, blocking escape routes.

Some Iraqi units, especially those placed along the anticipated coalition invasion route, put up a serious fight but they had no answer to the vastly superior firepower and mobility of the coalition. It was apparent after the first day that the land war would be in effect a walkover. Movement was rapid; the Iraqi response was marginal; coalition casualties were slight. There was minimal evidence of Iraq's much-vaunted artillery, let alone its chemical weapons capability. In fact chemical weapon stocks do not appear to have been issued to field commanders, perhaps because of Baker's warning to Aziz of retribution against the regime if they were used. Protective clothing and masks for chemical warfare had been noticed before hostilities, indicating that contingency plans for use had been made.[28]

Within less than forty-eight hours of fighting, the backbone of the Iraqi Army had been broken. The apparently formidable line of defence in Kuwait, the so-called 'Saddam line', collapsed as allied forces pushed through the Iraqi lines and stormed into Kuwait. Iraqi troops were surrendering *en masse*. There were stories of soldiers waving anything white in their possession and chanting 'MRE' (meals ready to eat – the US troops' rations), stories of troops desperately trying to give themselves up to pilotless drones, and of a lone soldier in a bogged-down vehicle being pulled out by an Iraqi tank and armoured vehicle and then receiving their surrender.[29] Republican Guard units were caught taking a cigarette break because colleagues in adjacent units had not been able to communicate to warn them of the impending attack.

At the same time allied forces were moving rapidly inside Iraq, in a determined thrust to reach the Baghdad–Basra highway and thus encircle the Republican Guard, deployed on Iraqi territory just north of the Kuwaiti border. More than 370 Iraqi tanks had been destroyed and American intelligence sources reported that at least seven Iraqi divisions – up to 100,000 men – were telling their supreme headquarters that they could no longer fight. By sunset on 26 February 30,000 prisoners had been taken and twenty-six Iraqi divisions had been destroyed or rendered ineffective. The rest of the Iraqi Army was largely in retreat with its command system destroyed. The coalition forces, however, had not yet cut off the Iraqi line of retreat.

During 25 February the Iraqis supposedly blocking the advance of the Marines and their Arab support had retreated into Kuwait City from where, with the occupation troops based there, they immediately planned to escape. By that evening the Marines were ten miles from the city and the next day they reached the outskirts. They now had to pace their advance with the Arab members of the coalition. The Egyptians were making good progress. On that Wednesday, they took an airfield close to the city and made their way into its southern outskirts in order to link up with the other Saudi-led Arab forces coming up from the north.

The commanders had been anticipating a prolonged siege of the city, with Arab forces assigned the task of gradually flushing out Iraqi troops from the built-up areas. The Kuwaiti commander had always doubted that the Iraqis would fight to the finish and had requested an alternative whereby his men would liberate the city. This became the plan. On the Thursday the Marines took the international airport early in the morning and then waited for the Arab forces to arrive. Some slipped into the city to make contact with the Kuwaiti resistance. The next day, 28 February, the Kuwaitis were ready formally to retake Kuwait City and the Marines stood by to let them pass.

Table 14: 'The left hook' order of battle

	XVIII CORPS	VII CORPS
Armoured	6th French Light Armoured Division	1st UK Division 1st Division 3rd Division
Mechanized	24th Division	1st Division
Airborne	101st Division 82nd Division	
Reconnaissance	3rd Regiment	1st Division 2nd Regiment
Attack helicopters	Battalion	Battalion
Artillery	Two battalions	Two battalions

Source: CENTCOM

CHAPTER 29

The Closing Whistle

On the morning of 24 February, officials in Washington waited first for news of the Marines' breaching operation. If they had faced stiff opposition, that would have served as a warning that the fight would be tough. In fact the early information from the Marine reconnaissance patrols reported finding their lines of advance virtually empty of Iraqi forces.

Later that morning in Washington (eight hours behind Kuwait), Cheney slipped into church beside the President to give him the hopeful preliminary reports. By the time the service was over and the President met with his aides to consider the situation, the news was even better. The advance was faster than anticipated and had been achieved with minimal casualties. Cheney could now report that the Marines had entered Kuwait, safely through the minefields, tank ditches and barbed wire at the cost of four killed in action. Colin Powell was already suggesting that the battle would be over by the Friday.

For his part, Saddam had no strategy for this stage of the war other than to get through it as quickly as possible with whatever he could salvage of his military power. As the land war developed, Iraqi political concessions came steadily and rapidly. Less than forty-eight hours after its start, around midnight 25 February, Baghdad Radio announced that the Iraqi troops in Kuwait had been ordered to withdraw 'in an organized way to positions they held prior to 1 August 1990'. 'This is regarded as practical compliance with UN Resolution 660,' it was explained. 'Our armed forces, which have proven their ability to fight and stand fast, will confront any attempt to harm them while they are carrying out their orders.'[1]

President Gorbachev called President Bush, informing him that Saddam no longer demanded the abolition of all UN resolutions as a condition of withdrawal. At the UN, Ambassador Vorontsov asked his colleagues on the permanent five for a timetable for withdrawal, arguing that this would produce a constructive response from Baghdad, although the Iraqi Ambassador had received no instructions.[2]

The Administration was not yet willing to let Saddam off the hook. 'We do not consider there is anything to respond to,' said Marlin Fitzwater, 'the war goes on.' The White House demanded that President Saddam Hussein 'personally and publicly' commit to a speedy withdrawal and that Iraq comply fully with the twelve UN Security Council resolutions.[3] According to Bush, Saddam was only interested in regrouping to fight another day. 'We have no choice but to treat retreating combat units as a threat.'

On 26 February the Security Council agreed to ask Dr Abd al-Amir al-Anbari for a clear commitment from Saddam with regard to all twelve resolutions. Moscow was now modifying opposition in line with the allies. Such a public humiliation was Saddam's worst possible scenario, no less alarming than the destruction of his forces. In a society where words most often substitute for deeds, and where loss of face is the gravest dishonour,[4] the public admission of a mistake as devastating as the Kuwaiti invasion threatened his future survival. The larger-than-life image of the infallible leader, on which his personal rule had depended for more than a decade, would be supplanted by that of the bungling leader whose poor judgement had brought nothing but suffering and indignity to his people. The carefully constructed barrier of fear and adulation which in the past had shielded him from criticism and accountability would be irrevocably destroyed.

In these circumstances the land war became a race between the coalition's determination to destroy as much as possible of the Iraqi military capability and Saddam's awareness of the need to accept all UN resolutions unequivocally. As the Iraqi forces were being decimated by the hour – on 26 February the allies reported the incapacitation of twenty-one of Iraq's forty divisions in the Kuwaiti theatre, and a day later eight more Iraqi divisions had been rendered ineffective – Saddam quickly softened his position.

Foreign Minister Aziz announced to the UN Iraq's readiness to rescind its official annexation of Kuwait, release all prisoners of war, and pay war reparations in return for an immediate cease-fire and an end to sanctions.[5] The proposal was immediately rejected by the Security Council, which remained adamant on Baghdad's compliance with all twelve UN resolutions. This compliance came shortly afterwards on 27 February, when Ambassador al-Anbari informed the Security Council that Baghdad was willing to abide by the remaining resolutions. The last Iraqi soldier had left Kuwait at dawn, he said, and there was no further justification for sustaining the international sanctions against Iraq.[6]

The Basra road

Almost as soon as the land war began, the Iraqis decided to pull troops out of Kuwait using the Republican Guard as a screen. Most Iraqi troops needed little encouragement to obey Saddam's command to withdraw. On the evening of 25 February the pull-out from Kuwait City began, sparing it at least the trauma of liberation through house-to-house fighting. Soon units of the Kuwaiti resistance were in control of most of the city. Soon too the roads leading north towards Basra were jammed with escaping vehicles, often crammed with plunder from Kuwait, caught by the volume of traffic and a route of roads and bridges that had already been well bombed.

The allies had intercepted the withdrawal order. They wanted the Iraqis out of the city before attacking, to avoid threats to civilian life and property and to discourage an urban defence which would be difficult to dislodge. However, allied blocking forces were not yet in place, and so retreating forces if left alone had a realistic chance of escape. Major-General Glosson, who had been in charge of targeting for the air war, received news that evening from informants in Kuwait City that the Iraqis were packing and preparing to leave. Nothing, however, was as yet showing up on JSTARS, the airborne tactical radar. Two hours later the picture changed. A large convoy was now moving north towards Basra on Highway 6. Kuwaiti officers assigned to the Tactical Air Control Centre assured their colleagues that this was solely the Iraqi military on the move, attempting to escape in the dark and then link up with Republican Guards. Other intelligence seemed to confirm this. Immediately Air Force and Navy fighter bombers which had been looking for Scud missiles were diverted towards Highway 6, but in bad weather they were unable to find and attack the convoy effectively. They reported back that they been fired on with anti-aircraft guns and shoulder-fired air defence missiles.[7]

Glosson ordered a dozen F-15Es, which could cope with the bad weather, to scramble and attack. He considered this to be a high-risk mission because it had to be improvised. The crews were tired and were being sent off against enemy forces without proper briefing. From 02.00 on 26 February the F-15Es bombed the front of the convoy near the Mutla Pass, a chokepoint on the road to Basra. They then flew south and attacked the rear. The convoy of some 1,000 vehicles was now trapped, with no alternative routes available. Many Iraqis did the sensible thing and fled: others tried to find a way out of the jam. Other retreating Iraqis had been found moving up the eastern highway parallel to Bubiyan island. They too were cut off by Navy jets.

The next morning the weather cleared. Waves of aircraft attacked the hopelessly vulnerable convoy – what had been presented as an orderly retreat was now a disorderly rabble. The convoy included senior officers. It was an attempt to escape with arms and weapons intact, as well as plunder, instead of surrendering. On the other hand, once the attack began they were given no opportunity to surrender. Instead, American aircraft queued in the skies to mount their attacks. Later that evening artillery from the Tiger Brigade of the US Second Armoured Division joined in. Hundreds of vehicles were destroyed and many casualties inflicted. The later descriptions from those involved suggested a blood sport – the Iraqis were like 'rabbits in a sack' or 'fish in a barrel', attacking them was comparable to a 'turkey' or a 'duck shoot' or 'clubbing baby seals'.

In straightforward military terms it was hard to know what the fuss was about. As General McPeak observed two weeks later, the best time to attack the enemy is when he is disorganized and in retreat. The alternative to never attacking a disorganized enemy was to 'wait until he is stopped, dug in, and prepared to receive the attack'. 'It's a tough business,' he continued, but 'our obligation is to our own people, and ... to end the war quickly in the most humane way possible'.[8] Ironically this episode did speed the war's conclusion but in an unexpected manner and largely because of its apparent inhumanity.

The closing whistle

As public attention focused on the diplomatic activity surrounding the question of a cease-fire at the United Nations, Powell, sensitive to the political mood, warned Schwarzkopf of the developing pressures: Schwarzkopf, for his part, warned that he needed more time to finish the job. Powell had always inclined to a minimalist definition of objectives since the start of the crisis. The objectives with which he and his fellow Chiefs-of-Staff had been working were to get the Iraqi Army out of Kuwait and restore the legitimate Government in such a way that Iraq could not launch a repeat performance. No senior figure in the Administration took the contrary view – that the war should be extended to the 'liberation' of Iraq, although that was certainly a practical possibility at that point. In the evening of 26 February (morning in Washington), after the day's events on the Basra Road, Powell discussed with Schwarzkopf the state of the campaign. Aware of its likely effects in Washington, Powell found the reports of the carnage disturbing and warned Schwarzkopf that a cease-fire could now not be far away. Schwarzkopf still wanted more time. If the cease-fire came, at least the two men could report an essentially successful campaign. The Marines were now on the outskirts of Kuwait City, the XVIII Corps were in the valley of the Euphrates and the VII Corps were making rapid progress against the Republican Guard. Powell went to the White House to see President Bush and his inner circle.[9] Sometime within the 'next day or two', he would be able to tell them that their objectives had been attained. Kuwait would be liberated and the Iraqi Army broken as a fighting force.[10]

At issue therefore was the extent of the destruction of the accessible Iraqi forces. The next morning Powell and Schwarzkopf again spoke. According to one report,[11] although Schwarzkopf knew that not all the roads out of Basra had been blocked he did not make this clear. Certainly in the triumphant 'how we did it' press briefing he gave at that time, generally considered to be a *tour de force*, he created a clear impression that the escape routes had been blocked.

Schwarzkopf noted how easy it would have been to get to Baghdad. There was only 150 miles distance and no opposition. 'If it had been our intention to overrun the country, we could have done it unopposed, for all intents and purposes.' This does not appear to have been entirely the case – Saddam had not neglected the potential need to defend Baghdad and had kept divisions in reserve for this task. Because this had not interested coalition intelligence, the extent of the Iraqi preparations was not well known.

The mission Schwarzkopf wished to accomplish was to 'make sure that the Republican Guard is rendered incapable of conducting the type of heinous act that they've conducted so often in the past'. Two Guard divisions with 700 tanks were still being engaged 'with their backs to Euphrates'. The 'gate is closed', he claimed, 'there's no way out'. By this, he explained, he did not want to suggest that nothing was escaping. 'Quite the contrary. What isn't escaping is heavy tanks, what isn't escaping is artillery pieces.' Unarmed Iraqis and civilian vehicles were getting out. There was, he admitted, a substantial Iraqi Army left north of the Tigris–Euphrates valley, but that was 'an infantry army, it's not an armoured army'. By this time, according to his figures, out of 5,880 tanks overall, of which 4,280 had been in the theatre of operations, 3,008 were confirmed destroyed.[12] Including the Republican Guard tanks about to be engaged, that meant that another 2,000 were still to be caught.

One journalist asked if he feared a cease-fire, 'that you will not be able to accomplish your ends, that there will be some political pressure brought on the campaign?' Schwarzkopf answered by stressing that he would have preferred it if the war had never started. 'We've accomplished our mission, and when the decision-makers come to the decision that there should be a cease-fire nobody will be happier than me.'[13]

If this was the message which Powell took to the White House at midday when he went to bring the President and his advisers up to date, then he could tell him that victory could be proclaimed. Kuwait was liberated and the Iraqi Army was breaking and running. When Bush asked if he needed another day, Powell replied that it was not necessary, that this would simply mean fighting stragglers. The prospect of being able to call a halt came as a relief to the civilians present. The morning news was full of the images of the 'highway of death' on the Basra Road. Politically the President had to judge whether the extra advantage to be gained by finishing off the remaining Iraqi units was worth the political costs of the continuing carnage.

There were already the first political calls to hold back. The military was becoming uncomfortable with unnecessary killing and saw little reason to accept additional American deaths. As Richard Haass later observed, using an American football analogy, 'we didn't want to be accused of piling on once the whistle had blown'.[14] If the war ended on a sour note, this could complicate post-war politics. Not all these pressures were yet much in evidence, but at this stage of the crisis the President and his advisers trusted their political antennae.

For all these reasons the President was now inclined to conclude the war. During the meeting Powell spoke to Schwarzkopf and indicated that a cease-fire might be declared soon, although the decision had not yet been taken. Then Schwarzkopf spoke to the President, apparently voicing no objections even though he later indicated that he would have preferred to have 'closed the door' so that no retreating units could escape.[15] Bush decided to end the war at midnight Washington time, 08.00 Saudi time. In symbolic terms this had the advantage of giving the land war exactly 100 hours' duration, and this appealed to Bush. In practical terms it also allowed a few hours of daylight the next morning in the Gulf to assess the situation on the ground.

Just after this, British Foreign Secretary Douglas Hurd arrived for a meeting with Bush. The senior British commander, Peter de la Billière, had already been told by Schwarzkopf of the imminent cease-fire. This caught him and other senior commanders by surprise. It seemed to make little sense when the last remnants of the Republican Guard were close to being caught. He reported back to Downing Street. As the 'loop had not been completely closed', a message was sent to Hurd to find out what was going on. Hurd, on being told that the military operation was essentially complete and that American pilots were becoming unhappy with being part of a 'slaughter', did not press the point. The Saudis too were unhappy but also did not feel able to object.[16]

At 16.00 the American television networks were asked for time that evening, and at 21.00 the announcement came that hostilities would cease in five hours' time.

The final battle

As news of an imminent cease-fire came through, the VII Corps was ordered to push forward as fast as possible to seal off Iraqi forces. Hours before the cease-fire was due to take effect, the 1st Infantry Division caught remnants of the Guard's Medina Division trying to get to Basra. The British had pushed through a number of bits and pieces of Iraqi divisions, although to their frustration they had not taken on the Republican Guard. Instead of attacking them they had been told to move east to cut off the Iraqi line of retreat. They moved to cut off the road to Basra, but by the time they reached it the Iraqis had already been stopped by the air assault.

Meanwhile, at midday on 27 February, the 24th Mechanized Infantry Division had seized Tallil and Jallibah air bases. Some twenty kilometres west of Basra it came across the Republican Guard's al-Faw and Adnan Infantry Divisions, Hammurabi Armoured Division and remnants of the Nebuchadnezzar Infantry Division. Altogether this force was made up of seven tank, five mechanized infantry and thirteen artillery battalions. The attack zone was a huge logistics and ammunition storage site composed of 1,300 bunkers full of munitions. In the ensuing battle, at least six battalions were destroyed and the rest broke and fled.[17] The Nebuchadnezzar Division appears to have escaped over the causeway of the Hawr al-Hammar inland lake.[18]

For the next day, the division was preparing an attack against remaining Iraqi forces. A massive artillery barrage began at 18.00 on the Wednesday evening, which was intended to intensify at 04.00 the next morning in preparation for an airborne attack an hour later. Half an hour before the pre-attack barrage was due to begin, news came of the cease-fire. It was not supposed to come into effect until 08.00, but the attack was aborted so as to avoid further American casualties: the artillery fire continued right up to the cease-fire.

From Basra, Iraqi troops could now flee up the highway alongside the Shatt al-Arab to al-Qurna. Another escape route – the causeway across the Hawr al-Hammar – was scheduled to be cut off by the 101st Airborne but it was left open and some equipment and troops passed through.

The 24th Division's own account shows, two days after the cease-fire, two Iraqi tank brigades to the south-west of Basra, another brigade of 200 trucks and forty armoured vehicles just to the south, and then a further infantry brigade of 200 vehicles on the other side of the Hawr al-Hammar. None of these were engaged. However, on the morning of 1 March there was a report that a battalion of T-72s was moving towards the division's sector. It appeared that remnants of the Hammurabi Armoured Division and elements of other forces were trying to escape to the north. When US troops were fired on as the Iraqis tried to move through the division's defensive sector, that was sufficient excuse. One hundred and eighty-seven enemy armoured vehicles, thirty-four artillery guns, 400 trucks, nine multiple rocket launchers and seven Frog missile systems were destroyed. The enemy soldiers fled on foot back into the 'Basra pocket'.

As Saddam wished to present his withdrawal as a voluntary act, he was initially reluctant to agree a cease-fire meeting, which would confirm the humiliating defeat. He eventually agreed after Moscow convinced him that he had no choice. Then the Iraqis kept on putting off the meeting on the grounds that they were not ready. On 3 March, Schwarzkopf together with General Khalid Ibn Sultan of Saudi Arabia met with Lieutenant-General Sultan Hashim Ahmad al-Jabburi, Iraq's Vice-Chief-of-Staff, accompanied by ten senior officers, at Safwan air base to agree a cease-fire. The British, French and other Arab commanders were there as observers. At the same time Security Council Resolution 686 set out the terms that Iraq had to agree before a formal cease-fire would be agreed. The main priorities were the immediate release of the 200 or so allied prisoners, return of goods taken from Kuwait and abducted Kuwaiti citizens, and help with the clearance of mines and booby traps. Most of the time the Iraqis listened in silence as General Schwarzkopf described the terms. They had yet to appreciate the extent of their defeat. Al-Jabburi appeared stunned when told that the allies had taken 58,000 prisoners and were still counting, and stunned again when he realized that the the US advance was well behind his lines.[19] They did have one request. The allies would not allow them to fly aircraft but could they use helicopters? With the roads shelled and bridges bombed there were no other forms of transport. Schwarzkopf agreed.

The reckoning

After the war US intelligence agencies conducted an intensive investigation of the battlefield and southern Iraq. Evidence obtained later suggests that the number of Iraqi tanks had been underestimated in the first place by about 270. This meant that while CENTCOM might have reasonably expected, especially after the additional battle of 2 March, to have destroyed all but about 400 of the Iraqi tanks, in fact around 700 remained. The initial estimate of armoured personnel carriers had been accurate but the reports of destruction had been exaggerated, so almost half the original total survived. The pre-war total of artillery had also been exaggerated. However, here the damage inflicted had been far greater than anticipated – barely 10 per cent of the pre-war total survived the war.[20]

In just over 100 hours, coalition forces captured over 73,700 square kilometres of territory. Fifteen per cent of Iraq was under coalition control. The Iraqi Army which had been in occupation had been effectively cut to pieces. No more than seven of the original forty-three Iraqi divisions were capable of operations. Coalition casualties were remarkably low – almost as much damage had been done by 'friendly fire' as by Iraqi fire. Almost a quarter of the American deaths and more than half the British had come in this form.[21] Another 138 were killed and 2,978 injured outside of battle, largely during the preceding months of Desert Shield. Nonetheless, after all the gloomy predictions of thousands of casualties, the total was remarkably small.

On the Iraqi side, calculations of casualties were impossible. CENTCOM had explicitly ruled out any of the 'body counts' which had been both a distasteful and wholly misleading feature of the Vietnam campaign. When pressed, a figure of 100,000 was plucked out of the air, with a margin of error of 50 per cent, but that was based largely on the fact that, compared to the projected numbers of Iraqi soldiers in the theatre, only a relatively small proportion had been accounted for as prisoners (64,000 were taken by the US, 17,000 by the Arab forces and 5,000 by the British). A year later revised estimates were as low as 10,000, largely because the evidence of mass death was slight and the numbers of Iraqi troops in the theatre had been dramatically reduced.

The Iraqis gave only one estimate, of 20,000 killed (of which about 1,000 then were civilians) and 60,000 wounded after twenty-six days of the air war. There is no reason to doubt this. Interrogation of prisoners revealed that in some units desertions exceeded casualties by ten to one, while casualties as a result of the bombing varied between 100 and 400 per division, which suggests another 4,000 dead. It is probable that at most another 10,000 died during the land war, making up to 35,000 in total, though this is based largely on circumstantial evidence. Despite the horrific images, most of the vehicles on the 'highway of death' were empty, and though there were other such highways the total casualties in these attacks were probably measured in hundreds rather than thousands.[22] There were no mass graves or large numbers of bodies. One report suggests that the Saudis buried 5,000 Iraqis.[23] However, the US said in late March that 444 Iraqi soldiers had been buried at fifty-five sites. The number reached 577 in June. Reporters asking around Iraqi villages found little evidence of a massive loss of young men, and the Iraqi health service was not inundated with dead and wounded.[24]

The battle had been one-sided and the victory complete. It was later judged to have been flawed by a final misjudgement of timing, by which Saddam's forces were allowed to escape before their route had been blocked. The problem of timing was in fact more fundamental. The envelopment of the Iraqi forces had been fast, but not so fast as the Marine-led drive on Kuwait City or Saddam's recognition that the game was up. If the Iraqis had resisted for longer then they would have been trapped. Instead they made a run for it and could only be stopped by methods which Washington found uncomfortable.

Table 15: Damage to Iraqi equipment

	ESTIMATE	PRE-WAR	DESTROYED OR CAPTURED	REMAINING
TANKS	War end	4,280	3,700	580
	Post-war	4,550	3,847	703
APCs	War end	2,870	1,856	1,014
	Post-war	2,880	1,450	1,430
ARTILLERY	War end	3,110	2,140	970
	Post-war	3,257	2,917	340

Sources: *New York Times*, 26 March 1991. Post-war figures are from US intelligence agencies; end of war figures (28 February 1991) from CENTCOM. *Final Pentagon Report*, p. 411.

Table 16: Coalition casualties

	US	COALITION	TOTAL
PEAK STRENGTH	541,000	254,000	795,000
KILLED IN ACTION	148	92	240
WOUNDED IN ACTION	458	318	776

CHAPTER 30
Saddam Survives

It had not quite been the 'mother of all battles' that Saddam had intended. Rather than flooding the West with thousands of body bags, he watched his army suffer a humiliating defeat while his country's economic and strategic infrastructure was systematically undone. As alarming, the formidable wall of fear with which he had so laboriously surrounded his subjects seemed to be crumbling under nationwide despair and frustration with his latest, ill-conceived adventure. When the cease-fire came, not a moment too soon, Saddam told his subjects that the cessation of hostilities was the result of their glorious stand against 'world imperialism':

> O Iraqis, you triumphed when you stood with all this vigour against the armies of thirty countries ... You have succeeded in demolishing the aura of the United States, the empire of evil, terror, and aggression ... The Guards have broken the backbone of their aggressors and thrown them beyond their borders. We are confident that President Bush would have never accepted a ceasefire had he not been informed by his military leaders of the need to preserve the forces fleeing the fist of the heroic men of the Republican Guard.[1]

Such rhetoric could not hide the magnitude of the defeat. Iraqis took matters into their own hands and, for the first time in Iraq's modern history, rose in strength against their unelected ruler. First to erupt was the southern city of Basra. The rebellion spread quickly to engulf the predominantly Shi'ite southern Iraq, including the holy cities of Najaf and Karbala. Many towns fell to the rebels, numerous armoured vehicles were reportedly destroyed, and some Republican Guard units were said to have surrendered. Fighting then moved to some Sunni cities and even reached Baghdad, where widespread clashes with the security forces and numerous 'hit and run' incidents were recorded.[2]

Before long the rebellion spread to the north. Swept by euphoric expectations of Saddam's demise, the Kurds decided to take their chance and assert their long-sought national rights. Their hopes were boosted by contacts with the US Administration which, to the Kurds' understanding, indicated a commitment to the removal of Saddam and to the protection of the Kurds against the central regime.[3] Consequently, in the early days of March, Kurdistan was also in flames. Within a fortnight the Kurdish leadership claimed to have liberated 95 per cent of Kurdistan and invited the various factions of the Iraqi opposition to set up a provisional government there. Although this invitation was not acted upon, some 300 delegates from twenty-three exiled opposition groups met in Beirut on 10 March, in an unprecedented attempt to co-ordinate a joint strategy against Saddam.

These were undoubtedly the most difficult moments in Saddam's long and violent career. He had encountered stark challenges to his personal rule before, but never such a devastating combination of international indignity and domestic chaos. Fortunately for him, not only did the Administration fail to provide military support for the Shi'ite and Kurdish uprisings, but the Western noose around Iraq seemed to loosen. The rebels were surprised. They had been encouraged by statements by coalition leaders urging the overthrow of Saddam by his own people, but they had failed to read the small print: the coalition was under no obligation to help.

Saddam's problem and the problem of Saddam

From the start of the war the coalition had used a twin formula to describe its attitude towards Saddam Hussein: it would not move directly against him but would be delighted if Iraqis did so. Thus Douglas Hurd told the House of Commons on the eve of the war: '. . . there is no hidden agenda. There is no intention to dismember Iraq. There is no intention to impose on Iraq a Government or President of our choice.' But then, not long after war began, John Major observed:

> I very strongly suspect that he may yet become a target of his own people ... It is perfectly clear that this man is amoral. He takes hostages. He attacks population centres. He threatens prisoners. He is a man without pity and, whatever his fate may be, I, for one, will not weep for him.[4]

George Bush used the same formula.

As the war progressed there were occasional hints about going further, often through stress on the need to 'restore peace and security', stipulated by the UN resolutions, which could be argued to give the coalition considerable latitude. Yet this phrase was generally considered to refer to removing Iraq's capacity to project military power, and especially weapons of mass destruction, beyond its borders, along with a drive for peaceful settlements of other regional disputes, rather than to the removal of the person whose past policies had so threatened regional peace and security. Particularly strong opposition to such an interpretation came from China and the Soviet Union, both of which had long championed the principle of non-interference in internal affairs, as they believed that it helped protect them from Western attempts to change their political structure.

Throughout the conflict the political pressure was to keep the war aims restricted. Thus the *New York Times* editorialized that wider objectives would mean higher casualties and grave political risks. Saddam's martyrdom could fuel regional unrest, while a weakened Iraq would be prey to separatists and neighbours. 'If Mr Bush is waging war in the Gulf for the sake of regional stability, then the most sensible war aims are limited ones.'[5] The only issue that almost led to a change in policy was the treatment of coalition prisoners of war, which raised again the question of putting Saddam on trial for war crimes. The White House said that Saddam would be held 'accountable', but this issue passed as the Iraqis apparently relented in their 'human shields' policy.

Public opinion was less restrained. In Britain a poll on the eve of the land war showed only 27 per cent wanting to march all the way to Baghdad. However, nine out of ten thought that Saddam should be brought to trial, with 70 per cent favouring assassination![6] In the United States it was reported that 71 per cent of the American people believed that the toppling of Saddam should be an allied goal, while only 29 per cent of respondents in a *Newsweek* survey believed that an Iraqi withdrawal with Saddam still in power would constitute a coalition victory.[7]

The Administration's rhetoric if not its policy had supported this assumption. George Bush spoke of a 'war against Saddam'. James Baker said that restoring peace and stability would 'be a heck of a lot easier if he and that leadership were not in power in Iraq'.[8] The most notable statement by Bush was the one made on 15 February, after the conditional offer of that day to abide by Resolution 660, in which he invited the Iraqi people to 'take matters into their own hands, to force Saddam Hussein the dictator to step aside'. This was widely interpreted as revealing the true Bush 'agenda' for the war. Precisely for that reason, the Administration took steps to confirm that its policy had not changed. On 20 February, the White House Deputy Press Secretary, Roman Popadiuk, insisted that 'We have never targeted or made Saddam Hussein an object of that mandate or this conflict.' He added: 'We support the territorial integrity of Iraq. We are not in this war to destroy

Iraq.' State Department spokesperson Margaret Tutwiler denied that 'the coalition has broadened or expanded or enlarged their goals', noting that the removal of Saddam Hussein from office or his trial for war crimes, 'was not part of a UN resolution'.[9]

The Administration wanted to see the back of Saddam but it was not prepared to do the deed itself. Even in the last days of the war, the arguments against making the removal of Saddam a war aim remained compelling: Bush's new world order did not require the restructuring of the Iraqi political system (or, for that matter, of any other domestic system), but was related to the international 'rules of the game'. This was a crisis about Iraq's violation of Kuwait and ability to violate again in the future, not about Saddam's repression of his own people. The overthrow of Saddam was not within the United Nations' mandate: nor did it accord with the preferences of other members of the coalition.

If Saddam happened to be caught in a command bunker then that would be fine, but there was a determination by civilian and military leaders alike not to be tempted into a trip to Baghdad to seize him. In the face of serious resistance the superior firepower of the coalition would not have been as much help in the city as it had been in the desert. Taking Baghdad could have led to a political quagmire in that any imposed replacement for Saddam could well have been perceived by Iraqis as yet another brutal interference by 'Western imperialism' in their domestic affairs. The Noriega experience warned against chasing Saddam Hussein himself around Baghdad. Others recalled the Korean War, when United Nations Forces under American command had not been satisfied with pushing back Communist North Korea to the 38th Parallel but had sought to liberate the North and pressed on to the border with China at the Yalu river, thereby provoking a disastrous Chinese entry into the war.

The non-interventionist rationale was summed up by Richard Cheney:

> If we'd gone to Baghdad and got rid of Saddam Hussein – assuming we could have found him – we'd have had to put a lot of forces in and run him to ground some place. He would not have been easy to capture. Then you've got to put a new government in his place and then you're faced with the question of what kind of government are you going to establish in Iraq? Is it going to be a Kurdish government or a Shia government or a Sunni government? How many forces are you going to have to leave there to keep it propped up, how many casualties are you going to take through the course of this operation?[10]

At any rate, it was hard to believe that Saddam could survive such a

413

battering and such a humiliation or that he would be much of a threat if he did. As the former US Assistant Secretary of State for Near Eastern Affairs, Richard Murphy, argued:

> If he survives, and is defanged, so what, why worry about it? He can make all the speeches he wants. A weakened Saddam with a weakened army and a weakened political reputation is maybe better for us if he is in power than if he is martyred. I don't think we want to get anywhere near Baghdad.[11]

Actively working towards the fragmentation of Iraq could cause more problems than it solved. It was a problem that those rising against Saddam were the least committed to the integrity of the Iraqi state. The Administration was apprehensive that a complete collapse of central authority in Baghdad would result in the country fragmenting, with the ensuing chaos sucking in Iraq's neighbours. There was, as Bush observed in January, something of a dilemma: 'We don't want to see a destabilized Iraq when this is all over. But we also don't want to see a continuation of this aggression. So we have a mix of problems.'[12] Ever since the Iranian revolution of 1979 and the ensuing 'hostage crisis' Shi'ites have been associated in American consciousness with avowed anti-Westernism and unbridled fanaticism. The spectre of a Shi'ite takeover in Baghdad was, therefore, anathema to American political thinking. There was a lack of appreciation of the socio-political diversity of the Shi'ite community and of the wide divide between Iranian and Iraqi Shi'ites (who had just fought each other ferociously for eight years). Little attention was paid to the hopes of the Kurds or the promises of the Shi'ites that they were grateful to the United States for weakening Saddam and that 'an Islamic government in Baghdad does not necessarily have to be similar to the Iranian system',[13] and more to Saudi concerns over the wider implications of a Shi'ite advance.

The Gulf monarchies, fearful of Iranian-supported radical Islamic movements, were loath to see Iran's influence enhanced by the rise of a Shi'ite regime in Baghdad.[14] The Governments in Ankara and Tehran were nervous about any notion of an independent Kurdish state, which, they feared, could fuel Kurdish separatism in their own countries. Only Syria continued to voice support for Saddam's removal and to extend significant support to the Kurdish (and to a lesser extent Shi'ite) struggle, but it was fighting a hopeless rearguard action.[15] Even the Israelis could see advantage in Saddam staying in power. With a new Iraqi dictator it might soon be 'business as usual' when it came to arms supplies. So long as Saddam was in power, Iraq would be isolated and excluded from regional power plays.

The Administration believed that only a firm hand could safely run Iraq's complex and volatile political system – someone like Saddam if not Saddam himself. This view ignored the extent that Saddam's 'firm hand', rather than acting as a unifying force behind the Iraqi state, had brought Iraq to the verge of disintegration. This had been apparent in the early 1970s at the time of a general uprising in Kurdistan and an extensive Iranian military intervention, in the 1980s taken up by a futile war against Iran, and yet again in his ill-conceived Kuwaiti adventure in the summer of 1990. In between these catastrophes, he had managed to alienate the Shi'ites and the Kurds, who together constituted some 80 per cent of the Iraqi population, from the Sunni community and the ruling Ba'th Party.

This mixture of concerns created a preference in the coalition for some public-spirited General changing his Government in the traditional Iraqi manner, with Saddam suffering the normal fate – a 'conventional' *coup d'état* rather than a popular revolution, an inside job, which required no outside support. Such expectations were not out of line with the general course of twentieth-century Iraqi history: all changes of regime in Baghdad, including the 1958 'revolution' which overthrew the monarchy and the Ba'th rise to power a decade later, had been effected by armed groups of sorts, with the Iraqi people acting as normally passive and rarely enthusiastic spectators.

There was an evident incentive for the Iraqi élite. The coalition indicated that it would be happy to deal with any Iraqi government, no matter how dismal the records of its individual members, so long as Saddam was not a member. The coalition had made it clear during the war that sanctions would continue after the fighting stopped, to ensure Iraqi compliance over outstanding issues such as compensation for Iraq's victims and the destruction of Iraq's chemical and nuclear weapons programmes. The compensation issue raised awkward memories of post-First World War reparations to the victorious powers and the role of the consequent economic burden in the collapse of the Weimar Republic. The coalition was aware of the dangers of imposing what would be a bitterly resented lifetime economic sentence on Iraq. So how seriously compensation claims were pressed would depend on whether Saddam stayed in power. The carrot for a prospective successor was sympathy when it came to the reconstruction of Iraq. Douglas Hurd made the link explicit:

> Iraq cannot be expected to be readmitted to the community of nations while it has a delinquent regime. Iraq needs leadership which will respect her commitments as a member of the United Nations and the Arab League.[16]

This strategy was controversial. Javier Perez de Cuellar openly argued against this rationale for sanctions: 'As Secretary-General, I cannot agree with measures that are aimed at overthrowing the government of a country which is a member of the United Nations . . . If the objective of pursuing sanctions is to topple the Iraqi regime, then I do not agree. I cannot agree.'[17] Indeed, he supported a resolution presented to the Security Council on 4 March by Yemen, Cuba, Ecuador, India and Zimbabwe, calling for the easing of sanctions relating to humanitarian goods. Unwilling to oppose such a measure but equally reluctant to relinquish the diplomatic initiative, the coalition agreed to speed food and relief supplies into Iraq in return for the withdrawal of the resolution. This kept the relaxation of sanctions under the control of the Sanctions Committee.

Following the publication of a report describing the gravity of the situation facing Iraqi women and children, the Sanctions Committee eased restrictions on humanitarian supplies. The Ahtisaari report on humanitarian needs in Kuwait and Iraq, completed on 20 March, concluded dramatically that:

> The recent conflict has wrought near-apocalyptic results upon the economic infrastructure of what had been, until January 1991, a rather highly urbanized and mechanized society. Now most means of modern life support have been destroyed or rendered tenuous. Iraq has, for some time to come, been relegated to a pre-industrial age, but with all the disabilities of post-industrial dependency on an intensive use of energy and technology.[18]

Despite this resistance, the Americans, British and French pushed through the 'mother of resolutions' – Resolution 687, passed by the Security Council on 3 April 1991 – which was the longest in the organization's history. It placed key aspects of Iraq's internal affairs under close supervision. In addition to having to accept the inviolability of the boundary with Kuwait, to be demarcated by an international commission, and UN peace-keepers on the border, it was to present the United Nations with full disclosure of all its chemical and biological weapons and facilities, its ballistic missiles stocks and production capabilities (over 150 kilometres range) and all nuclear materials, and then co-operate in their destruction. It was also to facilitate the return of all Kuwaiti property and agree to compensation to those foreign nationals and companies which had suffered as a result of the occupation of Kuwait. All sanctions remained in place for anything other than 'medicines and health supplies'. They were to be reviewed every sixty days, and Iraqi compliance with UN resolutions would be considered a key element of any decision to reduce or lift sanctions. No oil could be sold.[19]

So there was a strategy for dealing with Saddam, based on giving the Iraqi political élite every incentive to end his rule. Its success depended on the actions of people who had been only dimly identified. Those in a position to topple Saddam also tended to have a stake in the regime. The President had made sure that responsibility for his crimes was widely spread. He was also a pastmaster at identifying conspiracies well before they could make progress. Moreover, as the regime was dominated by Sunnis there was anxiety over the implications of a Shi'ite victory. A series of considerations of personal safety could well outweigh considerations of national interest.

Nonetheless, as the war drew to a close, few saw this strategy as controversial or even problematic. In March 1991 Bush was given an intelligence estimate predicting that Saddam would be out of office within a year, although even then there was some dissent by those who remained impressed by his control of both the military establishment and the Ba'th Party. The same message, however, also came from the Arab members of the coalition, who did not believe that Saddam could long survive the post-war turmoil in Iraq.

Saddam survives

The strategy was knocked off course by the revolution in Iraq. George Bush saw it as symptomatic of Saddam's vulnerability. 'With this much turmoil it seems to me that Saddam cannot survive ... people are fed up with him. They see him for the brutal dictator he is.'[20] However, unlike the sanctions-based strategy of economic carrots and sticks to encourage a transfer of power at the top, he had no strategy for dealing with an insurrection from below. Even if he had been comfortable with its implications for the shape of Iraq, any involvement meant unacceptable risks. From the start the White House was cautious in its response. 'We don't intend to get involved in Iraq's internal affairs,' said White House spokesman Marlin Fitzwater. 'We have these reports of fighting in Basra and other cities but it is not clear to us what the purpose or extent of the fighting is.'[21]

In forging a domestic consensus to support the action against Iraq, Bush had promised a strategy that would minimize American casualties and the risk of becoming entangled in a Vietnam-style quagmire. He had no intention of allowing his shining victory to be dimmed by a side-step into the treacherous marsh of Iraq's domestic politics and by risking a prolonged and embarrassing entanglement; rather, he sought to conclude the entire episode on a high note by returning US troops home as soon as possible.

The comprehensive nature of Iraq's military defeat, and the presumption

of his imminent downfall, in an ironic way helped Saddam. Had he succeeded in carrying out his threats and exacted an exorbitant human toll from
the coalition, he would have aroused its wrath to such an extent that his
position would have been made untenable. Since by its conclusion the war
had come to be seen in the West as a one-sided slaughter of hapless Iraqis,
the demonic aura that had surrounded Saddam during the crisis drained
away. Overnight he was reduced from being the 'most dangerous man in the
world' to a pathetic figure, a typical brutal Third World dictator struggling
for his personal and political survival. Since he no longer threatened Western lives or vital interests in any meaningful way, international interest in his
personal fortunes subsided as swiftly as it had risen following the occupation
of Kuwait. Having anxiously followed his every word and move for seven
tense months, there was immediate relief at the actual outcome of the crisis.
Attention was soon redirected back to Europe and the chronic situation of
the Soviet Union.

This combination of Saddam's deflated image and a reluctance to become
involved in a civil war gave him his opportunity. He needed coalition forces
to remain on the sidelines while he dealt with the insurrection. To remove
the military presence on Iraqi soil, he went out of his way to placate the allies
and to avoid any provocation that could lead to the renewal of hostilities.
Once he realized the severity of the internal challenge, he did not even
attempt to prevaricate with the United Nations as he had done so often in the
past. In a letter on 3 March to the President of the Security Council and to
the UN Secretary-General, Foreign Minister Aziz expressed Baghdad's
readiness to abide by Security Council Resolution 686, passed a day earlier,
which called *inter alia* for Iraq's renunciation of its annexation of Kuwait, its
acceptance in principle of legal liability for any loss, damage or injury caused
as a result of the occupation of Kuwait, the return of plundered Kuwaiti
assets and the release of captured civilians and prisoners of war.[22] Two days
later the Revolutionary Command Council issued an official decision rescin-
ding the annexation of Kuwait and all 'laws, decisions, regulations, instructions, directives and measures' issued in relation to Kuwait since 2 August
1990. This decision was accompanied by yet another letter from Aziz to the
UN on Iraq's decision to return immediately all the Kuwaiti assets seized
after 2 August, including 'quantities of gold, quantities of Kuwaiti bank-
notes, the museum's stocks, and civilian aircraft'.[23] He had little choice but
to go along with Resolution 687, although implementation soon came to be
directly related to his calculations of domestic vulnerability and the readiness
of the coalition to resort to armed force once again to ensure compliance.

For the moment his main concern was to keep the coalition off his back while he worked to reduce the threats to his personal rule. First he consolidated his inner circle. His deputy and brother-in-law, Izzat Ibrahim, was made Deputy Commander-in-Chief of the Armed Forces and sent to the south to supervise the suppression of the uprising there. Saddam's favourite son-in-law, Hussein Kamil Hassan al-Majid, was appointed Minister of Defence instead of Lieutenant-General Sa'di Tumah Abbas, who was made military adviser to the President. His ruthless henchman, Taha Yasin Ramadan, was made Deputy President. As a gesture of goodwill towards the Shi'ites and an indication of his intention to democratize the Iraqi political system, Saddam reshuffled his Cabinet. He gave up the premiership, in itself an exceptional act illustrating the depth of his plight, and promoted his longtime close associate, Sa'dun Hammadi – a Shi'ite – to this prominent role.[24]

To ensure the loyalty of the various security organs and to boost their shattered morale, Saddam announced a pay rise across the board. Members of the Republican Guard received a monthly increment of 100 dinars, while the rest of the armed forces and members of the security services received an increase of 50 dinars a month. Compulsory military service conscripts and reservists were awarded the more modest sum of 25 dinars. Those whose loyalty, in Saddam's perception, could not be bought were purged and some of them executed. During the three months after the war no fewer than fourteen senior commanders were removed, including the Head of Military Intelligence, Major General Wafiq Jasim al-Samarra'i, and the Chief-of-Staff Lieutenant-General Hussein Rashid, who was replaced by the commander of the Republican Guard, Lieutenant-General Iyad Khalifa al-Rawi. Last but not least, Ali Hassan al-Majid, Saddam's paternal cousin, was appointed Minister of Interior. Given his atrocious record, both as the gasser of the Kurds during 1987 and 1988 and as the brutal governor of Kuwait, Majid's nomination sent an unmistakable signal to the opposition of Saddam's grim determination to suppress the uprising at all costs.

It was not long before the Republican Guard was unleashed on the rebellion in the south. Eager to redeem themselves from the disgrace of the Gulf War, the Guard plunged into their new task with a degree of brutality that was exceptional even by the exacting standards of the regime. The holy cities of Najaf and Karbala were given a particularly harsh treatment. Thousands of clerics were arrested and hundreds were summarily executed. Any turbaned or bearded man who took to the street ran the risk of being rounded up, or even executed. People were tied to tanks and used as 'human shields' while women and children were indiscriminately shot. Western correspondents, taken later by the Iraqi authorities to see the 'liberated' Karbala, found the city 'as if it had been shaken by a powerful earthquake, with few schools, government buildings, private homes or clinics left intact'.[25]

By mid-March Saddam felt sufficiently confident to make his first televised address since the end of the war and to announce the suppression of the 'odious sedition' in southern Iraq. Then, in a warning that sent chills down the spines of those remembering the Iraqi atrocities in Kurdistan at the latter stage of the Iran–Iraq War, he called upon the Kurds to desist from their armed struggle. 'Those who are now carrying out division in the north,' he threatened,

> should remember that [similar acts in the past] brought only loss and destruction to our Kurdish people. If they persist in this game, their fate, God willing, will inevitably be the same as the fate of those who came before them.[26]

By now the Administration was starting to take notice. It warned that the use of helicopters violated the spirit if not the letter of the cease-fire agreement, but officials remained ambiguous when asked if they intended to do anything by way of response.[27] On 20 and 22 March two aircraft were shot down, as they were not allowed to fly at all under the cease-fire agreement. There was even some movement back of US heavy armour into southern Iraq to put pressure on Saddam. Colin Powell was quoted as warning Saddam 'to be a little careful how he goes about suppressing the various insurrections that are taking place'.[28] Yet on 26 March the Administration decided not to intervene in support of the rebels and this was made clear. At a meeting that day Powell made the case against attempting to down the helicopters on the grounds that this would be no more than 'empty symbolism', given the other firepower at Saddam's disposal. Because the helicopters were operating in the north well away from US forces it would have been potentially hazardous to send aircraft after them. The United States 'could almost get inexorably drawn into a mighty mess just defending yourself', Powell warned. Only Dan Quayle appears to have queried whether there was a moral obligation to the Kurds. Concerns about the fragmentation of Iraq and the rise of the Shi'ites had come to the fore and overrode other considerations.[29] Two days later a major offensive on Kurdish positions began. Soon Kurdistan's major cities fell to Government forces and thousands of fearful Kurds began fleeing to the mountains in a desperate attempt to escape the advancing Iraqi army.

In early April nearly 1 million refugees were concentrated along the Iranian and Turkish borders, and by the end of the month their number had exceeded 2 million. As allied forces were poised to leave the Middle East, having resolved the Kuwait problem, a new human tragedy on a grand scale was rapidly unfolding in this war-torn region.

Safe havens

Thus while the final touches were still being put to the 'mother of all resolutions', which represented the centrepiece of the coalition's solution to the 'Saddam problem', there was a vivid demonstration of his ruthlessness towards his own subjects. The merciless campaign against the Kurds aroused international indignation, strongly influenced by dramatic media coverage. As a result of the war, news organizations were still well represented in the area. Large numbers of Western reporters and television crews were soon in Kurdistan, relaying live from the Turkish–Iraqi border heart-rending scenes of refugees freezing and starving to death in the snowy mountains of Kurdistan at a reported rate of 1,000 people a day. [30]

Suddenly the Bush Administration found itself on the defensive, facing accusations of irresponsibility. Bush responded angrily:

> Do I think that the United States should bear guilt because of suggesting that the Iraqi people take matters into their own hands, with the implication being given that the United States would be there to support them militarily? That was not true. We never implied that.[31]

Yet, at the same time, Brent Scowcroft admitted that 'we did not expect the severity of the attacks on the Kurds'.[32]

The refugee problem was aggravated by the reluctance of the Turkish Government to accept a substantial influx. The refugees were prevented from penetrating into the countryside, and so were left exposed on the mountains. The sense that, once again, the Kurds had been left to their fate when they might have had good reason to expect material support touched the international conscience. On 5 April the UN Security Council passed a special resolution on the Kurdish issue – Resolution 688. The resolution condemned 'the repression of the Iraqi civilian population in many parts of Iraq, including most recently in Kurdish populated areas', and laid the ground for foreign interference in Iraqi domestic affairs by defining the activities of the regime as 'threatening international peace and security in the region' and calling upon Baghdad 'to allow immediate access by international humanitarian organizations to all those in need of assistance in all parts of Iraq.'[33]

Within days, a concentrated international effort, code-named Operation Provide Comfort, was in place, with transport aircraft and helicopters delivering large quantities of relief materials including food, clothes, tents, and blankets. But the mountain areas where the refugees to Turkey had gathered had poor roads which, in turn, had been rendered virtually impass-able by mud and rain. The large crates in which the aid was parachuted proved a risk to the refugees, some of whom were killed when they were unable to avoid them due to overcrowded conditions, ankle-deep mud and the speed of the crates' descent. The problem on the Iranian border was if anything worse. Iran already had more refugees than any other country in the world. The nearly 1 million Iraqi Kurds who arrived in 1991 were joining some 600,000 still in the country following past expulsions, as well as nearly 2.2 million Afghans who had sought refuge following the 1979 Soviet invasion of Afghanistan. Unlike Turkey, Iran did not prevent the new refugees from entering the country. However, delays at the border to enable Iranian soldiers to search the fleeing Kurds resulted in mounting numbers of deaths. As a result, before they were gradually moved into camps there were lines of Kurds stretching back fifty to eighty kilometres from the Iranian border. The West did not go out of its way to help the Iranians. Even though Tehran's role during the war was generally helpful to the coalition, and although the Americans and British were hopeful of Iranian help in the release of their hostages in Lebanon, they remained wary of the revolu-tionary regime.

The logic of the longer-term response to the refugee crisis was largely dictated by Turkey. It wanted the Kurds off Turkish soil as soon as possible – but *not* into a separate Kurdish state. The only alternative was some guarantee of safety for the Kurds within Iraqi borders, as President Ozal quickly pointed out. 'We have to get [the Kurds] better land under UN control,' he said on 7 April, 'and to put those people in the Iraqi territory and take care of them.'[34] Reviewing the relief operation in south-east Turkey, James Baker expressed sympathy for the 'suffering and desperation of the Iraqi people', saying that 'these people must be free from the threats, persecution and harassment that they have been subjected to by that brutal regime in Baghdad'. But at the same time he insisted that the United States would not 'go down the slippery slope of being sucked into a civil war'. The best that was offered the Kurds was that Saddam would recognize that economic sanctions would be sustained so long as he continued to repress his own people.[35]

In addition to the reluctance to make a long-term commitment to Kurdish security, there were also legal considerations. There was no dispute that humanitarian intervention on behalf of the Kurds would be morally correct; at the same time it appeared to contradict the sanctity of national borders, a principle over which the coalition had just fought a ferocious war. However brutal, the Iraqi Government was still the legal authority in Iraq, and the setting of international relief centres on Iraqi soil without its consent would constitute an 'interference in the internal affairs' of a sovereign country.

Public opinion turned out to be overriding. The French were the first to suggest that something should be done, but John Major came forward with the first concrete suggestion at a special summit of the heads of the European Community in Luxembourg on 8 April. He had been prompted by his predecessor, Margaret Thatcher, who had observed that, whatever 'the legal niceties', the Kurds needed 'not talk, but practical action'. Major developed his plan rapidly. It called for the creation of 'safe havens' for the Kurds in northern Iraq that would allow the refugees to return safely to their places of residence. The havens were envisaged to cover vast areas inside Iraq, including the key oil city of Kirkuk, and to be put under UN protection. Sanctions were to remain in place as long as Saddam continued to brutalize his own people. If Iraq violated the sanctuary of the havens, it could face international retaliation in accordance with UN Resolutions 687 (on the Gulf cease-fire) and 688.[36]

The Luxembourg summit had been called at the instigation of France to discuss what had been generally felt to be a weak Community performance during the Gulf War. Rather than get bogged down in an acrimonious post-mortem, Community leaders were relieved to be able to take an initiative in an area where the United States was dithering. President Mitterrand, apparently pleased with the lack of prior co-ordination with the United States, was exceptionally warm to the plan and praised it as 'a major advance for the political dimension of the community'. In addition to endorsing Britain's safe haven plan, the Community leaders pledged refugee aid of $185 million. As one European official remarked at the time: 'The Kurds saved the summit so we must save the Kurds.'[37]

The British Government had used this forum out of concern that the US was acting too slowly. Major and Bush spoke on Thursday 4 April on the passage of Resolution 688, but they reportedly did not discuss the safe haven concept. On the day of the summit, Douglas Hurd spoke to James Baker, but Baker, while personally concerned, could not deviate from the US policy of non-interference in internal Iraqi affairs. Though obviously irritated at not being consulted beforehand, the US Administration did not dismiss the British plan though they damned it with faint praise – it had 'some merits . . . at least worthy of consideration'. Yet even though Congressional pressure was building up,[38] President Bush would not rush. In a speech on 13 April, he still insisted that he 'did not want one single soldier or airman shoved into a civil war in Iraq that has been going on for ages'. There was, however, an increasing stress on not tolerating 'any interference in this massive international relief effort'.[39] Three days later, there was an abrupt about-turn, and the 'safe havens' concept was effectively embraced. On 16 April, Bush announced that, as part of 'a greatly expanded and more ambitious relief effort',

> I have directed the US military to begin immediately to establish several encampments in northern Iraq where relief supplies for these refugees will be made available in large quantities and distributed in an orderly manner.

Bush went out of his way to convince the American public that the 'safe havens' idea was fully commensurate with the existing US policy in the Gulf:

> All along, I have said that the United States is not going to intervene militarily in Iraq's internal affairs and risk being drawn into a Vietnam-style quagmire. This remains the case.

He promised that 'the administration of and security for these sites' would be turned over to the United Nations as soon as possible.[40]

Bush's anxiety to pre-empt criticism and to underscore the consistency of his Gulf policy was also evident by the rush of some Washington officials to claim parenthood for the safe haven plan. 'This is the United States' proposal,' argued White House spokesman Marlin Fitzwater, 'and President Bush presented it to the coalition in the last few days.'[41] Although this claim hardly conformed to reality, as the irritated British press pointed out, the Americans moved quickly and were soon co-ordinating with allies a joint policy on the safe havens. Soon some 5,000 American troops were deployed in northern Iraq, together with 2,000 British, 1,000 French and a small Dutch force.[42]

Not only had the persecution of the Kurds led to Western involvement in Iraq but it also put the 'Saddam problem' back on the agenda. European Foreign Ministers, at the prompting of German Foreign Minister Hans-Dietrich Genscher, judged Saddam 'guilty of genocide and war crimes' and proposed that he be called personally to account for crimes against Kurds as well as the invasions of Iran and Kuwait. Furthermore, Resolution 674 invited states 'to collate substantiated information in their possession or submitted to them on the grave breaches by Iraq ... and to make this information available to the Security Council', and such information was now available.

The key coalition members were not enthusiastic. France could not see how a prosecution could be brought, while the British wanted to pass the whole matter to the UN. The Americans meanwhile said that they were looking to Kuwait and other Arab countries for leadership on this issue, and admitted that it was 'not something that we have been actively moving on'.[43] There were the familiar problems with the idea: who would take the lead, where would the trial take place and under whose jurisdiction, not to mention the small matter of apprehending the criminal. If ideas about a Second Chamber of the International Court at the Hague to try states and individuals for breaches of international criminal law had been implemented, then a trial would be less problematic.[44] Most immediately, the UN Secretary-General saw it as a complication to his organization's efforts to get involved in assistance to the Kurds. He 'respected' the EC initiative and deemed it worthy of 'much study and reflection'. For the moment, however, 'I would like nothing to be done which would prejudice the humanitarian action to which we, the United Nations, are totally committed.'[45]

Still the 'Saddam problem'

Inevitably there were recriminations. Because so many people assumed, from the body language if not from the official statements, that the objective of the war was to remove Saddam, his continued presence served as a standing rebuke. The claim by Schwarzkopf that Washington had led him to end the war prematurely, and his complaint that he had been 'suckered' by the Iraqis at the first cease-fire talks at Safwan when he was persuaded to allow the use of helicopters, encouraged the view that this was responsible for Saddam's survival.

At the time the main concern was to retrieve the some 200 coalition prisoners of war, and little attention was given to the significance of provisions, in what was expected to be a very temporary agreement, on internal Iraqi politics. Saddam was certainly helped by the cease-fire, in that it allowed him to retrieve more of his forces than he might have dared to hope, but it would be a mistake to place all the blame for his survival on the fact that the war concluded a number of hours earlier than it might have done. Saddam had kept forces back to maintain internal order from the start of the war, and had been able to withdraw others even before the cease-fire was announced in addition to those who returned home afterwards. Nor was the Iraqi use of helicopters decisive. In practice, artillery was even more critical for breaking Shi'ite and Kurdish resistance.

It may be that short of a push to Baghdad there was little the coalition could have done. One analyst has argued that the 'rebellions were spontaneous, disorganized and poorly armed, and were no match for the firepower of the troops loyal to the regime. Also, very early on the revolts came to be seen to be inherently sectarian and secessionist.' Thus Saddam 'had the power and the will to extinguish the flames of revolt'.[46]

However, if the Administration wanted a pretext one could have been created, for few at the time were disposed to support Saddam. The evidence is that the Administration took a political and not a legal decision to remove any hint of support from the rebels. Saddam's calculations were eased immeasurably once he could be confident that the coalition would take a passive stance. The clarity of the disclaimers from the coalition of any connection with the uprising meant that he could move ruthlessly against his opponents, confident that there would be no external interference.

If it had not been for the brutal suppression of the Kurdish rebellion, Saddam's survival in power would not have appeared so significant. His ability to influence regional politics had been drastically reduced and his local power base severely weakened, even if the moment and manner of his collapse could not be predicted. The new evidence of his regime's inherent cruelty and the disclosures about his pre-war drive to acquire weapons of mass destruction revived the 'Saddam problem', just as he consolidated his power following the first post-war shocks to his regime.

The coalition could respond – with protection for the Kurds (which became more tenuous as time went on), rigorous enforcement of Resolution 687 and continued sanctions. President Bush stated bluntly on 21 May that 'we don't want to lift these sanctions as long as Saddam Hussein is in power'. Robert Gates, now Bush's nominee as Director of the CIA, reinforced the message: 'Iraqis will pay the price while he is in power. All possible sanctions will be maintained until he is gone. Any easing of sanctions will be considered only when there is a new government.'[47]

Saddam's country was wrecked, but he could make sure that those upon whom he depended were looked after. So long as he could hold down his domestic opponents, Saddam's basic strategy with the international campaign against him was to survive until it ran out of steam. To avoid direct confrontation with the coalition he exercised his considerable talent for procrastination and operated just below its level of tolerance. He bent when the 'safe havens' for Kurds were established on Iraqi territory and then later when he was unable to close every door to the UN weapons inspectors. However, as soon as he judged Washington or London to be distracted or weakened he tried to claw back concessions.

As he knew that he would not be let completely off the hook through the lifting of the economic embargo on Iraq, he used it as an excuse for the increasing misery of his people. The Security Council tried to get round this in July 1991 by authorizing a one-time sale of oil worth up to $1.6 billion, to buy foods and medicines for the Iraqi people and set up the compensation fund. Saddam refused to co-operate: it would mean conceding control over his revenues while enhancing UN authority in the country.

So long as he remained in power there was a keen sense of unfinished business. It was like an exasperating endgame in chess, when the winning player never quite seems to manage to trap the other's king even though the final result is inevitable. The timing of Saddam's departure, however, would be a function less of Western policy than of the workings of the Iraqi political system, which remained obscure. This meant that just as Saddam's ability to control this system for so long was surprising, his eventual downfall would also come as a surprise.

Conclusions

War is a brutalizing experience for all involved. Innocents suffer and young men die in combat, resources are wasted and the social and economic fabric of the countries involved is disrupted and sometimes impaired for years. It is also normally avoidable. A point can often be identified in the development of a conflict when firm action might have resolved a dispute coming to the boil or warned off a potential aggressor. In the aftermath of any war it is natural to look for such points in an effort to learn how to avoid similar tragedies in the future and to assign blame for the past. If wars are like road accidents, as historian A. J. P. Taylor argued, then more skilful 'driving' can surely help avert some of them.

With regard to the Gulf War the question tends to be posed in terms of flaws in the policy of the United States, and of the West more generally. Was Saddam given a 'green light' to invade Kuwait in July 1990? Should Bush have abandoned dependence upon sanctions so quickly? Were there opportunities for a diplomatic settlement which were wilfully ignored in the rush to war?

The origins of the conflict

Real responsibility lies with Saddam Hussein, for the origins of the crisis are to be found in his chronic political insecurity and the lengths to which this drove him. Saddam was very much a creation of the radical Arab politics of the 1960s and of the cruel Iraqi school in which he learned to survive and defeat all opponents. His insecurity reflected the internal hostility his repressive Government had generated, reinforced by a keen sense of being the special target of hostile Iran and Israel. At the start of 1990 his insecurity was aggravated by the fear of the democratic fallout from the collapse of communism, tensions generated, especially with Israel, as a result of his immense programme of military modernization, plus the severe economic difficulties resulting from the combined effects of this programme and the

428

aftermath of the war with Iran. These were largely home-grown pressures.

The West's culpability in this was complicity in the drive towards the acquisition of a lethal arsenal and a tolerance of Saddam's maltreatment of his own people and threats towards others, in the hope that he could be persuaded to acknowledge the need for political reform and moderate regional policies. For a time such an approach was not unreasonable, as occasionally he did nod in this direction. The mistake of Western countries was to stick with it even after it became apparent that such policies could not solve Saddam's immediate problems and when their own value to Saddam was being reduced. Eventually they became obliged to acknowledge the cumulative evidence of his drive for weapons of mass destruction and were no longer prepared to provide the credit to fund this and other ambitious projects. Yet they persisted with protestations of friendship and dialogue, which came increasingly to appear banal in the face of the fundamental crisis confronting Saddam's regime.

There were many strands to Saddam's insecurity, but the most pressing problem of the summer of 1990 was economic. He could not show his people any material gains from the war with Iran and the supposed victory of 1988, having run out of credit, and the oil price was down. The West could have eased this problem by new lines of credit but that would have been financially irresponsible unless Saddam agreed to hand his economy over to the International Monetary Fund, which he was desperate to avoid. His preferred response was to extort support from his Gulf neighbours, as he had done in the past.

The mistake in the Arab world as well as the West was not to recognize the desperation of Saddam's situation. Such a recognition should not have led to pressure on Kuwait and the United Arab Emirates to give generously to Iraq, although that would probably have been the result. As the Kuwaitis recognized, if Saddam was rewarded this time he would soon be back for more. They might have been more tactful, especially in the realm of honouring oil quotas or gratuitous snubs to Saddam's pride, but our judgement is that only a very large bribe would have persuaded Saddam to pull back his troops once he had determined on his campaign of intimidation.

The fault here, therefore, was in not warning Saddam away from the logic of this campaign. Saddam was well aware of the implications of America's post-cold-war pre-eminence, and sensitive to the possibility of its inter-ference in his dispute with Kuwait. It is not at all clear whether a tougher stance by the Bush Administration would have sufficed to stop Saddam. However, since the campaign was essentially a means to ensure his political survival, it would have made no sense whatsoever if its hazards came to outweigh its potential gains. Furthermore, even if Saddam, as many widely supposed, was 'only bluffing', then that was no reason for passivity. His threats and demands against Kuwait were still unacceptable. Extortion should not only become intolerable when the extorted refuses to comply and the threat is implemented. The importance of the principle of non-aggression could have been stated far more clearly than quiet comments about the inadvisability of solving disputes through force.

We have explained this failure in part as a consequence of the very real distractions resulting from the historic developments in Europe, which resulted in inattention to the brewing crisis and a failure to adjust policy. The old position on relations with Iraq had become irrelevant by July 1990, and to repeat it, as Ambassador Glaspie had little choice but to do when she met Saddam at the height of the crisis, was to reinforce an impression of indifference.

Despite this, it is important to emphasize the extent to which Western governments were taking their cues from friendly Arab states. Saddam deceived them all. As a result, when the bluff turned into aggression it was local fury at this deception which made it possible to forge a coherent international response firmly based on regional politics. Despite all the caricatures of the conflict as one between the Western and Arab worlds, the shock at the occupation of one Arab state by another and a recognition that this represented a profound challenge to regional stability created a receptive environment for a coalition with the West once George Bush determined that this aggression 'must not stand'.

Diplomatic options

The scope and intensity of the international response must have surprised Saddam, whose strategy from the start was to urge his fellow Arab states to resist the 'internationalization' of their local squabbles. Just as his deception infuriated other Arabs, so the unambiguous character of his aggression alarmed states which would not otherwise have expected to join with the United States in a confrontation with a leader so well versed in Third World rhetoric. But many small countries could well see the implications for their own security if predators were allowed to prosper. The respect of the sovereignty of states and the sanctity of national borders has long been a central principle of international order. The idea that it should be enforced by the international community as a whole can be traced back to President Woodrow Wilson's concept of collective security on which the League of Nations, and later the United Nations, were predicated. The main difference between the Gulf conflict and previous instances of collective action (such as Korea) lay in the unprecedented ability to respond to such a blatant challenge and to carry the response through to its logical conclusion.

From this point on, avoiding war meant persuading Saddam to withdraw from Kuwait. The coercive element of this effort was based on political isolation, economic sanctions and later the threat of war. In addition to these sticks there were also carrots, but their attraction to Saddam had always to be set against the costs to him of abandoning Kuwait in terms of both lost prestige and lost relief from his economic predicament. As Saddam told the Soviet envoy Yevgeny Primakov: 'The Iraqi people will not forgive me for unconditional withdrawal from Kuwait.'

At issue is not whether Saddam was at all interested in a political settlement. There are plenty of hints on the record of a readiness to talk about withdrawal if the price was right. The basic problem, as Saddam appears to have understood, is that his price could not be met. The coalition could not offer any carrots which could be presented as 'rewards' for aggression. Those available were therefore effectively trivial and Saddam responded accordingly.

Four basic types of carrots were on offer: (1) a possible change of regime in Kuwait; (2) serious negotiations with the Kuwaitis on economic and territorial questions; (3) progress on other regional disputes; (4) a promise that Iraq would not be attacked and American forces would leave the region following the evacuation of Kuwait. The variations in the proposals put before Saddam were largely in how far they went with each of these carrots. The British and Americans, for example, were prepared to go firm on (4), rejected (1) entirely, did not object to (2) and would do no more than hint on (3). The French and Russians were prepared to offer all four.

However, none of these carrots provided sufficient compensation for withdrawal from Kuwait, which all serious efforts at mediation demanded as the essential prior condition. The only possible exception was the promise of a change of regime in Kuwait, but this option was progressively removed as a result of UN resolutions which demanded the return of the previous government and denounced attempts to change the demographic and political structure of the emirate. All the other options would have meant little in practice and certainly would not have helped with the economic difficulties which drove Saddam to invade Kuwait, and were then made worse by the sanctions. Saddam knew that there would be no incentive for the al-Sabahs to concede anything once they had their country back. They would certainly never agree to ceding any of their country to Iraq, especially the more profitable parts. The Americans might promise to leave him alone and even withdraw most of their troops from the region, but they would be watching his every step from now on. It was not in Saddam's nature to trust the assurances of others.

The potential linkage with regard to the Palestine question, upon which many hopes were based, was phoney. Leaving aside the curious logic of highlighting the plight of the Palestinians by means of an occupation of another Arab state, the sort of proposals on offer would not necessarily have progressed the Palestinian cause. The coalition could not have delivered the requisite Israeli concessions. It is not hard to imagine the attitude of an Israeli Government which saw itself being set up as a sacrifice in order to appease Saddam. One of the post-war achievements of the Bush Adminis-tration was to convene, with the Russians as co-sponsors, a peace conference to address the Arab–Israeli dispute. This was exactly what had been pro-posed by those promoting 'linkage'. As might have been predicted, the talks were hard going, demonstrating how problematic the mere opening of such a conference would have been as a face-saver for Saddam.

Saddam never himself acted as if a diplomatic solution based on a combination of withdrawal from Kuwait and a face-saver was readily avail-able. He did not engage in an active search for an escape route. His response to the various formulas offered by anxious third parties and regional allies was generally dismissive. At no time did he ever spell out his conditions for withdrawal, other than to suggest that once all other problems in the Middle East had been dealt with the question of Iraq's new nineteenth province might also be addressed. The experience of the Arab–Israeli talks when they did take place indicated the pretext they would have provided for continual prevarication on his part as they failed to produce a result which justified any concession.

His 12 August proposal, from which he never wavered until forcible eviction from Kuwait faced him in mid-February, along with his approach to negotiations, suggests less a search for an immediate solution and more an attempt to divide and weaken the coalition confronting him and play for time. With time he could complete the incorporation of Kuwait into Iraq's structures, and with time international interest would wane and he would be able to obtain the sort of deal which was not on offer when he was at the centre of attention.

Economic sanctions

This also explains the limitations of sanctions as a coercive mechanism. A full trade embargo was implemented right from the start and enforced more rigorously than in any previous instance. Not waiting to see whether this might work to force Saddam out by itself disappointed those who saw this strategy as the best opportunity ever to demonstrate the primacy of economic measures in policing the international system. Sanctions would probably have been more effective if linked to a more promising diplomacy, but as we have noted, there was little obvious 'middle ground' upon which to build a deal. There was also a fundamental ambiguity at the heart of the sanctions strategy which was rarely acknowledged. Saddam's personal position could only be an indirect target of sanctions: they would work through their effects on ordinary Iraqis. Here was the dilemma. Was it moral to impose increasing misery on the Iraqi people when there was no guarantee that it would make the slightest difference to Saddam?

The sanctions undoubtedly posed a cost in terms of projects forgone and cracks in the infrastructure which foreign workers and spare parts could not be imported to mend. Saddam had to weigh these short-term inconveniences, eased by the plunder of Kuwait, against the long-term gains if he could hold on to the emirate. They would only have made a difference if they had undermined the political stability of Iraq. However, Saddam was in a position to divert available resources to his armed forces and those upon whom his political future depended. His capacity in this regard was underlined after the war, when he was able to hold on to power even with an infrastructure wrecked by war, UN interference in his internal affairs and the humiliation of defeat. It is arguable that, paradoxically, defeat made it easier for the Iraqi leader to resist the economic blockade than in the pre-war period. Having nothing to lose, he brutalized his people more ruthlessly than before; the damage caused by allied bombardments meant there was a ready-made scapegoat to blame for Iraq's economic plight. Nonetheless, Saddam's ability to hang on to power against such tremendous odds and despite the little love lost between him and his subjects (best illustrated by the popular uprisings in the wake of the war) provided a clear demonstration of the limitations of sanctions – even in circumstances where their implementation could be unusually watertight.

In the end sanctions were not judged to be sufficient in themselves to force Saddam to back down, at least during the time-frame in which it would also be possible to sustain the complementary political and military pressures, without which the sanctions themselves could not be maintained. Nonetheless their influence should not be disregarded: an international coalition could be forged around them in a way that would not have been possible in a rush to armed force, and this was also the means by which the United Nations was drawn into its central role. Five months of the embargo undermined the ability of Iraq to sustain a long war. A continued embargo provided the main means of exercising influence over post-war Iraq.

Military pressure

The next stage in the escalation of pressure was to give the military option extra prominence in order to demonstrate to Saddam the retribution he faced if he persisted with holding on to Kuwait. Given the one-sided nature of the eventual confrontation, it is not surprising that those aware of the full power of the American military machine could not understand Saddam's readiness to decide the issue of Kuwait through a trial of strength. Here it is evident that the problem was not only Saddam's misguided confidence, based on his defensive successes against Iran, but also the mixed signals from Washington including the 'mile for peace' initiative, which came over as reflecting American weakness, in the sense of deteriorating popular support.

Consequently, the Administration failed to convince Saddam of the seriousness of its intention. Until quite a late stage in the conflict the Iraqi leader remained confident that through a combination of bluster and inducements he might strengthen the peace camp in the West to such an extent that war would be averted. Even when, in late December 1990 or early January 1991, he reckoned that war was coming, he believed that he could and would be allowed to survive it. The only explicit threat to his personal rule, issued by James Baker during his meeting with Tariq Aziz in Geneva, related to Iraq's resort to non-conventional warfare. In abiding by this limitation, as he actually did, Saddam hoped not only to keep the allied war aims limited to Kuwait, but to emerge victorious from the conflict. As Aziz told Baker in Geneva, 'never has an Arab regime entered into a war with Israel and the United States and lost politically'.

Bush's best chance for making his threats stick was to convince Saddam that the consequences of retaining Kuwait would be devastating for his personal rule. Yet despite all the talk of a 'hidden agenda to get Saddam' and the retrospective presumption that this should have been top of the agenda, Bush could not do this. He feared that the cohesion of the wide and variegated coalition he had so laboriously assembled would be threatened if the removal of Saddam were to be made an explicit war aim; the Arab members of the coalition, for example, could not publicly agree to America's setting of such a goal, though in private (and, in the Syrian case, overtly as well) they pressed for Saddam's demise. Moreover, interference in Iraq's internal affairs ran counter to Bush's own concept of 'a new world order'.

He was no crusader for human rights, only for the cause of international norms of decency. Having challenged a state which had given itself the liberty to reshape violently the internal affairs of its neighbour, he had no intention of doing the same in Iraq, even under the cloak of international legitimacy (which, in any event, was not unequivocally there). Moreover, he was anxious about setting a goal which might not be attained. It would have raised the demands on the military operation and risked embarrassment if it was unsuccessful and Saddam slipped through the net, but also if it was too successful and Saddam achieved the status of a martyr.

The argument that an even tougher stance against Saddam in 1990 might have been more successful in averting war contrasts with the normal critiques of the diplomatic efforts of this period. We acknowledge the compelling reasons which would have made it difficult to adopt such a stance. Nor could there have been any guarantee that it would have worked. The basic difficulty with any coercive approach to such problems is that they depend for their success on their influence on the target's calculations. We believe that the key to Saddam's calculus is always his preoccupation with personal survival, but that is not always sufficient to predict his likely responses to alternative sources of pressure. Even with the benefit of hindsight, it is difficult to design an alternative approach to the challenge Kuwait's seizure posed which would not have compromised elementary principles of international law.

In January 1991 Saddam's basic miscalculation was to underestimate both American will and American capabilities. He was correct in judging his ability to survive the war, though, as in the Iran–Iraq War, he managed to escape by the skin of his teeth and it was his ill-conceived military strategy which almost led to his undoing. As aptly noted by General Schwarzkopf, Saddam proved to be neither a strategist nor a soldier. His poor understanding of military affairs, and his complete subordination of military strategy to the ultimate goal of protecting his regime, drove him to fight a political war, with one eye set on his post-war survival: key units were held back from the start for this purpose and he was clearly anxious that as many units as possible would get back to save the regime rather than make a gallant last stand. He was cautious when it came to initiatives, reluctant to hazard his air force, and did not want to commit the Republican Guard, Iraq's élite force, too forward positions because he dare not risk its loss.

War

This flawed strategy also reflected a fundamental misunderstanding of the main lessons of the Iran–Iraq War. Saddam's failure to distinguish between the coalition forces confronting him and the poorly equipped and ill-trained Iranian army led him to the mistaken belief that Iraq's defensive posture would suffice to inflict unacceptable pain on the enemy. No less importantly, he failed to appreciate the decisive role of airpower in the modern battlefield: he did not only have to look to the Arab–Israeli wars, where airpower often determined the outcome, for this lesson. It was the sustained Iraqi air campaign against civilian targets during the Iran–Iraq War which gradually led to the collapse of Iranian national morale in 1988. And if the zealous Iranians eventually broke down under the pressure of the not very effective Iraqi force, how could the less resilient Iraqis expect to withstand an onslaught of the most lethal aerial force assembled in modern history? Lastly, the substantial Iraqi desertions in the first months of the Iran–Iraq War, after Saddam had voluntarily surrendered the initiative to the Iranians, should have warned him of the consequences both of the lack of military initiative and of the collapse of morale.

The only coherent component of his war strategy was the Scud attacks against a non-participant in the war – Israel. In hurling his missiles against the Jewish state Saddam sought to trigger an Israeli retaliation which, he hoped, would either lead to the collapse of the anti-Iraq coalition, or drive the allies into a premature ground offensive in Kuwait, thus enabling Iraq to exact an exorbitant toll, or, even better, push the coalition to accept a cease-fire on terms favourable to him. Unfortunately for Saddam, though this scenario was by no means far fetched, it failed to materialize. The remarkably slight casualties caused by the missiles, the general recognition in Israel of the merits of restraint, the allied pressures on and inducements to Israel, and Arab determination not to play into Saddam's hands, all these shuffled Saddam's cards and left him with no adequate response to the allied onslaught.

Saddam was on the military defensive but on the political offensive. President Bush could go on to the military offensive but, simply because he was leading a disparate coalition rather than a unitary state, he was on the political defensive. This provided Saddam with his main strategic opportunity. The pattern of employment of US airpower was shaped by this political context. Direct military action was needed because Bush could not be sure that the cohesion of the coalition could withstand a long wait for sanctions to bite, and it had to be swift because the coalition, and Bush's support at home, would have been strained by a prolonged conflict. When it came to using airpower to undermine Saddam's ability to resist a ground offensive, Bush had to depend on international tolerance of the spectacle of a largely unopposed air bombardment continuing day after day. When he called for a cease-fire, it was because he was aware of a growing unease at the carnage inflicted upon Iraqi troops and because his basic objectives had now been achieved, even if the future of Saddam himself was left unresolved. Saddam by this time had been deprived of a strategy other than one of political survival. The blunting of his political offensive had exposed the weaknesses of his wholly inadequate military defence.

Could the coalition have achieved its objectives with a greater economy, and the air campaign on its own have decided the war? It is arguable that Iraq was already on the ropes when the land war began and that the opportunity to inflict pain on American forces did little more than provide Saddam with his main opportunity to counter the pain the US Air Force had undoubtedly inflicted on Iraq. Against this argument, three points can be made. First, if the Western military presence in Saudi Arabia had been smaller, then Saddam's opportunities to extend the war would have been greater. Second, an air offensive directed solely at purely military targets might not have moved Iraq, especially if it could counter with missile attacks against Israel and Saudi Arabia, however ineffectual they might be in strict military terms. To put pressure on Saddam required imposing real distress on the civilian population and there could have been no guarantee that Saddam could not have turned the consequential unease in the West to his political advantage. The USAF could not resist the opportunity to demonstrate a decisive strategic role, but the aspects of its campaign most directed against Iraq's economic and political structure seem to have been the least relevant to the ultimate victory. Third, it was the ground campaign that ensured rapid agreement to all UN resolutions. What is beyond doubt is that chronic inferiority in airpower is a strategic liability for which it is almost impossible to compensate in regular conventional warfare.

The Gulf War is viewed as the first real 'electronics war'. The sight of cruise missiles and smart bombs roaming to their destination with pinpoint accuracy has created a widespread impression of an uneven match between a high-tech power and a hapless, ill-equipped, and backward Third World army. However intriguing, this notion is largely misconceived. While the war clearly represents a military victory of an advanced over a developing society, the outcome was by no means a foregone conclusion. The Iraqi Army, it is true, proved to be a far cry from the formidable power portrayed in the West prior to the war, and it was inferior to the coalition forces in crucial technological respects, but the fact that it fought so badly was mainly the outcome of more 'traditional' factors, such as a poor combat performance along with an incompetent politico-military leadership and war strategy. There was never any doubt that the coalition would prevail, but an Iraqi strategy which imposed high battlefield costs on coalition forces and led to a protracted campaign offered Saddam some prospect of a much more favourable cease-fire as well as post-war reputation.

Objectives

Saddam was unfortunate to pick a unique period in international affairs. Had he invaded Kuwait a few years earlier, such wide-ranging collaboration would have been inconceivable; had he taken a limited action against Kuwait, he might have well got away with it; had he been a minor dictator in a remote area, perhaps few would have bothered over the plight of his victim, or more likely, a small punitive action might have redressed the situation. As things stood, a regional superpower swallowing its small neighbour in one of the world's most sensitive areas threatened both to reverse the Middle East's hesitant drift from war, make the world oil market virtually captive to the whims of a ruthless and unpredictable dictator, *and* challenge a basic rule of international order.

If the early efforts at coalition-building had been unsuccessful and the foundation for a military option not been created, initially in the form of the defence of Saudi Arabia, then the verdict of history may well have been that this was the point at which the international community gave up attempting to enforce its own norms. As it was the basic objective was achieved – Kuwait was liberated and its legitimate Government restored. The quarrel of those who believe that the war should not have been fought must be with the principle of non-aggression – on the grounds that Kuwait itself was not worthy of defence or that it was only being honoured for baser motives, such as oil, or that the principle had been breached so many times that it no longer counted for anything.

Oil played an important role in the conflict. Had it not been for oil, Kuwait might not have been invaded in the first place and Iraq would not have been able to afford the military power to do so and then challenge the world. The potential for Iraqi control over Saudi as well as Kuwaiti supplies (a possibility that went well beyond the question of whether Saddam planned a further invasion in August 1990) buttressed the readiness to take on Saddam. Oil influenced the evolution of the conflict in the wider sense of impacting on the emerging politico-economic international order. But concern over oil was not the West's exclusive preserve, so the idea that the conflict was a simple case of 'blood for oil' was misleading. In fact, the Western economies were far less affected by the Iraqi aggression than those of the Third World. As shown in this book, it was the weaker economies of the world, from East

438

Europe to Asia, to Africa, to the Middle East, which were worst afflicted by the Iraqi invasion. Many of these states were incapable of handling the adverse economic consequences on their own. Those who thought that oil provided justification for war could point to the consequential Saudi hegemony established over OPEC, thereby ensuring continuity of supply and stability of prices. The prices which peaked at $38.3 per barrel after the invasion hovered at $19.1 at the start of 1992, just below where they had been prior to the occupation.

By the time war came, the Bush Administration had concluded that an important advantage would be the opportunity to cut Iraq's military power down to size. It was less successful in the military campaign in this objective than was assumed at the time. However, the deficit, at least with regard to mass destruction capabilities, was made up in the enforcement of the cease-fire demands for the destruction of these capabilities.

Where the record is less clear is in the political effects of the war. When in January 1992 the first anniversary came of the Gulf War, the retrospective evaluations suggested that Saddam Hussein's remarkable survival after one of the most humiliating military defeats in contemporary history qualified the whole episode. An enormous military effort had been undertaken, and yet there was Saddam, still thumbing his nose at the international community. This was so much part of the prevailing view in the United States that one major account of the crisis prepared by the journal *US News & World Report* for the anniversary was entitled *Triumph Without Victory*.

The Administration could claim that it was unfair to be judged against an objective that had not been set, when those that had been set were all achieved. They could also point to the steady post-war erosion of Saddam's power base, with his at best tenuous hold over the main Kurdish areas to the north and Shi'ite to the south, a devastated economy still suffering under economic sanctions, the determined progress of the UN inspectors steadily uncovering more of Saddam's attempts to be able to terrorize the region, the regular reshuffles of his regime. Perhaps if, in President Bush's rhetoric, he had not been built up into such a monster all this would have sufficed, but for a monster it was not good enough. In the United States the survival of such a hated enemy seemed to bear no relation to the old practice of unconditional surrender and of removing the political source of aggression and not just its instruments. However, it would have been very difficult to hold the coalition together for larger objectives, nor could there have been any certainty that they could have been achieved. Where the Bush Administration could be faulted is in its cautious response to the post-war uprising, when Saddam was vulnerable and coalition passivity gave the impression of indifference to the fate of those who had been given vocal encouragement, if not material promises, to take arms against Saddam.

The wider political effects were also uncertain. With the memories of the 'triumph in the desert' overtaken by the gloomy realities of world recession, the 'new world order' had become a remote vision. Besieged by an intensifying mood of 'America first', President Bush had little to show to his constituents by way of a more orderly world. The collapse of the Soviet Union and the disintegration of Yugoslavia had not led so far to the triumph of liberal ideals there but, rather, to bitter internecine wars. The Middle East seemed as impermeable as ever to the winds of change. The harsh treatment of Palestinians in Kuwait demonstrated that the settling of scores was taking precedence over the modernization of the political structure. The Emir acted as if he could return to his pre-invasion ways. The Middle East's complex balance of power system produced another tilt: as Iraq went down Iran started to move up. The main conclusion drawn by the conservative Gulf states was that whatever they might do to defend themselves, the best option by far was to rely on the West. As a reward for its support to end the occupation of one country, Syria received a Western blank cheque to complete the satellization of Lebanon; Israel still occupied Arab territories seized in the 1967 war; Islamic fundamentalism remained potent, as did nationalist extremism.

However, there was another side to the ledger. The coalition had fully achieved the liberation of Kuwait, and at an unexpectedly low cost. More-over, the reversal of the Iraqi aggression had removed the most recent formidable threat to an orderly Middle East. Although the war was not fought over the principle of democratization but rather over the rule of law in international relations, and although Western-type democracy might not be far more akin to Middle Eastern peoples than communism used to be, there were encouraging signs of liberalization. Even the ultra-conservative Saudi regime seemed poised to widen, albeit to a limited extent, political freedoms and participation. Improved relations with Iran and Syria brought to an end the holding of Western hostages in Beirut. More importantly, the war allowed the peace process between Israel and the Arabs to move forward. It was not advancing in great leaps, for a nearly century-long legacy of acri-mony and distrust is not easy to erase. However, for the first time in their history, Israelis and Arabs were sitting at the negotiating table and discussing enduring peace, not only an *ad hoc* cease-fire, or armistice agreement. How this ledger will look in five or ten years' time is difficult to predict. The consequences of war are always many and the unanticipated effects over time tend to swamp the intended. It is unfair to demand of war that it do much more than right a wrong. It is not a natural means to a better world.

The Gulf War saw the return of the United States to a self-confident and an effective role at the heart of international affairs. While the 'Vietnam syndrome' might always have been exaggerated and misinterpreted, the display of US power in the Gulf had the effect of creating an image of overwhelming power. However, there was still a reluctance to get embroiled in civil wars, as seen in its refusal to get involved in the 'quagmire' of an Iraqi civil war of uncertain duration. Though the 'safe havens' involvement was of a circumscribed nature, and carried few risks of casualties, it illustrated the political complexities normally associated with this sort of activity including local suspicion, UN resistance and problems with defining objectives.

The risk of terrorism and the nature of the media coverage meant that the war touched people at home directly. Along with the more basic reasons of blood and treasure, it reinforced the requirement in democratic societies that any use of armed force must have extraordinary justification. This was found through the United Nations. The prominent role of the UN was helpful but by no means an anticipated feature of the crisis during its initial stages, and a formidable coalition could have been built outside of it, although its role was significant domestically in all Western countries. This role was made possible by active co-operation with the West by the Soviet Union and by more passive acquiescence from China. Whether these conditions will obtain in the future depends upon the general state of the international system.

Even then, without local regional interest and burden-sharing arrangements it is unlikely that Western states, and in particular the US, will be very adventurous in the future. While future adversaries may be less crude than Saddam Hussein, it is probable that action will still only be taken against a regime behaving in an unusually outrageous manner. The Gulf War may reinforce the basic predilection to stay clear of civil wars, rely on air superiority and fight land wars with the maximum mobility. Where there may be doubt is in the readiness to stick to limited objectives if faced with a Saddam-like figure in the future. One can imagine demands that this time we must not let the rascal escape.

However, the more demanding the objectives the greater the military risks involved. Despite its scale, or perhaps as a result of its scale, the coalition military operation could be geared to the minimization of risk by dedicating immense military resources to the attainment of a very clear objective. This had the inevitable consequence that the political conclusion was not as decisive as the military result, but at least what was achieved politically was important on its own. The uncertain lessons from this conflict result from the fact that in general future conflicts are likely to be politically much more complex from the start and, in consequence, carry with them a higher military risk. The West may not find many conflicts with principles so clear-cut, enemies so ready to take on Western military power on its own terms and circumstances so favourable to its application.

Notes

Introduction

1 President George Bush, State of the Union speech, 29 January 1991, United States Information Service (USIS).
2 President George Bush, speech at Air University, Maxwell Air Force Base, 13 April 1991 (USIS).
3 For a discussion of this debate see Lawrence Freedman, 'The Gulf War and the New World Order', *Survival*, Vol. 33, No. 3, May/June 1991.
4 Brian Lapping Associates for BBC 2, *The Washington Version*, shown on 16, 17 and 18 January 1992.

Chapter 1: New World, New Middle East?

1 Sermons delivered by Ayatollah Ruhollah Khomeini on 2 November 1979 and 11 February 1980, in F. Rajaee, *Islamic Values and World View: Khomeini on Man, the State, and International Politics*, Lanham, University Press of America, 1983, pp. 31, 48, 82–3.
2 Tehran Radio, 24 July 1982. Most, though not all, Arab and Soviet broadcast statements are taken from either the BBC's Summary of World Broadcasts or the American Foreign Broadcasts Information Service (FBIS).
3 Tehran Radio, 4 April 1983.
4 Ibid., 9 August 1982.
5 Ayatollah Ruhollah Khomeini, 'Islamic Government', in his *Islam and Revolution*, trans. H. Algar, Berkeley, Mizan, 1981, pp. 31, 48.
6 See Nikki Keddie and Mark Gasiorowski (eds.), *Neither East Nor West: Iran, the Soviet Union, and the United States*, New Haven, Yale University Press, 1990.
7 In February 1989 Ayatollah Khomeini issued a death sentence against the Indian-born British novelist Salman Rushdie and declared his book *The Satanic Verses* blasphemous. This move led to a deep crisis in Iran's relations with the European Community, including the recall of European diplomats from Iran and the recall of Iranian diplomats from EC countries.
8 Aryeh Naor, *A Government at War*, Jerusalem, 1986, p. 51 (Hebrew).
9 Zeev Schiff and Ehud Ya'ari, *Israel's Lebanon War*, London, Allen & Unwin, 1984, p. 304.
10 *Literaturnaya Gazeta, Radio Peace and Progress in Hebrew*, 31 May 1989 (emphasis added).
11 Interview by *Izvestiya*'s Middle East correspondent, Konstantin Geyvendov, with the Kuwaiti newspaper *al-Anba*, 12 September 1987. For Soviet–Syrian relations under Gorbachev, see Efraim Karsh, *Soviet Policy towards Syria since 1970*, London and New York, Macmillan and St Martin's Press, 1991, Chapter 10.
12 Iraqi News Agency (INA), 27 January 1990.

Chapter 2: Saddam's Crisis

1   Eliyahu Kanovsky, 'Economic Implications for the Region and World Oil Market', in Efraim Karsh (ed.), *The Iran–Iraq War: Impact and Implications*, London and New York, Macmillan and St Martin's Press, 1989, pp. 231–2.

2   See, for example, *al-Thawra*, Baghdad, 9 February, 21 June 1980.

3   For Saddam's attempts to contain the Iranian pressures in 1979 and in 1980 see Efraim Karsh and Inari Rautsi, *Saddam Hussein: A Political Biography*, New York and London, The Free Press and Brassey's, 1991, pp. 139–46.

4   For a detailed discussion of Saddam's decision to invade Iran see ibid., Chapter 6.

5   For this peace offer see Baghdad Radio, 28 September 1990.

6   On the shift in the Israeli position see J. Alpher, 'Israel and the Iran–Iraq War', in Karsh (ed.), *The Iran–Iraq War*, pp. 154–71.

7   *International Herald Tribune*, 27 November, 5 December 1984.

8   *Christian Science Monitor* (International Edition), 12–18 December 1988. Even though Israel was disillusioned with its longstanding alignment with the Lebanese Christians following the 1982 Lebanon War, it welcomed Iraq's military support to this community, which was still viewed as a counterweight to the Syrian and Iranian supported Shi'ite militias.

9   John Bulloch and Harvey Morris, *Saddam's War*, London, Faber and Faber, 1991, p. 89.

10   The revelations on the intelligence link come from Seymour Hersh of the *New York Times* (*International Herald Tribune*, 27 January 1992). Previously it had been assumed that the intelligence link did not open until 1984.

11   *International Herald Tribune*, 30–31 May 1992; *Financial Times*, 30–31 May 1992.

12   This episode has been thoroughly examined by Rep. Henry Gonzalez, chairman of the House of Representatives Banking, Finance and Urban Affairs Committee. He read many key documents into the *Congressional Record* on 2, 9 and 30 March 1992. See also Elaine Sciolino, *The Outlaw State: Saddam Hussein's Quest for Power and the Gulf Crisis*, New York, John Wiley, 1991, Chapter 8.

13   See, for example, *Economist*, 29 September 1990, pp. 19–22; *International Herald Tribune*, 25 September 1990; Judith Miller and Laurie Mylroie, *Saddam Hussein and the Crisis in the Gulf*, New York, Times Books, 1990, pp. 8–12; Bob Woodward, *The Commanders*, New York, Simon & Schuster, 1991, p. 239.

14   Authors' interview.

15   The discussion in this section draws on Karsh and Rautsi, *Saddam Hussein*, Chapter 9, and their article: 'Why Saddam Hussein Invaded Kuwait', *Survival*, Vol. 33, No. 1, January/February 1991, pp. 18–31.

16   Saddam's speech in Amman, *Amman Television*, 24 February 1990.

17   *Al-Thawra*, Baghdad, 2 March 1990.

18   Baghdad Radio, 5 January 1990.

19   Authors' interview with Richard Murphy, 1 November 1990.

20   INA, 29 March 1990.

21   Woodward, *The Commanders*, p. 201.

22   Baghdad Radio, 2 April 1990.

23   *Economist*, 20 September 1990.

24   Baghdad Radio, 2 April 1990.

25   INA, 7, 8 April 1990; Baghdad Radio, 19 April 1990.

26   Woodward, *The Commanders*, p. 201.

27   William Waldegrave, Minister of State at the Foreign Office, had warned the Iraqi Ambassador of 'grave consequences' for Anglo–Iraqi relations in the event of Bazoft being executed.

28   Dilip Hiro implies, on the basis of no more than the speculation of others, that Bazoft was spying and describes the details of Bazoft's life as 'unsavoury'. Dilip Hiro, *Desert Shield to*

Desert Storm: The Second Gulf War, London, Harper Collins, 1992, pp. 69–70.

29 Leonard Spector with Jacqueline Smith, *Nuclear Ambitions: The Spread of Nuclear Weapons 1989–1990*, Boulder, Colorado, Westview Press, 1990, pp. 191–2.

30 Kenneth Timmerman, *The Death Lobby: How the West Armed Iraq*, London, Fourth Estate, 1992, p. 335. This is the best source on Saddam's determination to build up his military industry and Western complicity.

31 *Congressional Record*, 16 March 1992, H-1278.

32 Pierre Salinger with Eric Laurent, *Secret Dossier: The Hidden Agenda Behind the Gulf War*, London, Penguin, 1991, p. 4.

33 Hearing before the Subcommittee on Europe and the Middle East of the Committee on Foreign Affairs, House of Representatives, *United States–Iraqi Relations*, 26 April 1991.

34 Timmerman, *The Death Lobby*, pp. 382–3; *Congressional Record*, 9 March 1992, H-111.

35 The transcript is reproduced in Michah L. Sifry and Christopher Cerf (eds.), *The Gulf War Reader: History, Documents, Opinions*, New York, Random House, 1991, pp. 119–21. The Senators later complained that this contained only small excerpts from a three-hour interview.

36 Timmerman, *The Death Lobby*, pp. 224, 353.

37 Ibid., p. 369.

38 Ibid., p. 309.

39 About half of the debt was owed to Arab Gulf states, Saudi Arabia and Kuwait in particular. Guaranteed trade debt to Western countries amounted to between $16 billion and $20 billion. Most of the rest were military debts, much of which was owed to the Soviet Union. See, for example, *Economist*, 30 September 1989, 4 August 1990; *The Middle East*, December 1989; *Independent*, 16 March 1990.

40 Karsh and Rautsi, *Saddam Hussein*, pp. 202–3.

41 Much of the following paragraphs is drawn from Charles Ebinger and John P. Banks, 'OPEC in 1990: The Failure of Oil Diplomacy' in David Newsom (ed.), *The Diplomatic Record 1990–91*, Boulder, Colorado, Westview Institute for the Study of Diplomacy, 1992, pp. 109–114.

Chapter 3: Iraq Confronts Kuwait

1 See INA, 7, 28 August 1990; Baghdad Radio, 8 August 1990.

2 For the text of the agreement, see J. C. Hurerwitz (ed.), *Diplomacy in the Near and Middle East*, Princeton, Van Nostrand, 1966, Vol. 1, pp. 218–19.

3 Cited in H. Batatu, *The Old Social Classes and the Revolutionary Movements of Iraq*, Princeton, Princeton University Press, 1978, p. 25.

4 Concluded on 29 July 1913, the British–Ottoman treaty restricted Ottoman sovereignty over Kuwait, recognized the autonomy of the Sheikh of Kuwait, and acknowledged Britain's special status in the principality. According to this agreement, the territory of Kuwait proper was to be delineated by a semi-circle to indicate the area within which the tribes were to be subordinated to Kuwait, and the Ottomans were not allowed to establish garrisons or undertake any military action in the sheikhdom without London's approval or to exercise administrative measures independently of the Sheikh of Kuwait. The agreement also stipulated for the inclusion of the Warba and Bubiyan islands, strategically located at the northern tip of the Gulf, within Kuwait's boundaries. However, as a result of the outbreak of the First World War the agreement was not ratified. For the text, see Hurerwitz (ed.), *Diplomacy in the Near and Middle East*, Vol. 1, pp. 269–70.

5 Majid Khadduri, *Socialist Iraq: A Study in Iraqi Politics since 1968*, Washington DC, The Middle East Institute, 1978, p. 155.

6 Ibid., p. 157.

7 *Observer*, 21 October 1990.

8   INA, 17, 20 February, 1 May 1990; Baghdad Radio, 20 February 1990; *al-Sharq al-Awsat* (London), 18 May 1990.
9   Baghdad Radio, 18 July 1990.
10 Salinger and Laurent, *Secret Dossier*, p. 37.
11 INA, 19, 26 June 1990; Saddam's interview with *Wall Street Journal*, 16 June 1990.
12 Salinger and Laurent, *Secret Dossier*, p. 61.
13 Baghdad Radio, 17 July 1990.
14 Woodward, *The Commanders*, pp. 206–7.
15 Baghdad Radio, 18 July 1990.
16 Ibid., 17 July 1990.
17 Authors' interview with Kuwaiti diplomats.
18 *International Herald Tribune*, 21–22 July 1990.
19 *Al-Qabas* (Kuwait), 20 July 1990; *al-Ray al-Amm* (Kuwait), 26 July 1990.
20 The Iraqi version is presented in Salinger and Laurent, *Secret Dossier*, p. 47. Aziz described it to Baker during their January 1991 Geneva meeting, the transcript of which was later released. INA, 9–13 January 1991. Mubarak's press conference, as broadcast by Cairo Radio, 8 August 1990. Mubarak also gave an interview to *US News & World Report*, entitled *Triumph Without Victory: The Unreported History of the Gulf War*, New York, Random House, 1992, p. 23 (hereinafter referred to as *Triumph Without Victory*).
21 Woodward, *The Commanders*, p. 207. April Glaspie indicated that her Embassy only 'picked up in Baghdad the first indication of military deployment to the south' on 20 July, which she interpreted as a response to the US request for moderation. It is an interesting question why the Baghdad Embassy was not apprised of the latest intelligence. Glaspie testimony, *Senate Foreign Relations Committee*, 20 March 1991.
22 Glaspie testimony, *Senate Foreign Relations Committee*, 20 March 1991.
23 *Economist*, 21 July 1990.
24 *Triumph Without Victory*, pp. 23, 31.
25 *International Herald Tribune*, 25 July 1990; *New York Times*, 23 September 1990. Cheney had intimated on 19 July that the American commitment made to Kuwait during the Iran–Iraq War was still valid.
26 Woodward, *The Commanders*, p. 210. See also MEP Survey, 3 August 1990; *Financial Times*, 25 July 1990.
27 See statement by Tariq Aziz, 23 July 1990, criticizing the Kuwaitis' readiness to 'internationalize' the issue and take it out of Arab hands, and also an article in *al-Thawra* (Baghdad), 22 July 1990. Rather curiously, the article compared this with the way that Kuwait had 'provided the cover and the justifications for the entry of foreign fleets in to Gulf waters', failing to mention that this particular Western intervention had made a major contribution to the Iraqi cause.
28 *Al-Thawra* opined on 25 July that 'no foreign power can protect he who conspires against the Arab nation and threatens its interests', and condemned the Kuwaiti leadership for its 'contacts and co-ordination with the United States'.
29 The Iraqis later released a transcript to demonstrate that the Ambassador showed understanding of Iraq's plight and indifference to its campaign against Kuwait. The Ambassador's own recollection was that Saddam knew the strength of the American position. The softness of her tone reflected the Iraqi dictator's assurance that Kuwait would not be invaded. For the Iraqi version see *International Herald Tribune*, 17 September 1990; *Economist*, 29 September 1990; *The Observer*, 21 October 1990; Salinger and Laurent, *Secret Dossier*, pp. 47–63. Ambassador Glaspie has claimed the Iraqi text to be only 80 per cent correct and has given her own version of the meeting. *Senate Foreign Relations Committee*, 20 March 1991; *House Foreign Affairs Subcommittee on Europe and the Middle East*, 21 March 1991. She accused the Iraqi Ministry of Information, 'which had a long history of doctoring and editing documents', of presenting a distorted account of the

meeting. However, she opposed the release of an American version of the meeting.

30 Glaspie admitted to having told Saddam that the United States had no opinion about Iraq's border dispute with Kuwait, but argued that such aloofness had been the main trait of US policy in the Middle East, where all Arab countries were beset by border disputes of one kind or another.

31 This was in the Ambassador's report back to Washington. *International Herald Tribune*, 13–14 July 1991.

32 Ibid.

33 Ibid.

34 *Financial Times*, 25 July 1990.

35 Ben Brown and David Shukman, *All Necessary Means: Inside the Gulf War*, London, BBC Books, 1991, p. 2.

36 Woodward, *The Commanders*, p. 212.

37 *International Herald Tribune*, 13–14 July 1991.

38 See, for example, *Financial Times*, 27 July 1990, reflecting briefings of the previous day, including the US report of the Glaspie meeting: 'Saddam was seeking to reassure us of his intentions . . . he was not looking to inflame hostilities with us.'

39 Salinger and Laurent, *Secret Dossier*, p. 64.

40 Colonel Sa'id Matar made this statement at a press conference on 2 March 1991. *International Herald Tribune*, 8 March 1991.

41 The meeting is described in Bulloch and Morris, *Saddam's War*, pp. 102–4.

42 Ebinger and Banks, 'OPEC in 1990' in Newsom (ed.), *The Diplomatic Record*, pp. 119–23.

43 Woodward, *The Commanders*, pp. 216–17.

44 This was reported by American officials to the Iraqis during the January 1991 Baker–Aziz meeting in order to show that King Hussein as well as Mubarak was passing on the message that Saddam did not intend to invade.

45 Authors' interview with Israeli military sources.

46 During the Iran–Iraq war, Kuwait had refused Iraq access to the islands for military use because it was fearful of further antagonizing Iran. Although no more than mudflats, the islands largely dominate the approaches to the Iraqi naval base in Umm Qasr and its port of Zubair. Their seizure, therefore, could significantly improve Baghdad's narrow access to the Gulf (of some ten miles wide) and make it less dependent upon a settlement with Iran on the contentious Shatt al-Arab. *Financial Times*, 2 August 1990.

47 *New York Times*, 23 September 1990.

48 Peter Turnley, 'The Road to War', *Newsweek*, 28 January 1991.

49 Eric Laurent, *Tempête du désert: les secrets de la Maison Blanche*, Paris, Olivier Orban, 1991, p. 27.

50 According to one account of the crisis, Saddam was probably serious about the negotiations but the Kuwaitis obstructed the summit by announcing three hours before the meeting was due to begin that the Emir himself would not be coming to Jeddah. This was 'a deadly insult' to Saddam, which forced him to cancel his scheduled trip to Jeddah and to send instead his number two, Deputy Chairman of the RCC, Izzat Ibrahim. Salinger and Laurent, *Secret Dossier*, p. 69. This assertion, however, is dubious. Not only had information about the composition of the Kuwaiti delegation been public for a few days, but the summit's level of representation (i.e. the Kuwaiti Crown Prince and Iraq's Deputy Chairman of the RCC) had already been agreed upon during Mubarak's mission to Baghdad (see, for example, Mubarak's press conference as broadcast by Cairo Radio, 8 August 1990; *Financial Times*, 28 July 1990). Furthermore, it is doubtful whether Saddam had ever intended to come to Jeddah, given his overriding preoccupation with his personal safety, on the one hand, and his longstanding resentment of Iraq's need to beg its tiny neighbour for financial support, on the other.

51 See a statement by a Kuwaiti official to Radio Monte Carlo, 1 August 1990. Heikal cites

what he claims to be the Crown Prince's negotiating instructions from the Emir, warning against being taken in by protestations of Arab solidarity, suspicious of Saudi motives and claiming 'We are more powerful than they imagine'. Mohamed Heikal, *Illusions of Triumph: An Arab View of the Gulf War*, London, Harper Collins, 1992, p. 181.

52 Salinger and Laurent, *Secret Dossier*, pp. 70–75.
53 Miller and Mylroie, *Saddam Hussein and the Crisis in the Gulf*, p. 20.
54 Authors' interview with Kuwaiti diplomats.
55 *International Herald Tribune*, 2 August 1990.
56 White House spokesman Roman Popadiuk stated: 'Obviously, coercion and intimidation have no function in this kind of dialogue. We are concerned, but we do look forward to the Arab neighbours of those two countries to continue the mediation efforts and to continue urging dialogue, and we're still hopeful that a second round will take place and that some kind of amicable agreement can be reached.'
57 The editors of *Time* magazine, *Desert Storm: The War in the Persian Gulf*, Boston, Little Brown & Co., 1991, p. 9.
58 Woodward, *The Commanders*, pp. 218–19.
59 *International Herald Tribune*, 25 September 1990.
60 Ibid.
61 M. Heikal, *Illusions of Triumph*, p. 192.

Chapter 4: Response to Invasion

1 *International Herald Tribune*, 4 March 1991. The same story appears in *Triumph Without Victory*, p. 36.
2 See, for example, Baghdad Voice of the Masses, 2 August 1990.
3 See, for example, statement by Abd al-Rahman al-Awadi, the Kuwaiti Minister of State for Cabinet Affairs, Cairo Radio, 2 August 1990.
4 *Triumph Without Victory*, p. 59; Woodward, *The Commanders*, pp. 232, 234; Beirut Radio, 3 August 1990.
5 Press conference with the Jordanian Prime Minister, Mudar Badran, Amman Radio, 5 August 1990. See also King Hussein's interview with PETRA (The Jordanian News Agency), 5 August 1990, and with NBC, 4 August 1990.
6 Mubarak's press conference, Cairo Radio, 8 August 1990.
7 INA, 3 August 1990.
8 See the comments of the Secretary-General of the Islamic Conference Organization (ICO), of which Iraq was a member state, on the day of the invasion, calling for Iraqi withdrawal. Riyadh Television, 2 August 1990. An official condemnation by the ICO was not issued until 4 August. Middle East News Agency (MENA) (Cairo), 4 August 1990.
9 Authors' interview with a Saudi diplomat.
10 Salinger and Laurent, *Secret Dossier*, p. 105; INA, 2 August 1990; Cairo Radio, 2 August 1990.
11 Authors' interview with a Saudi diplomat.
12 The Kuwaitis reciprocated by refusing to attend any summit on the Kuwaiti–Iraqi dispute at which Saddam was present. See Radio Monte Carlo in Arabic (Paris), 4 August 1990.
13 Woodward, *The Commanders*, p. 229. See also *International Herald Tribune*, 4 March 1991.
14 The Prime Minister liked to travel light. Charles Powell was the only adviser with her. In addition, press spokesman Bernard Ingham was present along with a duty clerk, two technicians, and the Special Branch. Mrs Thatcher did not like telephone diplomacy as much as President Bush, and she perhaps made half as many calls as he did. Her calls over the following days were to Commonwealth leaders, such as Bob Hawke of Australia, and to fellow members of the European Community, such as Lubbers of Holland, Andreotti of Italy and Kohl of Germany. The latter two were on holiday and took time to find. Her

concern was to encourage the Community to push ahead with sanctions. She also began some lobbying of Security Council members, such as Malaysia, and her own discussions with Arab leaders.

15 Thus Fred Barnes in *New Republic*, 3 September 1990, p. 14, spoke of Thatcher's critical influence and how Bush left with his 'spine stiffened'. Jean Smith, *George Bush's War*, New York, Henry Holt, 1992. Smith reinforces his position by erroneously citing Mrs Thatcher's 'This is no time to go wobbly' remark for this meeting rather than later in the month.

16 Filmed interview with Brent Scowcroft, Brian Lapping Associates, 10 December 1991.

17 Eagleburger had had no opportunity to talk to Baker and so was following his own instincts. It is an interesting question whether these instincts were more naturally hawkish than Baker's and whether the Secretary of State would have urged a more cautious line if he had been in Washington. There is no evidence to suggest that he would have materially differed from the line taken at this stage.

18 BBC Television, *The Washington Version*, 16 January 1992.

19 Ibid.

20 Secretary of State James Baker in BBC Television, *The Washington Version*, 16 January 1992. David Hoffman, 'Coalition Diplomacy', in David Newsom (ed.), *The Diplomatic Record 1990–91*, Boulder, Westview Institute for the Study of Diplomacy, 1992, p. 61.

21 On this issue see Thomas McNaugher, 'Walking Tightropes in the Gulf', in Karsh (ed.), *The Iran–Iraq War*, pp. 171–200.

22 Moscow Radio in Arabic, 19 July 1990.

23 Radio Peace and Progress in Persian, 24 July 1990.

24 Authors' interviews with Soviet academics and diplomats.

25 Tass, 2 August 1990.

26 Ibid.

27 *Izvestiya*, 13 August 1990.

28 See, for example, Vladimir Vinogradov's article in *Krasnaya Zvezda* on 3 August 1990. Without denying that Iraq's action was wrong, Vinogradov, a former Ambassador to Egypt and Iran and a longstanding hardliner, wondered 'why the United States risked taking such a step against Iraq'. 'One cannot help recalling,' he wrote, 'the invasion of Panama by US troops not so long ago, when Washington, according to the right of the strong, occupied the country which had refused to submit to its diktat. It is also possible to recall an event of longer ago – the freedom and sovereignty of the island state of Grenada trampled by the US interventionist's boot. In both cases, the attacker was condemned by the world community but nevertheless enjoyed the fruits of his criminal action. Is not Baghdad counting on the same thing?'

29 Filmed interview with James Baker, Brian Lapping Associates, 9 December 1991.

30 Jim Nichol, *Iraq–Kuwait Crisis: Soviet Response*, Washington DC, Congressional Research Service, 17 August 1990, p. 2.

31 Tass, 10 August 1990.

32 During 1990, in addition to the permanent members of the Security Council – China, France, the USSR, the United States and the United Kingdom – the ten non-permanent members were Cuba, Yemen, Canada, Finland, Colombia, Ethiopia, Malaysia, Ivory Coast, Zaïre and Romania.

33 The measures consisted of an embargo on oil exports from Kuwait and Iraq; appropriate measures aimed at freezing Iraq assets in the territory of member states; an embargo on sales of arms and other military equipment to Iraq; suspension of any co-operation in the military sphere with Iraq; suspension of technical and scientific co-operation with Iraq, and suspension of the application to Iraq of the System of Generalized Preferences. *European Community Statement*, 5 August 1990.

34 A Brazilian spokesman was quoted as saying: 'Today Brazil condemns the invasion but this

won't affect relations in the long term. There is no reason for a change. Brazil has important interests with Iraq and these will be maintained.' *International Herald Tribune*, 4–5 August 1990.

35 *Independent*, 6 August 1990.

36 A strict reading of Article 51 suggests that it is suspended as soon as the UN begins to take collective action to redress the grievance. One reason for inserting a reference to it in the sanctions resolution was intended to head off any attempt at this sort of interpretation.

Chapter 5: Desert Shield

1 James Blackwell, *Thunder in the Desert: The Strategy and the Tactics of the Persian Gulf War*, New York, Bantam Books, 1991, p. 86.

2 A monograph prepared by the Strategic Studies Institute at the US Army War College doubted whether in the foreseeable future Iraq would have the will or the resources to go to war. It presumed that Iraq's main target was Israel and made no mention of Kuwait. Stephen C. Pelletière, Douglas V. Johnson II and Leif R. Rosenberger, *Iraqi Power and US Security in the Middle East*, Strategic Studies Institute, US Army War College, Pennsylvania, 1990.

3 BBC Television, *The Washington Version*, 16 January 1992.

4 Woodward, *The Commanders*, pp. 241, 225, 237.

5 Heikal, *Illusions of Triumph*, p. 200.

6 *Wall Street Journal*, 6 August 1990.

7 *Triumph Without Victory*, p. 69.

8 Laurent, *Tempête du désert*, p. 40; the editors of *Time* magazine, *Desert Storm: The War in the Persian Gulf*, Washington DC, Little, Brown & Co., 1992, p. 26.

9 Woodward, *The Commanders*, p. 254; *Triumph Without Victory*, p. 74.

10 *Independent*, 4 August 1990.

11 Woodward, *The Commanders*, pp. 258–9, 264. According to the Pentagon, by this time a major resupply effort was under way. By the next day Kuwait was estimated to contain some 200,000 Iraqi soldiers backed by 2,000 tanks. Department of Defense, *Conduct of the Persian Gulf War: Final Report to Congress*, Washington DC, GPO, April 1992, p. 2. [Hereinafter referred to as *Final Pentagon Report*.]

12 See, for example, *International Herald Tribune*, 4–5 August 1990.

13 *Washington Post*, 9 August 1990.

14 INA, 3 August 1990.

15 *Wall Street Journal*, 6 August 1990.

16 BBC Television, *The Washington Version*, 16 January 1992.

17 On Saddam's meeting with Wilson see BBC Television, *The Washington Version*, 16 January 1992; filmed interview with Joseph Wilson, Brian Lapping Associates, 7 December 1991; Baghdad Radio, 6 August 1990; Salinger and Laurent, *Secret Dossier*, pp. 139–48. According to the *Washington Post* of 7 August 1990, during the meeting Saddam threatened to attack Saudi Arabia if it prevented the flow of Iraqi oil through its territory. This allegation was vehemently denied by the Iraqis. See, for example, INA, 7 August 1990.

18 BBC Television, *The Washington Version*, 16 January 1992; Woodward, *The Commanders*, pp. 267, 271.

19 Kelly later recalled that as the Deputies Committee was discussing how the announcement should be made it was discovered that a sergeant from McGuire Air Force base had asked for flight clearances for 530 tankers and cargo planes and laid out the entire deployment. BBC Television, *The Washington Version*, 16 January 1992.

20 Woodward, *The Commanders*, pp. 279–80.

Chapter 6: Middle East Alignments

1 Saudi Press Agency (SPA), 7 August 1990.
2 On the Syro–Iraqi rivalry, see Eberhard Kienle, *Ba'th v Ba'th*, London, I.B.Tauris, 1990.
3 *Guardian*, 15 August 1990; *Middle East International* (London), 31 August 1990.
4 J. Miller, 'Syria's Game', *New York Times Magazine*, 26 January 1992, p. 20.
5 *The Times*, 14 September 1990.
6 *Middle East International*, 31 August 1990.
7 *The Times*, 14 September 1990; Heikal, *Illusion of Triumph*, pp. 200–1.
8 Damascus Radio, 21 August 1991.
9 In mid-October the bodies of several hundred of General Aoun's supporters were found in Beirut, with their hands tied behind their backs and bullet-holes in their heads.
10 Heikal, *Illusions of Triumph*, pp. 202–3.
11 *Al-Akhbar* (Cairo), 20 August 1990.
12 *Al-Jumhuriya* (Cairo), 12 August 1990.
13 Cairo Radio, 21 August 1990; Heikal, *Illusions of Triumph*, p. 280.
14 In 1979, in an attempt to stem the mounting pressures of the revolutionary regime in Tehran, Saddam suddenly 'discovered' that he was a direct descendant of the Prophet. For Saddam's reply to Mubarak, see Baghdad Radio, 23 August 1990.
15 See his press conference as broadcast on Cairo Radio on 28 August 1990.
16 Baghdad Radio, 8 August 1990; Heikal, *Illusions of Triumph*, p. 226.
17 E. Lauterpacht, C. J. Greenwood, Marc Weller and Daniel Bethlehem, *The Kuwait Crisis: Basic Documents*, Cambridge, Grotius Publications, 1991, p. 90.
18 Of the twenty League members attending the Cairo Summit, twelve voted in favour of the decision while three (Libya, the PLO, and Iraq) voted against. For the text of the resolution, see Lauterpacht *et. al.*, *The Kuwait Crisis*, p. 294. See also *Independent*, 11 August 1990; *International Herald Tribune*, 11–12 August 1990.
19 Radio Monte Carlo in Arabic, 9, 10 August 1990; MENA (Cairo), 10 August 1990; *International Herald Tribune*, 10 August 1990.
20 Damascus Radio, 4, 7 August 1990.
21 Ann Mosely Lesch, 'Contrasting Reactions to the Persian Gulf Crisis: Egypt, Syria, Jordan and the Palestinians', *Middle East Journal*, Vol. 45, No.1, Winter 1991.
22 Baghdad Radio, 8 August 1990.
23 INA, 9 August 1990; Baghdad Radio, 8, 11 July 1990.
24 See, for example, INA, 18 September 1990; Baghdad Radio, 23 September 1990; *The Times* 24 September 1990.
25 Lauterpacht *et al.*, *The Kuwait Crisis*, p. 281; Baghdad Radio, 12 August 1990.
26 MENA, 13 August 1990.
27 Damascus Radio, 14 August 1990.
28 Testimony of Brigadier-General Dani Rothschild, Head of the Net Assessment Division of the Military Intelligence, before the Knesset's Foreign Affairs and Defence Committee a day after the occupation of Kuwait. *Hadashot* (Tel Aviv), 3 August 1990. See also the references of the Israeli Minister of Defence, Moshe Arens, to the crisis. *Ha'aretz* (Tel Aviv), *Jerusalem Post*, 3 August 1990.
29 *Ma'ariv* (Tel Aviv), *Israel in the Gulf War*, 29 March 1991, p. 26.
30 *Jerusalem Post*, *Ha'aretz*, 5 August 1990.
31 *International Herald Tribune*, 3 August 1990.
32 *Ha'aretz*, *Davar*, *Ma'ariv*, 3 August 1990.
33 *International Herald Tribune*, 18–19 August 1990.
34 Ibid., 3 August 1990.
35 *Jerusalem Post*, 12 August 1990; *Ha'aretz*, 17 August 1990. Sharon's scepticism regarding the sanctions' utility was shared by some military sources which assessed that between six

and twelve months were required for the sanctions to bring Iraq to its knees. *Jerusalem Post*, 29 August 1990.

36 Ibid., 3 August 1990.
37 *Ha'aretz*, 28 August 1990.
38 Ibid., 29 August 1990.
39 *Jerusalem Post*, 16 August 1990; *Ha'aretz*, 16, 29 August 1990.
40 *Jerusalem Post*, 22 August, 14 October 1990; *Ha'aretz*, 19 August 1990.
41 *Jerusalem Post*, 19 July, 13 August 1990; *Ma'ariv*, 5 August 1990; *Ha'aretz*, 5, 6 August 1990.
42 *Ha'aretz, Jerusalem Post*, 24 August 1990.
43 *Ma'ariv*, 10 August 1990.
44 *Jerusalem Post*, 17 September 1990.
45 *Ma'ariv*, 30 September 1990.
46 *Ha'aretz, Jerusalem Post*, 23 August 1990.
47 *Ha'aretz*, 15 August 1990.
48 *Jerusalem Post*, 7 September 1990; *Ha'aretz*, 6 September 1990. *Triumph Without Victory*, p.149.
49 For the Iraqi–Iranian correspondence over a political settlement, see *Kayhan International*, 29 September, 13 October 1990; Baghdad Radio, 15 August 1990.
50 Taha Yasin Ramadan's interview with *al-Tadamun* (London), 29 October 1990, pp. 20–24.
51 See, for example, Iranian News Agency (IRNA), 22 July 1990.
52 Cited by *Agence France Presse (AFP)*, 22 July 1990.
53 Tehran Television, 2 August 1990.
54 Tehran Radio, 8 August 1990.
55 IRNA, 9 August 1990.

Chapter 7: Sharing the Burden

1 *Independent on Sunday*, 9 September 1990.
2 John Sullivan in *Independent on Sunday*, 2 September 1990.
3 Transcript of speech given by Mrs Thatcher to the Aspen Institute on Sunday 5 August 1990.
4 Transcript of press conference given by Mrs Thatcher at Andrews Air Force Base, Washington, on Monday 6 August 1990.
5 *Independent*, 6 August 1990.
6 BBC TV News, 13.00, 8 August 1990.
7 This was somewhat ironic, as the Falklands campaign had also been preceded by a major defence review.
8 *The Times*, 7 September 1990; *Daily Telegraph*, 14 September 1990; *Financial Times*, 15–16 September 1990; *International Herald Tribune*, 15–16 September 1990; *Independent on Sunday*, 16 September 1990; *Independent*, 18 September 1990.
9 According to Pierre Marion, former national intelligence director, *International Herald Tribune*, 8 August 1990.
10 *Financial Times*, 10 August 1990.
11 'Preliminary Statement of M. François Mitterrand, President of the Republic, Following the Meeting of the Select Council (Elysée Palace, 21 August 1990)', *Ambassade de France à Londres Service de Presse et d'Information*.
12 *Le Figaro*, 23 August 1990; *Independent*, 23 August 1990; *International Herald Tribune*, 24 August 1990.
13 *Independent*, 14 August 1990.
14 Josette Alia and Christine Clerc, *La guerre de Mitterrand: la dernière grande illusion*, Paris, Olivier Orban, 1991, pp. 85–6.

15 Ibid., p. 96.
16 *Gulf Conflict: Communiqué from the Ministry of Foreign Affairs*, Paris, 27 August 1990.
17 *Guerre éclair dans le Golfe: la defense du droit*, Paris, Jean-Claude Lattes/Addim, 1991.
18 Alia and Clerc, *La guerre de Mitterrand*, pp. 105–6.
19 Article 2 of the Constitution says that: 'Apart from defence, the armed forces may be used only to the extent explicitly permitted by this Basic Law.' No article deals explicitly with deployment abroad except Article 24, which enables the Federal Republic to join an alliance 'to bring about a peaceful and lasting order in Europe and among the nations of the world'. It should be noted that although in practice the North Atlantic Treaty only mandates collective action within this area, it does not prohibit such an action outside this immediate area.
20 *International Herald Tribune*, 15, 16 August 1990.
21 Thomas Kielinger, 'The Gulf War and the Consequences from a German Point of View', *Aussenpolitik*, Vol. 42, No. 3, 1991.
22 *International Herald Tribune*, 10 September 1990.
23 The figure included DM1.6 billion in military equipment, including transport. Of this about half came from the stocks of the old National People's Army of East Germany. This would include protective devices against chemical weapons, as well as engineering equipment such as bridge-building materials. Another DM420 million was the German contribution to EC aid for the front-line countries, with another DM1.28 billion in direct support for Egypt, Turkey and Jordan. The biggest single component of this latter item was DM975 million for Egypt, of which DM775 million had already been allocated under the budgets for 1988, 1989 and 1990 but had then been frozen pending an accord on Egypt's debt rescheduling. *Financial Times*, 25 September 1990.
24 For background, see Courtney Purrington and A.K., 'Tokyo's Policy Responses during the Gulf Crisis', *Asian Survey*, Vol. 31, No. 4, April 1991.
25 *International Herald Tribune*, 14 August 1990.
26 Taizo Terashima, the Chairman of the Joint Staff Council, said: 'We are ready to go abroad any time and I am confident that the SDF is capable of carrying out whatever missions are required.' *Guardian*, 16 August 1990.
27 *Independent*, 22 August 1990. For the views of a supporter of backing the international coalition see Hiroyuki Kishino, *The Persian Gulf Crisis and Japan's Role*, Tokyo, International Institute for Global Peace, October, 1990.
28 *International Herald Tribune*, 31 August, 1–2 September 1990; *Independent*, 31 August 1990.
29 BBC Television, *The Washington Version*, 17 January 1992.
30 With regard to the funds to support the American military effort, Taizo Watanabe, the Foreign Ministry spokesman, explained that the delay was in part because Japan was not involved in the decision to send forces to the Gulf and so it needed to find out more before acting: 'We all understand and know that there was a need for urgent action. But when we are asked to pay the bill we have got to check the contents of the invoice.' *International Herald Tribune*, 15–16 September 1990.
31 See the testimony of Assistant Secretary Richard Solomon, House of Representatives, Subcommittee on Asian and Pacific Affairs of the Committee on Foreign Affairs, *Asian Response to the Crisis in the Persian Gulf*, 19 September 1990, pp. 41–2.
32 *International Herald Tribune*, 28 September 1990; *Daily Telegraph*, 28 September 1990.
33 A survey in *Mainichi* newspaper in late October showed 53 per cent of Japanese against the bill and 49 per cent judging that it violated the Constitution. It also showed a steep decline in support for the Government. *Independent*, 1 November 1990.
34 Gennadi Ilyichev of Soviet Foreign Ministry, cited by Novosti Information Agency, 10 August 1990.
35 Tass, 9 August 1990.

36 Tass, 23 August 1990.

37 Interview with Lt.-General Vladimir Nikitiuk, deputy departmental head at the General Staff of the USSR Armed Forces. *Izvestia*, 16 August 1990. According to some estimates, the figures were somewhat higher and ranged around 1,000 specialists. See Robert Freedman, 'Moscow and the Iraqi Invasion of Kuwait: A Preliminary Analysis', *Problems of Communism*, Vol. XL, July–August 1991.

38 *Izvestiya*, 26 September 1990. Hoffman, 'Coalition Diplomacy' in Newsom (ed.), *Diplomatic Record*, p. 64.

39 *Independent*, 26 September 1990.

40 Tass, 15 October 1990.

41 A. Vasilyev, 'Should We Send Our Boys to the Arabian Desert?', *Komsomolskaya Pravda*, 25 October 1990 (Tass translation).

Chapter 8: Saddam's Unwilling Guests

1 *Economist*, 22 December 1990, p. 80.

2 There had been an Israeli–Egyptian–Jordanian understanding to let Egyptians home through Israel, both through the Israeli port town of Eilat and across the Allenby Bridge into the West Bank and through Israel. However, the plan was abandoned after being leaked by Israel's newly instated Foreign Minister, David Levy. Neither Egypt nor Jordan was willing to collaborate openly with Israel at a time when Saddam was 'Zionizing' the conflict.

3 On one occasion the Jordanians asked that a refugee camp at Azraq be pulled down after they had given permission to the International Committee of the Red Cross, when they became fearful that it would pollute Amman's water supply.

4 *Independent*, 5 September 1990.

5 Baghdad was not making things any easier for itself by insisting that any evacuation vessels entering Iraqi ports must bring in food and medicines despite the fact that, in the absence of clear need, this would be a breach of the UN embargo. Nor would the Iraqis deal with the Red Cross (charged under the 1949 Geneva Convention with the protection of war victims), on the grounds that Iraq was not involved in an armed conflict and that it could not act to help foreigners in Kuwait as an occupied country because the latter was not occupied but was part of Iraq. Again, this behaviour did not create widespread sympathy for the Iraqi cause.

6 *International Herald Tribune*, 13 August 1990.

7 Ibid., 11–12, 13 August 1990.

8 Iraq's Ambassador to Austria, Rahim al-Kital, as cited by *Die Presse* (Vienna), 17 August 1990. The Iraqi Ambassador to Athens, Fatah al-Khazraji, carried the denial that Western nationals were held as hostages a step further by stating that all of them were free to leave Iraq and Kuwait by road via Jordan or Turkey. See Athens Radio, 7 August 1990.

9 *Independent*, 6 August 1990.

10 *International Herald Tribune*, 7 August 1990.

11 Radio Monte Carlo in Arabic (Paris), 14 August 1990.

12 This 'open letter' was also transmitted to the UN on the same day by Iraq's Permanent Representative. For the full text, see Lauterpacht *et al.*, *The Kuwait Crisis*, pp. 283–4; Baghdad Radio, 19 August 1990; INA, 21 August 1990.

13 *Independent on Sunday*, 19 August 1991. He added: 'The National Assembly has been co-ordinating with a number of state ministries and installations, which have the required accommodation facilities throughout the country from Zakho to al-Nida, including the Ministry of Oil, the Ministry of Military Industrialization, the armed forces and air bases and other ministries and institutions and the refinery complex in Kuwait and other places, so they are provided with the appropriate accommodation.'

14 Lauterpacht *et al.*, *The Kuwait Crisis*, p. 115.
15 Baghdad Radio, 18 August 1990.
16 Ibid., 19 August 1990.
17 INA, 19 August 1990. Later, when some ninety Swedes tried to leave Iraq on the basis of this statement, more than half, mainly men, were turned back at the border.
18 Ibid., 2 September 1990.
19 United Nations debate on Resolution on 664, 18 August 1990. In Lauterpacht *et al.*, *The Kuwait Crisis*, p. 110.

Chapter 9: From Embargo to Blockade

1 *International Herald Tribune*, 13 August 1990.
2 See Mark Lowenthal, *Naval Restriction of Commerce against Iraq: Historic Background, Implications and Options*, Congressional Research Service, 14 August 1990; Raymond Celada, *Blockade: Some International and Domestic Legal Implications*, Congressional Research Service, 15 August 1990.
3 The Foreign Office announced that a request from the legitimate Kuwaiti authorities would provide legal authority for a blockade, that such a request was expected, and that it would be granted promptly. *Independent*, 14 August 1990.
4 Roland Dannreuther, *The Gulf Conflict: A Political and Strategic Analysis*, Adelphi Paper 264, London, Brassey's for the IISS, Winter 1991/2, p. 30.
5 After the meeting it was reported that as a positive element Iraq seemed to accept that there could be a multinational force on Saudi soil. Tass, 21 August 1990.
6 The British also reported Iraqi aircraft in North Yemen, prepared to fly food to Baghdad. *International Herald Tribune*, 25–26 August 1990; *Independent*, 22 August 1990.
7 Present were Scowcroft, Gates, Cheney, Sununu, Powell and Eagleburger.
8 Thus one article suggested that the combination of Soviet military advisers and KGB agents operating through the Iraqi establishment must have provided Moscow with advance knowledge of the invasion, and also cited evidence of arms shipments reaching Baghdad as late as 7 August. *International Herald Tribune*, 23 August 1990. Moscow remained extremely sensitive to such accusations. It claimed that the Soviet vessel accused of taking military equipment to Iraq had turned round and headed for home before reaching its destination. Tass, 27 August 1990.
9 Without UN authority the rules of engagement for the ships were tricky. As any action would be politically charged, how much could be left to military discretion? What action would be taken against the tankers if they refused to stop? What sort of warning, with what calibre gun? What part of a fully laden supertanker should be targeted to avoid polluting the whole of the Gulf? How would the boarding take place?
10 Filmed interview with Sir Charles Powell, Brian Lapping Associates, 7 December 1991.
11 BBC Television, *The Washington Version*, 17 January 1992.
12 Tass, 24 August 1990. Coincidentally, this was the day that the evacuation of Soviet families from Kuwait was completed.
13 Salinger and Laurent, *Secret Dossier*, pp. 181–3; the Iraqi Foreign Ministry later complained that it received the letter only at 17.30 on 23 August, calling for a 'withdraw or not' reply by 19.30. *Independent*, 6 September 1990. See also Shevardnadze's comments on the Security Council vote on Resolution 665, Tass 25 August 1990.
14 For a discussion of the history of the Military Staff Committee, and some reflections of concern within the UN that the full UN machinery and the rights of small countries were being taken over by the permanent five, see David Cox (ed.), *The Use of Force by the Security Council for Enforcement and Deterrent Purposes: A Conference Report*, Toronto, Canadian Centre for Arms Control and Disarmament, 1991.
15 *Independent*, 27 August 1990.

16 These orders were intercepted by the US signals intelligence. *International Herald Tribune*, 28 August 1990.
17 *The Times*, 16 August 1990.
18 Willem Van Ekelen, 'WEU and the Gulf Crisis', *Survival*, November/December 1990; Michael Chichester, 'The Gulf: The Western European Union Naval deployment to the Middle East', *Navy International*, February 1991; Eric Remacle, 'What Future for European Security', *Contemporary European Affairs*, Vol. 4, No.1, 1991. A map of the dispositions appears in *Guerre éclair dans le Golfe*, Paris, Jean-Claude Lattes/Addim, 1991, p. 42.

Chapter 10: Poor Communications

1 The only serious communication between the two came in September, when the United States demanded a spot on Iraqi television to explain its position – as the Iraqis had free access to American television. Against expectations, the wish was granted. An eight-minute broadcast by the President was handed over to the Iraqis (in every conceivable format, as the technical capability of Iraqi television was not known). The objective was to get through to the 'street' – where the Arabists claimed support for Saddam was strongest – by stressing that the President had no quarrel with ordinary Iraqis. When it was finally broadcast, anti-American rallies were called in Iraq to occur at the same time.
2 *International Herald Tribune*, 22 August 1990.
3 INA, 28 August 1990.
4 Moscow told Saddam that Iraq 'has lost much, politically and morally, in the eyes of world public opinion by its illegal and inhumane action towards citizens of third countries'. Tass, 23 August 1990.
5 Saddam called Waldheim a 'particularly fair politician who could act as a mediator' in the crisis. *Independent*, 28 August 1990.
6 For the joint press conference, see Baghdad Radio, 25 August 1990.
7 Alia and Clerc, *La guerre de Mitterrand*, p. 71; *International Herald Tribune*, 20 August 1990.
8 *Preliminary Statement of M. François Mitterrand, President of the Republic, Following the Meeting of the Select Council*, Elysée Palace, 21 August 1990.
9 *Daily Telegraph*, 30 August 1990.
10 *International Herald Tribune*, 5 September 1990. An aide explained that he was warning that Israel might be brought into the conflict and that long-range ballistic missiles might be used.
11 Alia and Clerc, *La guerre de Mitterrand*, pp. 89–91.
12 INA, 23 August, 2 September 1990.
13 He portrayed this move as acquiescence to a request made by the former Algerian President, Ahmad Ben-Bella, during a visit to Baghdad. Ben-Bella had also been in touch with the French.
14 *Financial Times*, 17 September 1990.
15 *Independent*, 27 August 1990. Perez de Cuellar might also have been influenced by the reception accorded his predecessor, Kurt Waldheim.
16 Ibid., 31 August 1990.
17 *International Herald Tribune*, 3 September 1990.
18 Laurie Brand, 'Liberalization and Changing Political Conditions: The Bases of Jordan's 1990–1991 Gulf Crisis Policy', *The Jerusalem Journal of International Relations*, Vol. 13, No. 4, December 1991.
19 For a list of peace plans made during August, see *Guardian*, 6 September 1990.
20 Heikal, *Illusions of Triumph*, 256, 261–2.
21 Tass, 30 August 1990.
22 *International Herald Tribune*, 4 September 1990.

23 Heikal, *Illusions of Triumph*, p. 16.
24 *International Herald Tribune*, 6, 7 September 1990.
25 INA, 8 September 1990.
26 On the Helsinki summit see, *Economist*, 15 September 1990, pp. 91–2; *The Times*, 8 September 1990; *Sunday Times*, 9 September 1990; *Pravda*, 10 September 1990.

Chapter 11: Enter Linkage

1   See, for example, INA, 23 August, 2 September 1990.
2   Reprinted in Lauterpacht *et al.*, *The Kuwait Crisis*, pp. 287–8.
3   Laurent, *Tempête du désert*, p. 75.
4   *The Times*, 2 October 1990.
5   Baghdad Radio, 9 October 1990.
6   Filmed interview with Ambassador Thomas Pickering, Brian Lapping Associates, December 1991.
7   For a description of the week's events, see *Independent*, 13 October 1990.
8   *Independent*, 4 October 1990. M. Le Pen of the right-wing National Front, who had in his public utterances been extremely sympathetic to Iraq, offered himself but was denied a visa. The French clearly did not want an extremist speaking for France and gaining the credit for a major political coup. He did arrive later, though, as part of a delegation of European parliamentarians.
9   Alia and Clerc, *La guerre de Mitterrand*, p. 140.
10 Baghdad Radio, 22 October 1990.
11 INA, 23 October 1990.
12 Radio Monte Carlo in Arabic 24 October 1990; Baghdad International Service in English, 25 October 1990.
13 See his interview with *Le Figaro* on 7 November 1990.
14 See Edward Heath's testimony to the US House of Representatives, Hearings before the Committee on Armed Services, *Crisis in the Persian Gulf: Sanctions, Diplomacy and War*, 1991, pp. 741–3. Heath here and elsewhere made frequent reference to President Kennedy's attempt to help Nikita Khrushchev save face during the Cuban missile crisis.
15 In the same statement they also reaffirmed 'their total solidarity in achieving the freedom of all foreign citizens trapped in Iraq and Kuwait and denounce the unscrupulous use which Iraq is making of them with the sole and vain purpose of trying to divide the international community. They unreservedly condemn this manoeuvre which, carried out in contempt of the most basic humanitarian rules, can only complicate prospects for a solution to the crisis.' The European Council, *Declaration on the Gulf Crisis*, Brussels, 28 October 1990. In Lauterpacht *et al.*, *The Kuwait Crisis*, p. 314.
16 A former East German Parliamentarian, Brigitta Kohler, had secured the release of four German hostages at the start of October, as 'a gesture', according to the Speaker of the Iraqi Parliament, 'to show that the Iraqi people share the German people's joy at reunification'. *International Herald Tribune*, 6–7 October 1990.
17 *The Times*, 2 November 1990. Brandt himself discounted Genscher's view that he was not negotiating. 'It's obvious what humanitarian means,' he said, 'it means political efforts to find out if there is still an alternative to war.' *International Herald Tribune*, 6 November 1990.
18 The same day the Speaker of Iraq's National Assembly, Sa'di Mahdi Salih, said Iraq would free all hostages in return for an assurance of non-aggression. On 29 October there had been indications, following a visit by Gorbachev to Paris, that a Franco-Soviet commitment to solving the crisis by peaceful means would see the release of the hostages. *Financial Times*, 30 October 1990.
19 Ambassador Ryukichi Imai, *The Gulf Crisis and the Gulf War*, Tokyo, International Institute

of Global Peace, March 1991. The group advising Nakasone, which included senior Arab Middle Eastern specialists, the director of Japan's National Oil Corporation and the managing director of Sony, felt 'the need to show the world, and the Middle East in particular, that there was a powerful politician in Japan who was seeking to push a comprehensive resolution of the problem from a global perspective'.

20 See comments by Gennadi Gerasimov, Tass, 26 September 1990.

21 Radio Moscow in English, 5 September 1990.

22 This is Primakov's account. Yevgeni Primakov, 'The Inside Story of Moscow's Quest for a Deal', *Time*, 4 March 1991, p. 41.

23 Tass, 2 October 1990.

24 A few days after the meeting it was announced that 1,500 Soviet citizens in the country would leave within a month and that the remaining 140 military experts would be leaving as soon as their contracts expired. Tass, 10 October 1990. Primakov claims to have suggested the number, after first being told by Saddam that only 1,000 could leave, because this was the number of outstanding applications then at the Soviet Embassy. Primakov, 'The Inside Story', p. 42.

25 Ibid., p. 42.

26 The initial report from the Novosti News Agency was officially denied later in Moscow. See Tass, 16 October 1990. State Department spokeswoman Margaret Tutwiler observed that: 'The Kuwaitis themselves have said these islands and some of these subjects could be discussed at The Hague once two things happen – the return of their legitimate government and the complete withdrawal of [Iraqi] forces from Kuwait.'

27 Primakov, 'The Inside Story', pp. 47–8. Thatcher's attitude led Primakov to brand her as a potential obstacle to a settlement and stress the relative importance of President Mitterrand of France and Prime Minister Andreotti of Italy, with whom he also met.

28 The resolution was passed on 29 October.

29 *The Times*, 28 October 1990.

30 Primakov, 'The Inside Story', p. 48; and his full account, *Missions à Baghdad: Histoire d'une negociation secrète*, Paris, Seuil, 1991, p. 54.

31 On the Iraqi views on Primakov's visits, see INA, 4, 5, 6 October 1990; MENA (Baghdad), 5 October 1990; *al-Sharq al-Awsat* (London), 11 October 1990; Baghdad Radio, 27 October 1990.

32 Moscow Television, 31 October 1991.

33 *Independent*, 30 October 1990; *International Herald Tribune*, 30 October 1990; *Financial Times*, 31 October 1990.

34 Tass, 28 October 1990; *Izvestiya*, 31 October 1991.

35 Gorbachev: 'President Hussein should not base his calculations around the idea of dividing us, of creating a split among us . . . If he thinks like this, he is very wrong.'

36 *Independent*, 1 November 1990.

Chapter 12: The Oil Weapon

1 The Strategic Petroleum Reserve (SPR) was set up in late 1975 to protect the United States against the sort of dislocation caused by the oil embargo imposed by the Arab oil exporting countries in 1973–4. It can be used to cope with an actual or threatened 'severe energy disruption' or to meet US obligations in the event of International Energy Agency requests for emergency oil-sharing. In 1979–80, after the Iranian revolution, the SPR was only at 100 million barrels and was not considered large enough to be of service. However, during the years of oil glut it had gradually been built up. See Robert L. Bamberger and Lawrence C. Kumins, *The Strategic Petroleum Reserve and the Drawdown Dilemma*, Washington DC, Library of Congress, Congressional Research Service, 12 October 1990, p. 1.

2 Problems mentioned included the heaviness of much of the reserve oil which makes it unsuitable for many refineries, equipment problems at some of the reserve facilities, the possibility of speculators buying the reserves when released and hoarding it, and a possible shortage of tankers if a sudden draw-down was required. *Wall Street Journal*, 5 September 1990.

3 *Independent*, 28 September 1990.

4 For a discussion of these issues, see Bamberger and Kumins, *The Strategic Petroleum Reserve and the Drawdown Dilemma*.

5 E. Zhurabayev, 'The Oil Fever and Its Possible Aftermath for the Soviets', *Trud*, 23 October 1990.

6 *Independent*, 18 September 1990.

7 Deputy Foreign Minister Alexander Belonogov to Soviet Parliament's International Affairs Committee. Tass, 30 August 1990. A spokesman from the Soviet Ministry of Foreign Economic Relations later put the losses from trade with Middle Eastern clients at $6–7 billion. Cited in Zhurabayev, 'The Oil Fever'.

8 *Independent*, 19 November 1990.

9 *Financial Times*, 12 December 1990.

10 Turkey had estimated a trade loss of $4.5 billion by the end of year, Jordan $100 million each month and Egypt $2 billion per annum.

Chapter 13: The Food Weapon

1 US Department of State, *Current Policy No. 1302*, 25 September 1990.

2 On 10 September, Saddam offered free oil to any country that could arrange its own shipping. This was presented as a gesture of solidarity with poor countries badly hit by the effects of sanctions.

3 At the end of September a convoy of twenty-five Jordanian trucks loaded with 400 tonnes of Palestinian-financed food and medicine was paraded through the streets of Baghdad. It had been organized in Amman by a charitable group, the General Union of Voluntary Societies, and had not embarrassed the Jordanian Government by asking for permission to make its delivery. *International Herald Tribune*, 28 September 1990.

4 See, for example, Gary Hufbauer and Jeffrey Schott, *Economic Sanctions Reconsidered*, Washington DC, American Enterprise Institute, 1985.

5 This seems to assume a price of $100 a barrel, thereby giving weight to those who feared a commanding Iraqi position when it came to oil prices. *International Herald Tribune*, 1 September 1990. Aziz in *Middle East Economic Survey*, 27 August 1990.

6 Soybean meal, 100 per cent ; vegetable oil, 95 per cent; sugar, 93 per cent; corn, 90 per cent; wheat, 82 per cent; rice, 82 per cent; beef, 68 per cent; barley, 24 per cent; poultry, 10 per cent. See Susan B. Epstein, *The World Embargo on Food Exports to Iraq*, Washington DC, Library of Congress, Congressional Research Service, 25 September 1990, p. 1.

7 *Independent*, 11 September 1990.

8 The summary records of the Committee are reprinted in D.L. Bethlehem (ed.), *The Kuwait Crisis: Sanctions and their Economic Consequences*, Cambridge, Grotius Publications, 1991.

9 *International Herald Tribune*, 11 September 1990.

10 *Independent*, 12 September 1990.

11 *Financial Times*, 14 September 1990.

12 Baghdad Radio, 12 August 1990.

13 INA, 28 August 1990.

14 Baghdad Radio, 12 August 1990.

15 Ibid., 19, 22, 28 October 1990.

16 *New York Times*, 28 August 1990.

17 Cited in Susan B. Epstein, *The World Embargo on Food Exports to Iraq*, p. 5.
18 *Independent*, 2 September 1990.
19 *New York Times*, 14 September 1990; *Independent*, 8 September 1990.
20 *Guardian*, 29 August 1990.
21 'The Road to War', *Newsweek*, 28 January 1991, p. 62.; Brown and Shukman, *All Necessary Means*, pp. 18–19.
22 See testimony by William Webster, Director of Central Intelligence Agency, on 5 December 1990 in the US House of Representatives, Hearings before the Committee on Armed Services, *Crisis in the Persian Gulf: Sanctions, Diplomacy and War*, 1991, p. 113.
23 Kimberly Elliot, Gary Hufbauer and Jeffrey Schott, 'Judging from History, the Anti-Saddam Sanctions Can Work', *International Herald Tribune*, 11 December 1990.

Chapter 14: The Offensive Option

1 Carroll Doherty, 'Members Back Sending Troops to Gulf . . . But Worry about a Drawn-Out Crisis', *Congressional Quarterly*, 11 August 1990.
2 *Independent*, 22 August 1990.
3 Ronald O'Rourke, *Sealift and Operation Desert Shield*, Washington DC, Congressional Research Service, 17 September 1990.
4 *Independent*, 27 August 1990.
5 *International Herald Tribune*, 3 September 1990.
6 Ibid., 1–2 September 1990.
7 BBC Television, *Newsnight*, 7 September 1990. Hurd had sought earlier to dampen down the war scare. *The Times*, 24 August 1990. *Independent*, 29 August 1990.
8 *Financial Times*, 31 August 1990.
9 *Aviation Week and Space Technology*, 27 August 1990.
10 R.W. Apple of *New York Times* in *International Herald Tribune*, 8–9 September 1990.
11 See, for example, Taha Yasin Ramadan's statement, INA, 21 October 1990. Heikal, *Illusions of Triumph*, p. 259.
12 *The Times*, 27 September 1990; Woodward, *The Commanders*, p. 297.
13 Cited in BBC, Radio 4, 9 October 1990.
14 In *Atlanta Journal and Constitution*. See Woodward, *The Commanders*, pp. 307, 310, 313. On earlier planning see *Final Pentagon Report*, p. 84.
15 Woodward, *The Commanders*, pp. 304–5.
16 Filmed interview, Brian Lapping Associates, December 1991.
17 *Triumph Without Victory*, p. 166.
18 Ibid., p. 165. *Final Pentagon Report*, pp. 51–55.
19 This was, however, leaked to the press as a preferred option. *International Herald Tribune*, 24 September 1990.
20 *New York Times*/CBS poll, reported in *International Herald Tribune*, 15 October 1990.
21 Woodward, *The Commanders*, p. 312.
22 Filmed interview, Brian Lapping Associates, December 1991.
23 Woodward, *The Commanders*, pp. 319, 320.
24 *Sunday Times*, 2 September 1990; Heikal, *Illusions of Triumph*, p. 218.
25 In Britain there were daily and quite large interdepartmental meetings, co-ordinated at first by the Foreign Office and then by the Cabinet Office. The Overseas and Defence Subcommittee of Cabinet or OD (G) involved the Prime Minister, the Foreign Secretary, the Minister of Defence and the Attorney-General, with the Chancellor of the Exchequer present when required. However, Mrs Thatcher tended to prefer policy-making to be held tightly and to make decisions on the basis of informal discussions with the most relevant ministers, and also with her closest official adviser, Charles Powell, who performed the same role as Brent Scowcroft did for President Bush. Under John Major the system

became more formal. Britain's Parliamentary system meant that ministers were subjected to regular questioning, although apart from the emergency debate in September, Parliament was not sitting until late October (and was then preoccupied with the Europe issue and the challenge to Mrs Thatcher's leadership).

26　Brown and Shukman, *All Necessary Means*, p. 21.

27　President George Bush, News conference at the White House, 8 November 1990.

Chapter 15: The Great Debate

1　CBS/*New York Times* poll, 13–15 November 1990. Nationwide random sample of 1,370 adults, interviewed by telephone 13–15 November 1990. Source: CBS News, New York.

2　On the anti-war movement in the United States see Max Elbaum, 'The Storm at Home', in Phyllis Bennis and Michel Moushabeck (eds.), *Beyond the Storm: A Gulf Crisis Reader*, New York, Olive Branch Press, 1991. This book reflects the perspectives of the anti-war movement.

3　See, for example, prepared statement of Christopher Layne and Ted Galen Carpenter, US Senate, Hearings before the Committee on Foreign Relations, *US Policy in the Persian Gulf*, December 1990, p. 258.

4　Walid Khalidi, 'Why Some Arabs Support Saddam', in Sifry and Cerf (eds.), *The Gulf War Reader*, pp. 167–8.

5　Michael Walzer, 'Perplexed', *The New Republic*, 28 January 1991.

6　Noam Chomsky, 'The Use (and Abuse) of the United Nations', in Sifry and Cerf (eds), *The Gulf War Reader*, p. 309.

7　Murray Wass, 'What Washington gave Saddam for Christmas', in ibid.

8　Eqbal Ahmad, 'Introduction: Portent of a New Century', in Bennis and Moushabeck (eds.), *Beyond the Storm*, p. 18. Ahmad described the war as one to 'protect the conquests of Israel'.

9　In 1967 Israel's neighbours considered themselves to be in a state of permanent hostility with the Jewish state. The war saw a tremendous expansion in the area under Israel's territorial control, but subsequently it did relinquish the Sinai to Egypt in exchange for peace and normal diplomatic relations. Formal annexation was limited to East Jerusalem and the Golan Heights. The international community had not forced Israel off the West Bank and the Gaza Strip, but nor had it recognized Israeli control or forced the Arab states to reach a peaceful settlement with Israel, as stipulated by Security Council Resolution 242 of November 1967. There had been continual pressure on the Israeli Government to return to something close to the 1967 boundaries and, in late 1990, there were many hints that the search for a settlement would be stepped up in the aftermath of the Gulf crisis.

10　Tom Friedman, 'Washington's "Vital Interests"', *New York Times*, 12 August 1990. Reprinted in Sifry and Cerf (eds.), *The Gulf Reader*, pp. 203–6.

11　Text of speech by President George Bush, *Financial Times*, 9 August 1991.

12　BBC Television, *The Washington Version*, 17 January 1992. See also *Triumph Without Victory*, pp. 140–43.

13　President George Bush, *Address to Congress*, 11 September 1990.

14　See, for example, Edward Luttwak, 'Saddam and the Agencies of Disorder', *Times Literary Supplement*, 18 January 1991.

15　*Burdensharing Report Card on the Persian Gulf Crisis*, House Armed Services Committee, 14 November 1990. Aspin used six criteria – military participation, financial contribution, compliance with UN sanctions, political support, response time and special factors, including mitigating circumstances (which is why he was comparatively tolerant of Jordan).

16　Arthur Schlesinger Jr, 'White Slaves in the Persian Gulf', *Wall Street Journal*, 7 January 1991. Reprinted in Sifry and Cerf (eds.), *The Gulf Reader*.

17　William Pfaff, 'Mistakes in War-Making', *International Herald Tribune*, 20–21 October 1990.

18　Filmed interviews with Haass, Scowcroft, Gates, Cheney, Wolfowitz, Quayle; Brian

Lapping Associates, December 1991. Quayle confirmed that 'the President had already made up his mind on what he was going to do, before that meeting'.

19 *The Times*, 29 September 1990; *Wall Street Journal*, 1 October 1990; *International Herald Tribune*, 1 October 1990; Woodward, *The Commanders*, pp. 297, 299. One alternative interpretation was that the Iraqi behaviour might have been part of the preparation for a compromise. One American official was quoted as saying: 'While you can never be sure with the Iraqis – they may just like tearing things apart – it makes sense that if they planned to stay they wouldn't be carting away the entire Kuwaiti infrastructure. *MEP Survey*, 19 October 1990.

20 Alexander Cockburn, 'Beat the Devil', *The Nation*, 4 February 1991, later cast doubt on this story. It was explored by the US group Middle East Watch. See *Independent on Sunday*, 12 January 1992.

21 Amnesty International, *Iraq's Occupation of Kuwait*, 19 December 1990.

22 During the 1990 Congressional campaign, Bush observed of Saddam's treatment of the hostages: 'Many of them are reportedly staked out as human shields near possible military targets – something that even Adolf Hitler didn't do.' Compared with some of the things Hitler did do, of course, this is comparatively trivial.

23 This for example was the gravamen of Edward Luttwak's critique (see *Independent*, 27 August), 'Blood for Oil: Bush's Growing Dilemma'. This noted Bush's comparisons between Saddam and Hitler, and warned of 'an inconsistent set of goals and means': 'On the one hand, his real, though unofficial, goal of destroying the Saddam Hussein regime is the most extreme of ambitions in any confrontation. On the other hand, his chosen instruments of diplomatic pressure, economic blockade and military intimidation, are slow and uncertain. Saddam does not seem to be wilting because of his diplomatic isolation, he does not appear to be trembling before the military spectacle in Saudi Arabia, and the Iraqis may not revolt even if the shortages do become acute.'

24 Interview with Rick Atkinson of *Washington Post* reprinted in *International Herald Tribune*, 17 September 1990, p. 1. See also *Aviation Week and Space Technology*, 24 September 1990, pp. 16–18. On the Dugan episode see Woodward, *The Commanders*, pp. 290–96. In sacking Dugan, Secretary of Defence Richard Cheney observed: 'We never talk about the targeting of specific individuals who are officials in other governments. That is a violation of the executive order.' *International Herald Tribune*, 18 September 1990.

25 House of Representatives, Committee on Foreign Affairs, Hearings, *Crisis in the Persian Gulf*, 4 September 1990, p. 17.

26 *International Herald Tribune*, 18 October 1990.

27 Attributed to a 'European diplomat' describing attitudes in the Bush Administration by Judith Miller, 'And What If Saddam Really Pulled Out?', *International Herald Tribune*, 9 October 1991. For later uses see, for example, Peter Jenkins, 'War and Peace No Simple Issue', *Independent*, 25 October 1990, and the *New York Times* editorial 'The Dangers of Peace', in *International Herald Tribune*, 26 October 1990. It was still in use on the eve of the UN deadline. John J. Fialka and Gerald F. Seib, 'In This Scenario, Retreat by Saddam Would be Nightmare: Allies Fear Partial Withdrawal Could Turn Public Opinion and Preserve Iraqi Army', *Wall Street Journal*, 11 January 1991.

28 *International Herald Tribune*, 24 September 1990.

29 US Senate, Hearings Before the Committee on Armed Services, *Crisis in the Persian Gulf Region: US Policy Options and Implications*, 1990, p. 58.

30 For State Department views, see *Wall Street Journal*, 30 March 1990; see Warren H. Donnelly, *Iraq and Nuclear Weapons*, Congressional Research Service Issue Brief, 21 December 1990, p. 10; House of Representatives, One Hundred First Congress, Second Session, *United States–Iraqi Relations*, Hearings before the Subcommittee on Europe and the Middle East.

31 *Triumph Without Victory*, p. 134. After the war it was discovered that in April 1989 a

warning had been issued by a senior Energy Department official with regard to the Iraqi programme but that this had been dismissed as overstated by his superiors. *International Herald Tribune*, 21 April 1992.

32 *New York Times*, 30 November 1990. A Defence Intelligence Agency analysis was alleged to have said that Iraq could have a nuclear capability within two months. *Sunday Times*, 18 November 1990.

33 *International Herald Tribune*, 26 October 1990.

34 *Newsweek* interview, 8 October 1990.

35 *Independent*, 29 October 1990.

36 'This man is a loser. It is not for us to say what should happen to him within Iraq. That is for the people of Iraq who have suffered grievously through his eight-year war with Iran.' David Frost interview with Margaret Thatcher, *The Times*, 3 September 1990.

37 Ibid.

38 *Independent*, 25 October 1990.

39 Laurent, *Tempête du désert*, p. 77–80.

40 Woodward, *The Commanders*, p. 315.

41 *Speech to Los Angeles World Affairs Council*, 29 October 1990.

42 Filmed Interview, Brian Lapping Associates, December 1991.

43 CBS/*New York Times* poll, 13–15 November 1990. Nationwide random sample of 1,370 adults, interviewed by telephone 13–15 November 1990. Source: CBS News, New York.

44 Quoted in Warren H. Donnelly, *Iraq and Nuclear Weapons*, p. 10; See also, *International Herald Tribune*, 23 November 1990.

45 *Financial Times*, 27 November 1990.

46 William R. Graham in Senate Armed Services Committee, *Crisis in the Persian Gulf Region*, p. 542.

47 Richard Falk, 'How the West Mobilized for War', in John Gittings (ed.), *Beyond the Gulf War: The Middle East and the New World Order*, London, Catholic Institute for International Relations, 1991, p. 16.

48 David Albright and Mark Hibbs, 'Hyping the Iraqi Bomb', and 'Iraq's Bomb: Blueprints and Artifacts'. See also their 'Iraq's Nuclear Hide-and-Seek'. All in *Bulletin of the Atomic Scientists*, March 1991, January/February 1992 and September 1991 respectively. As more evidence came in it became apparent that the Iraqis were facing some severe bottlenecks which would have slowed progress.

49 Speech of 10 January 1991, reprinted in Sifry and Cerf (eds.), *The Gulf War Reader*. Moynihan's Chamberlainesque remark was out of keeping for a man who had complained for much of the 1980s about the Reagan Administration's disregard of international law.

50 Schlesinger, *Senate Hearings*, p. 116.

51 Michael Howard, 'Why UN Sanctions Are Better than a Prolonged War', *The Times*, 17 August 1990.

52 Michael Howard, 'Digging in for the Duration', *The Times*, 6 September 1990. By November, however, he judged that the West had been patient long enough! Michael Howard, 'On Balance, Bush Must Go to War', *The Times*, 5 November, 1990.

53 *International Herald Tribune*, 11–12 August 1990.

54 James Webb, 'Do War Advocates See the Pandora's Box?', *International Herald Tribune*, 24 September 1990.

55 Robert Fisk, 'A Gulf Trap Set to Close on America', *Independent*, 26 September 1990.

56 See testimony of Hermann Eilts, former US Ambassador to Egypt and Saudi Arabia, in House Hearings, *Crisis in the Persian Gulf*, p. 610.

57 Former Chairman of the Joint Chiefs of Staff, General David Jones, Senate Hearings.

58 He advocated the 'surgical and progressive destruction of Iraq's military assets', although he later admitted that the use of the word 'surgical' was unwise. *International Herald Tribune*, 20 August 1990. It might also be noted that the United States had proved itself in

the past perfectly capable of sustaining large-scale deployments for many years, as in Europe and Korea.

Chapter 16: Two Miles Forward, One Mile Back

1 *Official Record*, 6 September 1990.
2 *International Herald Tribune*, 24 September 1990.
3 Filmed interview with Robert Kimmitt, Brian Lapping Associates, December 1991. This does not mean, contrary to what has been argued in *Triumph Without Victory* (p. viii), that the need to bounce Congress into support was the only reason for going to the UN.
4 This did not use the word 'force' but instead recommended that UN members 'furnish such assistance to the Republic of Korea as may be necessary to repel the armed attack and to restore international peace and security in the area' (S/RES/83, 1950). The word force had been used in a peace-keeping resolution on the Congo in 1961 and the blockade of Rhodesia in 1966. Marjorie Ann Browne, *Iraq–Kuwait: The United Nations Response*, Washington DC, Congressional Research Service, 22 October 1990. See also Hans Arnold, 'The Gulf Crisis and the United Nations,' *Aussenpolitik*, January 1991. For a legal analysis see Christopher Greenwood, 'New World Order or Old? The Invasion of Kuwait and the Rule of Law', *Modern Law Review*, Vol. 55, No. 2, March 1992.
5 *Guardian*, 8 November 1990.
6 *International Herald Tribune*, 9 November 1990.
7 BBC Television, *The Washington Version*, 17 January 1992.
8 Yitzhak Shichor, 'China and the Gulf Crisis,' *Problems of Communism*, November–December 1991. See also Lillian Craig Harris, 'The Gulf Crisis and China's Middle East Dilemma', *The Pacific Review*, Vol. 4, No. 2, 1991.
9 On the same day Bush was with the troops in Saudi Arabia. His trip included Mubarak, Fahd and, notably, Asad of Syria.
10 The draft resolution was published in a number of newspapers. See, for example, *Independent*, 27 November 1990.
11 *International Herald Tribune*, 3 December 1990.
12 *The Times*, 1 December 1990.
13 Laurent, *Tempête du désert*, pp. 104–6.
14 Elizabeth Drew, 'Letter from Washington', *New Yorker*, 4 February 1991; *Washington Post*, 31 March 1991; *Independent*, 4, 15 December 1990; Woodward, *The Commanders*, p. 337.
15 *Financial Times*, 27 November 1990. This, they said, would update a bilateral deal signed in 1987, three months after the *Stark* episode in which an Iraqi aircraft had accidentally attacked an American warship, killing thirty-seven American sailors. Under this agreement, it was reported, Iraqi pilots gave a special call sign by which they could be identified by American warships without alerting the Iranians. As far as the Americans were concerned, this agreement had lapsed at the end of the Iran–Iraq War and they had no intention of entering into any bilateral contracts or giving away information on US deployments.
16 *Guardian*, 6 November 1990; *International Herald Tribune*, 11 November 1990.
17 Baghdad Radio, 4 December 1990.
18 John Simpson, *From the House of War*, London, Arrow Books, 1991, p. 252.
19 *International Herald Tribune*, 3 December 1990.

Chapter 17: Making a Date

1 *The Times*, 4, 5 December 1990.
2 *The Economist*, 8 December 1990, pp. 16, 85.
3 The Italian Foreign Ministry announced on 25 November that seventy Italians were to be

released. This followed the arrival of an aircraft loaded with twenty-five tons of medicines in Baghdad. Prime Minister Andreotti appears to have been the main figure arranging this, using his office to pay for the plane. The Foreign Office, which was generally taking a much harder line, does not seem to have been involved.

4   *Sunday Times*, 28 October 1990.
5   Patrick Cockburn in *Independent*, 7 December 1990.
6   The Iraqi communiqué said that the release was aimed to 'add more constructive measures in favour of peace and dialogue' and 'to weaken all the elements of evil nurtured by those who push evil to the prejudice of humanity'. The next day Information Minister Jasim said that the plan would be called off if war broke out.
7   Saddam's interview with Antenne 2 Télévision, Paris, 2 December 1990.
8   *The Times*, 28, 30 November 1990.
9   *Independent*, 9, 11 December 1990. These reports were later said to be Israeli disinformation.
10 See, for example, Riyadh Television, 2 December 1990; Cairo Radio, 2 December 1990.
11 Woodward, *The Commanders*, p. 336.
12 Riyadh Television, 31 November, 3 December 1990.
13 Tlas's interview with Abu Dhabi Radio, 1 December 1990; MENA, Cairo, 6 December 1990.
14 MENA, 3 December 1990; Cairo Radio, 5 December 1990.
15 *Al-Akhbar* (Cairo), 4 December 1990. See also *al-Ahram* (Cairo), 4 December 1990; Damascus Radio, 3 December 1990.
16 Israel's Educational Television, 2 December 1990; Israel Radio, 3 December 1990.
17 Israeli Television, 2 December 1990; Israel Radio, 3 December 1990.
18 Riyadh Radio, 2 December 1990; Israel Radio, 2 December 1990.
19 'Mission to Baghdad', *Economist*, 8 December 1990; *MEP survey*, 14 December 1990, No. 262.
20 *Financial Times*, 10 December 1990.
21 *International Herald Tribune*, 10 December 1990.
22 INA, 11, 16 December 1990.
23 Radio Monte Carlo in Arabic, Paris, 18 December 1990.
24 King Hussein's interview with Amman Television, 17 December 1990.
25 *Al-Dustur* (Amman), 1 December 1990; see also ibid., 6 December 1990; *al-Ra'i* (Amman), 30 November, 9 December 1990.
26 INA, 17 November 1990. In citing this interview as evidence of Saddam's readiness to negotiate seriously John Gittings gives the wrong impression that the President gave a straight 'yes' to the interviewer's question. Gittings, *Beyond the Gulf War*, p. 7
27 *International Herald Tribune*, 17 December 1990.
28 Baghdad Radio, 17 December 1990.
29 *International Herald Tribune*, 26 December 1990.
30 *Financial Times*, 11 December 1990.
31 *International Herald Tribune*, 11 December 1990; *Guardian*, 12 December 1990.
32 *Financial Times*, 17 December 1990.
33 *International Herald Tribune*, 27 December 1990.
34 *New York Times*, 31 December 1990.
35 *Independent*, 31 December 1990.
36 Ibid., 3 January 1991; *International Herald Tribune*, 3 January 1991.

Chapter 18: Showdown in Geneva

1   Baghdad Voice of the PLO, 8 January 1991. See also his interview with a Spanish television network, ibid.

2 *Al-Ra'i* (Amman), 2 January 1991.
3 See Salinger and Laurent, *Secret Dossier*, pp. 206–7; *Financial Times, Guardian*, 16 January 1991.
4 See, for example, Damascus Radio, 4 December 1990.
5 *Washington Post*, 11 January 1991. Baker is referred to in the article as a 'senior US official ... travelling on Baker's plane'. He has, however, since made the observation in public.
6 It was published in five parts by the Iraqi News Agency, starting on 9 January 1992. The text was reprinted in *FBIS-NES-92-009*, 14 January 1992. Aziz, however, gave a full account immediately afterwards in an interview with foreign correspondents, Jordan's Television in English, 9 January 1991.
7 BBC Television, *The Washington Version*, 18 January 1992.
8 Aziz's interview with foreign correspondents, Jordan's Television in English, 9 January 1991.
9 James Baker, filmed interview, Brian Lapping Associates, December 1991.
10 *Independent*, 10 January 1991.
11 Aziz's interview with foreign correspondents.
12 Heikal, *Illusions of Triumph*, p. 291.

Chapter 19: Deadline Diplomacy

1 *International Herald Tribune*, 20 December 1990.
2 *Triumph Without Victory*, pp. 194–5.
3 This was also evident in a rare contribution from Japan at this time when Kunio Katakura, one of the Japanese Foreign Ministry's longest-serving Arabists, met with Iraq's First Deputy Prime Minister, Taha Yasin Ramadan. Concluding that the Iraqis still took the deadline 'very lightly', Katakura came up with the traditional Arabist proposal of movement on the Palestinian issue and the extension of security guarantees to non-attack of Iraq by Israel as well as by the United States.
4 Nonetheless, in admonishing Saddam for this error they were prepared to point to differences between the Europeans and the United States, especially with regard to what Belgian Foreign Minister Mark Eysenks referred to as 'fundamental solutions for the post-crisis situation'.
5 Heikal, *Illusions of Triumph*, p. 286. Heikal suggests that the suspicion of conspiracy also extended to King Hussein.
6 Alia and Clerc, *La guerre de Mitterrand*, pp. 176–81. Details of the Pisani initiative appeared also in *Le Canard enchaîné*, 6 March 1991.
7 The following is based on Alia and Clerc, *La guerre de Mitterrand*, pp. 187–90, and an annexe which gives details of the Pisani plan.
8 Ibid., pp. 158–68
9 *Independent*, 4 January 1991.
10 Alia and Clerc, *La guerre de Mitterrand*, pp. 198–204.
11 Conference de presse de Monsieur le Président de la République, Paris, Palais de l'Élysée, 9 January 1991.
12 Alia and Clerc, *La guerre de Mitterrand*, pp. 215–17.
13 *International Herald Tribune*, 11 January 1991.
14 Alia and Clerc, *La guerre de Mitterrand*, pp. 211, 213.
15 Salinger and Laurent, *Secret Dossier*, p. 215.
16 A UN spokeswoman expressed irritation with this breach of the diplomatic code but did not challenge their general authenticity. A reasonably full version of the transcripts appeared in the *Independent*, 14 February 1991.
17 *Daily Telegraph*, 15 January 1991.
18 Alia and Clerc, *La guerre de Mitterrand*, pp. 221–39.

19 Ibid., pp. 221–39.
20 *Independent*, 15 January 1991. Heikal, *Illusions of Triumph*, p. 356.
21 *Financial Times*, 15 January 1991.
22 *Independent*, 16 January 1991.

Chapter 20: Saddam Prepares for War

1 Bulloch and Morris, *Saddam's War*, p. 11.
2 Baghdad Radio, 7, 24 December 1990; *al-Thawra* (Baghdad), 11, 12 December 1990; INA, 14, 20, 21 December 1990; AFP, 21 December 1990.
3 *Al-Qadisiya* (Baghdad), 20 December 1990.
4 INA, 13 December 1990.
5 Ibid., 14 January 1991.
6 Saddam had been reluctant to keep any senior commander in his post for sufficient time to build up a personal following or to get into a position where he could conspire with others.
7 On the military lessons of the Iran–Iraq War, see Efraim Karsh, *The Iran–Iraq War: A Military Analysis*, Adelphi Paper No. 220, London, International Institute for Strategic Studies, 1987.
8 INA, 19 November 1990.
9 See, for example, *International Herald Tribune*, 4 September 1990.
10 *Independent*, 12 January 1991; *Financial Times*, 12–13 January 1991. With regard to the air threat, Saddam claimed that enemy aircraft needed to get within three miles of their target to inflict damage, but that Iraq could shoot them down from eighteen miles away.
11 Baghdad Domestic Service, 17 January 1991.

Chapter 21: America Prepares for War

1 'This will not be a protracted drawn-out war. The forces arrayed are different; the opposition is different; the re-supply of Saddam's military would be very different; the countries united against him in the United Nations are different; the topography of Kuwait is different, and the motivation of our all-volunteer force is superb.' Text of George Bush's statement, 'Bush: "Go the Extra Mile for Peace"', *International Herald Tribune*, 1–2 December 1990.
2 Nationwide poll of 1,057 randomly selected adults conducted for *Washington Post*-ABC on 4–6 January, reported in the *Washington Post*, 8 January 1991.
3 See John Mueller, *War, Presidents and Public Opinion*, New York, John Wiley, 1973.
4 The British experience with the Falklands provided an interesting contrast. This was fought with a volunteer Army. The war lasted weeks rather than years and, apart from Argentina's initial seizure of the islands in April 1982 and some uncertainty after the sinking of the cruiser *General Belgrano*, the British Government at all times appeared to have the initiative, and international support. Prior to the start of hostilities public opinion appeared unsure whether the recapture of the islands was worth loss of life, but when losses occurred this reinforced determination to defeat the enemy. There was a substantial and articulate body of opinion, around a quarter of the population, opposed to resolving the dispute through armed force but there was an opposed view, with a comparable level of support although perhaps less articulate, urging the Government to adopt even stronger measures. See Lawrence Freedman, *Britain and the Falklands War*, London, Basil Blackwell, 1988.
5 Woodward, *The Commanders*, p. 349.
6 Peter de la Billière in BBC Radio 4, *The Desert War*, Part IV, 2 February 1992. Worst-case British estimates were of some 1,500 Army casualties out of a force of 25,000, assuming a 'head-on' attack against entrenched Iraqi positions. The British Government was less

troubled by the prospect of casualties than the American. *The Times*, 30 November 1990. Brigadier Patrick Cordingley, 'Operating with Allies', in *Command in War: Gulf Operations*, London, Royal United Services Institute, 1992, pp. 63–4.

7   See, for example, testimony by former Secretary of Defense James Schlesinger, Senate Hearings, *Crisis in the Persian Gulf*, p. 116. See also Admiral William Crowe, p. 229.

8   Some of these estimates were extraordinarily precise. For example, Joshua Epstein of the Brookings Institution calculated an optimistic case of fifteen days' intense combat with 3,344 casualties and 1,049 dead and a pessimistic case of 21 days with 16,059 casualties of whom 4,136 would be dead. See Joshua Epstein, *War with Iraq: What Price Victory?*, Washington DC, Brookings, January 1991. Colonel Trevor Dupuy gave a low of 300 American dead and 1,700 injured and a high of 3,000 dead and 15,000 injured. Trevor Dupuy, *How to Defeat Saddam Hussein: Scenarios and Strategies for the Gulf War*, New York, Warner Books, 1991. The Center for Defense Information, assuming an overland drive to Baghdad, came up with 10,000 dead: 'US Invasion of Iraq: Appraising the Option', *The Defense Monitor*, Vol. XIX, No. 8, p. 7. It is interesting to note that an article published on the eve of the land campaign and generally prescient with regard to its character and duration postulated 'probably less than 1,000 fatalities' among coalition forces. John Mearsheimer, 'Kuwait Can Be Liberated in a Week', *International Herald Tribune*, 9–10 February 1991.

9   The optimistic scenario involved an elegant envelopment operation that cut off the Iraqi forces in Kuwait, with no frontal dislodgement attacks, highly effective softening up operations by air power and even naval gunfire, any major Iraqi counter-stroke broken by air attacks before it could reach US forces, no Iranian 'revolutionary guard' volunteers joining the fighting 'when the US offensive reaches its necessary end-point at the borders of Iran', hundreds of thousands of Iraqi troops on each side of the US offensive thrust not attempting 'to converge against it, [even] if only by dribs and drabs, [even] if only to make good a retreat', all equipment working perfectly, operational plans cunning, tactics sound. See Senate Hearings, *Crisis in the Persian Gulf*, p. 325. Luttwak later admitted that he concocted his estimates: 'I was not going to give my real forecast of casualties . . . As an advocate, you only make forecasts when they are conducive to your advocacy.' *Washington Post*, 28 February 1991.

10   Senate Hearings, *Crisis in the Persian Gulf*, pp. 662–3, 664

11   House Hearings, *Crisis in the Persian Gulf*, p. 594.

12   *International Herald Tribune*, 20 December 1990.

13   There was little real difference here with many of those preferring a primary stress on the air campaign. Eliot Cohen, for example, argued that it would be wise to preserve the ground option while being prepared for the 'possibility that an air campaign might do the trick'. House Hearings, *Crisis in the Persian Gulf*, p. 391.

14   Major-General Robert Johnson noted in a briefing on 8 February 1991: 'This will not be like Vietnam. We can measure our success here because our objectives are to get the Iraqis out of Kuwait. That's measurable in terms of real estate somewhere down the road.' CENTCOM briefing, Major General Robert B. Johnson, Riyadh, Saudi Arabia, 8 February 1991.

15   *Independent*, 31 October 1990.

16   For example, Edward Luttwak, who expected that they would be fired said, 'So, I do not think the ten, twelve, fifteen Scuds you would expect – upgraded Scuds – would escape destruction in the first air strike. I would be amazed if they inflicted significant damage.' Senate Hearings, *Crisis in the Persian Gulf*, p. 348.

17   John Barry, 'The Nuclear Option: Thinking the Unthinkable', *Newsweek*, 14 January 1991.

18   *Washington Post*, 7 January 1991. See William Arkin, Joshua Handler, Damian Durrant, *US Nuclear Weapons in the Persian Gulf Crisis*, Washington DC, Greenpeace, January 1991.

19   *Independent*, 9 January 1991.

20 Admiral Crowe, Senate Hearings, *Crisis in the Persian Gulf*, p. 207. He suggested that the total campaign would take thirty-five to forty days. See also his article, 'On Jan. 15, We Must Stand United', *Washington Post*, 7 January 1991: 'I assume that the fighting will commence with an intensive air campaign. This effort should be structured to accelerate the quarantine's effects and soften the resistance to subsequent ground attack, if it proves necessary. We have never fought a country as isolated as Iraq. The results of a sustained and heavy air attack should be successful.'

21 Representative Les Aspin, *The Military Option: The Conduct and Consequences of War in the Persian Gulf*, 8 January 1991. Reprinted in US House of Representatives, Hearings Before the Committee on Armed Services, *Crisis in the Persian Gulf: Sanctions, Diplomacy and War*, p. 905.

22 Joan Biskupic, 'Constitution's Conflicting Clauses Underscored by Iraq Crisis', *Congressional Quarterly*, 5 January 1991.

23 Filmed interview, Brian Lapping Associates, December 1991.

24 Present at the meeting were Quayle, Scowcroft, Cheney, Powell and Eagleburger (Baker was on his European tour).

25 *Washington Post*, 8 January 1991. The poll was conducted with ABC News. It took place on 6 January and involved 1,057 randomly selected adults.

26 Together with Richard Perle, a conservative Democrat who had a high-profile position in the Pentagon under the Reagan Administration, and Ann Lewis, a liberal Democratic activist, Solarz was instrumental in setting up a Committee for Peace and Security in the Gulf.

27 See Les Aspin, *The Aspin Papers: Sanctions, Diplomacy, and War in the Persian Gulf*, Washington DC, Center for Strategic and International Studies, 1991.

28 Elizabeth Drew, 'Letter from Washington', *New Yorker*, 4 February 1991, p. 86.

29 The committee included Scowcroft, White House Chief-of-Staff John Sununu, legal adviser Boyden Gray from the White House, Stephen Solarz, representing the Foreign Affairs Committee, House Minority leader Robert Michel, and other senior Republican and Democratic Congressmen.

30 *Washington Post*, 9 January 1991.

31 Sam Nunn, 'War Should Be a Last Resort', *Washington Post*, 10 January 1991.

32 Drew, 'Letter from Washington', p. 88. The previous morning at a breakfast meeting, Cheney had told Congressmen, in effect, not to vote for the resolution if they did not think that the Administration was actually going to use force.

33 *Washington Post*, 11 January 1991.

34 William Webster, *Letter to Rep. Les Aspin*, Central Intelligence Agency, 10 January 1991.

35 Vice-President Quayle later recounted the arguments that he was using with wavering Senators: 'One, Saddam Hussein was not going to get out. Two, give the President the benefit of the doubt in a foreign policy matter. Three, don't let history record you being on the side of Saddam Hussein and against the American President . . . Public opinion polls show that there is support for what the President may have to do . . . And, finally, I talked about the 400,000 to 500,000 men and women that were in Saudi Arabia and in the area, prepared to achieve an objective. I recounted some of my personal conversations with them, that they were there, willing to do the job, they wanted to do the job, and they wanted to get it over with.' BBC Television, *The Washington Version*, 17 January 1992.

36 The six were John Breaux and Bennett Johnson from Louisiana, Howell Heflin and Richard Shelby of Alabama, Richard Bryan and Harry Reid of Nevada. John Sununu was in charge of an effort to stimulate lobbying on those Senators from inside the state. In the end all six voted with the White House. Gerald Seib, 'How President Bush Deftly Orchestrated Victory over Iraq', *Wall Street Journal*, 1 March 1991.

37 This was sponsored by Congressmen Richard Gephardt and Lee Hamilton. Foley had argued with the generally pro-force Foreign Affairs Committee that members should be

allowed to vote for an alternative policy rather than just against the President's policy. Foley, however, resisted pressures to make the vote a Party vote rather than an open vote. In practice this would have been hard to enforce and the attempt would have made it easier to dismiss a negative outcome as being partisan on a matter of great national interest.

38   The idea here was to broaden support for the resolutions through reference to key provisions of the war powers resolution and so assert the constitutional prerogatives of the House in such a way that the President was left with the flexibility he required.

39   The House voted again on 17 January and this time there was an overwhelming vote to support the President and the troops in the field.

40   Other members of the delegation included Rear Admiral Merill Ruck from the Strategic Policy and Plans Directorate of the Joint Chiefs-of-Staff, and Daniel Kurtzer, Deputy Assistant Secretary of State for Near Eastern Affairs.

41   *International Herald Tribune*, 27 December 1991.

42   Woodward, *The Commanders*, pp. 361–4; *New York Times*, 3 March 1991; *Jerusalem Post*, 13, 14 January 1991.

43   See Damascus Radio, 12 January 1991; MENA, 15 January 1991; Riyadh Radio, 15 January 1991.

Chapter 22: War by Appointment

1   As the Ambassador had been asked not to divulge the information, he went back to his office and locked the door so that he would not be tempted to do so.

2   Newsweek, *Secret History*, 18 March 1991.

3   General Merrill McPeak (US Air Force Chief-of-Staff), *The Air Campaign: Part of the Combined Arms Operation*, Washington DC, Department of Defense, 15 March 1991.

4   Department of the Air Force, *Reaching Globally, Reaching Powerfully: The United States Air Force in the Gulf War*, Washington DC, September 1991, p. 17.

5   McPeak, *The Air Campaign*.

6   Half belonged to the US Air Force, 16 per cent to the US Navy, 7 per cent to the Marines, and 27 per cent to allied forces. The number grew to 2,790 by the beginning of the ground offensive. See McPeak, *The Air Campaign*.

7   This used mainly the French Roland short-range missiles.

8   A useful description of the Iraqi system and the measures used against it is found in Norman Friedman, *Desert Victory: The War for Kuwait*, Maryland, Naval Institute Press, 1991, Chapter 8.

9   The main such centre was in Baghdad, with sub-centres located at Kirkuk, Nasiriya and Routba. Though hardened, the shelters were not in deep bunkers.

10   *Triumph Without Victory*, p. 229.

11   Gross exaggeration is not that unusual in air warfare. Had the Iraqi air defence batteries produced an accurate picture of their success rate, they would have been historically unique: air defences have a natural tendency to report every big flash in the sky as a 'kill'. Nor, for that matter, would the total losses claimed have been that surprising after some 7,000 sorties.

12   Department of the Air Force, *Reaching Globally*, p. 34.

13   The high RAF losses (by comparison) became the subject of some controversy in the UK. The Royal Air Force flew the second largest number of sorties after the USAF – 6,100 in total. It began the war with eighteen Tornado F3 fighters, forty-six GR1/1A strike/attack and recce aircraft, seventeen tankers, three Nimrods, twelve Chinooks, nineteen Pumas, seven Hercules and one BAe 125. Later they were joined by more Tornados and Buccaneers.

14   Reprinted in *International Herald Tribune*, 29 January 1991.

15   Schwarzkopf briefing, CNN, 30 January 1991.

16 The exact scope of the Iraqi exodus is unclear. The normal number quoted is 122, although the Iranians put the number lower. This may be explained by crashes, or by Iranian desire to retain most of the aircraft after the war. Commander-in-Chief McPeak gives a total figure of 157. One explanation for the difference may be that the 122 figure does not include those which left prior to the main exodus on Day 10.

17 An alternative explanation suggested that the escape of the Iraqi planes was linked to a coup attempt by senior Air Force officers against Saddam, after he had allegedly executed his Air Force and air defence commanders. A related version maintained that by sending his planes to Iran, Saddam removed a group of potentially rebellious officers who could, at a certain point, challenge his decision to prosecute the war. Finally, Iranian sources argued that the air exodus was, in effect, mass defection of Iraqi pilots who flew to Iran without Saddam's authorization. This last version was questioned by Western sources, which attributed it to Tehran's anxiety to avoid any taint of an Iraqi–Iranian collusion. That this scepticism was warranted could be inferred from the expansion of the exodus beyond the air force: before long Iraqi naval vessels also tried to escape to the Iranian haven. On the Iraqi flights to Iran, see *Sunday Times*, 27 January, *The Times*, 29 January 1991; *Financial Times*, 30 January 1991.

18 Baghdad Radio, 17 January 1991. To encourage people to hunt for allied pilots, the authorities announced that such an act 'would please God and would be a national honour'. For those Iraqis who still required a more earthly inducement, the Government promised a handsome reward of 10,000 dinars ($32,000) for any captured pilot; non-Iraqis were promised a smaller reward of 'merely' $20,000. Ibid., 19 January 1991.

19 Another pilot expressed his opposition to the unjust war in strong terms: 'Myself and the other pilots talked about what interest the United States had for going to war, and we could find none. This was before the war. And now, we wonder whether American blood can be so cheap in the eyes of our government officials.' Baghdad Radio, 23 January 1991.

20 *Independent*, 22 January 1991.

21 The Iraqis lost ninety combat aircraft, including the thirty-five air-to-air kills. There were in addition, six non-combat losses, and sixteen captured or destroyed by ground forces. In addition 141 aircraft are believed to have been caught in shelters, while 122 combat aircraft escaped to Iran, where they were impounded.

22 McPeak, *The Air Campaign*.

23 Aware of the propaganda value of a Saudi success, the command had pushed forward Saudi rather than American fighters.

24 This is the estimate given by the Chief-of-Staff of the US Air Force in his 15 March briefing. A report on the war by the Israeli daily *Ma'ariv* reached the same estimate. See *Israel in the Gulf War*, Tel Aviv, 29 March 1991, p. 41. Others put the figure at thirty-nine: see Martin Navias, *Saddam's Scud War and Ballistic Missile Proliferation*, London, Brassey's/ Centre for Defence Studies, University of London, August 1991, p. 21; or at thirty-eight, *Jane's Defence Weekly*, 6 April 1991.

25 W. Seth Carus, 'Missiles in the Third World: The 1991 Gulf War', *Orbis*, Vol. 35, No. 2, Spring 1991, p. 254.

26 Interview with General Schwarzkopf, NBC, 'Meet the Press', 20 January 1991.

27 *International Herald Tribune*, 29 January 1991.

28 CNN, Schwarzkopf briefing, 30 January 1991. The known targets connected with Scuds were the fixed missile bases, production sites near Fallujah, west of Baghdad, an underground fuel production site at al-Hillah, south of Baghdad, and a test site at Karbala to the south-west. Sa'd 16, the massive military complex in the north near Mosul, which was a centre for all manner of missile work, including on new systems, was also attacked.

29 Interview of American F-15 pilots with the Israeli daily *Yediot Acharonot*: 'A year has passed: a special magazine on the first anniversary of the war', Tel Aviv, 10 January 1992, pp. 9–10.

30 See Friedman, *Desert Victory*, pp. 172–7.

31 According to Brigadier-General John Stewart, Intelligence Officer of the 3rd US Army, the JSTARS was 'the single most valuable intelligence and targeting collection system in Desert Storm'. See *Operation Desert Storm: The Military Intelligence Story*, p. 31.

32 'Special Operations', *Army* (September 1991). The best available account of special forces operations in Iraq is given in Brown and Shukman, *All Necessary Means*, p. 84. An official British reference to the role of its special forces in the Scud hunt is found in 'Dispatch by Air Chief Marshal Sir Patrick Hine', *Second Supplement to The London Gazette of Friday, 28 June 1991*, p. G44.

33 *Armed Forces Journal International*, July 1991.

34 *Aviation Week and Space Technology*, 24 June 1991; 29 June 1992. Iraq claimed 819 missiles, of which 520 were shot at Iran, 93 fired during the war, 138 destroyed by the UN and a few used in tests.

35 McPeak, *The Air Campaign*.

36 Ibid.

37 The prominence of the 'Scud busting' effort in allied strategy can be inferred, *inter alia*, by its relation to the effort devoted to other types of targets: 2 per cent of the strategic air campaign was directed against Iraq's strategic air defence, 5 per cent against Baghdad's nuclear, chemical, and biological arsenal and production facilities, and 8 per cent against strategic targets including telecommunications centres, railroads and bridges, electrical power, and oil facilities.

38 This figure can be compared with 535 sorties against weapons production sites and 300 against Republican Guard positions during the same period.

39 Stewart, *Operation Desert Storm*, pp. 17–19.

40 *Independent*, 29 April 1991; *International Herald Tribune*, 8–9 June 1991.

Chapter 23: The Strategic Air Campaign

1 William Arkin, a former Army Intelligence officer working for Greenpeace, produced the most searching post-war analysis of the air campaign, including a trip to Iraq to examine the target sites. While some of his findings are controversial, few question his scrupulous approach to evidence. His views are presented in *Aviation Week and Space Technology*, 27 January 1992, and 'Arkin Briefing on Gulf War', *Inside the Air Force*, 17 January 1992.

2 *Defense Week*, 13 January 1992.

3 McPeak, *The Air Campaign*.

4 Ibid. Of these, 49,345 strike sorties were by coalition aircraft and the rest by American aircraft.

5 *Aviation Week and Space Technology*, 22 April 1991.

6 Department of the Air Force, *Reaching Globally*, p. 30; William Arkin in briefing gave a figure of forty-one; Simpson, *From the House of War*.

7 There were instances, though, where such bombardments had a significant impact on the general course of a war. During the Egyptian–Israeli War of Attrition (1968–70), the Israeli strategic bombardments brought President Nasser to the verge of resignation and forced him to plead for direct Soviet intervention to contain the Israeli air campaign. The extensive Iraqi air raids on Iranian cities during the Iran–Iraq War played a crucial role in breaking Iranian national morale, leading eventually to a cease-fire. See E. Karsh, 'Military Lessons of the Iran–Iraq War', *Orbis*, Vol. 33, Spring 1989, pp. 209–20.

8 Luttwak's proposed targets were weapons production and storage facilities, including those associated with Iraq's missile, chemical, biological, and nuclear ventures, as well as ammunition depots and POL (petroleum, oil, lubricants) storage sites, 'insofar as they are not greatly dispersed and well camouflaged'. This would not be a 'surgical strike' but rather a sustained air operation, with thousands of sorties over several days. Luttwak argued that

an option against ground forces had been undermined by allowing Saddam time to get his stores dispersed and his troops dug in so that now 'to destroy, say, 50 per cent of the Iraqi army some tens of thousands of sorties would be needed, in protracted air operations lasting some weeks, and which would entail the loss of dozens of aircrew in operational accidents alone'. Senate Hearings, *Crisis in the Persian Gulf*, pp. 325–6.

9   'An entirely plausible approach, if force becomes necessary, to execute air strikes against critical Iraqi installations, to achieve control of the air over Iraq and Kuwait. And then, over many weeks or even months, if necessary, to interdict the supply of Iraqi forces in Kuwait to the point where we could hope to force surrender without engaging the Iraqi Army on the ground.' He advised against engaging the Iraqi Army on the ground, and expressed doubts about the recent build-up of US forces. Ibid, p. 335.

10 Senate Hearings, *Crisis in the Persian Gulf*, pp. 268–9.

11 Richard McKenzie, 'A Conversation with Chuck Horner', *Air Force Magazine*, June 1991.

12 Colonel John A. Warden, *The Air Campaign: Planning for Combat*, Washington DC, National Defense University, 1988. See also Blackwell, *Thunder in the Desert*, p. 115; *Triumph Without Victory*, p. 266. For a post-war analysis along similar lines see Edward Luttwak, 'Victory Through Air Power', *Commentary*, August 1991.

13 Interview with Rick Atkinson of *Washington Post*, reprinted in 'A Prime US Air Force Target: Saddam Hussein', *International Herald Tribune*, 17 September 1990. See also *Aviation Week and Space Technology*, 24 September 1990, pp. 16–18. On the Dugan episode, see Woodward, *The Commanders*, pp. 290–96.

14 This list had been published in *Aviation Week and Space Technology*, 27 August 1990. See also House of Representatives Committee on Armed Services, Rep. Les Aspin and Rep. William Dickinson, *Defense for a New Era: Lessons of the Gulf War*, Washington DC, GPO, 1992, p. 86.

15 The debate is discussed in *Triumph Without Victory*, pp. 266–7.

16 For a sceptical view from the perspective of a Navy planner attached to the targeting cell in Riyadh, see Cdr J. Muir USN, 'A View from the Black Hole', *US Naval Institute Proceedings*, October 1991. One example cited was of a Navy proposal for a cruise missile strike against an airfield. While because of their lower yield warheads they would not be as effective as strike aircraft, they could have been launched early in the conflict. A moderate success rate then might have proved more valuable than higher success much later in the campaign, when the aircraft could be spared.

17 *New York Times*, 23 January 1991. Marlin Fitzwater, the White House spokesman, said in January: 'I don't think you would ever see George Bush going over targeting charts. He's not involved in that kind of micro-management.' *Los Angeles Times*, 14 February 1991.

18 Newsweek, *Secret History of the War*, 18 March 1991. Another source, however, quotes Glosson as saying that the statue had already been removed from the target list because 'arts and antiquities' cannot be attacked under international law. Brown and Shukman, *All Necessary Means*, p. 58.

19 Schwarzkopf, CENTCOM briefing, Riyadh, Saudi Arabia, 27 January 1991.

20 *International Herald Tribune*, 9–10 February 1991.

21 CENTCOM briefing, 27 January 1991.

22 Arkin *et al.*, *On Impact: Modern Warfare and the Environment (A Case Study of the Gulf War)*, Greenpeace, 1991, pp. 100–104.

23 Ibid.

24 Brown and Shukman, *All Necessary Means*, p. 57. British officials were also concerned that attacks on chemical and biological weapons could release dangerous substances to the winds. Of particular concern was one chemical target near the shrines of Karbala and Najaf. *Final Pentagon Report*, p. 128.

25 CNN, Schwarzkopf briefing, 30 January 1991. Bob Woodward reported an assessment that the capacity to develop and produce nuclear weapons had been destroyed, along with

about 50 per cent of chemical and biological weapons manufacturing capacity. *International Herald Tribune*, 29 January 1991.

26 CENTCOM, Desert Storm briefing, p. 70.

27 *International Herald Tribune*, 5 June 1991; *Financial Times*, 13 June, 1991; *The Times*, 14 June 1991; *Jane's Defence Weekly*, 13 July 1991, p. 62.

28 *International Herald Tribune*, 10 July 1991; *Independent*, 27 June 1991. Despite initial scepticism, these claims were soon verified by a series of UN inspections. Not only was Iraq closer to possessing the bomb than had been previously assumed, but it was proceeding in an unexpected way, simultaneously producing fissile material in three technologically distinct ways. These were enrichment by gas centrifuge, electromagnetic separation, and thermal diffusion, which had been used to produce a small amount of plutonium by cheating on safeguard inspections at the Tuwaitha reactor. Moreover, work on a hydrogen bomb appears to have been advanced. Iraq had purchased deuterium oxide (heavy water), and was both producing lithium 6 and designing computer software capable of predicting the effects of thermonuclear explosions. While a hydrogen bomb was still some years away, in the near term Iraq could use the material to boost the destructive potential of atomic weapons and thereby enhance the capability of small missile warheads.

29 *Financial Times*, 15 January 1992; *Independent*, 15, 16 January 1992.

30 See analysis by Barton Gellman of the *Washington Post* in *International Herald Tribune*, 24 June 1991. 518 sorties involving about 1,200 tons of ordnance were used against the oil targets. Crude oil production was not touched. Over 200 sorties were flown against electrical targets. Department of the Air Force, *Reaching Globally*, p. 30.

31 Ibid., pp. 30–32.

32 Ibid., p. 32.

33 *International Herald Tribune*, 29 January 1991. An earlier British briefing had claimed that 'oil-refining capacity has been reduced by 50 per cent'. Transcript of press conference given by Minister of State for Armed Forces, Archie Hamilton and General Alex Harley, London, 23 January 1991.

34 CNN, Schwarzkopf briefing, 30 January 1991.

35 General Norman Schwarzkopf, Brigadier-General Buster Glosson, CENTCOM briefing, Riyadh, 30 January 1991.

36 Lieutenant-General Thomas Kelly, US Department of Defense News Briefing, Washington DC, 11 February 1991.

37 CENTCOM, Desert Storm briefing, p. 70. *Aviation Week and Space Technology*, 27 April 1992.

38 Tony Capaccio, 'Despite Directives, Off-Limits Iraqi Power Plant Gear was Hit', *Defense Week*, 13 January 1992.

39 Ibid.; *Washington Post*, 28 January 1992; *Aviation Week and Space Technology*, 27 January 1992.

40 Department of Defense, *Conduct of the Persian Gulf Conflict: An Interim Report to Congress*, Washington DC, July 1991, pp. 2–5.

41 *Triumph Without Victory*, pp. 2–6. This account asserts that the bomb was developed specifically to target Saddam. This does appear to have been the case, although largely in the context of the threat issued by Baker to Aziz at Geneva as to the risk to the Iraqi regime if chemical weapons were used. On the bomb see *Final Pentagon Report*, p. 223.

42 General Merrill McPeak, Presentation to Senate Armed Services Committee, *FY 1992 Air Force Posture*, 19 March 1991, p. 1.

43 CNN, Schwarzkopf briefing, 30 January 1991. *Final Pentagon Report*, p. 200.

44 *New York Times*, 11 February 1991.

45 Arkin in *Aviation Week and Space Technology*, 27 January 1992.

46 General Norman Schwarzkopf, CENTCOM briefing, Riyadh, 18 January 1991.

47 *International Herald Tribune*, 18, 25 January 1991. *The Times*, 23 January 1991; *New York*

Times, 6 February 1991. A spokesman on 24 January gave a figure of ninety military personnel killed and 154 civilians.

48 Schwarzkopf, CENTCOM briefing, Riyadh, 27 January 1991.
49 British military briefing, Riyadh, 7 February 1991.
50 Statement by White House press spokesman Marlin Fitzwater, 13 February 1991; briefing by Air-Marshal Sir Patrick Hine, 16 February 1991.
51 Lieutenant-General Charles Horner, in charge of the air campaign, observed: 'You know some people are mad at CNN. I used it. Did the attack go on time? Did it hit the target? Things like that.' 'The Secret History of the War', *Newsweek*, 18 March 1991.
52 *Le Figaro*, 18 February 1991.
53 *Reaching Globally*, p. 32.
54 *Triumph Without Victory*, p. 273.
55 *The Times*, 14 February 1991; Brigadier-General Neal, CENTCOM briefing, 13 February 1991.
56 Arkin in *Aviation Week and Space Technology*, 27 January 1992.
57 *New York Times*, 14 February 1991; *Daily Telegraph*, 14 February 1991; *Independent*, 15 February 1991; *Sunday Times*, 17 February 1991; Brigadier-General Neal, CENTCOM briefing, 13 February 1991. Arkin *et. al.*, *On Impact*, p. 91; BBC Radio 4, 'The Storm Breaks', *The Desert Storm*, Part III, 26 January 1992. *The Final Pentagon Report* suggests that the facility was made available to the families of officers working in the bunker (pp. 0–14).
58 Newsweek, *Secret History*, 18 March 1991.
59 Aziz denied that the raid killed some relatives and officials close to Saddam. 'Nobody in my family was injured, nor were any of those from other members of the leadership.' However, this does not mean that the families of second-ranking officials were not among the victims. See *Washington Post*, 8 May 1991.
60 *Independent*, 17 January 1992. Arkin was given the same figures by the Iraqi Government.
61 BBC Television, *The Washington Version*, 18 January 1992.

Chapter 24: Saddam's 'Israeli Card' Fails

1 See, for example, INA, 9 August, 18 September 1990; Baghdad Radio, 8, 11 August, 23 September 1990.
2 See, for example, statements by Defence Minister Arens and Israel's Ambassador to the US, Zalman Shoval, *International Herald Tribune*, 27 December 1990; *Jerusalem Post*, 30 December 1990.
3 *Jerusalem Post*, 2 January 1991; *Ma'ariv*, 7 January 1991.
4 *New York Times*, *Ha'aretz* (Tel Aviv), 3 February 1991.
5 *Ma'ariv*, 30 December 1990.
6 Ibid., 30 December 1990, 13 January 1991.
7 *Jerusalem Post*, 19 September 1991; *Ha'aretz*, *International Herald Tribune*, 26 December 1991; 10 January 1992.
8 *Washington Post*, 10 January 1991.
9 *The Times*, 18 January 1991.
10 In the 1948 'War of Independence', Egyptian fighting aircraft bombed Tel Aviv. In the 1973 October War an Egyptian aircraft fired an air-to-ground Kelt missile against Tel Aviv, but the missile was intercepted by the Israeli Air Force.
11 *The Times*, 19 January 1991.
12 Dan Shomron, 'A Personal Report on the Gulf War', *Yediot Acharonot* (Tel Aviv), 8 September 1991.
13 *The Times*, 19 January 1991; *New York Times*, 3 March 1991.
14 In a press interview on the first anniversary of the war, Avihu Bin-Nun vehemently denied that he pushed for a retaliatory strike against Iraq. 'These stories are complete nonsense',

he said, 'the opposite was the case. I have been often criticized of presenting a too balanced picture in the Cabinet.' *Yediot Acharonot*, 'A Year Has Passed: Special Issue on the First Anniversary of the Gulf War', Tel Aviv, 10 January 1992, p. 7.

15 *Yediot Acharonot*, 'A Year Has Passed', pp. 2–3. Ze'ev Schiff, 'Israel after the War', *Foreign Affairs*, Spring 1991.

16 This fact was learnt by the Israelis well after the termination of hostilities, and revealed by Major General Bin-Nun in a press interview on the first anniversary of the war. It was also confirmed by the findings of Ben Brown and David Shukman, *All Necessary Means*, p. 63.

17 *Triumph Without Victory*, p. 245.

18 Ibid., pp. 248–50.

19 Televised interview, Brian Lapping Associates.

20 The editors of *Time*, *Desert Storm: The War in the Persian Gulf*, p. 162.

21 Interviews with Israeli military officials; Arens's interview with *Yediot Acharonot*, 'A Year Has Passed', pp. 2–3. See also 'Five Decisive Moments', *Time*, 11 March 1991, p. 33; 'The Secret History of the War', *Newsweek*, 18 March 1991, p. 24.

22 See, for example, *Ha'aretz* (Tel Aviv), 21, 29, 30 January 1991.

23 Ibid.

24 This was the assessment of Dr Avi Ben-Basat, a member of the executive directorate of the Bank of Israel. See *Ha'aretz*, 4 February 1991.

25 These loan guarantees, though, were not approved, leading to an angry response by the Israeli Ambassador in Washington, Zalman Shoval. After the war President Bush would make these guarantees conditional on the suspension of new Israeli settlements in the occupied territories.

26 *Ha'aretz*, 1 February 1991; *The Times*, 2 February 1991.

27 Radio Monte Carlo in Arabic (Paris), 16 January 1991.

28 For Syrian discussion of the damage caused to the Arab cause by Iraq, see, for example, *al-Ba'th*, 3 February 1991; *al-Thawra* (Damascus), 20 February 1991; Syrian Arab News Agency (SANA), 19, 21 January, 10 February 1991; Radio Damascus, 19, 20, 21 January 1991.

29 *Al-Thawra* (Damascus), 21 January 1991.

30 *The Times*, 21 January 1991.

31 Interviews with Syrian sources.

32 See, for example, *al-Thawra* (Damascus), 5, 9 February 1991.

Chapter 25: The Coalition Holds

1   This discussion of the environmental aspects of the war has benefited from William Arkin, Damian Durrant, and Marianne Cherni, *On Impact: Modern Warfare and the Environment (A Case Study of the Gulf War)*, a Greenpeace study prepared for a conference on 'A "Fifth Geneva" Convention on the Protection of the Environment in Time of Armed Conflict', London, King's College, June 1991.

2   This was not the first time that Saddam had proved willing to inflict horrendous ecological damage in order to bring about a quick ending to a war: in 1983 the Iraqi Army blew up the Norwuz oil platform, west of Iran's main oil export terminal at Kharg Island, causing the Iranian wells to leak for some eight months.

3   A bombing raid by F-111 aircraft destroyed two oil terminal pressure controls in a raid on 27 January, slowing the flow of oil into the Gulf.

4   In Britain, Dr John Cox, a chemical engineer and a supporter of CND, warned a conference in early January that a smoke cloud of nuclear holocaust proportions would shroud the Gulf after a war. This could threaten more than 1 billion people with starvation if it caused Asian monsoons to fail. Dr Abdullah Toukan, scientific adviser to King Hussein, predicted a one-off 15 per cent increase in emissions of carbon dioxide. David

Thomas, 'Oilfield Pollution: A Burning Issue', *Financial Times*, 9 January 1991. See also Neville Brown, 'The Blazing Oil Wells of Kuwait', *World Today*, Vol. 47, No. 6, June 1991.

5 Richard Williams, Joanne Hechman, Jon Shneeberger, *Environmental Consequences of the Persian Gulf War, 1990–1991*, Washington DC, National Geographic Society: 1991; Frederick Warner, 'The Environmental Consequences of the Gulf War', *Environment*, Vol. 33, No. 5, 1991.

6 David Thomas and Deborah Hargreaves, 'High Anxiety about Black Gold', *Financial Times*, 14 January 1991.

7 INA, 23 September 1990; *The Times*, 28 September 1991; *Wall Street Journal*, 1 October 1991; *Sunday Times*, 16 December 1991.

8 *Independent*, 5 January 1991; *Financial Times*, 5–6 January 1991.

9 He made this pledge in a speech on the seventieth anniversary of the Iraqi Army. See Radio Baghdad, 7 January 1991.

10 On 21 September President Bush had stated that he would hold Saddam 'directly responsible for terrorist acts', and James Baker warned Aziz to this effect during their Geneva meeting. *Washington Post*, 8 January 1991.

11 State Department, *Patterns of Global Terrorism 1991*, Washington DC, GPO, April 1992. *International Herald Tribune*, 4 March 1991.

12 Charles Smith, 'Loyalties under Fire', *Far Eastern Economic Review*, 24 January 1991.

13 General Mirza Aslam Beg's attitude, however, may have been more related to an American decision of October 1990 to suspend economic and military aid due to Pakistan's nuclear programme. Prior to that point Beg had been explicitly anti-Saddam. J. Mohan Malik, 'India's Response to the Gulf Crisis', *Asian Survey*, Vol. 31, No. 9, September 1991, p. 849.

14 Ibid., p. 860.

15 John Lloyd, 'The World Watches with Moral Unease', *Financial Times*, 19–20 January 1991.

16 However, this went down to 30 per cent if there was no UN approval. *Independent*, 24 November 1990.

17 Gallup for *Daily Telegraph*, 11 January 1991.

18 *Sunday Times*, 20 January, 3 March 1991.

19 Denis Healey, 'Still Time to Escape Armageddon', *Observer*, 6 January 1991. Reprinted in Brian MacArthur (ed.), *Despatches from the Gulf War*, London, Bloomsbury, 1991. This is a useful collection of contemporary British journalism. See also Jolyon Howarth, 'United Kingdom Defence Policy and the Gulf War', *Contemporary European Affairs*, Vol. 4, No. 1, 1991.

20 *The Times*, 23 January 1991.

21 The British role is described in Secretary of State for Defence, *Statement on the Defence Estimates: Britain's Defence in the 90s*, Volume 1 (Cmnd 1559-I, July 1991); Ministry of Defence, 'Dispatch by Air Chief Marshal Sir Patrick Hine GCB ADC FRAES CBIM RAF, Joint Commander of Operation Granby, August 1990–April 1991', *Second Supplement to The London Gazette of Friday, 28th June 1991*, No. 52589; House of Commons Tenth Report from the Defence Committee, Session 1990–91, *Preliminary Lessons of Operation Granby*, August 1991. The British operation was officially known as Granby.

22 General Sir Peter de la Billière, 'The Gulf Conflict: Planning and Execution', in *Command in War: Gulf Operations*, pp. 16–17. BBC Radio 4, *The Desert War*, Part IV, 2 February 1992.

23 Richard Leaver notes that the main Australian contribution was probably in intelligence-gathering, via the early warning and electronic intelligence facilities at Pine Gap and Nurrungar. 'Australia's Gulf Commitment: The End of Self-Reliance', *The Pacific Review*, Vol. 4, No. 3, 1991.

24 *International Herald Tribune*, 21 February 1991. A report by the auditor-general questioned

the preparedness of Canada's armed forces. It was revealed that a Second-World-War-era Bofors gun had had to be salvaged from a naval museum to help fit one of the ships. *Armed Forces Journal International*, January 1991.

25 *Ottawa Globe and Mail*, 27 October 1990.

26 Alia and Clerc, *La guerre de Mitterrand*.

27 *Le Monde*, 24 January 1991. The French strikes against equipment stores used AS-30 laser-guided missiles. It was pointed out that Iraq had bought 240 of these missiles, the French forces only 180.

28 The French war Cabinet involved President Mitterrand, Prime Minister Michel Rocard, Foreign Minister Jacques Dumas, Interior Minister Pierre Joxe, Defence Minister Jean-Pierre Chevènement (until he was replaced by Joxe), Mitterrand's aides Jean-Louis Bianco and Hubert Védrine, on the civilian side, and Admiral Lanxade, on the military side. Also present was General Schmitt, Chief of the General Staff, and the chiefs of the three services. Bianco was responsible for general organization and co-ordination. The group tended to meet each evening at 18.00. For a discussion of decision-making see Admiral Jacques Lanxade, 'Au coeur des conseils restreints de l'Élysée', *Guerre éclair dans le Golfe*.

29 Claire Trean, 'La Malaise de M. Chevènement', *Le Monde*, 21 January 1991. See also *Le Monde*, 22 January 1991. Alia and Clerc, *La guerre de Mitterrand*, pp. 303–6.

30 *Le Figaro*, 19 January 1991.

31 *International Herald Tribune*, 25 January 1991.

32 *Le Monde*, 30 January 1991.

33 *International Herald Tribune*, 6 February 1992.

34 *Wall Street Journal*, 6 December 1990.

35 Turgut Ozal, 'Turkey: An Unwanted War "Became Unavoidable"', *International Herald Tribune*, 23 January 1991.

36 Jim Bodegnar, 'Turkey's Role in the Gulf Conflict', *Middle East Economic Digest*, 8 February 1991; *Wall Street Journal*, 12 February 1991.

37 Theo Sommer, 'That Uneasy Feeling Again', *Newsweek*, 28 January 1991. Timothy Garton Ash, 'The Gulf in Europe', *New York Review of Books*, 7 March 1991.

38 *The Times*, 6 February 1991.

39 *Daily Telegraph*, 15 January 1991.

40 On this debate see Paul E. Gallis, *German Foreign Policy after the Gulf War: Implications for US Interests*, Washington DC, Congressional Research Service, 30 May 1991, p. 8. Kohl confirmed at the end of the war that Germany would have been committed to Turkey's defence had there been an Iraqi attack.

41 *The Times* 29 January 1991.

42 Ronald Asmus, 'Germany after the Gulf War', *A Rand Note*, Santa Monica, Rand Corporation, 1992, p. 17. See Helmut Schmidt in *Die Zeit*, 25 January 1991.

43 *Daily Telegraph*, 25 January 1991.

44 An extremely useful collection covering the policies of most European countries is in Nicolo Gresotto and John Roper, *Western Europe and the Gulf*, Paris, The Institute for Security Studies of WEU, 1992.

45 *The Times*, 29 January 1991.

46 *Guardian*, 31 January 1991. Italian pride was not helped by a US briefer observing that it would make little difference if Italian forces withdrew.

47 *Guardian*, 24 January 1991.

48 See letter by Belgian Ambassador to *The Times*, 6 March 1991.

49 *International Herald Tribune*, 26–27 January 1991.

50 *Daily Telegraph*, 23 January 1991.

51 *Financial Times*, 25 January 1991.

52 *Washington Post*, 24 January 1991.

53 *Aviation Week and Space Technology*, 11 November 1991. By this time $45 billion had

already been received. In addition the United States received $5.8 billion in fuel and other non-cash support, and wrote off $1.2 billion in military equipment lost in the war which would not be replaced. See also Stephen Daggett and Gary J. Pagliano, *Persian Gulf War: US Costs and Allied Financial Contributions*, Congressional Research Service, 5 June 1991.

54 Treasury and Civil Service Committee, *Cost and Economic Consequences of the Gulf War*, Minutes of Evidence, Wednesday 6 February 1991, Session 1990–1991.
55 *International Herald Tribune*, 31 January 1991.
56 *International Herald Tribune*, 6 February 1991; *Economist*, 16 February 1991.
57 Elsewhere in Asia the South Koreans found it possible to send a transport and a medical team as well as cash. Taiwan reportedly wanted to send the US $100 million, but the administration turned it down for fear of offending China.

Chapter 26: Preparing the Battlefield

1 INA, 18 January 1991.
2 Baghdad Radio, 20 January 1991.
3 Saddam's interview with Peter Arnett, 28 January 1991.
4 See, for example, Baghdad Radio, 31 January 1991.
5 See International Institute for Strategic Studies, *Strategic Survey, 1990–1991*, p. 74.
6 Department of the Air Force, *Reaching Globally*, pp. 44–5.
7 *The Times*, 1 February 1991.
8 The lack of air support may have come as an alarming revelation to the local Iraqi commanders, who were calling for air support during the battle.
9 On these expectations see Elizabeth Drew, 'Letter from Washington', *New Yorker*, 25 February 1991, pp. 91–2. She suggested that the optimum was encouraged by Arab Governments who could not believe that Saddam could withstand American military might for long.
10 *Daily Telegraph*, 24 January 1991.
11 *The Times*, 2 February 1991.
12 Speech by Les Aspin before the Democratic Business Council, 7 February 1991.
13 Brigadier General John Stewart, *Operation Desert Storm: The Military Intelligence Story: A View from the G-2*, US Army, April 1991, p. 17. *Final Pentagon Report*, p. 124.
14 Schwarzkopf, CENTCOM briefing, Riyadh, 27 January 1991.
15 Department of the Air Force, *Reaching Globally*, p. 41.
16 An attack on a bridge over the Euphrates in al-Nasiriyeh killed forty-seven civilians and wounded 102. *Independent*, 8 February 1991.
17 McPeak, *The Air Campaign*.
18 Schwarzkopf, CENTCOM briefing, Riyadh, 27 January 1991.
19 'Lessons of the Gulf War', in *Trust and Verify*, London, Verification Technology Information Centre, March 1991; Bhupendra Jasani, 'Keeping the Peace in Orbit', *Guardian*, 8 March 1991; *Aviation Week and Space Technology*, 4 February 1991.
20 Brigadier General M.T. Hapgood Jr, USMC, 'Experience: Handle with Care', *US Naval Institute Proceedings*, October 1991.
21 Stewart, *Operation Desert Storm*, p. 20. See also *Guardian*, 20 February 1991; *International Herald Tribune*, 22 February 1991. British and French assessments appear to have been somewhere in between. Brown and Shukman, *All Necessary Means*, p. 112.
22 US Senate, Hearings before the Committee on Armed Services, *Operation Desert Shield/ Desert Storm*, June 1991.
23 *International Herald Tribune*, 29 January 1991.
24 CNN, Schwarzkopf briefing, 30 January 1991. Brown and Shukman, *All Necessary Means*, p. 109.
25 Laurent, *Tempête du désert*, pp. 271–4.

26 See Stewart, *Desert Storm: The Military Intelligence Story*, p. 21.
27 Brigadier-General Richard Neal, USMC, CENTCOM briefing, Riyadh, 9 February 1991; 14 February 1991. The British Secretary of Defence, Tom King, claimed that the overall effect of the campaign had been to 'reduce the Iraqi battle winning capability by between something like 15–10 per cent'. He gave 'one assessment' of 600 tanks destroyed. Tom King, briefing, 8 February 1991. In this briefing he confirmed publicly the aim to destroy 50 per cent of Iraqi fighting capability before launching the ground war. CENTCOM were not pleased that this planning figure had reached the public domain because it could tie them down. In his briefing the same day, General Robert Johnston agreed, when asked, with King's assessment on tank kills but insisted that 'we are not dependent upon a given percentage to launch the ground attack'.
28 Schwarzkopf briefing, Riyadh, 27 February 1991. Horner interview, *Air Force Magazine*, June 1991.
29 See Lawrence Freedman, 'Allies Advance in the Psycholological Battle', *Independent*, 16 February 1991.

Chapter 27: Land War or Cease-Fire?

1   *Financial Times*, 18 January 1991; Tass, 17 January 1991.
2   Robert O. Freedman, 'Moscow and the Gulf War', *Problems of Communism*, July–August 1991, pp. 10–11.
3   Gorbachev's statement as broadcast by Moscow Television, 17 January 1991.
4   Tass, 17 January 1991.
5   The Iranian plan was believed to involve Iraqi withdrawal with an Islamic peace force and Islamic adjudication on the territorial and financial disputes between Kuwait and Iraq, an Islamic fund to help restore damage to the two countries, guarantees on Iraqi security, withdrawal of Western forces and pledges on the Palestinian issue.
6   *Daily Telegraph*, 11 February 1991.
7   Olga Alexandrova, 'Soviet Policy in the Gulf Conflict', *Aussenpolitik*, III, 1991, p. 233.
8   Other members were Deputy Foreign Minister Alexander Belonogov, who had always been less enthusiastic than Shevardnadze in supporting the coalition, Central Committee Secretary Valentin Falin, and Yevgeny Primakov, Vitaly Ignatenko and A. Chernyaev from the Presidential Office. See Tass, 17 January 1991; *Literaturnaya Gazeta*, 27 February 1991.
9   See, for example, statement by the Supreme Soviet Committee on International Affairs, Tass, 4 February 1991.
10 Laurent, *Tempête du désert*, pp. 252–8.
11 Tass, 9 February 1991.
12 AFP, 11 February 1991.
13 These included, *inter alia*, gestures on Kuwaiti–Iraqi relations and the resolution of other outstanding regional conflicts. Interview with *Pravda*, 15 January 1991.
14 Tass, 9 February 1991.
15 The meeting was attended by practically the entire Iraqi leadership, including Saddam's deputy, Izzat Ibrahim, First Deputy Premier Taha Yasin Ramadan, Foreign Minister Tariq Aziz, and Minister of Information Latif Nusseif Jasim. Baghdad Radio, 12 February 1991.
16 Yergeny Primakov, *Missions à Baghdad*, pp. 127–33.
17 Tass, 13 February 1991.
18 *The Times*, 14 February 1991.
19 Moscow Radio in English, 13 February 1991.
20 Baghdad Radio, 12 February 1991.
21 Ibid., 15 February 1991.

22 *Guardian*, 18 February 1991.

23 *The Times*, 16 February 1991.

24 Amman Radio, 16 February 1991. A similar position was expressed by PLO Chairman Yasser Arafat. Ibid.

25 *Tishrin*, 16 February 1991.

26 Riyadh Radio, 15, 17, 18 February 1991. See also Saudi Press Agency, 17, 18 February 1991. For a similar response from Egypt see, MENA (Cairo), Egyptian Space Channel, 15 February 1991.

27 See Freedman, *Moscow and the Gulf War*, p. 16.

28 *International Herald Tribune*, 16–17 February 1991; Tass, 16 February 1991.

29 Yevgeny Primakov, 'The Inside Story of Moscow's Quest for a Deal', *Time*, 4 March 1991.

30 There was a mistaken belief at the time that the real allied objection was motivated by the desire to continue the war until they had removed Saddam from office.

31 Alia and Clerc, *La guerre de Mitterrand*, pp. 352–71. The normal divisions emerged in the European Community when it met on the Tuesday, with the discussions somewhat awkward as only four members – Britain, France, Italy and Germany – had received details and they had all been asked to keep them confidential. They agreed to welcome the fact that the discussion was now about an Iraqi withdrawal.

32 *Wall Street Journal*, 21 February 1991.

33 *New York Times*, 22 February 1991.

34 *Sunday Times*, 24 February 1991.

35 *International Herald Tribune*, 23 February 1991; for analysis of the politics of the plan see *Financial Times*, 23–24 February 1991. For a Soviet perspective see Anatoly Repin, 'The Chance Has Been Missed', *Novosti Gulf Bulletin*, 27 February 1991.

36 Because so many countries were involved in this issue it was not one that the coalition members could decide to drop by themselves. It would have to go back to the United Nations. Economic sanctions also could only be lifted following a Security Council vote.

37 *Sunday Times*, 24 February 1991.

38 Arkin *et al.*, *On Impact*, pp. 66–7. Of Kuwait's 743 wells in seven fields, 363 were active producing wells and 380 were inactive.

39 Vipin Gupta, 'Meteosat Lifted Fog of War to Expose Reality in Gulf', *Defense News*, 18 March 1991.

40 Filmed interview, Brian Lapping Associates, January 1992.

41 After Gorbachev had had a similar call with John Major, Major's foreign policy adviser Charles Powell formed the opinion that he was as much sounding out reactions as forwarding proposals.

42 *The Times*, 23 February 1991.

Chapter 28: Land War

1 One alternative was through Bubiyan island, which had the risk of accidentally encroaching on Iranian territory or airspace; also, the beaches on the island were shallow and easily blocked and mined, the naval base at Umm Qasr was close at hand, and the island itself was of little importance even in getting access to the mainland (Blackwell, *Thunder in the Desert*, p. 154). Blackwell's account appears to be based on a debriefing of an Iraqi corps commander. Friedman suggests that the Marines' proposal was to avoid the defended Kuwaiti coast but to land up the Shatt al-Arab towards or beyond Basra. This, he notes, would have landed forces into the Iraqi rear and would not have required the potentially quite visible logistics preparation involved in the eventual plan. However, unless there was a link-up with a ground attack, the Marines could have been isolated and they would not have been able to cut off Iraqi troops by themselves (*Desert Victory*, p. 216).

2 Blackwell, *Thunder in the Desert*, pp. 156–7.

3   Ibid., p. 159.
4   These points are made in a valuable article by James Pardew, 'The Iraqi Army's Defeat in Kuwait', *Parameters*, Winter 1991–2. At the time of Desert Storm, Colonel Pardew was the Army's Director of Foreign Intelligence.
5   Stewart, *Operation Desert Storm*, p. 25.
6   Pardew, 'The Iraqi Army's Defeat', p. 22.
7   Neal briefing, 12 February 1991; see also *Middle East Policy Survey*, 15 February 1991.
8   BBC Television, *The Washington Version*, 18 January 1992.
9   See *Newsweek*, 'Secret History', 18 March 1991; *International Herald Tribune*, 19 March 1991; 16 January 1992.
10 *Newsweek*, 'Secret History', 18 March 1991.
11 Friedman, *Desert Victory*, p. 217.
12 See, for example, testimony of James Blackwell, House Hearings, *Crisis in the Persian Gulf*.
13 Leslie Gelb, 'Bush Needs Correct Answers to Some Tough Questions', *International Herald Tribune*, 12 February 1991.
14 As Schwarzkopf explained it: 'When the quarterback is desperate for a touchdown at the very end, what he does is, he steps behind the centre and every single one of his receivers goes way out and they all run down as fast as they possibly can into the end zone, and he lobs the ball.' CENTCOM briefing, 27 February 1991.
15 *Newsweek*, 'Secret History', 18 March 1991.
16 *Final Pentagon Report*, pp. 286, 292.
17 Ibid., p. 265.
18 Vice-Admiral Stanley Arthur and Marvin Pokrant, 'Desert Storm at Sea', Michael Paterman, 'The Navy Did Its Job', *US Naval Institute Proceedings*, Naval Review 1991, May 1991.
19 House of Commons, *Preliminary Lessons of Operation Granby*, p. 59.
20 Powell further observed: 'And it had nothing to do with laser range finders or TV cameras or fancy technology. It had to do with brave young kids, crawling at night and finding where these mines were. And then laying and hiding all day long. And then the next night, doing it again.' Filmed interview, Brian Lapping Associates, December 1991.
21 *Triumph Without Victory*, p. 367.
22 *Final Pentagon Report*, I-38, I-41.
23 *Newsweek*, 'Secret History' 18 March 1991; Col. Peter Langenus, 'Moving an Army: Movement Control for Desert Storm', *Military Review*, September 1991.
24 General Bernard Janvier, 'Trente-six heures pour vaincre', *Guerre éclair dans le Golfe*.
25 Schwarzkopf briefing, 27 February 1991.
26 *International Herald Tribune*, 19 March 1991. The VII Corps required 450 trucks of ammunition and 400 trucks of fuel per day. The figures for XVIII Corps were 400 and 480 respectively. Lt.-General William Pagonis and Major Harold Raugh, 'Good Logistics in Combat Power', *Military Review*, September 1991.
27 *Triumph Without Victory*, p. 335.
28 This was corroborated by debriefs of Iraqi prisoners of war.
29 Strobe Talbott, 'White Flags in the Desert', *Time*, 11 March, 1991.

Chapter 29: The Closing Whistle

1   Baghdad Radio, 25 February 1991.
2   *Guardian*; *The Times*, 26 February 1991.
3   *New York Times*, 26 February 1991.
4   R. Patai, *The Arab Mind*, New York, C. Scribner's Sons, 1976, pp. 104–5.
5   Baghdad Radio, 27 February 1991.
6   *The Times*, 28 February 1991.

7 This account draws on that found in Douglas Waller and John Barry, 'The Day Bush Stopped the War', *Newsweek*, 20 January 1992.

8 McPeak briefing.

9 Quayle, Cheney, Baker, Sununu, Scowcroft and Gates.

10 *Newsweek*, 10 January 1992, appears to suggest that this was the meeting where Powell made his recommendation for a cease-fire. However, the recommendation was not made until the next day. It is quite possible that he recorded his unease over the events on the Basra Road.

11 *Newsweek*, 20 January 1992.

12 In addition, 1,856 out of 2,870 armoured personnel carriers had been destroyed, as had been 2,140 artillery pieces out of 3,110.

13 Schwarzkopf briefing, Riyadh, 27 February 1991.

14 BBC Television, *The Washington Version*, 18 January 1992.

15 See Schwarzkopf's remarks in interview with David Frost, reported in *International Herald Tribune*, 28 March 1991.

16 See John Bulloch, 'How Bush Lost the Gulf War', *Independent on Sunday*, 8 December 1991. BBC Television, *Panorama*, 2 September 1991.

17 Major-General Barry R. McCaffrey, 24th Infantry Division (Mechanized), *Desert Shield and Desert Storm: Operations Overview*, US Senate Armed Services Committee, Washington DC, May 1991.

18 See Blackwell, *Thunder in the Desert*, p. 208. Schwarzkopf in his interview noted that Republican Guard units had already 'bugged out' before the main attack and crossed the Euphrates. *International Herald Tribune*, 28 March 1991.

19 *Conduct of the Persian Gulf Conflict: An Interim Report*, pp. 4–10.

20 *International Herald Tribune*, 26 March 1991.

21 *Triumph Without Victory*, p. 373. Eleven more Americans were killed when unexploded allied ordnance blew up on them, and a further eighteen were killed by unexploded enemy ordnance.

22 Anthony Cordesman, 'Rush to Judgement in the Gulf War', *Armed Forces Journal International*, June 1991.

23 Dannreuther, *The Gulf Conflict*, p. 57.

24 *International Herald Tribune*, 2–3 March, 18 March, 24 June 1991, 16 January 1992. Patrick Cockburn, 'Lower Death Toll Helped Saddam', *Independent*, 5 February 1992.

Chapter 30: Saddam Survives

1 Baghdad Radio, 28 February 1991.

2 On the uprisings in Iraq following the war, see Efraim Karsh and Inari Rautsi, *Saddam Hussein*, London, Futura, 1991, revised edition, Chapter 12.

3 Interview with Kurdish opposition sources.

4 *Official Record* (House of Commons), 15 January 1991; 22 January 1991.

5 *New York Times* editorial, reprinted in *International Herald Tribune*, 26–27 January 1991. He will be 'weakened anyway, and could be toppled without us'. Speech by Les Aspin before the Democratic Business Council, 7 February 1991. For Britain, see for example Gerald Kaufman, 'So Far and No Further', *Guardian*, 30 January 1991 (Kaufman was the Labour Party's Foreign Affairs spokesman).

6 NOP in *Sunday Times*, 24 February 1991. 1,064 people were interviewed on 21 February.

7 *The Times*, 26 February 1991.

8 On ABC TV. *Guardian*, 26 February 1991.

9 USIA report, 21 February 1991.

10 BBC Radio 4, 'The Desert War – A Kind of Victory', 16 February 1992.

11 *Guardian*, 28 February 1991.

12 Statement of 24 January 1991.

13 Interview by Hojjat al-Islam Muhammad Bakr al-Hakim, Head of the Tehran-based Supreme Council of the Islamic Revolution in Iraq (SCIRI) with *Anatoliya* (Ankara), 5 March 1991.

14 Interview with a Saudi official.

15 See, for example, Damascus Radio, 4, 5, 10 March 1991.

16 USIA, 28 February 1991; *Guardian*, 28 February, 2 March 1991; *International Herald Tribune* 1 March 1991; *Daily Telegraph*, 2 March 1991.

17 Quoted in *Guardian*, 2 March 1991.

18 *Report to the Secretary General on humanitarian needs in Kuwait and Iraq in the immediate post-crisis environment by a mission to the area led by Mr Martti Ahtisaari, Under-Secretary General for Administration and Management, dated 20 March 1991*, p. 5, para 8.

19 Resolution 687 (1991), adopted by the Security Council at its 2,981st meeting on 3 April 1991.

20 *International Herald Tribune*, 28 March 1991.

21 *Independent*, 8, 9 March 1991.

22 In his letter, though, Aziz expressed his grievance with the continuation of sanctions despite what he described as Iraq's adherence to previous Security Council resolutions. For the text of Aziz's letter, see *Financial Times*, 4 March 1991.

23 INA, 5 March 1991; *The Times*, 7 March 1990.

24 Other prominent Cabinet changes included the replacement of Foreign Minister Aziz and Information Minister Jasim by Ahmad Hussein Khudair and Hamid Yusuf Hammadi respectively.

25 *Observer*, 3 March 1991; *Sunday Times*, 10 March 1991; AFP (Paris), 22 March 1991.

26 Baghdad Radio, 16 March 1991. While commonly associated with the gassing of the town of Halabja, in which some 5,000 people perished, the Iraqi atrocities in Kurdistan were far more extensive and included, apart from the gassing of other villages, the razing of half of Kurdistan's settlements and the displacement of half a million Kurds.

27 *International Herald Tribune*, 20 March 1991.

28 *New York Times*, 23 March 1991.

29 *Washington Post*, 14 April 1991; Laurie Mylroie, 'How We Helped Saddam Survive', *Commentary*, July 1991.

30 See Nik Gowing, 'The Media Dimension I: TV and the Kurds', *The World Today*, July 1991, pp. 111–12.

31 Bush's News Conference, USIA, 16 April 1991.

32 *International Herald Tribune*, 15 April 1991. The Administration had anticipated a refugee problem following the war, and had even pre-positioned supplies in Turkey to cope with it, but these proved completely inadequate because of the unexpectedly wide scope of the phenomenon. Early US predictions of refugee numbers were 20,000. A January report for the UN High Commissioner for Refugees on post-war requirements for humanitarian assistance came closer to the mark, putting the number at 400,000.

33 For the text of the resolution, see United States Information Service (USIS), *European Wireless File, Gulf Issues Special*, 8 April 1991.

34 *Independent on Sunday*, 14 April 1991.

35 *International Herald Tribune*, 9 April 1991.

36 Resolution 687 was passed on 3 April. *Financial Times*, *Independent*, 9 April 1991; *International Herald Tribune*, 10 April 1991.

37 On the Luxembourg summit see, for example, *Financial Times*, 10 April 1991; *International Herald Tribune*, 9, 10 April 1991; *Independent on Sunday*, 14 April 1991.

38 On 11 April the Senate passed Resolution 99, recognizing a US 'moral obligation to provide sustained humanitarian relief for Iraqi refugees' and calling upon the President 'immediately to press the United Nations Security Council to adopt effective measures to

assist Iraqi refugees as set forth in Resolution 688 and to enforce . . . the demand in Resolution 688 that Iraq end its repression of the Iraqi civilian population'. Prior to Major's initiative, 45 per cent of Americans favoured aid to the rebels, but only half of these believed the US should use force on the Kurds' behalf. *International Herald Tribune*, 6–7 April 1991.

39 Speech delivered at the Air University at Maxwell Air Force Base, 13 April 1991, USIA, 15 April 1991. The second requirement in Bush's speech, though, did involve the dispatch of troops, if only on a highly restricted mission.

40 Bush news conference, 16 April 1991, USIA, 18 April 1991. See also *Financial Times*, 18 April 1991.

41 *Independent*, 19 April 1991.

42 USIS, *US Troops to Help Set up Refugee Camps in Iraq*, 18 April 1991; *Guardian*, 16 April 1991; *International Herald Tribune*, 18 April 1991.

43 *International Herald Tribune*, 16 April 1991.

44 This point was made by Lord Shawcross, Britain's Chief Prosecutor at the Nuremberg trials, who nonetheless thought that action should be taken against Saddam on an *ad hoc* basis. 'There's Only One Way to Deal with Saddam', *Observer*, 7 April 1991. See also Russell Goodman, 'Think Twice About Trying Saddam', *Armed Forces Journal International*, April 1991, and Adam Roberts, 'The Case for a War Crimes Tribunal', *Independent*, 1 March 1991.

45 *International Herald Tribune*, 17 April 1991.

46 Dannreuther, *The Gulf Conflict*, p. 63. For a contemporary analysis along these lines, see *Middle East Policy Survey*, 15 March 1991.

47 *International Herald Tribune*, 22 May 1991; *Independent*, 7 June 1991.

Bibliography

Official documents

United States
Department of Defense, *Conduct of the Persian Gulf Conflict: An Interim Report to Congress*, Washington DC, GPO, July 1991.
Department of Defense, *Conduct of the Persian Gulf War: Final Report to Congress*, Washington DC, GPO, April 1992.
Department of the Air Force, *Reaching Globally, Reaching Powerfully: The United States Air Force in the Gulf War*, Washington DC, September 1991.
Department of State, *Patterns of Global Terrorism, 1991: Report to Congress*, Washington DC, GPO, April 1992.
House of Representatives, Markup before the Committee on Foreign Affairs, One Hundredth Congress, Second Session, *Legislation to Impose Sanctions against Iraqi Chemical Use*, Washington, DC, GPO, 1988.
House of Representatives, Hearing before the Subcommittee on Europe and the Middle East of the Committee on Foreign Relations, One Hundred First Congress, Second Session, *United States–Iraqi Relations*, Washington DC, GPO, 1990.
House of Representatives, Markup before the Committee on Foreign Affairs, One Hundred First Congress, First Session, *Sanctions Against Iraq* Washington DC, GPO, 1990.
House of Representatives, Hearings and Markup before the Committee on Foreign Relations, One Hundred First Congress, Second Session, *Crisis in the Persian Gulf*, Washington DC, GPO, 1990.
House of Representatives, Hearing before the Subcommittee on Asian and Pacific Affairs of the Committee on Foreign Affairs, One Hundred First Congress, Second Session, *Asian Response to the Crisis in the Persian Gulf*, Washington DC, GPO, 1991.
House of Representatives, Joint Hearings before Subcommittees of the Committee on Foreign Affairs and the Joint Economic Committee, One Hundred First Congress, Second Session, *Persian Gulf Crisis*, Washington DC, GPO, 1991.
House of Representatives, Hearings before the Committee on Armed Services, One Hundred First Congress, Second Session, *Crisis in the Persian Gulf: Sanctions, Diplomacy and War*, Washington DC, GPO, 1991.
House of Representatives, Committee on Armed Services, Rep. Les Aspin and Rep. William Dickinson, *Defense for a New Era: Lessons of the Gulf War*, Washington DC, GPO, 1992.
House of Representatives, Hearing before the Subcomittee on Europe and the Middle East of the Committee on Foreign Relations, One Hundred First Congress, First Session, *United States–Iraqi Relations*, Washington DC, GPO, 1991.
House of Representatives, Report Prepared by the Subcommittee on Arms Control, International Security and Science of the Committee on Foreign Affairs, One Hundred Second Congress, First Session, *The Persian Gulf Crisis: Relevant Documents, Correspondence,*

Reports, Washington DC, GPO, 1991.
House of Representatives, Subcommittee on Europe and the Middle East of the Committee on Foreign Affairs, One Hundred Second Congress, First Session, *Developments in the Middle East, July 1990*, Washington DC, GPO, 1991.
Senate, Staff Report to the Committee on Foreign Relations, One Hundredth Congress, First Session, *War in the Persian Gulf: The US Takes Sides*, Washington DC, GPO, 1987.
Senate, Hearing before the Committee on Foreign Relations, One Hundred First Congress, Second Session, *United States Policy Toward Iraq: Human Rights, Weapons Proliferation, and International Law*, Washington DC, GPO, 1990.
Senate, Hearings before the Committee on Armed Services, One Hundred First Congress, Second Session, *Crisis in the Persian Gulf Region: US Policy Options and Implications*, Washington DC, GPO, 1990.
Senate, Hearings before the Committee on Foreign Relations, One Hundred First Congress, Second Session, *US Policy in the Persian Gulf*, Washington DC, GPO, 1990.
Senate, Hearings before the Committee on Foreign Relations, One Hundred First Congress, Second Session, *US Policy in the Persian Gulf*, parts 1 and 2, Washington DC, GPO, 1991.
Senate, Report from the Committee on Armed Services, One Hundred Second Congress, First Session, *Authorizing Supplemental Appropriations for Fiscal Year 1991 for the Department of Defense for Operation Desert Shield, etcetera*, Washington DC, GPO, 1991.
Senate, Staff Report to the Committee on Foreign Relations, *Civil War in Iraq*, One Hundred Second Congress, First Session, Washington DC, GPO, 1991.
Senate, Hearings before the Committee on Armed Services, One Hundred Second Congress, First Session, *Department of Defense Authorization for Appropriations for Fiscal Years 1992 and 1993*, Washington DC, GPO, 1991.

United Kingdom
Secretary of State for Defence, *Statement on the Defence Estimates, 1991* (Cm 1559-I&II), London, HMSO, 1991.
House of Commons, *Official Report*, Vol. 182, No. 25 (11 December 1990), London, HMSO, 1990.
House of Commons, *Official Report*, Vol. 183, No. 34 (15 January 1991), London, HMSO, 1991.
House of Commons, *Official Report*, Vol. 183, No. 133 (27 June 1991), London, HMSO, 1991.
House of Commons, Second Report from the Foreign Affairs Committee, Session 1987–8, *Current Policy Towards the Iran/Iraq Conflict* (HC 279-I&II), London, HMSO, 1988.
House of Commons, Tenth Report of the Defence Committee, Session 1989-90, *Defence Implications of Recent Events* (HC 320), London, HMSO, 1990.
House of Commons, Eleventh Report of the Defence Committee, Session 1990-91, *Statement on the Defence Estimates, 1991* (HC 394), London, HMSO, 1991.
House of Commons, Tenth Report of the Defence Committee, Session 1990-91, *Preliminary Lessons of Operation Granby* (HC 287), London, HMSO, 1991.
Supplement to the *London Gazette*, London, HMSO, 28 June 1991.

Books

Alia, Josette, and Clerc, Christine, *La guerre de Mitterrand: la dernière grande illusion*, Paris, Olivier Orban, 1991.
Bennis, Phyllis, and Moushabeck, Michel (eds.), *Beyond the Storm: A Gulf Crisis Reader*, New York, Olive Branch Press, 1991.
Bergot, Erwan, and Gandy, Alain, *Operation Daguet*, Paris, Presses de la Cité, 1991.
Bethlehem, D.L. (ed.), *The Kuwait Crisis: Sanctions and Their Economic Consequences*, Cambridge, Grotius Publications, 1991.

Blackwell, James, *Thunder in the Desert: The Strategy and Tactics of the Persian Gulf War*, New York, Bantam Books, 1991.

Brown, Ben, and Shukman, David, *All Necessary Means: Inside the Gulf War*, London, BBC Books, 1991.

Bulloch, John, and Morris, Harvey, *Saddam's War: The Origins of the Kuwait Conflict and the International Response*, London, Faber & Faber, 1991.

Cohen, Roger, and Gatti, Claudio, *In the Eye of the Storm: The Life of General H. Norman Schwarzkopf*, New York, Farrar, Straus & Giroux, 1991.

Dabezies, Pierre, *et al.*, *Crise du Golfe: Les Changements Stratégiques*, Paris, Fondation pour les Études de Défense Nationale, 1990.

Dunnigan, James F., and Bay, Austin, *From Shield to Storm: High-Tech Weapons, Military Strategy, and Coalition Warfare in the Persian Gulf*, New York, Morrow, 1991.

Dupuy, Col. Trevor N., Johnson, Curt, Bongard, David L., and Dupuy, Arnold C., *How to Defeat Saddam Hussein: Scenarios and Strategies for the Gulf War*, New York, Warner Books, 1991.

Fialka, John J., *The Hotel Warriors: Covering the Gulf*, Washington DC, Woodrow Wilson Center, 1991.

Friedman, Norman, *Desert Victory: The War for Kuwait*, Annapolis, Naval Institute Press, 1991.

Friedrich, Otto (ed.), *Desert Storm: The War in the Persian Gulf*, Boston, Time Books, 1991.

Gittings, John (ed.), *Beyond the Gulf War: The Middle East and the New World Order*, London, Catholic Institute for International Relations, 1991.

Gnesotto, Nicole, and Roper, John (eds.), *Western Europe and the Gulf*, Paris, Institute for Security Studies of WEU, 1992.

Graubard, Stephen R., *Mr Bush's War: Adventures in the Policies of Illusion*, New York, Hill & Wang, 1992.

Guerre éclair dans le Golfe: la défense du droit, Paris, Jean-Claude Lattes/Addim, 1991.

Heikal, Mohamed, *Illusions of Triumph: An Arab View of the Gulf War*, London, Harper Collins, 1992.

Hiro, Dilip, *Desert Shield to Desert Storm: The Second Gulf War*, London, Harper Collins, 1992.

Karsh, Efraim, and Rautsi, Inari, *Saddam Hussein: A Political Biography*, New York and London, The Free Press and Brassey's, 1991.

Kodmani-Darwish, Bassma, and Charouni-Dubarry, May, *Gulfe et Moyen Orient*, Paris, Institut Français des Relations Internationales, 1991.

Lauterpacht, E., Greenwood, C.J., Weller, Marc, and Bethlehem, Daniel (eds.), *The Kuwait Crisis: Basic Documents*, Cambridge International Documents Series Volumes I, II, III, Cambridge, Grotius Publications, 1991.

Laurent, Eric, *Tempête du désert: les secrets de la Maison Blanche*, Paris, Olivier Orban, 1991.

MacArthur, Brian (ed.), *Despatches from the Gulf War*, London, Bloomsbury, 1991.

Nair, Brigadier V.K., *War in the Gulf: Lessons for the Third World*, New Delhi, Lancer International, 1991.

Newsom, David D. (ed.), *The Diplomatic Record, 1990–91*, Boulder, Westview Press for Institute for the Study of Diplomacy, 1992.

Nolan, Janne E., *Trappings of Power: Ballistic Missiles in the Third World*, Washington DC, Brookings Institution, 1991.

Parrish, Lt.-Col. Robert D., and Andreacchio, Col. N.A., *Schwarzkopf: An Insider's View of the Commander and His Victory*, New York, Bantam Books, 1991.

Sackur, Stephen, *On the Basra Road*, London, *London Review of Books*, 1991.

Serrano, Andrew Smith, *Las claves de la guerra del Golfo*, Barcelona, Asesa, 1991.

Sciolino, Elaine, *The Outlaw State: Saddam Hussein's Quest for Power and the Gulf Crisis*, New York, Wiley, 1991.

Sifry, Michah, and Cerf, Christopher (eds.), *The Gulf Reader: History, Documents, Opinions*, New York, Random House, 1991.

Simpson, John, *From the House of War: John Simpson in the Gulf*, London, Arrow Books, 1991.
Smith, Jean Edward, *George Bush's War*, New York, Holt, 1992.
Summers, Col. Harry G. Jr, *On Strategy II: A Critical Analysis of the Gulf War*, New York, Dell, 1992.
Timmerman, Kenneth R., *The Death Lobby: How the West Armed Iraq*, London, Fourth Estate, 1992.
Tucker, Robert and Hendrickson, David, *The Imperial Temptation: The New World Order and America's Purpose*, New York, Council on Foreign Relations, 1992.
US News & World Report, *Triumph Without Victory: The Unreported History of the Persian Gulf War*, New York, Random House, 1992.
Watson, Bruce W. (ed.), *Military Lessons of the Gulf War*, London, Greenhill Books, 1991.
Williams, Richard, Heckman, Joanne, and Shreeberger, Jon, *Environmental Consequences of the Persian Gulf War, 1990–91*, Washington DC, National Geographic Society, 1991.
Woodward, Bob, *The Commanders*, New York, Simon & Schuster, 1991.

Monographs

Amnesty International, *Iraq's Occupation of Kuwait*, 19 December 1990.
Arkin, William M., Durrant, Damian, and Cherni, Marianne, *On Impact: Modern Warfare and the Environment: A Case Study of the Gulf War*, Washington DC, Greenpeace, 1991.
Arkin, William M., Handler, Joshua, and Durrant, Damian, *US Nuclear Weapons in the Persian Gulf Crisis*, Washington DC, Greenpeace, January 1991.
Asmus, Ronald 'Germany after the Gulf War', *A Rand Note*, Santa Monica, Rand Corporation, 1992.
Aspin, Les, *The Aspin Papers: Sanctions, Diplomacy, and War in the Persian Gulf*, Center for Strategic and International Studies, Significant Issues Series, Vol. XIII, No. 2, 1991.
Association of the United States Army, *The US Army in Operation Desert Shield: An Overview*, Arlington, Virginia, Institute of Land Warfare, June 1991.
Association of the United States Army, *Operations Desert Shield and Desert Storm: The Logistics Perspective*, Arlington, Virginia, Institute of Land Warfare, September 1991.
Browne, Marjorie Ann, *Iraq–Kuwait: The United Nations Response*, Washington DC, Congressional Research Service, 22 October 1990.
Center for Army Lessons Learned, *Winning in the Desert*, Newsletter No. 90-7, US Army Combined Arms Training Activity, Fort Leavenworth, Kansas, August 1990.
Center for Army Lessons Learned, *Winning in the Desert II: Tactics, Techniques and Procedures for Maneuver Commanders*, Newsletter No. 90-8, US Army Combined Arms Training Activity, Fort Leavenworth, Kansas, September 1990.
Center for Army Lessons Learned, *Getting to the Desert: Deployment and Selective Callup Lessons Desert Shield*, Newsletter No. 90-11, US Army Combined Arms Command, Fort Leavenworth, Kansas, December 1990.
Collins, John M., *Desert Shield and Desert Storm, Implications for Future US Force Requirements*, Washington DC, Congressional Research Service Report 91-361 RCO, 19 April 1991.
Cox, David (ed.), *The Use of Force by the Security Council for Enforcement and Deterrent Purposes: A Conference Report*, Canadian Centre for Arms Control and Disarmament, 1991.
Dannreuther, Roland, *The Gulf Conflict: A Political and Strategic Analysis*, London, Brassey's/International Institute for Strategic Studies, Adelphi Paper No. 264, Winter 1991/2.
Department of the Air Force, United States, *Air Performance in Desert Storm*, April 1991.
Donnelly, Warren H., *Iraq and Nuclear Weapons*, Washington DC, Congressional Research Service, 21 December 1990.
Epstein, Joshua M., *War with Iraq: What Price Victory?* Washington DC, Brookings Institution, Brookings Discussion Papers, 10 January 1991.
Foster, Edward, and Hollis, Rosemary, *War in the Gulf: Sovereignty, Oil and Security*, London,

Royal United Services Institute for Defence Studies, Whitehall Paper Series No. 8, 1991.

Gallis, Paul E. *German Foreign Policy after the Gulf War: Implications for US Interests*, Washington DC, Congressional Research Service Report 91-451, 30 May 1991.

Golan, Gallia, *Soviet Middle East Policy under Gorbachev*, Santa Monica, Rand/UCLA Center for Soviet Studies, March 1990.

Hudson, Michael C., and Picchi, Bernard J., *Crisis in the Persian Gulf: Political Causes and Oil Market Effects*, London, Saloman Brothers, October 1990.

Imai, Ambassador Ryukichi, *The Gulf Crisis and the Gulf War*, Tokyo, International Institute for Global Peace Special Report, March 1991.

Khalidi, Ahmad S., and Evron, Yair, *Middle East Security: Two Views*, Cambridge, Massachusetts, International Security Studies Program, American Academy of Arts and Sciences, Occasional Paper No. 3, May 1990.

Kishino, Hiroyuki, *The Persian Gulf Crisis and Japan's Role*, Tokyo, International Institute for Global Peace, Policy Paper, October 1990.

Knight, Richard, *The Gulf Crisis Chronology*, BBC World Service News Information and Reference Library, 1990/91.

Lesser, Ian O., *Oil, the Persian Gulf, and Grand Strategy: Contemporary Issues in Historical Perspective*, Santa Monica, Rand National Defense Research Institute, 1991.

McPeak, General Merrill, *The Air Campaign: Part of the Combined Operations*, Washington DC, Department of Defense, 15 March 1991.

Middle East Watch/Human Rights Watch, *Needless Deaths in the Gulf War: Civilian Casualties During the Air Campaign and Violation of the Laws of War*, Washington DC, 1991.

Navias, Martin, *The Spread of Nuclear, Chemical and Ballistic Missile Weaponry in the Middle East*, London, Institute of Jewish Affairs, Research Report No. 4, 1990.

Navias, Martin, *Saddam's Scud War and Ballistic Missile Proliferation*, London, Brassey's/Centre for Defence Studies, University of London, August 1991.

O'Rourke, Ronald, *Sealift and Operation Desert Shield*, Washington DC, Congressional Research Service Report 90-446 F, 17 September 1990.

Pelletière, Stephen C., Johnson, Douglas V. II, and Rosenberger, Leif R., *Iraqi Power and US Security in the Middle East*, Strategic Studies Institute, US Army War College, 1990.

Pelletière, Stephen C. and Johnson, Douglas V. II, *Lessons Learned: The Iran–Iraq War*, Strategic Studies Institute, US Army War College, 1991.

The Soref Symposium: American Strategy after the Gulf War, Washington DC, Institute of Near East Policy, 1991.

Shaw, Martin and Carr-Hill, Roy, *Public Opinion, Media and Violence: Attitudes to the Gulf War in a Local Population*, Hull, Report No.1, Gulf War Project, University of Hull, 1991.

Stewart, Brigadier-General John, *Desert Storm: The Military Intelligence Story: A View from the G-2*, US Army, April 1991.

Taylor, Paul and Groom, A.J.R., *The United Nations and the Gulf War 1990–91: Back to the Future?*, London, Royal Institute of International Affairs, 1992.

Towle, Philip, *Pundits and Patriots: Lessons from the Gulf War*, London, Institute for European Defence and Strategic Studies, 1991.

Whitehall Paper Series, *Command in War: Gulf Operations*, London, Royal United Services Institute for Defence Studies, 1992.

Willett, Susan, *The Gulf Crisis: Economic Implications*, London, Brassey's/Centre for Defence Studies, University of London, November 1990.

Journal articles

Adelman, M.A., 'After the Gulf War: Oil Fallacies', *Foreign Policy*, No. 82, Spring 1991.

Ajami, Fouad, 'The Summer of Arab Discontent', *Foreign Affairs*, Vol. 69, No. 5, Winter 1990/91.

Albright, David, and Hibbs, Mark, 'Hyping the Bomb', *Bulletin of Atomic Scientists*, March 1991.
Albright, David, and Hibbs, Mark, 'Iraq's Nuclear Hide-and-Seek,' *Bulletin of Atomic Scientists*, September 1991.
Albright, David and Hibbs, Mark, 'Iraq's Bomb: Blueprints and Artifacts', *Bulletin of Atomic Scientists*, January/February 1992.
Albright, Madeleine K., and Goodman, Allan E., 'US Foreign Policy after the Gulf Crisis', *Survival*, Vol. 32, No. 6, November/December 1990.
Alexandrova, Olga, 'Soviet Policy in the Gulf Conflict', *Aussenpolitik*, Vol. 42, No. 3, 1991.
Antal, Major John F., US Army, 'The Iraqi Army: Forged in the (Other) Gulf War', *Military Review*, Vol. LXXI, No. 2, February 1991.
Anthony, Ian, 'The Global Arms Trade', *Arms Control Today*, Vol. 21, No. 5, June 1991.
Arkin, William M., 'US Nukes in the Gulf', *The Nation*, 31 November 1990.
Arnett, Eric, 'Awestruck Press Does Tomahawk PR', *Bulletin of Atomic Scientists*, April 1991.
Arnold, Hans, 'The Gulf Crisis and the United Nations', *Aussenpolitik*, January 1991.
Arthur, Vice-Admiral Stanley, and Pokran, Marvin, 'Desert Storm at Sea', *US Naval Institute Proceedings, Naval Review*, Vol. 117, No. 5, May 1991.
Azzam, Maha, 'The Gulf Crisis: Perceptions in the Muslim World,' *International Affairs*, Vol. 67, No. 2, July 1991.
Begin, Ze'ev B., 'The Likud Vision of Israel at Peace', *Foreign Affairs*, Vol. 70, No. 4, Fall 1991.
Bolton, David, 'Did Saddam Want War?', *RUSI Journal*, Vol. 136, No. 1, Spring 1991.
Boxhall, Peter, 'The Iraqi Claim to Kuwait', *Army Quarterly & Defence Journal*, Vol. 121, No. 1, January 1991.
Bradshaw, David, 'After the Gulf War: the Kurds', *World Today*, Vol. 47, No. 5, May 1991.
Brand, Laurie A., 'Liberalization and Changing Political Coalitions: The Bases of Jordan's 1990–1991 Gulf Crisis Policy', *The Jerusalem Journal of International Relations*, Vol. 13, No. 4, December 1991.
Braun, Ursula, 'Epicentre Kuwait: The International Political Dimension of a Regional Conflict', *Aussenpolitik*, Vol. 42, No. 1, 1991.
Brown, Neville, 'The Blazing Oil Wells of Kuwait', *World Today*, Vol. 47, No. 6, June 1991.
Brugger, Bill, 'Was the Gulf War "Just"?', *Australian Journal of International Affairs*, Vol. 45, No. 2, November 1991.
Brzezinski, Zbigniew, 'Selective Global Commitment', *Foreign Affairs*, Vol. 70, No. 4, Fall 1991.
Bundy, McGeorge, 'Nuclear Weapons and the Gulf', *Foreign Affairs*, Vol. 70, No. 4, Fall 1991.
Calvocoressi, Peter, 'After Kuwait', *International Relations*, Vol. 10, No. 4, November 1991.
Caran, James, 'The Electronic Storm', *Air Force Magazine*, June 1991.
Carpenter, Ted Galen, 'The New World Disorder', *Foreign Policy*, No. 84, Fall 1991.
Carus, W. Seth, 'Missiles in the Third World: The 1991 Gulf War', *Orbis*, Vol. 35, No. 2, Spring 1991.
Carver, Jeremy P., 'The Gulf Crisis', *Boundary Bulletin*, Vol. 1, No. 1, 1991.
Chalabi, Ahmad, 'Iraq: The Past as Prologue?', *Foreign Policy*, No. 83, Summer 1991.
Chubin, Shahram, 'Post-war Gulf Security', *Survival*, Vol. 33, No. 2, March/April 1991.
Cigar, Norman, 'Iraq's Strategic Mindset and the Gulf War: Blueprint for Defeat', *The Journal of Strategic Studies*, Vol. 15, No. 1, March 1992.
Cohen, Avner, and Miller, Marvin, 'Nuclear Shadows in the Middle East: Prospects for Arms Control in the Wake of the Gulf Crisis', *Security Studies*, Vol. 1, No. 1, Autumn 1991.
Cooley, John K., 'Pre-war Gulf Diplomacy', *Survival*, Vol. 33, No. 2, March/April 1991.
Cordesman, Anthony H., 'No End of a Lesson: Iraq and the Issue of Arms Transfers', *RUSI Journal*, Vol. 136, No. 1, Spring 1991.
Cordesman, Anthony, 'Rushing to Judgement on the Gulf War', *Armed Forces International*, June 1991.
Craig, C.J.S., 'Desert Shield/Desert Storm: The Right Flank', *The Naval Review*, Vol. 80, No. 1, January 1992.

Crawford, Malcolm, 'After Saddam Hussein – What?', *World Today*, Vol. 46, No. 11, November 1990.

Dawisha, Adeed, 'The United States in the Middle East: The Gulf War and Its Aftermath', *Current History*, January 1992.

Deibel, Terry L., 'Bush's Foreign Policy: Mastery and Inaction', *Foreign Policy*, No 84, Fall 1991.

Draper, Theodore, 'The Gulf War Reconsidered', *New York Review of Books*, 16 January 1992.

Drew, Elizabeth, 'Letter from Washington', *New Yorker*, 4 February 1991.

Drew, Elizabeth, 'Letter from Washington,' *New Yorker*, 25 February 1991.

Drew, Elizabeth, 'Letter from Washington', *New Yorker*. 11 March 1991.

Duanzhi, She, 'Gulf War Implications Linger', *Beijing Review*, Vol. 34, No. 28, 15–21 July 1991.

Duncan, Colonel B.A.C., 'Cruelty and Compassion: an Englishman in Kuwait', *Army Quarterly & Defence Journal*, Vol. 121, No. 2, Gulf War Issue, 1991.

Eekelen, Willem van, 'WEU and the Gulf Crisis', *Survival*, Vol. 32, No. 6, November/December 1990.

Farer, Tom, 'After the Gulf War: Israel's Unlawful Occupation', *Foreign Policy*, No. 82, Spring 1991.

Freedman, Lawrence, 'The Gulf War and the New World Order', *Survival*, Vol. 33, No. 3, May/June 1991.

Freedman, Lawrence, and Karsh, Efraim, 'How Kuwait Was Won: Strategy in the Gulf War', *International Security*, Vol. 16, No. 2, Fall 1991.

Freedman, Robert O., 'Moscow and the Gulf War', *Problems of Communism*, Vol. XL, July–August 1991.

Fuller, Graham E., 'Respecting Regional Realities', *Foreign Policy*, No. 83, Summer 1991.

Fuller, Graham E., 'Moscow and the Gulf War', *Foreign Affairs*, Vol. 70, No. 3, Summer 1991.

Fursdon, Major-General Edward, 'UN Successes in 1990', *Army Quarterly & Defence Journal*, Vol. 121, No. 2, Gulf War Issue, 1991.

Garnham, David, 'Explaining Middle Eastern Alignments during the Gulf War', *The Jerusalem Journal of International Relations*, Vol. 13, No. 3, 1991.

Glass, David S., 'The UN Security Council II: Perception of Bias', *The World Today*, Vol. 46, No. 12, December 1990.

Glennon, Michael J., 'War and the Constitution', *Foreign Affairs*, Vol. 70, No. 2, Spring 1991.

Gore-Booth, David, 'The Middle East: Future Security Structures', *RUSI Journal*, Vol. 136, No. 3, Autumn 1991.

Gowing, Nik, 'The Media Dimension I: TV and the Kurds', *World Today*, Vol. 47, No. 7, July 1991.

Greenwood, Christopher, 'Iraq's Invasion of Kuwait: Some Legal Issues', *World Today*, Vol. 47, No. 3, March 1991.

Grimmett, Richard F., Pierre, Andrew J., and Leonard, James F., 'Forum: Post-War Window Opens for Middle Eastern Arms Control', *Arms Control Today*, Vol. 21, No. 5, June 1991.

'The Gulf Crisis', special issue of *Contemporary European Affairs*, Vol. 4, No. 1, 1991.

Halliday, Fred, 'The Gulf War and Its Aftermath: First Reflections', *International Affairs*, Vol. 67, No. 2, April 1991.

Halliday, Fred, 'Historical Antecedents to the Present Crisis', *RUSI Journal*, Vol. 136, No. 3, Autumn 1991.

Hamilton, Representative Lee H., 'Middle Eastern Arms Restraint: An Obligation to Act', *Arms Control Today*, Vol. 21, No. 5, June 1991.

Harris, Lillian Craig, 'The Gulf Crisis and China's Middle East Dilemma', *Pacific Review*, Vol. 4, No. 2, 1991.

Hayr, Sir Kenneth, 'Logistics in the Gulf War', *RUSI Journal*, Vol. 136, No. 3, Autumn 1991.

Herrmann, Richard K., 'The Middle East and the New World Order: Rethinking US Political Strategy after the Gulf War', *International Security*, Vol. 16, No. 2, Fall 1991.

Hill, Lieutenant Colonel Richard D., US Army, 'Depot Operations Supporting Desert Shield', *Military Review*, Vol. LXXI, No. 4, April 1991.

Hindell, Keith, 'The UN Security Council I: Filling the Gaps', *The World Today*, Vol. 46, No. 12, December 1990.

Horner, Lt.-General Charles, 'The Air Campaign', *Military Review*, September 1991.

Howe, Jonathan T., 'NATO and the Gulf Crisis', *Survival*, Vol. 33, No. 3, May/June 1991.

Howe, Jonathan T., 'Southern Guard', in Bruce George (ed.), *Jane's NATO Handbook, 1991–92*, London, Jane's Information Group, 1991.

Hunter, Air Vice-Marshal A.F.C., 'The Future of Air Power', *Army Quarterly & Defence Journal*, Vol. 121, No. 1, January 1991.

Indyk, Martin, 'Peace without the PLO', *Foreign Policy*, No. 83, Summer 1991.

Inman, Bobby R., Nye, Joseph S. Jr, Perry, William J., and Smith, Roger K., 'Lessons from the Gulf War,' *Washington Quarterly*, Vol. 15, No. 1, Winter 1992.

Irving, Group-Captain Niall, 'The Gulf Air Campaign – An Overview', *RUSI Journal*, Vol. 137, No. 1, February 1992.

Karsh, Efraim and Rautsi, Inari, 'Why Saddam Hussein Invaded Kuwait', *Survival*, Vol. 33, No. 1, January/February 1991.

Jahanpour, Farhang, 'A New Order for the Middle East?', *World Today*, Vol. 47, No. 5, May 1991.

Kedourie, Elie, 'Iraq: The Mystery of American Policy', *Commentary*, Vol. 91, No. 6, June 1991.

Kielinger, Thomas, 'The Gulf War and the Consequences from a German Point of View', *Aussenpolitik*, Vol. 42, No. 3, 1991.

Kemp, Geoffrey, 'The Gulf Crisis: Diplomacy or Force?', *Survival*, Vol. 32, No. 6, November/December 1990.

Krauthammer, Charles, 'The Unipolar Moment', *Foreign Affairs*, Vol. 70, No. 1, 1991.

Kyle, Keith, 'The Gulf War: Lessons of Suez', *The World Today*, Vol. 47, No 12, December 1991.

Kuniholm, Bruce R., 'Turkey and the West', *Foreign Affairs*, Vol. 70, No. 2, Spring 1991.

Langerus, Colonel Peter, 'Moving an Army: Movement Control for Desert Storm', *Military Review*, September 1991.

Law, David, 'The Alliance and Security in the Mediterranean and the Gulf Crisis', in Bruce George (ed.), *Jane's NATO Handbook, 1991–92*, London, Jane's Information Group, 1991.

Leaver, Richard, 'Australia's Gulf Commitment: The End of Self Reliance?', *The Pacific Review*, Vol. 4, No. 3, 1991.

Lesch, Ann Mosely, 'Contrasting Reactions to the Persian Gulf Crisis: Egypt, Syria, Jordan, and the Palestinians', *Middle East Journal*, Vol. 45, No. 1, Winter 1991.

Lidderdale, Gavin, 'The Analysis of Operation Granby', *Air Clues*, March 1992.

Luttwak, Edward, 'Victory through Air Power', *Commentary*, August 1991.

Mackenzie, Richard, 'A Conversation with Chuck Horner', *Air Force Magazine*, June 1991.

Malik, J. Mohan, 'India's Response to the Gulf Crisis', *Asian Survey*, Vol. 31, No. 9, September 1991.

Mandelbaum, Michael, 'The Bush Foreign Policy', *Foreign Affairs*, Vol. 70, No. 1, 1991.

Mason, R.A., 'The Air War in the Gulf', *Survival*, Vol. 33, No. 3, May/June 1991.

Massing, Michael, 'The Way to War', *The New York Review*, 28 March 1991.

Mayall, James, 'Non-intervention, Self-determination and the "New World Order"', *International Affairs*, Vol. 67, No. 2, July 1991.

Maynes, Charles Williams, 'Dateline Washington: A Necessary War?', *Foreign Policy*, No. 82, Spring 1991.

McKnight, Sean, 'The Forgotten War: The Iraqi Army and the Iran–Iraq War', *Small Wars & Insurgencies*, Vol. 2, No. 1, April 1991.

Moisi, Dominique, 'Le Quai d'Orsay et la crise du Golfe', *Pouvoirs*, No. 58, 1991.

Morse, Edward L., 'The Coming Oil Revolution', *Foreign Affairs*, Vol. 69, No. 5, Winter 1990/91.

Mortimer, Edward, 'Iraq: The Road Not Taken', *New York Review of Books*, 16 May 1991.

Muir, Cdr J., USN, 'A View From the Black Hole', *US Naval Institute Proceedings*, October 1991.

Muslih, Muhammad and Norton, Augustus Richard, 'Winning the Peace: The Need for Arab Democracy', *Foreign Policy*, No. 83, Summer 1991.

Myers, Major James E., US Army, 'Building the Desert Logistics Force', *Military Review*, Vol. LXXI, No. 4, April 1991.

Mylroie, Laurie, 'How We Helped Saddam Survive', *Commentary*, July 1991.

Newhouse, John, 'The Diplomatic Round', *New Yorker*, 15 February 1991.

Norton, Graham, 'The Terrorist and the Traveller: a Gulf Aftermath Assessment', *World Today*, Vol. 47, No. 5, May 1991.

'155 Miles into Iraq: The 101st Strikes Deep', *Army*, August 1991.

Otis, Pauletta, 'Political and Military Considerations of the Kurdish Case, 1991: A Window of Opportunity?', *Small Wars & Insurgencies*, Vol. 2, No. 1, April 1991.

Otenberg, M.A., 'Operational Implications of Middle East Ballistic Missile Proliferation', *Defense Analysis*, Vol. 7, No. 1, March 1991.

Pagonis, Lt.-General William, and Raugh, Major Harold, 'Good Logistics in Combat Power', *Military Review*, September 1991.

Palmer, Michael, 'The Navy Did Its Job', *US Naval Institute Proceedings, Naval Review*, May 1991.

Perry, William J., 'Desert Storm and Deterrence', *Foreign Affairs*, Vol. 70, No. 4, Fall 1991.

Pfaff, William, 'Redefining World Power', *Foreign Affairs*, Vol. 70, No. 1, 1991.

Phillips, Rheta S., 'Logistics Automation Support for Desert Storm', *Military Review*, Vol. LXXI, No. 4, April 1991.

Pipes, Daniel, 'Is Damascus Ready for Peace?', *Foreign Affairs*, Vol. 70, No. 4, Fall 1991.

Postol, Theodore A., 'Lessons of the Gulf War Experience with Patriot', *International Security*, Vol. 16, No. 3, Winter 1991/2.

Potter, William C., and Stulberg, Adam, 'The Soviet Union and the Spread of Ballistic Missiles', *Survival*, Vol. 32, No. 6, November/December 1990.

Purrington, Courtney, and A.K., 'Tokyo's Policy Responses during the Gulf Crisis', *Asian Survey*, Vol. 31, No. 4, April 1991.

Quandt, William B., 'The Middle East in 1990', *Foreign Affairs*, Vol. 70, No. 1, 1991.

Ranken, Michael, 'The Gulf War – Logistic Support and Merchant Shipping', *Naval Review*, Vol. 79, No. 3, July 1991.

Reed, Stanley, 'Jordan and the Gulf Crisis', *Foreign Affairs*, Vol. 69, No. 5, Winter 1990/91.

Reid, Major-General P.D., 'Tanks in the Gulf', *Army Quarterly & Defence Journal*, Vol. 121, No. 2, Gulf War Issue, 1991.

'The Road to War', *Newsweek*, 28 January 1991.

Rochlin, Gene I., 'The Gulf War: Technological and Organizational Implications', *Survival*, Vol. 33, No. 3, May/June 1991.

Rodman, Peter W., 'Middle East Diplomacy After the Gulf War', *Foreign Affairs*, Vol. 70, No. 2, Spring 1991.

Roberts, John, 'Oil, the Military and the Gulf War of 1991', *RUSI Journal*, Vol. 136, No. 1, Spring 1991.

Rubinstein, Alvin Z., 'New World Order or Hollow Peace?', *Foreign Affairs*, Vol. 70, No. 4, Fall 1991.

Russet, Bruce, and Sutterlin, James S., 'The UN in a New World Order', *Foreign Affairs*, Vol. 70, No. 2, Spring 1991.

Salomon, Lieutenant-General Leon, US Army, and Bankirer, Lieutenant-Colonel Harold, US Army, 'Total Army CSS: Providing the Means for Victory', *Military Review*, Vol. LXXI, No. 4, April 1991.

Sayigh, Yezid, 'The Gulf Crisis: Why the Arab Regional Order Failed', *International Affairs*, Vol. 67, No. 2, July 1991.

Schichor, Yitzhak, 'China and the Gulf Crisis', *Problems of Communism*, Vol. XL, November/December 1991.

Schiff, Ze'ev, 'Israel after the War', *Foreign Affairs*, Vol. 70, No. 2, Spring 1991.

Schofield, Richard N., 'The Question of Delimiting the Iraq–Kuwait Boundary', *Boundary Bulletin*, Vol. 1, No. 1, 1991.

Smith, Charles, 'Loyalties under Fire', *Far Eastern Economic Review*, 24 January 1991.

Smith, Major General Rupert, 'The Gulf War: The Land Battle', *RUSI Journal*, Vol. 137, No. 1, February 1992.

'Special Operations', *Army*, September 1991.

Starr, Joyce R., 'After the Gulf War: Water Wars', *Foreign Policy*, No. 82, Spring 1991.

Sterner, Michael, 'Navigating the Gulf', *Foreign Policy*, No. 81, Winter 1990–91.

Summers, Colonel Harry G., Jr, US Army, 'Leadership in Adversity: From Vietnam to Victory in the Gulf', *Military Review*, Vol. LXXI, No. 5, May 1991.

Taft, William H., IV, 'European Security: Lessons Learned from the Gulf', *NATO Review*, Vol. 39, No. 3, June 1991.

Tarr, David W., 'Coercive Diplomacy in the Gulf Crisis: Deterrence vs. Compellence', *Jerusalem Journal of International Relations*, Vol. 13, No. 3, 1991.

Taylor, William J., Jr, and Blackwell, James, 'The Ground War in the Gulf', *Survival*, Vol. 33, No. 3, May/June 1991.

Thorne, I.D.P., 'Adolf and Friends', *Army Quarterly & Defence Journal*, Vol. 121, No. 2, Gulf War Issue, 1991.

Van Evera, Stephen, 'American Intervention in the Third World: Less Would be Better', *Security Studies*, Vol. 1, No. 1, Autumn 1991.

Vuono, Carl E., 'Desert Storm and the Future of Conventional Forces', *Foreign Affairs*, Vol. 70, No. 2, Spring 1991.

Walker, Martin, 'Dateline Washington: Victory and Delusion', *Foreign Policy*, No. 83, Summer 1991.

Warner, Frederick, 'The Environmental Consequences of the Gulf War', *Environment*, Vol. 33, No. 5, 1991.

Yetiv, S.A., 'Persian Gulf Security: a Bivariable Analysis', *Defense Analysis*, Vol. 6, No. 3, September 1990.

Index

496